# A ROMAN PROVINCIAL CAPITAL AND ITS HINTERLAND
# THE SURVEY OF THE TERRITORY OF TARRAGONA, 1985-1990

# JOURNAL OF ROMAN ARCHAEOLOGY

## SUPPLEMENTARY SERIES NUMBER 15

GENERAL EDITOR: J. H. HUMPHREY

AN INTERNATIONAL JOURNAL

# A ROMAN PROVINCIAL CAPITAL AND ITS HINTERLAND

## THE SURVEY OF THE TERRITORY OF TARRAGONA, SPAIN, 1985-1990

by

**Josep-Maria Carreté, Simon Keay and Martin Millett**

with contributions from
Lurdes Burès, John Evans, Jeremy Taylor, David Williams & Cyndy Winter

ANN ARBOR, MI
1995

ISBN 1-887829-15-6

ISSN 1063-4304 (for the supplementary series)


This volume is published with the support of
THE BETTY MORGAN MAY MEMORIAL FUND.

This and other supplements to the *Journal of Roman Archaeology* may be ordered from:
JRA, 1216 Bending Road, Ann Arbor, MI 48103, U.S.A.
telephone (USA) 313 662 7132, telefax (USA) 313 662 3240,
*or from*
Oxbow Books, Park End Place, Oxford, OX1 1HN, England
telephone (U.K.) 1865-241 249, Telefax (U.K.) 1865-794 449.

# CONTENTS

# ACKNOWLEDGEMENTS

A project of this scale could not have been completed without the help and co-operation of a considerable number of organizations and individuals. Throughout the project S.K. and M.M. have received considerable support from their respective University Departments in Southampton and Durham. It included financial support, the use of equipment and facilities, and the granting of Research Leave. We would particularly like to acknowledge the generous support of Rosemary Cramp, Anthony Harding, Colin Haselgrove (at Durham), David Peacock, Brian Sparkes and Peter Ucko (at Southampton).

Funds for the project were provided in England by The British Academy, The Society of Antiquaries of London, The M. Alwyn Cotton Fund, The Craven Fund and The Universities of Durham and Southampton. Funding, permits, access to archives and encouragement also came from the Servei de Arqueologia, Departament de Cultura, Generalitat de Catalunya. Professors M. G. Fulford and J. J. Wilkes kindly acted as referees at various stages.

In Tarragona we received considerable help and much kindness from the mayors, local authorities and farmers throughout the area we examined. Particular help came from the staff of the TED'A especially Jaume Massó, Francesc Tarrats Bou and his staff at the Museu Arqueològic Nacional de Tarragona, Juan-Vianney Maria Arbeloa, Arqueòleg Territorial for the Province of Tarragona, Sr Corbella and family at Sabinosa, and Maximo. In addition the Universidad Autònoma and the Universidad Central de Barcelona provided student assistants. We are especially grateful to Xavier Dupré for his sustained encouragement and enthusiatic support throughout the project.

The principal members of the field team who deserve our greatest thanks were Nick Bradford, Manel Güell, Nina Keay, Mary and Tony Morse, John and Janet Schofield, Chris Unwin, and Cyndy Winter. Other members of the team in various years included: Lorraine Adams, Julio Agraz, Dominic Barker, Victoria Brandon, Lurdes Burès, Hugh Corrie, Matt Edgeworth, Mark Grahame, Joanne Higson, Judith Jones, Kathleen Knowles, Josep Maria Macías, Tracy Newman, Josep Maria Palet, Romola Parish, Keith Paulin, Ester Planas i Bout, María Puertolas, Josep Anton Remola, Jeremy Taylor, Rachel Tyson, Kate Wilson and Jimmy Wright.

Preparation of the publication was greatly assisted by Yvonne Beadnell and Nick Bradford (illustrations), Rachel Tyson, Graham Tilbury, Fraser Chalmers, Andrew Lloyd (data input and computing), and Kate Wilson (maps).

S.K., M.M.

## TERMINOLOGY

In the field we used the common Castilian terms for ceramic types and for describing the periods. The latter have been retained in some of the illustrations. The English equivalents for the terms are as follows:
Iberica = Iberian;
Republicana = Republican;
Alto Imperial = Early Imperial;
Bajo Imperial = Late Imperial.

# PREFACE

The present volume presents the results and analysis of the data from the survey conducted between 1985 and 1990. The survey used the techniques of field-walking to investigate the development of the classical landscape in the hinterland of *Tarraco,* the Roman provincial capital of *Hispania Citerior (Tarraconensis).* Several papers have discussed interim interpretations of our data (Keay 1987, 1991b; Keay *et al.* 1989; Keay & Millett 1991; Millett 1991a, 1991b); the present volume supersedes the earlier papers.

Our intention in preparing this report has been to combine the presentation and analysis of the information collected with a discussion of the research methods employed. Our results should provide significant insights into the archaeology of the classical period in Spain while the methods developed may be of wider interest to others working in field-survey archaeology, especially in other regions of the Mediterranean. Although many field-surveys have been conducted in the Mediterranean over the past 20 years, this is one of the first to be fully published. Our experiences may contribute to the debate about how field-survey data can best be used. Since this survey is in certain respects a pioneering effort, the decision has been taken to publish the evidence in considerable detail. It is hoped that others will be able to evaluate our results and re-interpret them where appropriate. Yet this volume is not intended as an entirely comprehensive study of the material collected in the survey. Information and discussion of the lithic material is to appear in a separate paper (Schofield *et al.* forthcoming) and studies using finds of the classical period to address broader questions are planned.

Chapter 1 summarizes previous research in the region and provides a gazetteer listing sites known before the survey began. There follows an historical discussion of the development of Tarraco and its hinterland (Chapter 2). The objectives of the survey, the geographical background, and methodology used are discussed in Chapter 3, with details of the methodology provided in Chapter 4. The evidence of the finds is presented in Chapter 5 and conclusions drawn about the identification and dating of new sites in Chapter 6. These data are evaluated in Chapter 7 and a classification of sites proposed in Chapter 8. All the data are used to evaluate the changing settlement patterns in Chapter 9. A broader discussion is provided in Chapter 10. The above format should allow readers with different interests to use the volume with relative ease.

All the material collected in the survey was retained and has been deposited in the Museu Nacional Arqueològic, Tarragona, together with copies of the survey records and rubbings of the decorated fine wares. Copies of the database and maps are retained by the authors.

The volume is a collective effort and should be seen as a joint work. Those responsible for the drafting of the individual chapters were: J.-M.C (with Lurdes Burès) Chapter 1; S.K. Chapters 2 and 5; S.K. and M.M. Chapters 3 and 10; M.M. Chapters 4, 6, 7, 8 and 9. The arrangement and mounting of the final pottery drawings was done by Nick Bradford; the bases for the distribution maps are by Pauline Fenwick and Kate Wilson, and the principal distribution maps were produced by M.M. from scanned images (using Adobe Freehand on an Apple Mac computer). The remaining illustrations are by Yvonne Beadnell.

Throughout the text we have endeavoured to follow a consistent use of Catalan for place-names and other terminology.

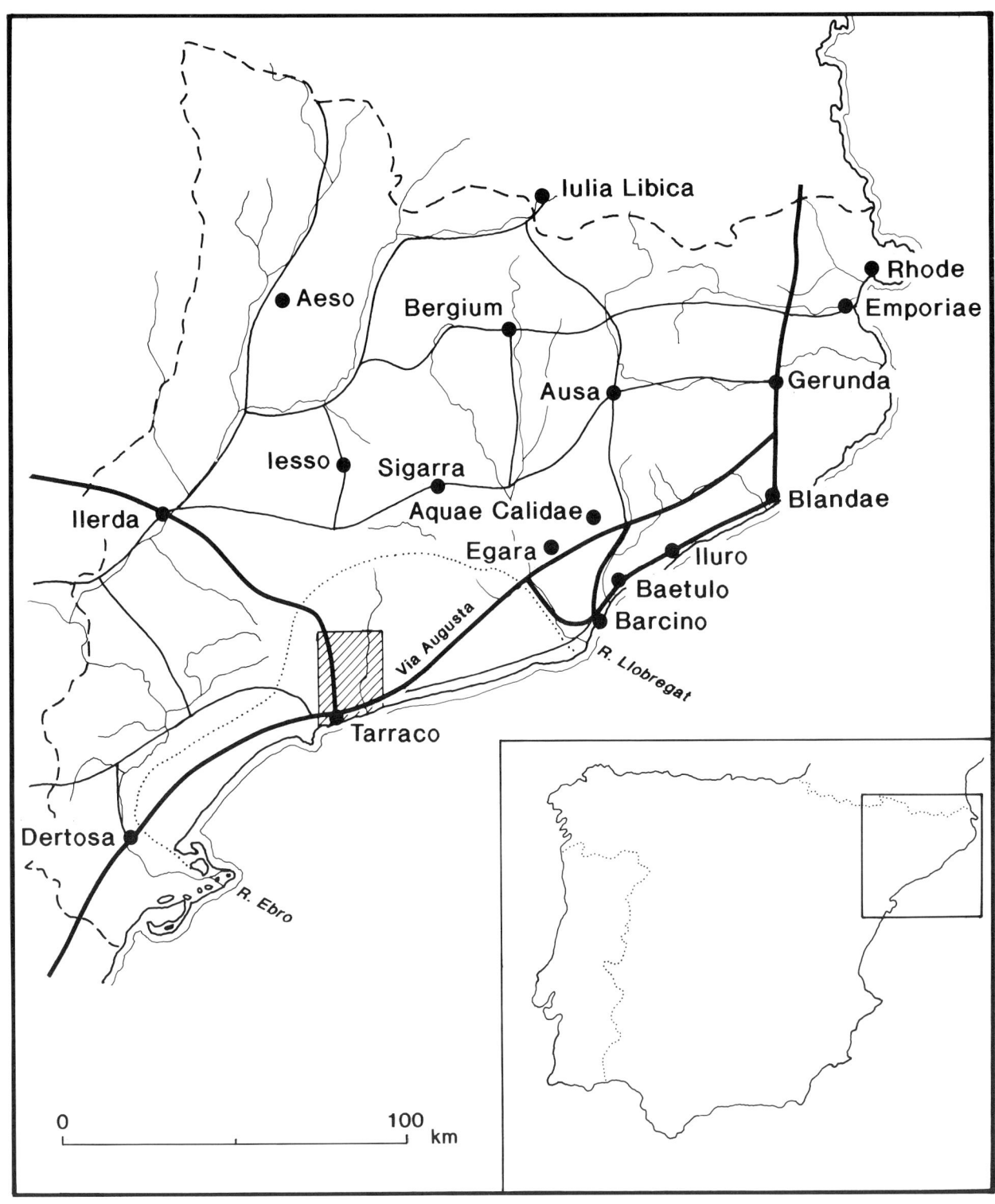

Fig.1.1. Location of the survey in relation to Roman topography. The area covered by fig.1.2 is hachured; the postulated limits of the *territorium* are marked by a dotted line.

# Chapter 1: HISTORY OF PREVIOUS RESEARCH IN THE TERRITORY OF TARRAGONA

The area covered by the *territorium* of Roman Tarraco, the *Ager Tarraconensis*, is imperfectly known (see p. 33). The survey focused upon land which lay towards its centre (fig. 1.1). Today this area, whose capital is Tarragona, is known as the *Camp de Tarragona* and is made up of smaller districts (*Comarques*). The *Camp* consists of the land lying between the pre-litoral mountain chain and the Mediterranean coast and is drained by the rivers Francolí and Gaià. This chapter, which analyses the ways in which Tarraco and its territory have beeen studied by archaeologists, provides the necessary background to an understanding of the historical development of the area. It concludes with a gazetteer of the Iberian and Roman sites in the region that were known before our survey began.

## PREVIOUS RESEARCH

Although it is a well defined geographical unit, previous studies of the *Camp de Tarragona* have been incomplete. They were either histories of individual towns packed with historical facts or descriptions of monuments, or articles about archaeological sites and individual finds. Until recently, there were few studies which discussed the historical evolution of the town and *Camp de Tarragona* as a whole and no analysis of the town/country relationships which conditioned the cultural landscape of the region.

Two groups of earlier scholars may be distinguished. The first, and by far the larger, comprises those who have published work on the city of Tarragona. Much of their work has appeared in academic publications and, by virtue of the collaboration of non-Catalan specialists, has achieved recognition in European circles. The second group has studied the countryside, producing specific studies of largely local interest. Their publications are town- or village-based and the work has been carried out largely by local archaeologists or connoisseurs. The dichotomy between the interests of those studying town and countryside has hindered the task of relating an understanding of Tarragona to that of its surroundings.

The town of Tarragona with its well-preserved Roman monuments caught the attention of specialists long before the birth of archaeology as a science, when interest in the classical world was renewed during the Renaissance. This is the context in which the book, *Libro de las grandezas y cosas memorables de la metropolitana insigne y famosa ciudad de Tarragona* by Lluis Pons D'Icart, was published in 1572. It covered a range of topics, describing the visible ancient monuments, airing opinions on the origins of the town, and discussing the lives of saints associated with the town and other legends. In his broad survey there are occasional references to outstanding monuments in the vicinity of the town, a chapter dedicated to the Torre dels Escipions, and another about 'buildings which are close to the town of Tarragona', such as Centcelles. In particular he focuses upon place-names.

The latter part of the 18th c., the era of illustrations and engravings, witnessed an upsurge in interest in the ancient monuments of the region. This was largely a product of the Catalan Neoclassic Movement which took an increased interest in classical monuments and artefacts. First attempts were made to restore monuments such as the triumphal arch at Berà and the aqueduct known as the Pont del Diable (Les Ferreres) in the vicinity of Tarragona. An interest in travelling and in ancient architectural remains inspired guide-books with drawings and engravings of monuments to illustrate the routes discussed. The *Voyage pittoresque et historique de l'Espagne* by A. Laborde (1806) is especially worthy of mention as it illustrates some of the principal monuments at Tarragona and in its countryside. Also important are the general historical works which appeared at the end of the 18th c., such as the *España Sagrada* of E. Flórez (1769; 1770).

From the 19th c., there was an upsurge of interest in the past. In the case of Tarragona it was enhanced by historical events, such as the destruction of the town during the war with France (1808-13) or the construction of the port. This increased interest soon led to the creation by the *Sociedad Económica Tarraconense de Amigos del País*, in the building known as the Antiga Audiencia (Dupré and Carreté 1993), of the archaeological collection that was to form the basis of the future *Museu Arqueològic*. The pieces came from earlier collections and, especially, from work undertaken in the lower part of the town in connection with the creation of a quarry during the construction of the port. Other important developments took place in 1844 with the formation of both the *Societat Arqueologica Tarraconense*, a forum for academics, erudite amateurs, and the collectors of antiquities, and the Provincial Monument Commissions, which aimed to ensure the preservation of the architectural and archaeological heritage.

One of the most important figures in the early history of research into ancient Tarragona was Bonaventura Hernández Sanahuja (1810-91). Among his prodigious scientific output are publications dedicated to monuments in the *Camp de Tarragona*, such as the Torre dels Escipions and Centcelles, as well as notes published in local newspapers about occasional discoveries in the countryside. His main interest, however, lay in the town and he attempted the first interpretation of the principal Roman monuments. He provided a rich legacy of information about monuments which he saw or was able to confirm at first hand (Massó and Soberanas 1992). Bonaventura described everything in minute detail, providing useful documentation for understanding monuments which subsequently have been altered or have changed. He played a crucial rôle both in archaeological work in the town and in the less extensive work done in the countryside, such as the restoration of the aqueduct of Les Ferreres. He was a member of the Provincial Monument Commission, Inspector of Antiquities, member of the *Cuerpo facultativo de archiveros, bibliotecarios y arqueólogos*, and served as director of the *Museu Arqueològic* from 1851 until his death in 1891.

In this first period archaeological work in the *Camp de Tarragona* focused almost entirely on the analysis of a number of well-known monuments. They were the villa and mausoleum of Centcelles, at which the now famous cupola mosaics were discovered in 1877, the arch of Berà, the aqueduct of Les Ferreres, and the Torre dels Escipions. The contribution of Agusti M. Gibert (1852-1928) is of particular importance for other parts of the *Camp*. Based at Vila-seca, a town close to Tarragona, at the end of the 19th c. his work focused upon the area of Vila-seca, Salou, La Pineda de Vila-seca (modern Vilafortuny), and La Canonja. A passionate lover of the sciences and history, he collected references to archaeological finds and archaeological sites and information supplied by others. His legacy survives in various articles published by the *Real Societat Arqueológica Tarraconense* in the *Buttleti Arqueològic* between 1921 and 1924 and in his book entitled *Ciutats focenses del litoral coseta. Excursions arqueològics* (Barcelona 1900). He had an excellent first-hand understanding of the region.

At the beginning of the 20th c. there was a strong 'noucentist' cultural current which aimed at retrieving as much as possible of the historic and material past. Many facets of cultural life, such as the plastic arts, literature, sculpture, architecture, language, and music, were enriched. In this context the *Institut d'Estudis Catalans* was created and the first large-scale research projects conducted on the cultural heritage of Catalunya. The excavations at Empúries by the architect and politician Puig y Cadafalch are a good example. This cultural movement soon resulted in the institutionalization of archaeology, ensuring that it was influenced by the political ideas and developments that were to dominate the history of Catalunya in the first half the 20th c.

In 1915 the *Servei d'Investigacions Arqueólogiques* of the *Institut d'Estudis Catalans* was created. Dependant upon the *Generalitat de Catalunya* it was directed by Pere Bosch Gimpera, a man who in some ways can be considered a driving force behind the development of archaeology as a modern science. He was also responsible for enacting the first legislation to regulate archaeological excavations, and for organizing archaeological research in Catalunya. Not only did Bosch Gimpera create a 'school' of archaeology; he also knew how to coordinate the efforts of those involved in research at the time. Two of these people were to have a key influence in the development of archaeology in both the *Camp* and the town, Mossen Joan Serra i Vilarò and Dr Salvador Vilaseca. They were his main assistants in the region and played a key rôle in the development of the archaeology at Tarragona from the 1920s until the 1970s. When Joan Serra Vilarò began work at Tarragona in 1925 he had already undertaken intensive activity in the region of Solsona on prehistoric, protohistoric and Roman remains. It included work on lowland dolmens, the Iberian hillforts at San Miquel de Sorba, and the *terra sigillata hispanica* workshops at Abella and Solsona. Curiously, his work at Tarragona concentrated almost exclusively on the town; it included the excavation of the early Christian basilica and cemetery, the forum of the colonia, the town wall (correctly dated for the first time), and the cathedral. (Perhaps he refrained from excavating prehistoric sites to avoid any conflict with Dr Vilaseca.) If there is a key figure in the study of the *Camp* it is Dr Salvador Vilaseca. Born in Reus in 1896, he studied medicine at Barcelona and Madrid but practised at his native town where he developed a consuming interest in archaeology, especially prehistory. His origins as a researcher are to be sought in the *Agrupaciò Excursionista de Reus* founded in 1915 in which the young Vilaseca was actively involved and through which he published his first article (Massó 1985). His work, which stretched from the 1920s to the 1970s, was dedicated principally to prehistory and marks an important stage in the understanding of, and method of working in, the archaeology of the *Camp de Tarragona* and Catalunya as a whole. His scientific precision was eulogized by Bosch Gimpera in the introduction to his book *La industria del silex a Catalunya. Les estacions tallers del Priorat i extensions* (Vilaseca 1936). Vilaseca was tireless in his surveys of the *Camp*, collecting all references to archaeological sites and undertaking excavations wherever he thought appropriate. His interest in archaeology was known by almost everyone in the region and during his professional or recreational visits to villages local inhabitants informed him about the 'ancient things' or artefacts they had found. Items were often given to him in gratitude for his medical services or out of kindness. The finds from his excavations and the many gifts were eventually to form the *Museu Municipal* of Reus of which he was Director until his death in 1975. Vilaseca also published prolifically and interpreted his finds within the context of the periods in question.

While these two were undertaking their research, the Spanish Civil War substantially modified the environment in which they worked. Some of their colleagues, like Bosch Gimpera, were forced into exile. While Serra Vilarò and Vilaseca continued their work the organizational and administrative framework had changed. Nevertheless they acted as a link between one period and the next. After the Civil War Bosch Gimpera was suceeded by Martín Almagro who in practice became responsible for official archaeology in Catalunya. Almagro knew how to use the institutions of the earlier period, such as the *Servei d'Investigacions*, to enable archaeologists to continue their work. However, from 1939 onwards archaeology lacked a rational structure and a coherent research policy, and the universities became disconnected from their regions and lost interest in saving the cultural heritage (MARC-7, 1986).

The Dictatorship created its own organization in 1949 with the installation of the *Comisaria General d'Excavaciones Arqueológicas* and a network of regional and provincial delegates. In the case of Tarragona the task of provincial delegate fell upon the Director of the *Museu Arqueològic*, which was dependant upon the *Museu Arqueològic* of Barcelona. In the 1940s and 1950s the little work that was done was concentrated at Barcelona. Despite this Samuel Ventura i Solsona, Director of the *Museu Arqueològic*, undertook excavations in the Roman amphitheatre at Tarragona between 1948 and 1957, funded by the William J. Bryant Foundation. In 1952 Sánchez Real and Nino Lamboglia excavated the fill of the Roman town walls. The *Camp*, however, was untouched.

The 1960s saw an economic re-awakening matched by an increase in archaeological activity. Working groups diversified and increased in number, more excavations were undertaken and more publications appeared. The State became more open to the collaborative efforts of foreign teams. In 1959 excavations began at the mausoleum of Centecelles and its mosaic was restored by a team under Helmut Schlunk, financed by the German Archaeological Institute at Madrid. In 1969 the same Institute began research in the upper terrace of the Roman town of Tarragona under the direction of Theodor Hauschild.

In 1966 Tarragona was declared a *Conjunt historico-artistic*.[1] This decree established that all of the town and its suburbs were subject to laws regulating archaeological excavations. The *Museo Arqueológico Provincial* (later the *Museu Nacional Arqueòlogic de Tarragona*) was held responsible for applying these norms and undertook numerous excavations. As most remain unpublished, much valuable information has been lost and our understanding of the town has suffered accordingly. The *Museu Arqueòlogic* at Tarragona, directed by M. Berges, undertook a series of excavations both at sites in the *Camp* such as Els Munts (1969), and in the town, where part of the circus was restored (1973). Despite this important activity, urban archaeology at Tarragona was neither sufficiently equipped nor adequately funded to cope with the challenge of urban redevelopment.

With the return of democracy (1975) and the restoration of Catalan political institutions (1979), both the National and the Catalan institutions concerned with cultural heritage were reorganized. This period raised expectations about the future of archaeology in the countryside and the city of Tarragona. In 1980 the *Servei d'Arqueologia de la Generalitat de Catalunya* was created.[2] On July 25, 1985 the *Patrimonio Historico Español* (Spanish historic heritage) law was passed. In 1981 a regulation for archaeological excavations in Catalunya controlled activities which impinged upon the historic heritage (this represented the resuscitation of part of the earlier law of 1933). The Generalitat created a decentralized organization in which a central rôle was played by regional archaeologists. It was their responsibility to ensure the protection of the historic heritage which lay in the *Comarques* under their jurisdiction.

A regional archaeologist for the town of Tarragona was appointed in December 1981. The *Servei d'Arqueologia* undertook excavations which had been agreed upon with the *Consell del Patrimoni Cultural* (successor to the *Comision Provincial del Patrimonio Histórico Artístico*) prior to granting a municipal licence to contractors to build. However the particular problems of Tarragona meant that this mechanism was inadequate: thus, special excavation and conservation plans were developed, beginning with work in the Roman Circus (Dupré, Massó, Palanques and Verduchi 1988) and culminating in the creation of the TED'A (*Taller Escola d'Arqueología* or 'archaeological workshop-school') in 1986. Although this was only a temporary initiative it marked a revolution in the organization of archaeology at Tarragona, since for the first time excavation was organized within a rational and scientific framework. This development ran parallel with the wider involvement of town councils in archaeology in Catalunya during recent years and with the growing importance of urban archaeology.

In rural archaeology the death of Vilaseca spelled the end of continuous archaeological activity in the *Camp*. His labours had greatly increased the number of known sites, provided precise documentation of finds, and centralized casual finds. Fortunately this information is accurately recorded in a large number of publications. Sadly, his work was not continued. Archaeological research in the *Camp* stagnated for two decades. New discoveries are only made where stable research groups exist. Vilaseca's tradition is continued only by Dr Josep M. Fullola's team in the Serra del Monsant, which lies outside the *Camp*. Otherwise the panorama of archaeological activity in the area up to the 1980s has been disappointing,

1    Decree 652/1966 of 10 March 1966 published in the *Boletín Oficial del Estado* 69.
2    Decree 295/180 of 4 December 1980, *Diari oficial de la Generalitat de Catalunya* 105, 7 January 1981.

particularly for prehistory; as a result the *comarcas* of Tarragona are omitted altogether from the discussion of certain chronological periods in general works for Catalan audiences. One response came in 1988 when a team of palaeo-ecological researchers was formed in the School of Prehistory, Ancient History and Archaeology of the *Facultat de Filosofia i Lletres* of the University of Tarragona. Recognizing the importance of sites and the lack of systematic research into the prehistory of the region, they began a research programme into the Quaternary period (Carbonell *et al.* 1986).

In 1982 the *Servei d'Arqueologia de la Generalitat de Catalunya* decided to enlist the help of the *Inventari del Patrimoni Arqueològic* to monitor the state of archaeological research and the conservation of sites, and to help regional archaeologists to preserve the archaeological heritage. The lists produced, commonly known as *Cartes Arqueològiques*, were for regional use and were intended as an exhaustive list of known sites. To compile them the literature was searched, a non-intensive survey of each area and its sites conducted, and contact made with amateurs, academics and treasure-hunters familiar with the region (Castells 1988). The information provided by these *Cartes Arqueològiques* is very useful at an institutional level but their value as research tools is limited since an intensive survey of the whole territory of the map of a particular region could not be made, thus many sites are unrecorded. The *Cartes Arqueològiques* are useful reference works at the onset of a study of a given region, but they say little about ancient settlement-patterns. Nevertheless, this systematic knowledge of sites has permitted control to be exercised over fieldwork. Following the creation of the *Serveis Territorials* rescue excavations were undertaken at a range of sites in the *Camp*. They dated to the prehistoric (Timba d'en Banys and Mas d'en Mario), Iberian (El Vilar and Santa Ana de Castellvell) and Roman (L'Esquirol, Creixell, Els Munts, La Llosa, El Moro, Montroig, Mas de Rofes, Mas dels Frares, Vila-rodona and Villalonga del Camp) periods (Arbeloa 1990b; AA VV 1993). In the best cases these excavations have produced publications about specific sites, sometimes with the aim of creating a broader context.

We should also note a number of individuals with different perspectives and interests who have worked in isolation and without official support and yet have greatly increased our understanding of the *Camp*. Some local amateurs and specialists have dedicated themselves to studying the origins of their town or its surroundings, as has been the case with Vila-rodona (Martínez Larriba 1979; 1980) or Riudoms (Romero 1984). Special recognition is due to J. Massó Carballido who stands out as a specialist in the historiography of the archaeology of Tarragona and the *Camp*, particularly for the Roman period. He has published studies on a number of different towns in the *Camp*, such as Reus (Massó 1978), Constantí (Massó 1990a), Alcover (Massó 1987), Cambrils (Massó 1990b), and has carried out excavations at a number of sites. Attention should also be given to a small group of researchers who have undertaken, or are currently engaged in, research into a particular area at a specific period. Ester Ramón has been working on the Iberian period of the Baix Camp (Ramón 1988; 1989; 1990) and Josep M. Miró (1990) has specialized in the Neolithic. However, there has been no overall study of the *Camp* in the Roman period, so that there could be no direct comparison with what is known about the Roman town. The only attempt at this kind of approach, albeit from a perspective centered on the analysis of the cadaster, is that by J. M. Gurt and A. Marqués (1988), but the results are still unpublished. Amongst the few works which attempt to relate town and country are one focusing upon the Iberian settlement (Ramón 1989) and the excavations at the site of Iberian Tarragona. The excavations reveal that there was a substantial settlement as early as the 5th c. B.C. This has allowed a reassessment of town-country relations in the Iberian period and their subsequent development under the Roman Republic (Aderias, Burès, Miró & Ramón 1994).

Another area of research which draws on a broad territorial framework concerns the manufacture of ceramics. This was the aim of a state-sponsored research programme called *Officina*. It generated articles specifically concerned with the *Camp* but now has stopped, despite evident interest in the theme and the many important extant remains (Juan Tovar,

Bermúdez, Massó and Ramón 1989). Another project focused upon the water supply in the *Camp*, specifically the aqueducts of Roman Tarraco (Cortés 1988; 1993), a theme which draws together town and country albeit from a limited perspective.

The developments of the 1990s have principally affected the town with the break-up of the organization and infrastructure that had been built up during the 1980s and the dissolution of the team which had worked steadily through a period of institutional disorder. Excavations at different sites in the *Camp* have continued, but many have been rescue projects (Parc de Port Aventura, Vallmoll, amongst others) and only a few have been designed primarily for research (Callipolis, La Llosa). Most are unpublished.

In short, there has been a great disparity between work undertaken in the town and in the country. The reason may lie in the overwhelming attraction of the town of Tarragona to traditional researchers. The town of Tarragona is not yet well known and there remain many gaps in our knowledge, but it has been studied from a range of perspectives, such as architecture (circus, amphitheatre, forum, walls etc.), epigraphy, ceramics, sculpture, numismatics etc. (see chapter 2). While much of the countryside has not suffered excessively from development in recent years, the town has not been spared and has witnessed major conflicts over conservation strategies. In the *Camp* only the occasional site, like the mausoleum at Centcelles, has been studied in detail. Other sites have been excavated, although partially and often by amateurs, during rescue campaigns or in summer seasons. Most of the publications are little more than notes. The disparity in the number of rescue excavations in town and country is striking, and the shortage of those in rural areas has impeded progress in research.

One might be tempted to think that this situation is characteristic of Catalan archaeology, but this is not the case, as can be seen from other counties. It almost seems as if the town's rôle as a provincial capital has dominated research interests to the point that its surrounding territory has been forgotten. Our understanding of a small town like Iluro (Mataró), thanks to the work by Prevosti (1981), is quite full, and has served as a springboard for future research. There have also been some territorial studies in areas adjacent to the *Camp*, such as that in the Lower Penedès (Miret, Sanmartí and Santacana 1986; Genera 1980).

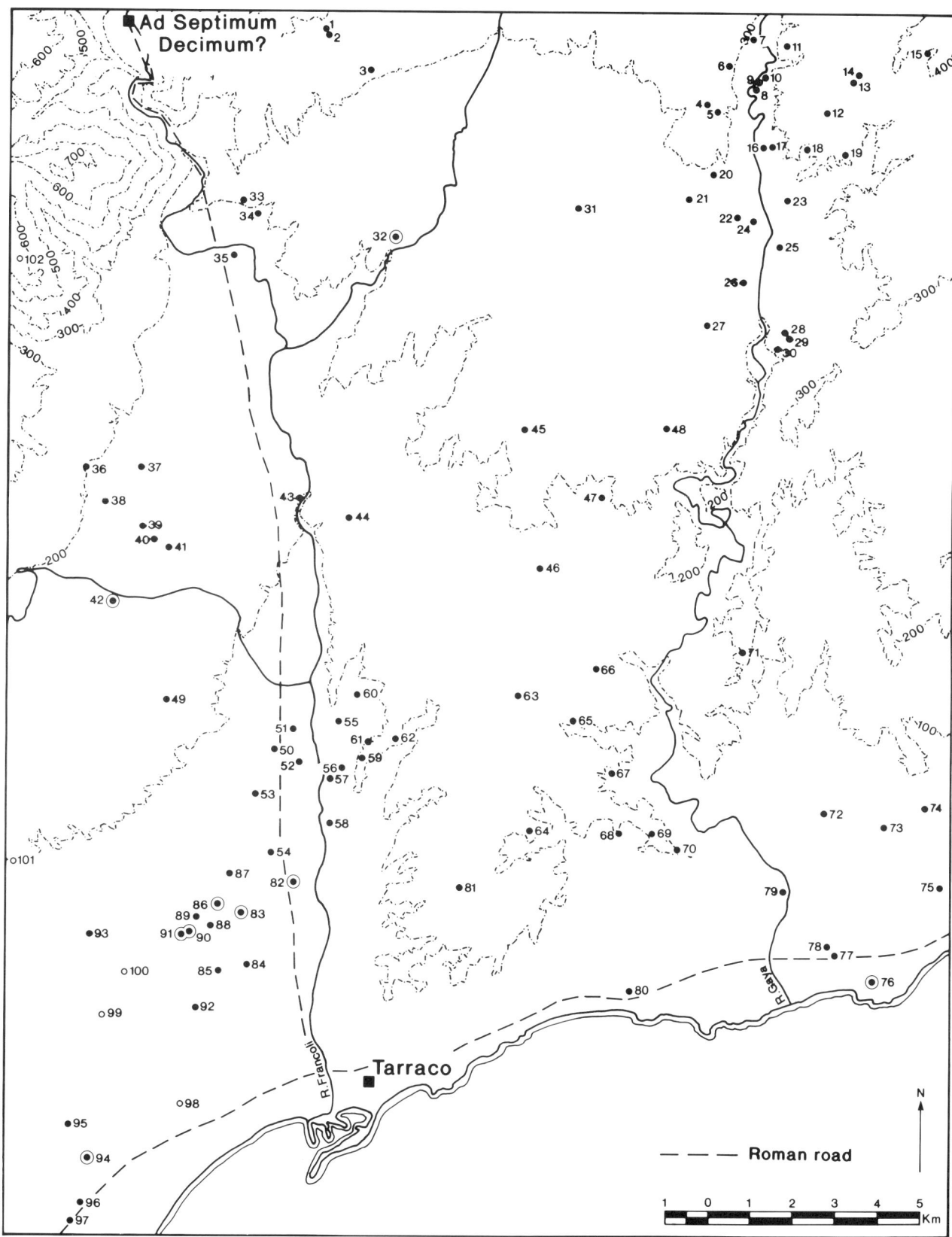

Fig.1.2. Topography of the territory of Tarraconensis showing the location of previously known sites (for a gazetteer listing the previously known sites see Table 1.1). Open circles denote sites whose precise location is uncertain; concentric circles indicate the more important sites.

Table 1.1    Settlement and cemetery sites in the survey area known prior to the survey. (see Illus.1.2)

| Map number | Description | Terme Municipal | References | Geology (Illus.3.4) | Soils (Illus.3.5) | Situation (see text) | Situation (see text) |
|---|---|---|---|---|---|---|---|
| 1 | Forn de Fontscaldes I (La Coma): pottery kilns. Iberian-Early Imperial. | Valls | Colominas Roca 1915-20, 602-05 | 3 | - | E | E |
| 2 | Forn de Fontscaldes II: pottery kilns. Roman. | Valls | | 3 | - | E | E |
| 3 | Vil.la de Fontscaldes: settlement without structures. Roman. | Valls | | 3 | - | E | E |
| 4 | Les Planes. Mas d'en Gori: settlement without structures. Republican. | Vila-rodona | Martínez 1982, 46 | 3 | - | E | E |
| 5 | Mas d'en Vives II: settlement without structures. Republican-Early Imperia | Vila-rodona | Martínez 1982, 48 | 3 | - | E | E |
| 6 | Les Planes II: settlement without structures. Roman? | Aiguamúrcia | | 6 | - | D | D |
| 7 | Mas d'en Bellot: settlement without structures. Republican. | Aiguamúrcia | | 1 | - | B | B |
| 8 | Font Cervellona: uncertain. Roman. | Vila-rodona | Vilaseca 1953, 368 | 1_6 | - | B | B |
| 9 | Font Cervellona: villa. Iberian-Early Imperial. | Vila-rodona | Martínez 1982, 10-13 | 1_6 | - | B | B |
| 10 | Els Vinyets: villa. | Vila-rodona | Martínez 1982 | 1_6 | - | B | B |
| 11 | Els Pons: settlement without structures. Republican. | Vila-rodona | Martínez 1982, 26 | 6 | - | E | E |
| 12 | Carretera de Vila-Rodona a Canferré: cemetery. Republican-Early Imperia | Vila-rodona | Martínez 1982, 38-40 | 6 | - | E | E |
| 13 | L'Alzinet: settlement without structures. Iberian-Republican. | Vila-rodona | Martínez 1982, 32-34 | 6 | - | F | F |
| 14 | Palomoses I: settlement without structures. Iberian-Republican. | Vila-rodona | Martínez 1982, 30 | 6 | - | F | F |
| 15 | Mas de Piedratita: settlement without structures. Iberian-Early Imperial. | Vila-rodona | Martínez 1982, 36-38 | 12 | - | D | D |
| 16 | Forn de la Finca del Gorí: villa and cremation cemetery. Republican. | Vila-rodona | Martínez 1982, 17 | 1 | - | B | B |
| 17 | Cal Mas: villa, columbarium and pottery production site. Early Imperial. | Vila-rodona | Martínez 1982, 15-17; Cortés et al. 1985 | 6_1 | - | B | B |
| 18 | Aubellons: settlement without structures. Iberian-Republican. | Vila-rodona | Martínez 1982, 42, 55 | 6 | - | D | D |
| 19 | Les Pinatelles: settlement without structures. Iberian-Early Imperial. | Vila-rodona | Martínez 1982, 44 | 6 | - | D | D |
| 20 | Les Planes de la Serra: inhumation cemetery. Iberian-Republican. | Vila-rodona | Martínez 1982, 50 | 5 | - | E | E |
| 21 | Planes del Porta: settlement without structures. Roman. | Vila-rodona | Martínez 1982, 52 | 5 | 4D | E | E |
| 22 | Mas del Barberet: villa. Republican-Early Imperial. | Vila-rodona | Martínez 1982, 18-20 | 5 | 3C | B | B |
| 23 | Horta Avall: settlement without structures. Republican. | Vila-rodona | Martínez 1982, 20-22 | 5 | 4D | C | C |
| 24 | La Serra: settlement without structures. Republican. | Vila-rodona | Martínez 1982, 22 | 1 | 3C | B | B |
| 25 | Vilardida: villa. Iberian to Late Imperial. | Montferri | Navarro 1969-70 | 5_1 | 4D | B | B |
| 26 | Casetes: settlement without structures. Roman. | Brafim | | 1_6 | 3C | B | B |
| 27 | El Vilà. Roman. | Brafim | Vives i Porta nd. | 5 | 4D | F | F |
| 28 | Les Hortes de Montferri: cremation cemetery. Early Imperial. | Montferri | | 5_6 | 4D | B | B |
| 29 | Mas Ravell: inhumation cemetery. Early Imperial. | Montferri | Navarro 1969-70 | 5 | 4D | F | F |
| 30 | Tervicosa: settlement without structures. Iberian. | Montferri | | 5_1 | 4D | F | F |
| 31 | Alió: settlement without structures. Republican. | Alió | | 6 | 4D | G | G |
| 32 | El Vilar: Iberian settlement. | Valls | Fabra i Salvat & Burguete i Recasens 1986 | 6 | 1A_2B | D | D |
| 33 | La Cantera: settlement without structures. Roman. | Valls | | 3 | 3C | D | D |
| 34 | Coll Roig: settlement without structures. Iberian. | Valls | Vilaseca 1968 | 3 | 3C | D | D |
| 35 | Pont de Goi: settlement without structures. Early Imperial. | Alcover | | 6 | 4D | B | B |
| 36 | Partida de Vilassec: pottery and tile kiln. Roman. | Alcover | | 3 | 4D | E | E |
| 37 | El Degotall: settlement without structures. Iberian-Republican. | Alcover | Barbara i Camafort 1982 | 3 | 2B | D | D |
| 38 | Mas d'en Burguet: funerary monument. Roman. | Alcover | Vidal i Rosich 1897 | 3 | 4D | E | E |
| 39 | El Cogoll II: funerary monument. Roman. | Alcover | Vidal i Rosich 1897; Puig i Cadafalch 1931 | 3 | 4D | E | E |
| 40 | El Cogoll I: villa. Early - Late Imperial. | Vilallonga del Camp | Dupré & Julia 1984 | 3 | 2B | E | E |

Table 1.1    Settlement and cemetery sites in the survey area known prior to the survey. (see Illus.1.2)

| Map number | Description | Terme Municipal | References | Geology (Illus.3.4) | Soils (Illus.3.5) | Situation (see text) | Situation (see text) |
|---|---|---|---|---|---|---|---|
| 41 | El Cogoll: funerary monument. Roman. | Vilallonga del Camp | Puig i Cadafalch 1931 | 3 | 2B | E | E |
| 42 | Parets Delgada: villa. Late Imperial. | La Selva del Camp | Guitart 1936; Gorges 1979, T.44 | 3 | 2B | B | B |
| 43 | Ribera del Francolí: settlement with structures. Roman. | La Masó | | 1 | 1A | B | B |
| 44 | Els Garrafols: settlement with structures. Iberian. | Vallmoll | Vilaseca 1968 | 6_5 | 4D | G | G |
| 45 | Camí de Valls: uncertain. Roman. | Nulles | | 5_6 | 4D | E | E |
| 46 | Les Domenges: villa. Iberian-Roman. | Renau | | 5 | 4D | D | D |
| 47 | Les Cabeses: villa and burials. Roman. | Vilabella | | 5_6 | 4D | F | F |
| 48 | Vilabella: settlement without structures. Roman. | Vilabella | | 7 | 4D | G | G |
| 49 | Mas Vallets: villa. | Pobla de Mafumet | | 2 | 3C | E | E |
| 50 | Mas Sardà: cemetery. Roman. | Pobla de Mafumet | | 2_1 | - | B | B |
| 51 | Repsol Químiques: villa. | Pobla de Mafumet | | 1 | - | B | B |
| 52 | Mas Sardà: villa. | Pobla de Mafumet | | 1 | - | B | B |
| 53 | Mas Blanc I: settlement. | Pobla de Mafumet | | 2 | - | B | B |
| 54 | Los Argilos: settlement. Iberian. | Constantí | | 2 | 3C | G | G |
| 55 | Les Vinyes Grans: villa. | Perafort | | 6 | 4D | D | D |
| 56 | Pont de Codony: villa. Iberian | Perafort | | 5 | 4D | C | C |
| 57 | Mas Blanquet: settlement. Iberian-Roman. | Perafort | | 5 | - | B | B |
| 58 | Pont del Tupí/Mas Garrut: villa. | Perafort | | 5_1 | 4D | B | B |
| 59 | Les Comes: settlement. Iberian-Republican. | Perafort | | 7 | 4D | G | G |
| 60 | Els Vinyers: settlement. Iberian. | Perafort | | 5 | 4D | G | G |
| 61 | La Barquera: villa. | Perafort | | 5_7 | 4D | D | D |
| 62 | Sitges de Perafort: villa. | Perafort | | 5_7 | 4D | D | D |
| 63 | Sitja de la Carretera: settlement. Iberian. | El Catllar | | 7 | 4D | F | F |
| 64 | La Quadra de Vilet: villa. | El Catllar | | 7_5 | - | F | F |
| 65 | Mas d'en Bevenat: villa. Iberian-Roman. | El Catllar | | 7_5 | 4D | D | D |
| 66 | Mas Moragues: villa | El Catllar | | 7 | 4D | C | C |
| 67 | Mas d'en Ros: villa | El Catllar | | 7_5 | 4D | C | C |
| 68 | Els Cocons: villa. | El Catllar | | 7 | - | D | D |
| 69 | Del Costat del Camp de Ter: settlement. Iberian. | El Catllar | | 7_9 | - | C | C |
| 70 | Els Pedregalets: villa. | Riera de Gaia | | 7 | - | G | G |
| 71 | Corral del Maginet: settlement. Iberian. | Vespella de Gaia | | 7 | - | D | D |
| 72 | La Nou de Gaia: villa and cemetery. | La Nou de Gaia | | 7 | 4D | C | C |
| 73 | Coll de Creus: Iberian settlement, Roman villa and cemetery | Pobla de Montornès | | 7_5 | 4D | F | F |
| 74 | Turó de l'Ermita de Montornès: settlement. Iberian. | Pobla de Montornès | | 7_5 | 4D | G | G |
| 75 | El Moro/Els Antigons: villa. Republican - Early Imperial. | Torredembarra | Terré 1987; Gorges 1979, T.54 | 5 | - | E | E |
| 76 | Els Munts: large villa. Early - Late Imperial. | Altafulla | Berges 1977; Gorges 1979, T.03 | 7 | - | F | F |
| 77 | Costat del Poble: villa. | Altafulla | | 7 | - | G | G |
| 78 | Altafulla església: villa. | Altafulla | Gorges 1979, T.04 | 7 | - | G | G |
| 79 | Fàbrica d'Alabastres: villa. Imperial. | Riera de Gaia | | 1_10 | 2B | B | B |
| 80 | Torre dels Escipions: funerary monument. Early Imperial. | Tarragona | Hauschild, Mariner & Niemeyer 1966 | 5 | - | G | G |

Table 1.1     Settlement and cemetery sites in the survey area known prior to the survey. (see Illus.1.2)

| Map number | Description | Terme Municipal | References | Geology (Illus.3.4) | Soils (Illus.3.5) | Situation (see text) | Situation (see text) |
|---|---|---|---|---|---|---|---|
| 81 | Manous: settlement. Iberian | Altafulla | Hauschild & Arbeiter 1993 | 7_5 | - | G | G |
| 82 | Centcelles: large villa. Republican-Late Imperial. | Constantí | Hauschild & Schlunk 1986; Gorges 1979, T.18 | 1 | 2B_3C | B | B |
| 83 | Sant Pol: villa. Late Imperial. | Constantí | Papiol 1973-74, 256; Gorges 1979, T.27 | 2 | - | E | E |
| 84 | Rivdarenas I: villa. Early - Late Imperial. | Constantí | Papiol 1973-74, 253; Gorges 1979, T.22 | 2_4 | - | D | D |
| 85 | Les Gavarres I: settlement. Iberian. | Constantí | Papiol 1973-74, 253-54; Gorges 1979, T.24 | 2 | - | F | F |
| 86 | La Creu de Salom/Mas de Serapi: villa. Republican-Late Imperial | Constantí | Papiol 1973-74, 251-52; Gorges 1979, T.20 | 2 | 4D | D | D |
| 87 | Mas d'en Bosc: settlement. Roman. | Constantí | Papiol 1973-74, 251; Gorges 1979, T.19 | 2_6 | 3C | C | C |
| 88 | Camí d'Almoster a Tarragona/Riudarenas II: villa. | Constantí | Papiol 1973-74 | 2 | 4D | A | A |
| 89 | Mas dels Frares/d'en Solé Bas: villa. | Constantí | Papiol 1973-74, 253; Gorges 1979, T.23 | 2 | 4D | A | A |
| 90 | Ermita de Sant Llorenç: villa. Republican - Early Imperial. | Constantí | Papiol 1973-74, 252-53; Gorges 1979, T.21 | 2 | 4D | E | E |
| 91 | Sant Llorenç: villa. Late Republican-Early Imperial. | Constantí | Papiol 1973-74, 252-53; Gorges 1979, T.21 | 2 | 4D | E | E |
| 92 | Les Gavarres II: settlement. Iberian - Early Imperial. | Constantí | Papiol 1973-74, 253-55; Gorges 1979, T25 | 2_4 | 4D | C | C |
| 93 | La Boella: villa. Roman. | Reus | Massó 1978, 32 | 3 | 4D | E | E |
| 94 | Cal.lipolis (La Pineda): villa | Vila-seca | Gorges 1979, T53 | 2 | - | E | E |
| 95 | Villa dels Aragalls: villa | Vila-seca | | 2 | - | E | E |
| 96 | Muebles Aterco. Iberian-Roman | Vila-seca | | 2 | - | E | E |
| 97 | Corral del Baló: settlement. Iberian-Roman | Tarragona | AIEC 5, (1913-14), 865ff.; MMAP 3 (1942), 195 | 8 | - | F | F |
| 98 | Fincasa Rafael: cemetery. Late Imperial | Reus | | 2_4 | - | E | E |
| 99 | Mas Pujols: settlement. Iberian-Roman | Reus | | 2_3 | 4D | E | E |
| 100 | Els Antigons: villa, amphora kiln & cemetery. Republican-Early Imperial | Reus | Massó 1978, 31; Gorges 1979, T.35 | 2_3 | 4D | E | E |
| 101 | Les Grasses: settlement. Roman. | Reus | Massó 1978, 31; Gorges 1979, T.37 | 3 | 2B | E | E |
| 102 | La Lloera | Alcover | Massó 1987, 37-56 | 12 | - | G | G |

PREVIOUSLY KNOWN SITES IN THE AREA

The sites known in the area prior to the present survey are listed in Table 1.1 and mapped on fig. 1.2. The listing draws on the *Cartes Arqueològiques* which are held in the Sevei d'Arqueologia of the Generalitat de Catalunya in Barcelona; they are the source of the information where no other reference is given. Further details of certain of the better known or more important sites are provided below. For convenience they are listed in the same order as they appear in the gazetteer (Table 1.1).

*El Vilar or Valls Railway Station (Valls). Gazetteer no. 32*

An important Iberian site covering an area of about 400 by 350 m in the vicinity of the Railway station (Valls-Vilanova) on a small rise some 230 m above sea-level and beside the valley of the Barranco Seco (fig. 1.3). Virtually nothing is known about its internal organization or chronological development, except that it imported high-status Attic red-figure pottery, black glaze pottery from the kilns at Rhode (Roses), Punic Maña D amphorae, Iberian painted fine-wares, as well as coarse-wares, metalwork, loom-weights and rotary kilns. They suggest a chronology between the 4th and 2nd c. B.C.

References: Fabra i Salvat and Burguete i Recasens 1983; 1986; Arbeloa 1990a.

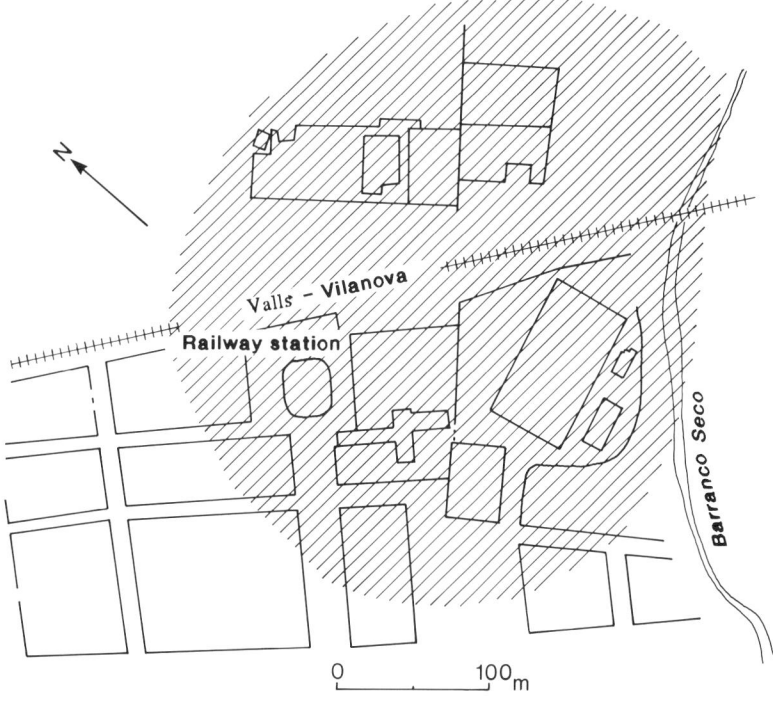

Fig.1.3. Plan of the Iberian site of El Vilar (Valls).

*El Cogoll (Alcover). Gazetteer nos. 39-41*

An important site best known for its two square funerary towers (fig. 1.4B). Built from concrete and covered with a limestone veneer they evidently belonged to a substantial villa, of early imperial date, which is largely unknown. However, it is possible that Dressel 2-4 wine amphorae were manufactured at kilns discovered close by. Recent excavations in the immediate vicinity have uncovered a building (17 by 5.8 m) of basilical plan (fig. 1.4A). The form of the apse suggests that it may have been a church attached to a late-Roman villa. It may reuse an earlier bath-building. A number of late-Roman tile and slab burials have been located in the vicinity.

References: Massó 1987; Puig y Cadafalch 1931; Dupré and Julià 1984.

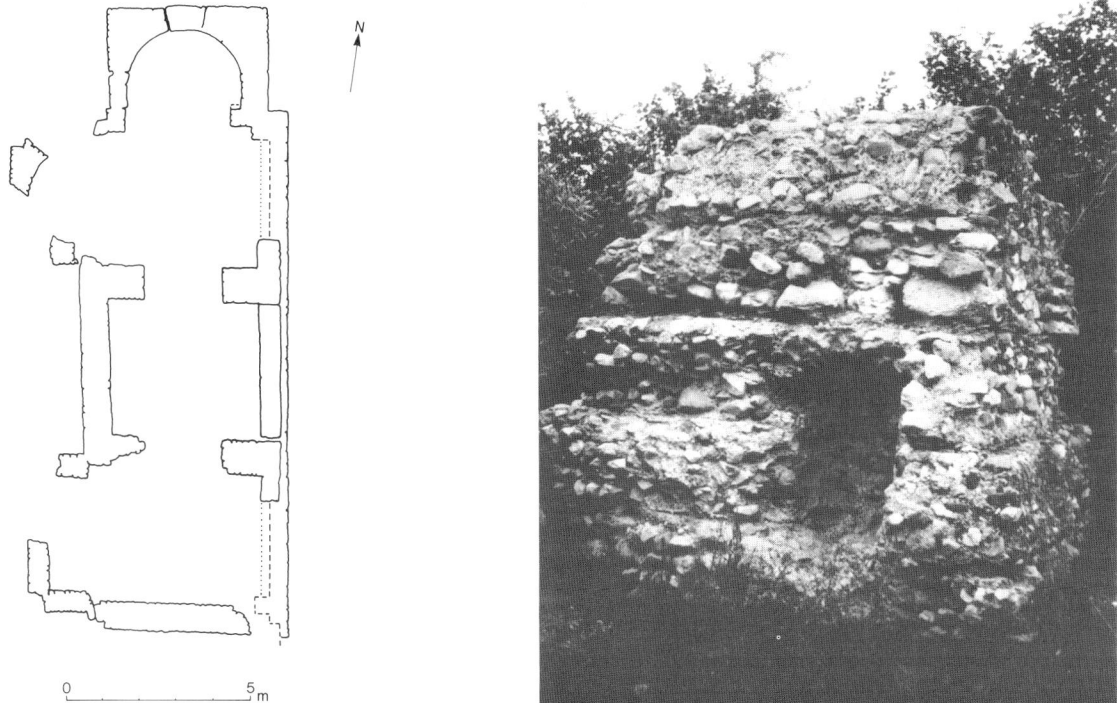

Fig.1.4A. Plan of excavated basilica #40 at El Cogoll (Alcover)   Fig.1.4B. The funerary monument (#41).

*Parets Delgada(La Selva del Camp). Gazetteer no. 42*

Situated on the banks of a small tributary of the river Francolí. Excavations in 1935 uncovered part of a luxurious peristyle villa adjacent to the Ermita, comprising 8 rooms with mosaic floors adjacent to a long passage (fig. 1.5). The site is best known for its mosaics, dated to the 3rd c.; they are mostly polychrome with floral and geometric motifs. Fragments of marble sculptures and column capitals have also been found. Nothing is known about the chronological development of the site.

References: Guitart 1936; Gorges 1979, 417-18 (T.44)

*El Moro (Torredembarra). Gazetteer no. 75*

Covers an area of *c*.600m² by the side of the Barranc of Subanolas, not far from the line of the Via Augusta, to the east of Tarragona. Work at this site (1984) is unfinished. There is only a partial picture of what was undoubtedly a complex building. A *sondage* towards the centre of the site revealed an early phase in the late 2nd/early 1st c. B.C., in which a Tuscan-style column capital was reused in construction: the first Roman phase may have begun earlier. To this same Republican phase belong *opus signinum* floors with white marble tessera decoration. This suggests that a Roman-style residential building was attatched to a farm by the late 2nd c. B.C. This part of the site underwent a change in the Augustan period. At roughly the same time in another part of the site small baths (fig. 1.6) with concrete vaults and a white mosaic floor were constructed. The site as a whole seems to have been abandoned towards the end of the 1st and beginning of the 2nd c. A.D.

Reference: Terré 1987

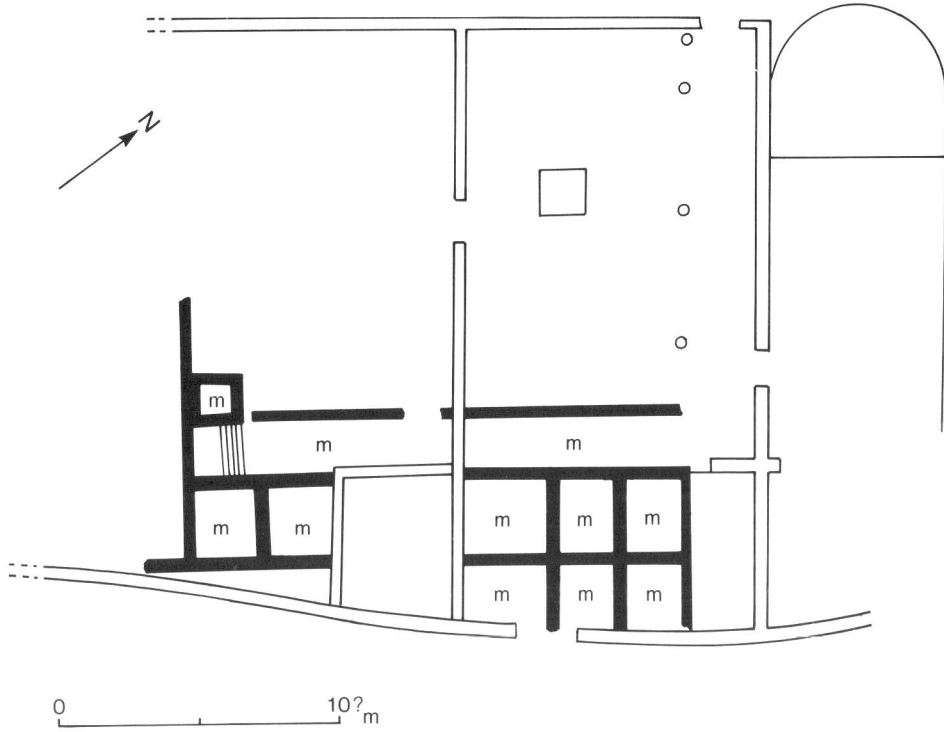

Fig.1.5. Plan of the excavated villa at Parets Delgada (La Selva del Camp) #42 (m = mosaic).

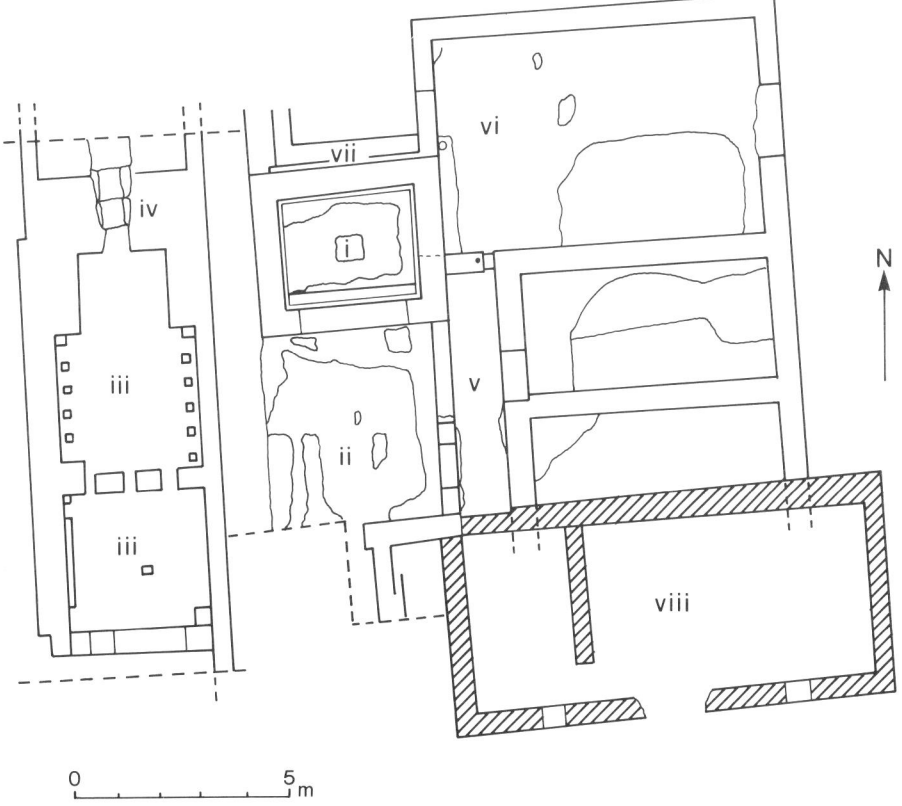

Fig.1.6. Plan of the excavated early imperial bath-buildings at the villa of El Moro (Torredembarra) #75.

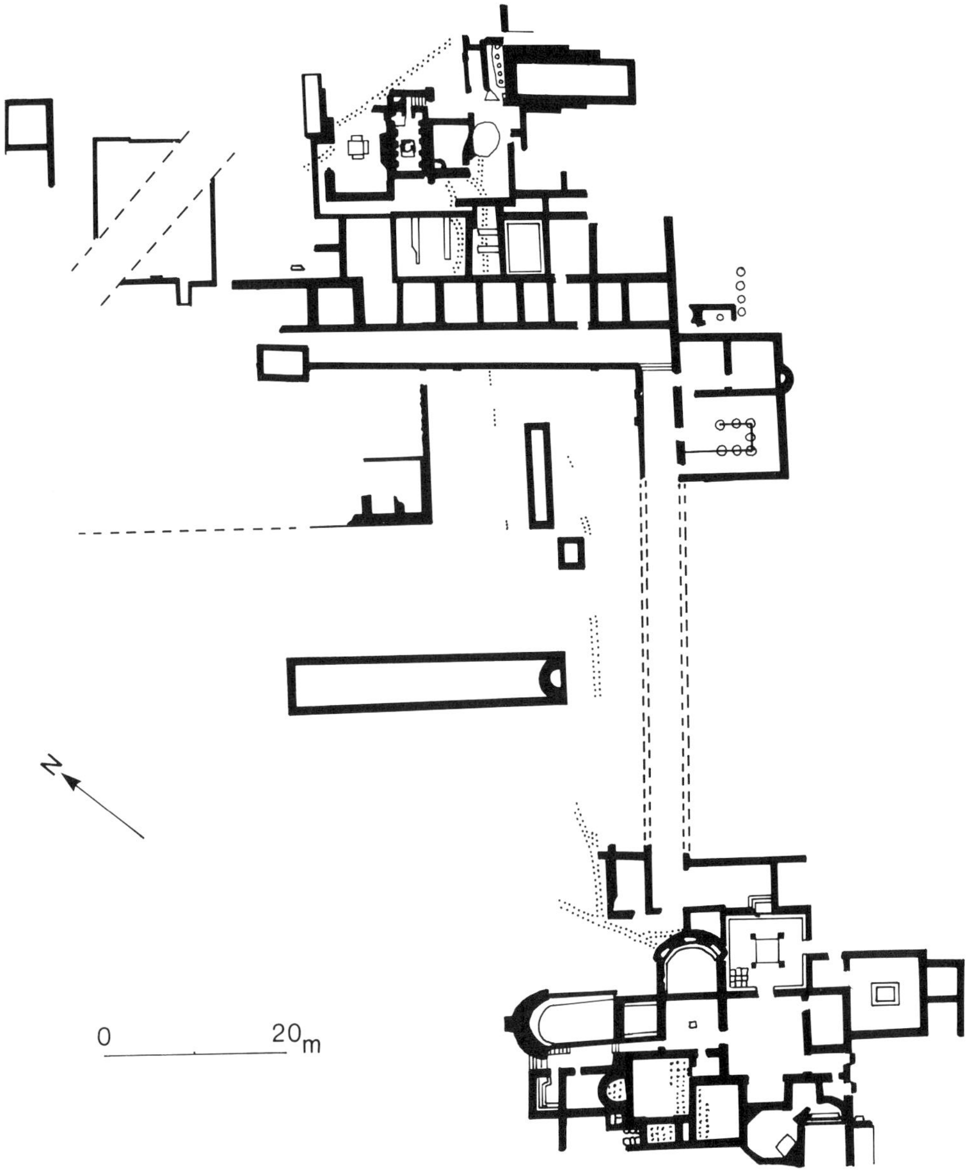

# Chapter 1

Fig.1.7A. Plan of the excavated villa of Els Munts (Altafulla) #76.

Fig.1.7B. Central part of the villa of Els Munts #76 from NW.

*Els Munts* *(Altafulla). Gazetteer no. 76*

Lies on a small knoll overlooking the sea some 12 km NE of Tarragona. The existence of this villa has been known since the 16th c. and intermittent archaeological work was done in the 1960s, 1970s and 1980s but most remains unpublished and the history of the site is difficult to unravel. It appears that it was founded in the 1st c. A.D. and remained occupied until the 6th or 7th c. That part of the central area of the villa which has been excavated covers some 127 by 110 m (figs. 1.7A-B). Further structures and a quarry exist in the vicinity. The *villa urbana* comprises a residential area with gallery, adjacent rooms, and baths at the E end. The *villa urbana* is linked by a corridor to a major bath to the south-west, closer to the sea. Polychrome mosaics have been found throughout the *villa urbana*, both figured and geometric, and have been dated to the first half of the 3rd c. A number of marble sculptures and architectural fragments cover a broad chronological span, attesting to the wealth and importance of the site. During the late empire the site seems to have been particularly important. A third set of baths was found down by the sea. Little is known about the *villa rustica*, although cisterns have been found on the N part of the hill and there are other installations in the vicinity of the residential area.

References: Berges 1969-70; 1970; 1977; Gorges 1979, 407-8 (T.03)

*Centcelles* *(Constantí). Gazetteer no. 82*

A multi-period rural site on the first terrace of the river Francolí a few kilometres to the east of Constantí and undoubtedly close to the Roman road from Tarraco to Ilerda. The site has been known since the 16th c. but was the object of archaeological study only in the late 1950s (fig. 1.8). Five periods of occupation have been distinguished. Little is known of the Republican phase (2nd-1st c. B.C.). However between the 1st and 3rd c. A.D. a large working farm *c.* 80 by 30 m was built, comprising a small residential area and a large enclosure for the storage of agricultural products in *dolia*. In the 3rd c. a new agricultural building was constructed, straddling the W wall of the earlier enclosure. The site was completely replanned (90 m long) towards the middle of the 4th c. Only the N end of the site is well known. Here the new building was aligned E-W and cut across the earlier site. In an initial phase it comprised two domed chambers and a bath suite. Before this was completed, however, the project was modified, one of the domed chambers being converted into a mausoleum and the baths being altered. It is one of the most important late Roman and early Christian monuments in Iberia, known mainly for the rich figured mosaics of the dome and its wall-paintings.

References: Schlunk and Hauschild 1962; Schlunk 1988; Arbeiter and Korol 1988-89; Gorges 1979, 411-12 (T.18)

*Els Antigons* *(Reus). Gazetteer no. 100*

A poorly understood site lying 6 km E of Tarragona. There is a range of walls and *opus spicatum* floors, and reports of drains. Two kilns for the manufacture of Dressel 2-4 wine amphorae were discovered. There is no evidence for mosaics, although marble sculptures are known. It seems to have been occupied between the 1st and 5th c. A.D.

References: Massó 1978; Miró 1988; Gorges 1979, 416 (T.35)

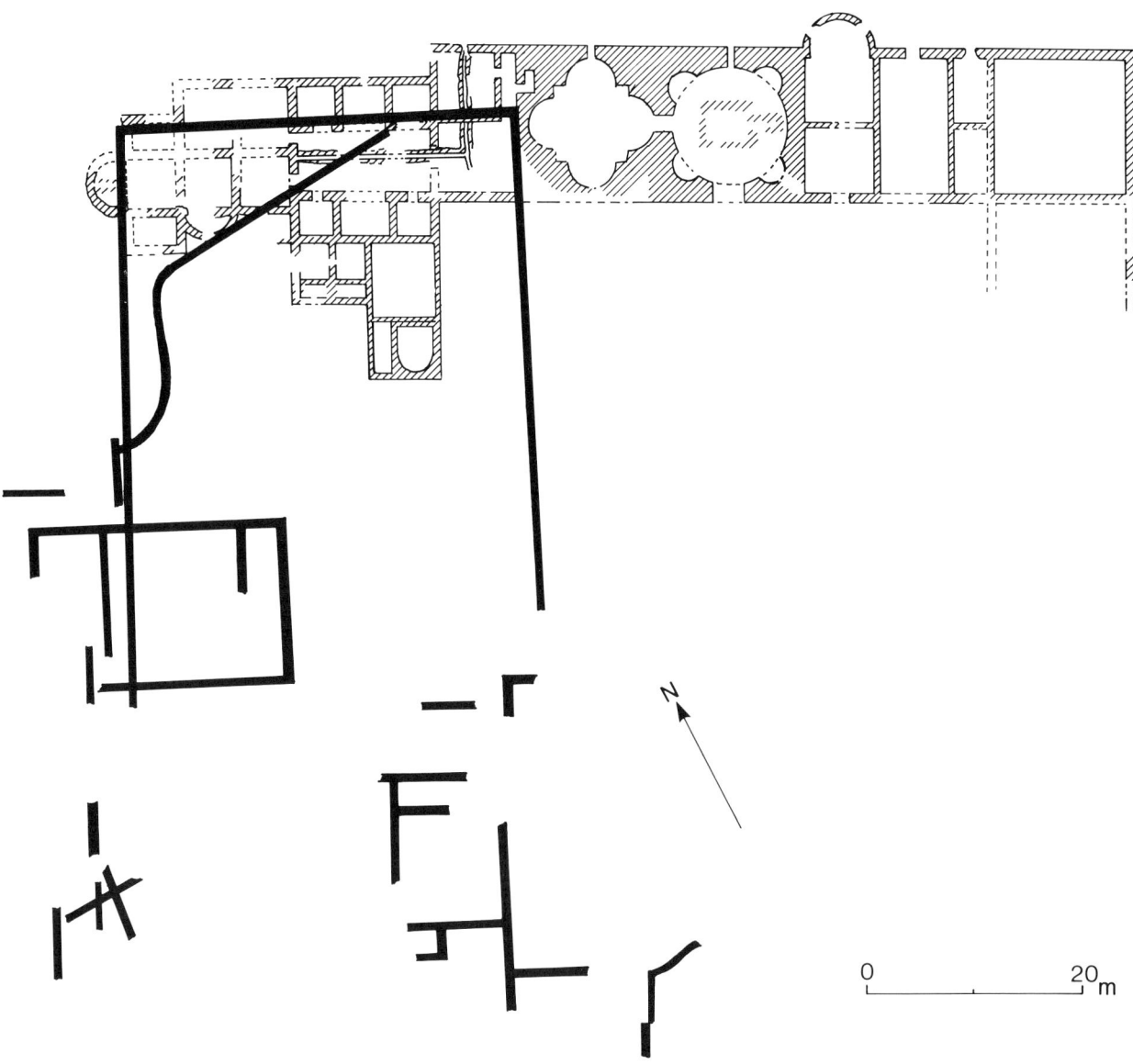

Fig.1.8. Plan of the excavated features at Centcelles (Constantí) #82. Features in black are from the pre-4th c. phase; shaded features are of the 4th-c. reconstruction.

# Chapter 2: TARRACO AND ITS TERRITORY IN ANTIQUITY

## INTRODUCTION

In the first three centuries A.D. Tarraco was one of the leading towns in the western Mediterranean and capital of the largest province in the western empire. The previous chapter has shown that, although our understanding of Tarraco has advanced in recent years, it has been studied for the most part in isolation from its surrounding territory. Also, Roman rural settlement has been of marginal interest to archaeologists working in the area. This has created an imbalance of knowledge which fails to promote an understanding of the symbiosis now generally understood to have characterized town and country in the Roman world. It is precisely this imbalance which the survey has sought to redress.

This chapter attempts to provide a synthesis of the available archaeological evidence for Tarraco and its territory in antiquity. It considers the broader archaeological context of the survey and especially those problems which are susceptible to analysis through systematic survey.

Recent research in Iberia has underlined the importance of the long-term perspective when examining social, economic and cultural change during the Roman period. Consequently the boundaries of this synthesis are not limited to the period from 218 B.C. to A.D. 475/76; they extend back to the genesis of the Iberian peoples whose settlement patterns were to be influenced by the foundation of Tarraco, and they conclude with the Arab invasions of 716.

## PREHISTORIC BACKGROUND

The increasing social complexity and other changes which characterize the Bronze Age in this part of Iberia were in large measure the result of ensuring access to metal resources and of the development of technology for the manufacture of bronze. For much of the period (1800-700 B.C.), communities inhabited caves and shelters, such as at Cova Josefina (Escornalbou) in the Baix Camp. Analogy with the region around Lleida to the east suggests that towards the middle Bronze Age small proto-urban communities may have begun to develop in the low-lying lands of the Francolí and Gaià valleys. They would have been small hamlets of some 20 houses articulated by a central street (Rovira and Santacana 1982, 99-102). The chance discovery of lowland sites dating to this period, as at El Quart (Reus) near Reus airport (Massó 1978, 15), suggests that small settlements of this kind are still to be found.

In the course of the first millennium B.C. the inhabitants of the region came into contact with new customs and iron technology. Between c.1100 and c.659 Urnfield cemeteries made their appearance in this region, as in other regions in NE Spain, the lower and middle Ebro valley, and the Valencian region to the south (Almagro Gorbea and Ruíz Zapatero 1993, 501-7). These Late Bronze Age cemeteries exhibit an abrupt change in burial custom, the bodies of the deceased being burnt and the ashes placed in characteristic urns. Traditionally the advent of the Urnfields has been linked to waves of migrating peoples whose more distant cultural origins were thought to lie in central Europe but who enjoyed close cultural links with southern France, northern Italy and possibly central Europe (for example, Savory 1968). Along the lower and middle Ebro the Urnfield 'populations' are understood to have formed the cultural substratum of the 'Celtic' populations later mentioned by classical sources. Recent opinion has been more careful in its interpretation of the archaeological evidence and its relationship to the historical sources (Ruíz Zapatero 1985). The earliest Urnfields in the Tarragona region date to around 1100 and little is known about associated habitation sites apart from storage pits or caves. The appearance of the Urnfields is usually associated with an intensification of agriculture (Almagro Gorbea 1986a, 385-93). How far this may have been true for the communities in our study-area is impossible to say. Ceramics of this period are rarely reported and the lack of survey makes any attempt at precision impossible.

For the uplands at least, the picture changes with the more recent Urnfields of the earlier first millennium B.C. The conventional hypothesis is that growing population pressure gave rise to the emergence of small, stable nucleated settlements, like those at El Mola (Tivissa) (Vilaseca 1943) and La Mussara (Baix Camp) (Rovira and Santacana 1982). These walled enclosures (c.50 by 100 m) with small stone and mudbrick houses lay in the uplands to the west of the study area. They were the focus of scattered communities with a long tradition of transhumance. Their economies were largely pastoral (Rovira and Santacana 1982, 91-102) although arable agriculture had begun to play an important part. In this sense sites like La Mussara represent the gradual process of upland communities becoming more sedentary. Some upland sites continued in occupation into the Iberian period, as the discovery of Late Bronze Age material (750-600) in the lowest levels of the settlement of Coll Alt (Tivissa) (Sanmartí and Padrò 1976-78) indicates.

## THE IBERIAN PERIOD

Towards the end of this period the region came under the influence of overseas colonists, essentially the Greeks, which gradually led to its 'Iberization' — the formation of the Iberian peoples known to us from the historical sources in the 6th c. (Sanmartí and Padrò 1976-78). In cultural terms this brought the more general use of iron, the manufacture of wheel-turned pottery, the emergence of nucleated 'urban' settlements, and the development of the Iberian script. In social terms, the Iberian peoples of NE Spain could perhaps be considered complex-chiefdoms (cf. Collis 1984, 19 ff.) particularly in the period immediately prior to the Roman conquest in the late 3rd c. The relevance of this model for southern Catalunya has been borne out by research in the Terra Alta region S of the Ebro (Arteaga, Padrò and Sanmartí 1990, 155 ff.); it has been suggested that there was a hierarchical system of defended hill-top settlements which focused upon a 'central' settlement at Sant Antoni de Calaceit.

Recent research suggests that the first contacts between the peoples of the region and foreign colonizing groups may have been with the Phoenicians as they attempted to develop trading posts along the lower Ebro valley (Sanmartí and Padrò 1976-78, 161-62). The first phase of sustained cultural change, however, followed the foundation of the Greek colony at Emporion (Empúries) at the end of the 6th c. It has been suggested that the consequent boost to commercial activity in NE Iberia may have precipitated the growth of urban settlements further north, like the Illa d'En Reixach (Girona) and the Penya del Moro (Barcelona), but it seemed to evoke no response in the region between the Llobregat and the Ebro until the late 6th c. onwards, with the foundation of the Iberian settlements at the Puig de la Nau (Benicarlo, Castelló), Alorda Park (Calafell: Sanmartí and Santacana 1992) and the Moleta del Remei (Alcanar-Montsia: Grácia, Munilla and Pallarès 1988) and the penetration of Greek pottery to the interior through such sites as Coll de Moro (Rafel and Blasco 1994). Recent research has suggested that in this early stage of 'Iberization' the region of southern Catalunya was culturally homogeneous and may perhaps be identified with a single historically-attested people, the Ilaraugates, who are to be distinguished from their northern neighbours the Misgetes (Padrò and Sanmartí 1993).

During the 5th c. the region saw increasing cultural complexity and the spread of nucleated Iberian settlements. They are situated on hilltops or low prominences in lowland areas, and are classed as urban by many archaeologists. The lack of survey and excavation in the region of Tarragona means that little is known about subsequent cultural development during the 4th and earlier 3rd c. At this time settlements elsewhere in S and E Spain were destroyed while others were refounded. This may be symptomatic of the 'crisis' which is understood to have affected many parts of the Iberian world at the end of the 4th c. (Ruiz and Molinos 1992, 271-75). It has been suggested that it came about as a result of the establishment of the Hispano-Carthaginian treaty of 348 (Polyb. 3.1.24) and a subsequent interruption of the high-status black-glaze Greek pottery, which had played a crucial rôle in the prestige-goods economies of the Iberian settlements (Rouillard 1991, 114-86). Although the evidence is thin, there are some grounds for suggesting that the Tarragona region may have undergone significant change at this time. Few sites have been excavated sufficiently to provide any reliable information even though some of them, like Tarragona and El Vilar (Valls), are known to have been importing Greek pottery. However, excavations at La Moleta del Remei (Alcanar-Montsia) suggest that that site was abandoned at this time (Grácia, Munilla and Pallarès 1988). Moreover, survey work further north in the lower Penedès suggests that the smaller sites so typical of the Iberian landscape did not appear until the 4th c. (Sanmartí, Santacana and Serra 1984, 7-10).

By the 3rd c. the people of the Ilauaragates may have been fragmented into smaller regional peoples whose names have not survived (Padrò and Sanmartí 1993). It is only by the late 3rd-early 2nd c. that the classical authors speak of the Cossetani/Cessetani, Ilergaones and Ilergetes.

The settlement pattern of the Tarragona region is imperfectly known owing to the lack of systematic survey. As is true for later periods, settlement may have been quite dense. There is good reason to think that there was a hierarchical settlement pattern appropriate to a complex chiefdom in this low-lying region, similar to that in the upland area of the Terra Alta. This stands in contrast to the better-known regions further north. It is borne out to some degree by what we know of the settlement pattern in the region of the Baix Penedès to the NE of our study area (Sanmartí and Santacana 1987) where there seem to be two classes of settlement. On the one hand there are the more numerous smaller sites, known mostly from the discovery of occasional scatters of pottery on low-lying land or on knolls. One example at L'Argilera (Calafell), dating to the 4th c., was located on a small elevation close to fertile agricultural land (Sanmartí, Santacana and Serra 1984). It was interpreted as a small grain storage site probably lying close to a small habitation site of some kind (Sanmartí, Santacana and Serra 1984, 7-10). The other class of site, located on low hills, like Alorda Park (Calafell: J. Sanmartí and Santacana 1992), is less common.

In the study area, several larger-scale settlements are known, such as those at El Vilar (Valls: Fabra i Salvat and Burguete i Recasens 1986), Santa Ana de Castellvell (Baix Camp) (Ramón and Massó 1994) and Tarragona (Miró 1988; Adserias et al. 1994) in the low-lying lands of what would be the territory of Tarraco, El Castellet de Banyoles (Tivissa) in the uplands overlooking the Ebro to the west, and Alorda Park (Calafell: Sanmartí and Santacana 1992) and Adarrò (Vilanova i Geltrù: López and Fierro 1988) in coastal areas further north. Little is known about their layout. All were relatively small and seem to have comprised a loose arrangement of rectangular houses and streets. Only El Castellet de Banyoles was defended. Located on a promontory overlooking the Ebro it was cut-off from the mainland by substantial defences with diamond-shaped bastions (Serra Ràfols 1941). Recent excavations have begun to show that the most important settlement in the region was probably that lying below the lower town of Tarragona (Miró 1988; Adserias et al. 1994), in the shadow of the large rocky bluff now dominated by the standing buildings of mediaeval Tarragona (fig. 2.1 and 2.2). The site occupies a key position on the Mediterranean coast at the mouth of the river Francolí and would have acted as a place for exchange between foreign traders and the peoples of the hinterland. Its earliest occupation dates to the 5th c. It would become the heart of the lower town of early imperial Tarraco. Possibly it should be identified with Cissis mentioned by Livy (21.60) in connection with events in 218. Little is known about its internal layout. In terms of material culture, all communities used the characteristic plain and (more rarely) wheel-turned painted Iberian finewares together with the bag-shaped Iberian amphorae. Hand-thrown coarse-wares are rarer while imported Attic black- and red-figure pottery and occasional Massiliote wine amphorae appear at the larger sites (listed in Rouillard 1991).

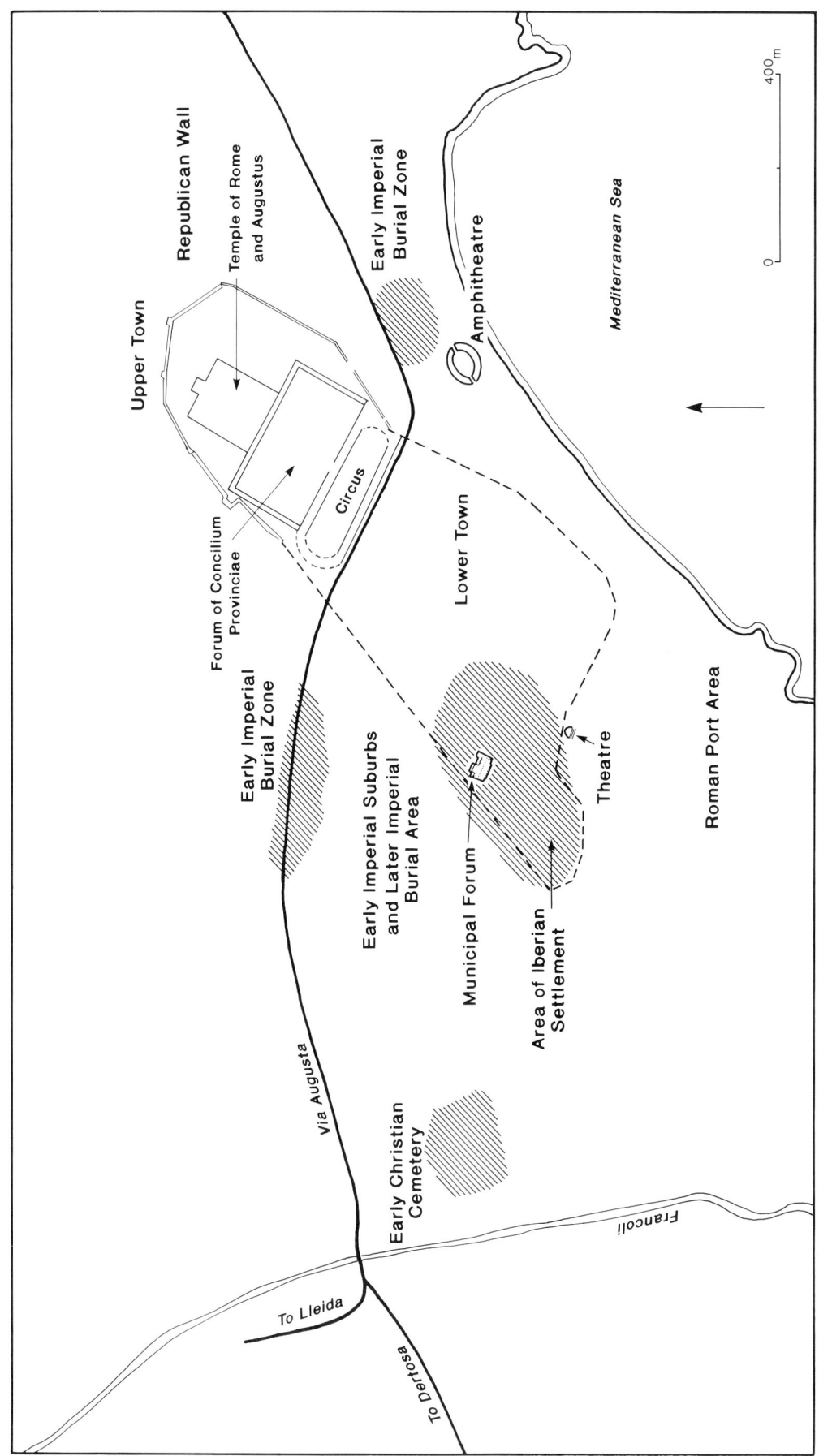

Fig.2.1. Plan showing the principal known features of Tarraco.

THE ROMAN PERIOD

*The Republic*

There is little doubt that the arrival of Rome represented a watershed in the region's cultural development. The Romans arrived in 218 during the opening stages of the Second Punic War against Carthage. In that year Cnaeus Cornelius Scipio disembarked at Emporion (Empúries) in the first stages of Rome's counter-strike against Carthaginian interests in Iberia. He marched south towards the Ebro with two legions, Roman citizen cavalry, 14,000 allied infantry, and 1600 allied cavalry. After initially defeating the Carthaginian general Hanno in a battle near the Ebro and taking the town of Cissis (Tarragona?), the Romans suffered a defeat at the hands of another Carthaginian general, Hasdrubal, who had made a rapid strike to the N side of the Ebro (Livy 21.60-61 with commentary in Richardson 1986, 35-42). Scipio left a garrison at Tarraco and after 209 the settlement played a key rôle in Rome's war against those Iberian peoples allied to Carthage (J. Martínez 1982-83, 79 ff.).

In the course of the later 3rd, 2nd and 1st c. B.C. the effect of the Roman presence at Tarraco was to enhance its importance locally and throughout the peninsula. The topography of the town was transformed. The cyclopean and ashlar walls which still crown three sides of the upper town (fig. 2.1) were initially constructed by Rome towards the end of the 3rd or beginning of the 2nd c. (Hauschild 1988; Aquilué, Dupré, Massó and Ruiz de Arbulo 1991) as a bridgehead for the control of Roman territory to the north of the Ebro in her struggle with Carthage. The importance of the town may be illustrated by a range of silver and bronze coins bearing the Iberian name KESSE referring to the political centre of the Cessetani, probably to be identified with Tarraco (Villaronga 1983). There is consensus that they were issued at Rome's behest although opinions vary as to when they were first minted. The two possibilities are the late 3rd (bronze)/early 2nd c. (silver) (Villaronga 1983), or some in the first half of the 2nd c., possibly even as late as the 150s (both metals) (Crawford 1985, 84-102).

As Tarraco (Pliny, *NH* 3.4), Tarragona assumed a pre-eminent rôle in the development of Roman military policy in the province of Hispania Citerior. It was pivotal to Roman strategy during the war with Carthage (218-205) and the two revolts against Roman control (206 and 197-95). The location of the town on the Mediterranean coast and a short distance N of the Ebro ensured that it was a major supply base and winter-quarters for the Roman legions and Italic allies during the early wars in Celtiberia in 180 (Livy 40.39.3) and probably during the later Celtiberian Wars of 155-33. It is probable that the troops were bivouacked in the fortified area of the upper town, while the Iberian settlement in the lower town became the focus for the growing Roman community. In the later 2nd c. the wall was extended and both parts of the settlement may have been united into a single community (Aquilué and Dupré 1986). Little is known about the interior of the town at this date (Ruiz de Arbulo 1990) although it has been suggested that there may have been a forum in the lower town by the first half of the 1st c. B.C. (Dupré forthcoming 1995). However, it should not be forgotten that, like Carthago Nova to the south, Tarraco was an important economic centre. In the first instance it would have acted as a major supply base for Roman troops in Hispania Citerior served by the *liberti* of freeborn Italians or Roman citizens who would probably have formed *collegia* or s*ocietates publicanorum* (their inscriptions have been found at the town, e.g. *RIT* 5). At the same time the availability of Italian wine, table-wares and other prestigious imports would have been attractive to the inhabitants of the town and the surrounding territory (Keay 1990, 127-29).

By the end of the century (120-110) the regional importance of Tarraco was confirmed with the construction of a network of roads (in general Mayer and Rodà 1986). The principal road, the Via Domitia, ran from Narbo in Gallia Transalpina across the Pyrenees and down through modern Catalunya along the pre-littoral depressions of the Vallès and the Penedès before reaching the coast N of Tarraco; then it probably crossed the Ebro in the vicinity of modern Tortosa before heading south. Another road reached up the coast towards the Llobregat and

Fig.2.2. The upper town of Tarragona from the NE.

then north via the site of the future setlement of Aquae Calidae (Caldes de Montbui) into the territory of the Ausetani close to the site of the future Auso (Vich: *IRC* I nos. 175, 176, 11). It had been built by the governor M. Sergius. Another road, the work of the governor Q. Fabius Labeo (*IRC* II no. 89), ran westwards into the territory of the Ilergetes towards Ilerda and the middle Ebro valley, while another (of uncertain date) ran south towards the lower Ebro.

Subsequently little is known of the town prior to the mid 1st c. B.C. It seems not to have taken sides in the Sertorian wars (82-72) and, although the inhabitants were quick to swear allegiance to the victorious Pompey, they changed to Caesar after the battle of Ilerda (49) in the Civil War. Tarraco was granted the status of *colonia* shortly before or after the death of Caesar (somewhere between 45 and 27: Alföldy 1991, 31).

*The early empire*

The *Colonia Iulia Urbs Triumphalis Tarraco* (figs. 2.1 and 2.2) was chosen by Augustus as the administrative capital of the province of *Hispania Tarraconensis* in 27 (Alföldy 1991, 55). To all intents and purposes it acted as the capital of the Roman world in 26-25 when Augustus stayed there to recover from an illness (Dio 53.25). It was also capital of the *Conventus Tarraconensis*, one of the 7 assize districts into which the province was divided during the course of the 1st c. A.D. Some time after *c*.2 B.C. and until A.D. 22/23 Tarraco issued bronze and brass coins bearing portraits of the imperial family and symbols of the imperial cult (Burnett, Amandry and Ripollès 1992, 102-5). The rich collection of inscriptions from the town (Alföldy 1975, and see also Alföldy 1969) provides a full record of various provincial governors and officials who resided at the town, the cosmopolitan character of the more élite members of the population (Etienne and Fabre 1979; Alföldy 1991), and their different religions (Alföldy 1993).

The historical record for subsequent centuries is poor. In recent years, however, archaeology has begun to compensate. It is now clear that the Augustan period ushered in an important period of urban development which was to last well into the 2nd c. A.D. The lower town was completely replanned with an orthogonal street-grid and provided with a range of major public buildings. The most important of these was the forum, whose basilica was excavated in the 1920s (Serra Vilaró 1932; Mar and Ruiz de Arbulo 1986). Nothing survives of the forum area itself or its complement of temples. However, it is generally accepted (Fishwick 1982) that the altar put up by the citizens of Tarraco in 2 B.C. (Quint., *Inst.* 6.3.77) would have been located in

Fig.2.3. The foundations of the S side of the Flavian circus in the upper town; the arena lay beneath the building in the background to the left.

the forum, as would the temple to the Divus Augustus sanctioned by Tiberius in A.D. 15 (Tac., *Ann.* 1.78). Recent research has hinted at the strongly ideological flavour of the complex, with statues commemorating members of the imperial family and of the municipal élite (Koppel 1985) from the Julio-Claudian period onwards, while an honorific arch possibly commemorated Augustan military victories (Koppel 1990). A short distance to the south, overlooking the port, lay the theatre (Berges 1982), whose rich sculptural decoration had similar ideological overtones. Much of the building of this early phase in the monumentalization of Tarraco was executed in a local limestone which was quarried some 6 km to the NE at El Medol (Carreras and Garriga 1991). Marble was rare and not used in any quantity until later in the 1st c. A.D. Further north in the town, just S of the modern Rambla Nova, excavations recently uncovered what has been identified as the *schola* of the *collegium fabrum* of Tarraco (Koppel 1988). This building, of the mid 2nd c., had a peristyle opening onto *triclinia* and a *nymphaeum* adorned with a range of statues, including a bust of the tutelary deity Minerva and a statuette of the *genius collegii*. Apart from some houses/shops adjacent to the forum (Serra Vilaró 1932; Balil 1973) little is known of intra-mural housing. Much of the evidence was destroyed by the 19th-c. quarrying away of its E sector for the rebuilding of the port and by the rapid urbanization of the lower town at the beginning of the 20th c. However, early excavations and rescue work undertaken in the 1980s have made it clear that in the course of the first two centuries A.D. private residences, particularly large villas, were built outside the walls on the flat ground between the W edge of the town and the river Francolí.

By contrast, the upper town seems to have remained largely an administrative centre. The Augustan period is little known apart from the discovery in the 1980s of a large official building of unknown function immediately SW of the Torre de Pilatos (Dupré and Subias 1993). However, the Flavian period saw all of the area within the Republican walls terraced to permit the construction of a huge architectural complex. It comprised two main elements. The first, covering 7.6 ha, consisted of an upper rectangular precinct and Temple to Rome and Augustus (fig. 2.1); it opened onto a lower and wider rectangular enclosure which was almost certainly the forum of the *Concilium Provinciae Hispaniae Citerioris* (TED'A 1989). Statue pedestals commemorating high priests (*flamines*) of the provincial imperial cult were set up within the enclosed area of the forum (Alföldy 1973) — a privilege to which they were entitled upon concluding their term of office. Both of these enclosures and the temple were richly decorated in Carrara and (more rarely) Proconnesian marble (Pensabene 1993). The second element was a circus (fig. 2.1) built parallel to the S face of the forum but at a lower level again (Dupré, Massó, Palanques and Verduchi 1988). Much of its structure is still encased within the mediaeval buildings of the upper town. However, excavations in the 1980s have done much to elucidate it. The upper two terraces at least were planned as a single architectural complex, with construction beginning early in the reign of Vespasian. The circus may have been added later, possibly under Domitian (fig. 2.3). The complex as a whole was destined to serve as precinct of the imperial cult (upper terrace), meeting-place of the provincial council (middle terrace), and as a setting for public shows, imperial anniversaries, celebrations, and formal communications from the governor to the populace (circus).

There were at least three main areas of burial of high-status individuals at early imperial Tarraco. One was located on flat ground a short distance from the river Francolí to the west of the town, a second straddled the Via Augusta as it approached the town from the W, and a third ranged along the S side of the Via Augusta as it left its E gate (TED'A 1987, 181-91). The latter, however, had only a limited life since at the beginning of the 2nd c. an amphitheatre was built overlooking the sea-shore (TED'A 1990). Occasional burials are known further afield, such as the funerary tower of the Torre dels Escipions (1st c. A.D.) (fig. 2.4), standing by the side of the Via Augusta some 6 km from Tarraco (Hauschild, Mariner and Niemeyer 1966).

Fig.2.4 (left). 'Torre dels Escipions', early imperial funerary monument, #80.
Fig.2.5 (right) Augustan arch at Berà, built straddling the Via Augusta.

The preeminent geopolitical position of Tarraco was emphasized as the town became a major hub of communications. It was a major stop on the Via Augusta which ultimately linked Rome with Gades in Hispania Ulterior. The Via Augusta constituted an upgrade of the Republican Via Domitia and largely followed the same route. It ran southwards from the Coll de Perthus in the Pyrenees, crossed the Llobregat at Martorell, continued down the length of the Penedès, and entered our study area near El Vendrell. From this point it followed the coast to Tarraco (fig. 1.2), and then continued SW until it reached Dertosa (Tortosa). *Mansiones* are recorded at Palfuriana (El Vendrell?), Oleastrum (L'Hospitalet de l'Infant), Sub Saltu (El Coll de Balaguer) and Tria Capita (L'Ampolla) (Pallí 1985; Morote 1979). The exact path of the road is imperfectly known except for a short stretch on either side of the Augustan triumphal arch at Berà (fig. 2.5; Dupré 1986 and 1994), and the possibility of a stretch in the region of El Perellò (Izquierdo 1988-89).

Tarraco was also the starting-point for the major road (*Iter* 452 of the Antonine Itinerary) running to Ilerda, Osca and, ultimately, Caesaraugusta (Roldán 1973). It ran northwards up the W bank of the Francolí to the pass at the Estret de la Riba and up to Espluga de Francolí, before heading on to Ilerda (fig. 1.2). The route taken by the road is suggested by the discovery of a *milliarium* on the left bank of the Francolí at El Morell (Baix Camp) (Montón Broto 1976-77) and a stretch of the road bed has been found a short distance to the south of La Riba (López i Vilar 1990). In this northern sector the road was metalled in some parts and cut into the rock in others. One *mansio* lay on its route at *Ad Septimum Decimum* (possibly to be identified with Vilaverd), 17 Roman miles to the north of Tarraco, and another at *Ad Novas* (possibly Vinaixa), 13 Roman miles further north.

The full extent of the *territorium* of Tarraco is not known. It has been suggested that its northern limit was marked by the Roman arch at Berà (Nierhaus 1964). However, recent work has suggested that it may have lain further north, on the edge of the Garraf Massif close to the intersection of the rivers Anoia and Llobregat at Martorell (*Ad Fines*), where a substantial Roman bridge was built by legionary veterans of VI Victrix, IIII Macedonica and X Gemina during the reorganization of the road system in this region between 16-13 and 8 B.C. (*IRC* I.1).

In the south the *territorium* of Tarraco abutted that of Dertosa (Tortosa), which lay on the lower Ebro. The limit may well have been at the point where the Serra de Tivissa meets the sea at L'Hospitalet de L'Infant (Alföldy 1991, 50 ff.).

To the west, the limit of the *territorium* may have lain somewhere between Valls and Montblanc. That part of the territory close to Tarraco (Baix Camp, Alt Camp and Tarragonès) and at the heart of the *territorium* has never been the subject of an in-depth study. It has been suggested that stretches of the area were centuriated (Gurt and Marqués 1988), possibly early in the Roman period, but this suggestion is largely based upon a study of mediaeval and post-mediaeval road alignments whose relationship to the Roman landscape is impossible to gauge.

A large number of Roman sites are known from casual finds and occasional small-scale surveys in many parts of the territory. They may indicate that the highly fertile soils of the Baix Camp were more densely settled than the Alt Camp or Tarragonès. However, the absence of systematic survey in the region makes it impossible to take these results at face value; the same may be said for their chronology, which is 'impressionistic' at best (see Table 1.1). Without systematic surface survey one is clearly unable to gain any idea of the density of rural settlement or its development. Indeed, to gain an idea of the process of rural development in the hinterland of Tarraco, one has to look at recent work done in the Penedès, some distance to the NE (Miret, Sanmartí and Santacana 1991) but still probably within the territory of Tarraco. Here there is a clear picture of continuity from the Iberian into the Republican period. Native sites were abandoned gradually in the course of the 2nd and 1st c. B.C. The first Roman rural sites did not appear before the second half of the 2nd c. B.C. (Miret, Sanmartí and Santacana 1991, 47-50). Excavations at L'Argilera (Calafell) have shown that prior to their abandonment some of the native farms had begun to undergo a process of transformation (Sanmartí, Santacana and Serra 1984, 16-22), both in terms of their material culture (import of Italic wine amphorae and black glaze table wares) and in their productive capacity.

Nevertheless, the potential for the study of rural settlement in the central part of the *Ager Tarraconensis* is clear. Excavations at the site of El Moro (Torredembarra) uncovered parts of a villa purported to be of Republican date (Terré 1987; see p.20 and fig. 1.6), while excavation beneath the late Roman complex at Centcelles (Constantí; p.23 and fig. 1.8) revealed a substantial rectangular structure with an enclosure for *dolia* of early imperial date (Hauschild and Arbeiter 1993). Another early imperial site has been excavated at the Velodrom (Montroig). Both seem to be farms, with no developed *villa urbanus*. There are also reports of scattered sites in the central part of the *Ager Tarraconensis* as well as throughout the *territorium* as defined above (see Table 1.1).

At sites such as these wine would have been produced, a significant proportion of it destined for export. Discussions about the economy of eastern Spain often mention Tarraconensian wine, which found markets around the western Mediterranean and parts of north-western Europe. Tarraconensian wine is generally assumed to have originated in Laietania to the north. However, the state of research into wine production in the Tarragona region is backward compared to the areas further north (the modern provinces of Barcelona and Girona) and to the south (the region of Saguntum and Denia). The quality of that produced in the territory of Tarraco in the 1st c. A.D. was lauded by Martial (13.108) and in recent years a number of kilns producing transport amphorae for wine have been found in the rich soils of the Baix Camp. We may note, though, that published evidence for production in the later 1st c. B.C. is non-existent; the characteristic Pascual 1 and Tarraconense 1 types seem to be absent from these sites. This is curious given the likely stimulus to production of the growing town of Tarraco during the later 1st c. B.C. The known kilns at the Mas de Coll, La Boada, Els Antigons, Mas de L'Antoni Corts, Timba del Castellet, and Molins Nous seem to have been active largely in the 1st and possibly 2nd c. A.D., producing primarily Dressel 2-4 types (J. Miró 1988, 51-54). Amphora kilns have also been located in the upland area of Tivissa (J. Miró 1988, 55), where, unusually, Pascual 1 amphorae are attested alongside a range of early imperial types.

Significant areas of the territory would probably have been in the hands of the *Antistii*, *Licinii* and other élite families known to us from inscriptions discovered at Tarraco. However, few major estate centres, or *villae*, are known. One is the large and impressive site at Els Munts (Altafulla), which is situated on a rocky bluff overlooking the sea a few kilometres NE of Tarraco (p. 23 and fig.1.7A). It may have been owned by Caius Valerius Avitus, a native of Augustobriga (Muro de Agreda, Soria Province) who was moved to Tarraco during the reign of Antoninus Pius (*RIT* 923). Long galleries and polychrome mosaics have been discovered. Its historical sequence is still poorly understood (Berges 1977; Gorges 1979) but important early and late imperial phases are probable. The existence of other important early imperial *villae* is suggested by substantial *mausolea*, such as those in the vicinity of Villalonga del Camp (Tarragonès), Alcover (Baix Camp) and Vila-rodona (Alt Camp; fig. 2.6) (see Table 1.1).

*The late imperial and Visigothic periods*

Traditionally this period has been seen as one of rapid decline in the urban fabric of Tarraco, coinciding with a period of architectural splendour in the countryside. In the days before the advent of systematic excavation it was all too easy to relate the former to the depredations of the invading Franks in 261/62 (Orosius; Sánchez Real 1957; cf. Keay 1981). However, an important series of rescue excavations by the TED'A during the 1980s has provided a clearer picture, pointing to a gradual transformation of the town as it took on a leading administrative and spiritual rôle into the Visigothic period from the late 5th c. (Keay 1991a; forthcoming). This is most evident in terms of material culture. Analysis of ceramics and coins from excavations in the late Roman town points to a remarkably vibrant commercial life

Fig.2.6. Early imperial *columbarium* at Cal Mas, Vila-rodona, #17.

well into the 6th c., and contacts with many parts of the Mediterranean (Keay 1984; Remola 1989). The discovery of an inscription (*RIT* 1075) mentioning an *archisynagogus* confirms the existence of a Jewish community at Tarraco in the late antique period.

Following the Diocletianic reorganization Tarraco remained capital of Tarraconensis, although the area of the province was reduced. In 410 the usurper Gerontius made it capital of the *Diocesis Hispaniarum* for his appointee, Maximus (Arce 1988, 116-21). Tarraco's new status, however, was short-lived. Tarraco also played an important spiritual role. By 418/19 Tarraco had become the metropolitan bishopric for the province, a position which it retained to the end of the 7th c. An inscription set up in honour of eastern emperors in 468/472 (*RIT* 100) testifies that its secular Roman authority lasted down until the final years of Roman control (after the 'Germanic' invasion of 409 Tarraconensis was to remain the last province under Roman control until the dissolution of the western empire in 476). Tarraco was finally captured by the Visigothic general Hedelfredus and the *dux Hispaniarum* Vincentius during their conquest of eastern Tarraconensis between 470 and 475 (*Gallic Chronicle* p.664, 651, XVI; D'Abadal i de Vinyals 1969, 39-45).

During the Visigothic period (475-711) and the short Ostrogothic interregnum (507-73) Tarracona, as Tarraco was now called, retained its importance largely by virtue of its rôle as metropolitan bishopric and head of the ecclesiastical 'province' of Tarraconensis. A church council was held at Tarracona in 516. The bishops of Tarracona attended church councils at Toletum (Toledo) down to the end of the 7th c. (Vives 1963). It was a mint for the gold *trientes* introduced by Leovigild (568-86) which were struck until the reign of Akhila (710-13) (Miles 1952). In time, though, it may have been surpassed in regional fiscal importance by Barcino (Barcelona) and in 'national' importance by Toletum (Toledo), which eventually became the capital of the unified Visigothic kingdom of Hispania (Collins 1983). By the time of the Arab invasions of Spain, Tarracona had become insignificant. Its inhabitants were too few in number to mount an adequate defence and the town was captured in 716 by Al-Hurr (Recasens 1975, 30-46). It was Caesaraugusta (Zaragoza) rather than Tarracona which became capital of the Upper March of Al-Andalus (Esco, Giarlt and Senaca 1989, 12-16). As there is virtually no archaeological evidence for any Islamic occupation, it seems that Tarracona was abandoned almost immediately. It only regained importance upon its refoundation by the Christians in the 1140s (Recasens 1975, 47-85).

The process of urban transformation at Tarraco may have begun as early as the 2nd c. A.D. At that date a suburban house W of the town began to be abandoned (TED'A 1987, 94 ff.). Others were abandoned towards the end of the 3rd c. (Keay 1984, 26). More significantly the upkeep of the theatre was suspended towards the end of the 2nd c., prior to a change in function in the 3rd (Aquilué, Dupré, Massó and Ruiz de Arbulo 1991, 51 ff.). The amphitheatre, however, was to continue in use until the 5th c. In 217/18 Elagabalus funded the reconstruction of its seating banks, *pulpitum* and *podium* (Alföldy 1990). Evidence for new public works in the 4th c. is rare. One inscription records the construction of the *porticus Iovis* (possibly in the municipal forum in the lower town) which was dedicated to the joint emperors Diocletian and Maximian (*RIT* 91), while another refers to the restoration of some public baths, the *thermae Montanarum*, by the provincial governor in the early 4th c. (*RIT* 155). Early excavations of the basilica in the lower forum suggest that it was destroyed during a fire in the later 4th c.; municipal consciousness was evidently at a sufficiently low ebb for it to remain in ruins and subsequently be used for occasional burials (Keay forthcoming; Serra Vilaró 1932). The same was true for some of the surrounding buildings.

The available evidence suggests that the lower town was progressively abandoned in the course of the 4th c. At the same time, much of the extramural area between the town walls and the Francolí (fig. 2.1) was turned into a cemetery or series of cemeteries (TED'A 1987 for a discussion). The largest was excavated by Serra Vilaró in the 1930s during the construction of the Tobacco Factory; it comprised well over 2000 burials (Serra Vilaró 1928; 1929; 1930; 1935). The burials ranged from less frequent high-status *mausolea* and elegant marble sarcophagi to more common, modest burials in amphorae and beneath tiles. A basilica, probably a *martyrium*, was built in the mid 5th and continued in use until the 6th or 7th c. While many of the people buried in the cemetery would have come from Tarraco, it is possible that others might have come from country areas or further afield in order to be buried close to the church.

The population seems to have slowly withdrawn into the more enclosed area of the upper town. The loss of the town's pre-eminent administrative rôle led to major topographical changes in the upper town. First, the public monuments decayed. In the second half of the 5th c., for instance, the provincial forum was gradually robbed of standing monuments, inscriptions and statues (Rodà 1990). Then, towards the middle of the century, the forum paving-blocks were robbed, the enclosure was used as a rubbish dump, and one of its angle towers (Antiga Audiencia) passed out of use (Dupré and Carreté 1993). The area of the forum was then converted into an ecclesiastical centre. The Visigothic cathedral was probably built within the shell of the Temple to Rome and Augustus and a possible episcopal palace (*episcopium*) was constructed against the outer face of its precinct wall (Aquilué 1993b). Outside the town on low ground overlooking the sea, a basilica was built in the late 6th c. within the ruins of the amphitheatre (fig. 2.7; TED'A 1990). The damage wrought by mediaeval robbing and the increasing rarity of pottery datable to the 6th c. and 7th c. make it impossible to trace the development of the town later into the Visigothic period. Our evidence is largely restricted to occasional sculptures, metalwork, and literary evidence (Palol 1953; Recasens 1975).

For many scholars the late Roman period in the hinterland of Tarraco is characterized by the emergence of large and luxurious residential villas belonging to élite landowners. This picture is common to many parts of the western Mediterranean. Its empirical basis here, however, is still lacking. Late Roman sites are known from the central area of the territory (Table 1.1) but their identification has been just as fortuitous as those of early imperial or Republican date and they tell little about the development, density or areas preferred for rural settlement from the 3rd to 5th c. All that can be said is that there is no evidence for local amphora production after the 2nd c., suggesting that wine was no longer being produced for export and that, if it continued to be produced, it was for local consumption. It suggests that surplus agricultural potential was being channelled into areas which are not traceable archaeologically. The picture is no clearer in the Penedès region further north (Járrega 1992).

Fig.2.7. The Visigothic basilica in the arena of the amphitheatre at Tarragona. The standing walls belong to the Romanesque church.

All that can be said is that late-antique rural sites do seem to be less numerous than their early imperial counterparts, and that known examples appear to be on a luxurious scale. The best known cluster relatively close to Tarraco in the Baix Camp and Tarragonès, suggesting that the town was still perceived to be an important part of social and political life. The earliest date to the 3rd c. and are to be found at Parets Delgades (La Selva del Camp; see p.20 and fig. 1.5) and Cal.lipolis (Vilaseca; Table 1.1 no. 94). They are best known for their polychrome mosaics, which depict geometric and floral motifs, and fishes, respectively. Unfortunately, only the partial plan of the former survives, revealing little about its organization. A site of similar date with no mosaics was discovered at La Llosa (Cambrils) (Macias and Ramón 1994). Other villas of the 4th c. are present in the central area of the territory but have either not been excavated or remain unpublished. The most important is undoubtedly Els Munts (Altafulla) in the Tarragonès (see p.23 and fig. 1.7A) and although it has yielded an extremely rich array of late mosaics and late-antique sculpture nothing has yet been published. Other significant sites are known at El Vilarenc (Calafell: Gorges 1979, 410 ff.) and Porporas (Reus: Gorges 1979, 415).

The most famous late Roman 'villa', however, is the enigmatic complex of Centcelles (Constantí), built towards the middle of the 4th c. on the site of an early imperial farm on the left bank of the Francolí (see p.23 and fig. 1.8). Traditionally it is seen as the villa of a late

Roman élite, possibly even imperial, landholder. This may be true of its initial constructive phase towards the middle of the 4th c. However, before it was completed, the structures were modified and it was converted into a *mausoleum* with strongly ideological overtones. The rich figured mosaic decoration of its standing cupola depicts scenes from the New Testament and a late Roman hunt, one of the figures of which has been identified with the emperor Constans who was thought to have been buried here after his defeat by Magnentius at the battle of Helena (Elne) in southern Gaul in 350. More recently, however, a new analysis of the whole cupola mosaic suggests that it may have been the work of the usurper Magnentius. In an attempt to rehabilitate himself in the eyes of Constantius II after the defeat and death of Constans, he commissioned artists to depict a fictional 'Tetrarchy' above Constans' tomb. Thus the cupola mosaic can be understood as a purely ideological statement in which Magnentius and Constantius II are depicted as the two Augusti with Vetranio and Decentius as the two Caesars (Arbeiter and Korol 1988-89).

These classes of establishment, however, are rare and were owned by people whose resources may well have been based in other provinces. This, coupled with the absence of systematic fieldwork in the area, means that they tell us little about the character of the agricultural economy of late Roman Tarraco. Far less is known about the Visigothic period. Even though it may be possible to posit the continuity of certain sites like Centcelles, the archaeological difficulty of dating sites later than the 6th c. makes it virtually impossible to document 'Visigothic' villas or farms. There is virtually no archaeological or historical evidence for the countryside of Tarracona between the later 6th-early 7th c. and the mid 12th c. It reappears in the historical record only after 1149 with the systematic settlement of small groups of people in the countryside after the reconquest of the region from the Arabs (Recasens 1975, 69-85). The foundation dates of many of these settlements are known from documentary sources; they can be identified with the small villages which still abound in the Alt Camp, Baix Camp and Tarragonès.

## Chapter 3: BACKGROUND TO THE FIELD SURVEY

GEOGRAPHICAL BACKGROUND[1]

The Roman city of *Tarraco* lies on the Mediterranean coast of Catalunya approximately 100 km south of Barcelona (ancient Barcino) (fig. 1.1). The modern industrial town lies in a rich agricultural area occupying the area between the coast and the mountains of the Serralada Pre-litoral. Its agricultural hinterland is divided into 3 *comarcas*, the *Alt Camp*, the *Baix Camp*, and the *Tarragonès*, which are themselves divided into *termes municipales* (parishes). Our survey was confined to the *Tarragonès* and the *Alt Camp*. Each of the detailed maps (figs. 6.2-6.33) shows the boundaries and names of the *termes municipales* studied.

The topography of the region is dominated by the Serralada Pre-litoral which separates the broad coastal plain from the Depressió Central around Lleida. The mountains rise to 1201 m in the Muntanyes de Prades *c.*35 km NW of Tarragona. This mountain chain is cut by a gorge of the river Francolí at Estret de la Riba due N of Tarragona, providing a natural route to the interior. The survey area lies between the coast and the foothills of the mountains and is drained by two N-S rivers, the Francolí and the Gaià (fig. 3.1) The land generally slopes gently from the mountains towards the coast. The maximum elevation in the survey area reaches about 300 m asl in Transect 4, north of Valls. In the eastern part of the study area the landscape is dominated by a plateau bounded to the E by the comparatively narrow valley of the Gaià and its small tributaries. The plateau narrows to a ridge which meets the sea at Tarragona; on it the Roman monuments of the upper town are situated (fig. 2.2). To the east of Tarragona there is little land below 100 m, although the coastal plain widens again towards Torredembarra. By contrast, in the western part of the survey area the river Francolí flows through a broad plain, the Depressió Valls-Reus, below its confluence with the Barranc de Sant Francesc south of Valls (figs. 3.2-3.3). The drainage system of the Francolí includes a series of seasonal streams (*barrancs*) which drain both the mountains to the NW and the plateau to the E. Despite its size, the course of the Francolí is comparatively stable, as witnessed by the Roman sites like Centcelles which lie immediately beside it on the first terrace. Nevertheless, down-cutting has created localized deep cuttings in the river bed.

The geology of the survey area, summarized in fig.3.4 (IGME 1973a; IGME 1973b), is dominated by three principal features which were produced by folding and faulting during the Alpine orogeny when the collision of the African with the Eurasian plate resulted in the formation of the coastal mountain chain. In the NW part of the study area the Horst Priorat-Gaià mountains are composed predominantly of Triassic dolomites, although complex faulting has also resulted in the outcrop NW of Valls of limited areas of Palaeozoic rocks of the Silurian, Devonian and Carboniferous eras. The second block of older rocks comprises the predominantly Jurassic limestones of the Bonansa Massif just E of the Gaià. A further minor anticline with a fault on its S side forms the ridge of Lower Cretaceous and Jurassic limestones and dolomites which runs inland NE from Tarragona. Between these blocks of older rocks is the Depressió Valls-Reus created by faulting during the Alpine uplift, which raised the blocks to its SE and NW, effectively creating a minor rift valley. This depression, the SW continuation from the Penedès of the Depressió Pre-litoral, dominates the survey area and is filled with coarse Tertiary and Quaternary sedimentary deposits. The river valleys of the Francolí, Gaià, and their tributaries cut through them and were filled with alluvial deposits derived from the erosion of the adjacent mountains. These deposits are thin and discontinuous, although there are occasional deeper pockets and more substantial accumulations towards the coast, especially in the Gaià valley.

The survey area has a classic Mediterranean climate with a maximum mean summer tem-

---

1     The information on soils and geology draws on fieldwork by Dr. R. Parish in 1989.

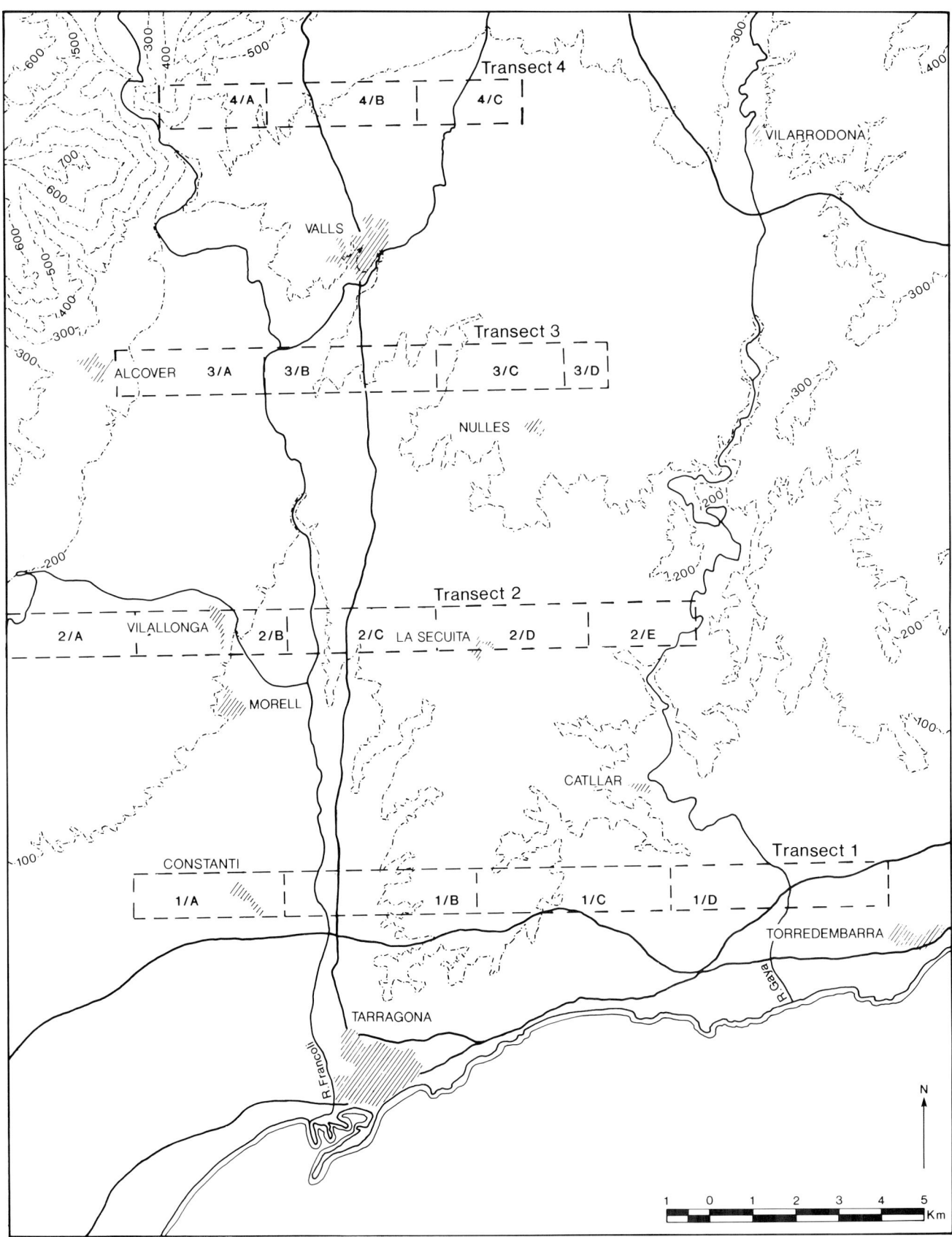

Fig.3.1. Topography of the territory, showing the location and numbers of the transects for fieldwalking.

Fig.3.2. Landscape looking W towards Alcover along transect 3. The Francolí valley and the Depressió Reus-Valls appear in the centre of the photograph.

Fig.3.3. Landscape looking S across the survey area from the Col de Lilla in the Serralada Pre-litoral. Road N240 is visible at the centre of the photograph.

perature of 24°C in July and a minumum winter average of 9°C in January. The mean annual rainfall is between 600 and 800 mm. Some rain falls in most months. There is generally less than 20 mm per month in June and July. The wettest period is the autumn, with the maximum in September, which averages 90 mm. These average figures mask the nature of the precipitation, which is often characterized by violent late-summer thunderstorms. Torrential rain creates localized flooding and results in rapid erosion and down-cutting in the valleys. As a result, settlement tends to avoid the valley floors. Both rainfall and temperature tend to decrease with distance from the coast, although the effect of this on climate in the survey area is negligible.

The basic character of all the soils in the region is similar but there are obvious local variations. All are Brown Soils although those in the Depressió Valls-Reus and on the N part of the plateau between Valls and Vila-rodona tend to be richer and deeper than those on the

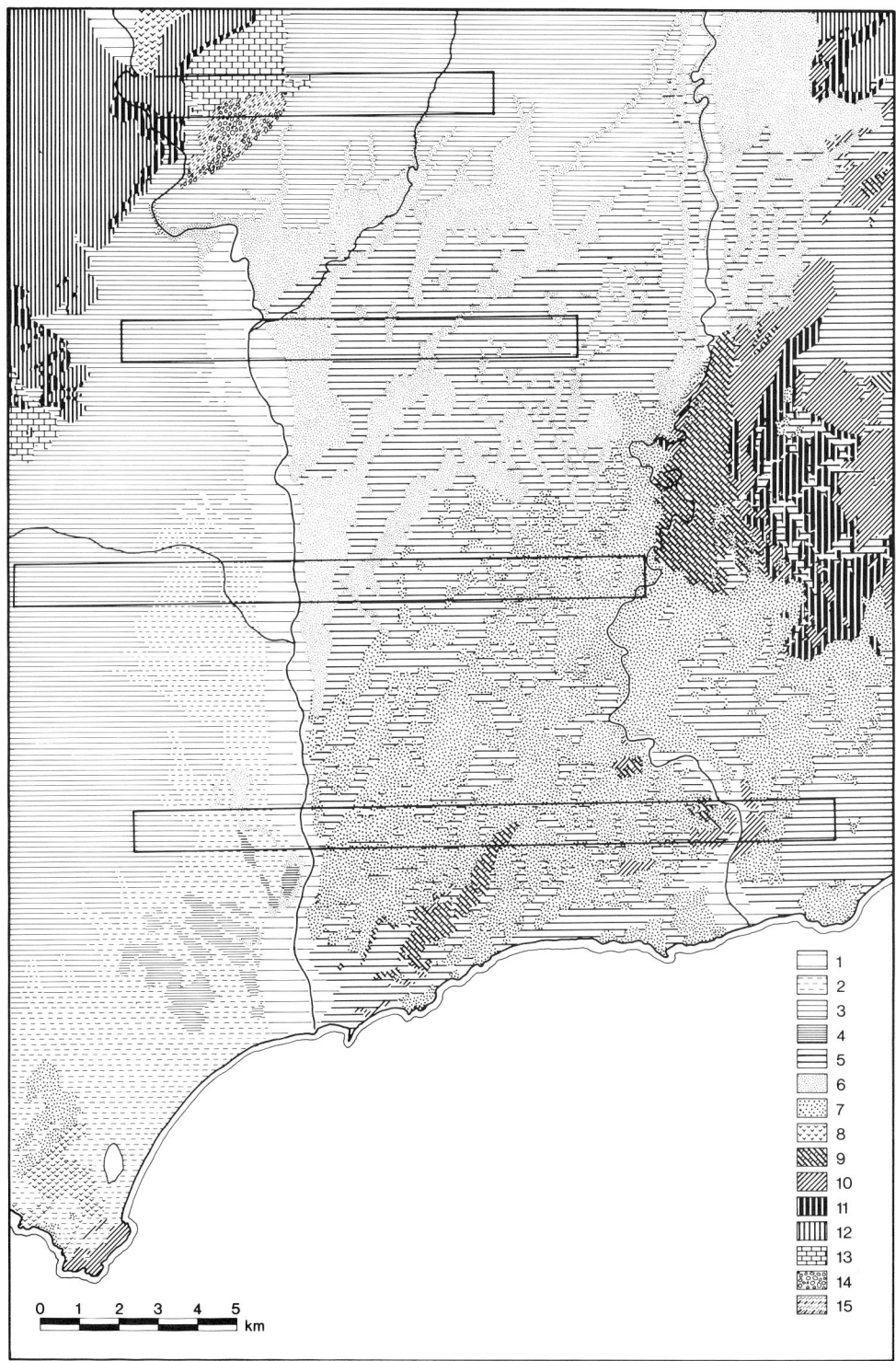

Fig.3.4. Geology of the territory, with the location of the transects.
*Key*: 1 -Quaternary, gravels and clayey sils; 2 -Quaternary, angular gravels with clayey-silt matrix; 3 - Quaternary, angular and poorly sorted conglomerates; 4 - Quaternary, calcareous crust; 5 - Quaternary, crusts, silts and soils; 6 - Tertiary, fluvial and lacustrine conglomerates, sands, clays, detrital limestones and marls; 7 - Tertiary, limestones; 8 - Tertiary, limestones, dolomites and grey clays; 9 - Cretaceous, limestones, red clays and sands; 10 - Jurassic, recrystallized dolomites; 11 - Triassic, dolomitic marls; 12 - Triassic, dolomites and dolomitic limestones; 13 - Carboniferous, slates, sandstones, conglomerates and andesite; 14 - Devonian, marmorial limestones; 15 - Silurian, schists and fine-grained grey slates with quartz veins.

Fig.3.5. Soils of the territory based on the work of Cobertera (1986), with the location of transects. The area to the N of that shown was not covered in Cobertera's published survey; blank areas were not mapped. Key: 1 - soils of highest fertility; 2 - soils of good fertility; 3 - soils of average fertility; 4 - soils of low fertility; 5 - soils of lowest fertility.
A - soils with very important agriculture; B - soils with important agriculture; C - soils with adequate agriculture; D - soils with poor agriculture; E - soils with very poor agriculture or abandoned.

ridge NE of Tarragona, which are also stonier and more calcareous. On all the higher ground the soils tend to be thin and stoney, since rates of soil production are low whilst exposure and the steep slopes facilitate the stripping of loose surface deposits. In the limestone areas solution-weathering occurs; it produces most of its products in solution and so does not contribute to soil formation. These types of process tend to concentrate clastic material (including artefacts) within the soil matrix, thus 'compressing' the timespan represented in an individual soil. The high summer temperatures in the region result in the widespread development of a calcareous crust (a pan which results from the concentration of calcium carbonate just below the surface as moisture within the soil migrates towards the surface and evaporates). This crust is most evident in areas of *maqui* vegetation where it has had an adverse effect upon agriculture.

Recent research on the soils in the survey area to the south of Valls (Cobertera 1986) has provided a classification based on their agricultural potential and current utilization. The results of this work are shown in fig. 3.5 which maps soil fertility on the basis of Cobertera's field research and chemical analyses. This has shown that over most of the E part of the survey area the soils are of relatively low fertility, although there are pockets of better land in the Gaià valley and on the coastal strip. The soils to the west of the Francolí and around Valls (within the Depressió Valls-Reus) are more mixed but generally of class 3 or better. The largest area of land of class 1 lies W of the Francolí around Villalonga del Camp.

The area around Tarragona is now dominated by urban sprawl and light industry. Between settlements in its immediate environs there is now little agricultural activity and many areas which were once farmed are covered with regenerated *maqui* scrub. This type of landscape, broken by occasional arable fields, also dominates the ridge of higher ground running inland NE from the city. The Francolí valley immediately E of Morrell is dominated by a large petro-chemical refinery (Repsol) with its associated industries.

Elsewhere, the region is heavily cultivated with a range of crops grown on all but the steepest slopes, which are generally wooded. The higher ground of the inland areas is largely arable, with cereal crops grown in open fields. These areas are also heavily exploited for almond trees which are grown widely spaced so that the land between can be ploughed and planted with fodder crops. In areas of older planting there are also olives and carobs, while limited areas of walnuts and fruit trees are found as more recent plantings. Vines are widely grown throughout the survey area, although they are most common between elevations of about 100 and 200 m. They are mostly planted in rows about 5 m apart and are grown relatively low. Most are trained along wires up to about 1.5 m in height in the Guyot fashion or grown without wire but trained 'En Vaso'. The lowest ground in the region where water is sufficient for their needs is densely planted with hazelnuts; the lower lands in the Francolí valley are dominated by hazelnut groves. Large-scale irrigation schemes were under development in the late 1980s especially in the area around Vilallonga del Camp to enable the areas of hazelnut cultivation to be extended.

AIMS AND OBJECTIVES

In recent years field survey has begun to make a major contribution to our understanding of the classical world. For many contemporaries the Roman empire was perceived to have been 'a world of cities' (Aelius Aristides); *urbanitas* and Roman urban form were sought after and adopted by communities in differing degrees and in varying intensities throughout the empire. The majority of its inhabitants, however, lived, worked, and died in the countryside. Nowhere has the balance between urban and rural been more clearly revealed than in the South Etruria survey (summarized by Potter 1979) which revealed the great density of rural settlement in the area N north of Rome throughout antiquity.

The survey of classical landscapes has made great strides since the completion of the South Etruria survey, partially through surveys designed to record sites but principally through research projects. As a result we now have a better understanding of a wide range of regions and environments throughout the Roman Empire (see, for example, Keller and Rupp 1983; Macready and Thompson 1985; Barker and Lloyd 1991). This has generated a new range of questions about the nature of Roman settlement and economy and the relationship between town and country (e.g., Rich and Wallace Hadrill 1991).

The aims of the survey were two-fold. First, we set out to analyse the pattern of settlement from the pre-Roman Iron Age (Iberian) period (6th/5th c. B.C.) through the Roman period (late 3rd c. B.C. onwards) into late antiquity (3rd c. A.D. onwards). The landscape around ancient Tarraco was ideal for modern survey techniques. Its territory had the potential to answer a range of questions of importance not only to our understanding of the region but also of the western empire as a whole. As a leading administrative centre it was sensitive to political and cultural change. The impact of the foundation of Tarraco upon the native settlement pattern in its hinterland would contribute to an understanding of the nature of early Roman towns in the Mediterranean (Keay 1987). The emergence of the city as provincial capital of Tarraconensis from the late 1st c. B.C. onwards would raise questions about the relationship of a provincial capital to its agricultural hinterland and, by implication, with more distant regions. Apart from the survey of the *territorium* of Iol Caesaraea (Leveau 1984) and some work around Carthage (Greene 1992), provincial capitals have not been the subject of study in any western province. Equally important was the transitional period of late antiquity during which Tarraco gradually ceded its administrative importance to other centres. The traditional picture of urban decline contrasted with rural renaissance, often put forward for late-Roman towns in the western empire, has also been invoked for Tarraco and needed to be tested.

The following aspects of the relationship between Tarraco and its hinterland seemed to be susceptible to analysis through systematic surface survey:

*Prehistoric period*
How far did the Iberian settlement pattern which preceded the establishment of Tarraco represent a break with Late Bronze Age traditions?

*Protohistoric period*
What was the character of Iberian settlement in the region? In particular, what was the economic relationship of rural settlements to the major centres in the region, how far were there preferred geographical areas of settlement, and what was the density of Iberian rural settlement?

*Republican period*
To what degree was the emergence of Tarraco as a strategic centre and town matched by changes in the rural settlement pattern? This might be gauged by estimating the balance between the abandonment of Iberian sites and the foundation of new ones; changes in the density and/or areas of settlement, which might provide an index of agricultural intensification; and the degree of economic contact with Tarraco as reflected in the distributions of imported and locally-produced ceramics.

*Early imperial period*
How far was the greatly increased concentration of power and wealth resulting from Tarraco's rôle as provincial capital reflected in the rural settlement pattern? This might be measured through increased nucleation of rural sites in areas of earlier settlement as land passed into the hands of élites based in Tarraco; by analysing the degree to which Tarraco emerged as the focus of wealthier sites; by estimating whether there was a tendency for the density of sites to increase on the more marginal soils as the demands of the town on its territory grew; and by assessing the degree of self-sufficiency in cash crops (wine and olive oil) at rural sites as reflected in the volume of imported foodstuffs.

*Late imperial period*
To what extent is the traditional picture of urban decline matched by a rural renaissance relevant to this region? This might be gauged by estimating how far the proximity of Tarraco

continued to be an important determinant in the location of higher-status sites; by establishing whether there was continued nucleation of settlements as late-Roman landowners absorbed smaller land holdings and controlled more land; by noting how far it is possible to speak in terms of continued rural settlement through periods of major political change, such as the invasions of the 3rd and later 5th c.; and by estimating the extent to which rural sites continued to receive imported pottery redistributed from Tarraco.

Our second set of objectives was methodological. We sought to develop an archaeological 'language' with which to record and interpret the results of field-survey data. The techniques used to record and interpret such data have varied from region to region and from archaeologist to archaeologist. This makes any satisfactory synthesis of evidence for rural settlement in the Mediterranean almost impossible to achieve. Furthermore, these methodologies have often made untested and even unquestioned assumptions. So far only the evidence from Greek surveys has been the subject of an analysis which has attempted to overcome these difficulties (Alcock 1993). Many surveys in the Mediterranean have been concerned simply with the mapping of sites, some of them visible structures, others simply scatters of surface material. The area selected for survey is often haphazardly chosen within that which is presumed to fall within the territory of an ancient town (usually within modern administrative boundaries). The recording techniques used have often been assumed to be unproblematical, and the criteria for the identification of sites seen as self-evident. Evidence is recorded and the sum total of sites at different periods in a region mapped to provide a guide to changing population densities.

In recent years the simplicity of these approaches has come under increasing scrutiny. Sites are rarely self-evident. It is often difficult to be certain what a surface scatter represents, or even to define its boundaries. 'Off-site' material (Foley 1981) is increasingly being recognized as having relevance to our understanding of farming communities in the classical as well as in the prehistoric periods. Finally, it has begun to be appreciated that, as the volume of pottery in circulation varies between periods (Millett 1985; 1991a), both the definition of sites and the estimation of past population levels requires a systematic and sensitive methodology. Our survey attempted to develop methodologies which were sensitive but sufficiently robust to cope with the large quantities of pottery that are characteristic of Mediterranean surveys.

We aimed to develop two sets of methodologies:
1. to analyse distributions of finds so as to identify potential settlement sites in order to facilitate comparisons between periods.
2. to make inter-site comparisons of field-survey pottery assemblages (which are essentially unstratified) so that they could be used to address the historical questions posed.

RESEARCH DESIGN

Full details of the methods used during the survey and analysis of finds are provided in Chapter 4. Here we outline our approach in relation to the objectives just described. The general area chosen for the survey is shown in fig. 1.1. It represents only a portion of the lands that formed the *territorium* of Tarraco. It would have been impractical to cover the whole of that area at any reasonable level of intensity within a 5-year project with fieldwork occupying only about one month each year. The boundaries for the limited area studied were determined by three issues. The natural topography suggested that the core area around the city could be defined as the coastal plain and the valleys of the Francolí and Gaià. A landscape block encompassing these features provided a study area of 22 by 28 km (with its NW corner at 41° 20′ 04" 2 N / 1° 08′ 49" 5 E). This was felt to be sufficiently large to enable us to make reasonable generalizations. Finally the necessity of obtaining an annual permit meant that our activities had to be confined within the boundaries of specified *comarcas*. The area defined had the administrative advantage of being confined to the *Alt Camp* and *Tarragonès* whilst excluding the *Baix Camp*.

The decision was made from the outset to examine sample transects across the landscape since these were easier to locate in the field than random squares. An examination of other field-surveys suggested that a transect width of 1 km was likely to be most appropriate. This width provided sufficient scope for finding sufficient ploughed fields free of crops and for obtaining reasonable areas of contiguous fields within the transects. Although stratified random samples of areas provide statistically reliable samples of the whole landscape, they are most suited to the investigation of regions about which little is previously known (Cherry *et al.* 1979). As there was already much information available about the topography of the area in the Roman period, a random sampling strategy was felt to be inappropriate. Thus, regular transects were used. Since our aim was to examine the interaction between town and country, these transects were regularly spaced 5 km apart moving inland from Tarragona (fig. 3.1). This structured our sample to address the question of the changing relationship between Tarragona and its immediate hinterland. This research design also gave relatively good coverage of a variety of landscape types, geological deposits, and soils within the study area, as well as providing sections across the valleys of the Francolí and Gaià in their different reaches.

Our initial aim was for each transect to be of equal length E-W across the study area in strips delineated by the 1-km grid lines used on the 1:25,000 maps of the *Mapa Topográfica Nacional de España* published in 1983 by the *Instituto Geográfico Nacional*. Experience in 1985-86 led to a decision to reduce the lengths of the transects to those shown on fig. 3.1. First, it soon became clear that very large quantities of finds were being recovered, thereby increasing the time needed for field-walking and processing. This made it impossible to cover at the planned intensity the 88 km² originally envisaged. Since our intention was to retain a good density of coverage and our objectives required us to collect all finds and process them in detail, the solution was to reduce the total area sampled. In order to retain as good a coverage as possible, in particular with respect to distance from the city, it was decided to reduce the length of the transects rather than reduce their number.

In practice this decision was made easier by the second problem, that of availability of maps. In 1985 field-walking began using the 1:25,000 maps supplemented by vertical air photographs available through the *Institut Cartogràfic de Catalunya*. The limited resolution of the maps created difficulties in identifying particular field boundaries that were altered due to changes in crop regime. During the 1985 season we learned of the publication by the *Institut Cartogràfic de Catalunya* of a 1:5,000 map series produced from satellite images. It was decided to adopt these maps as the base for our work since they showed topography and field boundaries in admirable detail. The coverage of the study area, however, was incomplete as the maps were being produced for one *terme municipal* at a time, starting with the most heavily populated. This had a twofold effect. First, as survey had to be limited to areas for which the maps were available, some transects had to be truncated, especially in upland areas. This removed the W end of Transect 4 and the E parts of Transects 2-4, leaving the coverage shown in fig. 3.1. However, the details provided in Chapters 7 and 9 show that coverage of different landscape types remained adequate. The second effect was that several of the published maps were incomplete, blank areas being left for the *termes municipals* that had not yet been plotted. The result of this curious situation is that some areas shown on our transect maps (figs. 6.2-6.33) lack topographical information. These unmapped areas have been treated as being outside the sample for the purposes of the analysis.

Within the transects chosen we visited each area and began by attempting to walk any field which was available and had sufficient soil visibility. This included not only ploughed fields but those which had thin stubble, sparse *maqui*, or trees. Our normal season fell in September. This generally precluded the walking of hazelnut groves.[2] Our final season was

---

2    Nuts are collected by being allowing to fall to the ground and then swept up or collected with indus-

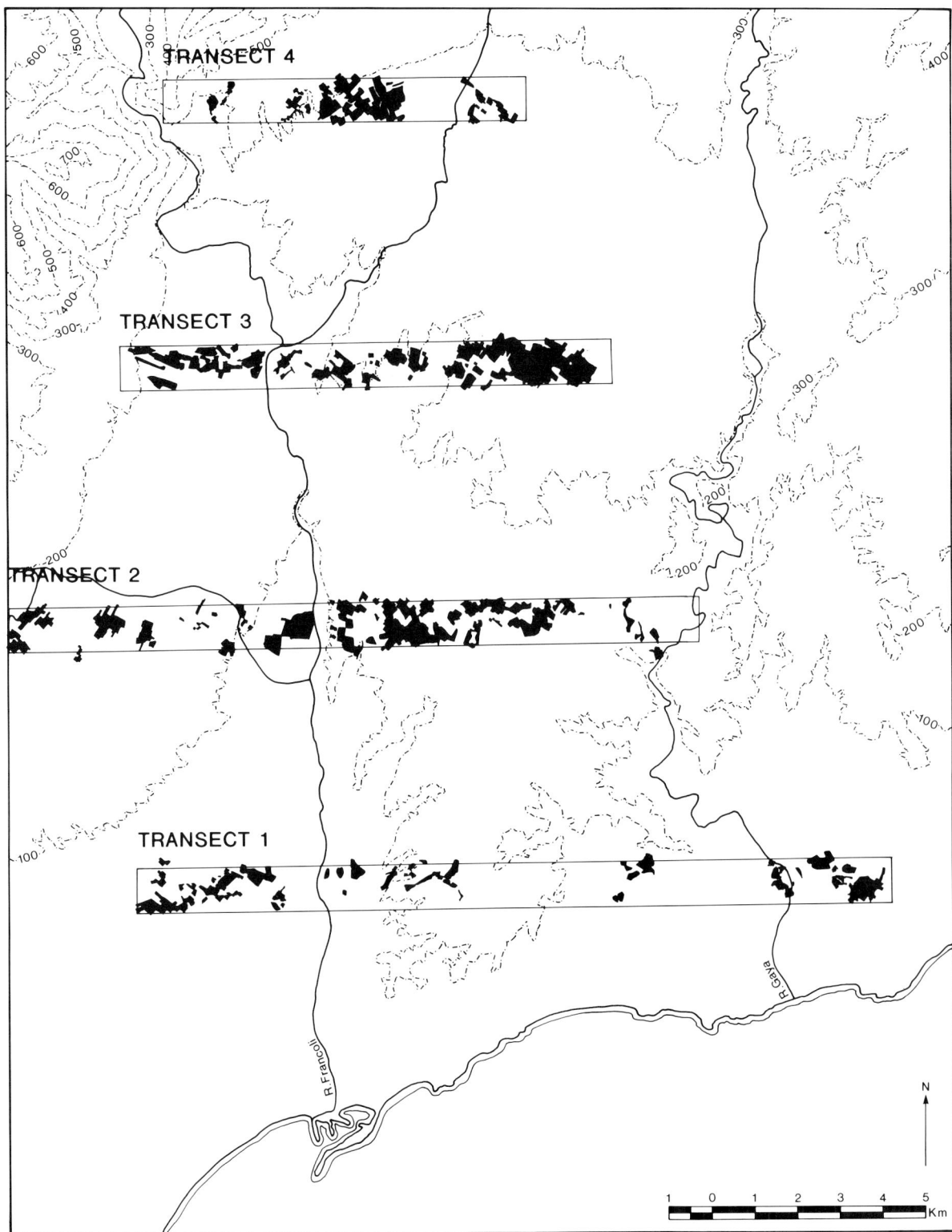

Fig.3.6. Topography of the territory, showing the transects with the areas walked in black.

trial vacuum-cleaners. The producers of this high-value crop were particularly sensitive about the possibility of their nuts being stolen in our polythene bags or being trodden into the ground with the result that they could not be picked up by the vacuum-cleaners.

undertaken in the spring to allow lower lying areas to be sampled more fully. Access to other areas was not uniformly easy because of different types of land use (including modern settlement and industry, areas of dense *maqui* and forest) and farmers unwilling to permit us on to their land. Out of the total of 53.7 km² encompassed by the modified transects, we were eventually able to walk a total of 11.32 km² or a sample of 21.07%. The distribution of the fields walked is shown on fig. 3.6 and in Table 3.1. It will be noted that in some areas coverage continued beyond the transect boundaries. This resulted either from the need to obtain coverage in areas where few fields were available or because a site spread beyond the edge of our transect.

Table 3.1: Proportions of field-walked land in the different transects

| Zone | Transect size (ha) | Area walked (ha) | Percentage coverage |
|---|---|---|---|
| Transect 1 | 1,770 | 199.96 | 11.29 % |
| Transect 2 | 1,600 | 386.41 | 24.15 % |
| Transect 3 | 1,150 | 372.99 | 32.43 % |
| Transect 4 | 850 | 172.18 | 20.26 % |
| *Totals* | *5,370* | *1,131.54* | *21.07 %* |

Our aim was to achieve the highest possible coverage, spread as evenly as possible. To this end coverage was curtailed in areas where it was possible to look at almost every field in order to increase the size of sample examined in the areas of less coverage. Since fields were numbered consecutively as walked, the interested reader should be able to reconstruct our order of working from the transect maps. While additional weeks of fieldwalking would have enabled us to increase the total coverage, we are reasonably confident that the areas covered are both representative of the study area and sufficiently large to permit soundly based conclusions to be drawn.

Each field examined was given a reference number and two record sheets completed for it (figs. 3.7 - 3.8). They were adapted from forms used in England by the Wessex Archaeological Committee (Fasham *et al.* 1980). In the event they did not prove entirely suitable and additional details (e.g., the type of crop and the size of the field in ha) were added. The boundaries of each field walked were marked on overlays to the 1:5,000 maps and the field record numbers recorded on them. The overlays were annotated with details of any particular concentrations of material noted. These maps form the basis for the transect-by-transect maps provided in Chapter 6. Table 3.2 lists the numbers of the fields walked in each season. Details of the field-working methods and techniques of analysing finds are discussed in Chapter 5.

Table 3.2: Fields walked in each season

| Year | Month | Field numbers |
|---|---|---|
| 1985 | September | 1-62 |
| 1986 | September | 100-293 |
| 1987 | September | 300-535 |
| 1988 | September | 600-885 |
| 1989 | September | 900-1053 |
| 1990 | April | 1100-1254 |

Note: the subdivision of several fields (see list in Appendix 4) meant that 1085 fields were eventually walked.

Throughout this report the transect numbers 1 to 4 and their subdivisions are used both for description in the text and for reference to the illustrations. Fig. 3.1 shows the location of the transect subdivisions, detailed topographical maps of which are included in Chapter 6. The correlation between these figures and the 1:25,000 and 1:5,000 maps are provided in Table 3.3.

Table 3.3:

Correlation of the sample transects and their subdivisions with the published maps

| Fig. no. | Transect subdivision | 1:25,000 IGN sheet | Grid references on IGN sheet | 1:5,000 ICC sheets |
|---|---|---|---|---|
| 6.2 | 1A | Tarragona (473-I) | 347.5-351 E / 4557-4558 N | 266 - 137 |
| 6.4 | 1B | Tarragona (473-I) | 351-355.5 E / 4557-4558 N | 267 - 137 & 268 - 137 |
| 6.6 | 1C | Tarragona (473-I) & Torredembarra (473-II) | 355.5-360 E / 4557-4558 N | 269 - 137A & 269 - 137B |
| 6.8 | 1D | Torredembarra (473-II) | 360-365 E / 4557-4558 N | 270 - 137 |
| 6.10 | 2A | Morrell (446-III) | 344.5-347.5 E / 4563-4564 N | 265 - 134 |
| 6.12 | 2B | Morrell (446-III) | 347.5-351 E / 4563-4564 N | 266 - 134 |
| 6.14 | 2C | Morrell (446-III) | 351-354.5 E / 4563-4564 N | 267 - 134 |
| 6.16 | 2D | Morrell (446-III) | 354.5-358 E / 4563-4564 N | 268 - 134 |
| 6.18 | 2E | Morrell (446-III) & Roda de Bará (446-IV) | 358-360.5 E / 4563-4564 N | 269 - 134 |
| 6.20 | 3A | Valls (446-I) | 348.5-351 E / 4569-4570 N | 266 - 131 & 266 - 132 |
| 6.22 | 3B | Valls (446-I) | 351-355 E / 4569-4570 N | 267 - 131 & 267 - 132 |
| 6.24 | 3C | Valls (446-I) | 355-358 E / 4569-4570 N | 268 - 131 & 268 - 132 |
| 6.26 | 3D | Valls (446-I) | 358-359 E / 4590-4570 N | 269 - 131 & 269 - 132 |
| 6.28 | 4A | Valls (446-I) | 348.5-351 E / 4575-4576 N | 266 - 129 |
| 6.30 | 4B | Valls (446-I) | 351-354.5 E / 4575-4576 N | 267 - 129 |
| 6.32 | 4C | Valls (446-I) | 354.5-357 E / 4575-4576 N | 268 - 129 |

Note:    IGN = Instituto Geográfico Nacional, Madrid
         ICC = Institut Cartogràfic de Catalunya, Barcelona

Proprietario                          Nº de campo
                                      Parroquia
Direccion

Telefono                              Ref. de carta
                                      Nombre de campo
                                      Extension de campo

Geologia superficial

Pendiente                             Elementos naturales

Limites

Terraplenas

Tierra

Co-ordenadas de la carta

Referenceias documentarias            Fotos aerias

Tipo de investigacion:                Fecha
  Andando / Apeo / Geofisica /
  Excavacion

Fig.3.7. Documento de Campo

Fecha de la prospección              Nº de Campo

¿Las coordenadas, cuadros y limites del campo estan marcado
sobre la carta?

Visibilidad        Bueno / Regular / Malo

Condiciónes de la tierra al momento de prospección:
                        1. Mojada / Húmedo / Seco
                        2. **Arada** degastada / non-degastada /
                        gradada / sembrada / arbolado / otra
                        – descripción
                        3. Si sembrada, describe la condición del
                        cultivo – no aún visible / visible / exposa
                        4. Luz constante / sol con sombra
¿Hay indicaciónes que el arada recientamente ha cortada el
subsuelo?                  Si / No

Intento de prospección – **investigación** preliminar / detallada /
otra

Metoda de prospección – LINEA: distancia entre investigadores    ;
                        dirección
                        CUADRO: tamaño de cuadro   ; distancia
                        entre investiagadores en el cuadro

Nº linea / cuadro:        Nombre de investigador:

Fig.3.8. Documento de Prospección a Diario.

# Chapter 4: SURVEY METHODOLOGY

The overall strategy has been introduced in Chapter 3. Here the intention is to provide details of the working methods, first the field methods, then the techniques of processing finds, and lastly how the data were mapped and potential sites identified. Detailed treatment of individual finds is given in Chapter 5; sites will be considered in Chapter 6. Visible structural remains in the survey area were rare; thus the evidence for sites generally comprises pottery and construction materials. Therefore we had to develop a methodology for identifying sites from surface material alone.

## FIELD METHODS

Modern agricultural fields were selected as the basic units for the collection of finds. Where the fields were exceptionally large and could be readily subdivided by features identifiable on the maps, this was done. Each field was walked in lines by individual walkers spaced at intervals of c.5 m. The distance between walkers was not precisely measured, but, as most of the team members were experienced, any variation in spacing was relatively insignificant. The ground conditions were recorded for each field (figs. 3.7-3.8). The influence that ground conditions had on results is discussed in Chapter 7. It is estimated that the field of vision of any individual walker is 2 to 2.5 m wide, with the result that the spacing produced a coverage of 40-50% of field surfaces. There is no doubt that when concentrations of finds were encountered the intensity of observation increased initially but declined with weariness if very large volumes of material had to be collected. This probably had a marginal effect on the volume of finds recovered, but there is no evidence that this was significant.

Each walker was instructed to place in a polythene bag any cultural material found on the surface in their line. In most fields the finds were gathered into a single bag marked with the field number after walking had been completed, since the primary collection units were the individual fields. Most of the fields within the area walked were relatively small (average area 1.04 ha), with the result that the level of resolution obtained was felt to be adequate. On occasions the material from individual lines was kept separately, the lines being distinguished by reference letters recorded on sketch maps on the record sheets. This was not often done as it slowed considerably the processing and recording of finds. We came to the conclusion that it was preferable to obtain broad coverage of the landscape rather than collect detailed information about every site located. In the case of a few selected sites more detailed survey work was undertaken (Chapter 7). The non-destructive nature of the survey makes it possible for future workers to undertake detailed studies of sites identified should it be felt worthwhile.

Although the fieldwalkers were instructed to collect all cultural material, post-mediaeval ceramics were sorted and discarded without being recorded either just after a particular field had been walked or at a preliminary stage in the processing. Fieldwalkers thus learned not to collect the more obviously modern material. There was considerable debate about this practice. The possibility that mediaeval material inadvertently was missed was investigated by the detailed examination of samples of the discarded finds. Although it would be foolish to insist that such pottery was never overlooked, we are convinced that this was not often the case.

The other problem encountered in the field was the varying ability of walkers to collect material other than pottery. As a forthcoming study of the lithics will show, there are discernible patterns within the distributions recovered; thus a reasonable sample seems to have been collected. However, there is little doubt that, since most walkers were more attuned to looking for ceramics, lithics and metal objects are probably under-represented. All the metal objects were recovered by the same two experienced members of the team; they were also the most expert at recovering lithics.

PROCESSING METHODS

The finds collected in the field were taken to the base in Tarragona for processing. All the material taken from the fields was washed and dried in the open air before being sorted. As all the pottery, flint, and other objects (except tile) were destined for museum collections, each piece was marked with its field number and later rebagged and boxed. These finds were kept grouped by field and were boxed according to the *terme municipal* from which they came.

Once the finds were sorted into categories (pottery, lithics, tile, and others) they were classified and recorded, initially by simple lists but after the first two seasons on standardized record sheets (fig. 4.1). The following procedures were followed:

•*Pottery* was first sorted into broad fabric types based on groups already established for the region. Distinctive fabrics which could not be readily attributed to known sources were sampled and ascribed to a running fabric series. Subsequently it was possible to propose regions of origin for a number of these fabrics either through the discovery of sherds of distinctive form, or through a programme of fabric analysis (see Appendix 2). A residue of mainly small sherds could not be given a source and was recorded generically (as coarse pottery, amphora, etc.). Each fabric from each field was counted and weighed before the rims and sherds of distinctive decoration or form were re-examined. Many could be identified using established typologies. Relief decorated and stamped sherds of terra sigillata were rubbed with graphite on tissue paper to record their schemes. Selected sherds, primarily little-known forms, were drawn before being replaced in bags destined for the museum.

•*Lithics* were passed to John Schofield who drew and recorded them. Important pieces were photographed before being returned to the museum boxes. His analysis will appear elsewhere.

•*Tile* presented more difficulties since, although there was surprisingly little, the pieces generally were small and Roman material almost indistinguishable in form and fabric from mediaeval and post-mediaeval pieces. In rare instances we found larger fragments which were diagnostically Roman. All but the definitely modern tile was recorded by count and weight before being discarded. The quantification almost certainly over-estimates the amount of Roman brick and tile found.

•*Other material* (coins, small finds and stone objects) were rare. They were recorded by photography and drawing before being deposited in the museum. The small quantities of glass were merely counted; none was distinctive or of outstanding quality.

The catalogues produced by these means form the basis of the discussions in Chapter 6. Copies of the full catalogues are kept with the finds at the Museu Nacional Arqueòlogic de Tarragona and are also held by the authors.

MAPPING THE DATA

It was clear from an early stage in the survey that the whole area was strewn with considerable quantities of ancient material, chiefly pottery. Indeed, a total of 94,206 sherds (1922.446 kg) was collected, producing a mean value of 83 sherds or 1.69 kg per hectare walked. The material was neither evenly distributed across the landscape nor equally common at all periods. Whilst some variations in distribution appeared to result from changes in the pattern of settlement, other factors also contributed. In particular there appeared to be evidence for
(a) variations in the volume of pottery supplied and used at different periods;
(b) changes in the distribution mechanisms which had brought it to the area, and
(c) alterations in the ways in which rubbish (including the pottery) had been discarded before it entered the archaeological record.
The material collected was mapped to facilitate both the observation of changes through time and the identification of concentrations of finds which might relate to buried settlements. However, the issues discussed above could not be ignored. It was therefore decided to separate the process of mapping pottery distributions from their interpretation. For mapping it was decided not to use an arbitary scale (e.g., less than 10 sherds per line; 10-50 sherds; more than 50 sherds, etc.); instead, we chose to establish scales for the mapping in accordance with observed

CAMPO:
LINEA:

| | SHERD NO | R | H | WT. (Kg) | TO DRAW |
|---|---|---|---|---|---|
| Anfora masaliota | | | | | |
| Gris emporitana | | | | | |
| Campaniense A | | | | | |
| Campaniense B | | | | | |
| Campaniense C | | | | | |
| C. común itálica (Q) | | | | | |
| Anfora púnica (102) | | | | | |
| Anfora ebusitana (3) | | | | | |
| Anfora ibérica (14/16) | | | | | |
| Anfora ibérica (20) | | | | | |
| Cerámica fina ibérica (14/16) | | | | | |
| Cerámica fina ibérica ( ) | | | | | |
| Anfora itálica (1) | | | | | |
| Anfora itálica (4) | | | | | |
| Anfora itálica (5) | | | | | |
| Anfora itálica (6) | | | | | |
| Anfora itálica (7) | | | | | |
| Anfora itálica ( ) | | | | | |
| Anfora itálica ( ) | | | | | |
| Anfora itálica ( ) | | | | | |
| Anfora itálica ( ) | | | | | |
| Anfora itálica ( ) | | | | | |
| Anfora tarraconense (12) | | | | | |
| Anfora tarraconense (13) | | | | | |
| Anfora tarraconense ( ) | | | | | |
| Anfora de la Bética (97) | | | | | |
| Anfora de la Bética (32) | | | | | |
| Anfora sudgálica (37) | | | | | |
| Paredes finas | | | | | |
| T.S. Sudgálica | | | | | |
| T.S. Itálica | | | | | |
| T.S. Hispánica | | | | | |
| T.S. Clara A | | | | | |
| SUB-TOTAL | | | | | |

Fig.4.1a. Record sheet for finds recovered on the survey.

| | SHERD NO | R | H | WT. (Kg) | TO DRAW |
|---|---|---|---|---|---|
| T.S. Clara C | | | | | |
| T.S. Clara D | | | | | |
| Anfora africana bajoimperial (102) | | | | | |
| Anfora oriental bajoimperial ( ) | | | | | |
| Anfora bética bajoimperial (104) | | | | | |
| Anfora misc. ( ) | | | | | |
| Anfora misc. ( ) | | | | | |
| Anfora misc. ( ) | | | | | |
| Anfora misc. ( ) | | | | | |
| Anfora misc. ( ) | | | | | |
| Anfora misc. ( ) | | | | | |
| Anfora misc. ( ) | | | | | |
| Anfora misc. ( ) | | | | | |
| C. comm. (K) | | | | | |
| C. comm. (19) | | | | | |
| C. comm. (13) | | | | | |
| C. comm. (MN) | | | | | |
| C. comm. misc. ( ) | | | | | |
| C. comm. misc. ( ) | | | | | |
| C. comm. misc. ( ) | | | | | |
| C. comm. misc. ( ) | | | | | |
| C. comm. misc. ( ) | | | | | |
| C. comm. misc. ( ) | | | | | |
| C. comm. misc. ( ) | | | | | |
| Tegula | | | | | |
| Silex | | | | | |
| Otros | | | | | |
| - | | | | | |
| - | | | | | |
| - | | | | | |
| SUB-TOTAL | | | | | |
| TOTAL | | | | | |

Fig.4.1b. Continuation of Record sheet for finds recovered on the survey.

variations in the densities. In this way it was hoped that the processes of mapping and identification of potential sites would be more rigorous and open to reassessment.

Analysis was undertaken by stages. In the first instance we intended to identify the principal concentrations of finds at different periods. The aim was to calculate the average density of pottery for each period across the whole landscape and to identify the fields in which concentrations were considerably greater than this mean (for a preliminary statement of these ideas see Millett 1985; 1991a). The stages in this analysis (summarized in Table 4.1) will now be considered step by step:

Table 4.1. Procedure for Processing Data to Produce Scales for Mapping

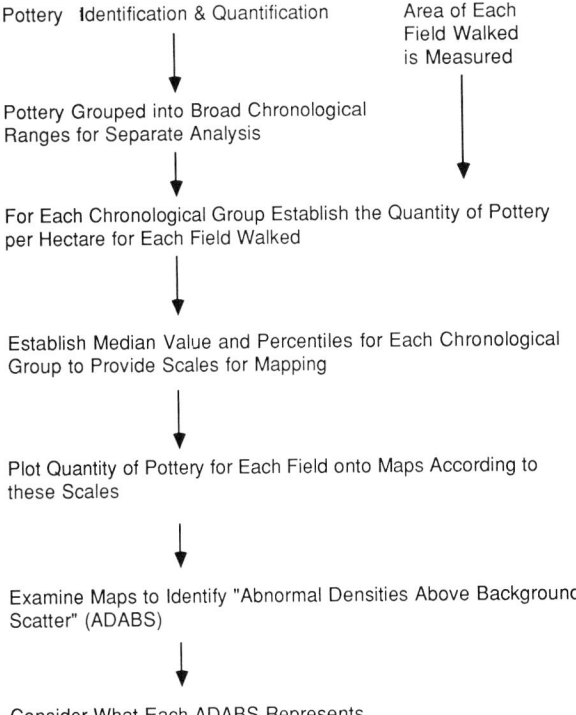

**1.** The pottery fabrics characterized and dated by S.K. were grouped in 4 chronological phases for the purposes of the analysis. The ranges of these ceramic phases are as follows:

*Iberica* (Iberian: 6th/5th to 1st c. B.C.)
*Republicana* (Republican: late 3rd to 1st c. B.C.)
*Alto Imperial* (High Empire: 1st-2nd c. A.D.)
*Bajo Imperial* (Late Empire: 3rd-6th c. A.D.)

The fabrics assigned to these broad phases are noted on the lists in Appendix 4. The phases are crucial since they allow us to group the ceramics into manageable chronological categories that are compatible with the general history of this part of the western empire. The aim was also to maximize the number of dated pottery types included so as to ensure that sufficiently large quantities of material were present for the results to be usable. The four phases minimized the number of chronologically undiagnostic fabrics, although they comprised up to *c.*40% of groups (see Appendix 4).[1]

---

1    This material was generally made up of coarse wares which were indistinct or too fragmentary to be assigned to known production centres.

We should stress that the chronological phases are drawn from the ceramic data rather than imposed from the historical sources. For example, Italic black glaze (Campanian ware) can be assigned confidently to the Republican period. Italic red-gloss wares (*terra sigillata italica*) is assigned to the early imperial period which technically begins in 27 B.C., although production of the fine ware had begun some years earlier. Similarly, all African cooking wares were assigned to the early imperial period even though some may well have continued into the late empire.

Possible overlaps of this kind were few and have a negligible overall effect. The ceramic phases can be used to examine the overall patterns of pottery distribution across the area through time. They proved useful as a means of producing scales for the overall mapping, but for the more detailed studies of pottery distributions and dating of sites (Chapters 6 and 9) the more subtle chronologies of individual, closely-dated types have been preferred.

The most difficult problem of overlap between one phase and another concerns the productions defined as *Iberica* and *Republicana*. Iberian material first appears in the 6th/5th c. and continues until the 1st c. B.C., even though significant typological changes occurred (see Chapter 5). There is no evidence that Iberian ceramics ceased to be manufactured in the later 3rd c.; their continuation into the late 1st c. B.C. is well attested and symptomatic of indigenous cultural continuity into the Roman period in this and other parts of Iberia. There was a clear overlap with Republican wares which appear in the late 3rd c. and disappeared at the same time as the Iberian productions. It would have been easy to group together both classes of pottery and class them simply as 'pre-imperial', but it was felt important to maintain a distinction. As fig. 4.2 shows, there are differences between the density distributions of these two fabrics. Those classified as *Iberica* have a wider and denser distribution than those grouped as *Republicana*. This distinction is also visible in the mapped distributions.

Two explanations seem possible. It may be that the presence or absence of pottery grouped as *Iberica* or *Republicana* reflects cultural preferences on the part of the rural populations. Alternatively, it may be that some sites with *Iberica* alone were earlier than those which also had *Republicana*. This is particularly true of sites 1.11, 1.12 and 3.13 where the typology of rims suggests occupation principally between the 6th/5th and 3rd c. B.C. (Appendix 6). The implications of this problem are explored in Chapter 10.

**2.** It was decided to use the individual fields as sample units for the mapping of distributions. They had to be measured before they could be used to establish the pottery densities. Therefore we overlay gridded paper on 1:5,000 maps and counted the numbers of squares covered. (Had we been starting our survey today we would have employed a GIS system to do this and other tasks automatically.) Given the map scales and the 1 mm squares used, the level of precision produced by this tedious method was very high and is easily consistent with the presentation of field sizes to two significant decimal places (i.e. to within 100 m$^2$).

**3.** The quantities of pottery from each of the 4 broad chronological divisons were totalled for each field and divided by the field area to produce a density per hectare.

**4.** The data (fig. 4.2) demonstrate that the ranges of pottery density values do not have a Normal Distribution; therefore it was decided to plot the densities on the maps using a scale based on the median rather than the mean.

The median is the middle value in the distribution when all are ranked. In our survey there were 1085 fields; thus the value of the median of any group is that of the 543rd when ranked. In our study this scaling was extended by subdividing the scale into 10% ranges (10 percentile). Thus the value of the top 10 percentile is that of the 109th field from the top; that of the second or 20 percentile is the 217th from the top, etc. Thus the densities of the pottery found within the survey area defined the scales used to plot the maps. Had there been no variation in the volume of pottery supply, the values of the median and percentiles for the different periods would have been the same. This method has the advantage that, regardless of the absolute quantities of pottery present, it is possible to compare one period with another because it defines, for instance, the highest

Chapter 4

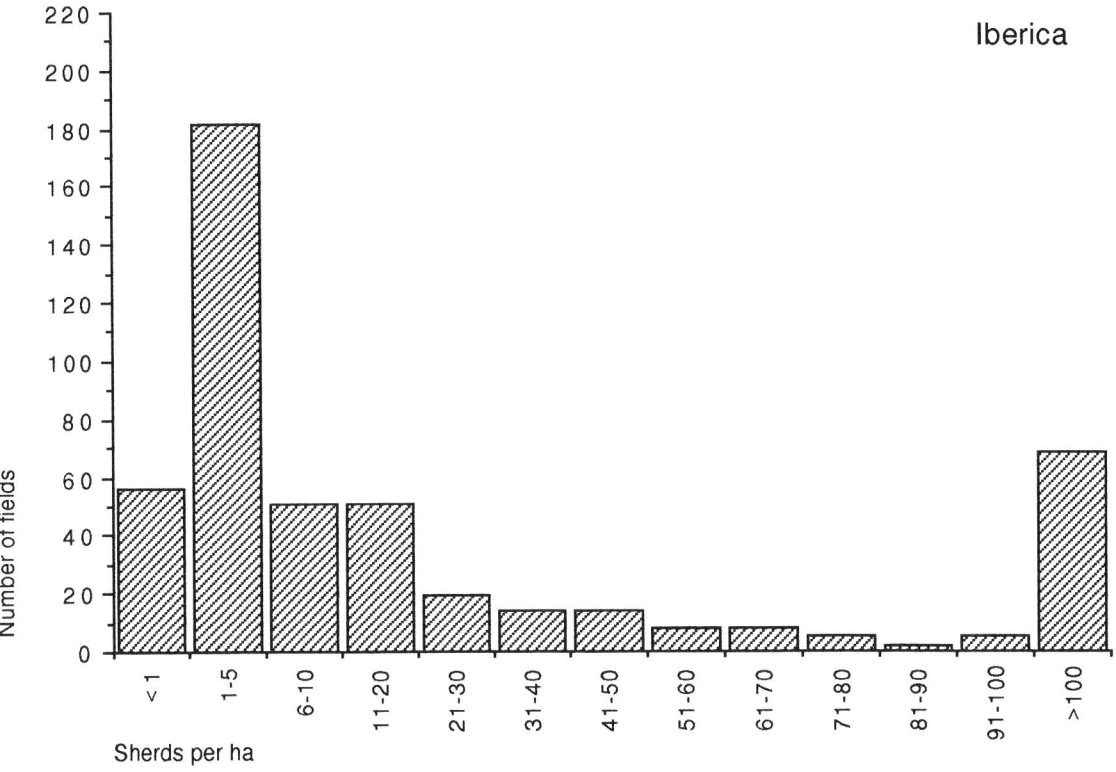

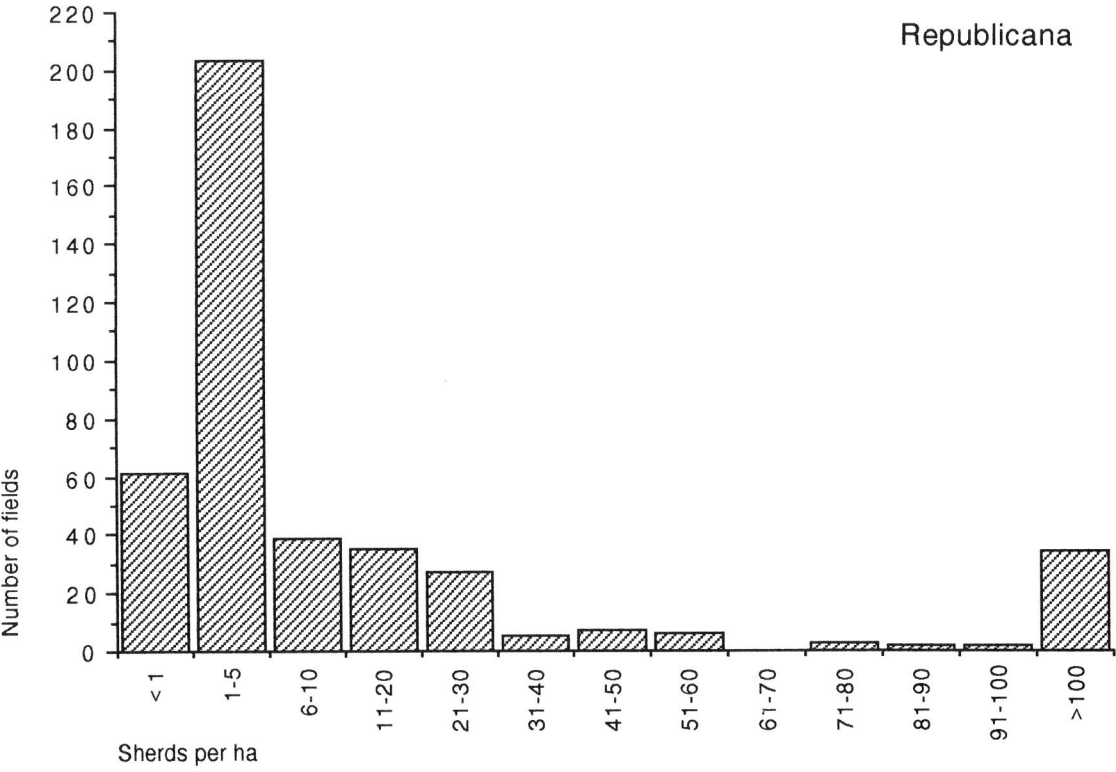

Fig.4.2. Graphs showing the ranges of pottery density (in sherds per ha for each field) as recorded for each ceramic phase. (For clarity the numbers of fields without pottery are omitted: they are Iberian 580; Republican 634; Early Imperial 731; Late Imperial 981).

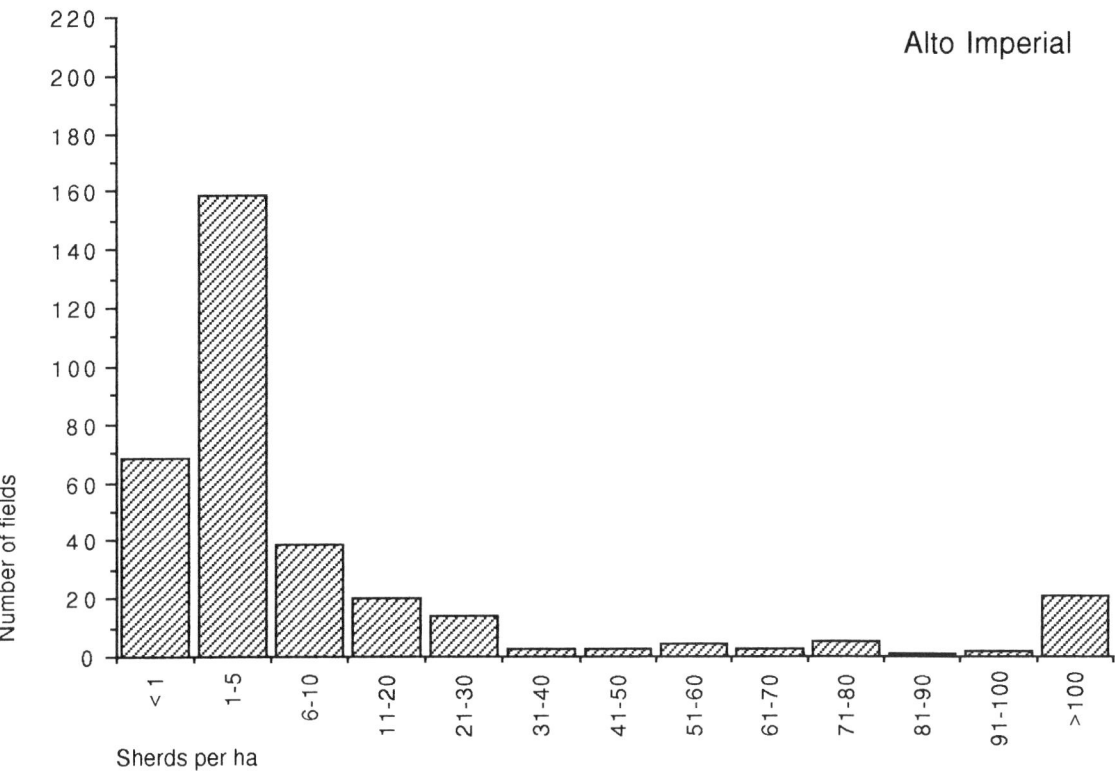

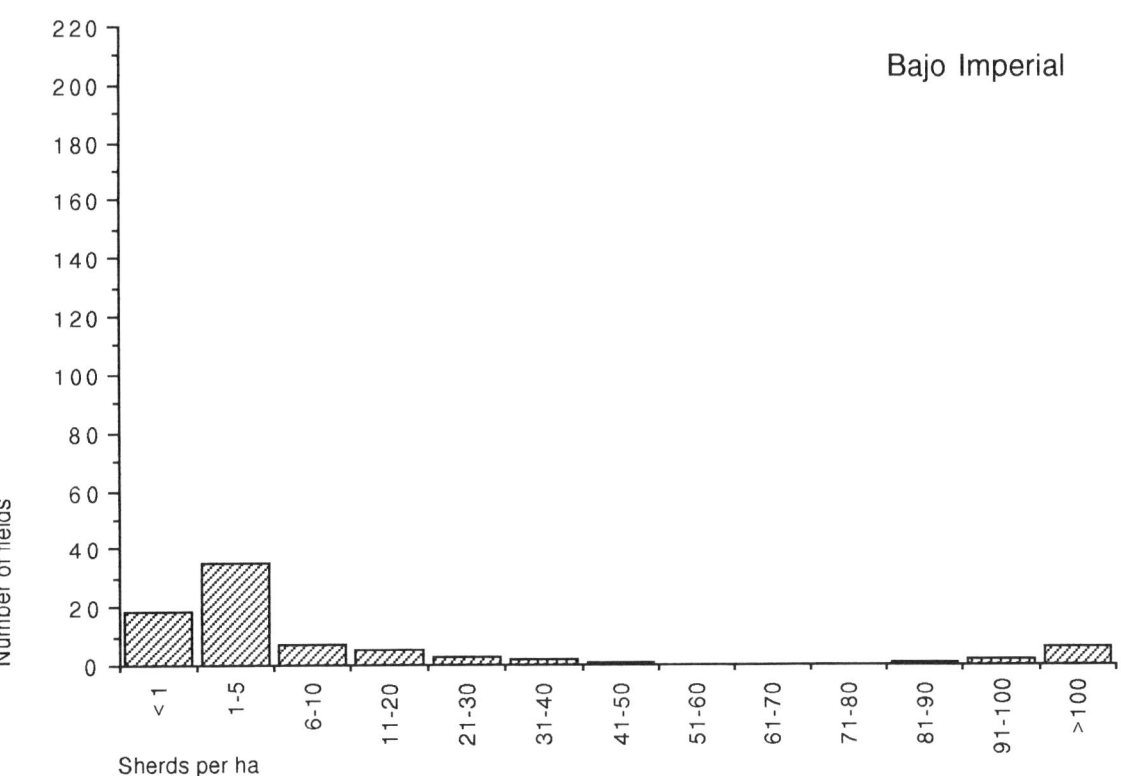

Fig.4.2 continued.

10% of the values for each period. It should be remembered that the method simply enables us to make valid comparisons by defining the areas of high density. It does not in itself provide a method for explaining how a particular concentration of material was formed. That requires making an archaeological judgement on each case (see Chapter 6).

The scales for the four broad chronological phases were defined in this way by running the sherd numbers through a simple routine on the SPSSX program on a computer at Durham University. Sherd numbers rather than weights were used because these were felt to provide a better measure given the nature of the material gathered by field-walking. As there was a 95% correlation between the two measures, one can reasonably be taken as proxy for the other. The results are shown in Table 4.2. These show that, since more than half the fields in any one phase produced no pottery, the value of the median is always 0. The observed variation in the frequency of pottery means that the scales used for the maps begin at the 40 percentile for the Iberian material and the 30 percentile for the Republican and Early imperial periods. There was so little material from the Late Empire that the presence of any pottery at all places it within the top 10% range. The resulting problem is discussed below.

Table 4.2.  Scales from the Survey

| Percentiles: | IBERIAN | | REPUBLICAN | | EARLY EMPIRE | | LATE EMPIRE | |
| | Sherd | Wt | Sherd | Wt | Sherd | Wt | Sherd | Wt |
|---|---|---|---|---|---|---|---|---|
| 50 | 0.0 | 0.0 | 0.0 | 0.0 | 0.0 | 0.0 | 0.0 | 0.0 |
| 40 | 0.9 | 0.009 | 0.0 | 0.0 | 0.0 | 0.0 | 0.0 | 0.0 |
| 30 | 2.5 | 0.034 | 1.4 | 0.050 | 0.3 | 0.003 | 0.0 | 0.0 |
| 20 | 8.0 | 0.128 | 3.7 | 0.170 | 1.9 | 0.041 | 0.0 | 0.0 |
| 10 | 41.9 | 0.648 | 12.6 | 0.630 | 6.1 | 0.229 | 0.0 | 0.0 |
| Median | 0.0 | 0.0 | 0.0 | 0.0 | 0.0 | 0.0 | 0.0 | 0.0 |
| Mean | 56.7 | 0.750 | 12.4 | 0.603 | 10.2 | 0.341 | 4.1 | 0.092 |
| Standard deviation | 411.8 | 5.103 | 65.5 | 3.259 | 79.9 | 2.715 | 68.8 | 1.464 |

| NOTES | 1. | The percentile ranges are numbered from the highest downwards (ie 10 percentile = the top 10% of the values) |
|---|---|---|
| | 2. | All values **sherds-per-hectare** or **kg-per-hectare** |
| | 3. | Results are based on 1085 fields |

**5.** The scale shown in Table 4.2 was used to plot the density of pottery in each of the fields walked for each of the four ceramic phases. The results (figs. 6.2-6.33), which are reviewed in detail in Chapter 6, were used to identify 'abnormal densities above background scatter' (henceforth 'adabs'). These were defined as areas which showed one or more adjacent fields in the top 10 percentile. Clearly these 'adabs' might have resulted from a number of factors, only one of which was the presence of a buried settlement site. Other processes, like agricultural manuring, will be considered in Chapter 7. Since it was not possible to evaluate each of the 'adabs' through excavation or geophysical survey, our identification of those that may represent sites remains subjective. In a few instances, however, these conclusions were supported either by the observation of remains such as floors and walls within exposed sections or through testing by geophysical survey (see Chapter 7).

The criteria used for the tentative identification of 'adabs' as sites were based on the spatial and chronological coherence of the patterns observed. In general those areas where there was a distinctive cluster of fields in the top 10 percentile that remained in that range through two or more contiguous ceramic phases were considered likely to be settlement sites. It will be clear from an examination of the transect maps (figs. 6.2-6.33) that there were relatively few 'adabs' which did not fulfil these criteria. For the most part they identify chronologically and spatially coherent clusters of fields that are identified and numbered as settlements. Where there are problems of interpretation they are analysed in the descriptions of the transects in Chapter 6.

METHODOLOGICAL PROBLEMS

The results produced by the methods just described are generally coherent and we believe that they stand up to critical scrutiny. Nevertheless, both practical and philosophical problems raised by the methods should serve as a caution to others contemplating using our results or applying the methods. These problems relate first to confidence in our measurements and second to anomalies created by the scales in certain circumstances.

The methods used are based on the aggregate densities of material collected by the individual walkers within the collection units. It will be evident to those who have been involved in fieldwork that the efficiency of collection is affected by factors ranging from the available light and degree of surface visibility to the experience of the walkers. Some of these have been the subject of an exhaustive consideration by Shennan (1985). We will consider them in Chapter 7.

Before arriving at archaeological conclusions based on the patterning observed, we must be sure that the degree of bias created by the above factors was sufficiently minor to ensure that our maps do not simply show the collection biases. The danger of results being influenced by the abilities of individual walkers (cf. Haselgrove 1985, 21-35) is reduced in this survey by the simple process of aggregating the finds by fields. Nevertheless, our results have been carefully compared with the original field records so that we can be satisfied that such problems are of only marginal importance. (Individual instances where we have identified problems will be considered during the discussion of the transects in Chapter 6.) If biases had been of sufficient magnitude, correction factors could have been applied before the scales were calculated — for instance, to compensate for varying surface visibility. This proved unnecessary, and anyone considering it would need to exercise extreme caution in establishing the magnitude of any correction factors applied. Our preference has been to examine each apparent anomaly individually and to seek sensible explanations in our records of field conditions.

The second set of problems concerns the method of applying scales. It must be remembered that the method simply facilitates the identification of the highest concentrations of material in a given ceramic phase, thus making comparisons between the different phases possible. The highest 10% of the values (or 108 fields) in each phase has been mapped with the highest density value. It is important to recognize that, although this makes comparison easy and thus moves beyond the use of purely arbitrary scales, the boundary chosen (10%) is still subjectively imposed. There is no reason to suppose that the top 10% of fields are any more important than, say, the top 11% or 15%. The method is fairly useful provided it is used as a guide to interpretation rather than as an absolute scale, but it does create particular problems in two of our phases.

Our work has shown that there were major variations in the quantities of pottery in circulation in different periods (fig. 4.2). The significance of this will be discussed in Chapter 9. Here it is important to note that in certain periods, such as the Bronze Age or the Mediaeval Period, when the area was almost certainly occupied, there are no known concentrations of ceramics. For these periods it is clear that our methodology proved inadequate. In the late-Roman period pottery was in circulation although evidently scarce; this also provides a test for the methodology. Any field containing even a single sherd of pottery of this period automatically falls in the top 10%, since less than 108 fields contained any pottery of this period. This makes it difficult to distinguish between a casual loss and a site which utilized so little pottery that it is represented on the surface by only a single sherd. This problem can only be overcome by examining each findspot in the context of other evidence to consider how it is best interpreted. In the case of the late-Roman material it proved useful to distinguish on the transect maps (figs. 6.2-6.33) between fields with only a single sherd and those with higher densities. In periods with such a low overall density of finds further work is needed to evaluate potential sites. It should also be noted that there is an increased probability of missing further sites which have similarly low densities of finds.

This problem also highlights an issue relevant to other phases when there may have been sites at the lower end of the settlement hierachy occupied by people with little or no access to goods such as pottery. Their settlements thus fall below the 'adabs' threshold. This difficulty is not easy to overcome, particularly in phases when pottery was generally abundant. In our survey Iberian material is the most widespread and its overall distribution suggests that the landscape was quite densely populated. Although it might be doubted that there were settlements which did not have access to pottery during this period, it is certainly conceivable that the 10% cut-off excludes some settlements that were materially poorer. This illustrates how important it is to consider the overall patterns of ceramic distribution in order to assess whether concentrations of lower density have sufficient spatial coherence and chronological consistency to be considered as potential settlement sites.

If these methods were used mechanistically they could result in an entirely misleading picture. In phases of ceramic abundance 10% of all fields would be automatically considered sites, while in phases of ceramic shortage any pottery at all would be taken to represent a site. We hope that by using the method as a guide and by applying archaeological judgement any circularity of argument has been avoided. Even if it has not, sufficiently detailed data have been presented to permit others to reinterpret them.

# Chapter 5: ANALYSIS OF FINDS

This chapter presents the primary evidence from the survey. The principal section on the pottery is followed by shorter sections on the other ancient finds.

## THE POTTERY

Ceramics are without doubt the most abundant archaeological evidence for settlement patterns in the protohistoric and classical periods. Our survey was no exception, and a total of 1.922 metric tonnes was collected over the 6 years.

The treatment of pottery by archaeologists has varied considerably from survey to survey. In some cases only the most 'interesting' or 'chronologically significant' pieces are recorded, with some notation about their frequency. In other cases, a more detailed listing is given but little more than a subjective opinion about whether the 'assemblages' are representative of the overall surface collection. The theoretical stance of this survey has been to accept that there is an implicit relationship between surface and sub-surface archaeology (Haselgrove 1985), and that much of the material collected derives from archaeological deposits brought to the surface by agricultural activities. We also recognize that there are difficulties in distinguishing sites from off-site materials (see Chapter 4). Nevertheless, it was hoped that statistical treatment of surface materials would enable sites and off-site material in the landscape to be distinguished more systematically. Therefore from the start it was decided to collect all the surface material that corresponded to our objectives. The ceramics were treated as if derived from excavated contexts. After an initial sorting in the field to eliminate modern material, all pottery from each field was bagged together. It was washed at Tarragona and identified on a field-by-field basis. Initially it was divided into the classes of fineware, coarseware, amphora, and tile. Each class was then subdivided into individual products identified on the basis of fabric. At this stage a 'running' fabric series was created, all rim, base, handle and body sherds being ascribed to a particular fabric. The fabrics and forms were then recorded by count and weight. Sherds required for drawing were removed and later returned. Some well-known imported fabrics could be readily identified. Most local fabrics had to be characterized, first by eye and in some cases later by petrological thin-section of selected samples.

The totals for each field were recorded on a form (fig. 4.1) (data based on this quantification are to given in Appendix 4). They were then used in the next stage of the analysis (Chapter 6). By these methods all the pottery found during each season was completely identified by the end of the season.

### Typology

The shortage of published archaeological sequences from the Tarragona region meant that no single ceramic typology was available as a basis for studying our material. Most of the finewares were imports and could be classified according to the standard works of Morel (1981), Oswald and Pryce (1920), and Hayes (1972). As they were fragmented and did not offer any new typological information, they are not listed but given in Appendix 4 in the site-by-site list of identified pottery types. Our strategy was to concentrate upon illustrating those sherds whose typological development is not well established, or where there was significant typological variation. For coarse wares and amphorae the most useful recent work is the study of late-Roman deposits at Tarragona (TED'A 1989). To compensate for the absence of local typologies for the Iberian, Roman Republican and early imperial periods, use was made of typologies from neighbouring areas, particularly the province of Girona and the region of Valencia, both of which belong to the same broad cultural region.

Each type description is followed by a list of sites from which they came, the fabric number (see the fabric descriptions in Appendix 1), and the dating evidence. The presence and absence of types on individual sites in the survey area is listed in Appendix 6.

For convenience the following abbreviations are used in the typology:

| | | | |
|---|---|---|---|
| Almagro | Almagro Basch 1955 | Ostia | Ostia III |
| Africana | Ostia III | Aguarod | Aguarod 1991 |
| Aranegui-Pla | Aranegui and Pla 1981 | Pereira | Pereira 1988 |
| Beltrán | Beltrán Lloris 1970 | PE | Ramón, J. 1981 |
| Cintas | Cintas 1950 | Py | Py 1978 |
| Gauloise | Laubenheimer 1985 | Ribera | Ribera 1982 |
| Keay | Keay 1984 | Tripolitana | Ostia III |
| Mañá | Mañá 1950 | Van der Werff | Van der Werff 1978 |
| Mata-Bonet | Mata and Bonet 1992 | Vila-roma | Fabrega 1989 |
| | | Will | Will 1982 |

In the illustrations the vessel number is followed first by the number of the field (C = Campo) in which it was found, and second by its fabric reference (F = fabric).

# AMPHORAE

AMPHORAE OF PRE-IMPERIAL DATE (6th-mid 1st c. B.C.)

Iberian Production

*Type 1: Iberian amphora/ Ánfora Boca Plana*

Overall these amphorae date to between the 5th c. and the end of the 1st c. B.C. and are characteristic of the Iberians. Ultimately the form was derived from Phoenician prototypes, but it was manufactured widely along the coast of Mediterranean Iberia, from Languedoc to Andalusia. Kilns have been discovered in the territory of Tarraco (Colominas Roca 1915-20) and in the *Pais Valenciano* (Ribera 1982). The amphorae have a long tapering, piriform body, a hollow base, and lug handles on the shoulder. They are characterized by a rounded shoulder, no neck, and a circular mouth with a poorly pronounced or non-existent rim. Within this general type variations in the rims have allowed several variants to be characterized. The content of these amphorae is not known, although fish sauce may be one of various possibilities (see Appendix 3).

An attempt has been made to group the material from the survey into categories based upon differences in rim detail. Where possible, they follow the sub-types established by Ribera (1982). His were based upon a limited number of complete vessels whereas ours were largely rim fragments. Consequently, a decision was taken to publish a large number of rim fragments, and to try and match them *grosso modo* with Ribera's typology. A clear match is often not possible. However, we hope that it will facilitate re-analysis of the data in the future when more excavated sequences are available. At the moment the dating of the rims should be treated with caution. The rims are described first, followed by the handles and bases found.

A      Rims
Found at sites: 1.2, 1.4, 1.6, 1.8, 1.9, 1.11, 1.12, 1.13, 1.14, 2.2, 2.3, 2.4, 2.6, 2.7, 2.9, 2.10, 3.1, 3.3, 3.4, 3.9, 3.10, 3.11, 3.13, 3.15, 3.16, 3.17, 3.18, 3.19, 4.1, 4.2, 4.3, 4.4, 4.5, 4.6.

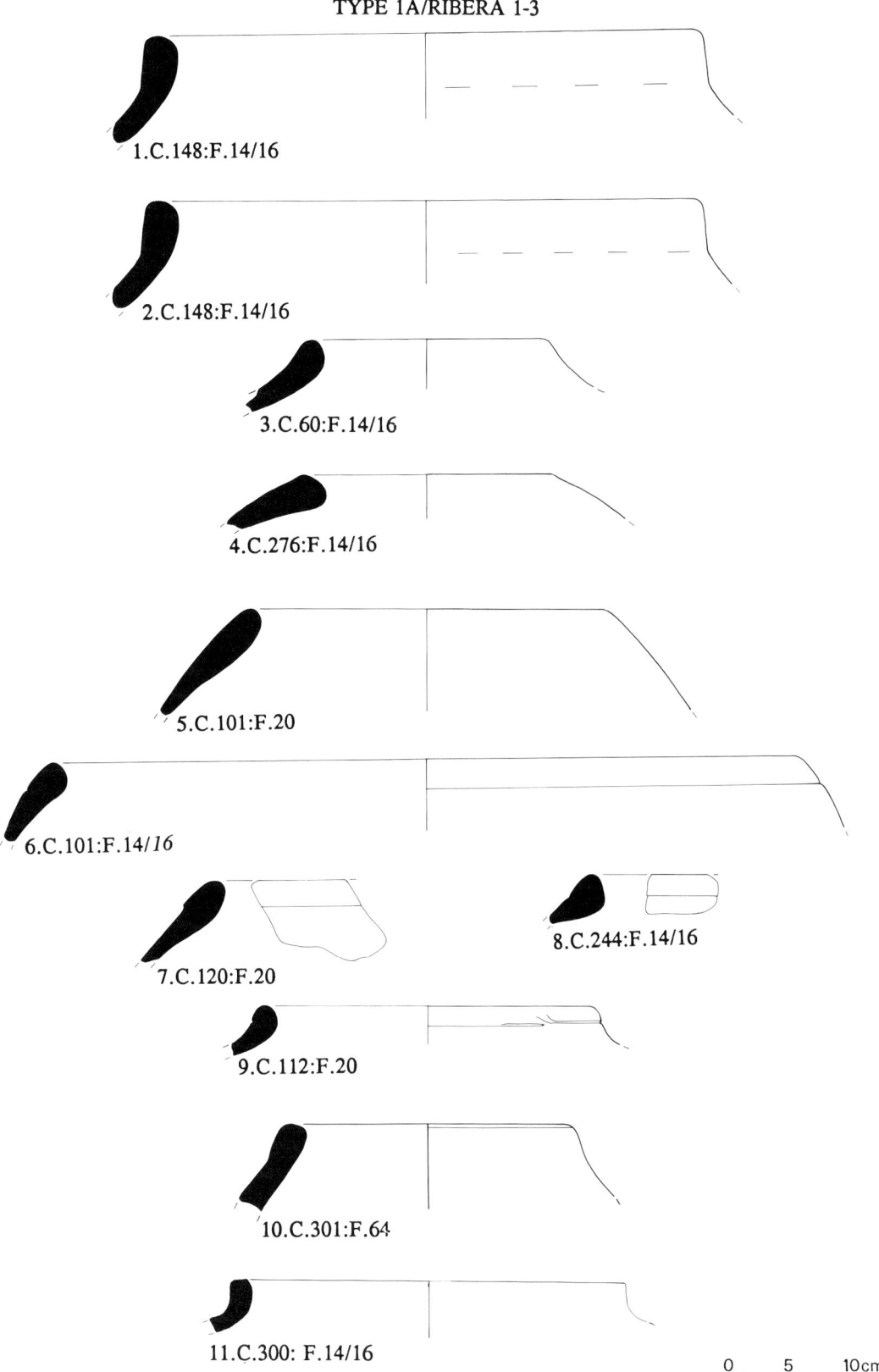

1.C.148:F.14/16

2.C.148:F.14/16

3.C.60:F.14/16

4.C.276:F.14/16

5.C.101:F.20

6.C.101:F.14/16

7.C.120:F.20

8.C.244:F.14/16

9.C.112:F.20

10.C.301:F.64

11.C.300: F.14/16

0    5    10cm

*Type 1A/ Ribera I-3* (Fig. 5.1)
Characterized by a virtually non-existent rim.
Sites: especially 1.6, 1.9, 1.13, 3.19.
Fabrics: 14/16, 20, 64.
Date: between the late 5th and early 2nd c. B.C. (Ribera 1982, 104 ff.).

Fig. 5.1 Amphorae of pre-imperial date. Iberian productions.

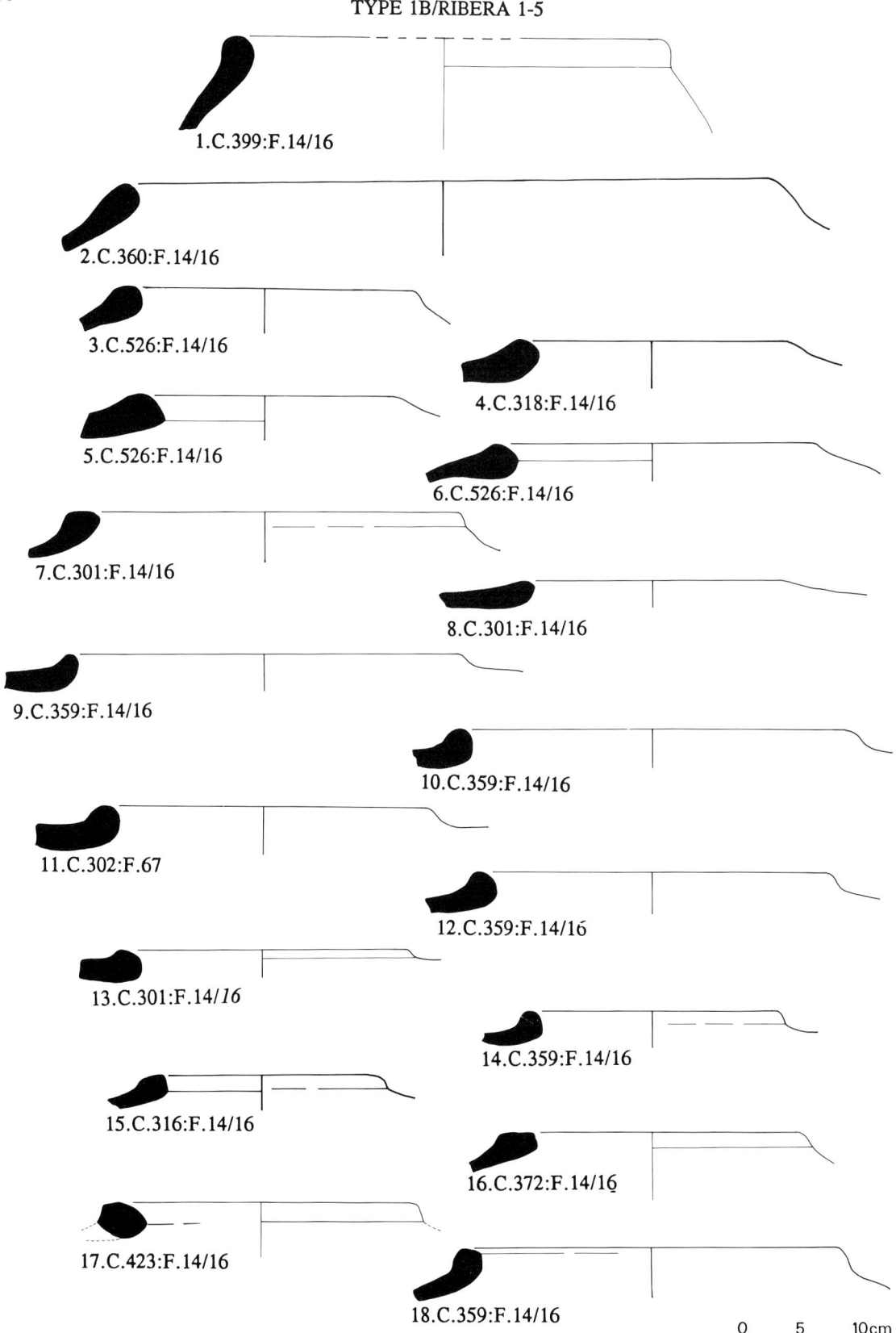

1.C.399:F.14/16

2.C.360:F.14/16

3.C.526:F.14/16

4.C.318:F.14/16

5.C.526:F.14/16

6.C.526:F.14/16

7.C.301:F.14/16

8.C.301:F.14/16

9.C.359:F.14/16

10.C.359:F.14/16

11.C.302:F.67

12.C.359:F.14/16

13.C.301:F.14/16

14.C.359:F.14/16

15.C.316:F.14/16

16.C.372:F.14/16

17.C.423:F.14/16

18.C.359:F.14/16

0    5    10cm

Fig. 5.2 Amphorae of pre-imperial date. Iberian productions.

*Type 1B/ Ribera I-5* (Fig. 5.2)
As Type 1A but with a more pronounced rim.
Sites: especially 2.7, 2.9, 3.13, 3.15, 3.16, 3.17, 3.18, 3.19.
Fabrics: 14/16, 20 and 67.
Date: later 3rd to later 1st c. B.C.

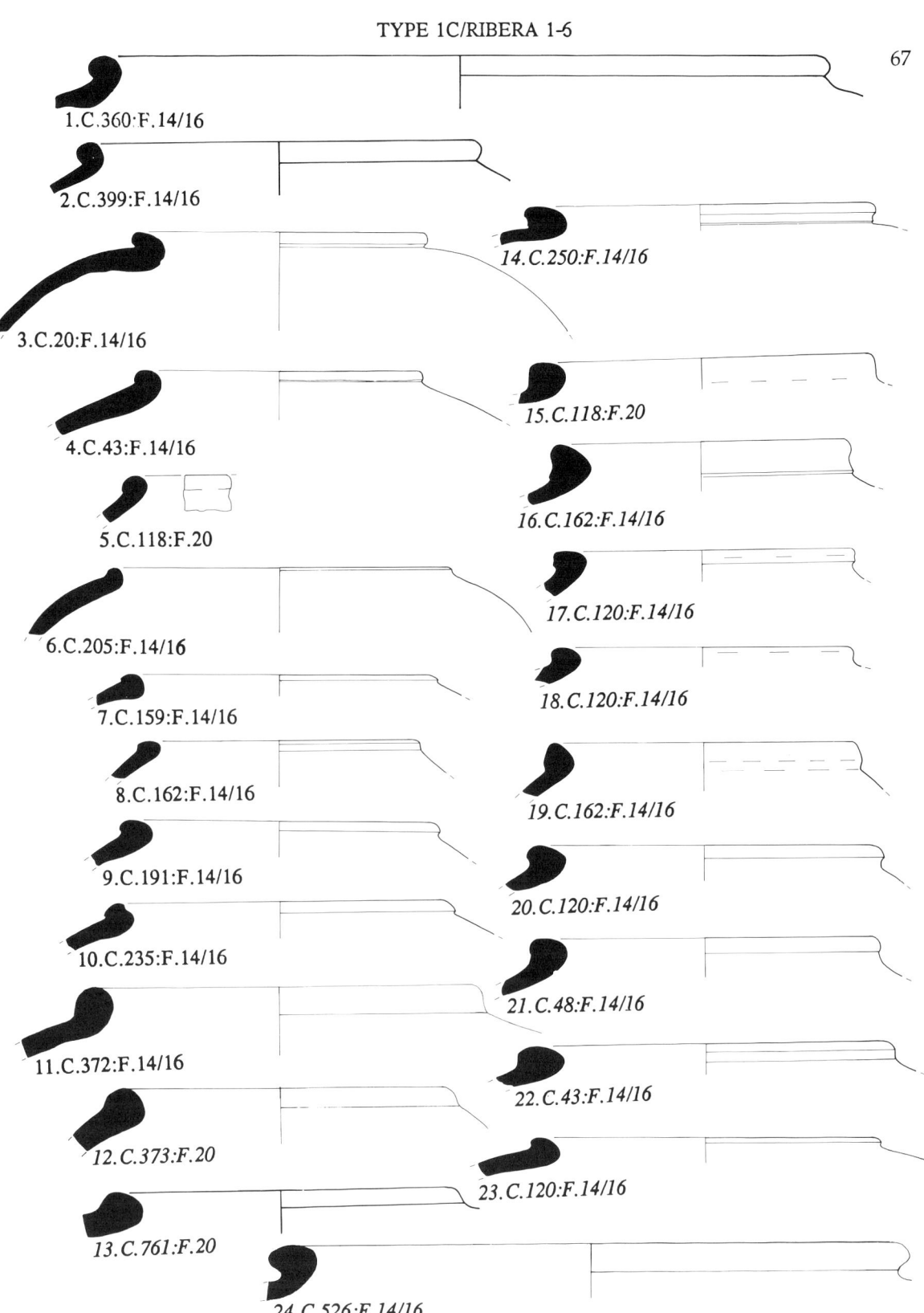

1.C.360:F.14/16

2.C.399:F.14/16

3.C.20:F.14/16

4.C.43:F.14/16

5.C.118:F.20

6.C.205:F.14/16

7.C.159:F.14/16

8.C.162:F.14/16

9.C.191:F.14/16

10.C.235:F.14/16

11.C.372:F.14/16

12.C.373:F.20

13.C.761:F.20

14.C.250:F.14/16

15.C.118:F.20

16.C.162:F.14/16

17.C.120:F.14/16

18.C.120:F.14/16

19.C.162:F.14/16

20.C.120:F.14/16

21.C.48:F.14/16

22.C.43:F.14/16

23.C.120:F.14/16

24.C.526:F.14/16

Fig. 5.3 Amphorae of pre-imperial date. Iberian productions.

0    5    10cm

*Type 1C/ Ribera I-6* (Fig. 5.3)
As Type 1B but with the rim becomes 'rolled' and has a round/elliptical section with an undercut.
Sites: especially 1.4, 1.6, 1.8, 1.12, 1.13, 1.14, 2.3, 2.7, 3.11, 3.15, 3.16, 3.17.
Fabrics: 14/16 and 20.
Date: late 3rd to later 1st c. B.C.

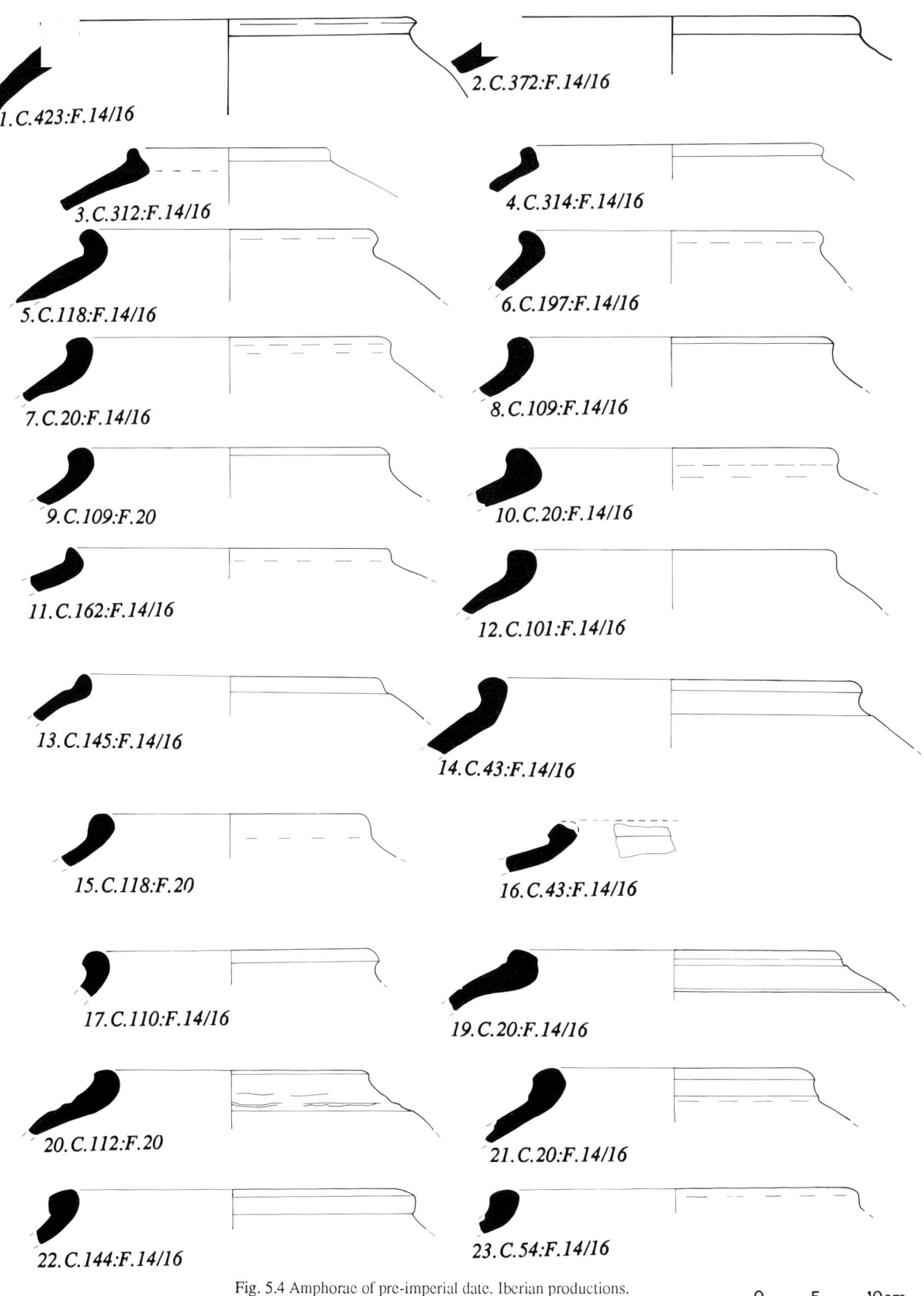

Fig. 5.4 Amphorae of pre-imperial date. Iberian productions.

0    5    10cm

*Type 1D/ Ribera I-1* (Figs. 5.4-5.5)
Similar to Type 1C but the rim is slightly higher, with less of an undercut, and has a pronounced internal 'lip'.
Sites: especially 1.2, 1.4, 1.6, 1.11, 1.12, 1.13, 2.9, 3.9, 3.10, 3.11, 3.13, 3.15, 3.19, 4.1, 4.4.
Fabrics: 14/16 and 20.
Date: early 5th to the later 4th c. B.C.

TYPE 1D/RIBERA 1-1 (Cont)

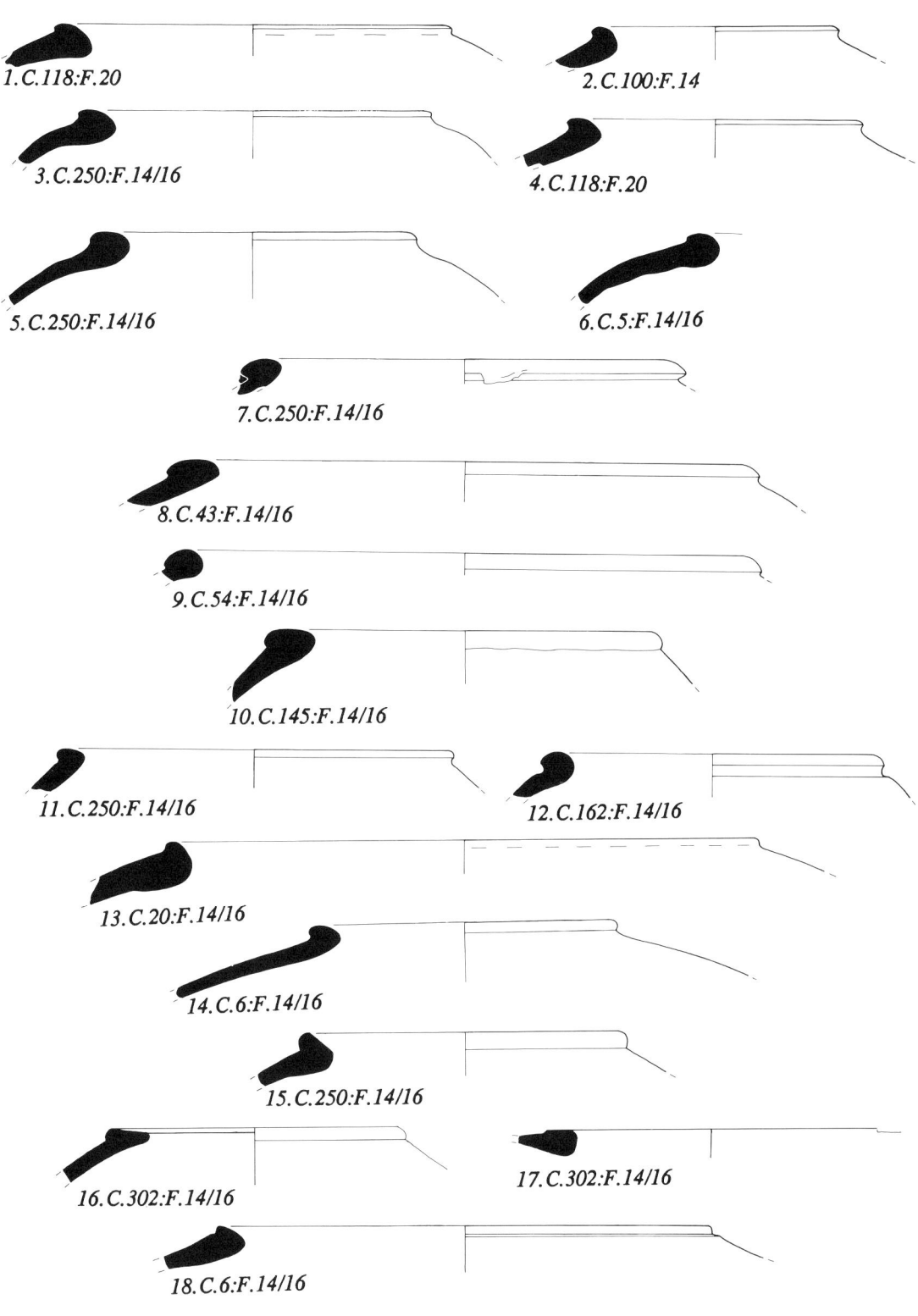

1. C.118:F.20

2. C.100:F.14

3. C.250:F.14/16

4. C.118:F.20

5. C.250:F.14/16

6. C.5:F.14/16

7. C.250:F.14/16

8. C.43:F.14/16

9. C.54:F.14/16

10. C.145:F.14/16

11. C.250:F.14/16

12. C.162:F.14/16

13. C.20:F.14/16

14. C.6:F.14/16

15. C.250:F.14/16

16. C.302:F.14/16

17. C.302:F.14/16

18. C.6:F.14/16

Fig. 5.5 Amphorae of pre-imperial date. Iberian productions.

0    5    10cm

Types 1E-F (not used)

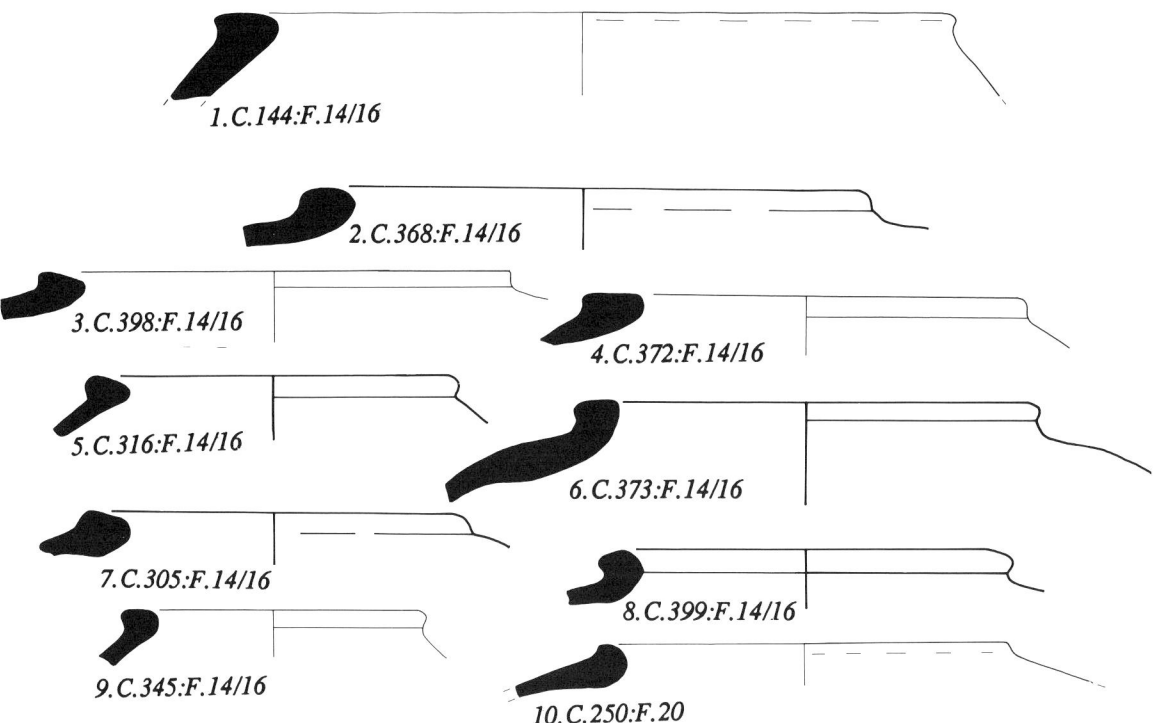

Fig. 5.6 Amphorae of pre-imperial date. Iberian productions.

*Type 1G/ Ribera I-2* (Fig. 5.6)
Similar to Type 1D but the rim has a sharper and more triangular profile.
Sites: especially 1.2, 1.13, 2.9, 3.11, 3.15, 3.16, 3.18, 3.19.
Fabrics: 14/16 and 20.
Date: mid 4th to mid 3rd c. B.C.

*TYPE 1H/ RIBERA 1-1*

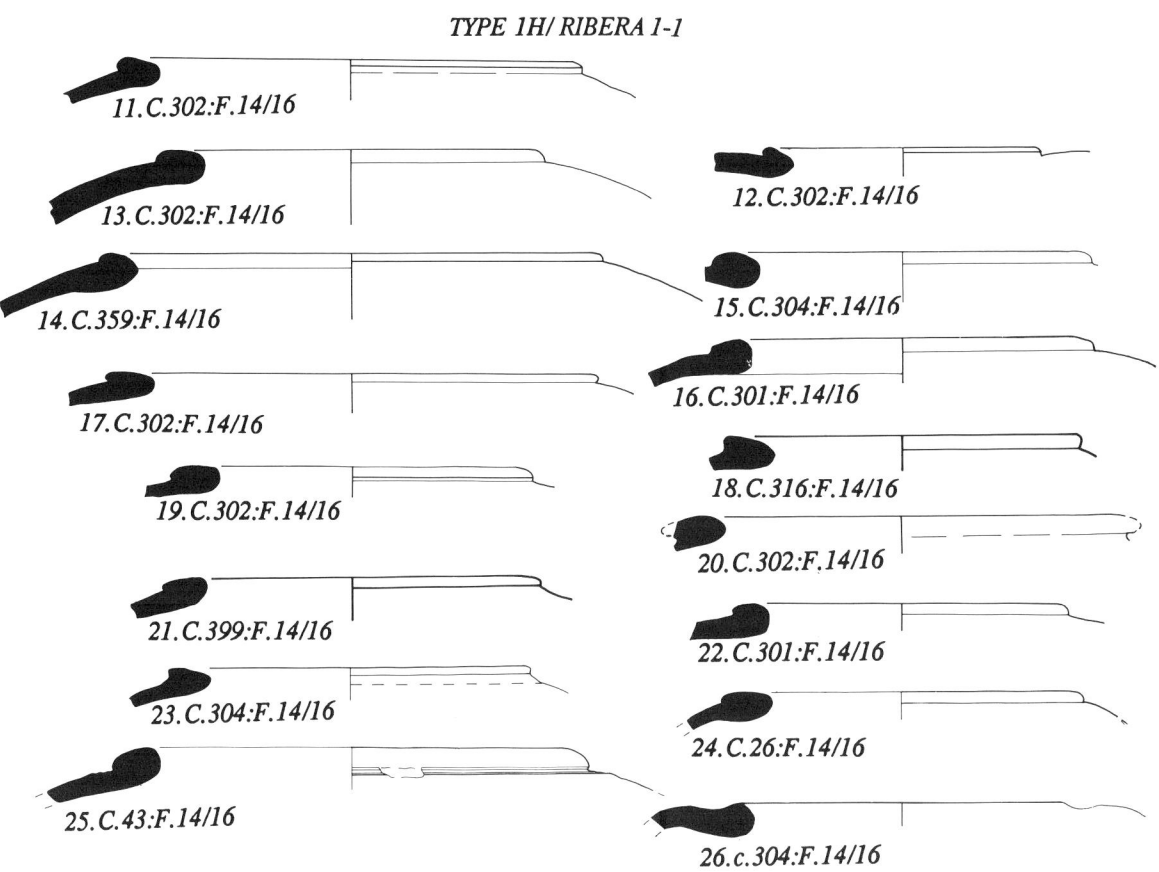

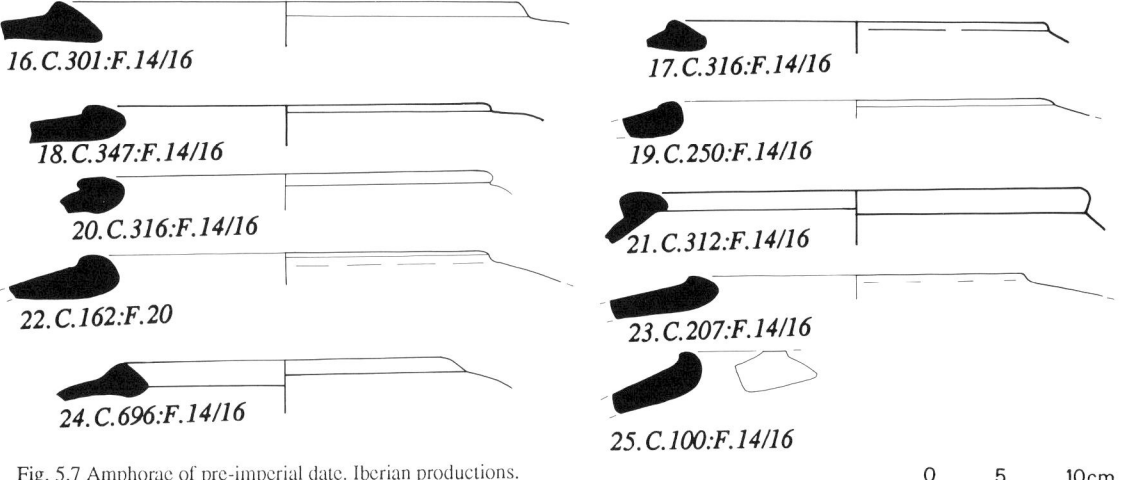

1. C.398:F.14/16
2. C.372:F.14/16
3. C.359:F.14/16
4. C.302:F.14/16
5. C.368:F.14/16
6. C.372:F.14/16
7. c.497:F.13
8. C.366:F.14/16
9. C.526:F.14/16
10. C.312:F.14/16
11. C.301:F.14/16
12. C.367:F.14/16
13: C.312:F.14/16
14. C.373:F.14/16
15. C.526:F.14/16
16. C.301:F.14/16
17. C.316:F.14/16
18. C.347:F.14/16
19. C.250:F.14/16
20. C.316:F.14/16
21. C.312:F.14/16
22. C.162:F.20
23. C.207:F.14/16
24. C.696:F.14/16
25. C.100:F.14/16

Fig. 5.7 Amphorae of pre-imperial date. Iberian productions.

0    5    10 cm

*Type 1H/ Ribera I-1* (Figs. 5.6-5.7)
Similar to Type 1G except that the rim has a more rounded profile and, in some cases, is more coarse.
Sites: especially 1.4, 1.6, 1.12, 2.6, 2.7, 2.9, 2.10, 3.11, 3.13, 3.15, 3.16, 3.17, 3.18, 3.19.
Fabrics: 13 and 14/16.
Date: early 5th to the later 4th c. B.C.

72

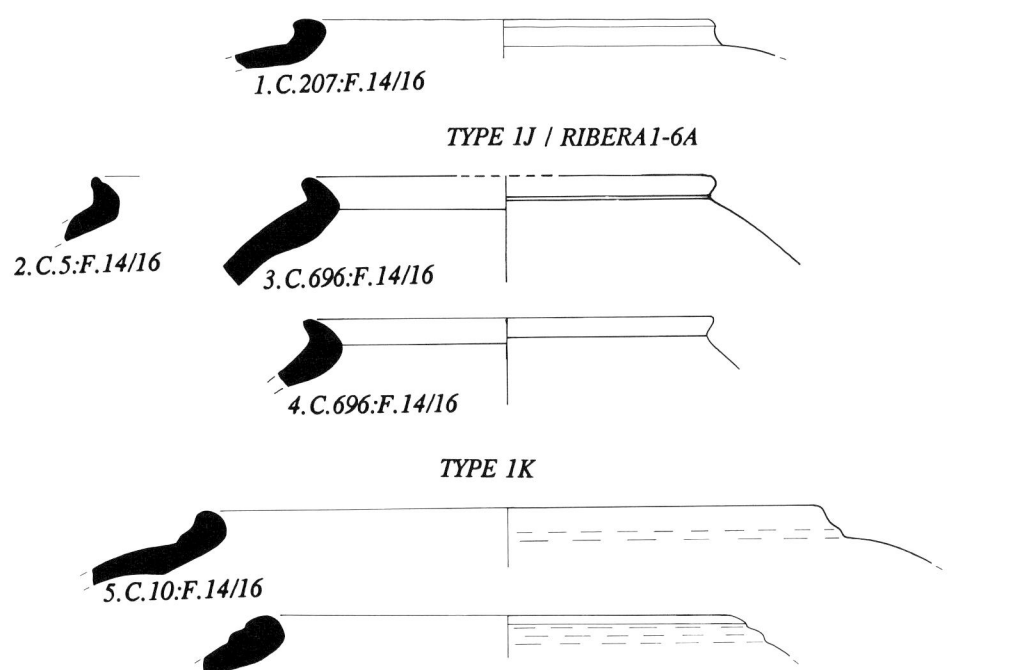

TYPE 1i / RIBERA 1-6

1. C.207:F.14/16

TYPE 1J / RIBERA 1-6A

2. C.5:F.14/16    3. C.696:F.14/16

4. C.696:F.14/16

TYPE 1K

5. C.10:F.14/16

6. C.17:F.14/16

Fig. 5.8 Amphorae of pre-imperial date. Iberian productions.

*Type 1I/ Ribera I-6* (Fig. 5.8)
An elevated rim lip with a sharp undercut.
Fabric: 14/16.
Date: late 3rd to later 1st c. B.C.

*Type 1J/ Ribera 1-6A* (Fig. 5.8)
A more pronounced version of Type 1I.
Sites: especially 2.9, 3.9.
Fabric: 14/16.
Date: late 3rd to later 1st c. B.C.

*Type 1K* (Fig. 5.8)
A rim characterized by a ridge running around the base of its outer face.
Site: especially 3.19.
Fabric: 14/16.
Date: 5th to the end of the 1st c. B.C.

*TYPE 1L*

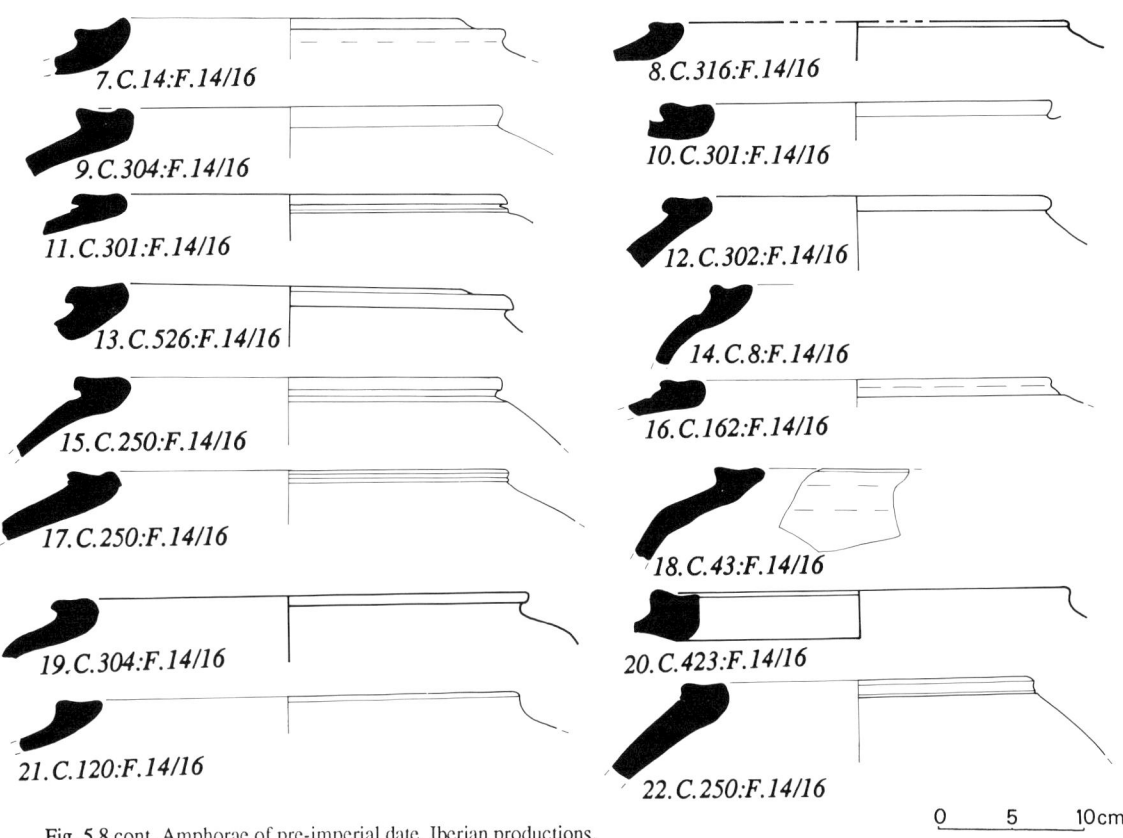

7.C.14:F.14/16
8.C.316:F.14/16
9.C.304:F.14/16
10.C.301:F.14/16
11.C.301:F.14/16
12.C.302:F.14/16
13.C.526:F.14/16
14.C.8:F.14/16
15.C.250:F.14/16
16.C.162:F.14/16
17.C.250:F.14/16
18.C.43:F.14/16
19.C.304:F.14/16
20.C.423:F.14/16
21.C.120:F.14/16
22.C.250:F.14/16

0   5   10cm

**Fig.** 5.8 cont. Amphorae of pre-imperial date. Iberian productions.

*Type 1L* (Fig. 5.8-5.9)
A variant of the above in which the ridge becomes more pronounced. In some cases it develops an undercut and appears effectively as a flange.
Sites: especially 1.2, 1.4, 1.6, 1.13, 1.14, 2.4, 2.7, 2.9, 2.10, 3.11, 3.13, 3.15, 3.16, 3.17, 3.18, 3.19.
Fabric: 14/16.
Date: 5th to the end of the 1st c. B.C.

74

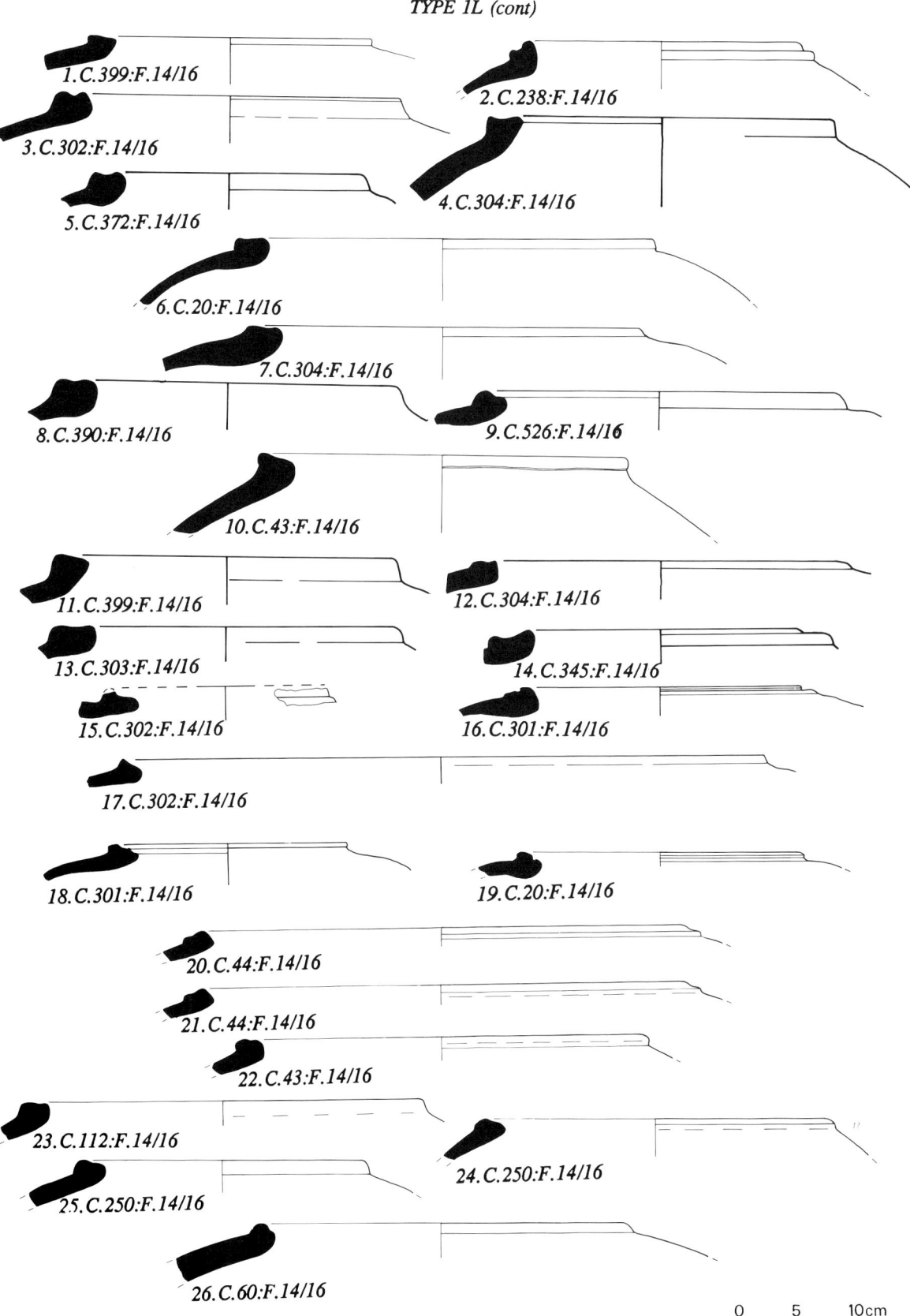

1. C.399:F.14/16
2. C.238:F.14/16
3. C.302:F.14/16
4. C.304:F.14/16
5. C.372:F.14/16
6. C.20:F.14/16
7. C.304:F.14/16
8. C.390:F.14/16
9. C.526:F.14/16
10. C.43:F.14/16
11. C.399:F.14/16
12. C.304:F.14/16
13. C.303:F.14/16
14. C.345:F.14/16
15. C.302:F.14/16
16. C.301:F.14/16
17. C.302:F.14/16
18. C.301:F.14/16
19. C.20:F.14/16
20. C.44:F.14/16
21. C.44:F.14/16
22. C.43:F.14/16
23. C.112:F.14/16
24. C.250:F.14/16
25. C.250:F.14/16
26. C.60:F.14/16

0    5    10cm

Fig. 5.9 Amphorae of pre-imperial date. Iberian productions.

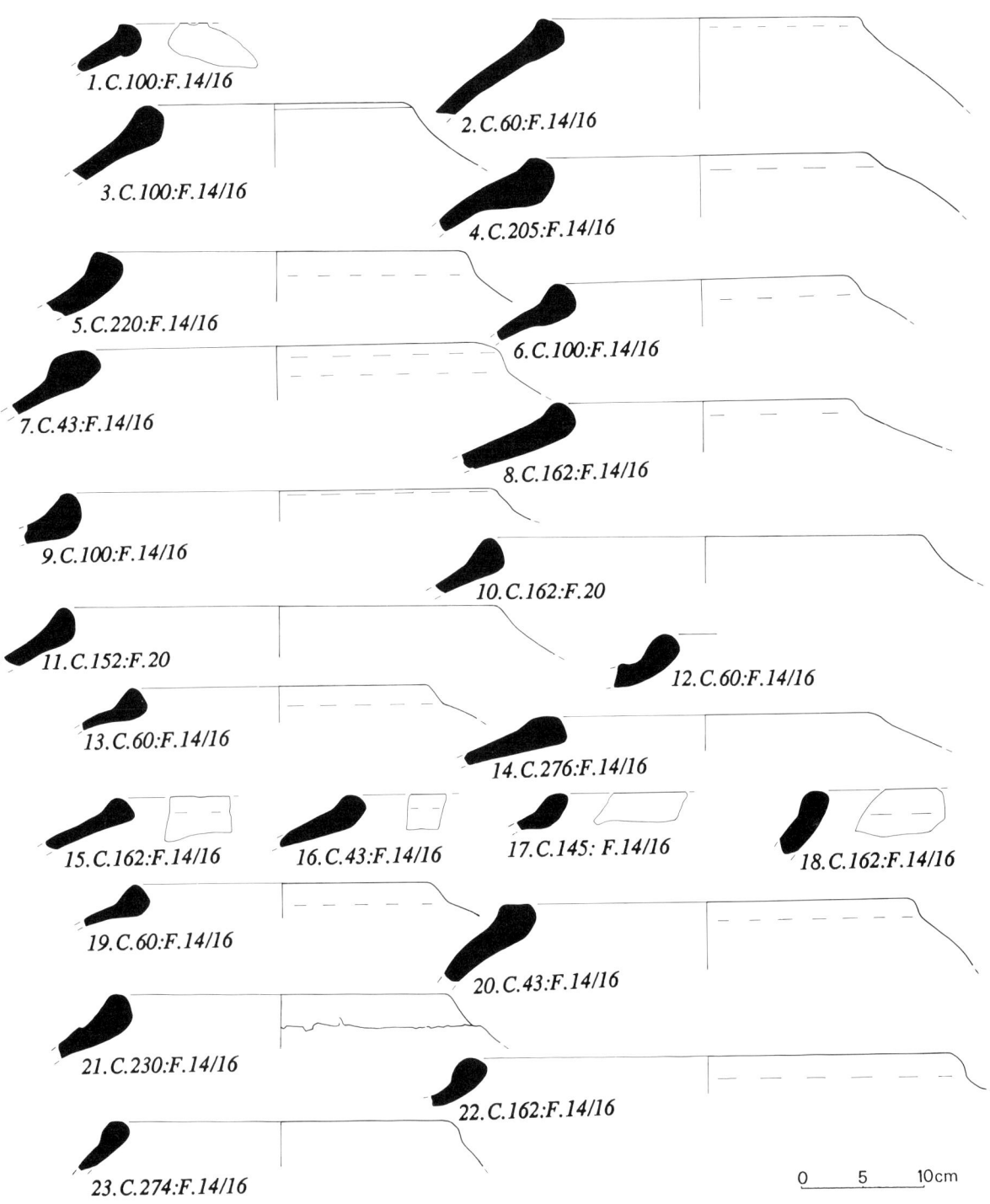

1. C.100:F.14/16
2. C.60:F.14/16
3. C.100:F.14/16
4. C.205:F.14/16
5. C.220:F.14/16
6. C.100:F.14/16
7. C.43:F.14/16
8. C.162:F.14/16
9. C.100:F.14/16
10. C.162:F.20
11. C.152:F.20
12. C.60:F.14/16
13. C.60:F.14/16
14. C.276:F.14/16
15. C.162:F.14/16
16. C.43:F.14/16
17. C.145: F.14/16
18. C.162:F.14/16
19. C.60:F.14/16
20. C.43:F.14/16
21. C.230:F.14/16
22. C.162:F.14/16
23. C.274:F.14/16

0 5 10cm

Fig. 5.10 Amphorae of pre-imperial date. Iberian productions.

*Type 1M/ Ribera I-5* (Fig. 5.10)
Similar to Type 1A but the outer face of the rim is sufficiently developed to be visible and the inner face is more pronounced.
Sites: especially 1.2, 1.4, 1.6, 1.8, 1.9, 2.9, 3.11, 3.15.
Fabric: 14/16 and 20.
Date: later 3rd to later 1st c. B.C.

*TYPE 1N*

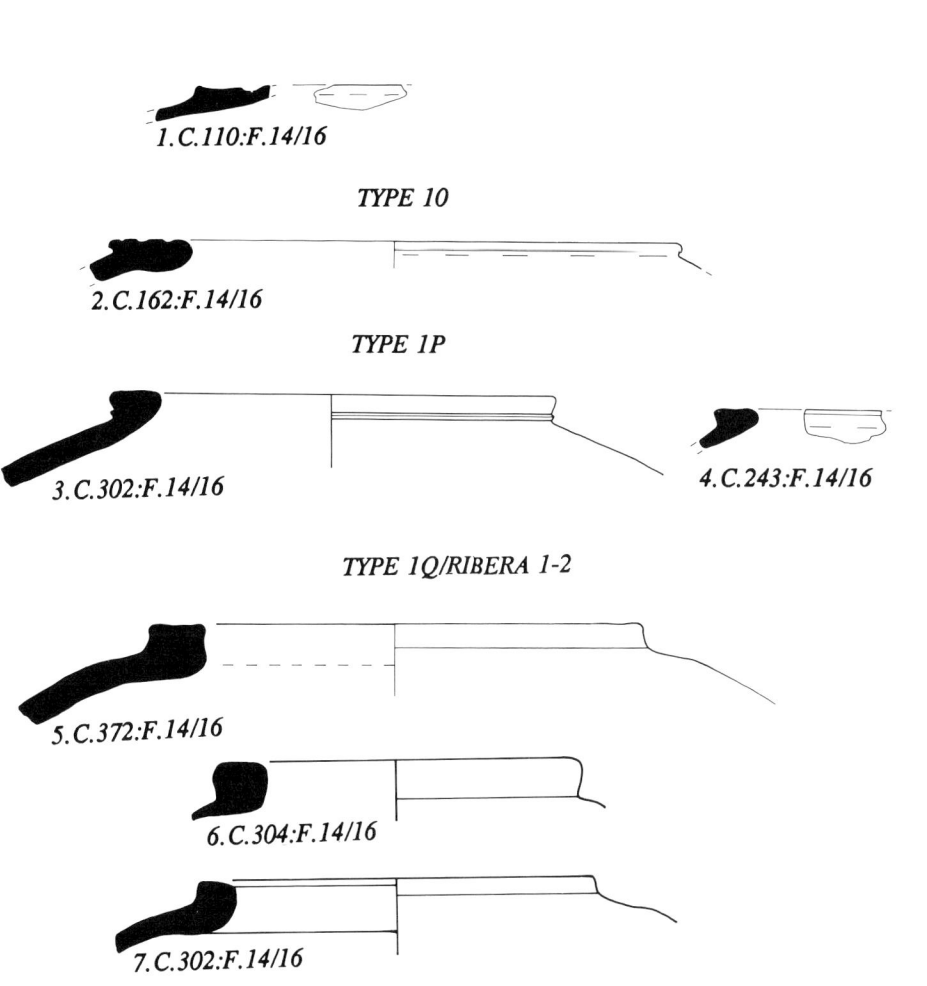

*1. C.110:F.14/16*

*TYPE 10*

*2. C.162:F.14/16*

*TYPE 1P*

*3. C.302:F.14/16*          *4. C.243:F.14/16*

*TYPE 1Q/RIBERA 1-2*

*5. C.372:F.14/16*

*6. C.304:F.14/16*

*7. C.302:F.14/16*

*8. C.373:F.14/16*

*9. C.399:F.14/16*

*10. C.304:F.14/16*

*11. C.109:F.14/16*

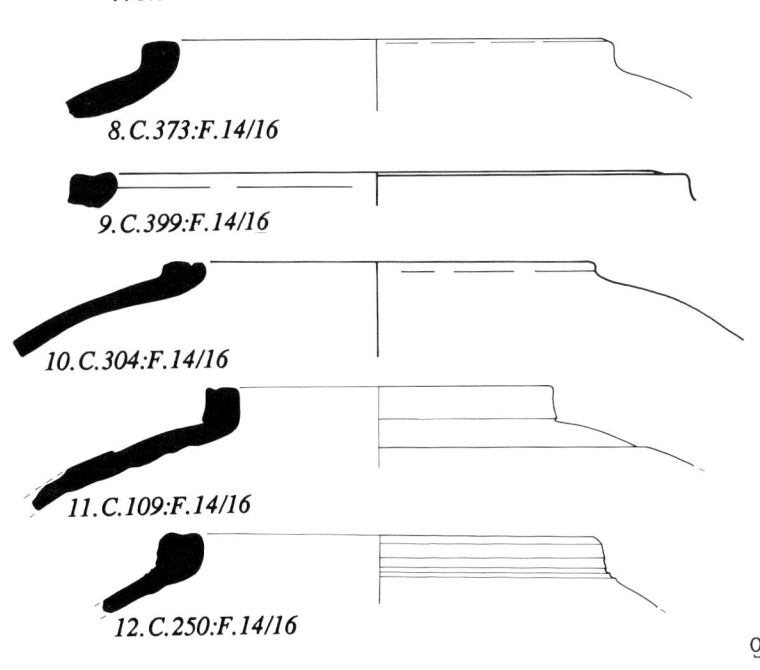

*12. C.250:F.14/16*

0     5     10cm

Fig. 5.11 Amphorae of pre-imperial date. Iberian productions.

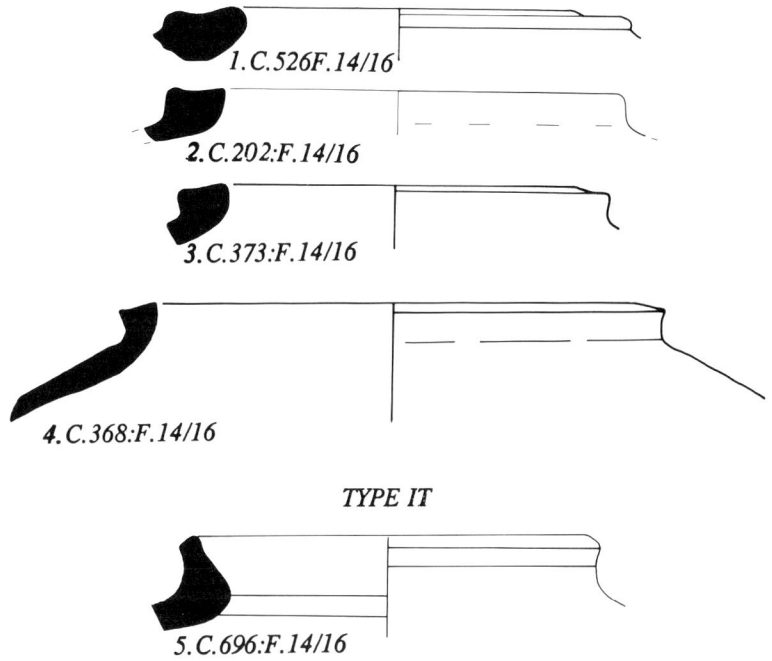

*1.C.526F.14/16*

*2.C.202:F.14/16*

*3.C.373:F.14/16*

*4.C.368:F.14/16*

*TYPE IT*

*5.C.696:F.14/16*

Fig. 5.12 Amphorae of pre-imperial date. Iberian productions.

*Type 1N* (Fig. 5.11)
A very degraded version of Type 1M.
Sites: especially 1.11, 2.9.
Fabric: 14/16.
Date: 5th to the end of the 1st c. B.C.

*Type 1O* (Fig. 5.11)
A more developed version of Type 1N with the inner face of the rim more prominent.
Sites: especially 1.4, 2.9.
Fabric: 14/16.
Date: 5th to the end of the 1st c. B.C.

*Type 1P* (Fig. 5.11)
The rim develops a distinctive round-triangular profile.
Sites: 3.16, 3.19, 4.4.
Fabric: 14/16 and 20.
Date: 5th to the end of the 1st c. B.C.

*Type 1Q/ Ribera I-2* (Figs. 5.11-5.12)
Characterized by a distinctive 'square' profile.
Sites: 1.11, 1.13, 2.3, 2.7, 2.9, 3.4, 3.13, 3.15, 3.16, 3.17, 3.19.
Fabric: 14/16.
Date: earlier 4th to mid 3rd c. B.C.

*Type 1R and 1S* (not used)

*Type 1T* (Fig. 5.12)
A coarser version of Type 1M.
Site: 2.9.
Fabric: 14/16.
Date: 5th to the end of the 1st c. B.C.

78

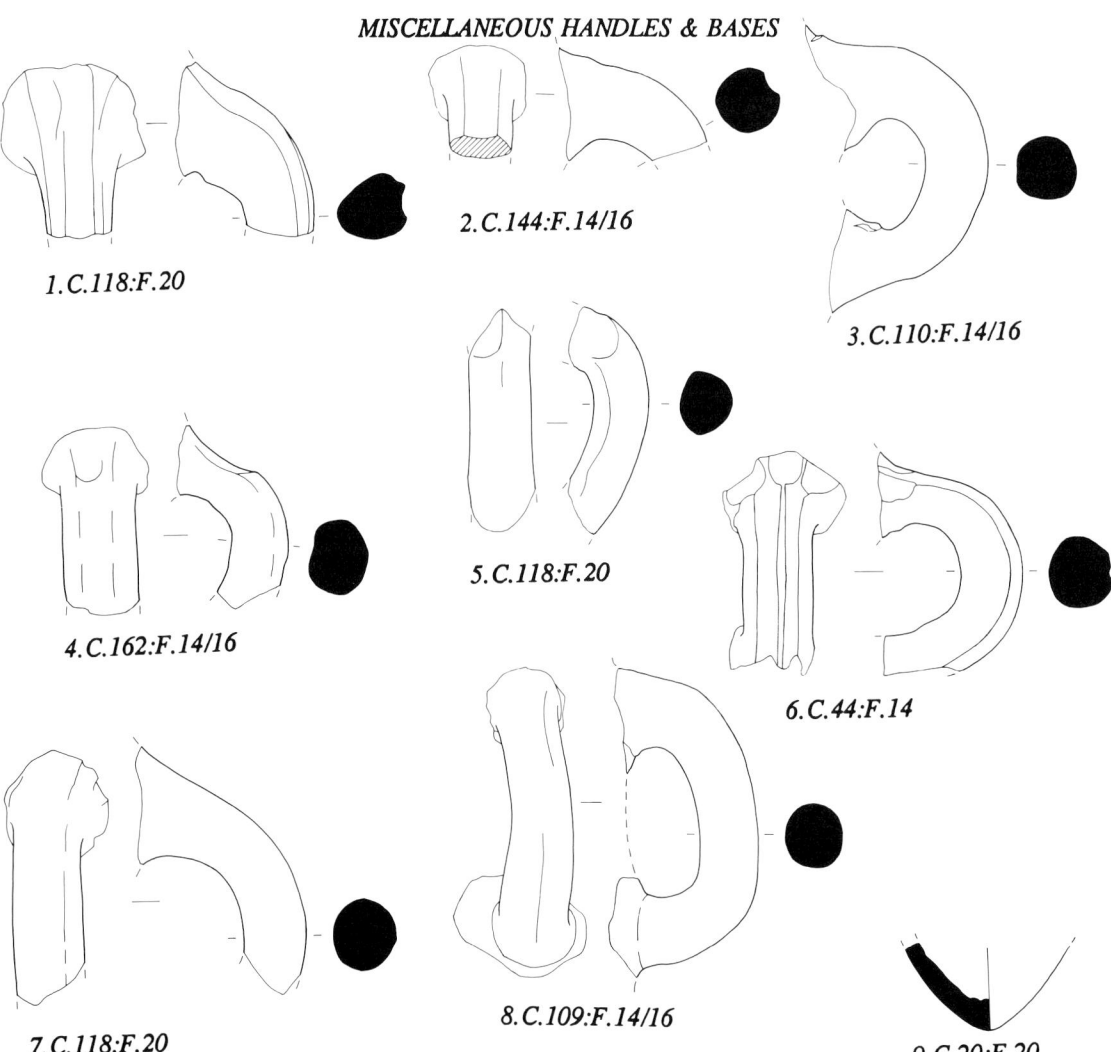

MISCELLANEOUS HANDLES & BASES

1. C.118:F.20

2. C.144:F.14/16

3. C.110:F.14/16

4. C.162:F.14/16

5. C.118:F.20

6. C.44:F.14

7. C.118:F.20

8. C.109:F.14/16

9. C.20:F.20

Fig. 5.13 Amphorae of pre-imperial date. Iberian productions.

B.     Handles

They cannot be separated on chronological grounds; consequently a representative selection has been illustrated (Fig. 5.13).

Fabrics: 14/16 and 20.

C.     Base

Only one example was found, presumably because these lend themselves easily to abrasion in the ploughsoil and are largely unrecognizable in field-survey collections (Fig. 5.13).

Fabric: 20

*TYPE 2/IBERIAN MANUFACTURE MAÑA D/CINTAS 315-6*

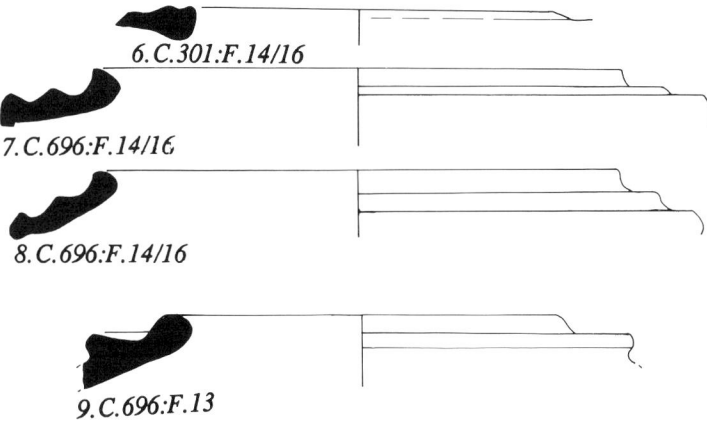

6.C.301:F.14/16

7.C.696:F.14/16

8.C.696:F.14/16

9.C.696:F.13

*TYPE 3/IBERIAN MANUFACTURE MASSILIOTE AMPHORA*

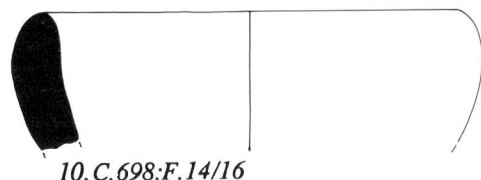

10.C.698:F.14/16

**Fig.** 5.12 cont. Amphorae of pre-imperial date. Iberian productions.

0    5    10cm

*Type 2/ Iberian manufacture Mañá D/ Iberian manufacture Cintas 315-316*
See under Type 8.
Site: 2.6.
Fabrics: 13, 14/16.
Date: earlier 4th to earlier 2nd c. B.C.

*Type 3/ Iberian manufacture Massiliote Amphorae / Py Rim type 1 or 2* (Fig. 5.12)
It appears to be an imitation of a Massiliote wine amphora (see Type 9), although the absence of the lower part of the rim makes this identification uncertain.
Found only on off-site scatters.
Fabric: 14/16.
Date: probably between 525 and 450 B.C.

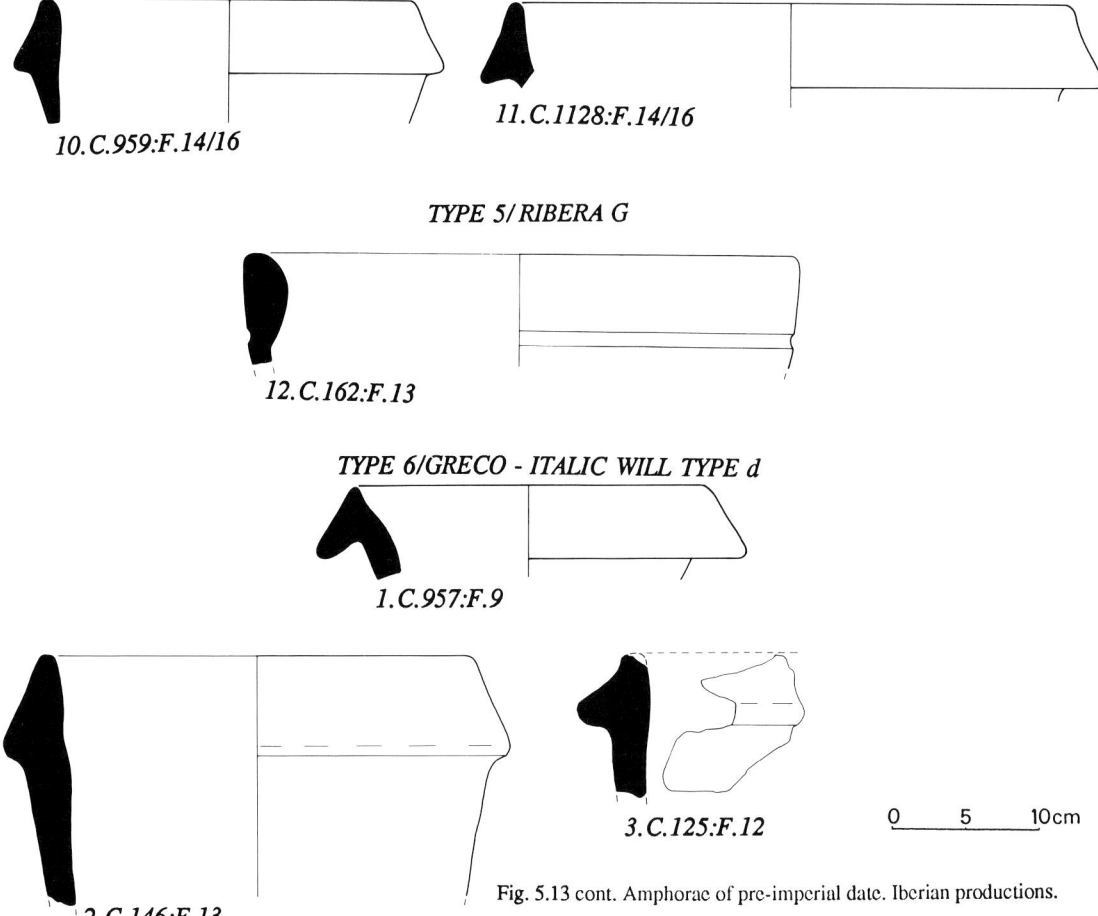

TYPE 4/IBERIAN MANUFACTURE DRESSEL 1A

10.C.959:F.14/16    11.C.1128:F.14/16

TYPE 5/ RIBERA G

12.C.162:F.13

TYPE 6/GRECO - ITALIC WILL TYPE d

1.C.957:F.9

2.C.146:F.13    3.C.125:F.12    0    5    10cm

Fig. 5.13 cont. Amphorae of pre-imperial date. Iberian productions.

*Type 4/ Iberian manufacture Dressel 1A Amphorae* (Fig. 5.13)
See description under Roman amphorae Type 17 (below). As they share the same fabric with the typical Iberian amphora Type 1, they are grouped with 'Iberian' types. Type 4 amphorae are to be distinguished from amphorae of the same type that were manufactured in fabric 9, which was the forerunner of the 'Tarraconensian' amphora fabric of the late Republic and early empire (see Types 23-26 below).
Sites: 3.6, 4.4.
Fabrics: 14/16.
Date: later 2nd to mid 1st c. B.C.

*Type 5/ Ribera Type G* (Fig. 5.13)
Overall Ribera G is characterised by a short, ribbed, cylindrical body with a base which tapers quickly and may terminate in a re-entrant foot. It has no neck and the rim has a pronounced internal ridge. Lug handles are affixed immediately below the rim. The form of this amphora falls broadly within a class of possibly southern Spanish amphorae noted at sites in Andalucia, between Huelva and the Punta de la Nao. Overall they date to some time within the 4th, 3rd and 2nd c. B.C. However, the characteristics of this example are closely comparable with late examples from the camps of Valdevorrón and Molino at Numantia, dated to 133 B.C. (Sanmartí 1985b). The type may have carried olive oil. Although a southern Spanish origin has been suggested, the fabric suggests that it may have been manufactured in the territory of Tarraco.
Site: 1.4.
Fabric: 13.
Date: second half of the 2nd c. B.C. An example of this type has been discovered in a context of 150-125 B.C. at Tarraco (Aquilué 1993, fig. 56.7)

*Type 6/ Greco-Italic Will Type d* (Fig. 5.13)
For description of the type see Type 16 below. The rim sherds are characterized by pronounced triangular rims. Analysis of the fabric points firmly to an origin in the territory of Tarraco and possibly in Laietania (around Barcelona) to the north.
Site: 4.4.
Fabrics: 12, 13, 98.
Date: first half of the 2nd c. B.C.

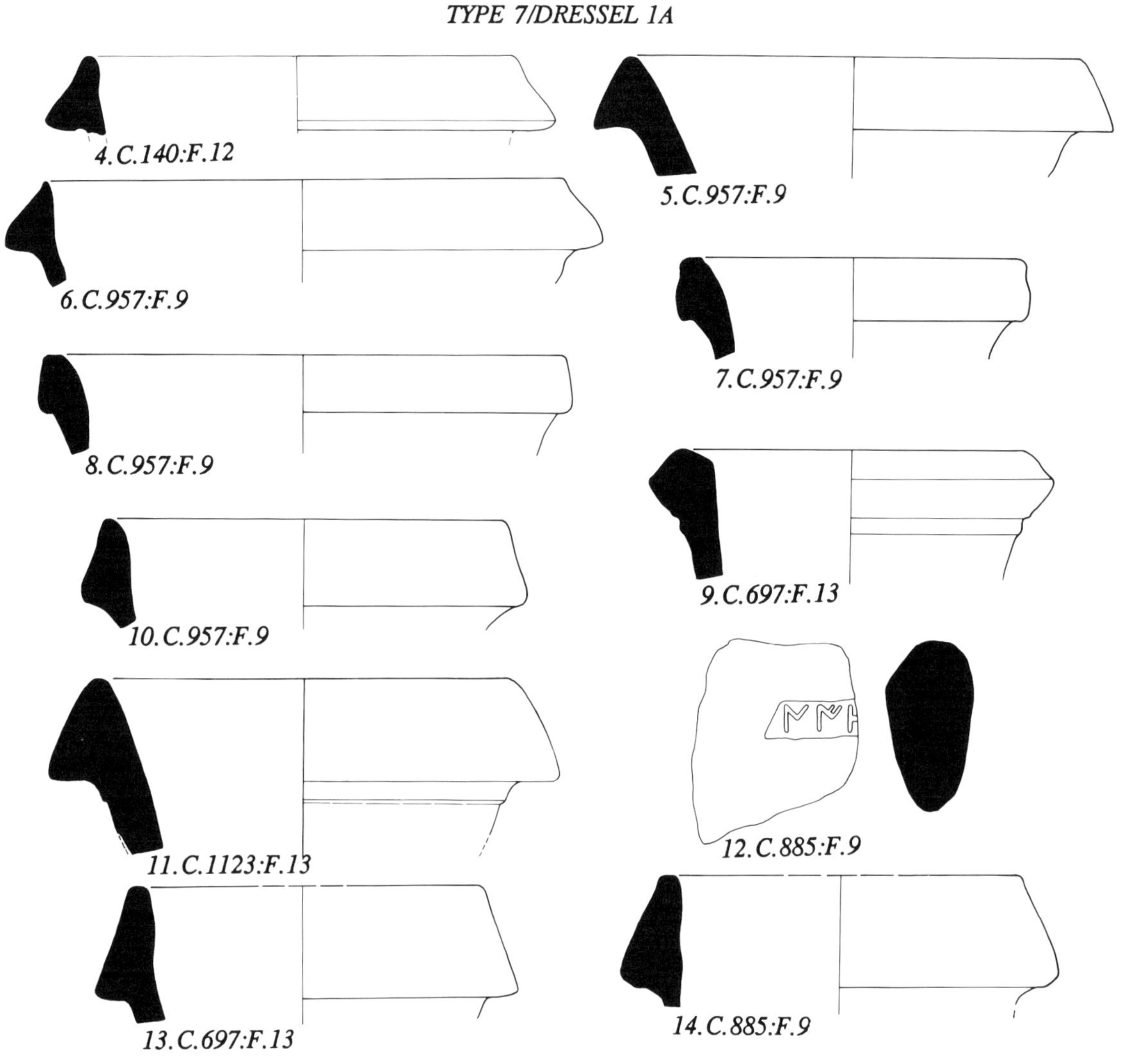

TYPE 7/DRESSEL 1A

4.C.140:F.12

5.C.957:F.9

6.C.957:F.9

7.C.957:F.9

8.C.957:F.9

9.C.697:F.13

10.C.957:F.9

11.C.1123:F.13

12.C.885:F.9

13.C.697:F.13

14.C.885:F.9

0    5    10cm

Fig. 5.14 Amphorae of pre-imperial date.

*Type 7/ Dressel 1A* (Fig. 5.14)
For description of the type see Type 17 below. The rim sherds are characterized by a less pronounced triangular rim than Type 6. Analysis of the fabric points firmly to an origin in the territory of Tarraco. Gas chromatographic analysis of Fabric 9 (Appendix 3) suggests that Types 7, 8 and 9 may have carried fish sauce; yet this seems unlikely in terms of the form, which imitates a wine amphora, and the distribution towards inland parts of the survey area.
Sites: 2.6, 2.9, 3.5, 4.2, 4.4.
Fabrics: 9, 12, 13, 98.
Date: between *c.*130 and the mid 1st c. B.C.

82

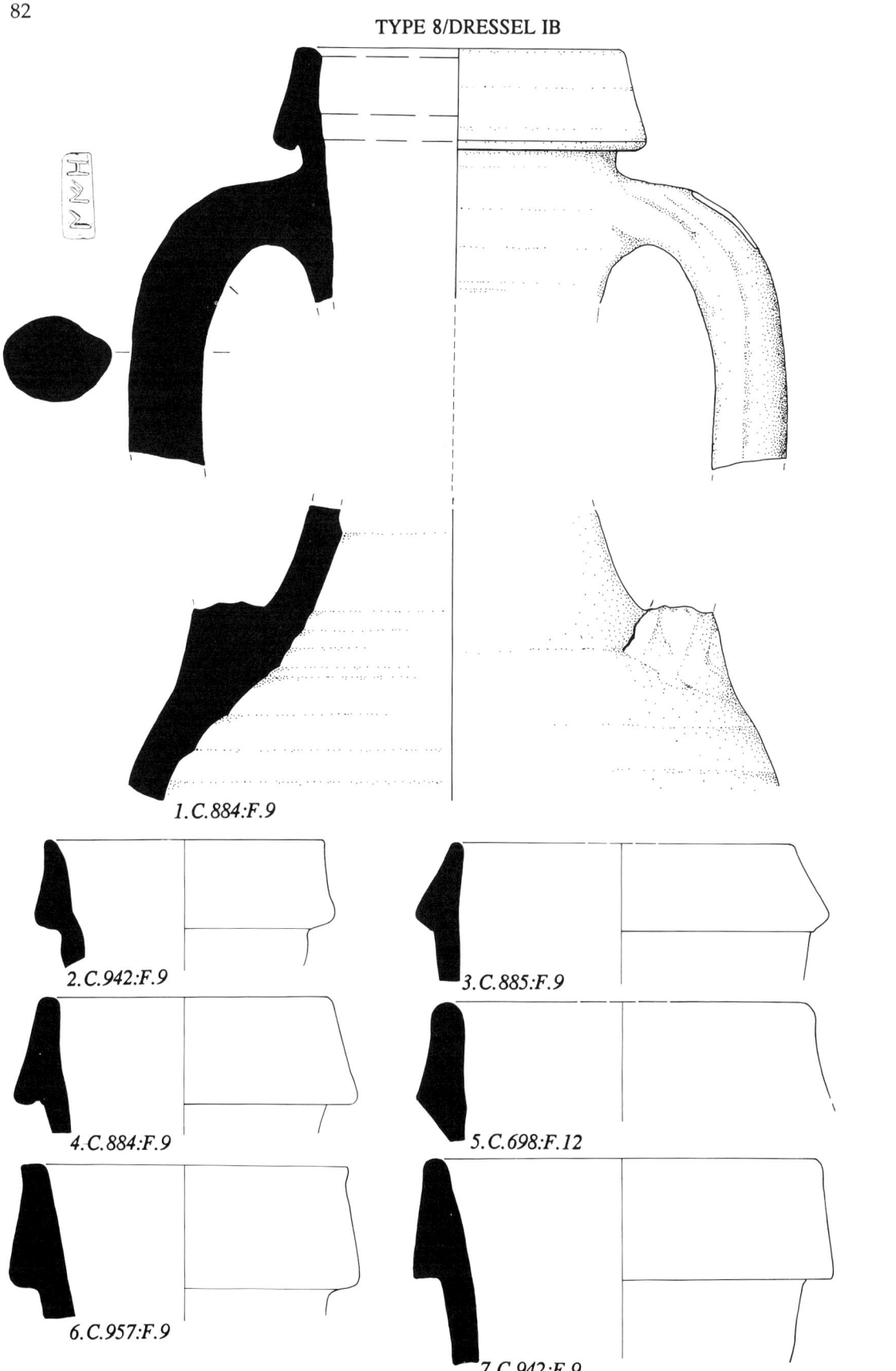

1.C.884:F.9

2.C.942:F.9

3.C.885:F.9

4.C.884:F.9

5.C.698:F.12

6.C.957:F.9

7.C.942:F.9

0    5    10cm

Fig. 5.15 Amphorae of pre-imperial date.

*TYPE 8   DRESSEL 1B*

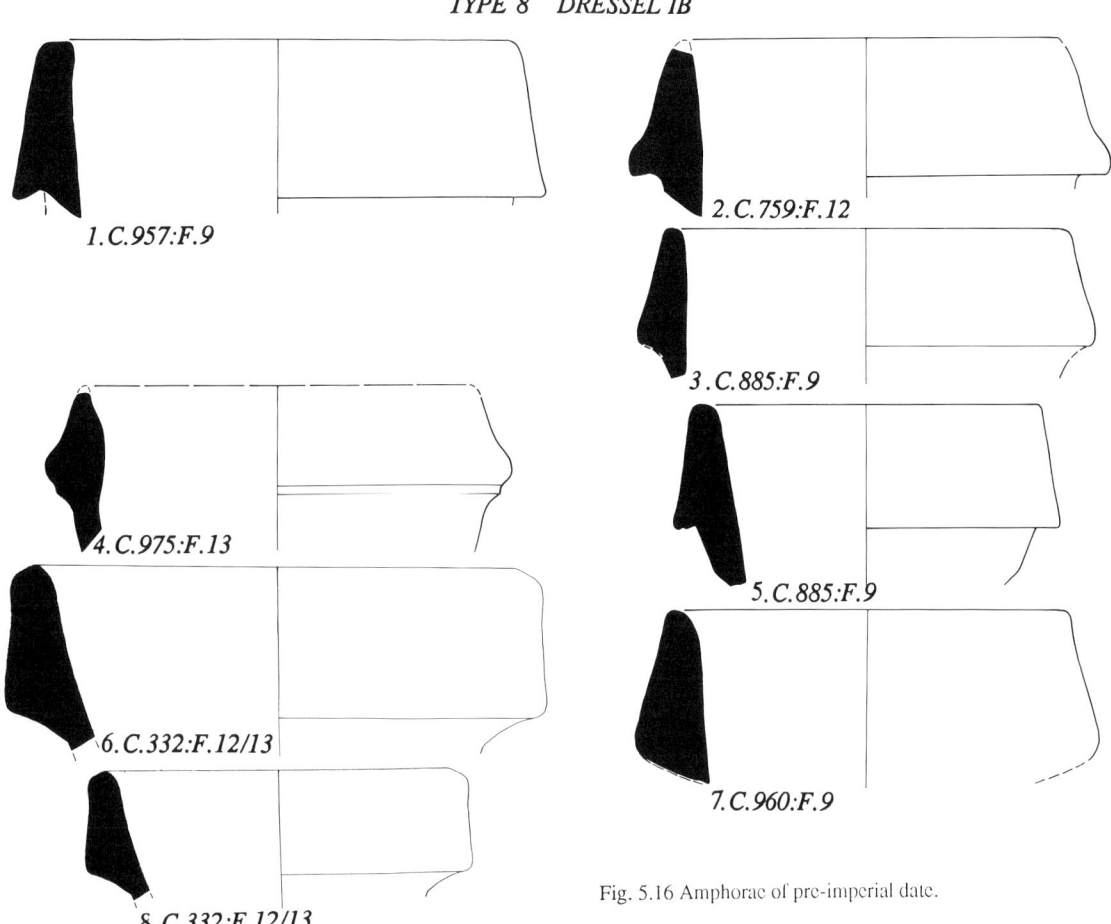

1. *C.957:F.9*

2. *C.759:F.12*

3. *C.885:F.9*

4. *C.975:F.13*

5. *C.885:F.9*

6. *C.332:F.12/13*

7. *C.960:F.9*

8. *C.332:F.12/13*

Fig. 5.16 Amphorae of pre-imperial date.

*Type 8/ Dressel 1B* (Figs. 5.15-5.16)

For description of the type see Type 18 below. The rim sherds are taller than those of Type 7 and have an almost flat internal face. Analysis of the fabric points firmly to an origin in the territory of Tarraco and possibly in Laietania further north. The regional origin is further confirmed by two name stamps in Iberian characters. Similar vessels with fabric 9 have been found further north in Laietania. Contrary to recent suggestions (Miró 1988, 60 ff.), they are probably products of the territory of Tarraco.

Sites: 2.3, 2.9, 4.1, 4.2, 4.4.

Fabrics: 9, 12, 12 or 13.

Date: beginning to some time after the mid 1st c. B.C.

Epigraphy: Two handles from separate amphorae (from Campos 884 and 885) were found to be stamped with the same 3 Iberian letters within a rectangular cartouche. This is unparalleled in the area of the survey (see Figs. 5.14, 5.15, 5.68 and 5.69). Parallels have been found on a *dolium* at Azaila (Beltrán Lloris 1976, lams. LXX and LXXI) in the lower Ebro valley and on an unclassified amphora stamp at Enserune in Languedoc (Jannoray 1955, pl. LIII.3). The closest, however, was the Iberian stamp ($ƚ N ⟨$ [ ... ]) found on an amphora of type 24, in levels of 50-40 B.C. at Zaragoza (Aguarod 1992). The letters translate as N I O (Maluquer 1968) and there are no known parallels (Velaza 1991); the significance of these letters is not clear. The fact that there are 3 letters should not lead one to posit an Iberian equivalence with Roman *tria nomina*.

TYPE 9    DRESSEL 1C

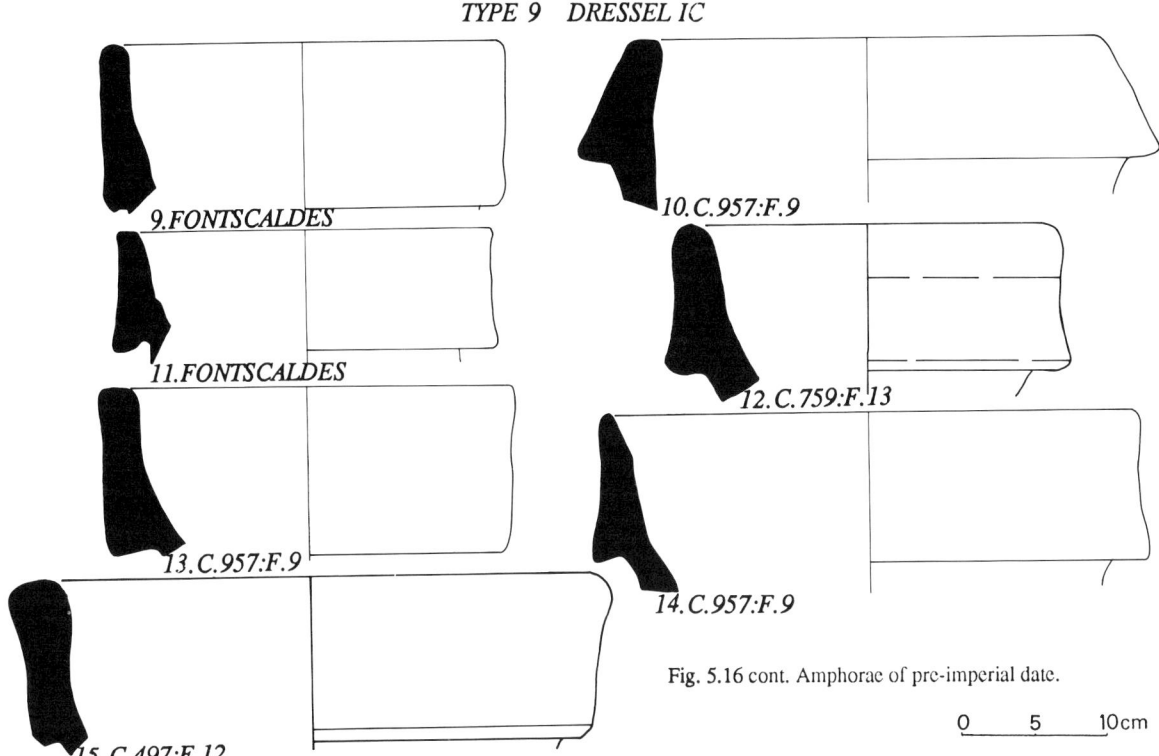

9.FONTSCALDES

10.C.957:F.9

11.FONTSCALDES

12.C.759:F.13

13.C.957:F.9

14.C.957:F.9

15.C.497:F.12

Fig. 5.16 cont. Amphorae of pre-imperial date.

0    5    10cm

*Type 9: Dressel 1C* (Fig. 5.16)
For description of the type see Type 19 below. The rim sherds are characterized as similar to those of Type 8, except for a concave internal face. Analysis of the fabric points firmly to an origin in the territory of Tarraco.
Sites: 2.3, 4.4.
Fabrics: 9, 12, 13.
Date: between the late 2nd and early 1st c. B.C.

Miscellaneous inscribed sherds (Fig. 5.18)
Anepigraphic graffiti were found on 3 separate body sherds of Iberian amphora.
Site: 3.16.
Fabric: 14/16.
Date: no evidence.

85

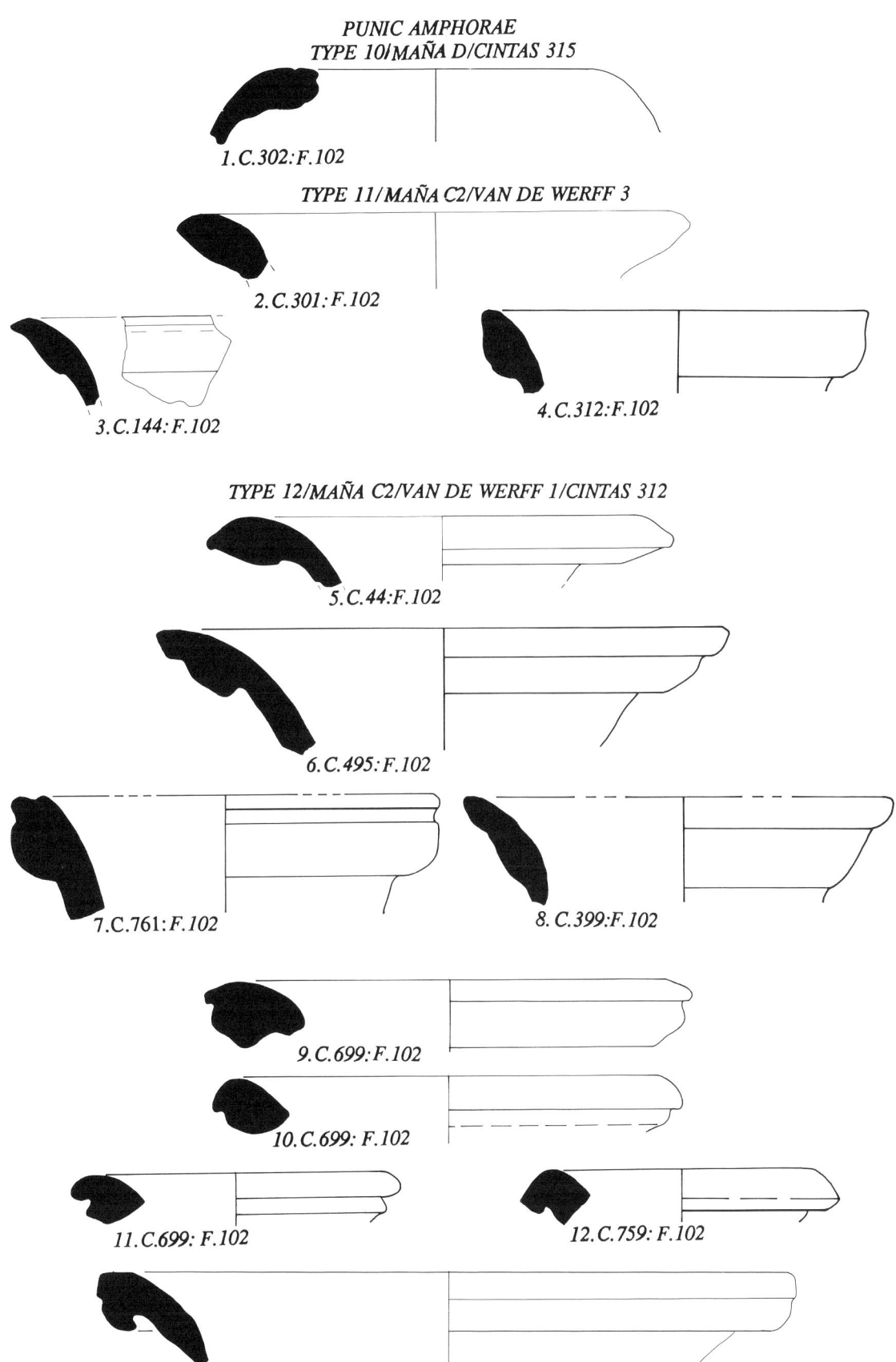

Fig. 5.17 Amphorae of pre-imperial date. Punic Amphorae.

86

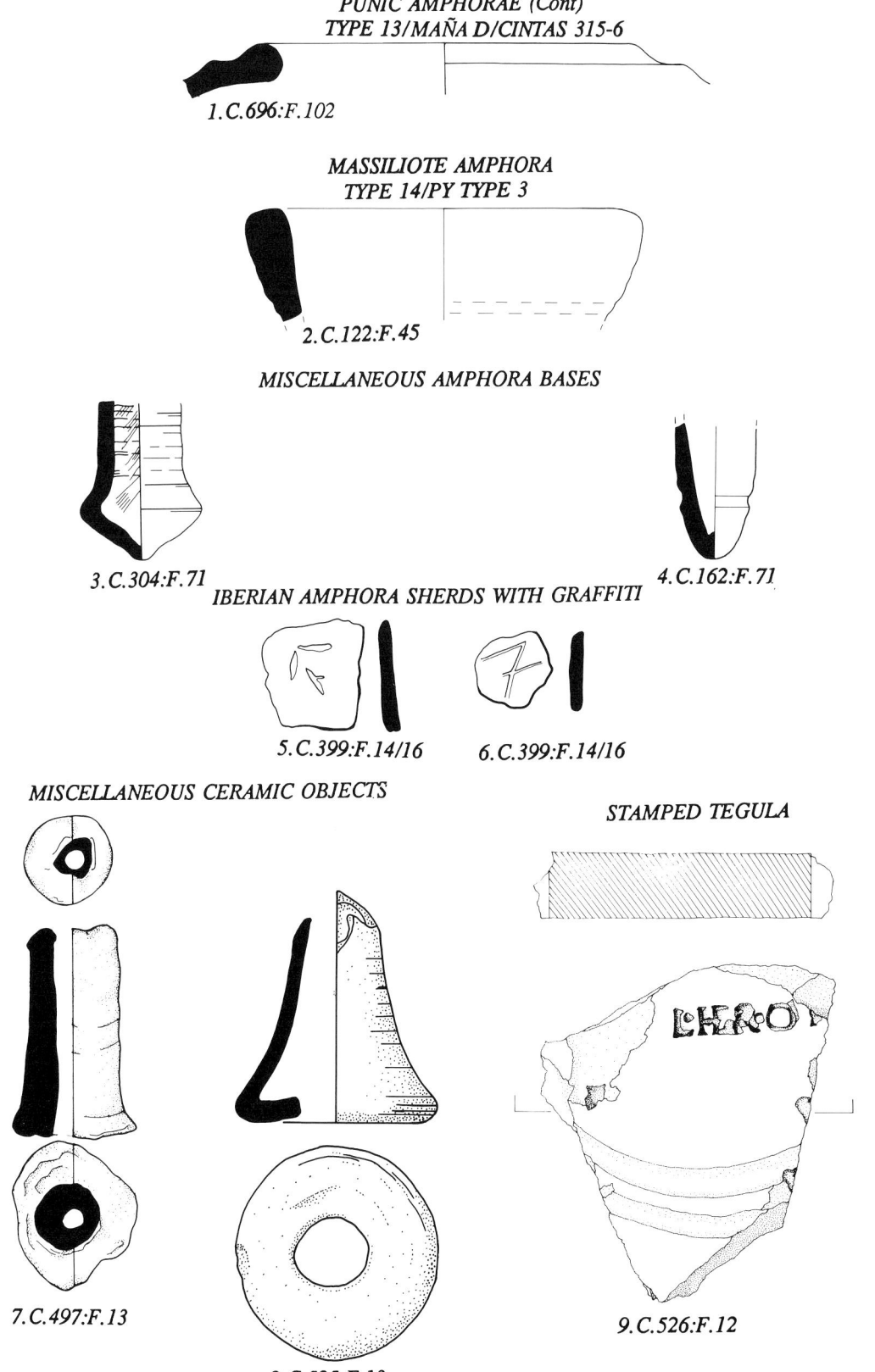

PUNIC AMPHORAE (Cont)
TYPE 13/MAÑA D/CINTAS 315-6

1.C.696:F.102

MASSILIOTE AMPHORA
TYPE 14/PY TYPE 3

2.C.122:F.45

MISCELLANEOUS AMPHORA BASES

3.C.304:F.71

4.C.162:F.71

IBERIAN AMPHORA SHERDS WITH GRAFFITI

5.C.399:F.14/16

6.C.399:F.14/16

MISCELLANEOUS CERAMIC OBJECTS

STAMPED TEGULA

7.C.497:F.13

8.C.525:F.13

9.C.526:F.12

0    5    10cm

Fig. 5.18 Amphorae of pre-imperial date. Punic and Massiliote Amphorae and miscellaneous sherds.

Punic Production

*Type 10/ Hole-Mouthed amphora/ Mañá D/ Cintas 315* (Fig. 5.17)
Characteristic of the 4th to mid 2nd c. B.C., their principal centre of manufacture seems to have been Carthage (Peacock 1986; Riley 1979, 91-467). They are cylindrical amphorae similar in form to Iberian Type 1, but the internal lip of the vessel is more pronounced (see analysis in N. Keay 1989).
Site: 3.19.
Fabric: 102.
Date: 4th to mid 2nd c. B.C.

*Type 11/ Van der Werff 3 / Mañá C2* (Fig. 5.17)
Characteristic of the period between the early 2nd c. and the end of the 1st c. B.C. They are cylindrical amphorae with a long tapering base, lug-handles on the shoulder, and a tall neck which splays outwards and terminates in an overhanging rim. These were manufactured in Morocco; kiln sites are known at Kouass, Sala, and Volubilis. They probably carried fish-sauce (Van der Werff 1978; Ribera 1982).
Sites: 2.3, 2.9, 3.19, 4.4.
Fabric: 102.
Date: late 2nd c. until end of the 1st c. B.C./1st c. A.D.

*Type 12/ Van der Werff 1 / Mañá C2 / Cintas 312* (Fig. 5.17)
Characteristic of the period between the early 2nd c. B.C. and the end of the 1st c. B.C. They are similar to Type 6 but the neck terminates in a double-lipped overhanging rim.
Sites: 1.2, 2.3, 2.6, 2.9, 3.16, 3.19, 4.4.
Fabric: 102.
Date: late 2nd c. B.C. until the end of the 1st c. B.C./1st c. A.D.

*Type 13/ Mañá D / Cintas 315-316* (Fig. 5.18)
Overall they date to between the earlier 4th and earlier 2nd c. B.C. The complete form consists of a long cylindrical body terminating in a characteristic developed base (Ribera 1982). Its most characteristic feature is the mouth, which lies within ridged concentric rings sharply offset from the body. This is an Iberian form but the fabric shows it was manufactured in North Africa.
Site: 2.9.
Fabric: 102.
Date: earlier 4th to earlier 2nd c. B.C. An example was discovered in a context of 150-125 B.C. at Tarraco (Aquilué 1993, fig. 56.8).

Massiliote Production

*Type 14/ Py Rim Type 3* (Fig. 5.18)
Overall they date to between the late 6th and mid 5th c. B.C. (Py 1978). They comprise squat piriform amphorae with button base, short neck, splayed neck, and an everted concave rim. They were manufactured in the region of Massalia and probably carried wine.
Site: 1.2.
Fabric: 45.
Date: between 500 and 450 B.C.

Miscellaneous Amphora Bases (fig. 5.18)

Two hollow pointed amphora bases of unknown type.
Sites: 1.4, 3.19.
Fabric: 71.
Date: unknown but possibly pre-Roman.

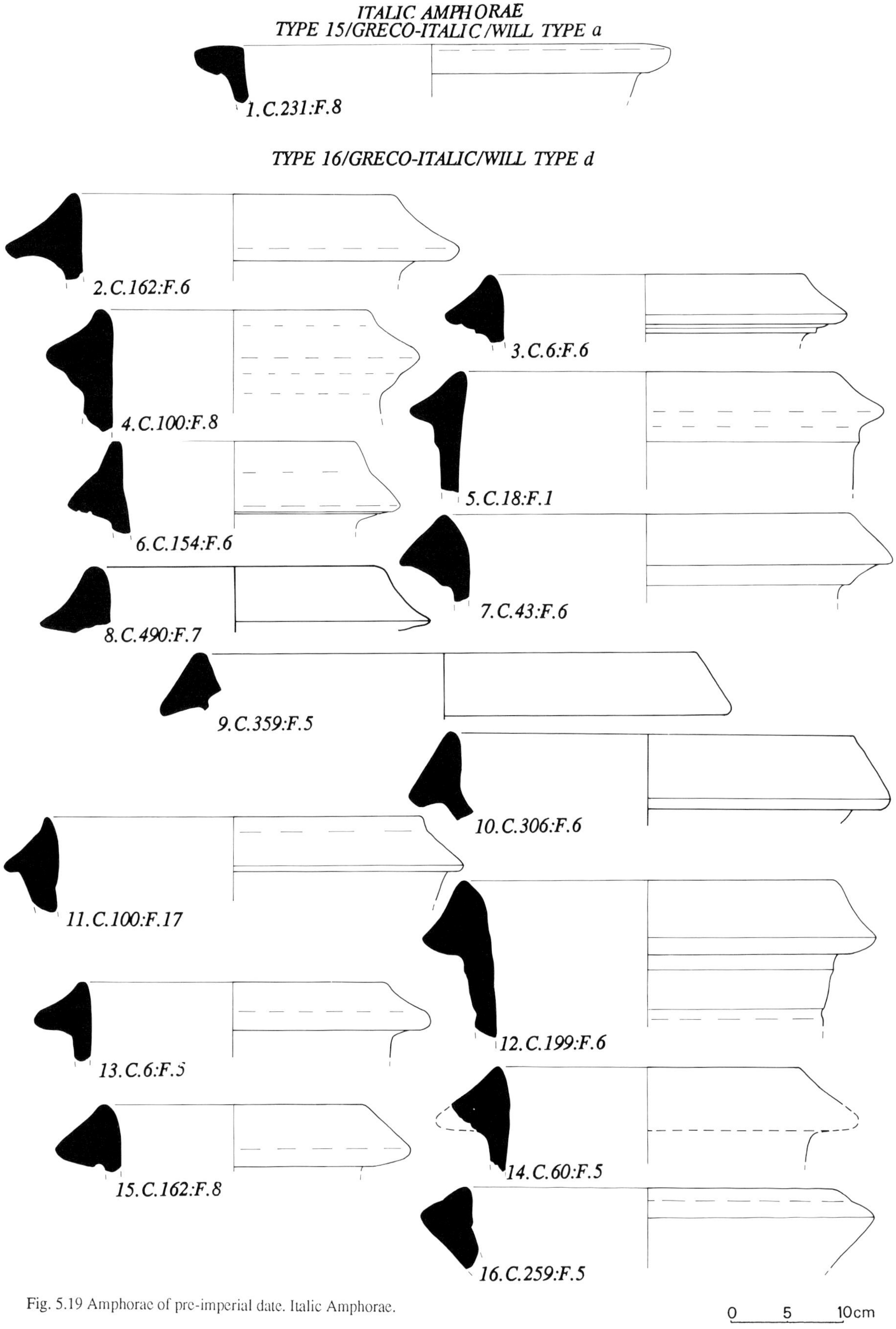

88

ITALIC AMPHORAE
TYPE 15/GRECO-ITALIC/WILL TYPE a

1.C.231:F.8

TYPE 16/GRECO-ITALIC/WILL TYPE d

2.C.162:F.6

3.C.6:F.6

4.C.100:F.8

5.C.18:F.1

6.C.154:F.6

7.C.43:F.6

8.C.490:F.7

9.C.359:F.5

10.C.306:F.6

11.C.100:F.17

12.C.199:F.6

13.C.6:F.5

14.C.60:F.5

15.C.162:F.8

16.C.259:F.5

Fig. 5.19 Amphorae of pre-imperial date. Italic Amphorae.

0     5     10cm

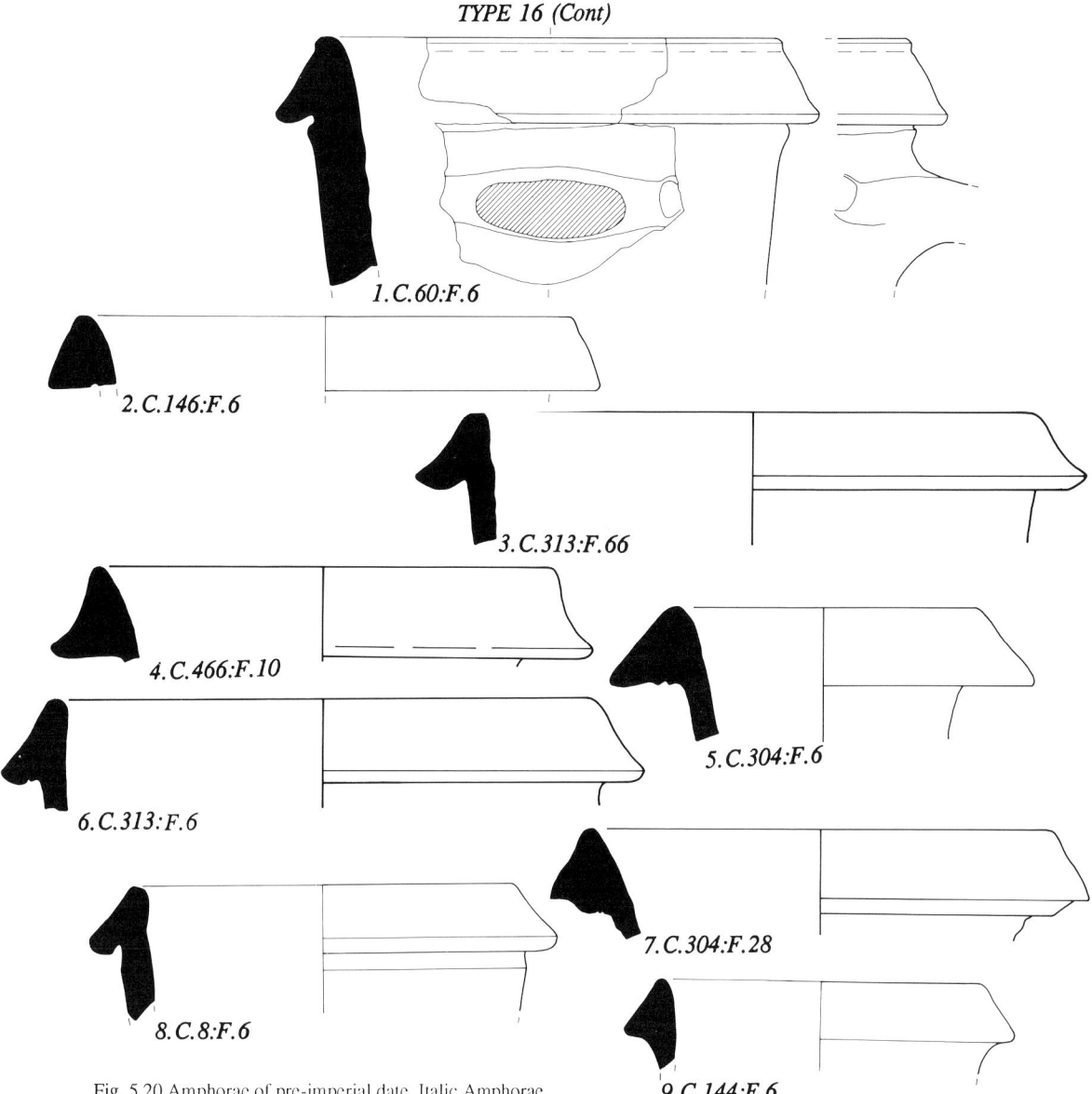

TYPE 16 (Cont)

1. C.60:F.6
2. C.146:F.6
3. C.313:F.66
4. C.466:F.10
5. C.304:F.6
6. C.313:F.6
7. C.304:F.28
8. C.8:F.6
9. C.144:F.6

Fig. 5.20 Amphorae of pre-imperial date. Italic Amphorae.

## Italic Production

Listed under this heading are those forms which are normally associated with Italic production of the Republican period. Thin-section analysis (Appendix 2) has shown that the more common fabrics (3, 5, 6, 7, 8) are definitely of Italian origin. Others which share this form and are not local are assumed to be Italic. Future discoveries of kilns in other parts of the western Mediterranean may indicate otherwise, although that seems unlikely.

*Type 15/ Greco-Italic / Will Type a* (Fig. 5.19)
The form consists of a pear-shaped body with a stubby foot, convex neck, flexed handles and triangular rim. It may possibly be an example of Will's subvariant A (Will 1982). Overall this variant of the Greco-Italic form is thought to have been manufactured in Sicily and/or the Aegean. A visual inspection of the fabric, however, suggests an Italian origin for this fragment.
Found only in off-site scatters.
Fabric: 8.
Date: later 4th to early 3rd c. B.C.

*Type 16/ Greco-Italic / Will Type d* (Fig. 5.19-5.20)
Characteristic of the period 200 to 150 B.C. (Will 1982). The form is largely similar to that of Type 15, except that the rim has a more developed triangular section. An attempt has been made to separate them from Dressel 1A (Type 17 below). However, this distinction is more successfully made with semi-complete vessels. As all the fragments here are rim sherds, the chronological difference implied in the separation between Types 11 and 12 should be treated with caution. The form is considered to have been made near Cosa and Pompeii. The range of fabrics and their analysis (Appendix 2), however, suggests a variety of different production centres in Italy.
Sites: 1.2, 1.4, 1.6, 1.8, 1.10, 1.13, 2.3, 3.9, 3.11, 3.16, 3.17, 3.18, 3.19.
Fabrics: 1, 5, 6, 7, 8, 10, 17, 28 and 66.
Date: first half of the 2nd c. B.C.

*TYPE 17/DRESSEL 1A*

10.C.60:F.6

11.C.8:F.6

12.C.162:F.6

13.C.60:F.6

14.C.5:F.6

15.C.243:F.6

**Fig.** 5.20 cont. Amphorae of pre-imperial date. Italic Amphorae.

0    5    10cm

*Type 17/ Dressel 1A* (Figs.20-27)

Characteristic of the period between *c*.130 B.C. and the mid 1st c. B.C. (Tchernia 1986, 42-53; Peacock and Williams 1986, 86-88). They represent a development of Type 16. They consist of a cylindrical body, with stubby foot, sharply defined shoulder, tall and gently everted neck, flexed handles, and a triangular rim. The examples from the survey consisted of rim sherds only. They exhibited a large range of variation within the broadly defined type Dressel 1A. It was decided to publish a large number of illustrations in case future work defines regional Italian variants within the type. They carried wine and were manufactured at a range of kiln sites in Tuscany and Campania. Dispersed manufacture in Italy is borne out by the range of fabrics characterized (Appendix 2).

Sites: 1.2, 1.4, 1.6, 1.10, 1.12, 1.14, 2.1, 2.3, 2.4, 2.6, 2.7, 2.8, 2.9, 2.10, 3.2, 3.5, 3.9, 3.13, 3.16, 3.17, 3.18, 3.19, 4.1, 4.4, 4.5.

Fabrics: 1, 4, 5, 6, 7, 8, 10, 26, 28, 31, 40, 41, 44, 45, 65, 66, 69, 70, 73, 76, 78, 84 and 86.

Date: between *c*.130 and the mid 1st c. B.C. The form has been discovered in a context of 150-125 B.C. at Tarraco (Aquilué 1993, fig. 56.4-6).

91

TYPE 17 (Cont)

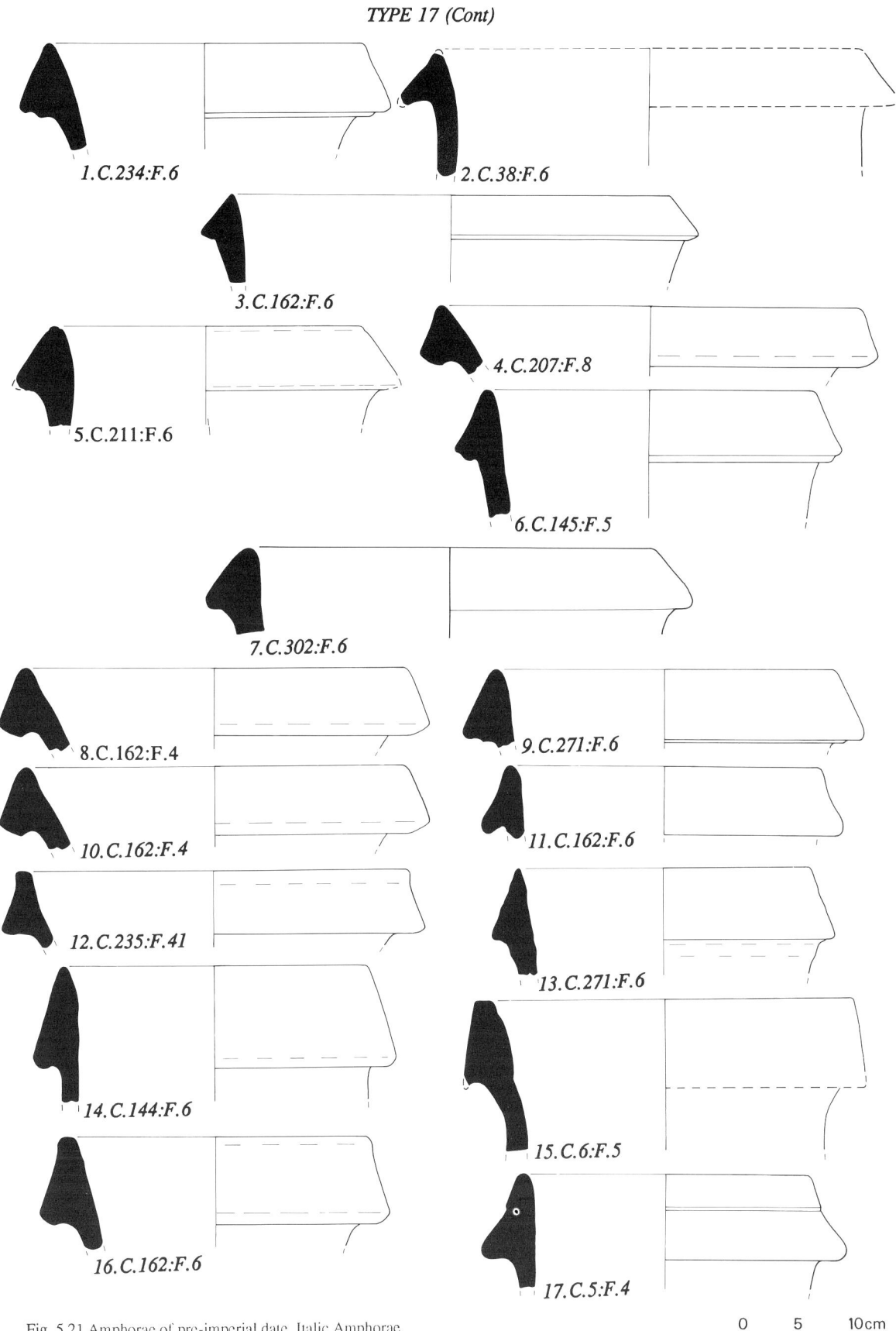

1.C.234:F.6
2.C.38:F.6
3.C.162:F.6
4.C.207:F.8
5.C.211:F.6
6.C.145:F.5
7.C.302:F.6
8.C.162:F.4
9.C.271:F.6
10.C.162:F.4
11.C.162:F.6
12.C.235:F.41
13.C.271:F.6
14.C.144:F.6
15.C.6:F.5
16.C.162:F.6
17.C.5:F.4

Fig. 5.21 Amphorae of pre-imperial date. Italic Amphorae.

0    5    10cm

92

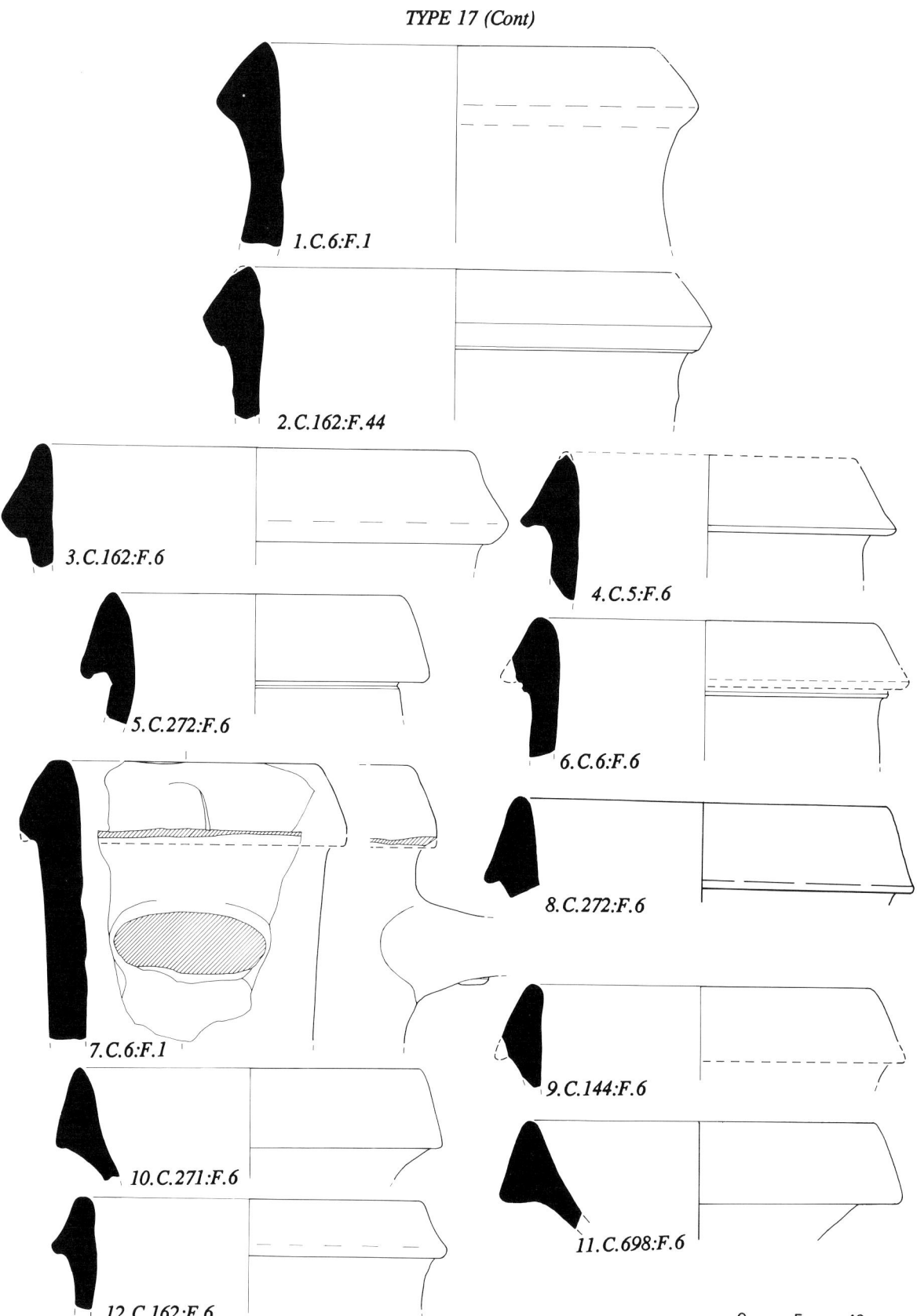

1.C.6:F.1

2.C.162:F.44

3.C.162:F.6

4.C.5:F.6

5.C.272:F.6

6.C.6:F.6

7.C.6:F.1

8.C.272:F.6

9.C.144:F.6

10.C.271:F.6

11.C.698:F.6

12.C.162:F.6

0    5    10cm

Fig. 5.22 Amphorae of pre-imperial date. Italic Amphorae.

*TYPE 17 (Cont)*

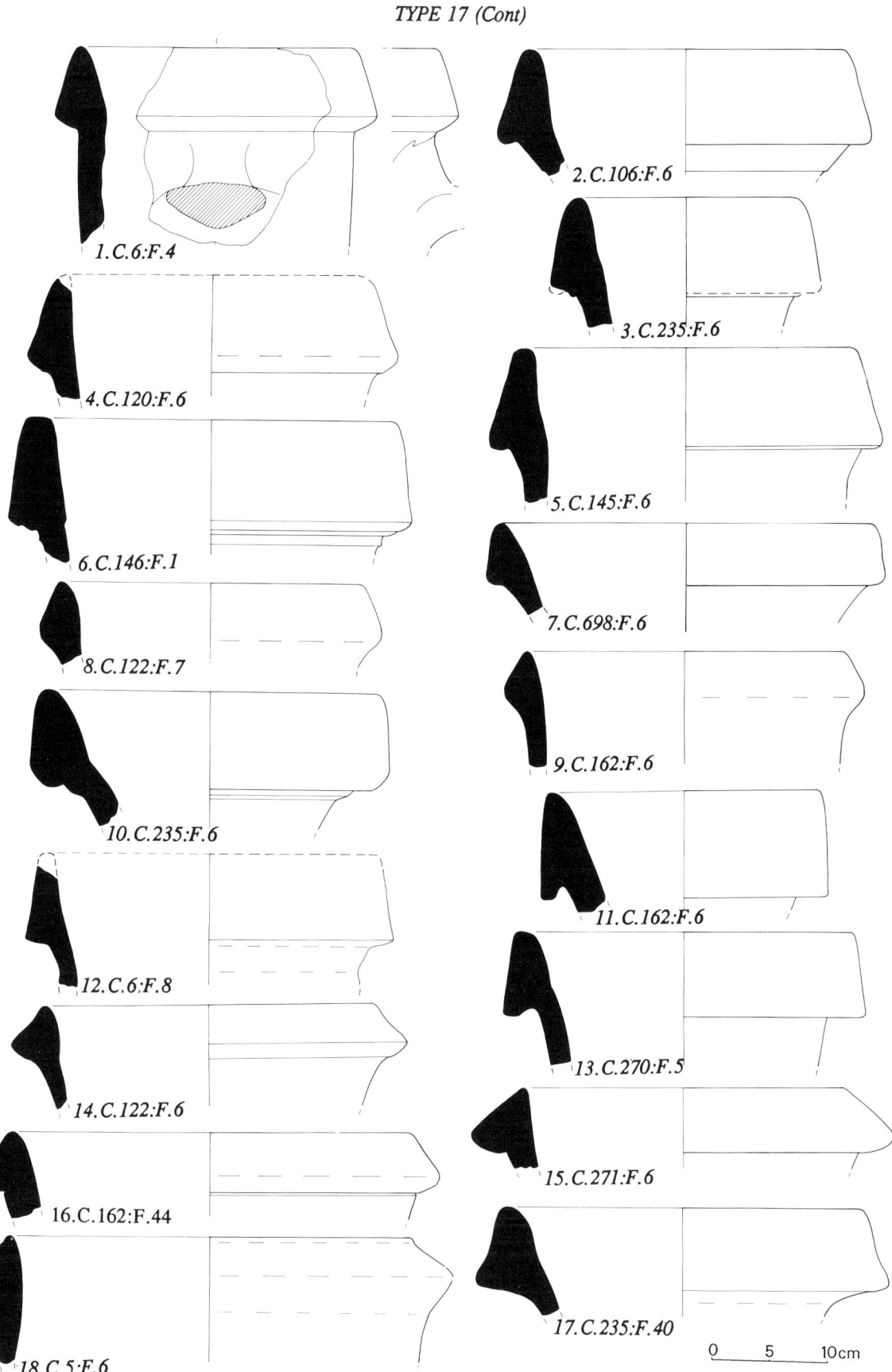

1.C.6:F.4
2.C.106:F.6
3.C.235:F.6
4.C.120:F.6
5.C.145:F.6
6.C.146:F.1
7.C.698:F.6
8.C.122:F.7
9.C.162:F.6
10.C.235:F.6
11.C.162:F.6
12.C.6:F.8
13.C.270:F.5
14.C.122:F.6
15.C.271:F.6
16.C.162:F.44
17.C.235:F.40
18.C.5:F.6

0    5    10cm

Fig. 5.23 Amphorae of pre-imperial date. Italic Amphorae.

94

*TYPE 17 (Cont)*

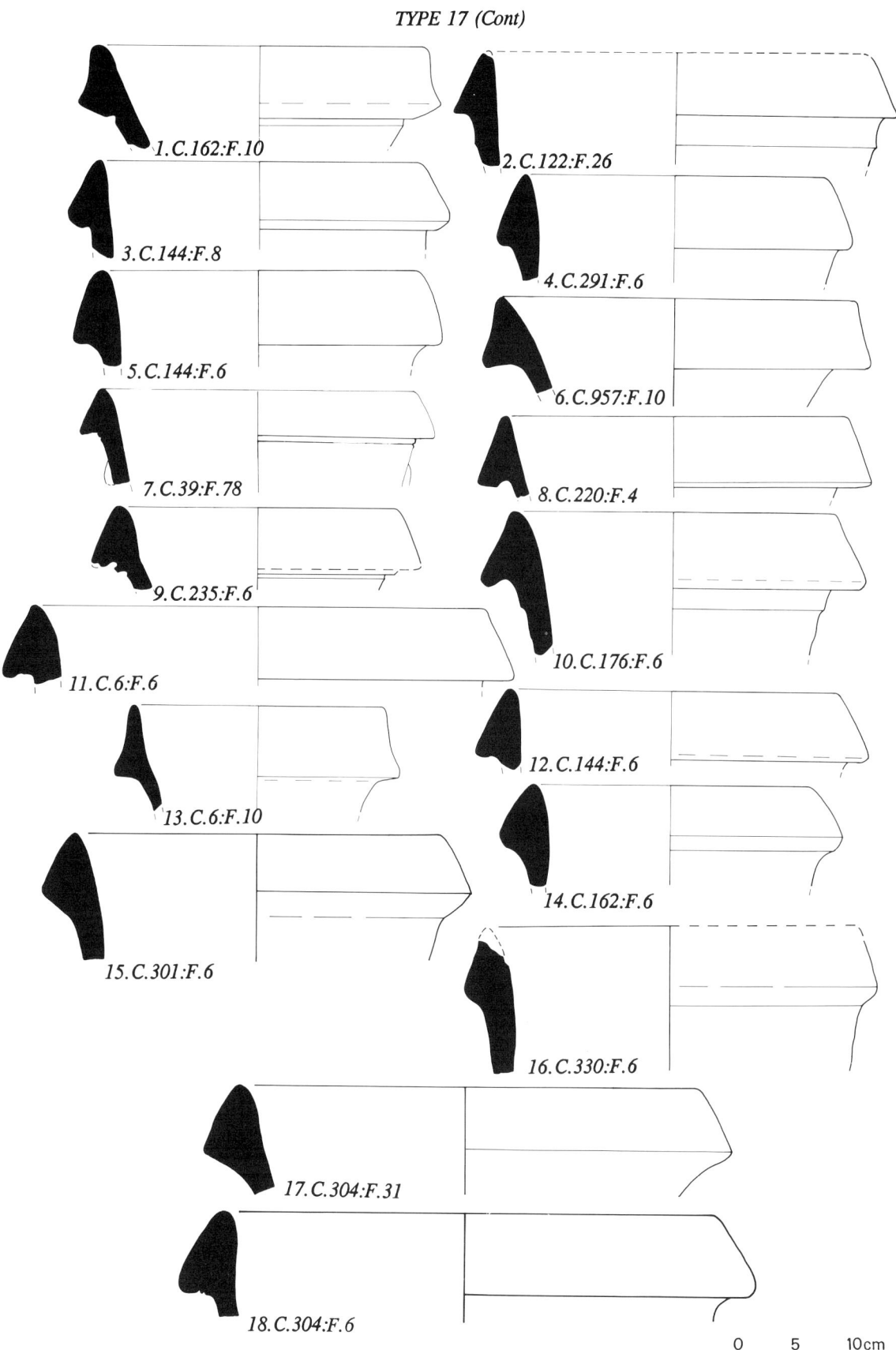

1. C.162:F.10
2. C.122:F.26
3. C.144:F.8
4. C.291:F.6
5. C.144:F.6
6. C.957:F.10
7. C.39:F.78
8. C.220:F.4
9. C.235:F.6
10. C.176:F.6
11. C.6:F.6
12. C.144:F.6
13. C.6:F.10
14. C.162:F.6
15. C.301:F.6
16. C.330:F.6
17. C.304:F.31
18. C.304:F.6

0      5      10cm

Fig. 5.24 Amphorae of pre-imperial date. Italic Amphorae.

95

TYPE 17 (Cont)

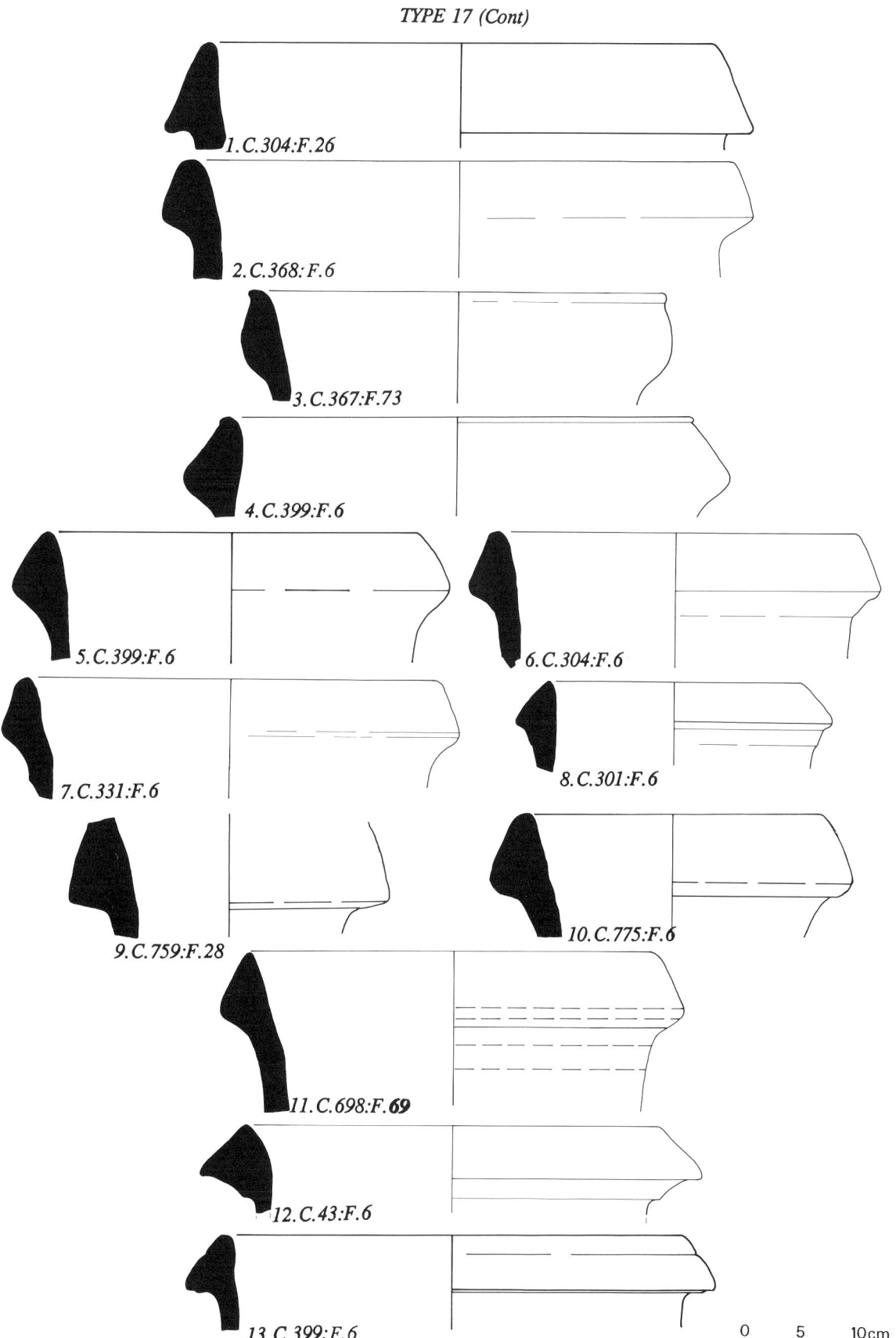

Fig. 5.25 Amphorae of pre-imperial date. Italic Amphorae.

96

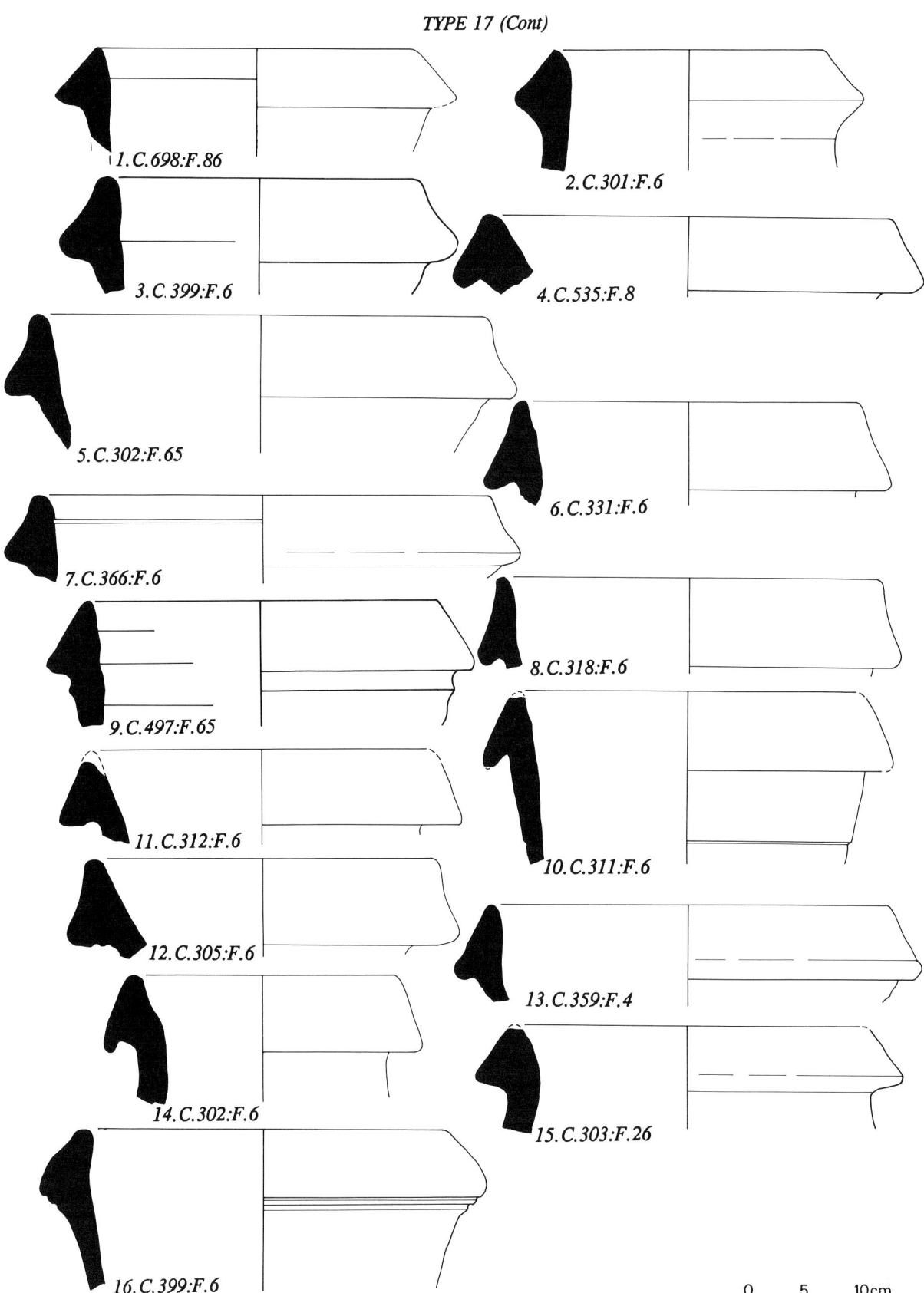

Fig. 5.26 Amphorae of pre-imperial date. Italic Amphorae.

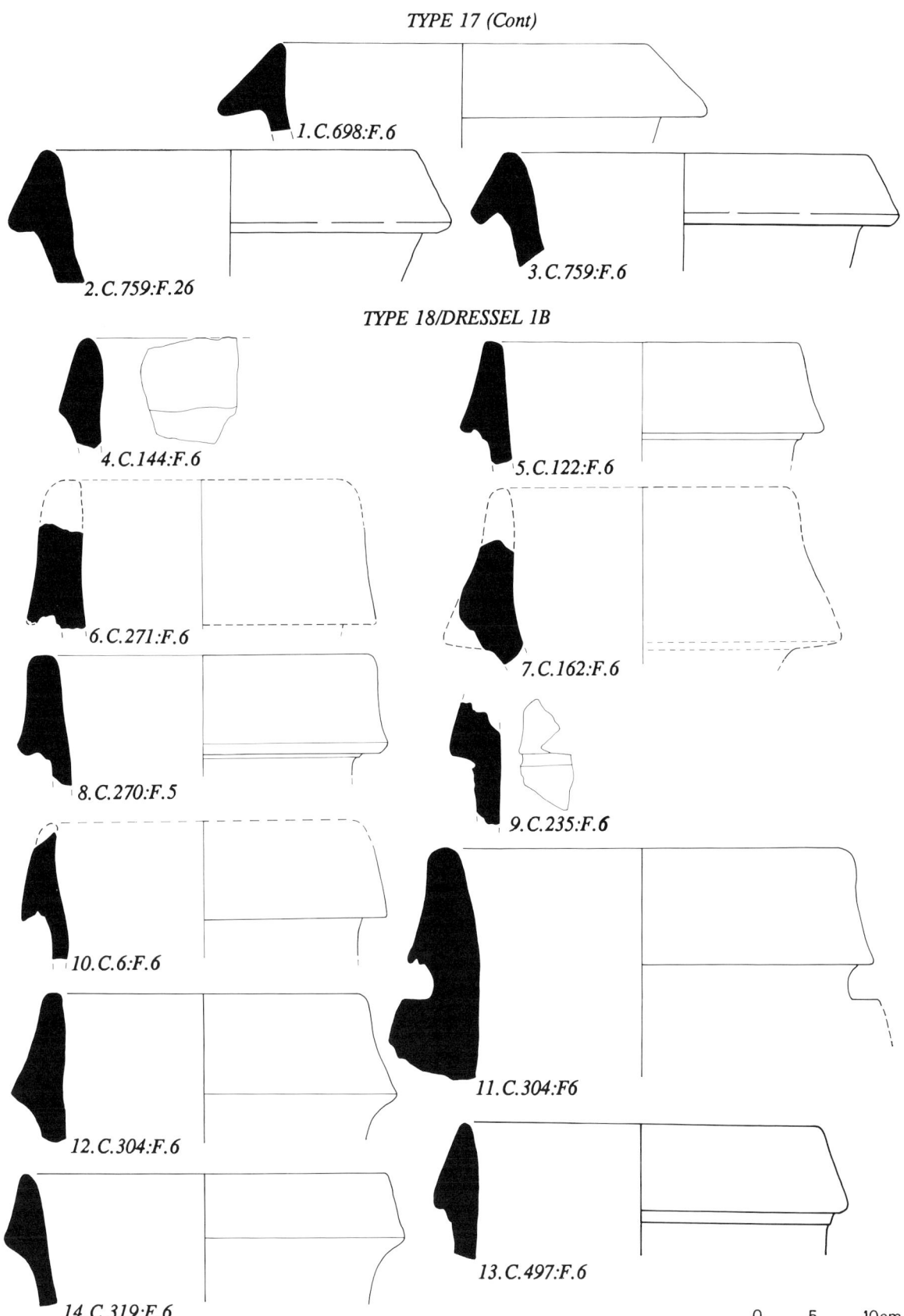

*TYPE 17 (Cont)*

*1.C.698:F.6*

*2.C.759:F.26*

*3.C.759:F.6*

*TYPE 18/DRESSEL 1B*

*4.C.144:F.6*

*5.C.122:F.6*

*6.C.271:F.6*

*7.C.162:F.6*

*8.C.270:F.5*

*9.C.235:F.6*

*10.C.6:F.6*

*11.C.304:F6*

*12.C.304:F.6*

*13.C.497:F.6*

*14.C.319:F.6*

0    5    10cm

Fig. 5.27 Amphorae of pre-imperial date. Italic Amphorae.

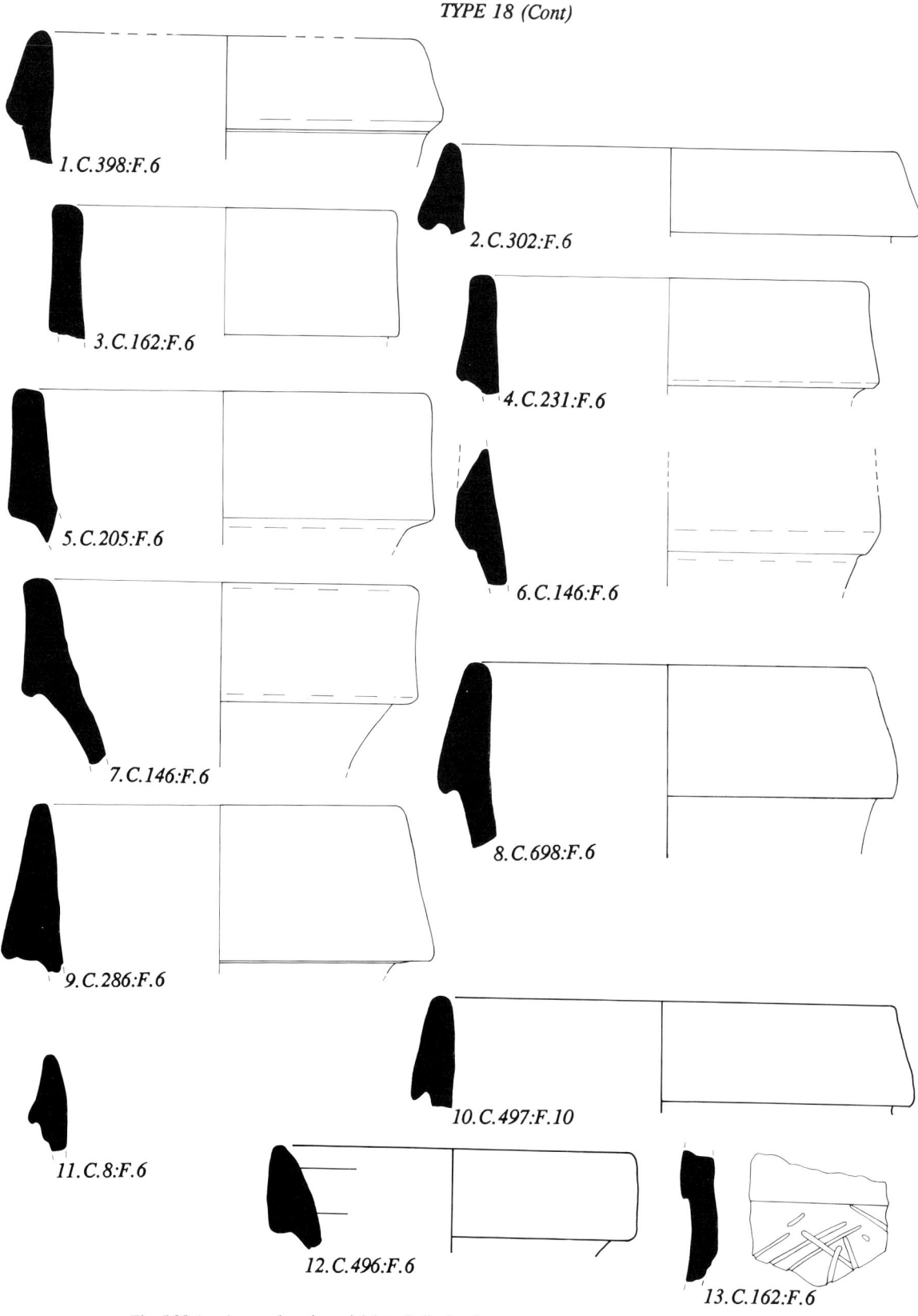

1. C.398:F.6
2. C.302:F.6
3. C.162:F.6
4. C.231:F.6
5. C.205:F.6
6. C.146:F.6
7. C.146:F.6
8. C.698:F.6
9. C.286:F.6
10. C.497:F.10
11. C.8:F.6
12. C.496:F.6
13. C.162:F.6

Fig. 5.28 Amphorae of pre-imperial date. Italic Amphorae.

0    5    10cm

*Type 18/ Dressel 1B* (Fig. 5.27-5.28)
Characteristic of the period between the beginning and some time after the mid 1st c. B.C. (Tchernia 1986, 312-20). The form is broadly similar to Type 17 but the rim is taller with an almost flat internal face. A large number of examples is illustrated for the same reasons as Type 17. Dressel 1B amphorae carried wine manufactured in Campania, Etruria and Latium.
Sites: 1.2, 1.4, 1.6, 1.8, 1.9, 1.10, 1.14, 2.3, 2.6, 2.9, 2.10, 3.9, 3.16, 3.19, 4.1.
Fabrics: 1, 5, 6, 8, 10, 40, 89, 90.
Date: beginning of 1st c. B.C. to after the middle of the century.

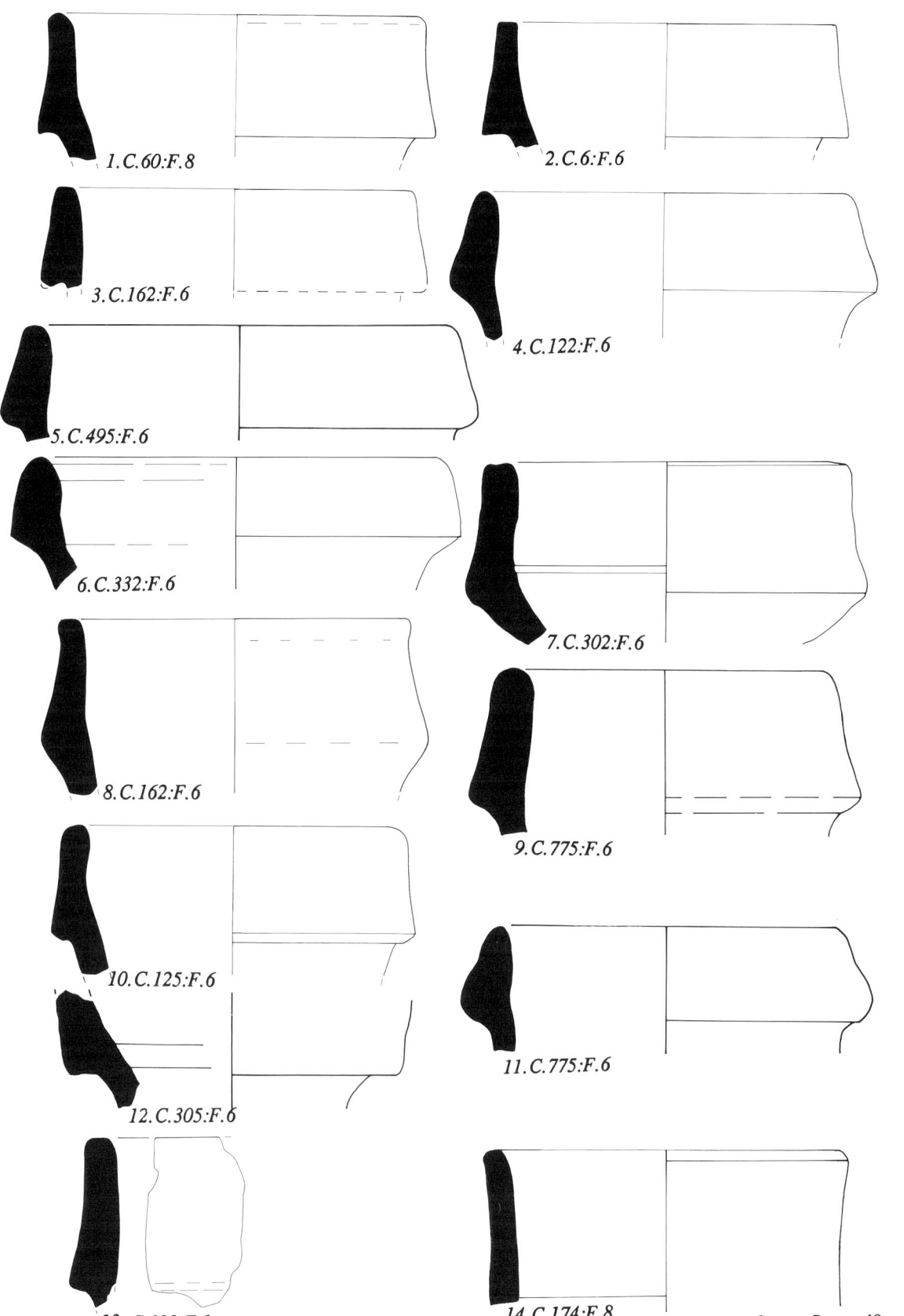

Fig. 5.29 Amphorae of pre-imperial date. Italic Amphorae.

*Type 19/ Dressel 1C* (Fig. 5.29)

Characteristic of the late 2nd and early 1st c. B.C. (Beltrán Lloris 1970). The form is similar to that of Types 17 and 18. However, the shoulder is less pronounced, giving the vessel a tapering appearance, the handles are ribbed, and the rim is characterized by a distinctive concave internal face. Dressel 1C carried wine manufactured principally in Campania and, possibly, Etruria.

Sites: 1.4, 2.3, 2.6, 2.7, 2.9, 2.10, 3.9, 3.16, 3.19.

Fabrics: 1, 6, 8, and 40.

Date: between the late 2nd and early 1st c. B.C.

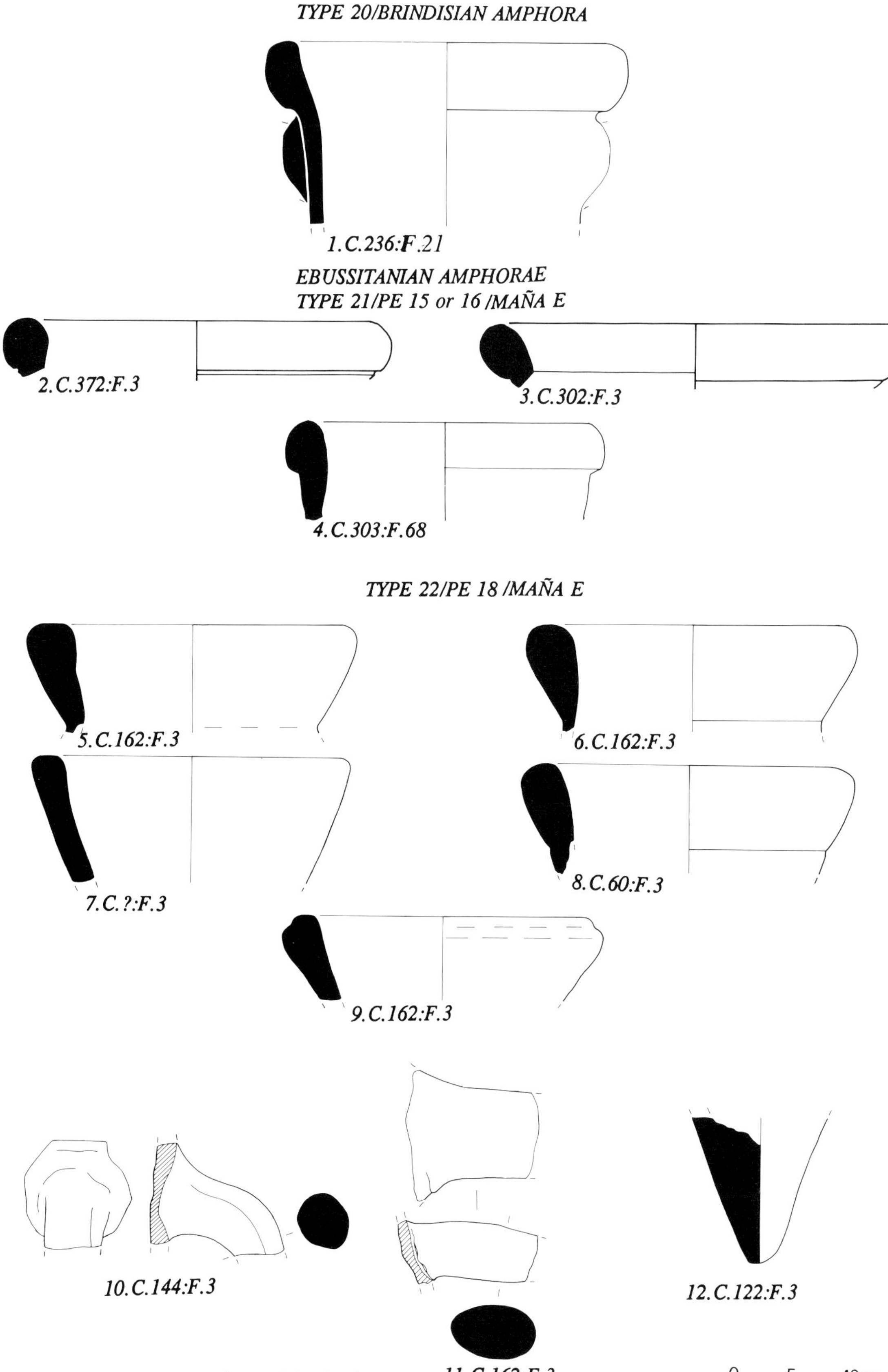

*TYPE 20/BRINDISIAN AMPHORA*

*1.C.236:F.21*

*EBUSSITANIAN AMPHORAE*
*TYPE 21/PE 15 or 16 /MAÑA E*

*2.C.372:F.3*

*3.C.302:F.3*

*4.C.303:F.68*

*TYPE 22/PE 18 /MAÑA E*

*5.C.162:F.3*

*6.C.162:F.3*

*7.C.?:F.3*

*8.C.60:F.3*

*9.C.162:F.3*

*10.C.144:F.3*

*11.C.162:F.3*

*12.C.122:F.3*

0    5    10cm

Fig. 5.30 Amphorae of pre-imperial date. Other Amphorae.

*Type 20/ Brindisian amphora* (Fig. 5.30)
This type probably dates from the late 2nd to mid 1st c. B.C. (Peacock and Williams 1986, 82-83; Cipriano and Carre 1989). The complete form consists of a squat piriform body with a 'button' base, squat neck, pronounced rim, and handles which are round in section. They were manufactured along the Adriatic coast, although it has been suggested that one variety, stamped M. Tuccius Galeo, may have been manufactured along the Adriatic coast (Cipriano and Carre 1989, 74-77). Brindisian amphorae carried olive oil and possibly wine.
Site: 1.14.
Fabric: 21.
Date: late 2nd to mid 1st c. B.C.


Ebussitanian Production

*Type 21/ PE 15 or 16 / Mañá E* (Fig. 5.30)
These vessels have a distinctive form comprising a long tapering and gently curved base topped by a tall neck which gradually tapers inwards towards a narrow point immediately below the rim. The rim has a circular section. Lug handles are present halfway up the neck. The form has its origins in the Phoenician/Punic tradition of amphora production at Ebusus (Ramón 1981, 107 ff.). The type probably carried olive oil (ibid. 129).
Sites: 3.13, 3.15, 3.19.
Fabrics: 3, 68.
Date: 305-255 B.C. (PE 15) or 245-195 B.C. (PE 16).

*Type 22/ PE 18 / Mañá E* (Fig. 5.30)
Vessels of these types are broadly similar in form to Type 21. It is distinguished by its gently curved/rounded base and rim with triangular section (Ramón 1981, 102 ff.). It carried olive oil.
Sites: 1.2, 1. 4, 1.12.
Fabric: 3.
Date: 130/120 B.C. until the end of the 1st c. B.C./beginning of the 1st c. A.D.

Miscellaneous handles and bases (Fig. 5.30)

A number of handles and bases which could not be ascribed to any particular Ebussitanian form were also found at a range of sites and in off-site scatters.

102

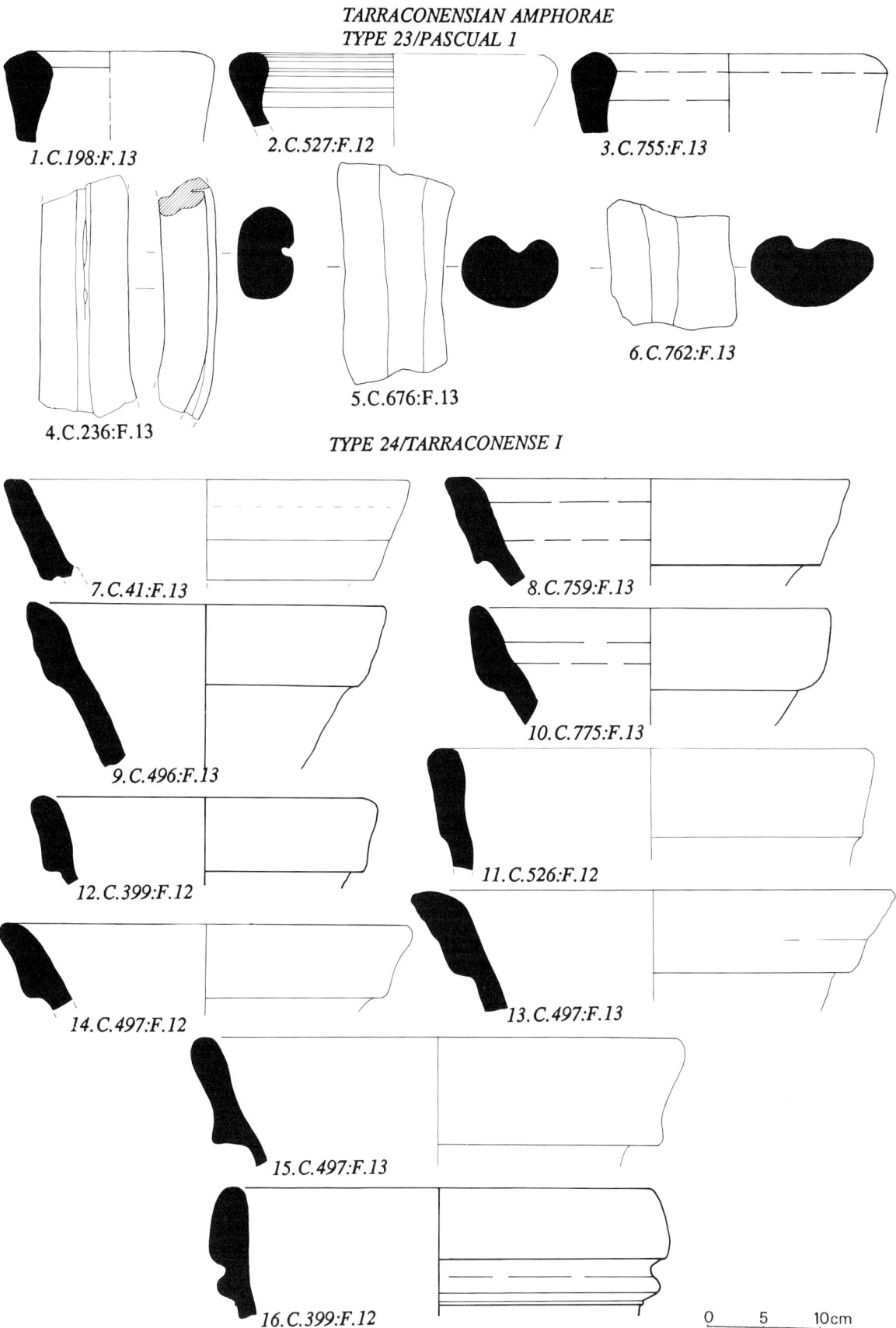

Fig. 5.31 Amphorae of early imperial date. Tarraconensian Amphorae.

AMPHORAE OF EARLY IMPERIAL DATE (MID 1st c. B.C. - LATE 2nd c. A.D.)

Tarraconensian Production

*Type 23/ Pascual 1* (Fig. 5.31)
A regional adaptation of Dressel 1C. It has a pear-shaped body with cylindrical foot and rounded shoulder. The handles were affixed a short distance below the rim and on the shoulder, with a characteristic groove running along the outside. The rim was tall and everted, quite often with a pronounced rounded ridge running around the inside (Miró 1988, 70-78). This form was manufactured at kiln sites in Laietania, although the fabric of our pieces shows that they were manufactured in the territory of Tarraco. Pascual 1 amphorae transported wine.
Sites: 1.8, 1.14, 2.3, 2.6, 2.7, 2.9, 2.10, 3.9 and 3.10.
Fabrics: 12 and 13.
Date: mid 1st c. B.C. until the first or second decade of the 1st c. A.D.

*Type 24/ Tarraconense 1/ Laietana 1* (Fig. 5.31)
This form was a regional adaptation of Italic oil-carrying forms such as Lamboglia 2 and the Brindisian amphorae (here Type 20). They are quite tall (*c.*0.80 m) ovoid/cylindrical vessels, with a stubby base and squat cylindrical neck. The rim varies but tends to be well defined and gently everted. The handles are attatched a short distance below the rim and have a groove running along the outside (akin to Type 23). One rim from Campo 399 (F.12, Fig. 5.31.16), distinct from the others, is characterized by a pronounced ridge running around the neck below the rim. The contents are not known, although wine is possible (Nolla and Solias 1984-85). Analysis of the fabric suggests that the form was manufactured in the territory of Tarraco as well as further north in Laietania. An example with an Iberian rim stamp has been found at Salduie (Zaragoza) (Aguarod 1992).
Sites: 2.3, 2.6, 2.7, 2.10 and 3.16.
Off-site scatters: 41.
Fabrics: 12 and 13.
Date: last quarter of the 1st c. B.C. until the first or second decade of the 1st c. A.D. No stamps were found on the survey examples, although Latin names are known elsewhere (Nolla and Solias 1984-85).

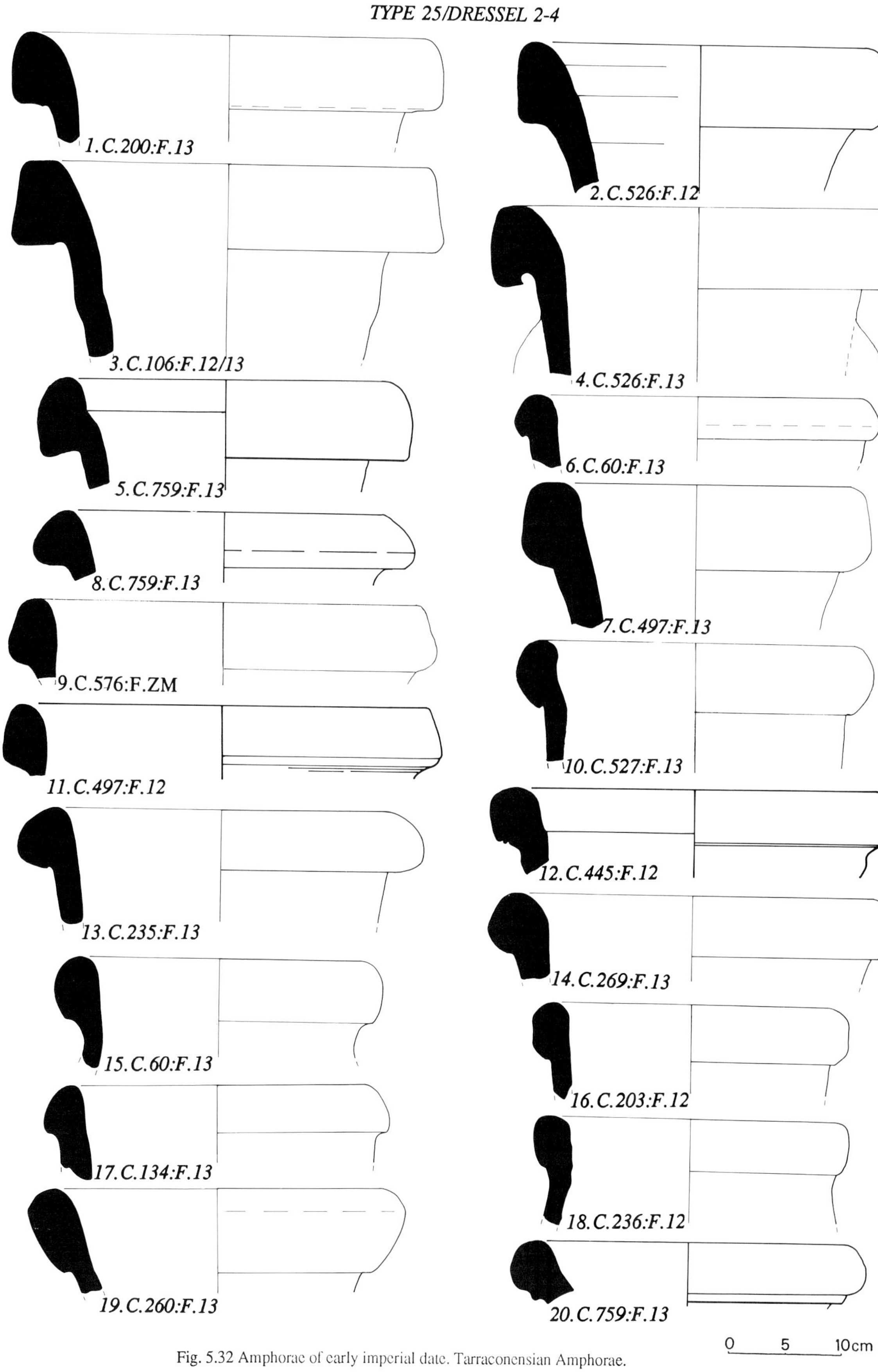

TYPE 25/DRESSEL 2-4

1.C.200:F.13

2.C.526:F.12

3.C.106:F.12/13

4.C.526:F.13

5.C.759:F.13

6.C.60:F.13

8.C.759:F.13

7.C.497:F.13

9.C.576:F.ZM

10.C.527:F.13

11.C.497:F.12

12.C.445:F.12

13.C.235:F.13

14.C.269:F.13

15.C.60:F.13

16.C.203:F.12

17.C.134:F.13

18.C.236:F.12

19.C.260:F.13

20.C.759:F.13

0    5    10cm

Fig. 5.32 Amphorae of early imperial date. Tarraconensian Amphorae.

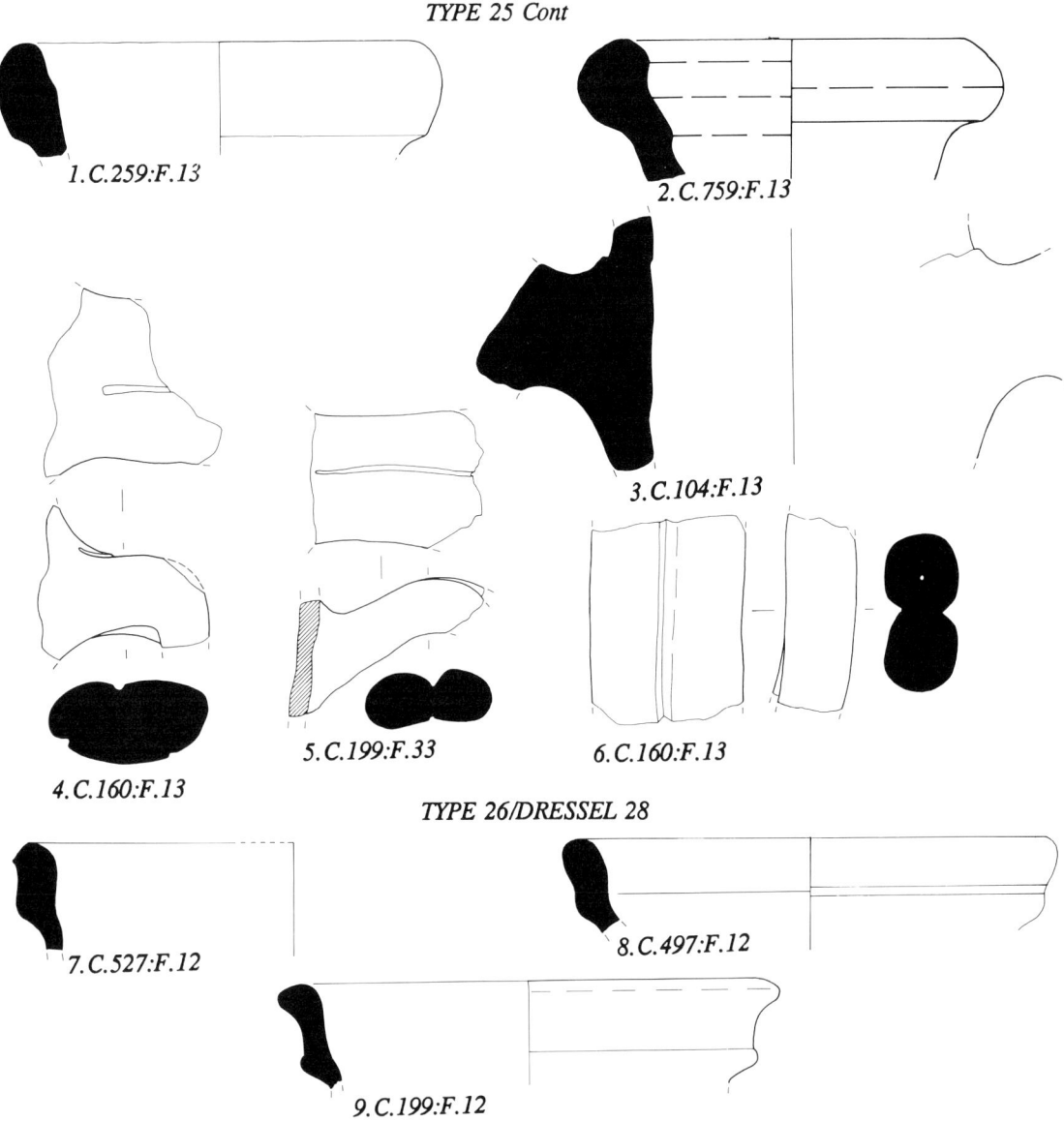

TYPE 25 Cont

1.C.259:F.13

2.C.759:F.13

3.C.104:F.13

4.C.160:F.13

5.C.199:F.33

6.C.160:F.13

TYPE 26/DRESSEL 28

7.C.527:F.12

8.C.497:F.12

9.C.199:F.12

**Fig.** 5.33 Amphorae of early imperial date. Tarraconensian Amphorae.

*Type 25/ Dressel 2-4* (Figs. 5.32-5.33)
As Type 36 (below). A regional imitation of a type developed in Italy. A range of rim sherds was recovered during the survey, exhibiting some variation in the basic form, from squarish to round. The form was manufactured at many kiln sites found in the hinterland of towns such as Emporiae, Baetulo, Barcino, Tarraco, and Saguntum (Miró 1988). The fabric of the examples from the survey reveals that some were made in the territory of Tarraco, whilst others were manufactured further north in Laietania. They carried wine.
Sites: 1.3, 1.4, 1.6, 1.8, 1.14, 2.2, 2.3, 2.6, 2.7, 2.9, 3.5, 4.2, 4.3 and 4.4.
Fabrics: 12, 13, 33 and ZM.
Date: between the first decades of the 1st and the very beginning of the 2nd c. A.D.

*Type 26/ Dressel 28* (Fig. 5.33)
A relatively small pear-shaped vessel. It has a flat bottom and ring-foot, handles with furrows, and a distinctive rim with concave external and convex internal faces. It is manufactured widely in the western empire, particularly in Tarraconensis and Gallia Narbonensis (Peacock and Williams 1986, 149 ff.). The fabric suggests that they were manufactured in Laietania (see Pascual 1977; also Miró 1988, 96-97). The form may have transported wine.
Sites: 2.6, 2.7 and 4.4.
Fabric: 12.
Date: late Augustan to the first half of the 2nd c. A.D.

TYPE 27/BELTRÁN I

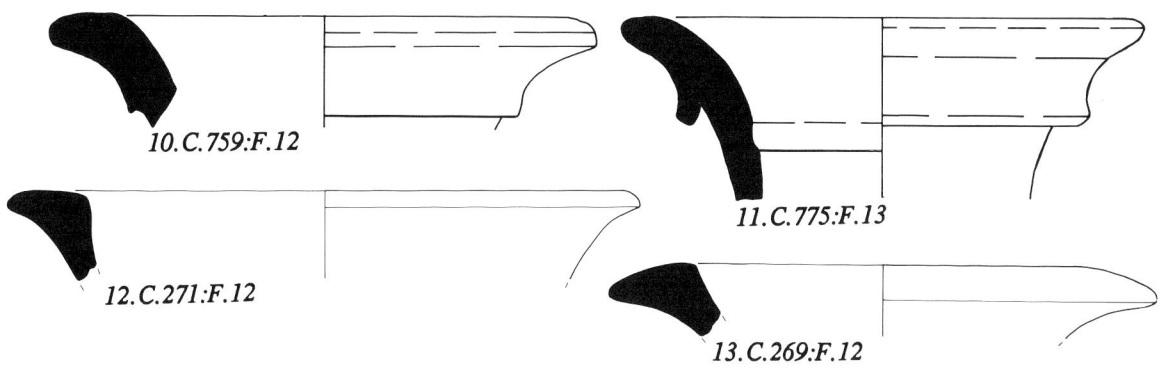

10.C.759:F.12

11.C.775:F.13

12.C.271:F.12

13.C.269:F.12

Fig. 5.33 cont. Amphorae of early imperial date. Tarraconensian Amphorae.

0    5    10cm

*Type 27/ Beltrán I* (Figs. 5.33-5.34)
As Type 31 (below). Analysis of the fabric of the sherds from the survey suggests that they were manufactured in the territory of Tarraco and possibly in Laietania. This complements evidence for production at the Pla de Aumedina de Tivisa (Mora d'Ebre: J. M. Nolla *et al.* 1980), and elsewhere in NE Tarraconensis (Miró 1988, 99-116). In the Baetican examples fish-sauce was the principal content. The contents of our examples is unknown although fish-sauce is a possibility (in light of fish vats at Els Munts and near Salou).
Sites: 2.3, 3.5 and 4.4.
Fabrics: 12 and 13.
Date: first quarter of the 1st c. A.D.

*Type 28/ Beltrán IIB* (Fig. 5.34)
As Type 31 (below). Analysis of the fabric suggests an origin in the territory of Tarraco and possibly in Laietania. The content is unknown although fish-sauce is a possibility (in light of fish vats at Els Munts and near Salou).
Site: 4.1.
Fabrics: 12 and 13.
Date: possibly Tiberian/Claudian to the mid 2nd c. A.D.

*Type 29/ Dressel 20* (Fig. 5.34)
As Type 33 (below). Analysis of the fabric suggests an origin in the territory of Tarraco. The content is unknown although in Baetica the form was used to transport olive oil.
Sites: 2.9 and 4.1.
Fabric: 13.
Date: beginning of the 1st to the mid 3rd c. A.D.

*Type 30/ Africana 1/ Keay IIIB*
As Type 38 (below). The fabric of the sherd from the survey points to manufacture in the territory of Tarraco.
Site: 4.4.
Fabric: 13.
Date: later 2nd to early 4th c. A.D.

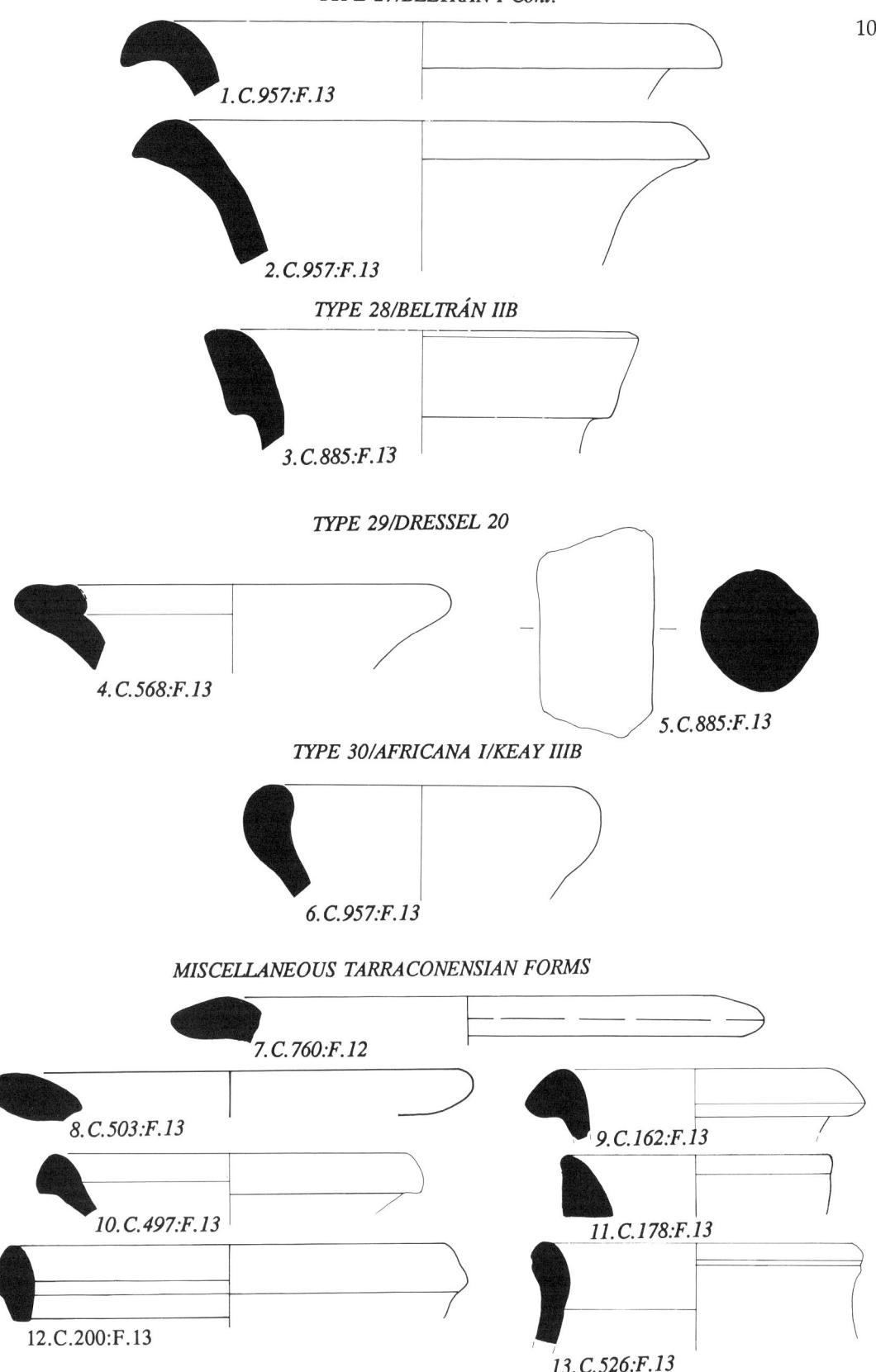

TYPE 27/BELTRÁN I Cont:

1. C.957:F.13

2. C.957:F.13

TYPE 28/BELTRÁN IIB

3. C.885:F.13

TYPE 29/DRESSEL 20

4. C.568:F.13

5. C.885:F.13

TYPE 30/AFRICANA I/KEAY IIIB

6. C.957:F.13

MISCELLANEOUS TARRACONENSIAN FORMS

7. C.760:F.12

8. C.503:F.13

9. C.162:F.13

10. C.497:F.13

11. C.178:F.13

12. C.200:F.13

13. C.526:F.13

Fig. 5.34 Amphorae of early imperial date.

0   5   10cm

*Miscellaneous Forms* (Figs. 5.34-5.35)
A range of Tarraconensian amphora rims and bases for which no obvious parallel has been found.
Found at various sites and in off-site scatters.
Fabrics: 12 and 13.

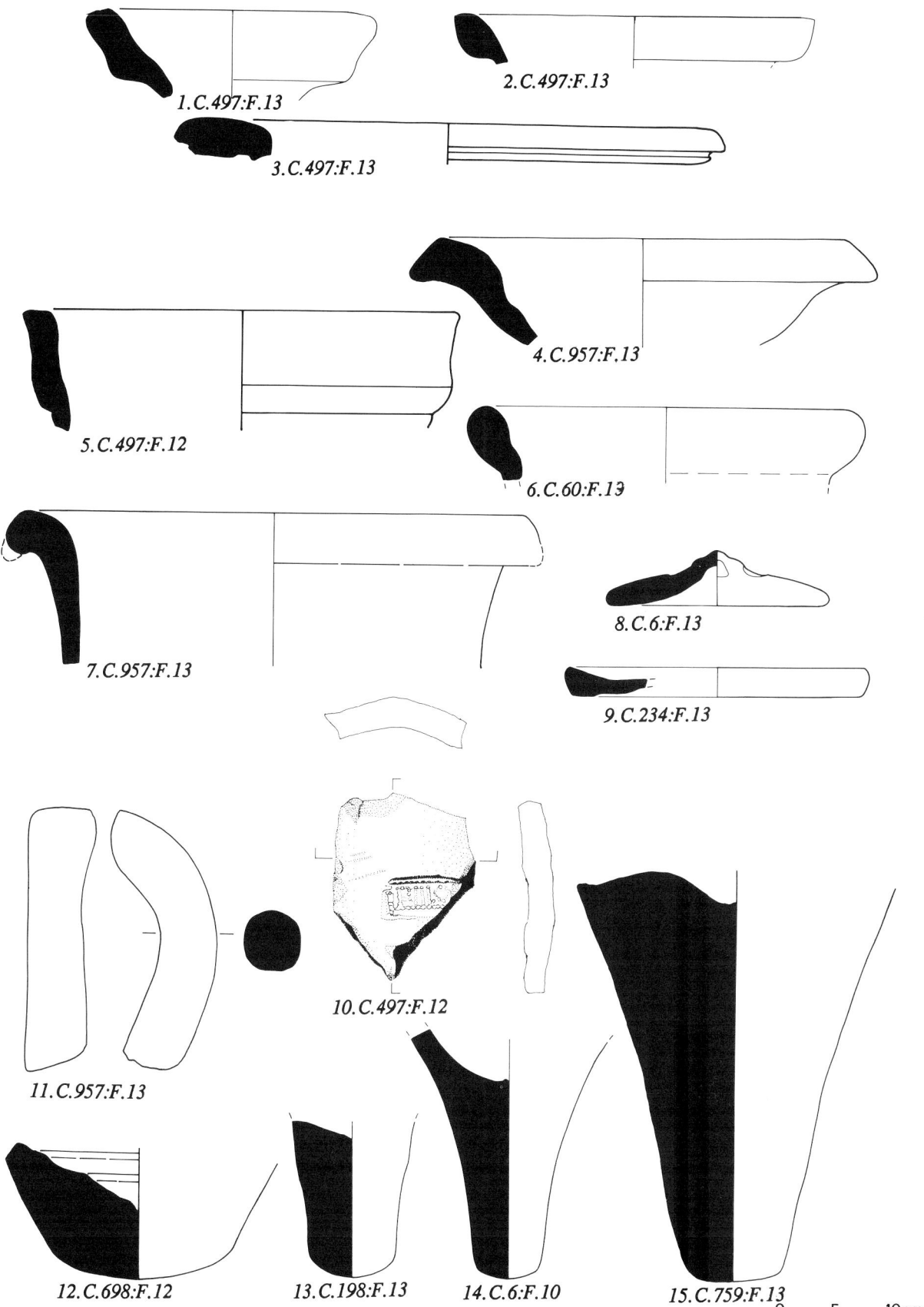

1. C.497:F.13
2. C.497:F.13
3. C.497:F.13
4. C.957:F.13
5. C.497:F.12
6. C.60:F.13
7. C.957:F.13
8. C.6:F.13
9. C.234:F.13
10. C.497:F.12
11. C.957:F.13
12. C.698:F.12
13. C.198:F.13
14. C.6:F.10
15. C.759:F.13

0   5   10cm

Fig. 5.35 Amphorae of early imperial date.

*Miscellaneous stamps* (Fig. 5.35)
Although many of the Tarraconensian amphora types were stamped (Pascual 1977; Miró 1988), only one stamp was found during the survey (Campo 497). It may possibly read PHILOD within a rectangular cartouche composed of dots. A similar example was found on the neck of an early imperial Tarraconensian amphora at the kiln of Sot del Camp (Sant Vincents de Montalt, Mataró: Pascual 1977, fig. 17.6 and 18.6). Fabric: 12.

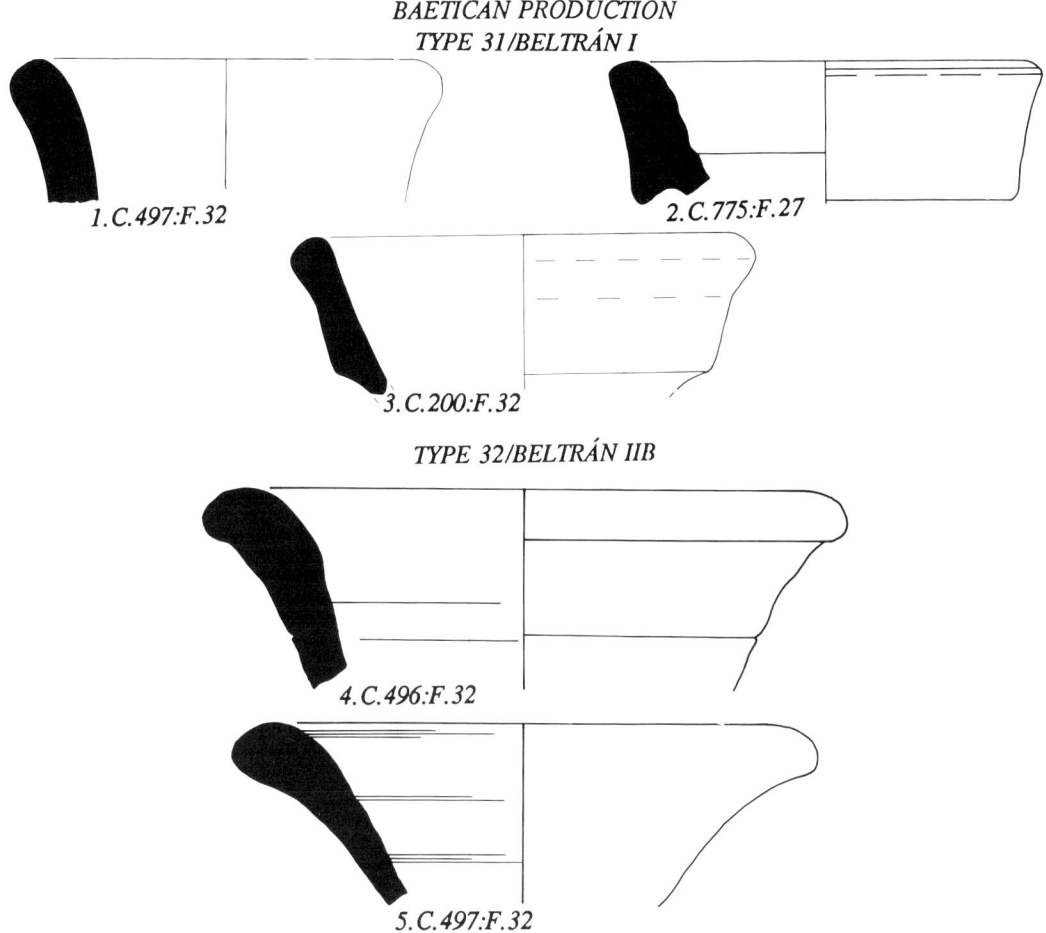

Fig. 5.36 Amphorae of early imperial date. Baetican production.

## Baetican Production

*Type 31/ Beltrán I* (Fig. 5.36)
These vessels are quite tall, having a pear-shaped body with a pronounced base. The neck is quite tall; the flexed handles have a furrow down the outside. The distinctive everted rim has concave outer face and is undercut (Beltrán Lloris 1977). They were manufactured primarily along the Mediterranean coast of Baetica and possibly elsewhere in the western empire (Peacock and Williams 1986, 118). They carried fish sauce.
Sites: 2.5, 2.10 and 3.5.
Fabrics: 27 and 32.
Date: late 1st c. B.C. until the late 1st c. A.D.

*Type 32/ Beltrán IIB* (Fig. 5.36)
A long pear-shaped body with long tapering foot (hollow or solid). The neck is a continuation of the body and tapers inwards to form a characteristic rim that splays outwards. The handles are long and reach their highest point immediately below the lip

of the rim. The type was manufactured principally along the Mediterranean and Atlantic coasts of Baetica and carried fish sauce (Beltrán 1977).
Sites: 2.2, 2.3, 2.6 and 4.4.
Fabric: 32.
Date: Tiberian/Claudian to the mid 2nd c. A.D.

*Type 33/ Dressel 20* (Fig. 5.36)
Characterized by a globular body, with button base, sharply bent oval/round sectioned handles, and an internally concave rim (Peacock and Williams 1986, 136-40). Recent research has suggested that the rim profile alters through time (Martin Kilcher 1983). They were manufactured along the banks of the Guadalquivir and Genil valleys in Baetica, and carried olive oil.
Site: 2.2.
Fabric: 97.
Date: the second decade of the 1st until the mid 3rd c. A.D.

*TYPE 33/DRESSEL 20*

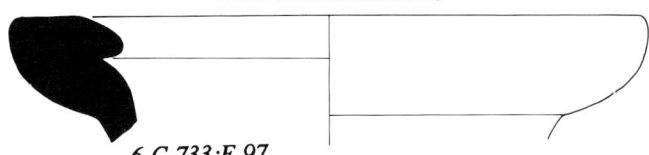

6.C.733:F.97

*S. GAULISH PRODUCTION*
*TYPE 34/DRESSEL 2-4*

7.C.250:F.39

8.C.397:F.37

*TYPE 35/GAULOISE 4*

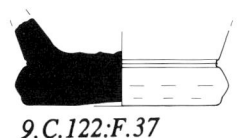

9.C.122:F.37

**Fig. 5.36** cont. Amphorae of early imperial date. Baetican production.

0    5    10cm

## South Gaulish Production

*Type 34/ Dressel 2-4* (Fig. 5.36)
As Type 36 (below). An analysis of the fabric suggests that they were manufactured in S. Gaul (see Laubenheimer 1989). The form carried wine.
Sites: 1.13 and 4.4.
Fabrics: 37 and 39.
Date: end of the 1st c. B.C. until some time in the course of the 1st c. A.D.

*Type 35/ Gauloise 4* (Fig. 5.36)
A piriform-shaped body, whose tapering body terminated in a characteristic base with a small foot-ring. The neck is short and everted, terminating in a thick rounded rim. The flexed handles with a groove running along the outer face are crudely attached to the neck. The type is characteristic of S. Gaul (Laubenheimer 1985), although it was also produced in other parts of Gaul (Laubenheimer 1989, 132 ff.). It probably carried wine.
Sites: 1.2, 1.8 and 4.4.
Fabric: 37.
Date: mid 1st to mid 2nd or beginning of the 3rd c. A.D.

## Italic Production

*Type 36: Dressel 2-4* (Fig. 5.37)
This form was first manufactured in Campania, Latium, and Etruria following a prototype from the island of Kos that was widely imitated in different parts of the empire (Tchernia 1986; Peacock and Williams 1986, 105-6). The form comprises a piriform body with a stubby cylindrical base, sharply defined shoulder, and tall, gently everted neck with round-section rim. A characteristic feature is the bifid handles, attached a short distance below the rim and on the shoulder (Tchernia and Zevi 1971, 35 ff.). The fabric of the sherds collected during the survey suggests that they were manufactured in Campania. The type transported wine.
Sites: 1.6 and 3.9.
Fabrics: 6, 6A and 85.
Date: later 1st c. B.C. until the mid 2nd c. A.D.

*Miscellaneous Italic amphorae* (Fig. 5.37)
A range of miscellaneous rims and handles for which an Italian origin is suggested by the fabric but for which no obvious parallel has been found.
Found at a range of sites.
Fabrics: 6, 7, 25, and 29.

AMPHORAE OF LATE IMPERIAL DATE (late 2nd - early 6th c. A.D.)

North African Production

*Type 37/ Tripolitana III/ Keay XI* (Fig. 5.38)
Comprised a tall wide cylindrical body with curved base and characteristic conical foot. The neck was short and squat and the rim everted with an 'S' profile. The type was manufactured at a number of kiln sites in the hinterland of the coastal towns of Lepcis Magna, Sabratha and Oea (Keay 1984, 133-36). It transported olive oil.
Sites: 1.14, 2.6, 2.7 and 3.19.
Fabrics: 80 and 103.
Date: between the 2nd c. and the second half of the 3rd c. A.D.

*Type 38/ Africana 1B/ Keay IIIB* (Fig. 5.38)
This type comprised a narrow cylindrical body with a stubby base, a small neck, small 'ear-shaped' handles, and a characteristic rim with pronounced convex outer and concave inner faces (Keay 1984, 100 ff.). It was manufactured in Byzacena (Tunisia) and carried *garum* and olive oil.
Sites: 2.7, 2.8 and 3.5.
Fabric: 102.
Date: later 2nd to early 4th c. A.D.

*Type 39/ Africana IIA/ Keay IV* (Fig. 5.38)
A tall wide cylindrical body with short solid foot and short conical neck. The handles have a characteristic circular profile and elliptical section while the rim is slightly rounded. The type was manufactured in Byzacena (Keay 1984, 110-14). It carried olive oil, and/or possibly fish sauce.
Sites: 1.6 and 2.7.
Fabric: 102.
Date: between the late 2nd/early 3rd and mid 4th c. A.D.

*Type 40/ Africana IIB/ Keay VBis* (Fig. 5.38)
Similar to Type 38 but the profile of the rim differed in having a squarish section and gentle offset. The type was manufactured in Byzacena (Keay 1984, 115-18). The content is unknown although olive oil or fish sauce may be presumed.
Sites: 1.6, 2.7 and 2.8.
Fabric: 102.
Date: between the late 2nd and the early 4th/5th c. A.D.

*Type 41/ Africana IID/ Keay VII* (Fig. 5.38)
Similar to Types 39 and 40 but the rim is a poorly defined continuation of the neck with a gentle bulge on its inner face and the trace of a lip on the upper outer lip. The type was produced in the vicinity of towns like Leptiminus and Hadrumetum in Byzacena (Keay 1984, 121-26). It transported olive oil and fish sauce.
Sites: 1.14, 2.7 and 4.4.
Fabric: 102.
Date: between *c.*230 and the mid 4th c. A.D.

114

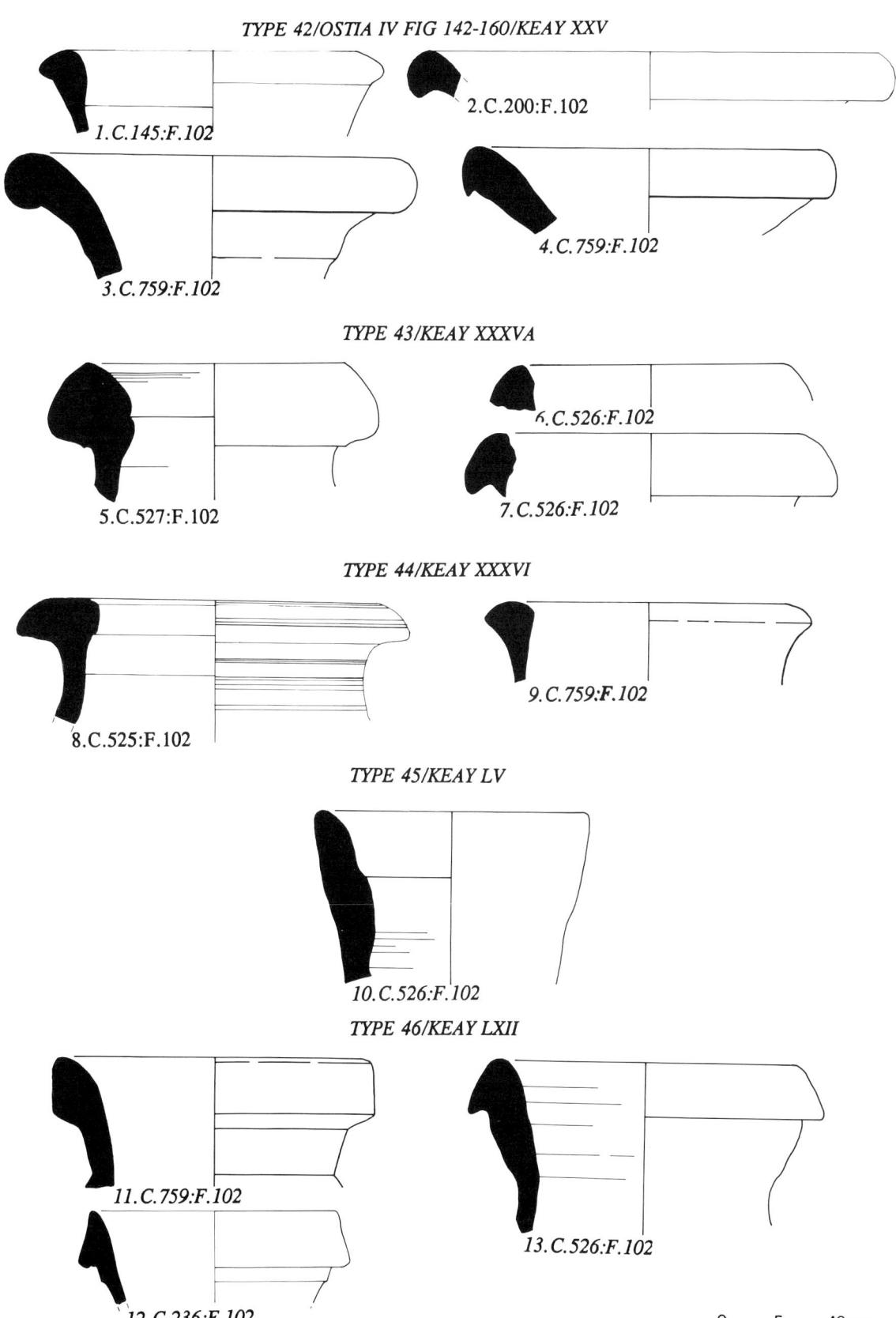

TYPE 42/OSTIA IV FIG 142-160/KEAY XXV

1.C.145:F.102

2.C.200:F.102

3.C.759:F.102

4.C.759:F.102

TYPE 43/KEAY XXXVA

5.C.527:F.102

6.C.526:F.102

7.C.526:F.102

TYPE 44/KEAY XXXVI

8.C.525:F.102

9.C.759:F.102

TYPE 45/KEAY LV

10.C.526:F.102

TYPE 46/KEAY LXII

11.C.759:F.102

12.C.236:F.102

13.C.526:F.102

0    5    10cm

Fig. 5.39 Amphorae of late imperial date. North African production.

115

*Type 42/ Ostia IV, Fig.142-160/ Keay XXV* (Fig. 5.39)
Comprises a range of narrow bodied cylindical amphorae of varying heights. The lower part of the amphora tapers to form a long foot, while the upper part tapers inwards to form a tallish conical neck. The rim type varies but is generally everted, with pronounced lip and occasionally an undercut or offset. The type was produced in Byzacena (Keay 1984, 184; Manacorda 1977, 171 ff.). Its content is unknown although olive oil is a possibility.
Sites: 1.2, 2.3 and 2.7.
Fabric: 102.
Date: between the last quarter of the 3rd and the middle of the 5th c. A.D.

*Type 43/ Keay XXXVA* (Fig. 5.39)
A wide bodied cylindrical amphora, with tapering base and conical neck. The handles are thick with an elliptical section while the rim has a circular section and pronounced overhang and undercut (Keay 1984, 233-40). It was produced in Byzacena and may have carried olive oil.
Sites: 2.3 and 2.7.
Fabric: 102.
Date: between the mid 5th and end of 6th c. A.D. (Keay 1984; Bonifay 1986).

*Type 44/ Keay XXXVI* (Fig. 5.39)
Similar to Type 43 but the rim is more flange-like. The type was produced in Byzacena and may have carried oilve oil (Keay 1984, 240-45).
Site: 2.3.
Fabric: 102.
Date: between the early/mid 5th and the end of 6th c. A.D. (Keay 1984; Bonifay 1986).

*Type 45/ Keay LV* (Fig. 5.39)
A wide-bodied cylindrical amphora with a long solid foot. The neck is cylindrical and is characterized by having combed decoration (usually horizontal). The rim is indistinguishable from the neck apart from a pronounced groove running around its interior face. The handles join the vessel on the shoulder and half-way up the neck. The type was produced in Byzacena and may have carried olive oil (Keay 1984, 289-93).
Site: 2.7.
Fabric: 102.
Date: between the later 5th and 7th c. A.D. (Keay 1984; Bonifay 1986).

*Type 46/ Keay LXII* (Fig. 5.39)
A wide-bodied cylindrical amphora. It has a pointed foot with a characteristic offset separating it from the lower body of the vessel. The neck is conical and sometimes slightly bulbous. The rim is also characteristic, being everted, well defined in relation to the neck and with a marked overhang. Three variants of the rim were distinguished: Keay LXII variant a (Fig. 5.39.13: Campo 526), Keay LXII variant i (Fig. 5.39.11: Campo 759), and Keay LXII variant m I (Fig. 5.39.12: Campo 236). The type was manufactured in Byzacena and may have carried olive oil (Keay 1984, 309-50; Peacock *et al.* 1990; Dore and Schinke 1992).
Sites: 2.3 and 2.7.
Fabric: 102.
Date: generically between the third quarter of the 5th and the 7th c. A.D. (Keay 1984; Bonifay 1986).

*Type 47* (not used)

116

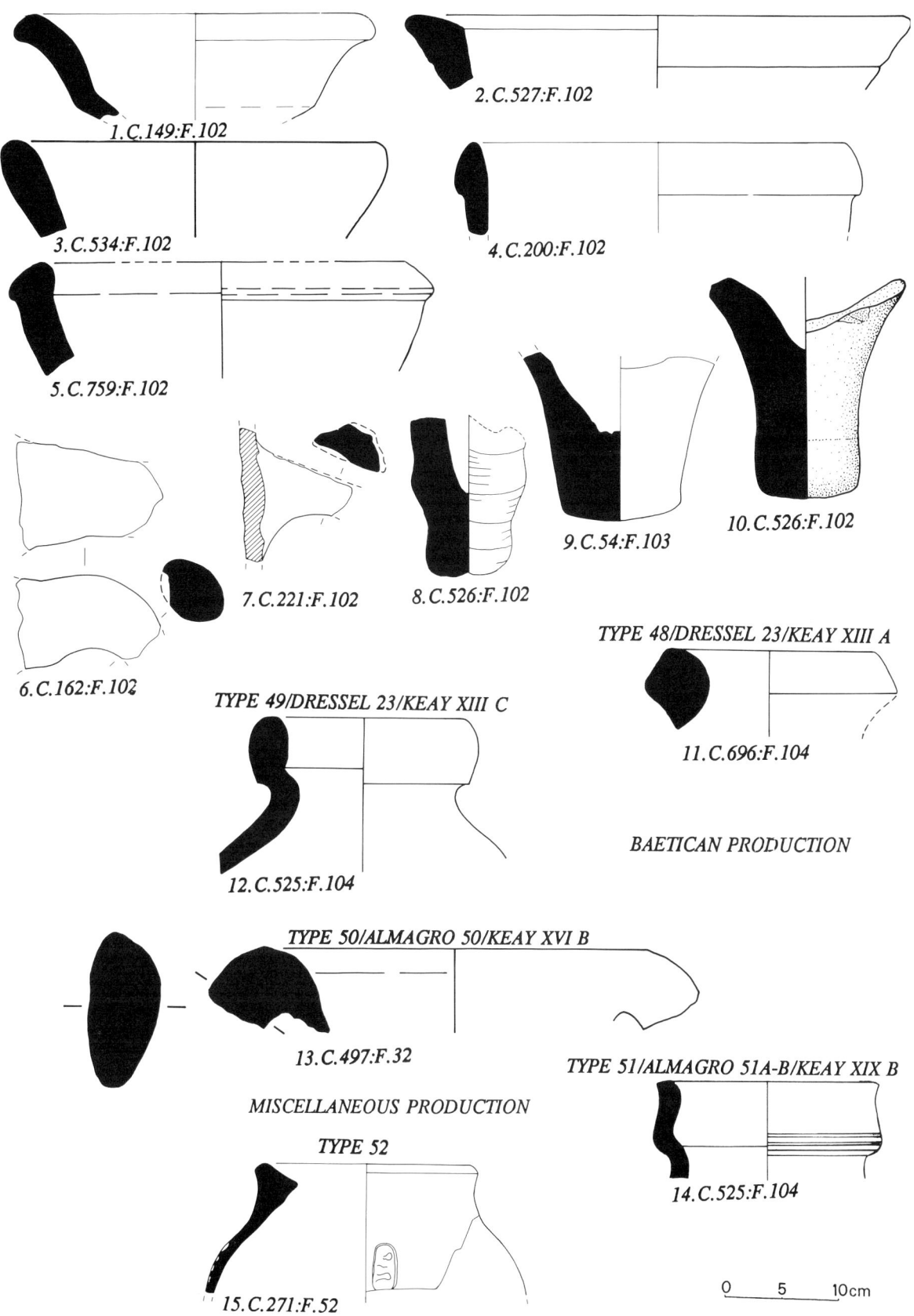

Fig. 5.40 Amphorae of late imperial date.

*Miscellaneous North African forms* (Fig. 5.40)
A range of rims, bases and handles which could not be readily ascribed to any particular type.
Found on several sites and in off-site scatters.
Fabrics: 102 and 103.


## Baetican Production

*Type 48/ Dressel 23/ Keay XIIIA* (Fig. 5.40)
A small version of Dressel 20 (Type 33 above). It has a small pear-shaped body with a small rim triangular in section, two small handles oval in section and a small foot. It was manufactured in the Guadalquivir valley (Baetica) and carried olive oil (Keay 1984, 140-46; Carreras and Williams forthcoming; Bonifay 1986).
Site: 2.9.
Fabric: 104.
Date: later 3rd to 4th c. A.D.

*Type 49/ Dressel 23/ Keay XIIIC* (Fig. 5.40)
Same form as Type 48. The rim differs, however, in having a convex outer face and pronounced undercut.
Site: 2.7.
Fabric: 104.
Date: later 3rd to later 4th or early 5th c. A.D.

*Type 50/ Almagro 50/ Keay XVIB* (Fig. 5.40)
A cylindrical/sack-shaped body which tapered inwards sharply to a hollow short foot. The upper part of the body tapered inwards before everting to form a thickish jutting rim with overhang. The handles are affixed to the rim and the shoulder and have an elliptical profile. The type was probably manufactured in southern Spain and may have transported fish-sauce (Keay 1984, 149 ff.).
Site: 2.6.
Fabric: 32.
Date: between the later 2nd and the mid 4th c. A.D.

*Type 51/ Almagro 51A-B/ Keay XIXB* (Fig. 5.40)
A tapering piriform body with small foot. The neck is short and conical, often with turning-marks evident. It terminated in a small rim with a characteristic 'S' shaped section. The handles have a rounded profile with characteristic grooves running along the outer face (Keay 1984, 156). South Spanish origin. Nothing is known of its contents.
Site: 2.7.
Fabric: 104.
Date: between the first quarter of the 3rd and the mid 5th c. A.D.


## Miscellaneous Possible Late Roman Amphorae

*Type 52* (Fig. 5.40)
A distinctive vessel with a poorly pronounced rim and no neck. Typologically it bears some similarity to the late-Roman Gaza amphora, Almagro 54 (Keay 1984, 278-85). However, the fabric suggests that it may be otherwise.
Site: 1.10.
Fabric: 52.
Date: No evidence.
Epigraphy: there is a stamp on the shoulder but it is indistinct.

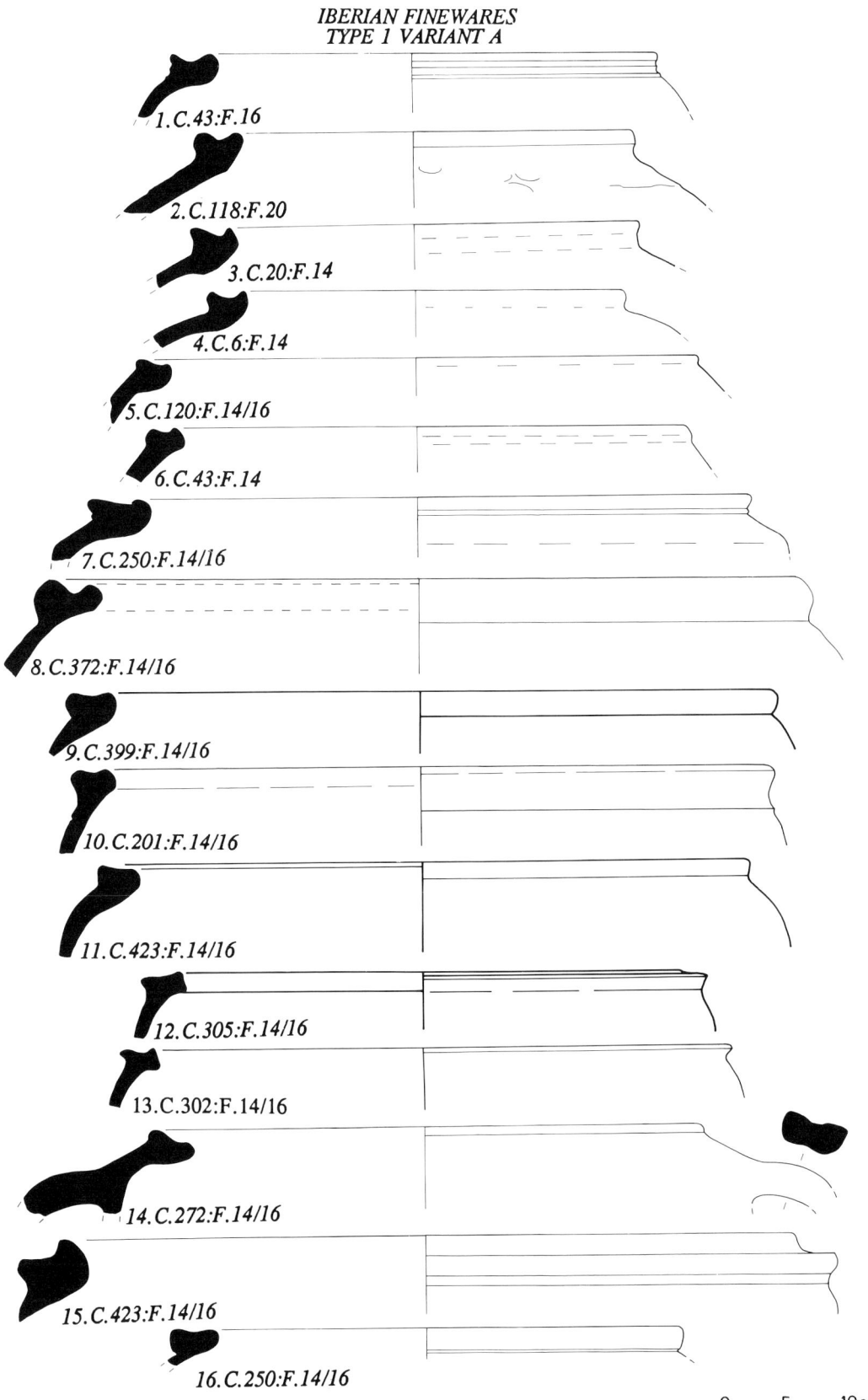

IBERIAN FINEWARES
TYPE 1 VARIANT A

1.C.43:F.16

2.C.118:F.20

3.C.20:F.14

4.C.6:F.14

5.C.120:F.14/16

6.C.43:F.14

7.C.250:F.14/16

8.C.372:F.14/16

9.C.399:F.14/16

10.C.201:F.14/16

11.C.423:F.14/16

12.C.305:F.14/16

13.C.302:F.14/16

14.C.272:F.14/16

15.C.423:F.14/16

16.C.250:F.14/16

0    5    10cm

Fig. 5.41 Finewares. Iberian production.

TYPE 1 VARIANT A *(Cont)*

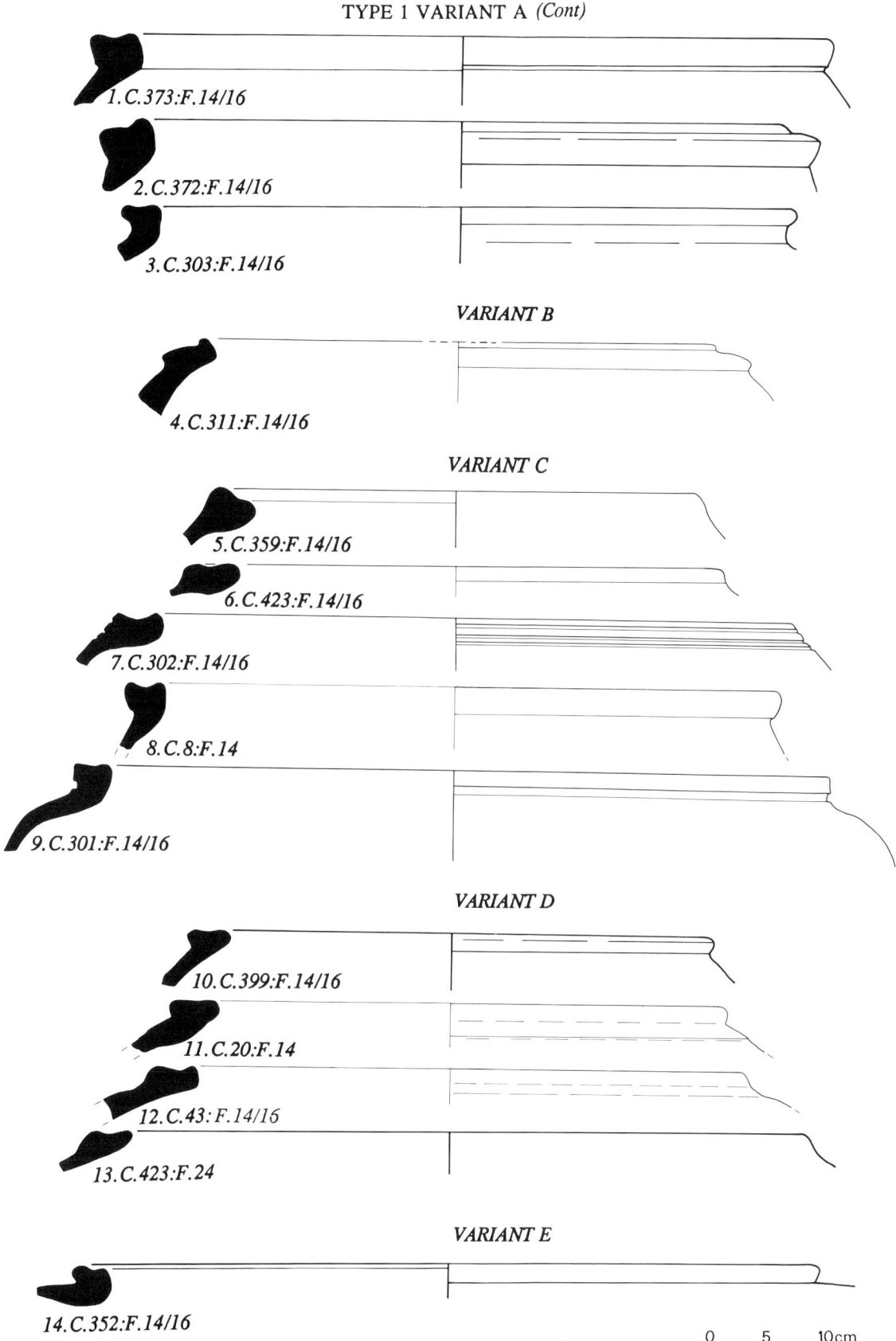

*1.C.373:F.14/16*

*2.C.372:F.14/16*

*3.C.303:F.14/16*

*VARIANT B*

*4.C.311:F.14/16*

*VARIANT C*

*5.C.359:F.14/16*

*6.C.423:F.14/16*

*7.C.302:F.14/16*

*8.C.8:F.14*

*9.C.301:F.14/16*

*VARIANT D*

*10.C.399:F.14/16*

*11.C.20:F.14*

*12.C.43: F.14/16*

*13.C.423:F.24*

*VARIANT E*

*14.C.352:F.14/16*

0    5    10cm

Fig. 5.42 Finewares. Iberian production.

120

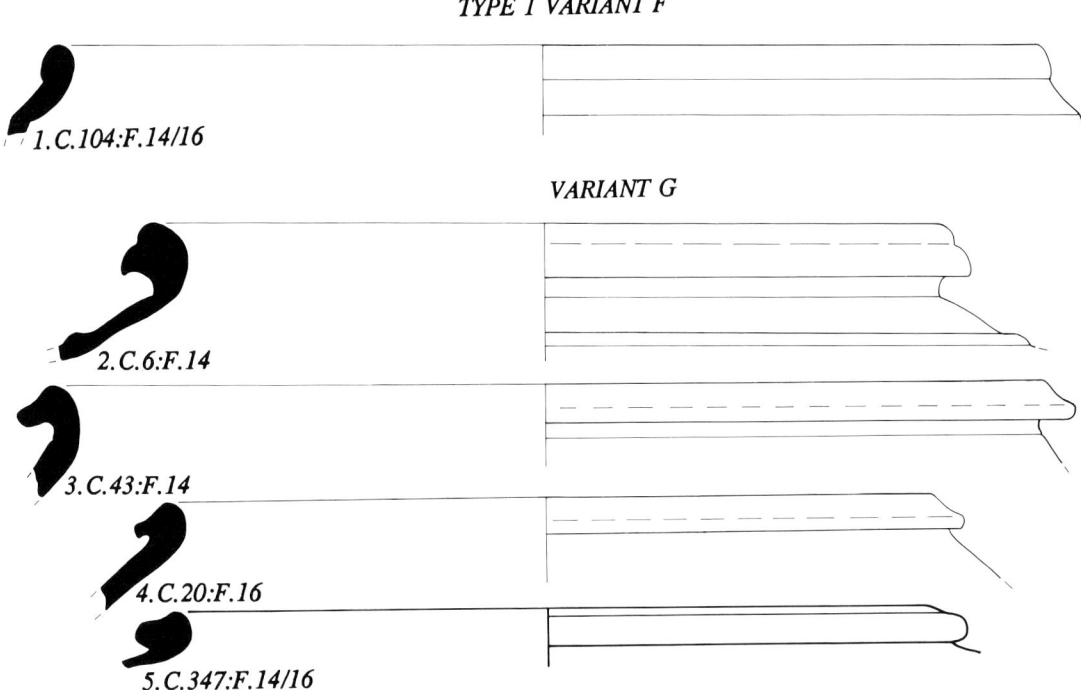

TYPE 1 VARIANT F

1.C.104:F.14/16

VARIANT G

2.C.6:F.14

3.C.43:F.14

4.C.20:F.16

5.C.347:F.14/16

**Fig.** 5.43. Finewares. Iberian production.

Iberian Production

They are identified by cross-reference to typologies from excavations in Catalunya and Valencia.

*Type 1/ Pereira Sieso 11/ Mata-Bonet Tipo 2.1 or 3.1/ Aranegui-Pla 21 or 25/ Sanmartí 1992, fig.1.6* (Figs. 5.41-5.43)
A tall cylindrical storage vessel with a gently curved base (2.1), no neck, a wide mouth and lug handles attached immediately below the the rim. A variant (3.1) has a flatter base and a spout at the lower part of the body. Seven rim variants (A-G) were identified amongst the survey material.
Sites: 1.13, 2.3, 2.6, 2.9, 3.9, 3.11, 3.13, 3.15, 3.16, 3.17, 3.18, 3.19, 4.2, 4.3, 4.4 and 4.5.
Fabrics: 14, 16, 14/16, 20, and 24.
Date: 3rd c. B.C. onwards, possibly around 200 B.C.

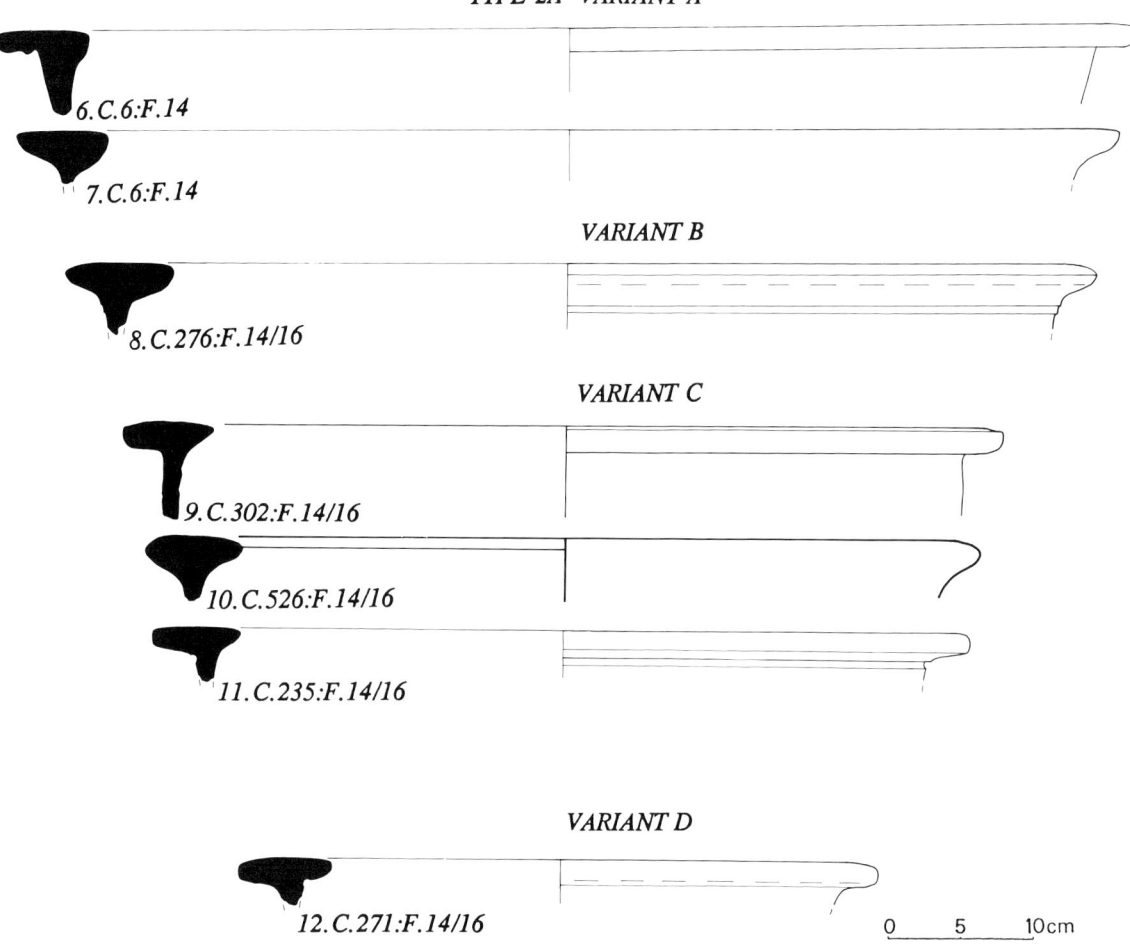

Fig. 5.43 cont. Finewares. Iberian production.

*Type 2* (Figs. 5.43-5.44)
Five variants of rims (A-E) whose fragmentary state do not permit a definite identification. They can be attributed to one of two possible forms.
Either:
*Kalathos/ Mata-Bonet II.Tipo 7.1.2 or 7.2.1/ Aranegui-Pla 17/ Sanmartí 1992, fig.4*
A multi-functional container for storing and exporting a range of products. It is a bag-shaped/cylindrical vessel with wide mouth and a flange-like rim.
Or:
*Hemispherical Bowls (Lafuente 1992, fig.3b)*
A characteristic hemispherical bowl with small foot and rim identical to that of the kalathos. They are characteristic of the production at Fontscaldes.
Sites: 1.8, 1.9, 1.10, 1.13, 1.14, 2.1, 2.3, 2.6,, 2.7, 2.8, 2.9, 2.10, 3.1, 3.2, 3.9, 3.11, 3.15, 3.19, 4.2, 4.3, 4.4 and 4.5.
Fabrics: 12, 14/16 and 20.
Date: The kalathoi are characteristic of the late 3rd, 2nd and possibly 1st c. B.C. The bowls have been dated to around 200 B.C.

122

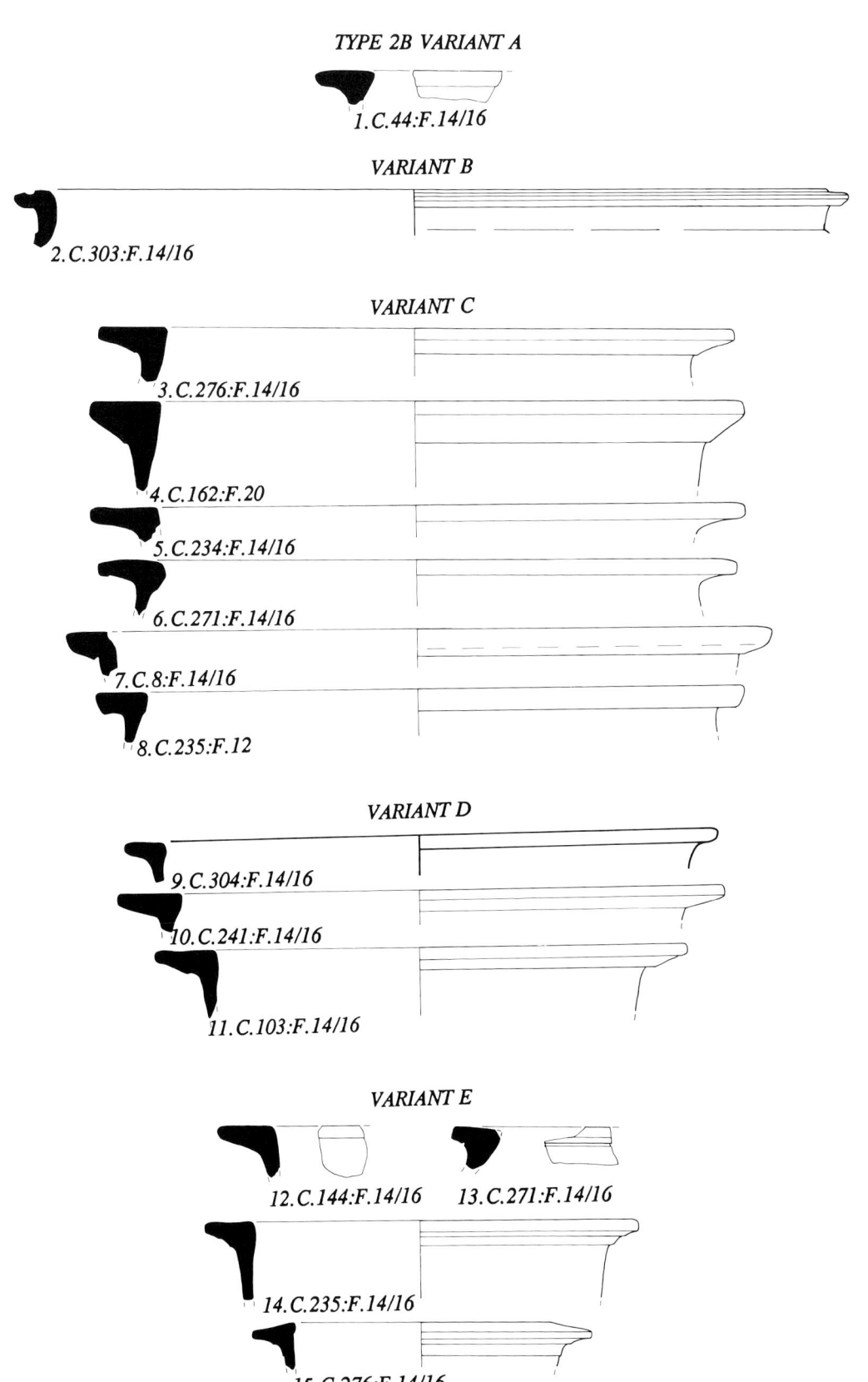

TYPE 2B VARIANT A

1.C.44:F.14/16

VARIANT B

2.C.303:F.14/16

VARIANT C

3.C.276:F.14/16

4.C.162:F.20

5.C.234:F.14/16

6.C.271:F.14/16

7.C.8:F.14/16

8.C.235:F.12

VARIANT D

9.C.304:F.14/16

10.C.241:F.14/16

11.C.103:F.14/16

VARIANT E

12.C.144:F.14/16          13.C.271:F.14/16

14.C.235:F.14/16

15.C.276:F.14/16

0     5     10cm

Fig. 5.44 Finewares. Iberian production.

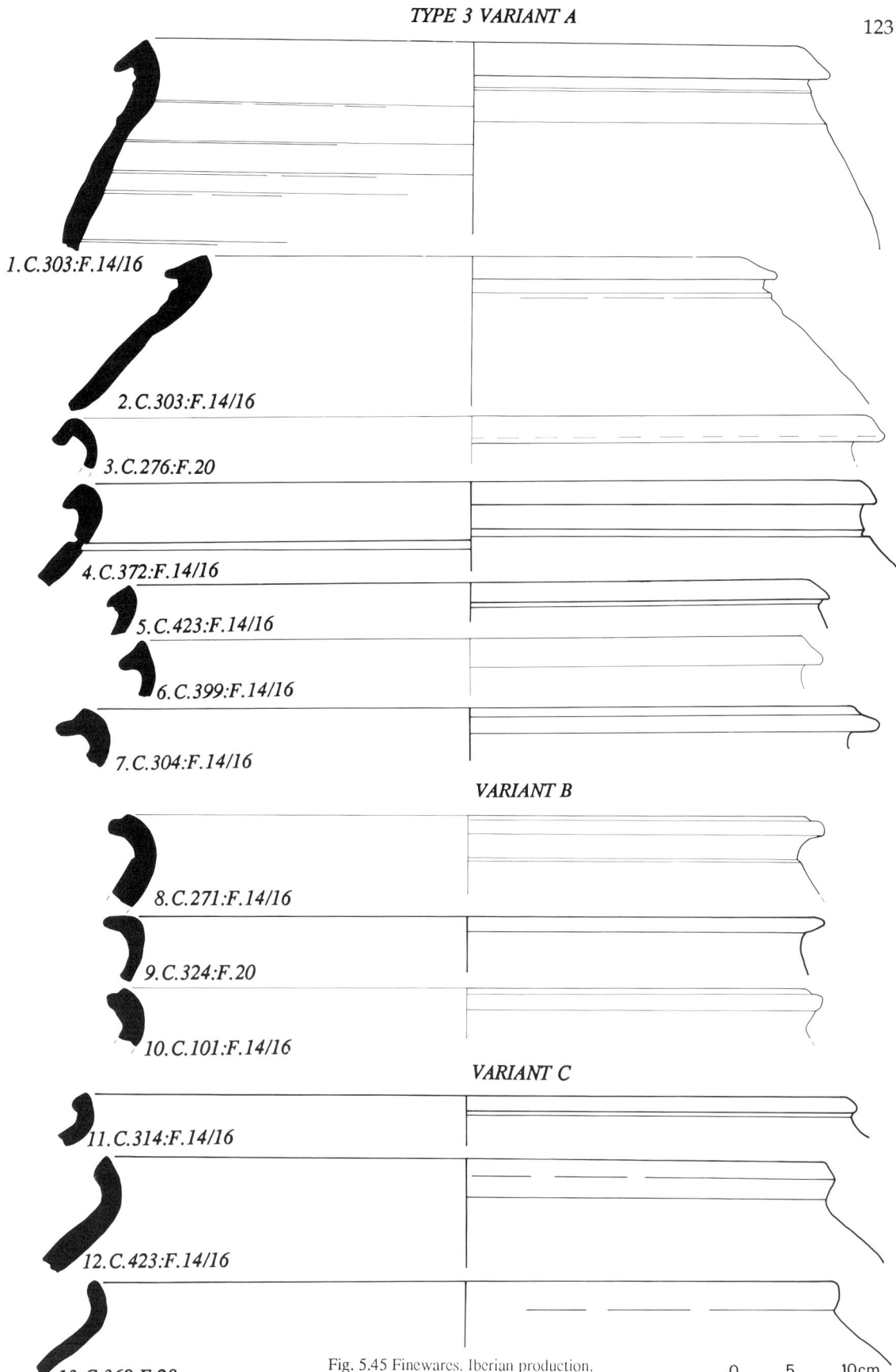

1. *C.303:F.14/16*

2. *C.303:F.14/16*

3. *C.276:F.20*

4. *C.372:F.14/16*

5. *C.423:F.14/16*

6. *C.399:F.14/16*

7. *C.304:F.14/16*

**VARIANT B**

8. *C.271:F.14/16*

9. *C.324:F.20*

10. *C.101:F.14/16*

**VARIANT C**

11. *C.314:F.14/16*

12. *C.423:F.14/16*

13. *C.368:F.20*

Fig. 5.45 Finewares. Iberian production.

0  5  10cm

*Type 3/ Aranegui-Pla 23/ Sanmartí 1992, fig.1.4-5* (Figs. 5.45)
A large storage or transport vessel (*c.*60 cm), comprising a bag-shaped body with rounded base and characteristic everted rim ('coll de cigne'). Three variants (A-C) based upon differences in rim details were distinguished.
Sites: 3.13, 3.16, 3.19 and 4.4.
Fabrics: 14/16 and 20.
Date: 5th(?) to late 3rd and possibly early 2nd c. B.C.

124

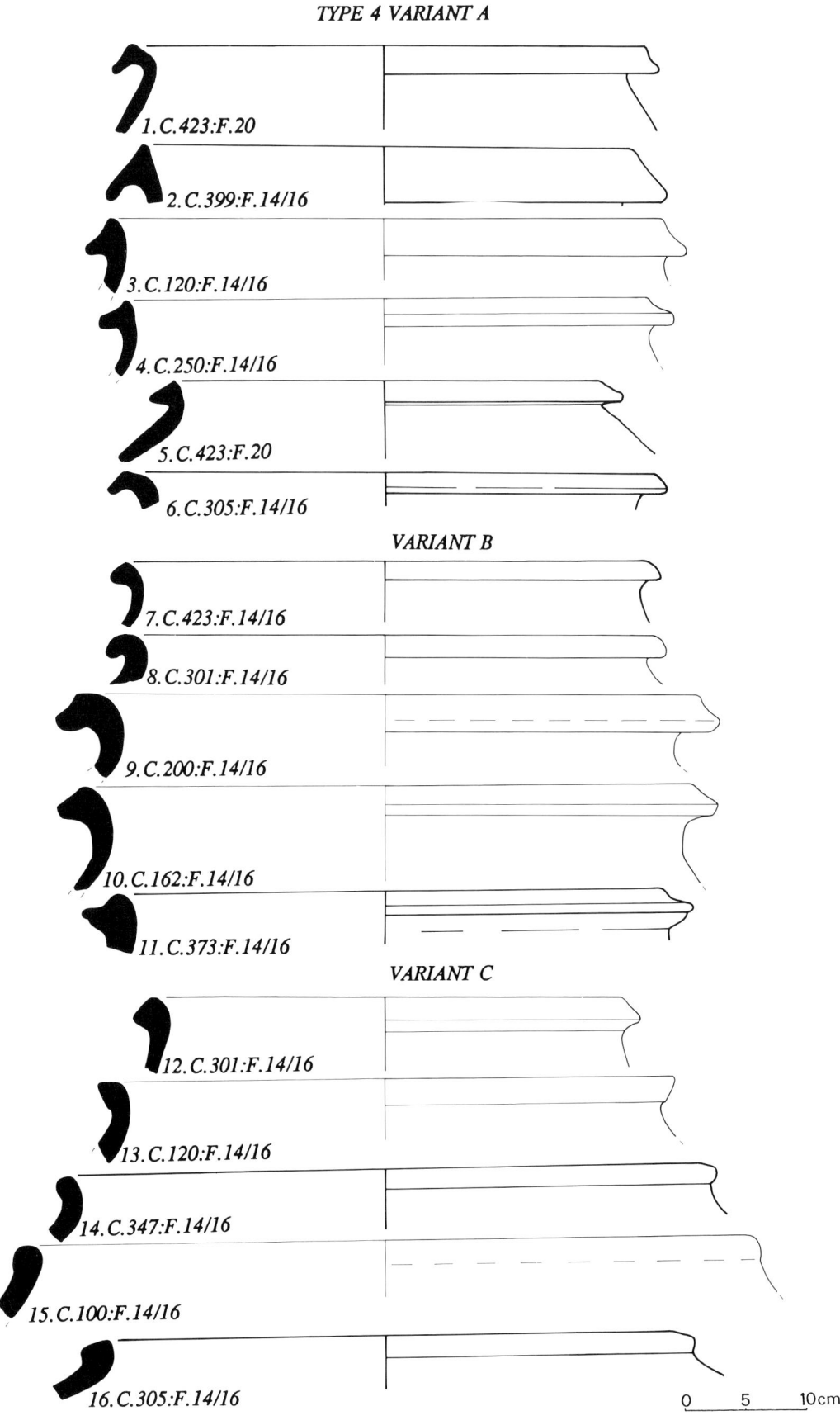

TYPE 4 VARIANT A

1.C.423:F.20

2.C.399:F.14/16

3.C.120:F.14/16

4.C.250:F.14/16

5.C.423:F.20

6.C.305:F.14/16

VARIANT B

7.C.423:F.14/16

8.C.301:F.14/16

9.C.200:F.14/16

10.C.162:F.14/16

11.C.373:F.14/16

VARIANT C

12.C.301:F.14/16

13.C.120:F.14/16

14.C.347:F.14/16

15.C.100:F.14/16

16.C.305:F.14/16

0     5     10cm

*Type 4/ Aranegui-Pla 23/ Sanmartí 1992, fig.1.4-5* (Fig.5.46).
A smaller version of Type 3 (40-63 cm). Three variants (A-C) were distinguished.
Sites: 2.10, 3.3, 3.13, 3.15, 3.16, 3.18 and 3.19.
Fabrics: 14/16 and 20.
Date: as Type 3?

Fig. 5.46 Finewares. Iberian production

TYPE 5 VARIANT A

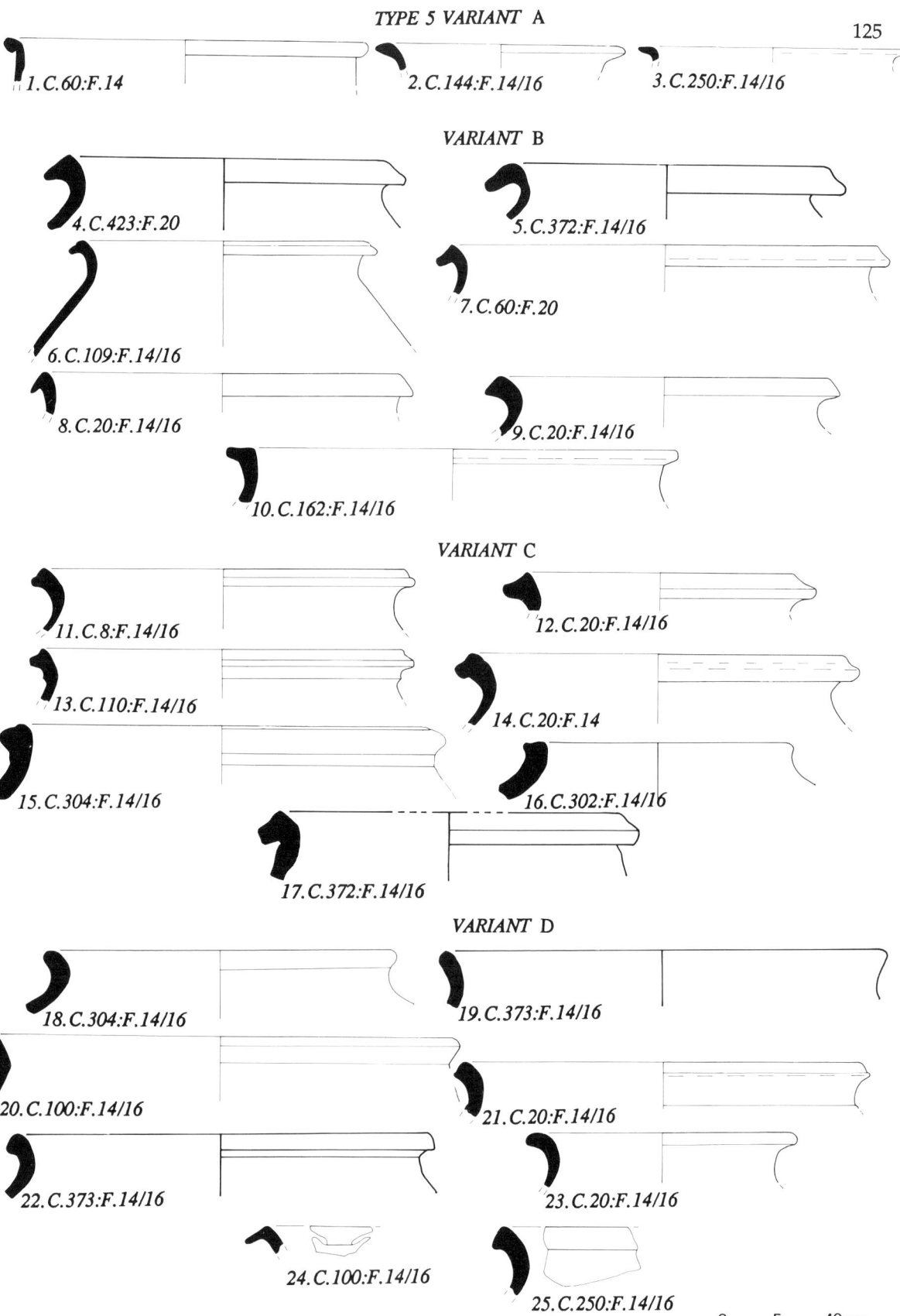

1. C.60:F.14
2. C.144:F.14/16
3. C.250:F.14/16

VARIANT B

4. C.423:F.20
5. C.372:F.14/16
6. C.109:F.14/16
7. C.60:F.20
8. C.20:F.14/16
9. C.20:F.14/16
10. C.162:F.14/16

VARIANT C

11. C.8:F.14/16
12. C.20:F.14/16
13. C.110:F.14/16
14. C.20:F.14
15. C.304:F.14/16
16. C.302:F.14/16
17. C.372:F.14/16

VARIANT D

18. C.304:F.14/16
19. C.373:F.14/16
20. C.100:F.14/16
21. C.20:F.14/16
22. C.373:F.14/16
23. C.20:F.14/16
24. C.100:F.14/16
25. C.250:F.14/16

0    5    10cm

*Type 5: Aranegui-Pla 23/ Sanmartí 1992, fig.1.4-5* (Fig. 5.47)
The smallest version of Type 3 (*c.*30-35 cm). Four variants (A-D) were distinguished.
Sites: 2.9, 3.9, 3.13, 3.15, 3.19 and 4.4.
Fabrics: 14/16 and 20.
Date: as Type 3?

Fig. 5.47 Finewares. Iberian production.

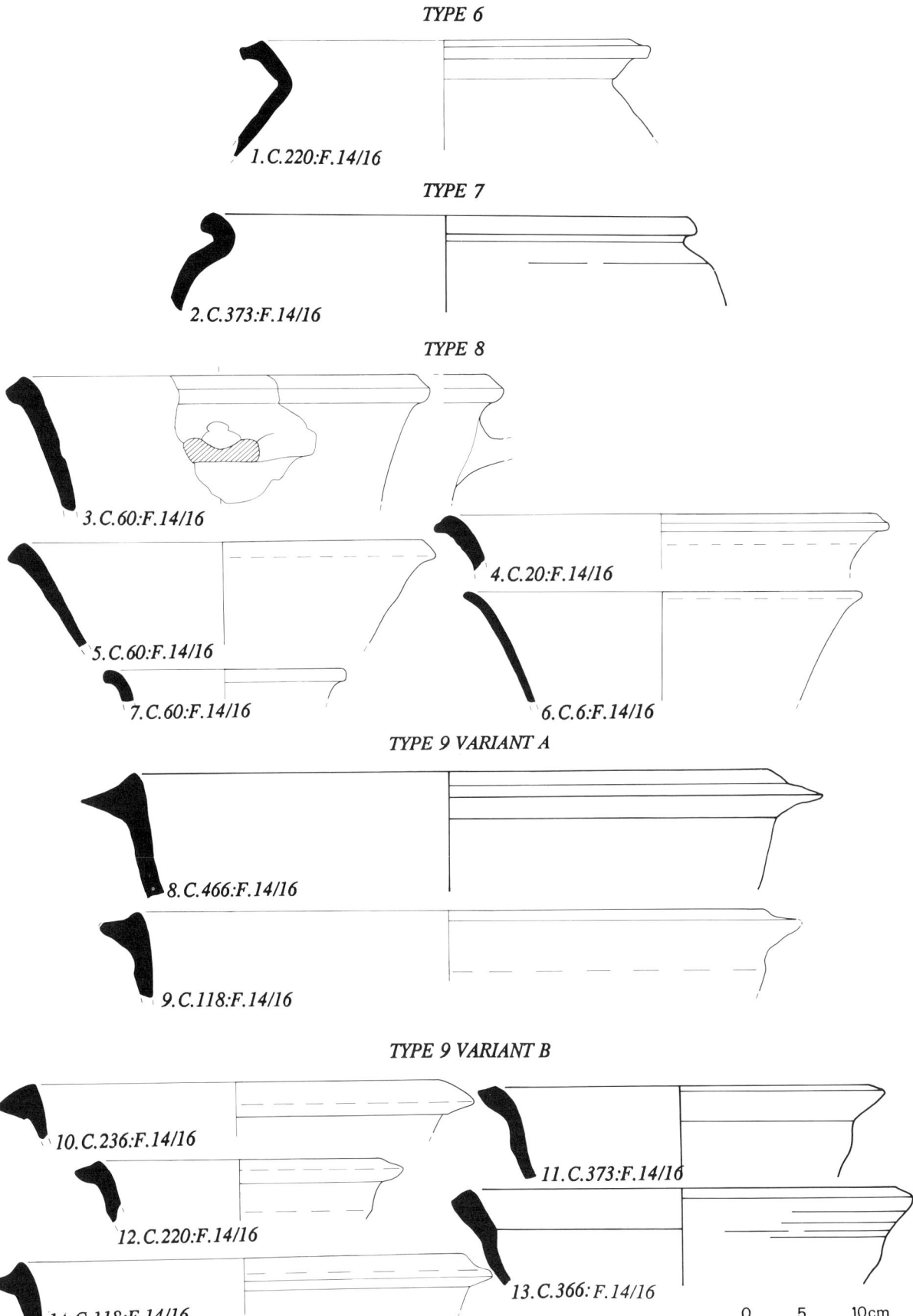

TYPE 6

1.C.220:F.14/16

TYPE 7

2.C.373:F.14/16

TYPE 8

3.C.60:F.14/16

4.C.20:F.14/16

5.C.60:F.14/16

7.C.60:F.14/16

6.C.6:F.14/16

TYPE 9 VARIANT A

8.C.466:F.14/16

9.C.118:F.14/16

TYPE 9 VARIANT B

10.C.236:F.14/16

11.C.373:F.14/16

12.C.220:F.14/16

13.C.366:F.14/16

14.C 118:F.14/16

0    5    10cm

Fig. 5.48 Finewares. Iberian production.

*Type 6* (Fig. 5.48)
A form similar to Type 5 but with a more everted neck which forms a flange.
Sites: 2.1 and 3.9.
Fabric: 14/16.
Date: as Type 3?

*Type 7* (Fig. 5.48)
A more developed form of Type 5 with a 'rolled' rim and virtually no neck.
Sites: 3.15 and 4.4.
Fabric: 14/16.
Date: as Type 3?

*Type 8/ Aranegui-Pla 1c (B)* (Fig. 5.48)
Trumpet-shaped necks which sometimes have a pronounced rim, belonging to a bottle-shaped form. One example had a flattened bifid handle.
Sites: 1.8 and 3.9.
Fabric: 14/16.
Date: late 5th to early 3rd c. B.C.

*Type 9* (Fig. 5.48)
Casserole with gently everted wall and a rim with triangular section. There appear to be two different sizes.
Sites: 3.15 and 3.16.
Fabric: 14/16.
Date: the discovery of a similar sherd at the site of L'Argilera (Sanmartí, Santacana and Serra 1984, 78 Lám. 32 nr.234) suggests a possible date in about the later 2nd c. B.C.

128

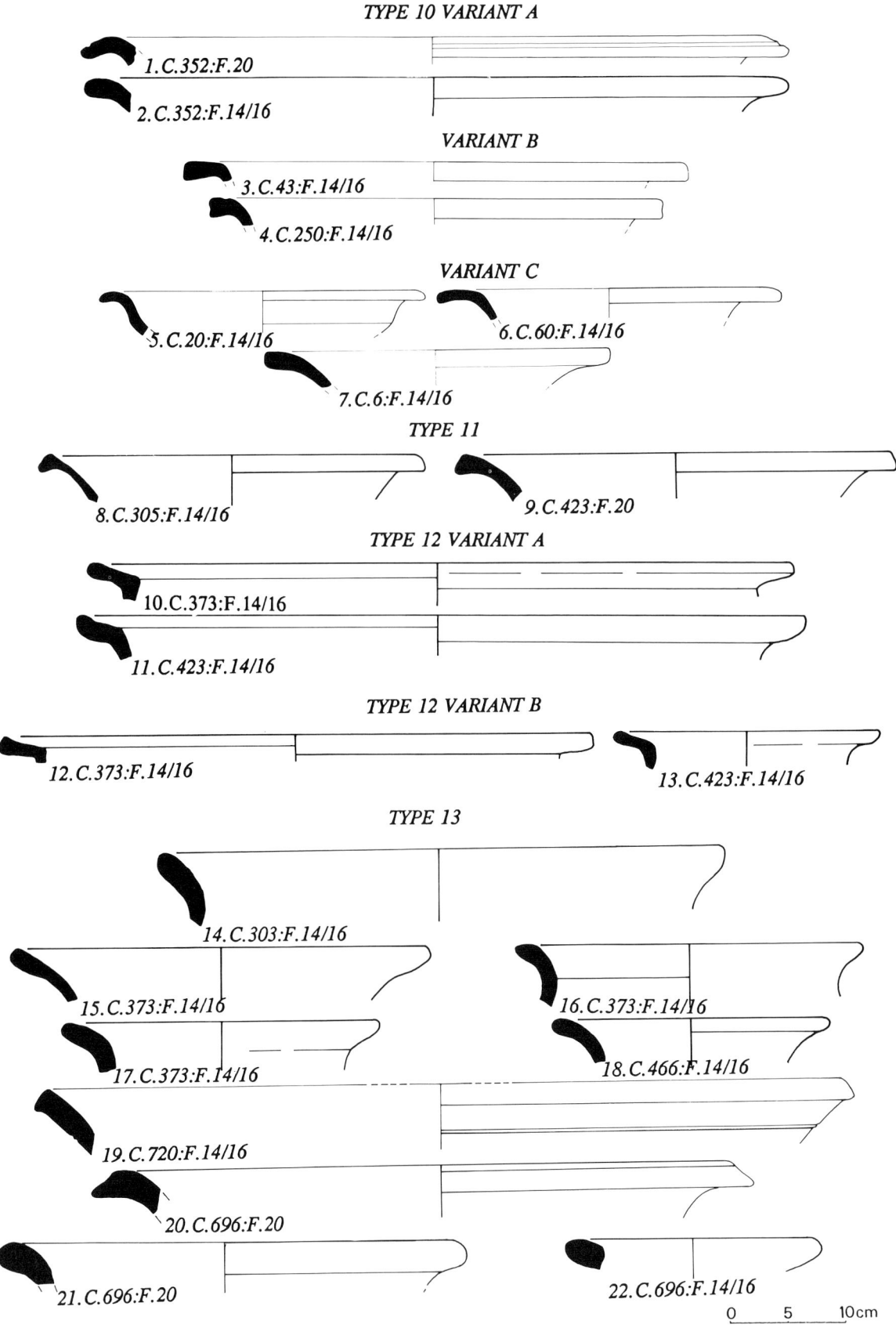

TYPE 10 VARIANT A

1.C.352:F.20

2.C.352:F.14/16

VARIANT B

3.C.43:F.14/16

4.C.250:F.14/16

VARIANT C

5.C.20:F.14/16

6.C.60:F.14/16

7.C.6:F.14/16

TYPE 11

8.C.305:F.14/16

9.C.423:F.20

TYPE 12 VARIANT A

10.C.373:F.14/16

11.C.423:F.14/16

TYPE 12 VARIANT B

12.C.373:F.14/16

13.C.423:F.14/16

TYPE 13

14.C.303:F.14/16

15.C.373:F.14/16

16.C.373:F.14/16

17.C.373:F.14/16

18.C.466:F.14/16

19.C.720:F.14/16

20.C.696:F.20

21.C.696:F.20

22.C.696:F.14/16

0    5    10cm

Fig. 5.49 Finewares. Iberian production.

*Type 10/ Mata-Bonet Grupo VI Tipo 1 or 2/ Aranegui-Pla Tipo 11a or 11b* (Fig. 5.49)
Flange belonging to a bowl-shaped form, possibly imitating the Greek kylix or skyphos.
Sites: 1.14, 2.6, 3.9, 3.13 and 3.18.
Fabrics: 14/16 and 20.
Date: late 5th to early 3rd c. B.C. (Aranegui-Pla 1979, 75).

*Type 11/ Mata-Bonet 1992 Class A Grupo 1 Tipo 2.2.1 or 2.2.2/ Aranegui-Pla Tipo 18 and 19* (Fig. 5.49)
Sharply everted neck with rim-flange probably belonging to a storage vessel with a pear-shaped body.
Sites: 3.13 and 3.19.
Fabrics: 14/16 and 20.
Date: typical of the 6th c. B.C. (Mata and Bonet 1992, 128)

*Type 12/ Sanmartí 1992, fig.6.2* (Fig. 5.49)
Characteristic everted flange with rounded outer face and convex interior face.
Sites: 3.1, 3.13 and 3.15.
Fabric: 14/16.
Date: around 200 B.C. (Sanmartí 1992, 36).

*Type 13* (Fig. 5.49)
A loose collection of sherds sharing everted and rounded rims.
Sites: 2.9, 3.15, 3.19 and 4.6.
Fabrics: 14/16 and 20.
Date: around the later 2nd c. B.C. (Sanmartí, Santacana and Serra 1984, 30-31 Lám.11.70 and 42.343)

130

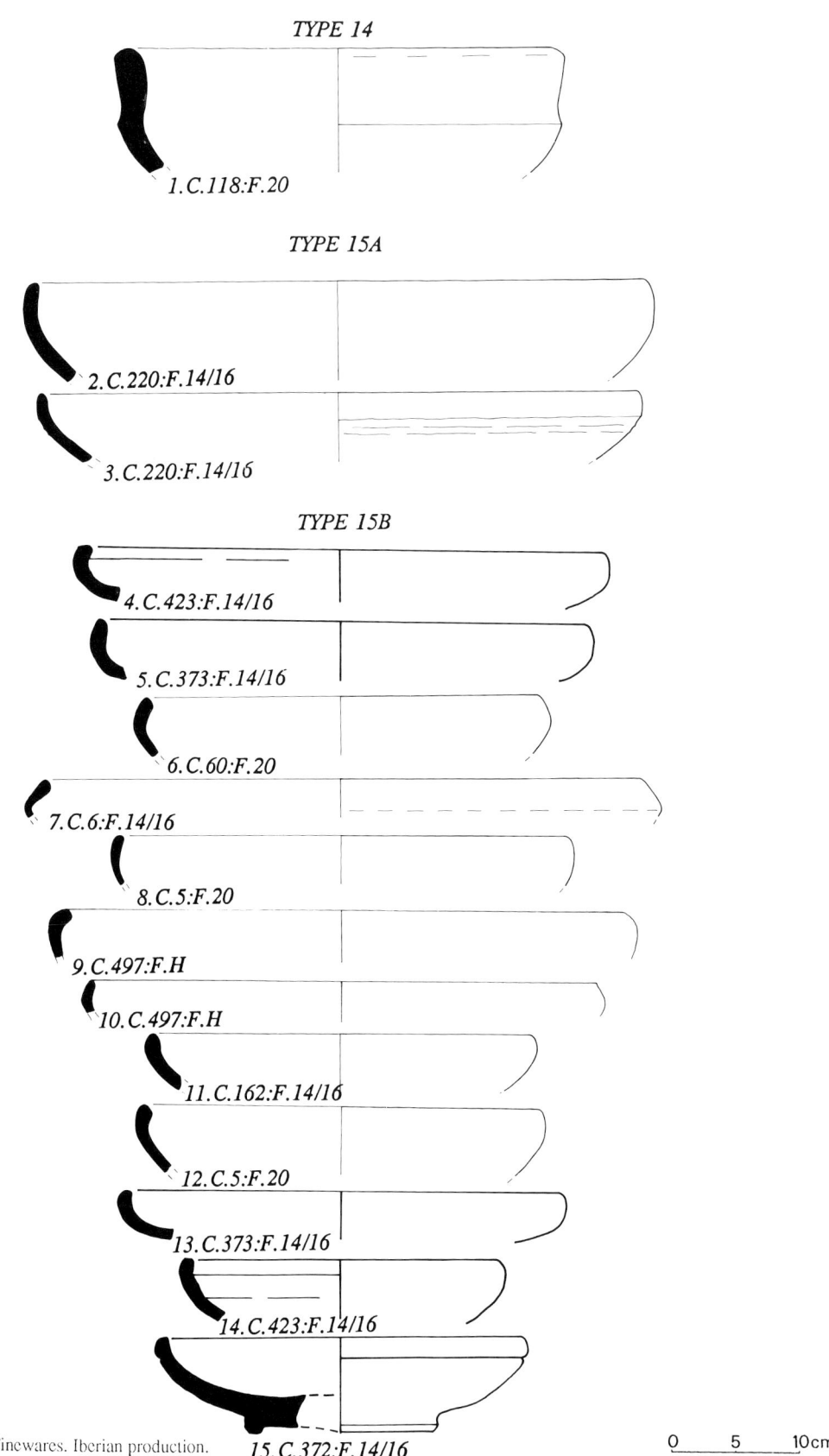

TYPE 14

1. C.118:F.20

TYPE 15A

2. C.220:F.14/16

3. C.220:F.14/16

TYPE 15B

4. C.423:F.14/16

5. C.373:F.14/16

6. C.60:F.20

7. C.6:F.14/16

8. C.5:F.20

9. C.497:F.H

10. C.497:F.H

11. C.162:F.14/16

12. C.5:F.20

13. C.373:F.14/16

14. C.423:F.14/16

15. C.372:F.14/16

Fig. 5.50 Finewares. Iberian production.

0    5    10 cm

*Type 14* (Fig. 5.50)
Distinctive bowl with clearly defined shoulder and rim.
Site: 1.12.
Fabric: 20.
Date: no evidence.

*Type 15/ Mata-Bonet 1992 Clase A Grupo VI Tipo 6.1/ Aranegui-Pla Forma 10a ('open') and 10b ('closed')* (Fig. 5.50)
Simple bowl comprising two varieties: in Variant 15A the rim is relatively 'open', while in 15B the rim is more 'closed'.
Sites: 2.9, 3.9, 3.13, 3.15 and 3.16.
Fabrics: 14/16, 20 and H.
Date: late 5th to early 3rd c. B.C.

*Type 16* (Fig. 5.51)
Bowl with flange-like rim with triangular section.
Sites: 2.7, 3.16, 3.19 and 4.4.
Fabrics: 14/16 and X.
Date: no evidence.

*Type 17: Ros Sala 1989 Lip Type 7* (Fig. 5.51)
Wide casserole or open dish characterized by a flange-like rim.
Off-site scatter only.
Fabric: 20.
Date: 2nd c. until the end of the 1st c. B.C./mid 1st c. A.D. (Ros Sala 1989, 88-90).

*Type 18/ Mata-Bonet Clase A Grupo II Tipo 11/ Aranegui-Pla Tipo 20* (Fig. 5.51)
A situla or jug characterized by a handle which crosses the mouth of the vessel perpendicularly.
Sites: 2.4, 2.7, 3.16 and 3.19.
Fabric: 14/16.
Date: 5th to 2nd c. B.C. (Mata and Bonet 1992, 131; Sanmartí, Santacana and Serra 1984, 55 Lám.9.57).

*Type 19/ Aranegui-Pla Tipo 21* (Fig. 5.51)
Upstanding rim with ridge running around the neck, probably belonging to a storage jar.
Sites: 2.6, 2.9, 3.15, 3.19 and 4.4.
Fabric: 14/16.
Date: some time after the 4th c. B.C. (Aranegui and Pla 1981, 81).

*Type 20 / Mata-Bonet Grupo III Clase A 4.1.1 (2)* (Fig. 5.51)
Wide-mouthed vase with gently splayed rim, tall and gently conical neck, and well defined shoulder with hemispherical body.
Found in an off-site scatter.
Fabric: 14/16.
Date: present in Iberian contexts from the 6th c. B.C. onwards (Mata and Bonet 1992, 133) until the 2nd and 1st c. B.C.

*Type 21* (Fig. 5.51)
Distinctive carinated bowl with re-entrant vertical rim.
Site: 2.7.
Fabric: ZO.
Date: a similar form was found in possible 3rd- and 2nd-c. B.C. contexts at the Iberian settlement of L'Alorda Park (Sanmartí and Santacana 1986, Fig.136.4).

132

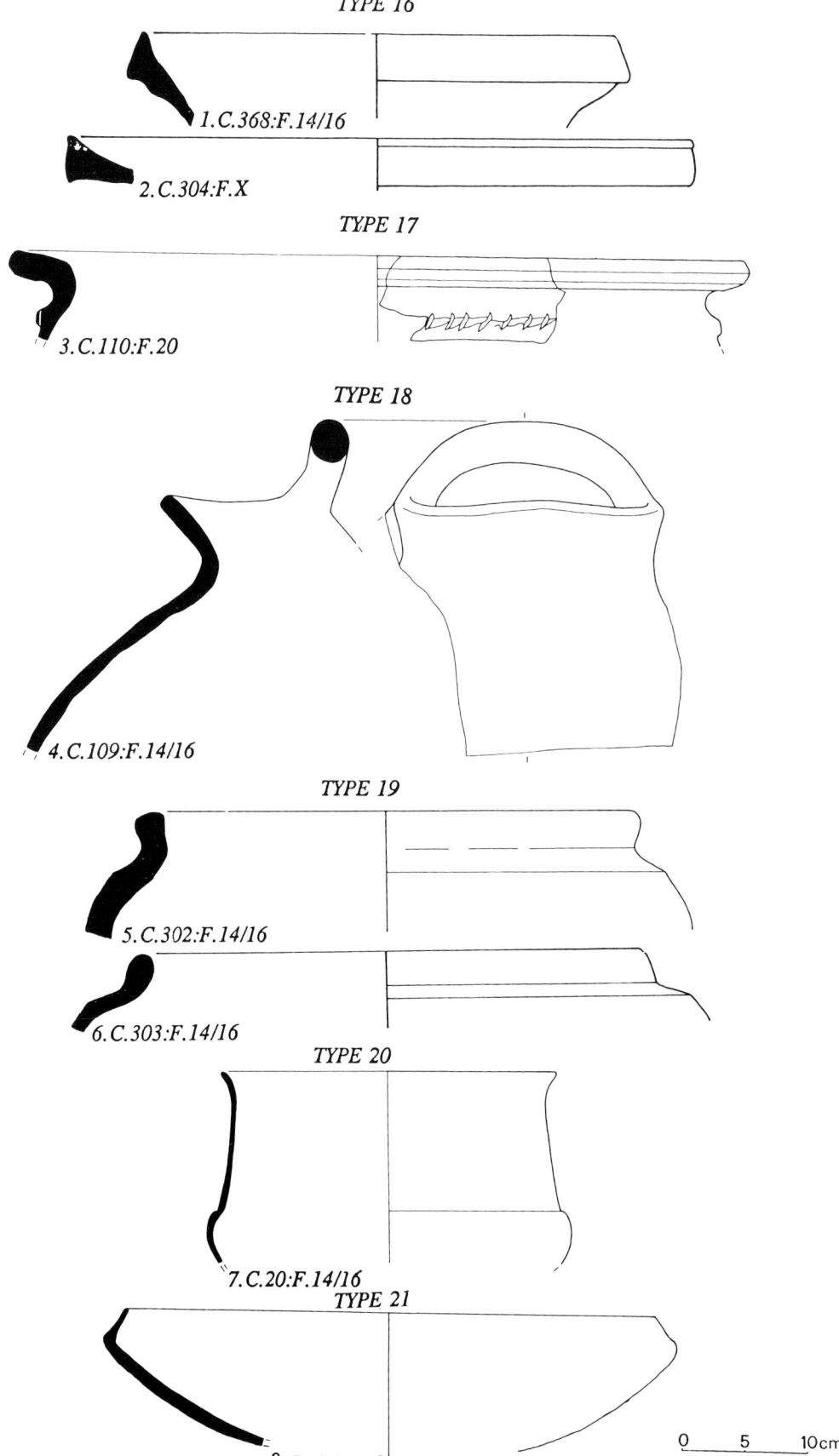

TYPE 16

1.C.368:F.14/16

2.C.304:F.X

TYPE 17

3.C.110:F.20

TYPE 18

4.C.109:F.14/16

TYPE 19

5.C.302:F.14/16

6.C.303:F.14/16

TYPE 20

7.C.20:F.14/16

TYPE 21

8.C.526:F.ZO

0    5    10cm

Fig. 5.51 Finewares. Iberian production.

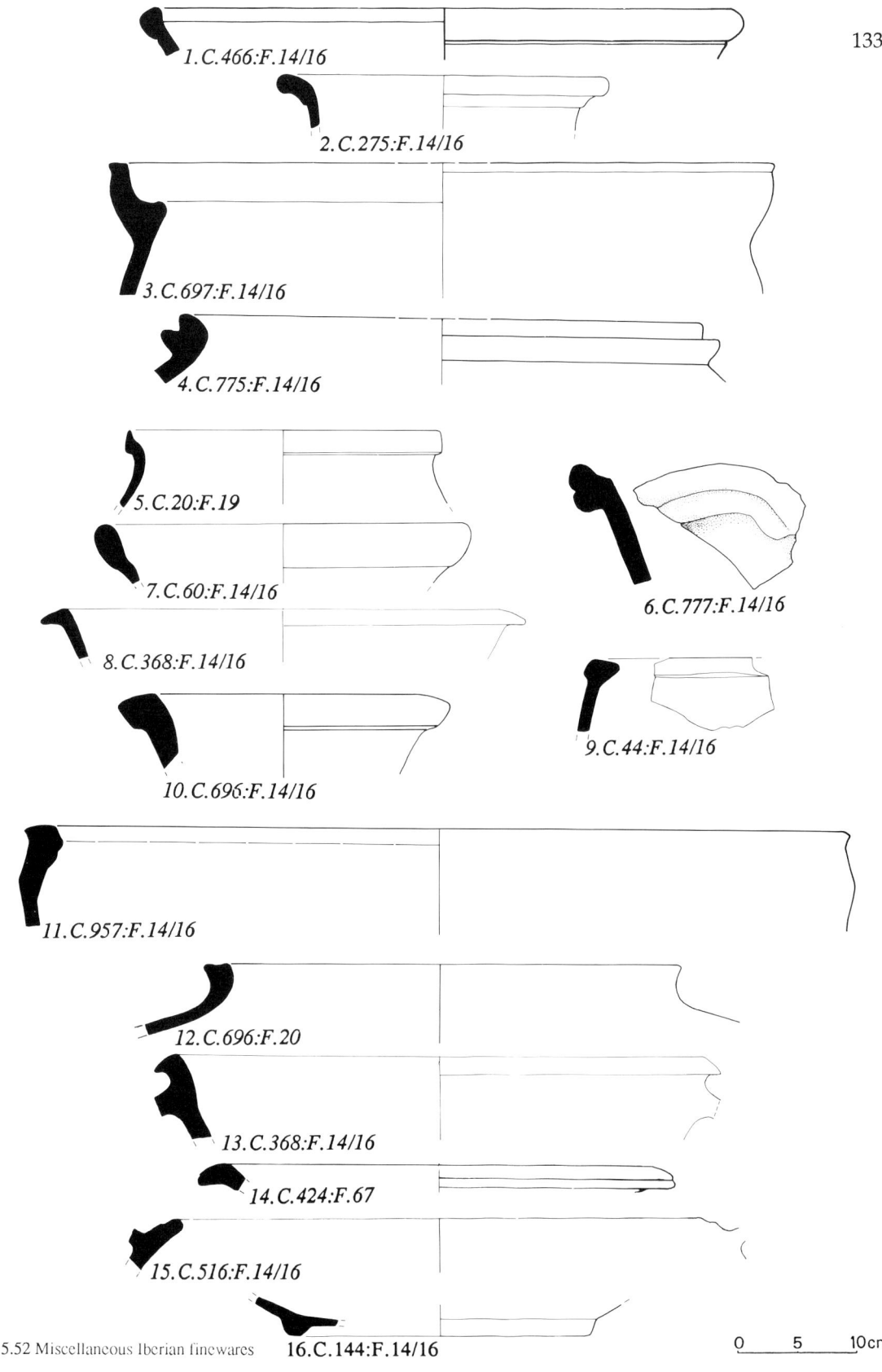

1. C.466:F.14/16
2. C.275:F.14/16
3. C.697:F.14/16
4. C.775:F.14/16
5. C.20:F.19
7. C.60:F.14/16
8. C.368:F.14/16
6. C.777:F.14/16
10. C.696:F.14/16
9. C.44:F.14/16
11. C.957:F.14/16
12. C.696:F.20
13. C.368:F.14/16
14. C.424:F.67
15. C.516:F.14/16
16. C.144:F.14/16

0    5    10 cm

Fig. 5.52 Miscellaneous Iberian finewares

*Miscellaneous Iberian Fineware Rims* (Fig. 5.52)
Sixteen sherds too fragmentary to be definitely ascribed to any established type.
Found on sites and in off-site scatters.
Fabrics: 14/16, 19 and 20.
Dating: no evidence.

## MISCELLANEOUS IBERIAN FINEWARE HANDLES

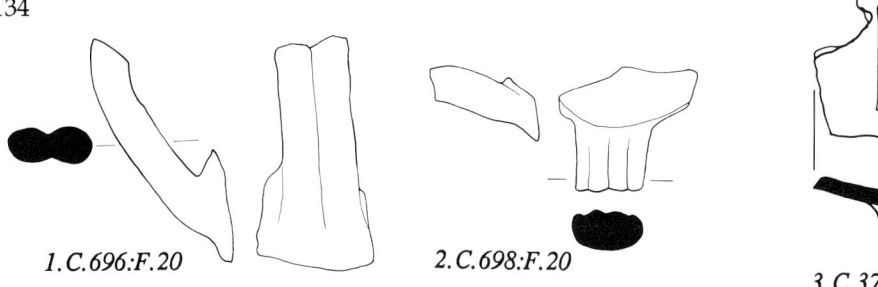

1. C.696:F.20          2. C.698:F.20          3. C.373:F.14/16

### MISCELLANEOUS PAINTED IBERIAN FINEWARE

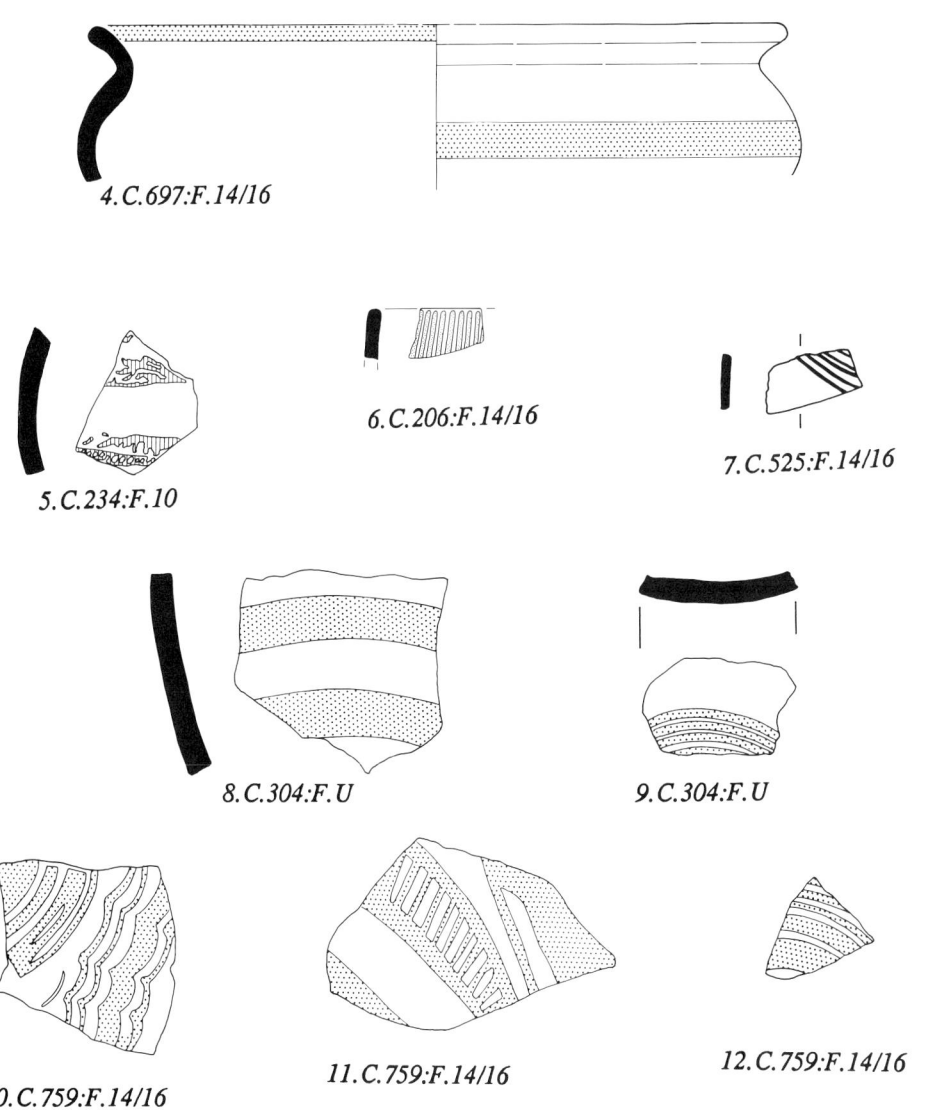

4. C.697:F.14/16

5. C.234:F.10

6. C.206:F.14/16

7. C.525:F.14/16

8. C.304:F.U          9. C.304:F.U

10. C.759:F.14/16          11. C.759:F.14/16          12. C.759:F.14/16

Fig. 5.53 Miscellaneous Iberian fineware handles and sidesherds          0    5    10cm

*Miscellaneous Iberian Fineware Handles* (Fig. 5.53)
Four handles which were too fragmentary to be ascribed to a particular type.
Found at a number of sites.
Fabrics: 14/16 and 20.
Date: no evidence.

*Miscellaneous Iberian Painted Fineware body sherds* (Fig. 5.53).
Eight miscellaneous sherds of painted Iberian fineware.
Found on a number of sites and in off-site scatters.
Fabric: 14/16.
Date: no evidence.

Italic Production

Campana A and other black gloss sherds are not illustrated; they are identified according to the standard typology (Morel 1981). Their ocurrence at sites in the survey area is given in Appendix 4.

Thin Walled Wares
Not illustrated. They are identified according to the established typologies of Mayet (1975), López (1977) and Puerta i López (1989). Their occurrence at sites in the survey areas is given in Appendix 4.

Terra Sigillata Italica
Not illustrated. It is identified according to the *Conspectus formarum* (Ettlinger *et al.* 1990) and Goudineau (1968). Their occurrence is noted in Appendix 4.

South Gaulish Production

Not illustrated. It is identified according to the standard typologies (Oswald and Pryce 1920). Their ocurrence at sites in the survey area is given in Appendix 4. Rubbings of decorated sherds may be found in the site archive deposited at the Museu Nacional Arqueològic de Tarragona.

Terra Sigillata Hispanica

Not illustrated. They are decorated in accordance with the standard typology (Mezquiriz 1961). Rubbings of decorated sherds may be found in the site archive deposited at the Museu Arqueològic de Tarragona. All identified sherds seem to have been products of the Tricio kilns (Garabito 1978) in the Rioja region.

North African Production

Not illustrated. They are identified according to the classifications by Hayes (1972) and (occasionally) Carandini (1981) within the broad categories of Sigillata Clara A, C and D established by Lamboglia (1958 and 1963). Their ocurrence at sites in the survey area is given in Appendix 4.

Narbonensian Production

Palaeochristian Orange Ware. Not illustrated. It is identified according to the standard typology (Carandini 1981). Its occurrence at sites in the survey area is given in Appendix 4.

## GLASS
Only one diagnostic fragment of ancient glass was found in the course of the survey (Fig. 5.54). It is too fragmentary to allow a form or date to be proposed.

## COARSE WARES

Iberian Production

This typology is based upon survey material cross-referenced to typologies from excavations within Catalunya. The aim has been to elucidate the chronology of individual pieces. It should be remembered, however, that Iberian hand-made pottery was manufactured between the 5th and later 2nd c. B.C. and that during this period there appears to have been little typological change (Gracia, Munilla and Pallarès 1988, 113). It is unwise to date this pottery more closely than between the 5th and later 2nd c. B.C.

*Type 1/ Gracia, Munilla and Pallarès 1988, 121, fig.3* (Fig. 5.54)
Rather tall everted rim belonging to a storage jar.
Site: 2.7.
Fabric: A.
Date: a similar fragment was discovered in 4th-c. B.C. contexts at the Moleta del Remei (Tarragona) (Gracia, Munilla and Pallarès 1988, 113).

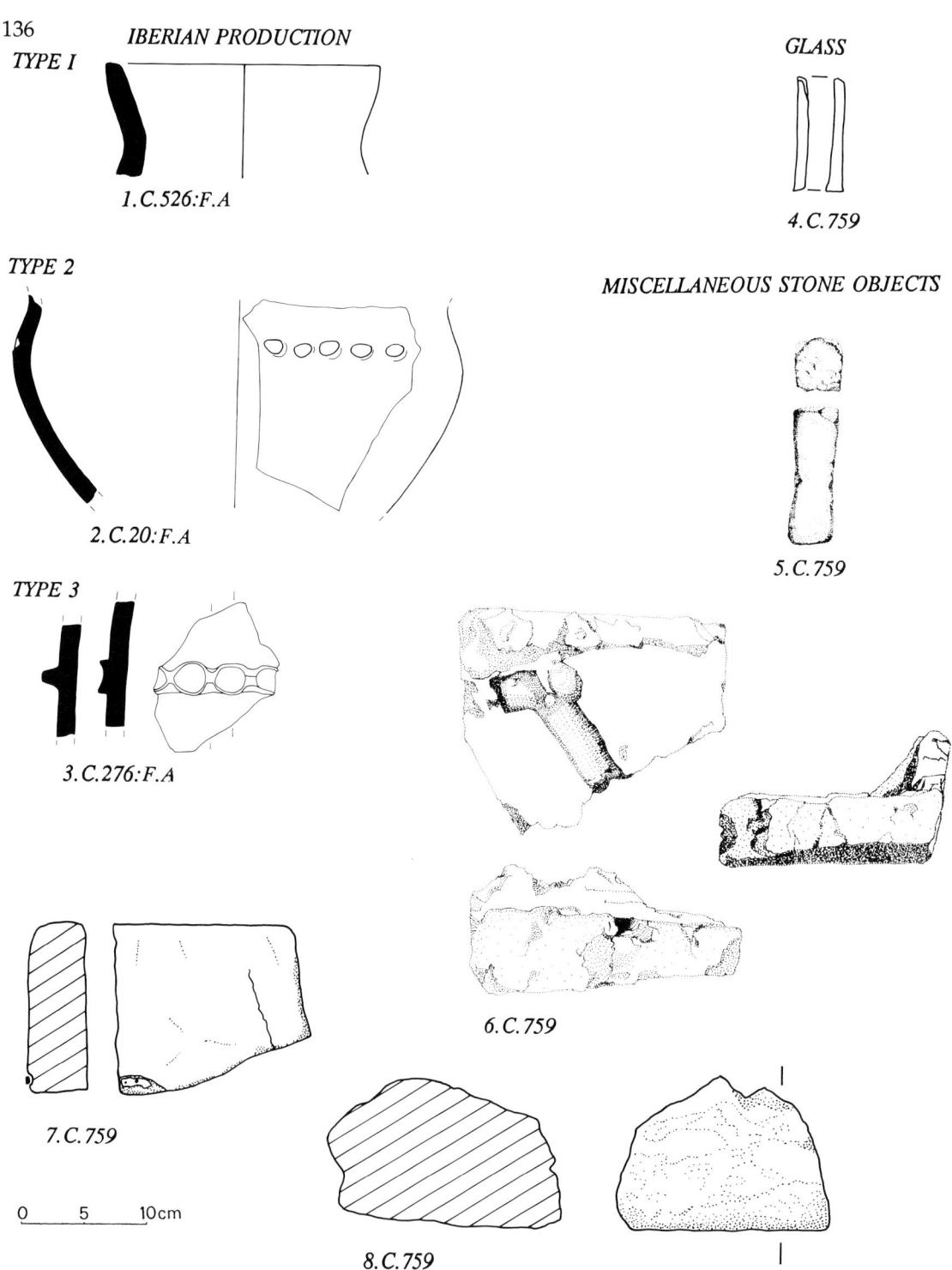

IBERIAN PRODUCTION

TYPE I

1.C.526:F.A

TYPE 2

2.C.20:F.A

TYPE 3

3.C.276:F.A

7.C.759

0    5    10cm

8.C.759

GLASS

4.C.759

MISCELLANEOUS STONE OBJECTS

5.C.759

6.C.759

Fig.5.54. Coarse Wares, Iberian production; glass; miscellaneous fragment; worked stone.

*Type 2/ Junyent 1972, fig.5 [M.77.76]* (Fig. 5.54)
Fragment of hand-thrown pottery wall with 'S'
profile and finger impressions around the shoulder.
Found in an off-site scatter.
Fabric: A.
Date: similar fragments are present in contexts of the
later 3rd to early 2nd c. B.C. (Junyent 1972).

*Type 3/ Sanmartí, Santacana and Serra 1984, Lám. 17.
113-114/ Dedet and Py Type FO 1 or IO 9* (Fig. 5.54)
A fragment of hand-thrown body wall with cord

decoration applied by continuous finger impressions.
It probably belonged to a wide-mouthed vessel.
Site: 1.9.
Fabric: A.
Date: similar fragments are present in contexts of the
last quarter of the 2nd and early years of the 1st c.
B.C. at L'Argilera (Sanmartí, Santacana and Serra
1984, 30-31; see also Dedet and Py 1975). Similar
fragments are present at the Moleta del Remei
(Tarragona) in contexts of the 2nd c. B.C. (Gracia,
Munilla and Pallarès 1988, 129 fig.71 etc.).

## Italic Production

The sherds belong to productions from the region of Campania and are present in stratified contexts at Roman and native sites within Catalunya from the early 2nd c. B.C. onwards (Nolla *et al.* 1990, 87). Recent excavations at Emporiae (Aquilué *et al.* 1984, 33) suggest that these imports to the region stop in the Augustan period. There is little typological development within the production as a whole and it is hard to identify a particular form with a specific date.

*Type 1* (Fig. 5.55)
Distinctive large bowl or mortarium with pronounced triangular rim.
Site: 1.10.
Fabric: 8.
Date: unknown but presumably some time between the 2nd c. B.C. and the Augustan period.

*Type 2* (Fig. 5.55)
Similar form to the above but smaller and finer.
Site: 2.6.
Fabric: Q.
Date: unknown but presumably some time between the 2nd c. B.C. and the Augustan period.

*Type 3* (Fig. 5.55)
Possible lid fragment.
Site: 1.8.
Fabric: Q.
Date: unknown but presumably some time between the 2nd c. B.C. and the Augustan period.

*Type 4* (Fig. 5.55)
Flat base of a dish with sharply everted wall.
Found only at off-site scatters.
Fabric: Q.
Date: a similar base was discovered in a context of the first half of the 1st c. B.C. (Sanmartí, Nolla and Aquilué 1987, fig.36.24).

*Type 5* (Fig. 5.55)
Large coarse bowl with flange.
Site: 3.11.
Fabric: Q.
Date: unknown but presumably between the early 2nd c. B.C. and the Augustan period.

*Type 6* (Fig. 5.55)
Small bowl with overhanging rim.
Site: 2.6.
Fabric: Q.
Date: unknown but presumably between the early 2nd c. B.C. and the Augustan period.

*Type 7* (Fig. 5.55)
Distinctive rim with pronounced lip belonging to a storage jar.
Site: 2.4.
Fabric: Q.
Date: unknown but presumably between the early 2nd c. B.C. and the Augustan period.

*Type 8* (Fig. 5.55)
Sharply everted rim belonging to an unknown form.
Site: 2.3.
Fabric: Q.
Date: unknown but presumably between the early 2nd c. B.C. and the Augustan period.

138

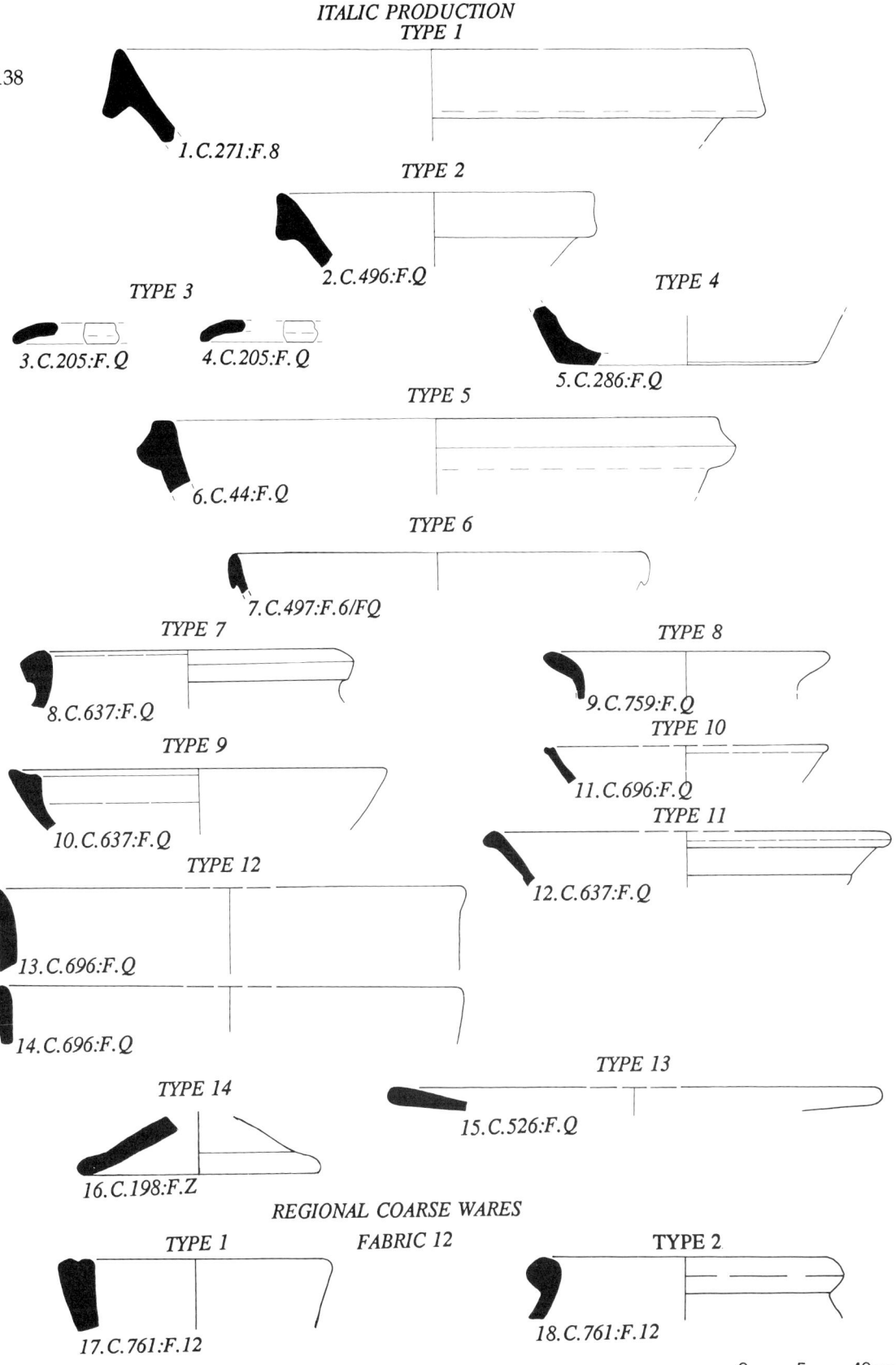

ITALIC PRODUCTION
TYPE 1
1.C.271:F.8

TYPE 2
2.C.496:F.Q

TYPE 3
3.C.205:F.Q
4.C.205:F.Q

TYPE 4
5.C.286:F.Q

TYPE 5
6.C.44:F.Q

TYPE 6
7.C.497:F.6/FQ

TYPE 7
8.C.637:F.Q

TYPE 8
9.C.759:F.Q

TYPE 9
10.C.637:F.Q

TYPE 10
11.C.696:F.Q

TYPE 11
12.C.637:F.Q

TYPE 12
13.C.696:F.Q
14.C.696:F.Q

TYPE 13
15.C.526:F.Q

TYPE 14
16.C.198:F.Z

REGIONAL COARSE WARES
FABRIC 12
TYPE 1
17.C.761:F.12

TYPE 2
18.C.761:F.12

0    5    10cm

Fig. 5.55 Coarse wares. Italic production; below, Regional production. Fabric 12.

*Type 9/ Aguarod Plato Forma 2* (Fig. 5.55)
Gently thickened, everted rim belonging to a flat-bottomed plate.
Site: 2.4.
Fabric: Q.
Date: between 40 and 10 B.C. (Aguarod 1991, 91).

*Type 10/ Aquilué 1993a, fig.4.19* (Fig. 5.55)
Bifid rim belonging to a dish with everted sides.
Site: 2.9.
Fabric: Q.
Date: from the first half of the 2nd c. on until as late as the Julio-Claudian period (Aquilué 1993a, 595).

*Type 11* (Fig. 5.55)
Small bowl with everted wall and pronounced rim.
Site: 2.4.
Fabric: Q.
Date: unknown but presumably between the early 2nd c. B.C. and the Augustan period.

*Type 12* (Fig. 5.55)
Straight-sided rim with rim virtually absent.
Site: 2.9.
Fabric: Q.
Date: a rather similar fragment was discovered in a context of the first half of the 1st c. B.C. at Emporiae (Sanmartí, Nolla and Aquilué 1987, fig.36.20).

*Type 13/ Aguarod Tapadera Forma 4* (Fig. 5.55)
Straight-sided lid with a barely perceptible rim.
Site: 2.7.
Fabric: Q.
Date: present at Emporiae in a context of the early 1st c. B.C. (Aquilué *et al.* 1984, 259 fig.8). Present at Celsa in an Augustan context (Aguarod 1991, 116).

*Type 14/ Aquilué et al. 1984, fig.103.18* (Fig. 5.55)
Site: 1.8.
Fabric: Z.
Date: A similar sherd appears in a context of the first half of the 1st c. B.C. (Aquilué *et al.* 1984, 248).

Regional Production

This typology is based upon survey material with cross-reference to material chiefly derived from excavations in Tarragona (Fàbrega 1989) and Girona (Casas *et al.* 1990). Analysis of the fabric has shown that the coarse pottery from the survey area was supplied from a number of different regions. They are probably all to be found within the Tarragona region. In an attempt to isolate them the pottery has been listed in typologies within each fabric group. As the material was very fragmented and recognizable forms were quite rare, individual 'types' were often represented by single sherds. In other cases 'types' comprise little more than convenient groupings of sherds with broadly similar morphological characteristics. As a coarse ware typology for the region is lacking, it was felt that this was the only way to proceed. An attempt has been made to provide dates for individual sherds. Given the nature of this material and the paucity of stratified deposits, however, it would be unwise to exaggerate the significance of the dates produced. Future excavations of stratified contexts, particularly at Tarragona, may be expected to develop this work

**Fabric 12**
*Type 1/ Casas et al. 1990, 251, fig.490* (Fig. 5.55)
Rim possibly belonging to a small single-handled jug. It may be an imitation of an African form.
Site: 2.3.
Date: a semi-complete jug with similar rim was discovered in contexts of the second half of the 2nd c. A.D. in Girona (Casas *et al.* 1990, 241 ff.).

*Type 2/ Vila-roma form 6.85* (Fig. 5.55)
Fairly narrow rim with circular profile, belonging to a small storage jar.
Site: 2.3.
Date: this form is very common (Vegas 1973, 11-14). Although there is a similar example in the mid 5th-c. deposit of Vila-roma at Tarragona (Fàbrega 1989, fig.106, 6.85), it is possible that the form was not specific to that period alone or, indeed, may have been residual there.

140

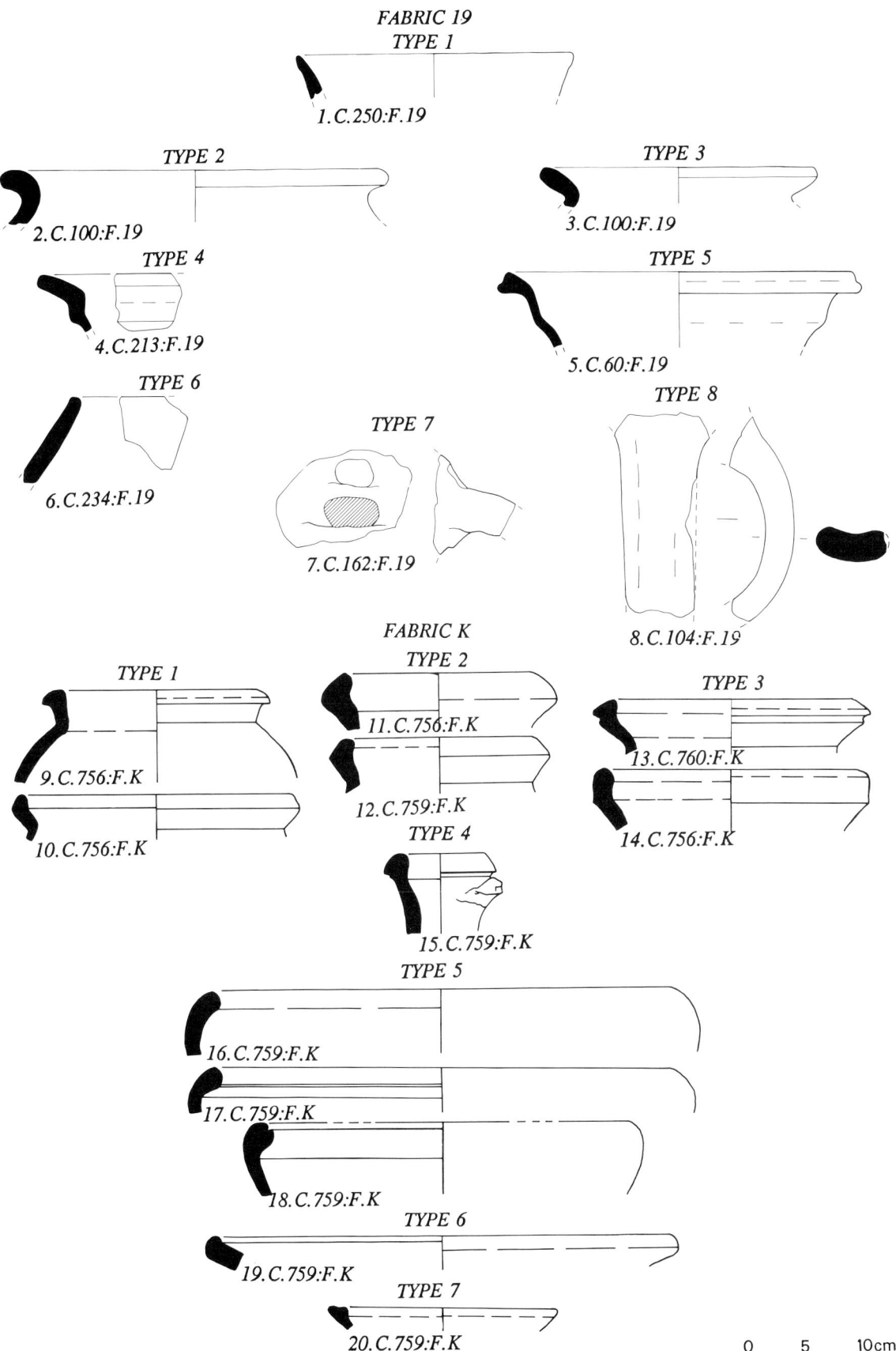

FABRIC 19
TYPE 1

1.C.250:F.19

TYPE 2

2.C.100:F.19

TYPE 3

3.C.100:F.19

TYPE 4

4.C.213:F.19

TYPE 5

5.C.60:F.19

TYPE 6

6.C.234:F.19

TYPE 7

7.C.162:F.19

TYPE 8

8.C.104:F.19

FABRIC K
TYPE 2

11.C.756:F.K

12.C.759:F.K

TYPE 1

9.C.756:F.K

10.C.756:F.K

TYPE 3

13.C.760:F.K

14.C.756:F.K

TYPE 4

15.C.759:F.K

TYPE 5

16.C.759:F.K

17.C.759:F.K

18.C.759:F.K

TYPE 6

19.C.759:F.K

TYPE 7

20.C.759:F.K

0    5    10cm

Fig. 5.56 Regional production. Fabric 19; below, Fabric K.

**Fabric 19**

*Type 1* (Fig. 5.56)
Everted rim belonging to an unknown type.
Site: 1.13.
Date: unknown.

*Type 2/ Vila-roma form 7.22* (Fig. 5.56)
Splayed rim with a rounded profile belonging to a medium sized jar.
Site: 1.6.
Date: this variant of jar rim comprised nearly 60% of all jar types with splayed rims in the mid 5th c. A.D. deposit at Vila-roma (Fàbrega 1989, 240). It seems reasonably certain, therefore, that the type was manufactured in the late empire. It is not certain, however, how far it represents a continuation from earlier periods.

*Type 3: Vila-roma form 6.42* (Fig. 5.56)
Simple everted rim belonging to a small storage jar.
Site: 1.6.
Date: this piece appears to be a small version of Vila-roma form 6.42 which was quite common among storage jar types in the mid 5th-c. A.D. deposit at Vila-roma (Fàbrega 1989, 213 ff.).

*Type 4* (Fig. 5.56)
Sharply everted rim with everted flange, possibly belonging to a jar or small amphora.
Found only in off-site scatters.
Date: no evidence.

*Type 5/ Casas et al. 1990, 357, fig.704* (Fig. 5.56)
Rim of a jar or small amphora with characteristic 'S' shaped profile and flange-shaped lip.
Site: 1.6.
Date: similar rims were found in contexts of the - second half of the 3rd c. A.D. in the province of Girona (Casas *et al.* 1990, 339-42).

*Type 6/* (Fig. 5.56)
Characteristic inturned neck with no rim.
Site: 1.14.
Date: no evidence.

*Types 7 and 8* (Fig. 5.56)
Miscellaneous handle types which cannot be easily ascribed to any particular form.
Sites: 1.6 and 1.7.
Date: no evidence.

**Fabric K**

*Type 1* (Fig. 5.56)
Rims with ovoid profile belonging to small storage jars. Complete unpublished examples have been found in Tarragona at excavations on the site of the Circus (Trinquet Vell 7.85A Neteja Sol) and are now in the Museu Arqueològic de Tarragona.
Sites: 2.3 and 4.4.
Date: unknown in the mid 5th-c. deposit at Vila-roma, the type may be early imperial.

*Type 2* (Fig. 5.56)
Similar rim but belonging to a jug or small amphora. A complete one-handled example has been found at the villa of Els Munts and is now in the Museu Arqueològic de Tarragona (Dep.Castell: E.III, II.74, unpublished).
Sites: 2.3 and 4.4.
Date: no evidence, although it may be early imperial.

*Type 3* (Fig. 5.56)
A variant of Type 2, with a wider rim.
Sites: 2.3 and 4.4.
Date: no evidence, although it may be early imperial.

*Type 4* (Fig. 5.56)
Rim with ovoid profile and handle attachment on the neck belonging to a bottle, probably with gently tapering body and flat bottom. Similar one-handled vessels have been found at unpublished excavations in the circus at Tarragona and are now in the Museu Arqueològic de Tarragona (Trinquet Vell.8. Neteja Sol 85a.455).
Site: 2.3.
Date: no evidence, although the nearest parallels are to be found in post-Augustan contexts in Girona (Casas *et al.* 1990, 191.392).

*Type 5* (Fig. 5.56)
Bowls with inturned rims.
Site: 2.3.
Date: they may date from the later 2nd c. A.D. onwards. Similar kinds of bowl are present in late 2nd-c. contexts at Girona (Casas *et al.* 1990, 263, fig. 521-23). At Tarragona the form appears in cooking-ware fabric in contexts of the mid 5th c. A.D. (Subias & Remolà 1989, fig. 119. 7.1-7.9).

*Type 6* (Fig. 5.56)
Plate with straight sides and pronounced lip. The complete form is unknown.
Sites: 2.3 and 4.1.
Date: no evidence, but probably early imperial.

*Type 7* (Fig. 5.56)
Small plate with bifid lip. The complete form is unknown.
Site: 2.3.
Date: no evidence, but probably early imperial.

142

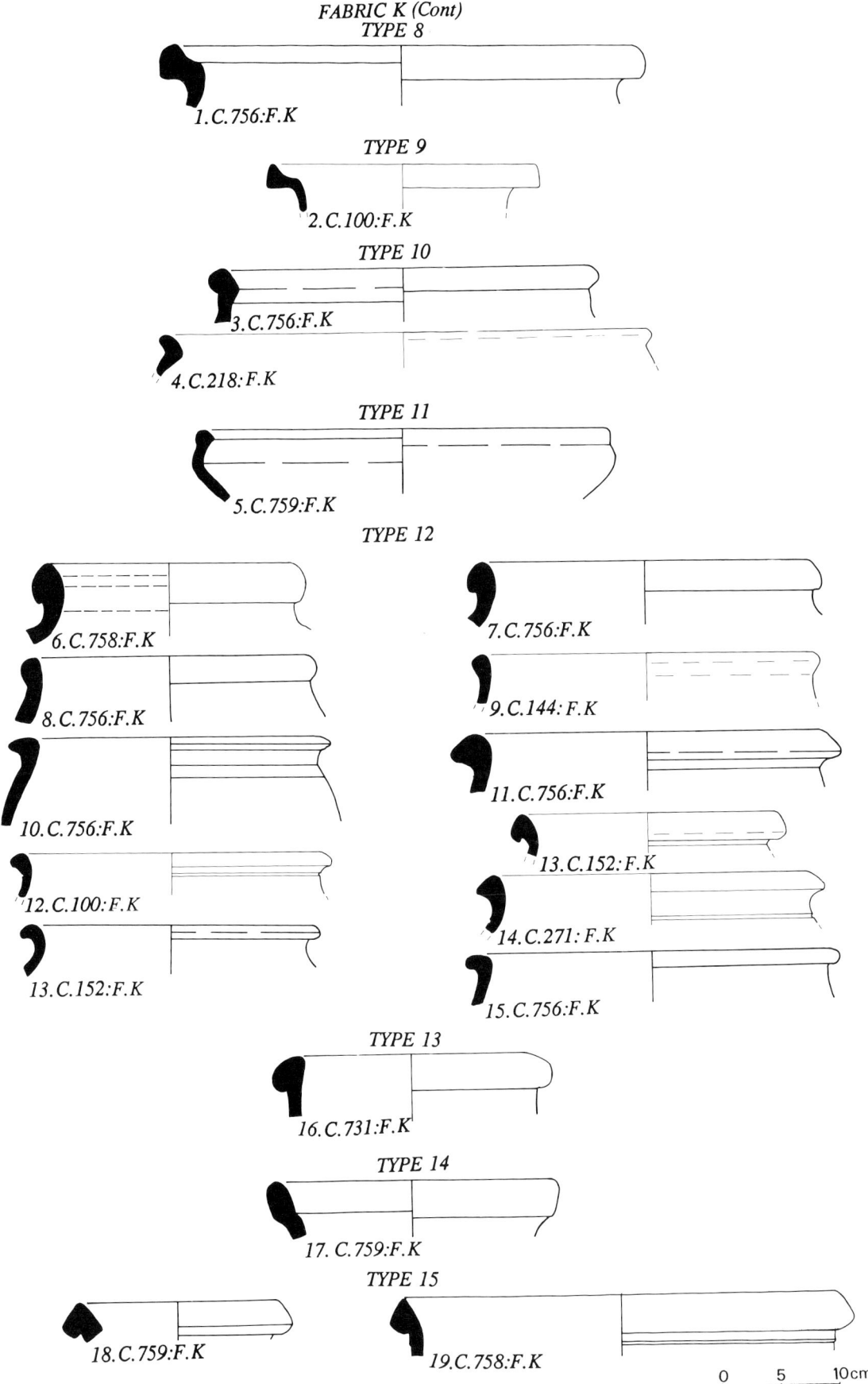

FABRIC K (Cont)
TYPE 8

1.C.756:F.K

TYPE 9

2.C.100:F.K

TYPE 10

3.C.756:F.K

4.C.218:F.K

TYPE 11

5.C.759:F.K

TYPE 12

6.C.758:F.K

7.C.756:F.K

8.C.756:F.K

9.C.144:F.K

10.C.756:F.K

11.C.756:F.K

12.C.100:F.K

13.C.152:F.K

13.C.152:F.K

14.C.271:F.K

15.C.756:F.K

TYPE 13

16.C.731:F.K

TYPE 14

17. C.759:F.K

TYPE 15

18.C.759:F.K

19.C.758:F.K

0    5    10cm

Fig. 5.57 Regional production. Fabric K (continued).

*Type 8/ Ostia III.321* (Fig. 5.57)
Casserole rim with a distinctive overhang and internal ledge for a lid. The form may derive from the African Cooking Ware form Ostia III, 321.
Site: 2.3.
Date: if the above attribution is correct this may be a form of the later 1st to mid 2nd c. A.D. (Aguarod 1991, 273).

*Type 9* (Fig. 5.57)
Similar style rim but it probably belongs to a jug.
Site: 2.3.
Date: no evidence, but probably early imperial.

*Type 10* (Fig. 5.57)
Casserole with curved/straight sides and a rolled rim.
Sites: 2.2, 2.3 and 4.4.
Date: no evidence, but probably early imperial.

*Type 11/ Casas et al. 1990, fig. 665/666* (Fig. 5.57)
Distinctive bowl with re-entrant wall and bead rim.
Site: 2.3.
Date: it is similar to the a bowl from contexts of the first half of the 3rd c. A.D. in the province of Girona (Casas *et al.* 1990, 329, fig. 665-66).

*Type 12* (Fig. 5.57)
Storage jars with a variety of rolled rims with circular section.
Sites: 1.2, 2.3, 2.9 and 4.4.
Date: no evidence, but probably early imperial.

*Type 13* (Fig. 5.57)
Pronounced rim belonging to a small amphora with a straight-sided neck.
Site: 2.2.
Date: no evidence, but probably early imperial.

*Type 14/ Vila-roma 6.116* (Fig. 5.57)
Everted neck of a small amphora with sharply offset rim and internal groove. It may belong to a two-handled vessel similar to Vila-roma form 6.116 (Fàbrega 1989, fig.110 6.118), with a narrow neck and sharply tapering neck.
Site: 2.3.
Date: the above parallel suggests that the form was at least current in the mid 5th c. A.D.

*Type 15* (Fig. 5.57)
Well-defined rims with triangular profiles.
Site: 2.3.
Date: no evidence, but probably early imperial.

144

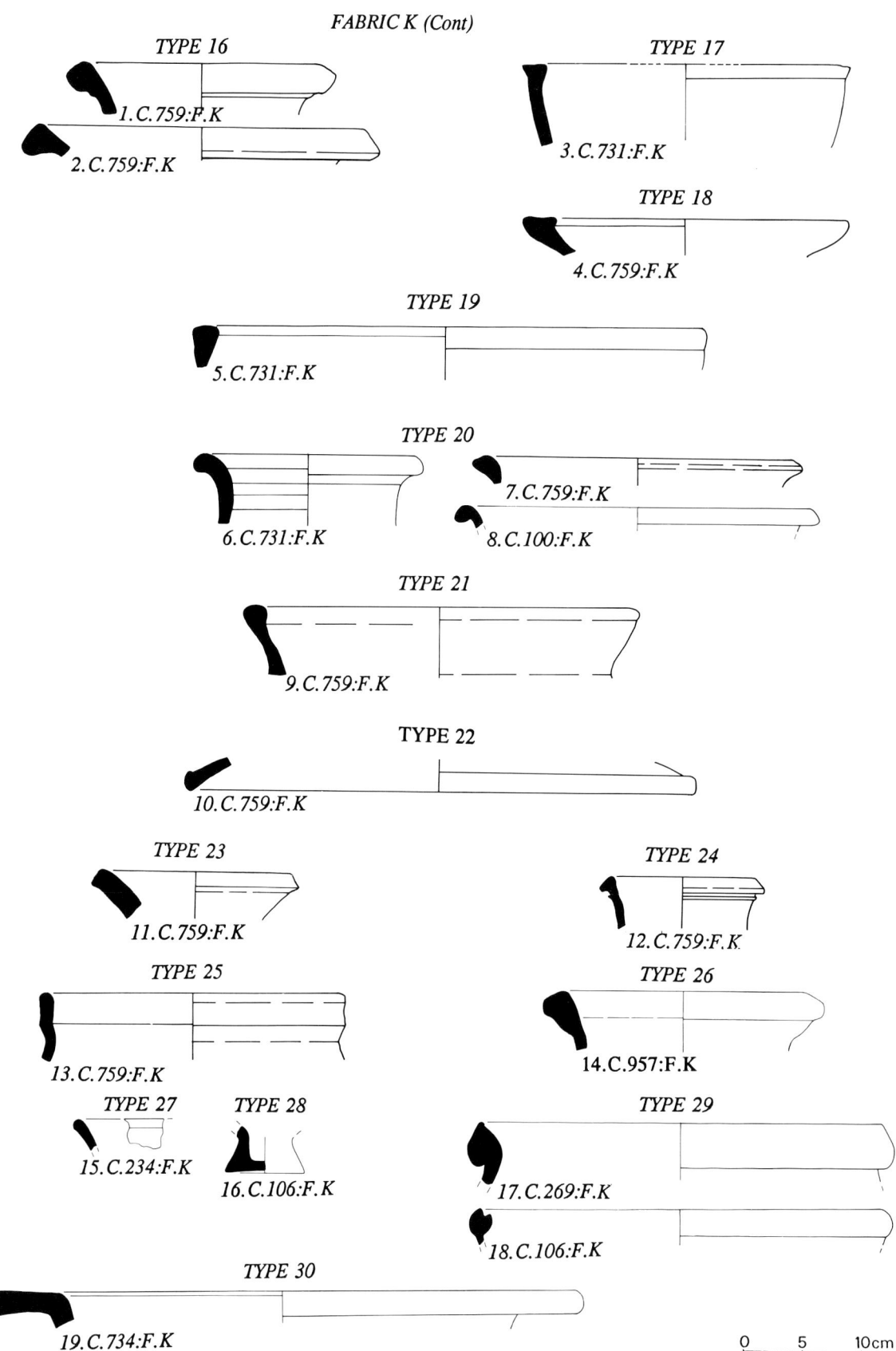

FABRIC K (Cont)

TYPE 16

1.C.759:F.K

2.C.759:F.K

TYPE 17

3.C.731:F.K

TYPE 18

4.C.759:F.K

TYPE 19

5.C.731:F.K

TYPE 20

6.C.731:F.K

7.C.759:F.K

8.C.100:F.K

TYPE 21

9.C.759:F.K

TYPE 22

10.C.759:F.K

TYPE 23

11.C.759:F.K

TYPE 24

12.C.759:F.K

TYPE 25

13.C.759:F.K

TYPE 26

14.C.957:F.K

TYPE 27

15.C.234:F.K

TYPE 28

16.C.106:F.K

TYPE 29

17.C.269:F.K

18.C.106:F.K

TYPE 30

19.C.734:F.K

0    5    10cm

Fig. 5.58 Regional production. Fabric K (continued).

*Type 16* (Fig. 5.58)
Sharply everted rim with circular section, belonging to a small amphora.
Site: 2.3.
Date: no evidence, but probably early imperial.

*Type 17* (Fig. 5.58)
Small bowl with steep sides and characteristic rim with flat-flange.
Site: 2.2.
Date: this form bears some similarity to sherds found in contexts of the first two decades of the 1st c. A.D. (Agraz *et al.* 1993, fig.82.92-95).

*Type 18* (Fig. 5.58)
Small bowl with a flat ledge running around the top and an internal groove.
Site: 2.3.
Date: similar bowls come from deposits dating to the first two decades of the 1st c. A.D. at Tarragona (Agraz *et al.* 1993, fig.83.115).

*Type 19* (Fig. 5.58)
Rim with triangular section possibly belonging to a large casserole dish.
Site: 2.2.
Date: no evidence but probably imperial.

*Type 20* (Fig. 5.58)
A variety of overhanging rims with circular section.
Sites: 1.6, 2.2 and 2.3.
Date: no evidence but probably early imperial.

*Type 21* (Fig. 5.58)
Vessel with a flaring wall and a rolled rim with round section. It may be a crude copy of African Red Slip Hayes 23 A or B. Alternatively, it may be a local shape similar to an example from recent excavations at the Antiga Audiència, Tarragona (Agraz *et al.* 1993, fig.84.113).
Site: 2.3.
Date: the above evidence suggests a date between the first two decades of the 1st c. and the early 3rd c. A.D.

*Type 22* (Fig. 5.58)
An imitation of the African Cooking Ware lid Ostia I form 20.
Sites: 2.2 and 2.3.
Date: some time between the early 1st c. and the second half of the 2nd c. A.D. (Aguarod 1991, 246).

*Type 23* (Fig. 5.58)
Small everted rim with triangular section.
Site: 2.3.

Date: no evidence, but probably imperial.

*Type 24* (Fig. 5.58)
Small rim with triangular section and undercut, belonging to a small jug.
Site: 2.3.
Date: no evidence, but probably imperial.

*Type 25* (Fig. 5.58)
Wide neck and simple rim belonging to an urn. The closest parallel is a cinerary urn from the Rubert cemetery at Emporiae (Casas *et al.* 1990, 177, fig.362).
Site: 2.3.
Date: the only evidence is the parallel cited which dates to the end of the 1st c. B.C. and beginning of the 1st c. A.D.

*Type 26* (Fig. 5.58)
Everted rim with circular section, belonging to a small amphora.
Site: 4.4.
Date: no evidence, but probably imperial.

*Type 27* (Fig. 5.58)
Small everted rim.
Site: 1.14.
Date: no evidence, but imperial.

*Type 28* (Fig. 5.58)
Small base with triangular profile.
Site: 1.6.
Date: no evidence, but probably imperial.

*Type 29* (Fig. 5.58)
Rims belonging to imitation African Cooking Ware forms Hayes 197.
Sites: 1.6 and 1.10.
Date: between the first half of the 2nd and the beginning of the 5th c. A.D. (Aguarod 1991, 281).

*Type 30* (Fig. 5.58)
A rim with extended flange.
Site: 2.2.
Date: a similar sherd was found during excavations at the Antiga Audiència, Tarragona in contexts of the first two decades of the 1st c. A.D. (Agraz *et al.* 1993, 102, fig.84.110).

146

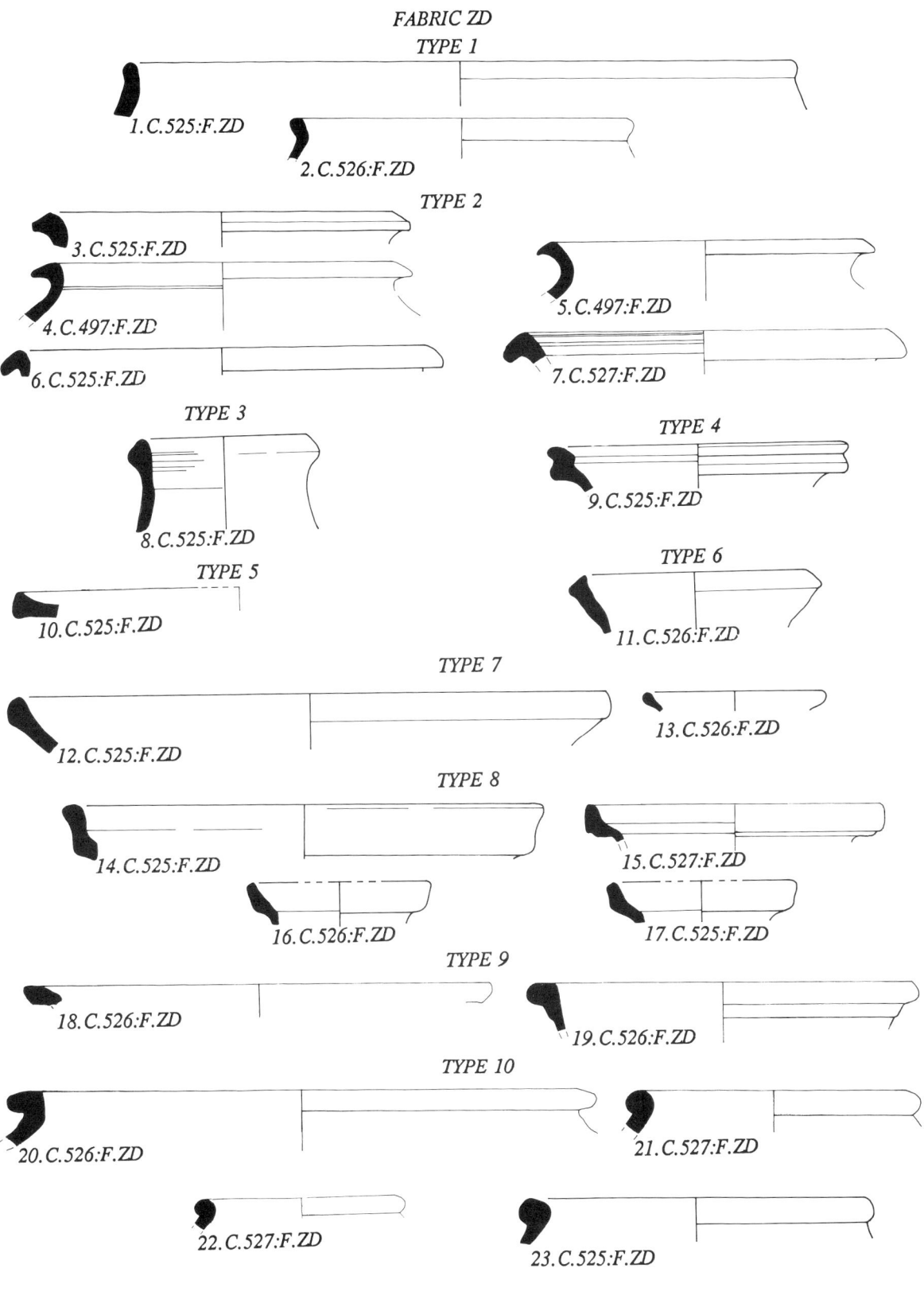

FABRIC ZD

TYPE 1

1.C.525:F.ZD

2.C.526:F.ZD

TYPE 2

3.C.525:F.ZD

4.C.497:F.ZD

5.C.497:F.ZD

6.C.525:F.ZD

7.C.527:F.ZD

TYPE 3

8.C.525:F.ZD

TYPE 4

9.C.525:F.ZD

TYPE 5

10.C.525:F.ZD

TYPE 6

11.C.526:F.ZD

TYPE 7

12.C.525:F.ZD

13.C.526:F.ZD

TYPE 8

14.C.525:F.ZD

15.C.527:F.ZD

16.C.526:F.ZD

17.C.525:F.ZD

TYPE 9

18.C.526:F.ZD

19.C.526:F.ZD

TYPE 10

20.C.526:F.ZD

21.C.527:F.ZD

22.C.527:F.ZD

23.C.525:F.ZD

Fig. 5.59 Regional production. Fabric ZD.

0     5     10cm

**Fabric ZD**

*Type 1* (Fig. 5.59)
Thin-walled storage jars with wide mouths.
Site: 2.7.
Date: a sherd similar to that from Campo 525 (Pl.65.1), in an Italian fabric, was discovered in a context of the first two decades of the 1st c. A.D. at the Antiga Audiència, Tarragona (Agraz *et al.* 1993, fig.84.125).

*Type 2* (Fig. 5.59)
Thin-walled storage jar with narrower mouth. The form bears some resemblance to Iberian shapes although the coarseness of the texture suggests that it is probably Roman. Similar forms were manufactured at the kiln of Fenals (Lloret de Mar, Girona) (Casas *et al.* 1990, 59, figs 17-19, 22-25; 60, figs. 27-28).
Site: 2.7.
Date: manufacture of the form at Fenals suggests a date between the later 1st c. B.C. and later 1st c. A.D.

*Type 3* (Fig. 5.59)
Wide neck of a small jar and rim with triangular section.
Site: 2.7.
Date: no evidence.

*Type 4* (Fig. 5.59)
A distinctive flanged rim with characteristic grooves running around its outer face and inside, it probably belongs to a jar.
Site: 2.7.
Dating: similar shapes are quite common in a context of the first two decades of the 1st c. A.D. at the Antiga Audiència, Tarragona (Agraz *et al.* 1993, fig. 83.97, 99, 102, 104, 107; fig. 84.108), as well as at some time after A.D. 60 (Agraz *et al.* 1993, fig.89.187). A similar sherd is also present in 1st-c. A.D. contexts in Girona (Casas *et al.* 1990, 195, fig. 400). It was absent from the mid 5th-c. deposit of Vila-roma.

*Type 5* (Fig. 5.59)
Rim fragment of a very shallow plate. It may be an imitation of the Italic coarse ware form 13 (Fabric Q).
Site: 2.7.
Date: no evidence.

*Type 6* (Fig. 5.59)
Everted rim with triangular section, belonging to a large jug or small amphora.
Site: 2.7.
Dating: no evidence.

*Type 7* (Fig. 5.59)
Rim of a lid or plate in two different sizes with a circular section. The larger of the two sizes resembles the African Cooking Ware lid Hayes 196.
Site: 2.7.
Date: not known, although if the larger of the two is an imitation of Hayes 196 a date between the early 1st and later 2nd c. A.D. may be appropriate.

*Type 8* (Fig. 5.59)
A family of similar rims whose defining characteristic is an everted face offset from the neck. There is no ready parallel although the smallest have parallels in Girona (Casas *et al.* 1990, 220, fig.438) and may belong to single-handled bottles.
Site: 2.7.
Date: the above parallel suggests that the form was current during the first half of the 2nd c. A.D.

*Type 9* (Fig. 5.59)
Broad-mouthed vessel with a stepped rim flange.
Site: 2.7.
Date: no evidence.

*Type 10* (Fig. 5.59)
Similar to Fabric 19 Type 3.
Site: 2.7.
Date: see Fabric 19 Type 3.

148

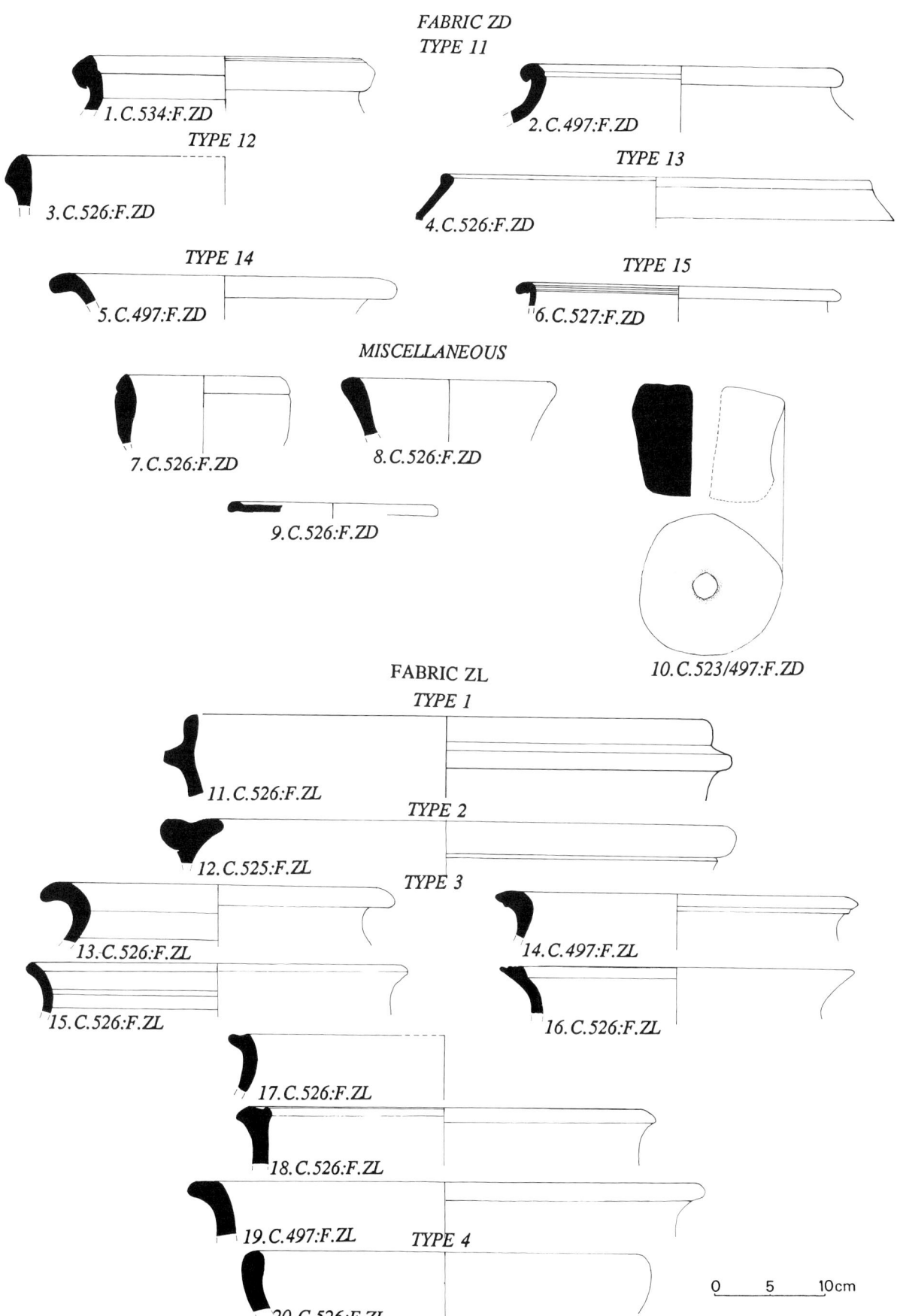

Fig. 5.60 Regional production. Fabric ZD (continued); below, Miscellaneous and Fabric ZL

*Type 11* (Fig. 5.60)
Similar to the storage jar discussed under Fabric K Type 12.
Site: 2.6.
Date: see Fabric K Type 12.

*Type 12* (Fig. 5.60)
Wide-mouthed casserole with triangular rim section and straight sides.
Site: 2.7.
Date: no evidence.

*Type 13* (Fig. 5.60)
Thin-walled storage vessel with re-entrant mouth rim with circular section, and straight sides.
Site: 2.7.
Date: no evidence.

*Type 14/ Casas et al. 1990, 251, fig.488* (Fig. 5.60)
Developed everted rim, probably belonging to a one-handled jug.
Sites: 2.6 and 2.7.
Date: the type occurs in contexts of the second half of the 2nd c. A.D. in Girona (Casas *et al.* 1990, 241-45).

*Type 15/ López 1989 form LIV* (Fig. 5.60)
Rather small bag-shaped bowl with thin walls and pronounced rim with grooves running around its inner face. There are similarities between this example and a product of a thin-walled production (López 1989 form LIV) which has been postulated in the region of Tarragona.
Site: 2.7.
Date: if the above parallel is correct, it dates between the last decade of the 1st c. B.C. and the early Flavian period (López 1989, 210-11). The same form has been found in a context of the first two decades of the 1st c. A.D. at the Antiga Audiència, Tarragona (Agraz *et al.* 1993, fig. 88.168).

*Miscellaneous sherds* (Fig. 5.60)
The complete shapes are difficult to establish and no parallels could be found. In addition one possible loom weight in fabric ZD is present.

**Fabric ZL**
*Type 1/ Casas et al. 1990, 329, fig.664* (Fig. 5.60)
Bowl with straight wall and a flange marking off a plain rim.
Site: 2.7.
Date: a very similar piece was found in contexts of the early 3rd c. A.D. at Puig Rodon (Corçà, Girona) (Casas *et al.* 1990, 328, fig. 664).

*Type 2* (Fig. 5.60)
A wide-mouthed jar with inturned rim; a thickened flange with circular profile runs around the shoulder. It is broadly similar to a jar manufactured at the coarse-ware production site at Fenals (Lloret de Mar, Girona) (Casas *et al.* 1990, 60, fig. 32).
Site: 2.7.
Date: the kiln at Fenals functioned during the later 1st c. B.C. and the earlier 1st c. A.D.

*Type 3* (Fig. 5.60)
Storage jars broadly similar to fabric ZD Type 2. Note the range in sizes and wall thickness.
Sites: 2.6 and 2.7.
Date: see fabric ZD Type 2.

*Type 4/ Vila-roma form 7.4* (Fig. 5.60)
Large bowl with thick wall and simple incurved rim.
Site: 2.7.
Date: occurrence of the form in some quantity in the Vila-roma deposit (Subias and Remolà 1989, 234 ff.) suggests that the form was at least current in the period 440-50.

150

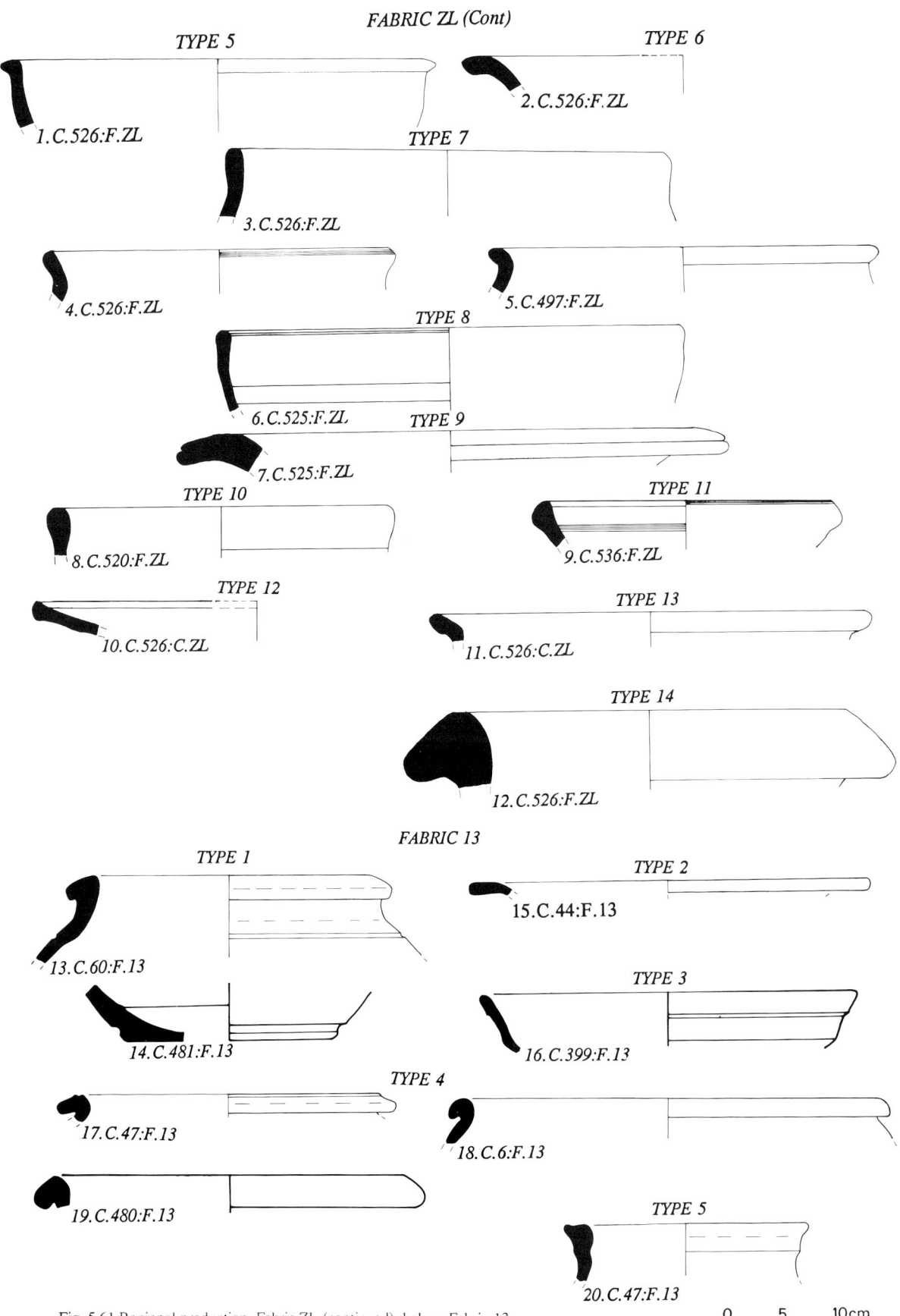

FABRIC ZL (Cont)

TYPE 5

1.C.526:F.ZL

TYPE 6

2.C.526:F.ZL

TYPE 7

3.C.526:F.ZL

4.C.526:F.ZL

5.C.497:F.ZL

TYPE 8

6.C.525:F.ZL

TYPE 9

7.C.525:F.ZL

TYPE 10

8.C.520:F.ZL

TYPE 11

9.C.536:F.ZL

TYPE 12

10.C.526:C.ZL

TYPE 13

11.C.526:C.ZL

TYPE 14

12.C.526:F.ZL

FABRIC 13

TYPE 1

13.C.60:F.13

14.C.481:F.13

TYPE 2

15.C.44:F.13

TYPE 3

16.C.399:F.13

TYPE 4

17.C.47:F.13

18.C.6:F.13

19.C.480:F.13

TYPE 5

20.C.47:F.13

Fig. 5.61 Regional production. Fabric ZL (continued); below, Fabric 13.

0    5    10cm

*Type 5/ Vila-roma form 7.11* (Fig. 5.61)
Gently everted wall, pronounced rim with triangular section; possibly it belongs to a casserole. A similar form was found at Tarragona, although in a coarser fabric (Fàbrega 1989, fig. 120 7.12).
Site: 2.7.
Date: the above context suggests that the form was at least current in 440-50.

*Type 6* (Fig. 5.61)
Rim probably from a one-handled jug similar to Fabric ZD Type 14.
Site: 2.7.
Date: see Fabric ZD Type 14.

*Type 7* (Fig. 5.61)
Thin- and thick-walled storage jars with wide mouths, as Fabric ZD Type 1.
Site: 2.7.
Date: as Fabric ZD Type 1.

*Type 8/ Casas et al. 1990, 351, fig. 694/695* (Fig. 5.61)
Bowl or deep plate with vertical wall and rounded rim.
Site: 2.7.
Date: similar sherds have been discovered in contexts of the second half of the 3rd c. A.D. (Casas *et al.* 1990, 350).

*Type 9/ Casas et al. 1990, 335, fig.678* (Fig. 5.61)
Flange belonging to a possible mortarium, with groove running around outer face.
Site: 2.7.
Date: a similar example was found in a context of the first (Casas *et al.* 1990, 335) and second (Casas *et al.* 1990, 372) halves of the 3rd c. A.D.

*Type 10/ Vila-roma form 7.19* (Fig. 5.61)
A form of possibly globular shape with a bead rim.
Site: 2.8.
Date: present in contexts of 440-50 at Tarragona (Fabrega 1989, 238).

*Type 11/ Vila-roma form 7.40?* (Fig. 5.61)
Trumpet-shaped rim of a small amphora or storage jar, with comb decoration running around the inner face. A fairly close parallel is perhaps to be found at Tarragona (Subias and Remolà 1989, 241-43).
Found in an off-site scatter.
Date: the parallel cited above would suggest that the form was current at least in 440-50.

*Type 12/ Imitation African Cooking Ware form Ostia I.261* (Fig. 5.61)

Simple rim with elliptical section.
Site: 2.7.
Date: the form which this imitates was manufactured between the mid 1st and the end of the 5th c. A.D. (Aguarod 1991, 250).

*Type 13* (Fig. 5.61)
No exact parallel, although the everted rim with triangular section is common to a range of shapes (jars, urns, etc.); one possibility is the Italic coarseware type Burriac 549 (Aguarod 1991, 85).
Site: 2.7.
Date: no evidence although if the above parallel is valid it may be characteristic of the 2nd to 1st c. B.C.

*Type 14* (Fig. 5.61)
Mortarium with coarse, overhanging flange.
Site: 2.7.
Date: broadly similar sherds have been found in Augustan (Casas *et al.* 1990, 157, fig. 344) and 1st-c. A.D. contexts in the province of Girona.

**Fabric 13**
*Type 1* (Fig. 5.61)
Storage jar with rolled rim and elliptical section, simple base with exterior groove. The form seems similar to Fabric K Type 12. A complete example of the latter was found in unpublished excavations at the Trinquet Vell in Tarragona and is now in the Museu Arqueològic de Tarragona (Trinquet Vell 7 85A Neteja Sol). This suggests that the base (Fig.5.61.17) belongs to this rim type.
Site: 1.6.
Date: as Fabric K Type 12.

*Type 2/ Casas et al. 1990, 269, fig. 536* (Fig. 5.61)
Rim flange belonging to a shallow plate.
Site: 3.11.
Date: this kind of vessel occurred in a context of the second half of the 2nd c. A.D. in the province of Girona (Casas *et al.* 1990, 268).

*Type 3/ Casas et al. 1990, 113, fig. 240* (Fig. 5.61)
Upper section of a carinated bowl with everted wall and an offset below the rim. It may be paralleled by a vessel from Girona with horizontal grooves on the exterior below the rim. It is also possible that it is an imitation of African Red Slip Ware Hayes 9B.
Site: 3.16.
Date: the example from Girona was discovered in late 3rd-c. contexts in conjunction with a large amount of residual late Republican and early imperial pottery (Casas *et al.* 1990, 112). If it is an imitation of the Hayes 9B, a date of the second half of the 2nd c. A.D. would be appropriate.

152

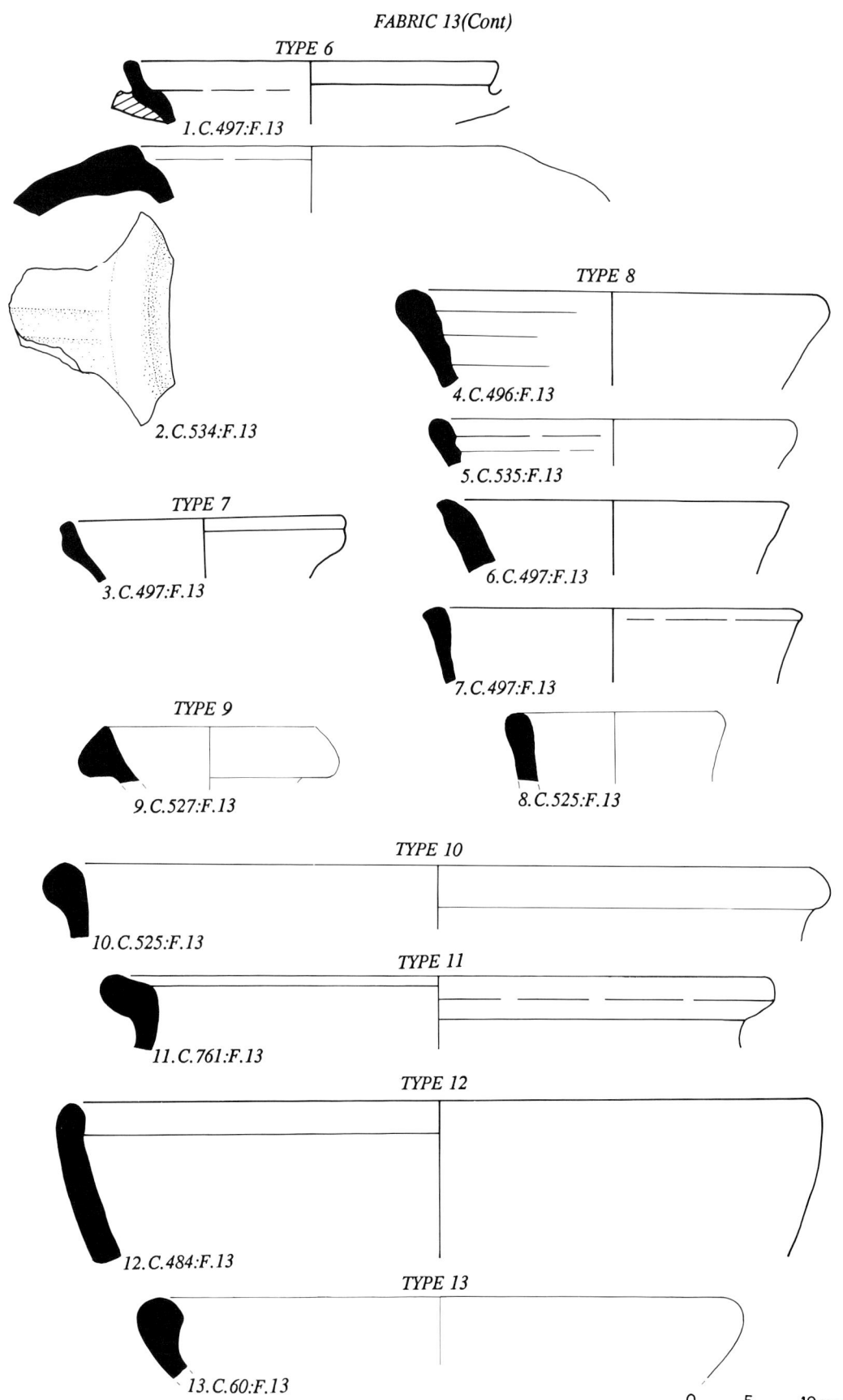

Fig. 5.62 Regional production. Fabric 13 (continued).

*Type 4* (Fig. 5.61)
Storage jars with rolled rim and circular section, similar to those of Fabric K Type 12.
Found only in an off-site scatter.
Date: see Fabric K Type 12.

*Type 5/ Casas et al. 1990, 321, fig. 659* (Fig. 5.61)
Distinctive rim of an unknown vessel type.
Found only in an off-site scatter.
Date: a larger version of this type was discovered in a context of the second half of the 2nd c. A.D. at Mas Gusó, Girona (Casas *et al.* 1990, 320).

*Type 6* (Fig. 5.62)
Rims and handles of a class of jug. The complete form is not known. However, the rim profile is similar to an example from Puig Rodon, Girona (Casas *et al.* 1990, 331, fig. 670). It is not clear, however, whether the published example definitely had no handle.
Site: 2.6.
Date: if there is any value in the parallel, the survey sherds might date to some time in the 3rd c. A.D.

*Type 7/ Casas et al. 1990, 221, fig. 438* (Fig. 5.62)
Everted rim with external groove belonging to a single-handled bottle.
Site: 2.6.
Date: a similar and complete example was discovered in a context of the first half of the 2nd c. A.D. at Emporiae (Casas *et al.* 1990, 220).

*Type 8* (Fig. 5.62)
A group of rims with similar characteristics, which may be variants by size of a single type. The salient characteristic is an everted face.
Sites: 2.6 and 2.8.
Date: a somewhat similar sherd from Emporiae (Casas *et al.* 1990, 237, fig. 481) has been classed as a *dolium* and ascribed to the second half of the 2nd c. A.D.

*Type 9* (Fig. 5.62)
Trumpet-shaped rim with triangular section belonging to a small amphora.
Site: 2.7.
Date: no evidence. but probably end of the Republic and early imperial.

*Type 10* (Fig. 5.62)
Rim with circular section, belonging to a large urn.
Site: 2.7.
Date: no evidence, but probably probably end of the Republic and early imperial.

*Type 11/ Casas et al. 1990, 299, fig. 624/625* (Fig. 5.62)
Wide-necked storage jar with prounced rim. Presumably it would have had two handles.
Site: 2.3.
Date: similar pieces were discovered at Pla de l'Horta and Puig Rodon in Girona in contexts of the second half of the 2nd c. A.D. (Casas *et al.* 1990, 298). 3rd-c. examples (Casas *et al.* 1990, 370-71, figs. 735-36) tend to have rims with a more triangular section.

*Type 12* (Fig. 5.62)
Deep bowl with gently incurved rim.
Found only in an off-site scatter.
Date: no evidence, but probably end of the Republic and early imperial.

*Type 13* (Fig. 5.62)
Shallow bowl with incurved rim.
Site: 1.6.
Date: no evidence, but probably end of the Republic and early imperial.

154

**Fabric ZM**

*Type 1* (Fig. 5.63)
Rim fragments in two different sizes which are similar to Fabric ZD Type 14.
Sites: 2.3 and 2.7.
Date: see Fabric ZL Type 14.

*Type 2* (Fig. 5.63)
Everted rim with concave outer face. The form is similar to a coarse-ware urn from Tolegassos (Casas *et al.* 1990, 145, fig. 318) and a late Emporitan Grey Ware vessel from Emporiae (Casas *et al.* 1990, 111, fig. 226).
Site: 2.3.
Date: the above parallels suggest an Augustan date.

*Type 3* (Fig. 5.63)
A sherd similar to Fabric K Type 12.
Site: 2.6.
Date: see Fabric K Type 12.

*Type 4* (Fig. 5.63)
A rim similar to Fabric ZL Type 11 (specifically the example from Campo 554).
Sites: 2.4 and 2.6.
Date: see Fabric ZL Type 11.

*Type 5* (Fig. 5.63)
Distinctive flanged rims, one of which had a 'forked' section.
Sites: 2.6 and 2.7.
Date: no evidence.

*Type 6* (Fig. 5.63)
A small and large version of Fabric ZD Type 8 (the large example comes from Campo 525).
Sites: 2.3 and 2.7.
Date: see Fabric ZD Type 8.

*Type 7* (Fig. 5.63)
A larger version of the form in Fabric K Type 11
Site: 2.6.
Date: as for Fabric K Type 11.

*Type 8* (Fig. 5.63)
Small bowl with re-entrant rim imitating Campanian Ware (Morel form 2765a).
Site: 2.6.
Date: probably some time in the late 3rd c. B.C.

*Type 9* (Fig. 5.63)
Distinctive container (bowl?) comprising an inturned rim with a groove running around the outer face.
Site: 2.7.
Date: no evidence.

*Type 10* (Fig. 5.63)
Rim of a mortarium with a pronounced flange.
Site: 2.7.
Date: the earliest parallel for this type comes from contexts of the second half of the 2nd c. A.D. at La Quintana, Girona (Casas *et al.* 1990, 317, figs. 648-49). The latest context comes from the Vila-roma deposit, Tarragona, dated to 440-50 (Fàbrega 1989, 207 ff.: form 6.23).

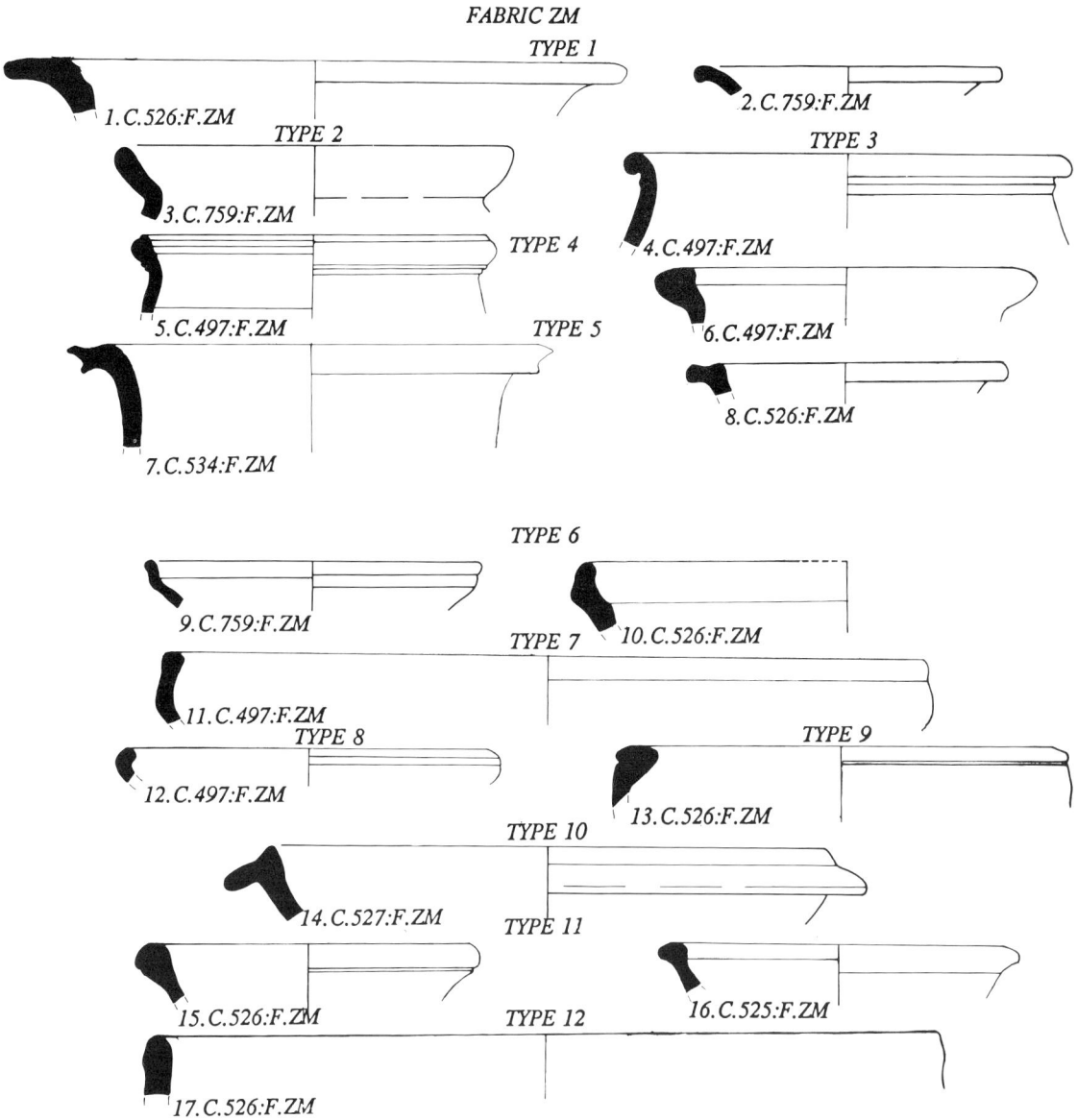

Fig. 5.63 Regional production. Fabric ZM.

*Type 11* (Fig. 5.63)
Rims similar to Fabric K Type 3.
Site: 2.7.
Date: see Fabric K Type 3.

*Type 12* (Fig. 5.63)
Large vessel of unknown function with vertical wall and barely perceptible rim.
Site: 2.7.
Date: no evidence.

## Miscellaneous Productions

Fabrics A, Z, ZB, ZE, ZO, ZZ.

These fabrics did not occur frequently enough to merit considering them a separate productions. They are included as identified fabrics in Appendix 4.

*Type 1* (Fig. 5.64)
Simple straight-sided vessel with no rim. In some ways the form resembles Fabric Q Type 12.
Fabric: ZZ.
Site: 2.9.
Date: no evidence, but see Fabric Q Type 12.

*Type 2* (Fig. 5.64)
Gently everted wall with rolled rim.
Fabric: A.
Site: 2.3.
Dating: no evidence.

*Type 3* (Fig. 5.64)
Everted wall of a bowl with a pronounced lip running around the interior of the rim. It is possible that this is an imitation of the African Red Slip Ware casserole Hayes 23B.
Fabric: KM.
Site: 2.3.
Date: if the above parallel is valid, a mid 2nd to early 3rd-c. A.D. date would be appropriate.

*Type 4* (Fig.5.64)
A larger version of Fabric K Type 6.
Fabric: A.
Found only in an off-site scatter.
Date: see Fabric K Type 6.

*Type 5* (Fig. 5.64)
Form similar to Fabric ZM Type 9.
Fabric: ZB.
Site: 2.7.
Date: see Fabric ZM Type 9.

*Type 6* (Fig. 5.64)
A more developed version of Fabric ZL Type 13, with an undercut beneath the rim.
Fabric: ZE.
Site: 2.8.
Date: see Fabric ZL Type 13.

*Type 7* (Fig. 5.64)
Form similar to Fabric K Type 2.
Fabric: ZO.
Site: 2.7.
Date: see Fabric K Type 2.

*Type 8* (Fig. 5.64)
Large straight-sided bowl with thickened rim and external groove.
Fabric: U.
Site: 3.19.
Date: no evidence.

*Type 9* (Fig. 5.64)
Flat base of a coarse ware vessel whose interior is characterized by a number of circular impressions.
Fabric: ZB.
Site: 2.7.
Date: no evidence.

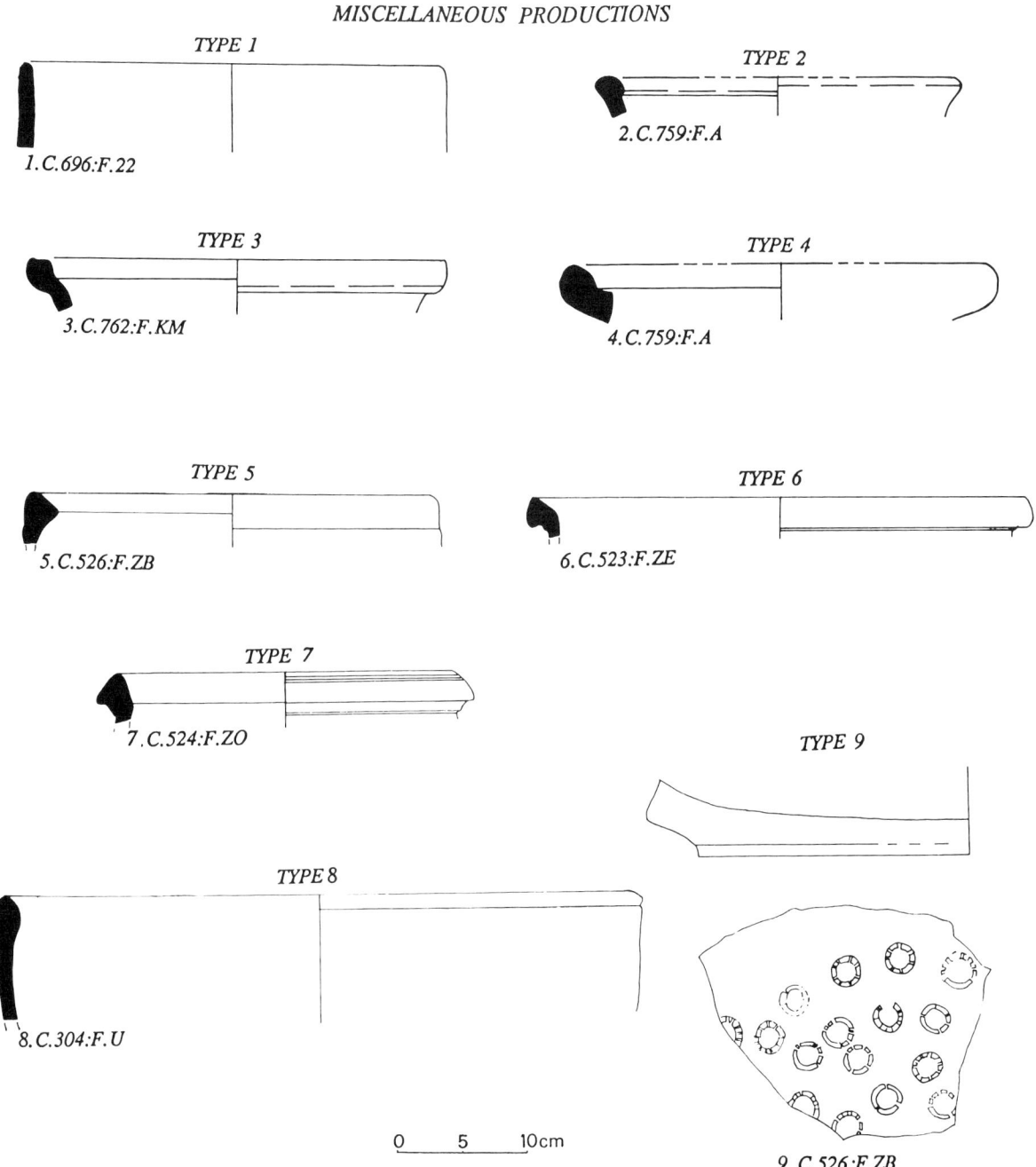

Fig. 5.64 Miscellaneous Regional Coarse Ware productions.

## North African Production

Not illustrated. They are identified according to the established typology of Hayes (1972) with changes to the dating by Carandini (1981). Their occurrence on sites in the survey area is detailed in Appendix 4.

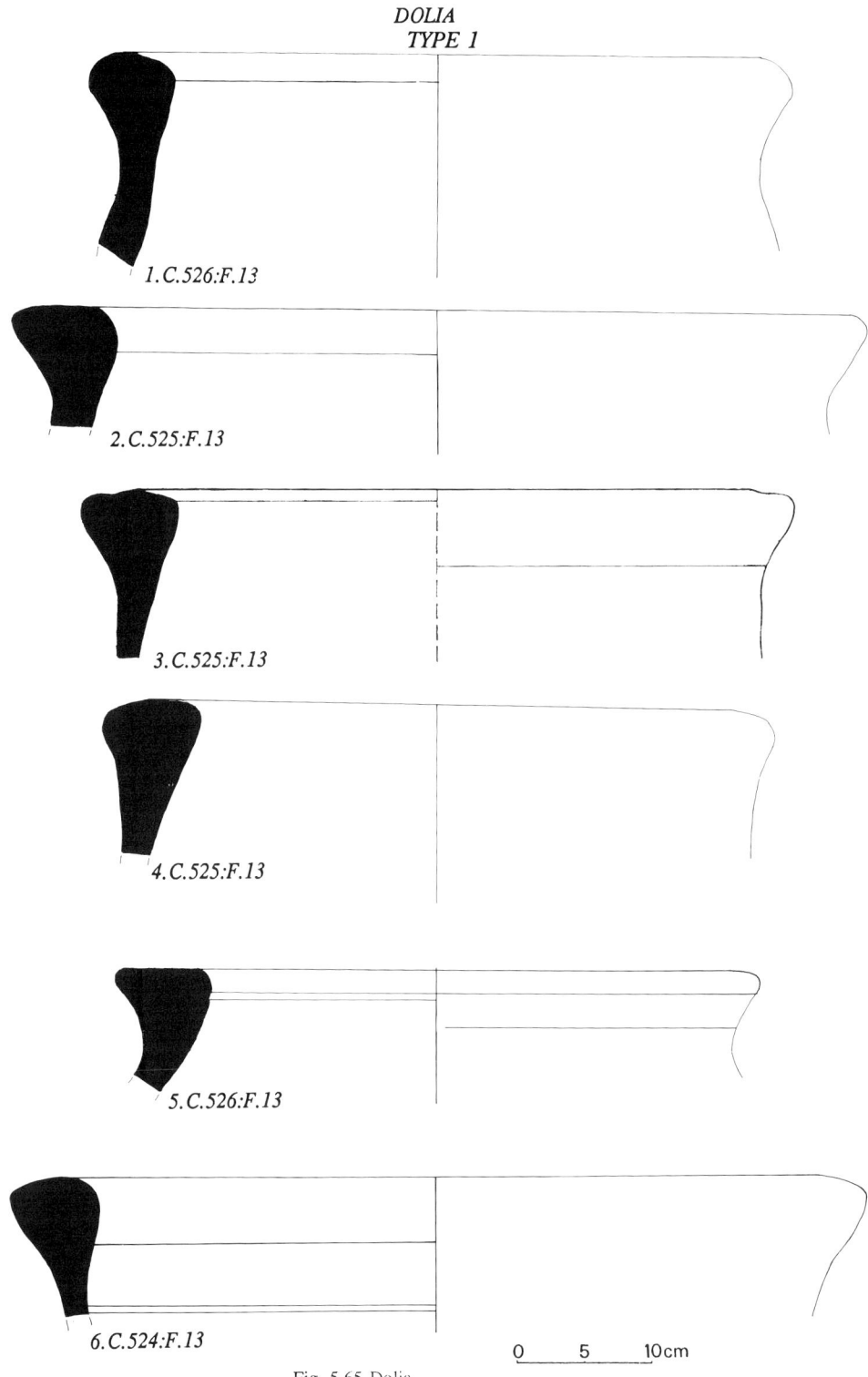

DOLIA
TYPE 1

1.C.526:F.13

2.C.525:F.13

3.C.525:F.13

4.C.525:F.13

5.C.526:F.13

6.C.524:F.13

0    5    10cm

Fig. 5.65 Dolia.

## DOLIA

The survey yielded a range of rim types of *dolia* (Figs. 5.65-5.66). There are few grounds for attempting a typological classification. Nevertheless, work in Girona does suggest broad differences between more upstanding rims (Type 1) of the Augustan period (Casas *et al*. 1990) and the squatter 'flange' types of the second half of the 3rd c. A.D.(Type 2). If this is sustained, it is possible that those in Fig. 5.66, from Site 2.7, Campos 526 and Site 2.9, 698, are later.

Fabrics: 12 and 13.

159

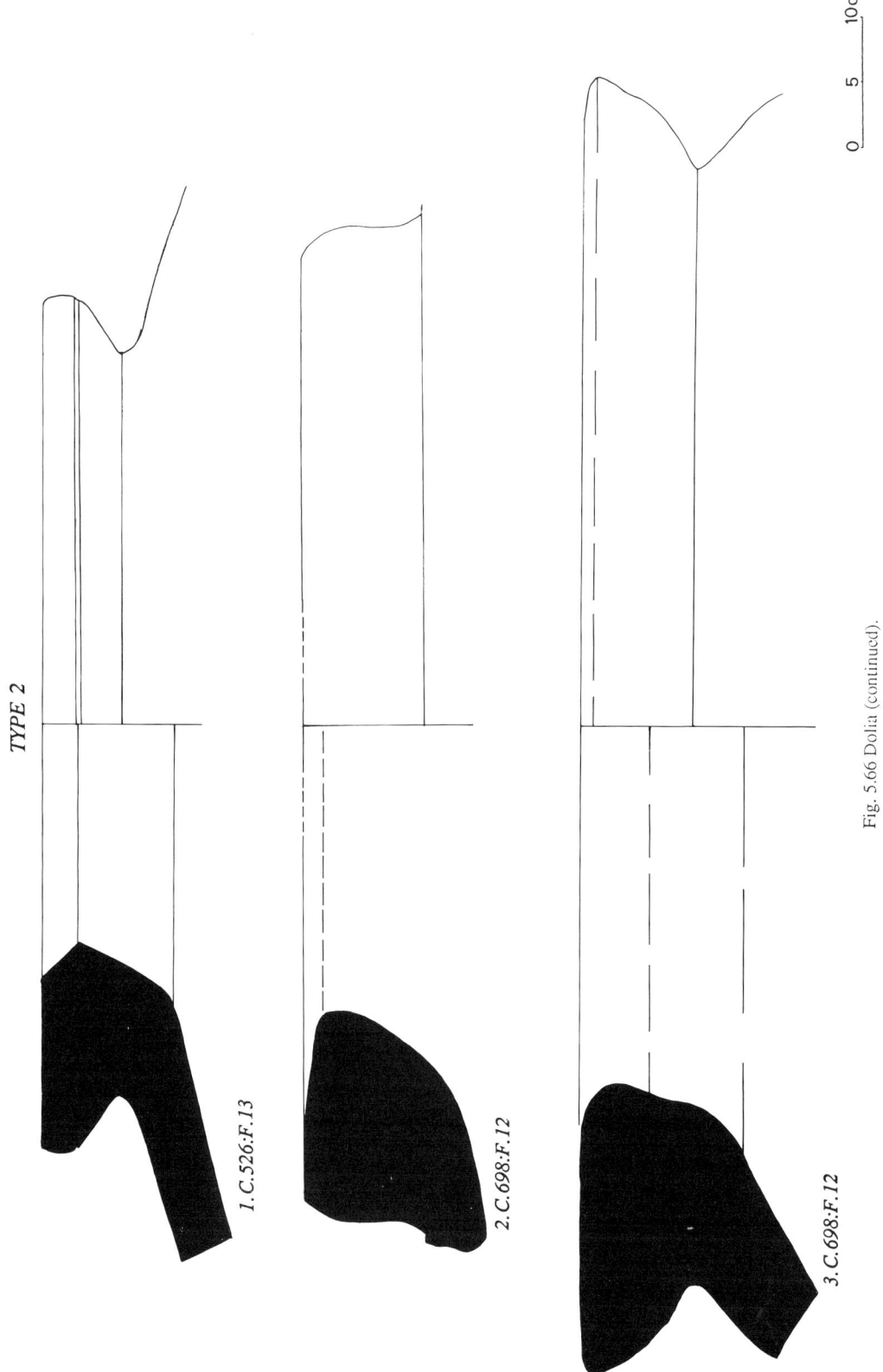

TYPE 2

1. C.526:F.13

2. C.698:F.12

3. C.698:F.12

Fig. 5.66 Dolia (continued).

0    5    10cm

160

## COMMENTARY

This is a rich array of ceramic material and provides a first typology for coarse wares and amphorae from a key part of the west Mediterranean littoral. Its value is compromised by the fragmentary state of the material, which has tended to ensure that amphorae and, to a lesser extent, coarsewares, were more recognisable than finewares. It is hoped that the form and fabric series will be enhanced by future excavations in the countryside and at Tarraco, and lead to adjustments in the proposed dating of individual forms.

The greatest value of the typology lies in the Iberian/Republican period since there is little comparative published Roman material from Tarraco itself (Aquilué 1993, 69-77; Vegas 1984-85). The material from the early imperial period is a valuable complement to what was known from Tarraco (Dupré and Carreté 1993), particularly with respect to coarsewares, despite the fragmentary nature of the material. The late imperial material is of less value given the recent publication of finds of the 4th, 5th and 6th c. from Tarraco (Keay 1984; Remolà 1989; Remolà 1993).

More detailed considerations of the typological and cultural implications of this material are reserved for future papers. However, several points can be made here:

### AMPHORAE

It is now clear that amphora production in the region of Tarragona had a long, possibly continuous, history. It began with examples (Type 1) that are well known elsewhere in eastern Spain and come in two distinct fabrics, together with imitations of forms manufactured elsewhere in the western Mediterranean (Types 2, 3 and 5). The former are generally understood to have been manufactured at Fontscaldes (Colominas Roca 1915-20; Tovar et al. 1986-87; Lafuente 1992) and possibly at sites 4.2-4.4. It should be noted, however, that no definite wasters were found at these sites. The content of Type 1 amphorae is still open to question; despite the gas-chromatographic evidence for fish-sauce (Appendix 3), normally they must have carried wine, possibly wine and grain.

The impact of Rome in cultural terms (especially through the large-scale import of Italic wine amphorae) can be measured in the adoption by native potters of an increasingly wide range of Roman forms and production techniques, as reflected in the fabrics. It is now possible to trace the outlines of the development. It began with a transitional stage in the manufacture of Iberian amphora Type 1 in the more coarse, 'Roman' style of fabric (13) and with typically Roman forms (Type 7) in an Iberian fabric (14/16). The first phase of the manufacture of Roman forms comprised wine amphora Types 6, 7, 8 and 9 in a fabric (9) which is transitional between the 'classic' Iberian (14/16) and Tarraconensian (12 and 13) fabrics. It should be noted, however, that an Iberian stamp suggests that ownership of production, or the estates upon which the wine was produced, was still in native hands. It seems probable that their production centre is to be found at sites 4.2-4.4 and at the kiln site of Fontscaldes, for overfired examples (not wasters) were found at both sites (fig. 5.16). The implication of a later 2nd to early 1st-c. B.C. date for the latter kiln is compatible with the revised chronology for the site (Lafuente 1992). The second phase is the first phase generally ascribed to Tarraconensian amphorae (Nolla and Solias 1984-85), generally dating to the mid 1st c. B.C. to early 1st c. A.D., and comprising Types 23 and 24 in the Tarraconensian fabrics (12 and 13). These are often ascribed to Laietania, the coastal region N of Barcelona. However, the fabric suggests that the examples from the survey were manufactured in the territory of Tarraco even though no kiln site has yet been found.

During the first two centuries A.D. production is dominated by Type 25, although a range of rarer forms was also manufactured (Types 26, 27, 28, 29 and 30). The kilns manufacturing some were known before the survey — at Mas de Coll, La Boada, Els Antigons, Timba del Castellet, and Molins Nous (Chapter 2), and further afield. Nevertheless, Tarraconensian amphorae of

Type 25 are rarely attested outside the region, undoubtedly reflecting an unfamiliarity with this production and its fabric among researchers in France, Spain and Italy. The tradition of amphora manufacture in the region is long and not simply a product of Roman influence. Its apparent disappearance in the course of the 2nd c. A.D. deserves attention and requires some explanation.

The main point of interest concerns imported amphorae. In the first instance one should note the great volume of Italic wine amphorae of Republican date (Types 15, 16, 17, 18 and 19). Careful characterization of the fabrics points to a wide range of suppliers, although the market at Tarraco was undoubtedly dominated by amphorae produced in the Bay of Naples (fabric 6). Otherwise, the range of imported types present on sites is fairly typical of the east coast of Spain generally, although the range of South Gaulish types is limited and Dressel 20 (Type 33) appears to be rare. Finally, late African types are supplied to rural sites in the survey area as they were to Tarraco until the late 6th-early 7th c. However, the absence of Roman types from the east Mediterranean is notable.

## COARSEWARES

Little can be said about local production given the fragmentary nature of the material. Nevertheless, if one assumes that each of the regional fabrics characterized is identified with a separate potter or workshop, it demonstrates that there would have been a number of relatively small-scale suppliers on local estates. It would be interesting to establish whether they were supplying Tarraco alone or whether their products were exported elsewhere along the Mediterranean coast.

The range of imported Italian coarsewares during the Republic is limited, which is curious given the range of Italian amphorae present. The same is true of the African Cooking Wares; Hayes forms 196 and 197 predominate, but the absence of other known variants is paralleled by the limited number of early African amphorae (Keay Type III, etc).

## FINEWARES

Little is new apart from the gathering of a good sample of the range of Iberian finewares current in the region during the Iberian/Republican period. Two kiln sites are known, at Fontscaldes and site 4.2-4.4. A recent analysis of material from the former (Lafuente 1992) suggests that this kiln functioned from at least the later 2nd c. B.C. until the 1st c. B.C. Apart from Iberian amphorae and the imitation Italian Types 6, 7, 8 and 9 it manufactured traditional Iberian fineware forms, kalathoi and hemispherical plates, and local imitations of Campana A. The material from Fontscaldes is often ascribed a very wide distribution. There are claims, for example, that Fontscaldes materials have been found at sites in southern France and Italy. In the survey only Type 2 was sufficiently similar to types known to have been produced at Fontscaldes to point to an origin there. It was manufactured in fabrics 14/16 and 20. The form was common throughout the survey. The fragmentary nature of the survey material makes it difficult to detect other forms of the Fontscaldes repertoire. Moreover, there is nothing about the Fontscaldes fabric to distinguish it from the predominant regional Iberian fabric 14/16. The available evidence suggests that Fontscaldes was probably one of a number of workshops throughout the area of the survey producing a range of different forms in a broadly similar fabric, and not unlike many others on the east coast during the 2nd and earlier 1st c. B.C.

The fragmentary state of the Roman material makes it difficult to assess variations from established typologies, which was one of the reasons why it was decided not to publish drawings. It is interesting to note, however, that sites in the survey continued to import African Red Slip until the 7th c., as did Tarraco itself. Nevertheless, one should perhaps note the absence of east Mediterranean sigillatas and late-Roman Phocaean Red Ware, all of which are attested at Tarraco.

## CERAMIC OBJECTS

1. Tegula stamped LHEROPT. This stamp is well known and can be expanded to read L(ucius) Herennius Opt(atus). Significant numbers have been found at the villa and production site for early imperial amphorae at Torre Llauder (Mataro) (Miró 1988, 37-40),N of Barcelona, and are quite common elsewhere in Catalunya, Rousillon, and Languedoc. The fabric suggests that it was produced in the Maresme (Barcelona) region.
   Fabric 12. Site 2.7, Campo 526 (Fig.5.18)
2. Kiln furniture. Fabric 13. Site 2.6, Campo 497 (Fig. 5.18)
3. Miscellaneous bell-shaped object. Fabric 13. Site 2.7, Campo 525 (Fig. 5.18)

## WORKED STONE

1. Border of a stone sill with a carved channel. Site 2.3, Campo 759 (Fig. 5.54)
2. Possible fragment of an inscribed plaque. Site 2.3, Campo 759 (Fig. 5.54)
3. Fragment of a stone ledge. Site 2.3, Campo 759 (Fig. 5.54)

## STONE ARTEFACTS

1. Hard limestone quern stone. Site 1.10, Campo 270. (Fig. 5.67.5)
2. Grey limestone trapetum. Site 1.10, Campo 270. (Fig. 5.67.2)
3. Small column base in yellow Medol limestone. Site 1.10, Campo 270. (Fig. 5.67.1)
4. Two grey limestone column shafts. Site 1.10, Campo 270. (Fig. 5.67.3, 5.67.4)

## COINS

1. Bronze 'As' of KESE (Villaronga 1983, issue 12). First half of 2nd c. B.C.

   Obverse: head of youth (r), spear point behind (l).

   Reverse: horseman holding palm and moving (r), below the legend 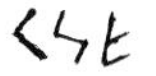

   Diameter 25 mm.

   Axes ↑↑

   Site 1.7, Campo 168.

2. Bronze 'As' of KESSE (Villaronga 1983, type uncertain). Probably 2nd c. B.C.

   Obverse: head of youth (r), otherwise worn.

   Reverse: horseman holding palm and moving (r), otherwise worn. Legend below illegible

   Diameter 24 mm.

   Axes ↑↑

   Site 1.10, Campo 270.

## MISCELLANEOUS SMALL FINDS

1. Ancient bronze fibula. Site 2.3, Campo 759. (Fig. 5.63.18)
2. Ancient bronze fibula. Site 2.3, Campo 759. (Figs. 5.63.20 and 5.70)
3. Inlaid plaque of uncertain date. Site 2.3, Campo 759. (Fig. 5.63.19)

***MISCELLANEOUS FINDS***

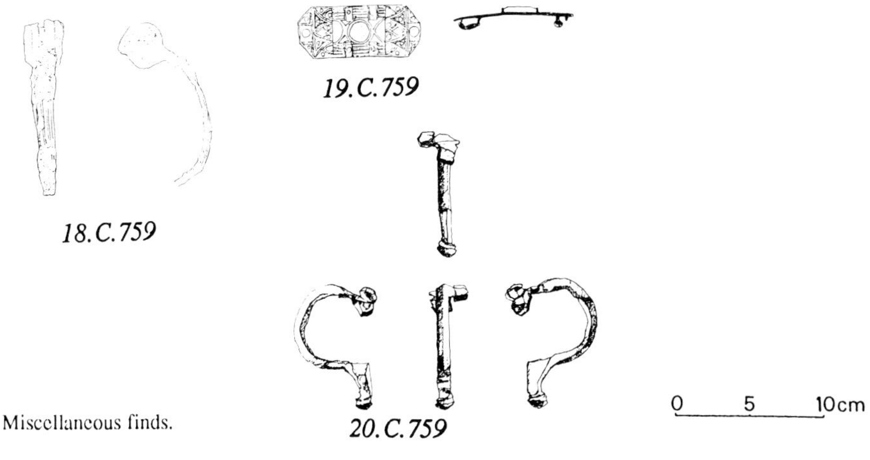
19.C.759
18.C.759
20.C.759
0 5 10cm

Fig.5. 63 cont. Miscellaneous finds.

163

STONE ARTEFACTS

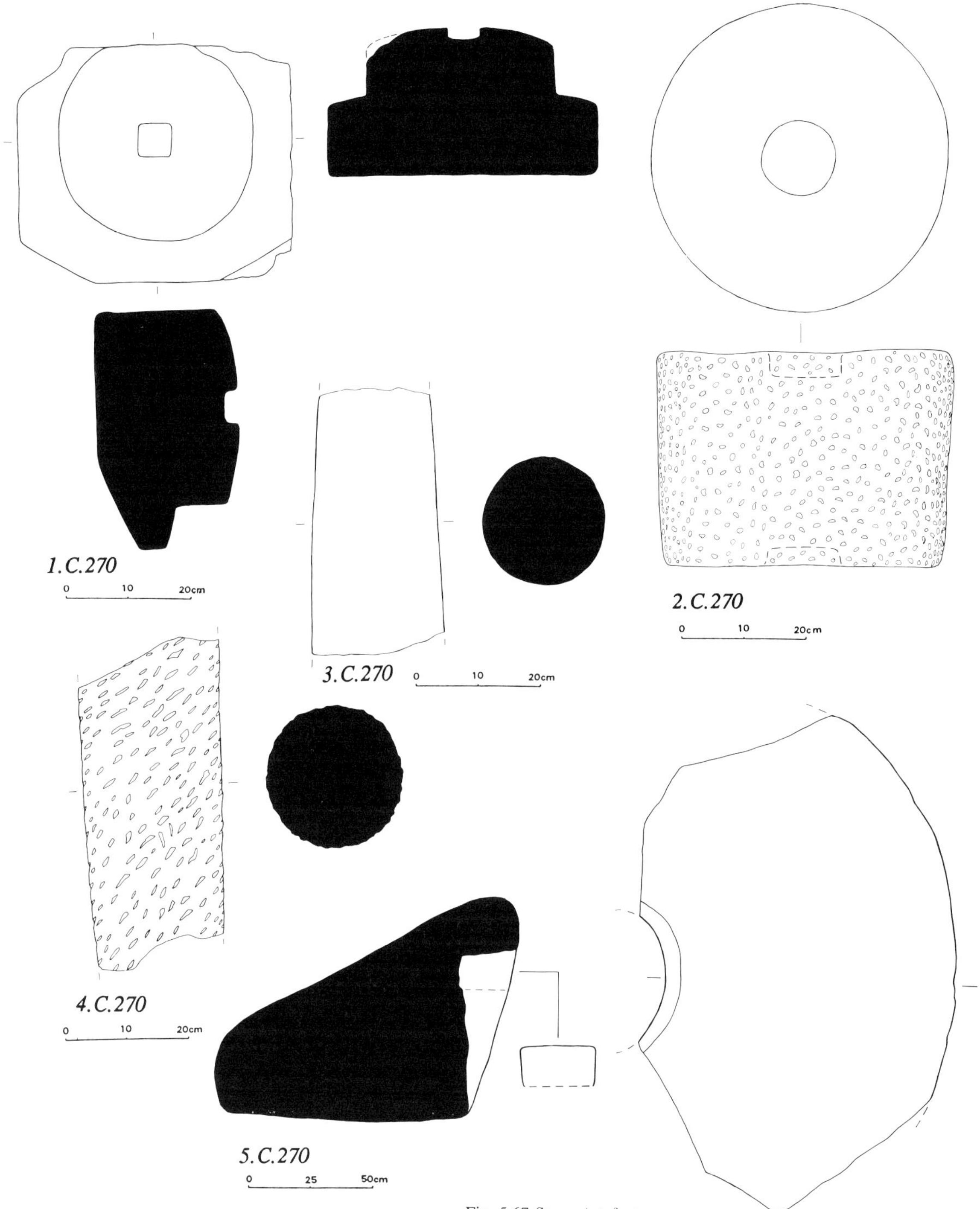

1.C.270

0    10    20cm

2.C.270

0    10    20cm

3.C.270    0    10    20cm

4.C.270

0    10    20cm

5.C.270

0    25    50cm

Fig. 5.67 Stone Artefacts.

# THE HUMAN BONES FROM SITE 2.3
## *By Cyndy Winter*

The human remains found on field 758 were in a pile in the northeast corner of the field. The pile also contained large amphora sherds, and the remains had presumably been placed there during agricultural work. Survey of this and the adjacent fields failed to reveal further human remains, although a large amount of recent animal bone was present.

The bones had clearly been weathered for some time, all showing a high degree of surface abrasion. The texture of the remains suggested repeated episodes of soaking and drying and all the bones were fragile, with a tendency to crumble. None was complete, but the breaks were not inconsistent with damage from being dragged to the surface in the recent past. Only limited measurements were possible, due to the breaks and the severe state of abrasion.

No attempt was made to date the material, which consists of 4 skull fragments, 1 clavicle, 1 humerus including the distal but not the proximal end, 1 ulna with distal end, 1 radius distal end, 1 vertebra, 4 pelvic pieces, 3 femur proximal ends, with a small amount of shaft, 1 femur shaft, and 1 femur distal end. On the basis of the pelves, at least three individuals are present.

Age assessment has been possible to some extent on the basis of epiphyseal fusion. All of the remains are of adults. There appears to be a female aged 20+, a male aged 20+, and an older male. It is not possible to rule out additional individuals being present.

The remains recovered are:

1. Left mastoid process, very heavy, with squamous part of temporal. Probably male.
2. Partial occipital with nearly obliterated coronal suture just visible.
3. Partial occipital with very open coronal suture visible.
4. Left clavicle, poor state of preservation, severely abraded and 'crumbling'. Measurements not possible.
5. Left humerus, distal end to surgical neck. Length approximaely 283 mm. Strongly defined deltoid tuberosity, epiphyseal fusion complete. The length of this bone would indicate a male, and would not be out of proportion on an individual over 1.8 m (6 feet) tall. It is, however, quite gracile, indicating poorly developed musculature.
6. Left ulna, distal end. Epiphyseal fusion complete.
7. Fragmentary left radius, distal end, epiphyseal fusion complete.
8. Complete fifth lumbar vertebra, poorly preserved, large.
9. Left upper pelvic fragment, including large partial acetabulum and strong inferior iliac spine.
10. Right pelvic fragment, including large ischial tuberosity, and wide partial greater sciatic notch. Probably not a pair to item 9 above. Probably female.
11. Right pelvic fragment, including partial iliac crest with lines of fusion visible, and narrow partial greater sciatic notch. Probably male aged 20+. Probably not a pair to item 10 above.
12. Left pelvic fragment, including wide partial greater sciatic notch. Probably female. Possibly pair to item 10 above.
13. Left femur proximal end, maximum diameter of head 32 mm, heavy greater trochanter and lesser trochanters. Line of epiphyseal fusion nearly obliterated. Probably male (on basis of robusticity of remains) aged 25+.
14. Left femur proximal end, maximum diameter of head 27 mm, trochanters quite light. Line of epipyseal fusion fairly visible. Probably female (on basis of size) aged 20+.
15. Right femur proximal end, maximum diameter of head 27 mm, very similar to item 14 above, probably same individual, probably female aged 20+.
16. Right diaphyseal femur, quite robust, possibly from same individual as item 15 above. Broken longitudinally, measurements not possible. Trace of lesser trochanter visible.
17. Right femur distal end. Bi-condylar breadth approximately 79 mm, epiphyseal fusion complete, not part of same bone as item 16 above.

Fig.5.68 Site 4.1, Campo 884. One of the Iberian stamps on a Type 8 amphora in fabric 9 (cf. fig.15.5).

Fig. 5.69 Site 4.1 Campo 885. The other Iberian stamp on a Type 8 amphora in fabric 9   (cf. fig. 5.15).

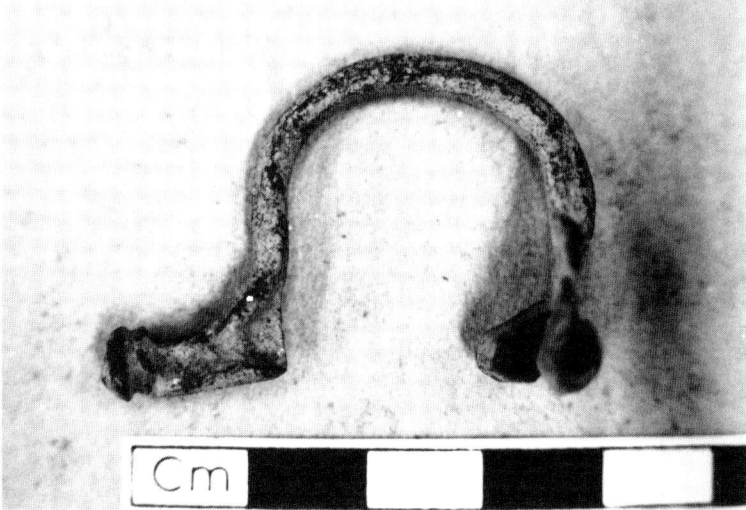

Fig.5.70 Site 2.3 Campo 759. Copper alloy brooch (cf. fig.5.63).

KEY for alternate figures in this chapter (6.3, 6.5, 6.7, etc.).

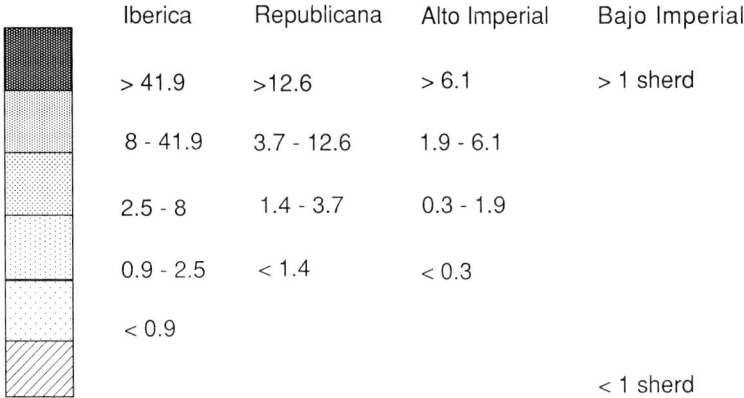

| | Iberica | Republicana | Alto Imperial | Bajo Imperial |
|---|---|---|---|---|
| | > 41.9 | >12.6 | > 6.1 | > 1 sherd |
| | 8 - 41.9 | 3.7 - 12.6 | 1.9 - 6.1 | |
| | 2.5 - 8 | 1.4 - 3.7 | 0.3 - 1.9 | |
| | 0.9 - 2.5 | < 1.4 | < 0.3 | |
| | < 0.9 | | | |
| | | | | < 1 sherd |

Fig.6.1. Scales used for mapping ceramic densities in the individual transects. For the methods used to establish the values, see p.57 ff. and Table 4.2.

# Chapter 6: THE IDENTIFICATION OF SITES

It has already been noted that one of the characteristics of this region is the rarity of structural remains in the countryside. Most of the sites in this survey were visible only through traces of ceramics and building materials on the surface. In this chapter the pottery distributions are examined in order to identify potential settlements. The distributions are described in relation to the geography of the transects, and individual problems of interpretation are discussed.

## TRANSECT-BY-TRANSECT DESCRIPTIONS

In order to present the evidence each transect has been divided into sections (Transect 1/A, Transect 1/B etc.) which will be discussed individually (for locations see fig. 3.1). Within each section of a transect a standardized presentation is followed. Three sets of maps are provided for each section:
(a) a simplified topographic map showing the location and numbering of each identified site;
(b) a plan showing the fields walked and the numbers assigned to them;
(c) a set of four maps showing the distribution of ceramics of the 4 *ceramic* phases.
Given the chronological overlap between certain pottery types, the term 'phase' is used in its broad sense. The scales used on the pottery distribution maps are those established in Chapter 4 (see Table 4.2 and fig. 6.1). The sets of maps are presented on facing pages to enable the reader to identify field numbers and compare the ceramic distributions with the conclusions drawn. Tables 6.1 - 6.4 (pp.212-14) summarize the fields identified as settlements. The sites themselves are numbered within each transect from W to E as Site 1.1, Site 1.2, etc.

The general pottery dating is based on the chronological ranges of the fabrics present; the more precise dates for each site are based on the occurrence of diagnostic forms. Since off-site scatters of pottery were widespread, forms dated outside the main range occasionally occur. Fuller details of the ceramic types found on each site are provided in Appendix 6.

Transect 1/A (figs. 6.2-6.3)

This area was relatively low-lying, mostly between 50 and 75 m asl. At the W end the ground gently slopes from NW to SE. It is cut by the valley of the Barranc de la Selva before rising to the ridge on which the town of Constantí is built. To the E of the town the ground falls to the terrace of the river Francolí at the E of this sector. The area is heavily cultivated and it was possible to achieve a good coverage. There was a relatively high background density of material, making the identification of sites and the definition of their boundaries difficult. The following have been identified:

*Site 1.1*

A very small 'adabs' evident only in the Republican phase. Some tile is present. The pottery shows that it was occupied during the 2nd and/or 1st c. B.C. This is perhaps the most doubtful potential site in transect 1/A as the surrounding area was mostly inaccessible for walking. It is situated on almost level ground.

*Site 1.2*

An extensive 'adabs' which is clearly evident in the Iberian and Republican phases, declined in the early empire, and disappeared by the late empire. The pottery forms span a range from the 5th c. B.C. to the late 3rd to mid 5th c. A.D. The fields were surrounded by others with relatively good visibility. There are some indications of a shift in focus towards the E in the early empire but there is little ambiguity over the general limits of the concentration. There was a also strong concentration of tile leaving little doubt that it was a settlement. The site lies

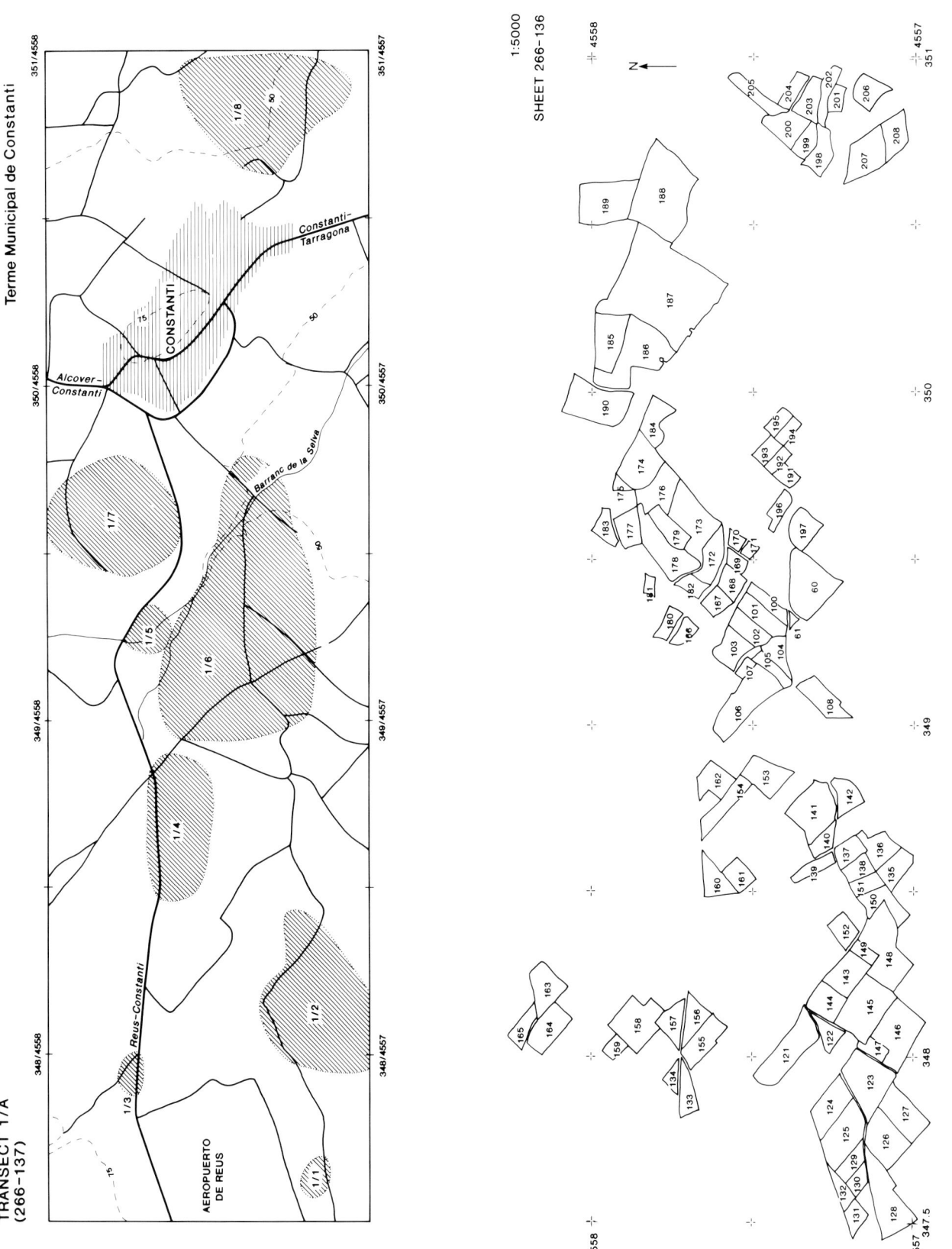

Fig.6.2. Transect 1/A: topography, site locations and field numbers.

1/A Iberica

1/A Republicana

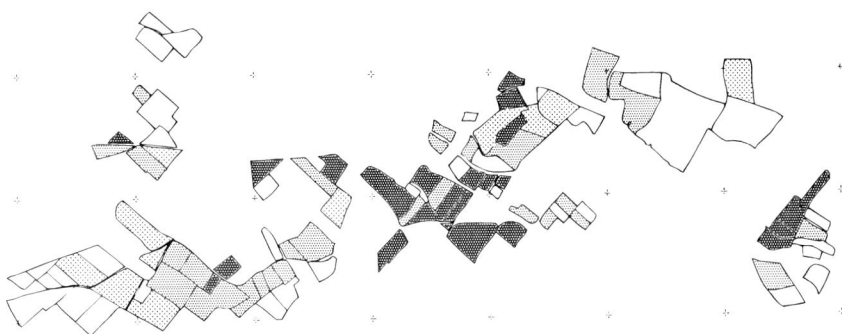

1/A Alto Imperial

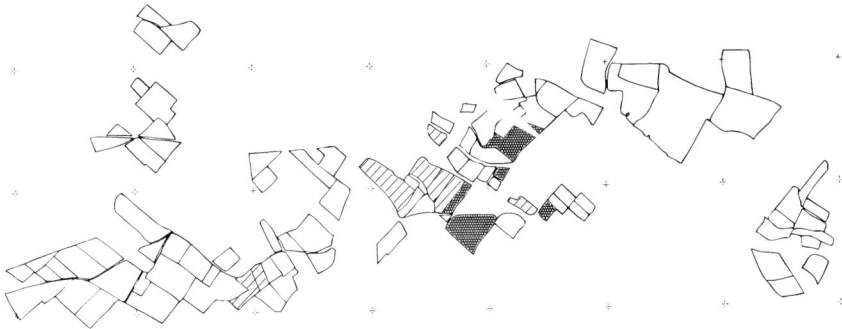

1/A Bajo Imperial

Fig.6.3. Transect 1A: densities of pottery.

on a minor ridge with the land falling away to N and S, and with a shallow valley immediately to the E. Its position dominates the immediate area despite the moderate topography.

*Site 1.3*

A small 'adabs' evident only during the early imperial phase. The pottery forms date to between the 1st and early 2nd c. A.D. The shortage of adjacent fields available for walking make it difficult to assess. A small concentration of tile is insufficient to confirm identification as a settlement. It lies on land which slopes very gently to the SE.

*Site 1.4*

A group of 'adabs' interspersed with fields which were not available for walking, making definition difficult. The concentration is strong through the Iberian, Republican and early imperial phases but absent during the late empire. The ceramic forms span the period from the 5th c. B.C. to at least the end of the 2nd c. A.D. The large assemblage of pottery suggests a substantial site. An ample collection of tile supports this identification. The site lies at the top of a slight slope with the ground falling away NE towards the barranc. The site to dominates the stream valley in a manner similar to other sites further E.

*Site 1.5*

A small 'adabs' which appears as a minor concentration through the Iberian and Republican phases, and continues at a lower intensity to the late empire. The ceramics suggest activity starting at some date between the 5th and 1st c. B.C., continuing into the later empire. Its core is separated from Site 1.6 by the barranc. Although it is difficult to judge, it may be considered part of Site 1.7. A small group of tile is insufficient to support its identification as a settlement. It is situated on the N side of the barranc on its flood plain. The ground rises fairly steeply behind the site to the NE. It is possible that soil containing the finds has eroded from the slope. On balance, there appears to be sufficient material present over time to support the identification of a small settlement.

*Site 1.6*

A substantial 'adabs' which runs from the Iberian phase to the late empire. The forms present suggest activity from the 5th c. B.C. to the 4th/ 5th c. A.D. A substantial concentration of tile supports the identification as a settlement. The sunken trackways which cut through it have exposed *opus signinum* floors and fragments of walls at the edges of fields 61 and 100. The site, now rather dispersed, was focused on the ridge; the highest densities are found in fields 60, 61 and the area immediately to the NW. It dominates the W side of the barranc, the land falling away gently to N, S and E. It is not clear to what extent the spread of material down the slopes is the result of original patterns of distribution rather than a product of modern erosion, but in view of the gentle slopes it is best to assume that it was orginally a large site. This site was previously known (see Table 1.1, Gazetteer no. 86)

*Site 1.7*

A rather unevenly concentrated collection of 'adabs' which appears to represent a large site. The surface visibility in these and surrounding fields was poor as most were abandoned and overgrown. This accounts for the uneven pattern of densities and the rather sparse finds. There is sufficient material to suggest occupation in both early and late imperial phases. Lesser concentrations during earlier phases may be no more than a background scatter. The pottery suggests activity from the 2nd c. B.C. to the 7th c. A.D. A coin dated to the first half of the 2nd c. B.C. (see p.162) was recovered from field 168. These densities coincide with a modest scatter of tile. The concentration lies on a bluff overlooking the barranc with the ground falling away to the S. Extensive erosion of the hilltop partly accounts for the uneven pattern of distribution.

*Site 1.8*

A strong concentration of 'adabs' through the Iberian, Republican and early imperial phases but with an absence of late imperial material. Other fields in the vicinity had poorer visibility but the concentration seemed fairly well defined. The ceramic forms suggest activity beginning in the early 5th c. B.C. and continuing until sometime just after the early 3rd c. A.D. A modest concentration of tile covers the same fields. Field 206 lay on top of the ridge but the other fields with the highest concentrations lay towards the bottom of the slope facing NE just above the terrace of the Francolí. It is possible that this results from downslope soil-movement, but the concentration suggests a settlement hereabouts.

Transect 1/B (figs. 6.4-6.5)

The W part of this sector crosses the terrace of the Francolí, which flows N-S here. The low-lying floodplain together with the broad terrace to its W are dominated by hazelnut groves which were not available for walking. To the E of the river the ground rises steeply to a plateau along the edge of which runs the Lleida-Tarragona road (N-240). Occasional cultivated plots amongst the *maqui* allowed limited walking in this zone. Broken higher land continues to the E but it is largely wooded. An area of lower ground is found within a minor valley near the centre of the transect but most of it had not been mapped at the 1:5,000 scale. On the higher land at the E end of the sector larger areas of cultivated land were available for walking. The broken character of the landscape, the high density of woodland, and the problem of lack of detailed maps meant that it was not possible to obtain a very full coverage of land walked in this part of the transect. Only one site was identified:

*Site 1.9*

A strong 'adabs' which remains through all four phases although strongest in the Iberian and Republican phases. The ceramic forms suggest that activity began in the 5th c. B.C. and continued up to the early 5th c. A.D. No tile was associated. Despite poor visibility in field 276 and the absence of adjacent cultivated land, the concentration was well defined and it seems likely that fields 275 and 276 represent its full extent. They lie on the edge of the plateau at the point where the ground falls steeply to the SE. There has been some soil movement caused by terracing but it does not appear to have moved the material far from its original position. This was a typical small settlement.

Transect 1/C (figs. 6.6-6.7)

Between Transects 1/B and 1/C where the wooded uplands reach as high as 150 m asl the landscape has not yet been mapped at 1:5,000. To the E the land falls to a lower level but it remains generally wooden and rugged. Only a single area of cultivated land was available for walking, in the vicinity of the Urbanització Pinalbert beside the Tarragona-El Catllar road. Only one site was located:

*Site 1.10*

A sharply defined 'adabs' which continues through the Iberian, Republican and early imperial phases, disappearing by the late empire. The ceramic forms suggest that activity began by the earlier 2nd c. B.C. and continued until at least the later 2nd c. A.D. A worn coin, probably of the 2nd c. B.C. (see p.162), was recovered from field 270. Architectural fragments found on the site and now in the garden of the farmhouse Mas Clarà appear to be Roman and suggest the presence of a substantial building. They comprise a square column base *c.*50 x 50 cm with a plain column (*c.*40 cm diameter) and two fragments of a plain column drum of slightly smaller diameter (see p.162). Almost no tile was recovered. The site lies at the summit of a hill situated at the S end of a ridge. The land falls away to the W, S and N, the fields being terraced to the S. This has resulted in some redeposition of material, but the distribution is still tightly defined.

172

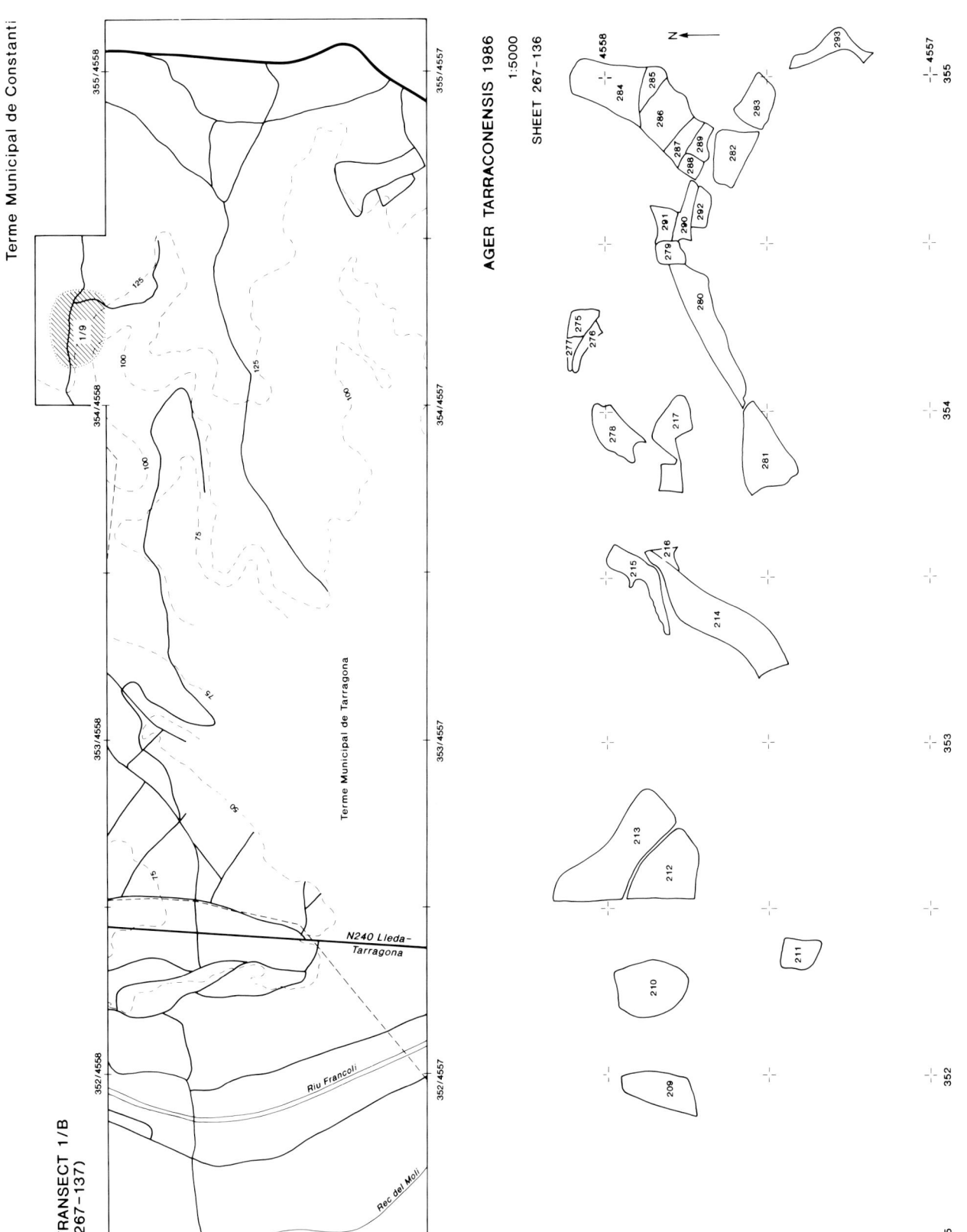

Fig.6.4. Transect 1/B: topography, site locations and field numbers.

173

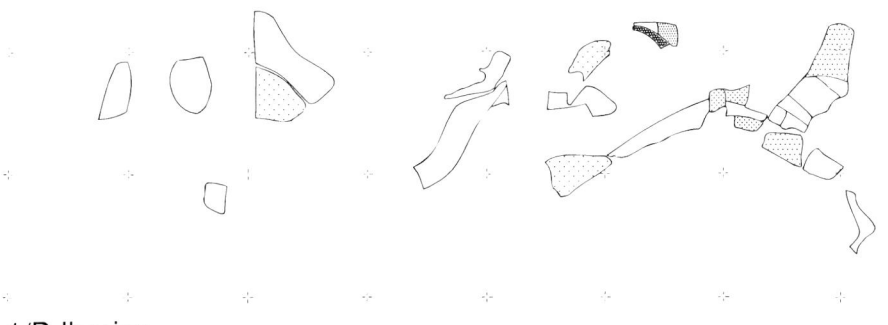

1/B Iberica

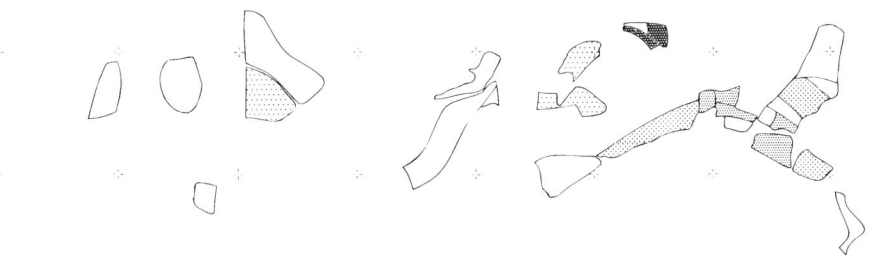

1/B Republicana

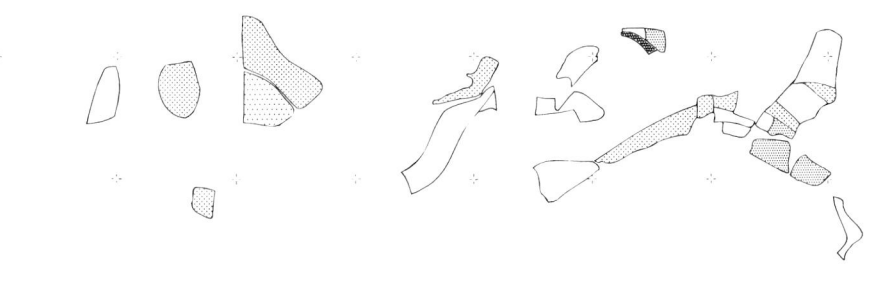

1/B Alto Imperial

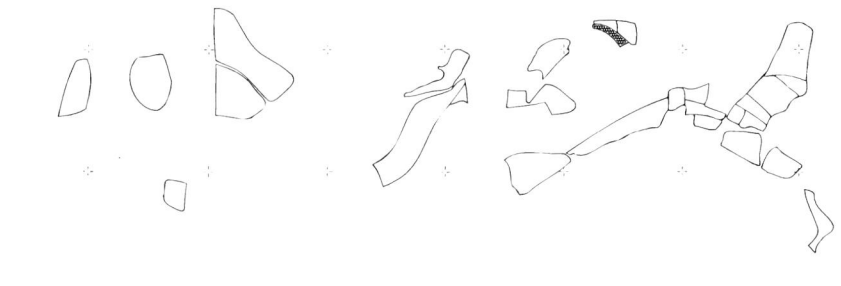

1/B Bajo Imperial

Fig.6.5. Transect 1B: densities of pottery.

174

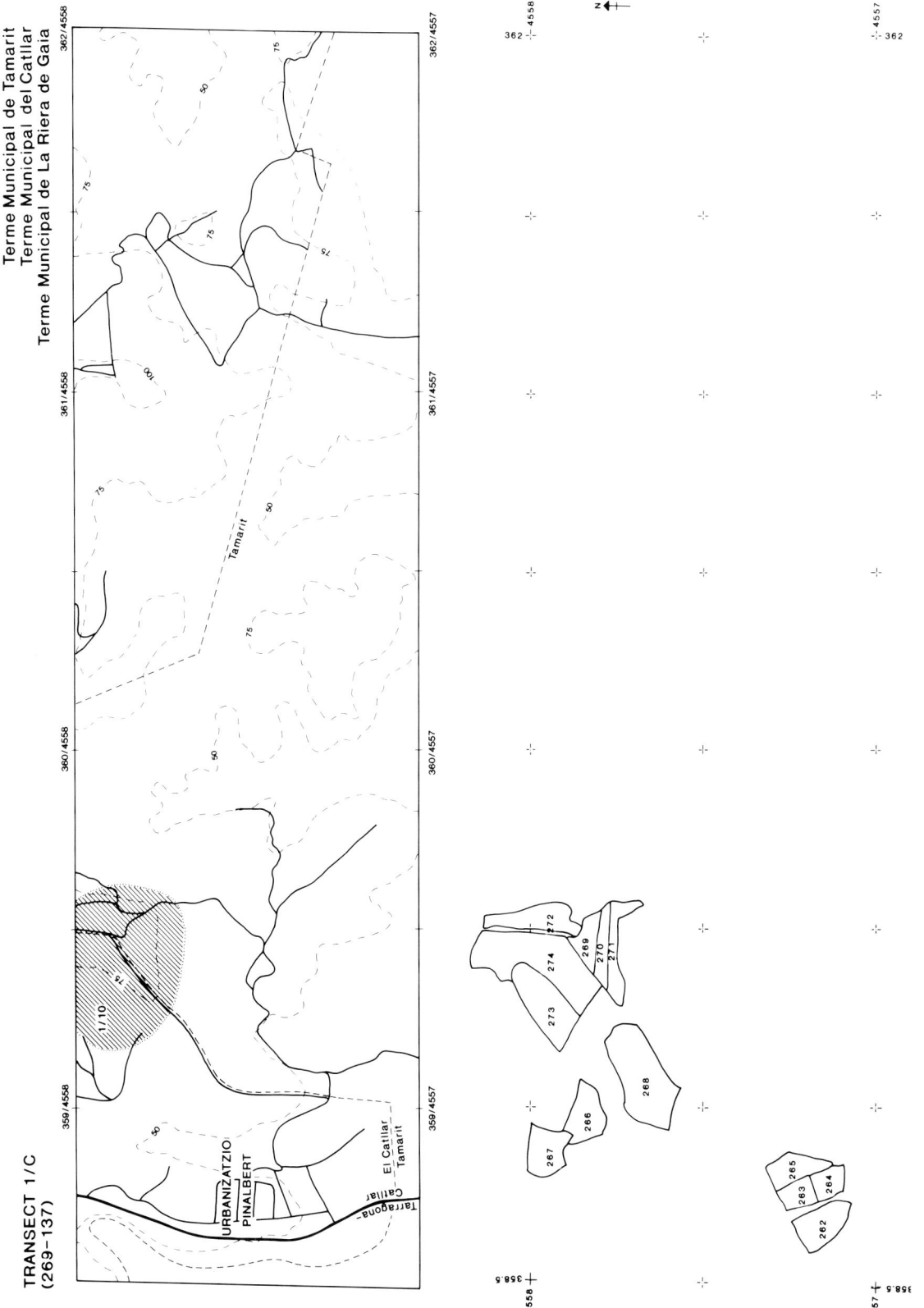

Fig.6.6. Transect 1/C: topography, site locations and field numbers.

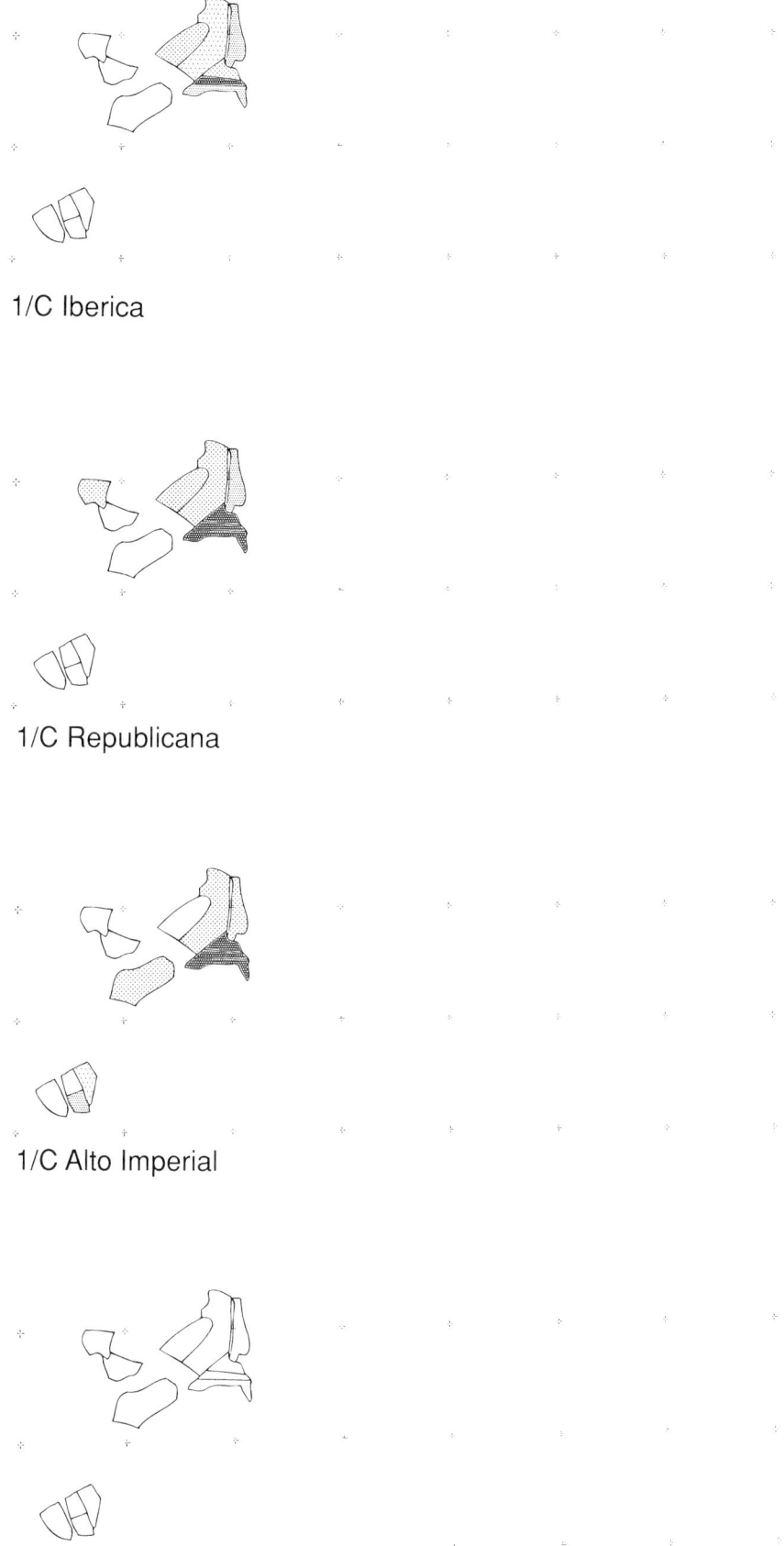

1/C Iberica

1/C Republicana

1/C Alto Imperial

1/C Bajo Imperial

Fig.6.7. Transect 1C: densities of pottery.

176

The bedrock of the hilltop immediately behind the farmhouse has been cut back to define a subrectagular platform c.1.8 m high. It measures c.40 m E-W by 100 m N-S and has evidently been used as a building platform. Without excavation it is impossible to establish its date, but as it forms the focus of the site it may well be Roman. The platform dominates the land to the S and has clear views to the coast. It would have made a fine situation for a villa, although its topography and dominant position may equally suggest a temple.

Transect 1/D (figs. 6.8-6.9)

At the E end of this sector the higher ground is cut by a loop of the river Gaià, the narrow valley of which provides a little arable land. The slopes to the W of the river were covered with small terraced fields, some of which we walked. To the E the land rose to a ridge before falling more gently SE towards the boundary of the Terme Municipal of Torredembarra. The higher ground and the fields on the E side of the Gaià valley were largely abandoned; former arable land covered in scrub provided poor visibility and few opportunities for walking. The slope facing SE was better cultivated, enabling us to achieve a reasonable density of coverage. The following sites were located:

*Site 1.11*

A small and relatively well-defined 'adabs' which appears to represent a small settlement. It is strongly defined in the Iberian phase, with less intensive concentrations of Republican and early imperial material. The ceramic forms suggest activity from the 5th c. B.C. to 1st c. A.D. There was virtually no associated tile. The site is located on the edge of the higher ground, on a slope facing E above the terrace of the Gaià.

*Site 1.12*

An 'adabs' with a large concentration of Iberian pottery, a lesser amount of Republican and early imperial material, and a couple of sherds dating to the late empire. The principal concentration was in field 118 with further pottery on the uphill, N edge of field 120. It seems likely that a settlement of similar scale to Site 1.11 had been dispersed downhill by erosion. The late imperial material may be related to the previously-known site beside the main road just SE of field 120 (Table 1.1 Site 79). The pottery forms suggest that activity began some time after the early 5th c. B.C. and continued to the 1st c. A.D. Only a very small amount of tile was associated with the pottery. The site was located on the S side of the ridge dominating a hollow facing SE on the slope above the Gaià.

*Site 1.13*

An 'adabs' that is most evident in the Iberian phase, with a lesser concentration in the Republic and early imperial phases. Despite the poor visibility in these recently abandoned fields, it seems a good candidate for another small settlement. The pottery recovered is largely confined to the period from the 5th to the 2nd or 1st c. B.C. There is also a small quantity of material of the 1st c. A.D. Almost no tile was associated. It lies just below the top of the ridge on an E-facing slope above good agricultural land.

*Site 1.14*

A densely concentrated 'adabs' that remains as a focus through all four phases. The pottery spans a range from the 5th c. B.C. to 5th c. A.D. A minor concentration of tile focused upon field 235. There is little doubt that it represents another small settlement. This conclusion is supported by the evidence of the geophyscial survey (see Chapter 7). The site is located on a S- and SE-facing slope which is now terraced. Despite some earth movement there is little evidence that finds have moved significantly.

*Possible site*

A minor concentration of pottery in field 220 may also represent a small settlement of the

Iberian period as visibility in this area is poorer than average, but it is not secure.

Transect 2/A (figs. 6.10-6.11)

This is lower ground within the Depressió Valls-Reus at an elevation of 150-200 m asl. It lies just S of the Riera de la Selva, a major tributary of the Francolí. The ground slopes gently from NW to SE with minor undulations created by the former seasonal streams. The whole area is heavily cultivated and there is widespread irrigation. As most of the land is used for hazelnuts, only limited areas could be walked. They were largely barren, and only one site was found.

*Site 2.1*

This 'adabs' lay just S of the boundary of the transect in an island of open ploughed land. Since the team was ejected from the field when only about 50% of it had been walked, the recorded densities represent a minimum value. The concentration was clearly defined and did not continue into the fields to the N which had equally good visibility. The 'adabs' appears in the Republican phase and continued to the late empire. There is a slight concentration of Iberian material but it lies below the 10 percentile range; had we been able to walk the whole field, it is probable that it would have exceeded this value. The limited number of pottery forms recovered suggest that activity began before the late 3rd c. B.C. Very little tile was recovered. Nevertheless, there is little doubt that it was a small settlement. It was situated in a dominant location on a slight ridge overlooking a barranc to the S.

*Potential sites*

Another minor concentration of Republican material in field 863 may suggest a site nearby but its centre was not located. Similarly a very light scatter of late imperial material in several fields in the NE part of the Transect may suggest a site nearby.

Transect 2/B (figs. 6.12-6.13)

The low-lying land of Transect 2/A continues across this sector which lies mostly between 150 and 100 m asl. It is crossed towards its E end by the Riera de Vilallonga (the eastwards continuation of the Riera de la Selva). On the land just above the stream on its W bank is the town of Vilallonga del Camp. At the extreme E end of the sector the edge of the Francolí terrace is reached. The land is heavily cultivated and widely irrigated. As hazelnut plantations restricted access only small areas could be walked.

No definite sites were located in this sector although a minor concentration of early imperial material in field 821 may suggest a site nearby. More difficult to evaluate are the three sherds of late imperial pottery in fields 800 and 801 on a hillock overlooking the E bank of the stream. The fields were overgrown and had poor visibility. In the absence of supporting evidence from other periods it is difficult to identify this as a settlement although it clearly deserves further investigation under better conditions. Its slightly elevated location above a stream is similar to that of other identified sites.

Transect 2/C (figs. 6.14-6.15)

The W part of this sector lies on a terrace of the Francolí just S of its confluence with the Riu Glorieta. On the E bank of the river is a much narrower terrace before the land rises steeply to a ridge at *c.*110 m asl. On the E side of that ridge the ground slopes gently to the SE and is crossed by the Lleida-Tarragona road (N-240). At the foot of the slope lies the deeply-cut valley of the Torrent del Bogatell. Above the stream on its E side is the village of Els Garidells. The land rises again behind the village to reach an elevation in excess of 125 m before sloping away to the SE. As the area was well cultivated with a mixture of vines, arable and tree crops, it proved possible to walk a reasonably good sample of the area. The fields were fairly densely covered in pottery and 3 sites were noted:

178

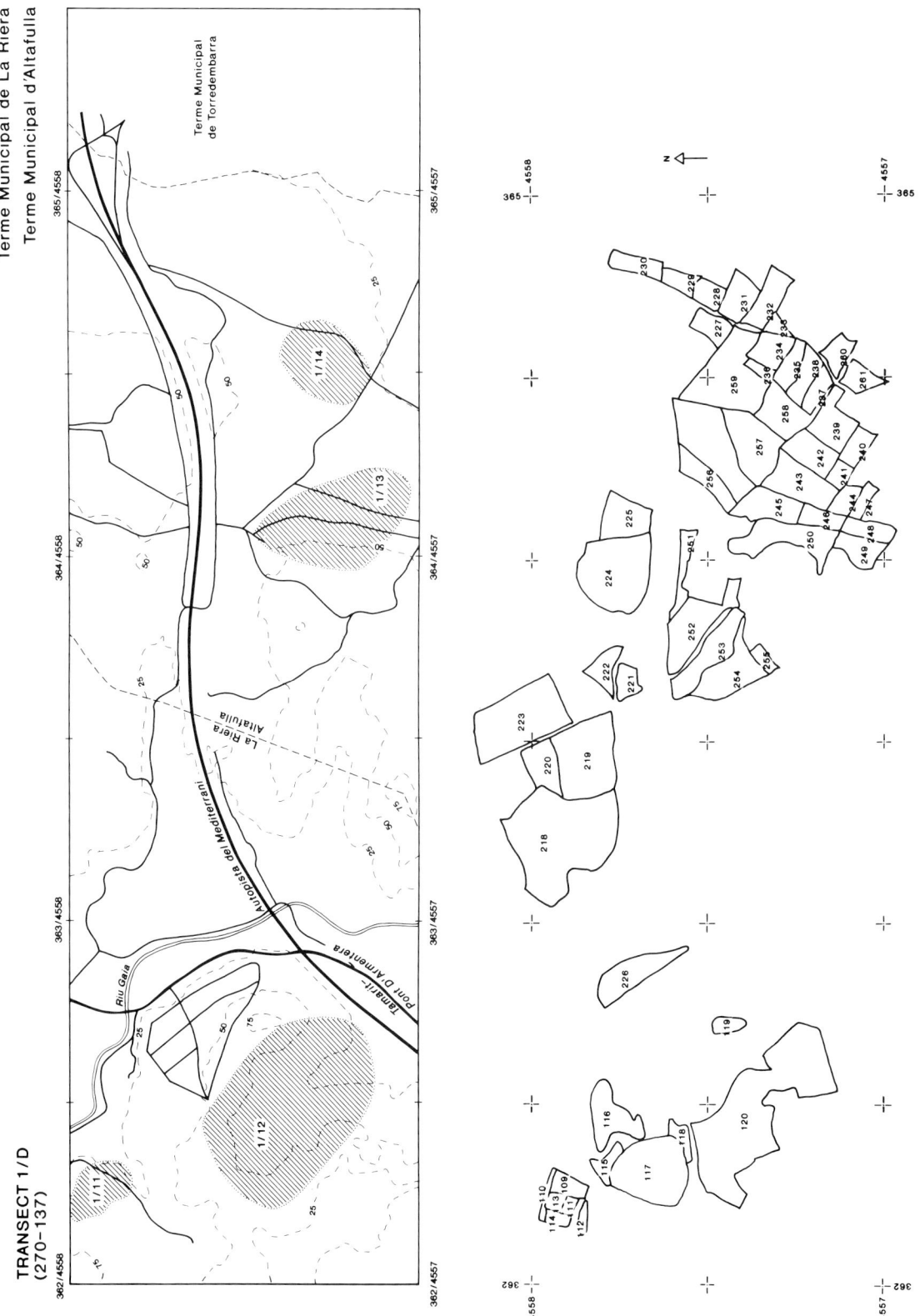

Fig.6.8. Transect 1/D: topography, site locations and field numbers.

1/D Iberica

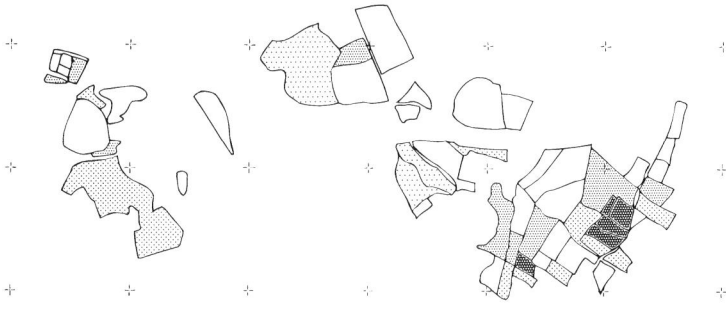

1/D Republicana

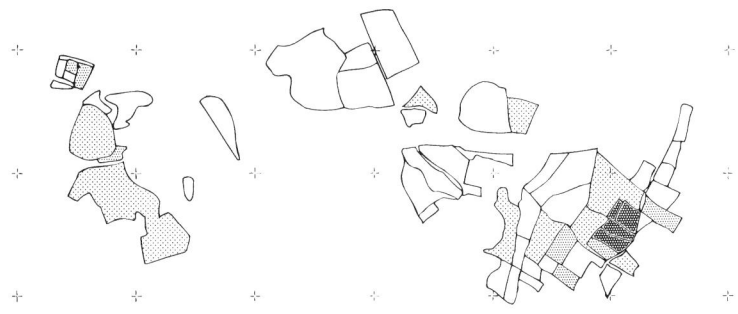

1/D Alto Imperial

1/D Bajo Imperial

Fig.6.9. Transect 1D: densities of pottery.

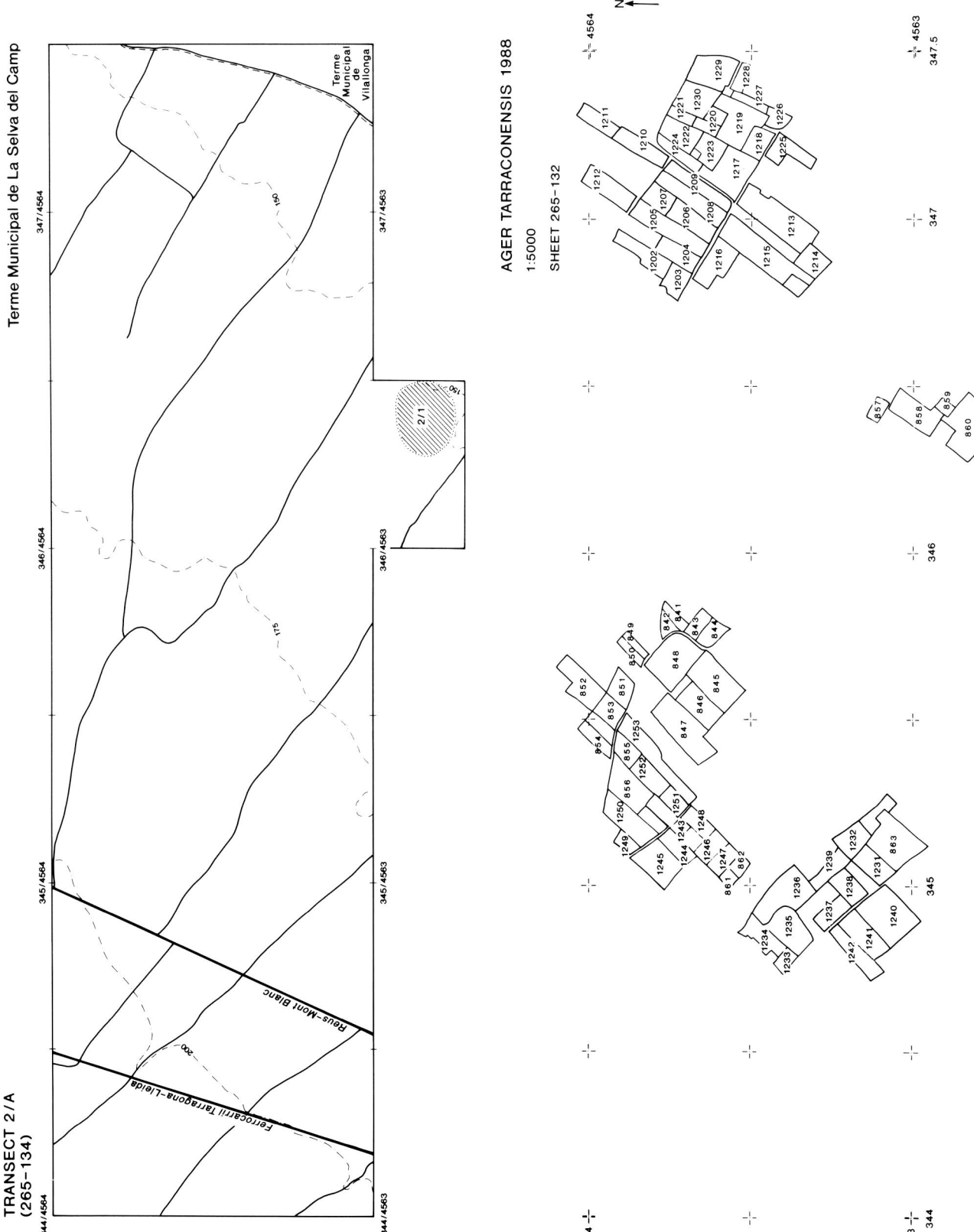

Fig.6.10. Transect 2/A: topography, site locations and field numbers.

181

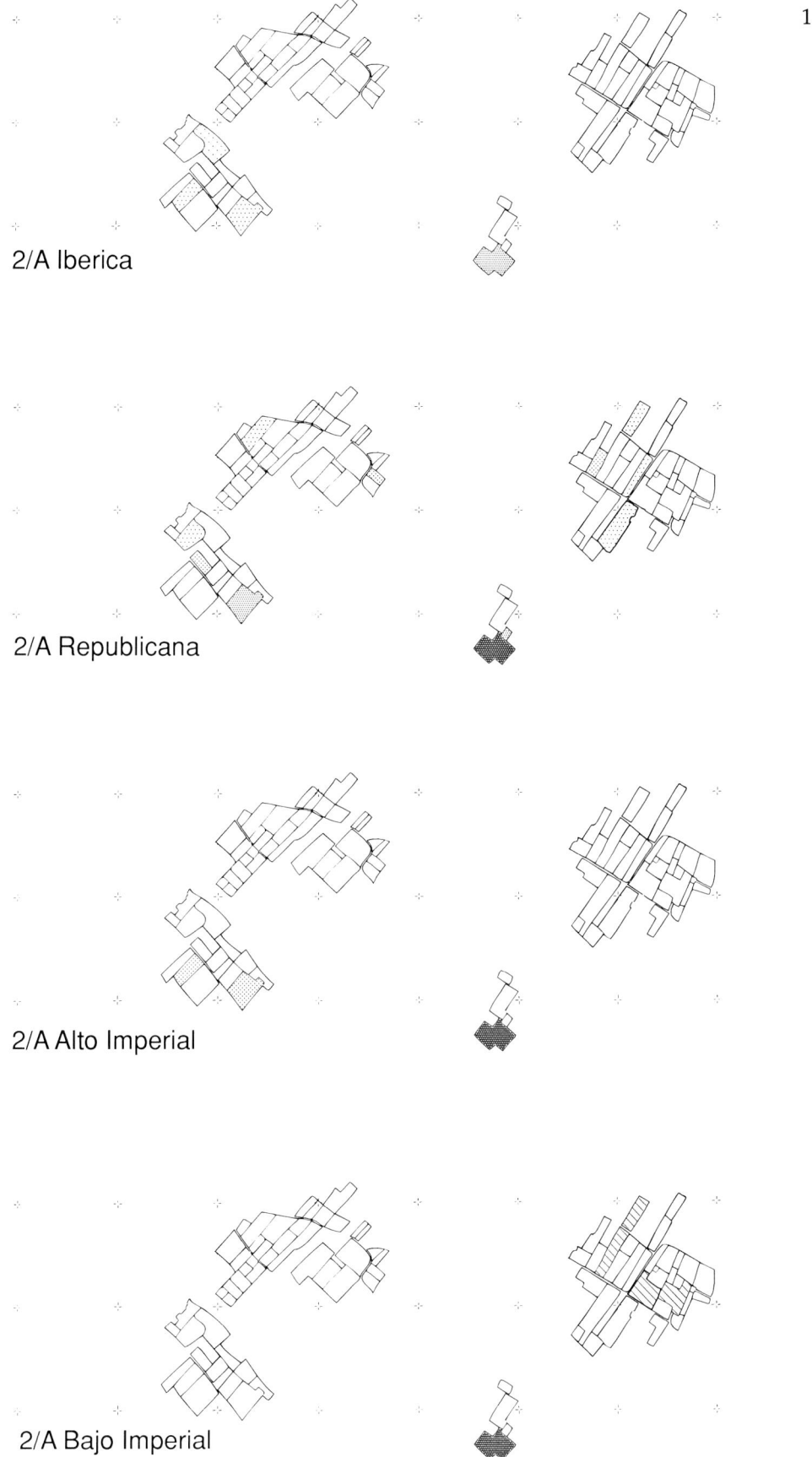

2/A Iberica

2/A Republicana

2/A Alto Imperial

2/A Bajo Imperial

Fig.6.11. Transect 2A: densities of pottery.

182

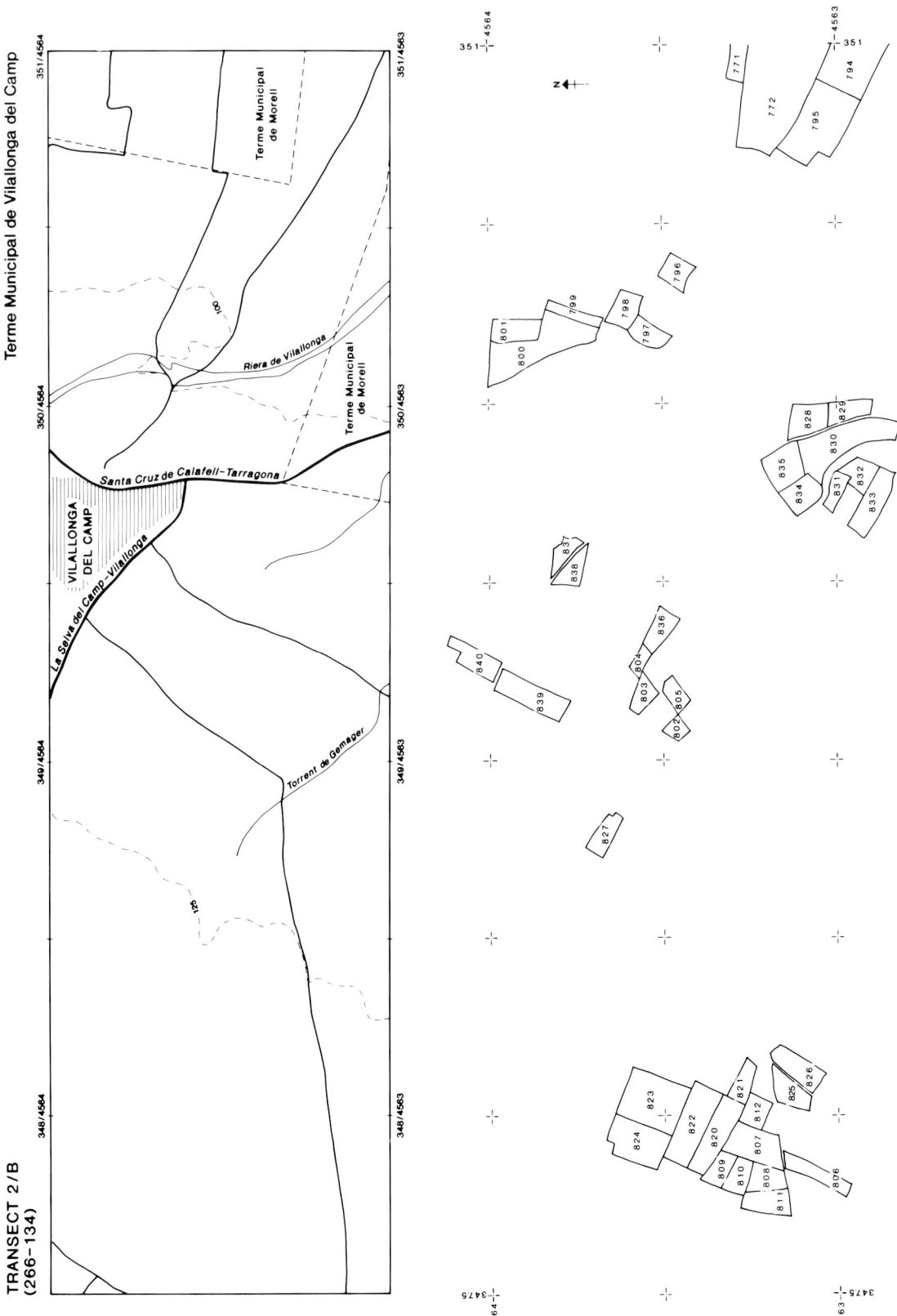

Fig.6.12. Transect 2/B: topography, site locations and field numbers.

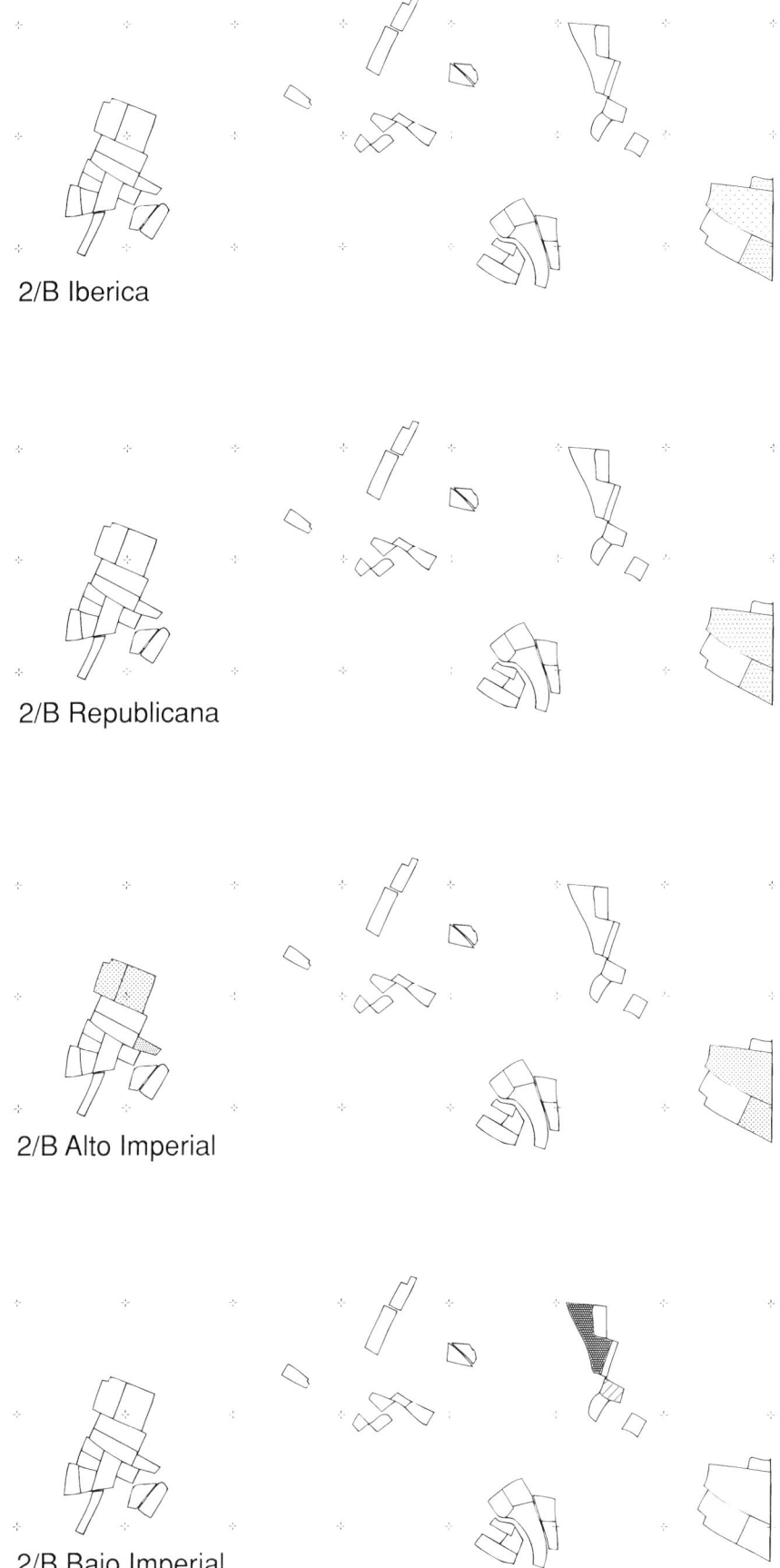

2/B Iberica

2/B Republicana

2/B Alto Imperial

2/B Bajo Imperial

Fig.6.13. Transect 2B: densities of pottery.

184

Fig.6.14. Transect 2/C: topography, site locations and field numbers.

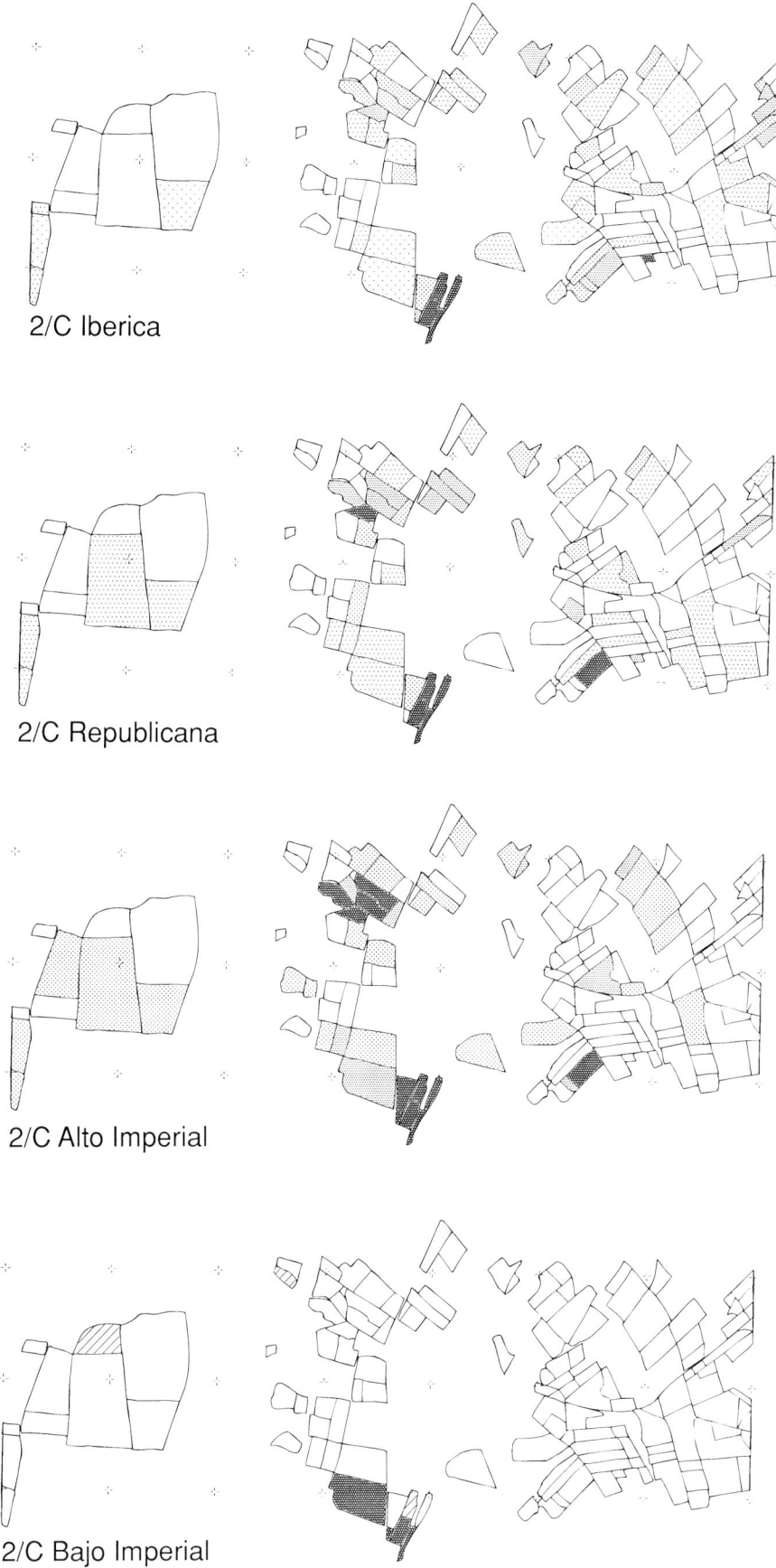

2/C Iberica

2/C Republicana

2/C Alto Imperial

2/C Bajo Imperial

Fig.6.15. Transect 2C: densities of pottery.

*Site 2.2*

A small 'adabs' which first appears during the Republican phase. It achieved its maximum extent during the early empire. The forms span a range from the 5th c. B.C. to late 2nd/early 5th c. A.D. A small amount of tile was associated with the pottery. These fields form a fairly tight cluster within an area of good visibility and are best interpreted as a small settlement. It lies on ground which slopes gently towards the S and SW.

*Site 2.3*

A strongly defined 'adabs' which lies partly outside the transect. It produced very high densities of material from the Iberian to late imperial phases, with the main focus in fields 758 and 759. The density of material points towards the presence of a settlement. However, bones from at least three human skeletons (see p.164) together with substantial fragments of *tegula* and amphora recently disturbed by the plough suggest that there was also a cemetery. There were probably late-Roman *tegula* and perhaps amphora burials similar to those found in at the Tobacco Factory (del Amo 1979-89) and the Parc de la Ciutat in Tarragona (TED'A 1987). The presence of cemeteries associated with rural settlements is known at several late-Roman sites in the region (Table 1.1) as well as at sites in NE Spain and elsewhere in the west Mediterranean.

The pottery forms span a range from the 3rd c. B.C. to the 7th c. A.D. It is difficult to judge whether the substantial quantities of tile from these fields were all associated with burials or whether some derive from the roofs of buildings in the settlement. The site lay on the extreme edge of the valley of the Bogatell and was cut into by terracing along its E side. The area of the site was relatively flat but it enjoys a clear view over the valley which opens out immediately to the S.

*Site 2.4*

A rather diffuse 'adabs' which is evident through the Iberian to early imperial periods. It consists of two fields with reasonably good visibility. Field 637 appears to be the core of a small settlement, although the Iberian concentration is in field 648. The pottery forms span the 5th to the end of the 1st c. B.C. No tile was associated. The site lies on a gentle slope facing SE.

Transect 2/D (figs. 6.16-6.17)

The W end of this sector is marked by a ridge (above 125 m) upon which the village of Vistabella is situated. This ridge is separated from a higher one to the E by a small valley running NE-SW. On this ridge stands the village of La Secuita. To the E the ground rises again to a maximum of *c*.185 m at its boundary with the *terme municipal* of El Catllar. On the E side of this ridge is the Pont d'Armentera-Tarragona road and the village of Argilaga. From the road the land slopes away to the E. The SE corner of this sector has not yet been mapped at 1:5,000. Most of the area comprised small fields with a variety of vines, arable and tree crops, which permitted good field-walking coverage. Four sites were located:

*Site 2.5*

A small 'adabs' of low density is confined to field 533. Poor visibility caused by overgrown scrub on this and adjacent fields may account for its uncertain identification but it appears to be a small settlement of the early and late imperial phases. Better visibility might have raised the densities above the 10 percentile in the earlier phases. The only chronologically diagnostic form dates to the late 1st c. B.C. - late 1st c. A.D. No tile was associated. The settlement lies just below the top of the ridge on a gentle slope facing E.

*Site 2.6*

An 'adabs' of very high density was clear through the Iberian and early imperial phases. The core of the site lay in fields 496 and 497, and the highest concentrations of pottery belonged to the early empire. The pottery forms range from the 5th c. B.C. to mid 5th c. A.D. Substantial concentrations of tile leave no doubt that this was a settlement. It lay on the N side of the valley on land which faced SSW.

*Site 2.7*

A very high concentration of material formed an 'adabs' from the Iberian to the late imperial phases. Fields 525, 526 and 527 formed the core. The most marked concentration was in the late empire. The pottery forms recovered range from the 5th c. B.C. to later 7th c. A.D. During the late empire the scatter merges with that of Site 2.8 and it is not impossible that the two formed part of a single larger settlement. Substantial concentrations of tile were found in the fields at the core of this 'adabs'. Fragments of *opus signinum* were reused in modern field walls. The site lay in a dominant location on a knoll overlooking the valley to the W and S.

*Site 2.8*

This 'adabs' lies N of Site 2.7 and merges with it in the late imperial phase. It first emerges as a visible concentration in the early empire, when it has a lower density concentration than Site 2.7 — not easily explained as due to problems of visibility. The much lower concentration at that period makes it doubtful as a settlement. The ceramic forms run from the late 3rd c. B.C. to the early 5th c. A.D. Almost no tile was associated, possibly suggesting that it might have been a midden. It is located on and around a knoll which dominates the valley to the N and W.

*Site 2.9*

Another high density 'adabs' lay just E of the present town of Argilaga. The core of the distribution lay in field 696 and appears to have been spread down the slope to the S, perhaps the result of agricultural erosion. A modest concentration of tile and a few fragments of *opus signinum* were found in field 696. The 'adabs' remains concentrated through all four phases and evidently points to a settlement. The pottery forms recovered span the period from the 5th c. B.C. to the 4th c. A.D. This conclusion is supported by the evidence of the geophysical survey (see Chapter 7). The site is located on a distinct E-W ridge which dips steeply to the E. It was not clear whether the site continued to the W beneath the village.

Transect 2/E (figs. 6.18-6.19)

The land in this sector was largely overgrown with scrub and woodland and access was difficult. The ground rose to almost 200 m in the centre of the N part of the transect. It generally sloped S, reaching a minimum elevation of less than 75 m in the Gaià valley. The slope is cut on the W by the valleys of the Torrent de Renau, on the E by the Barranc de La Rasota, and the Gaià (which forms the boundary of the *terme municipal* and thus of the mapped area). The area below *c.*120m is shown as a reservoir (the 'Embalse de Gayá') on the 1983 edition of the 1:25,000 IGN map. However, the present water level lies well below the 100 m-contour and the land above *c.*105 m seems never to have been flooded. Only small pockets of agricultural land are present, used to cultivate vines. Thus our sample was very limited and only one site was found.

*Site 2.10*

This 'adabs' lay beyond our transect to the S. It consisted of a clearly defined concentration of the Iberian to early imperial phases. The pottery ranges from the 5th c. B.C. to the early 3rd c. A.D. Only a small quantity of tile was associated. The 'adabs' was evidently a small settlement. It lay on a ridge between the valleys of the two barrancs just above their confluences with the Gaià, in a dominant position on the relatively level ground just above the valley.

188

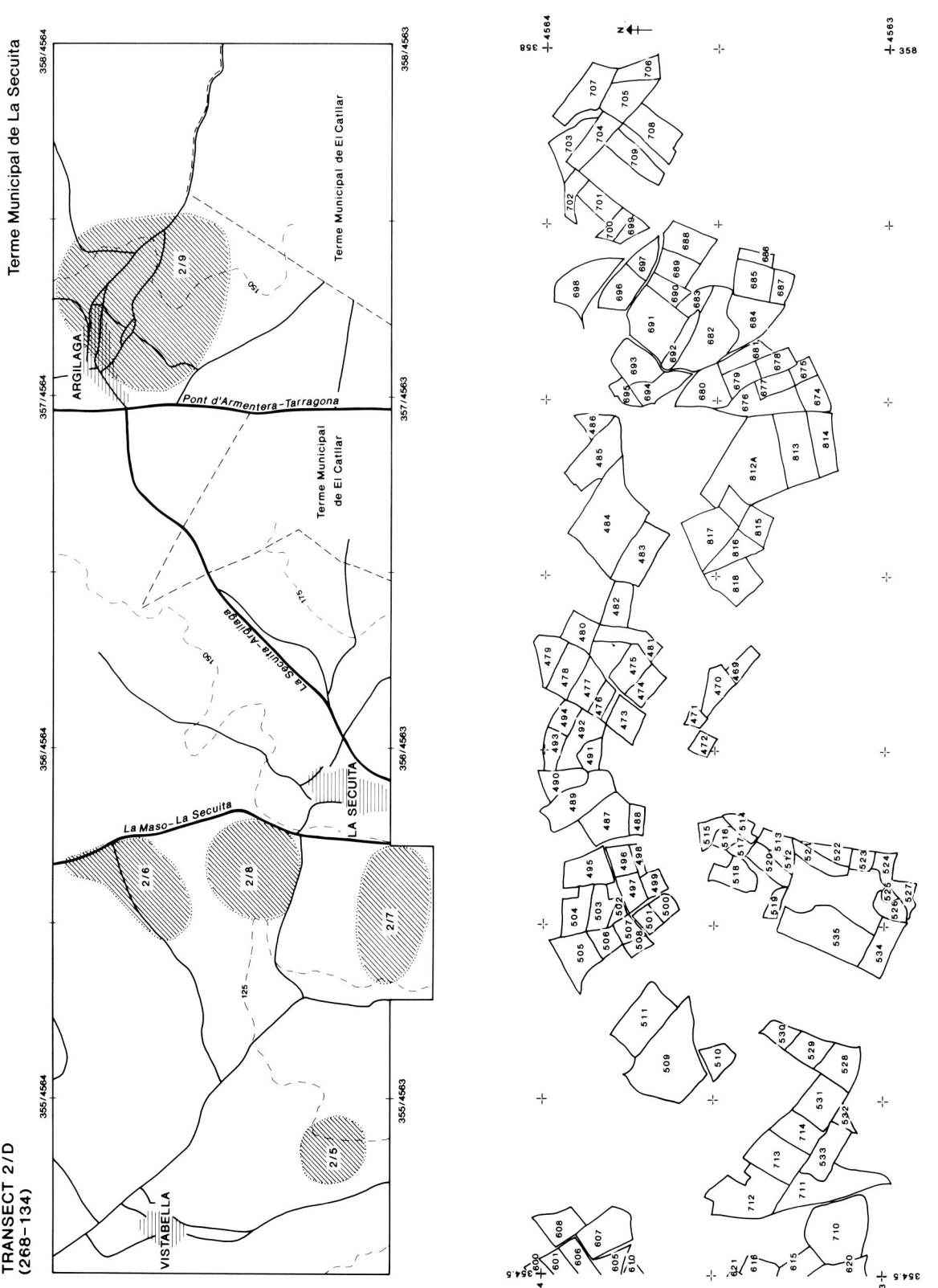

Fig.6.16. Transect 2/D: topography, site locations and field numbers.

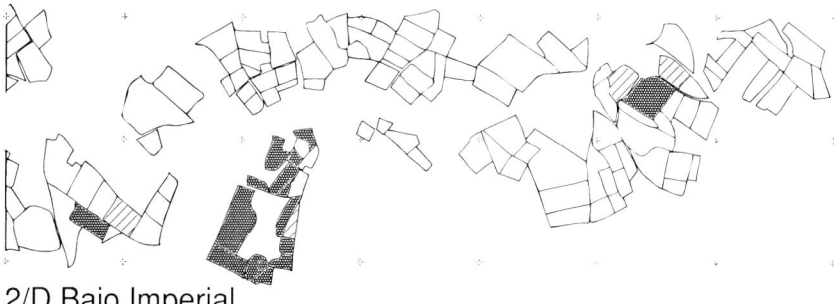

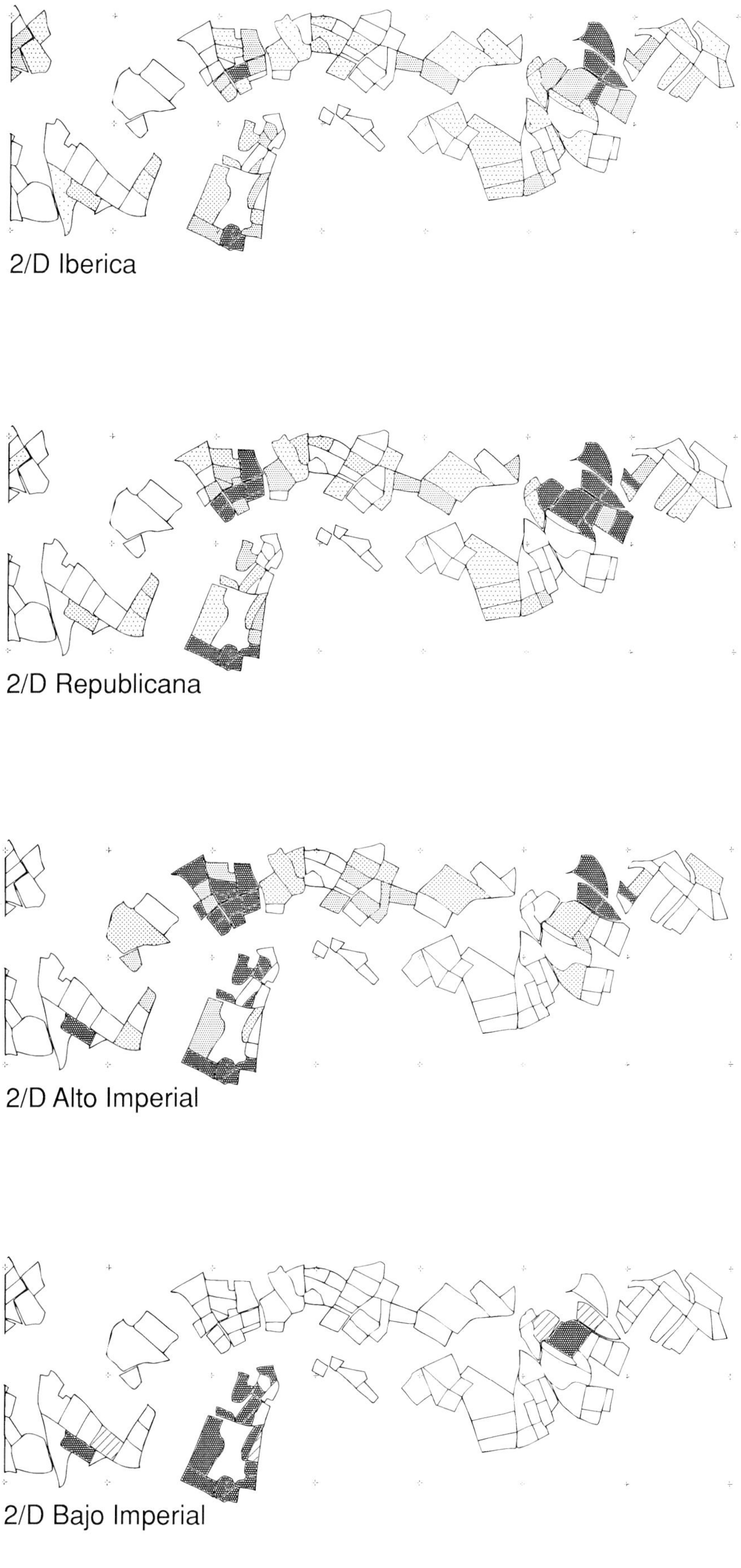

2/D Iberica

2/D Republicana

2/D Alto Imperial

2/D Bajo Imperial

Fig.6.17. Transect 2D: densities of pottery.

190

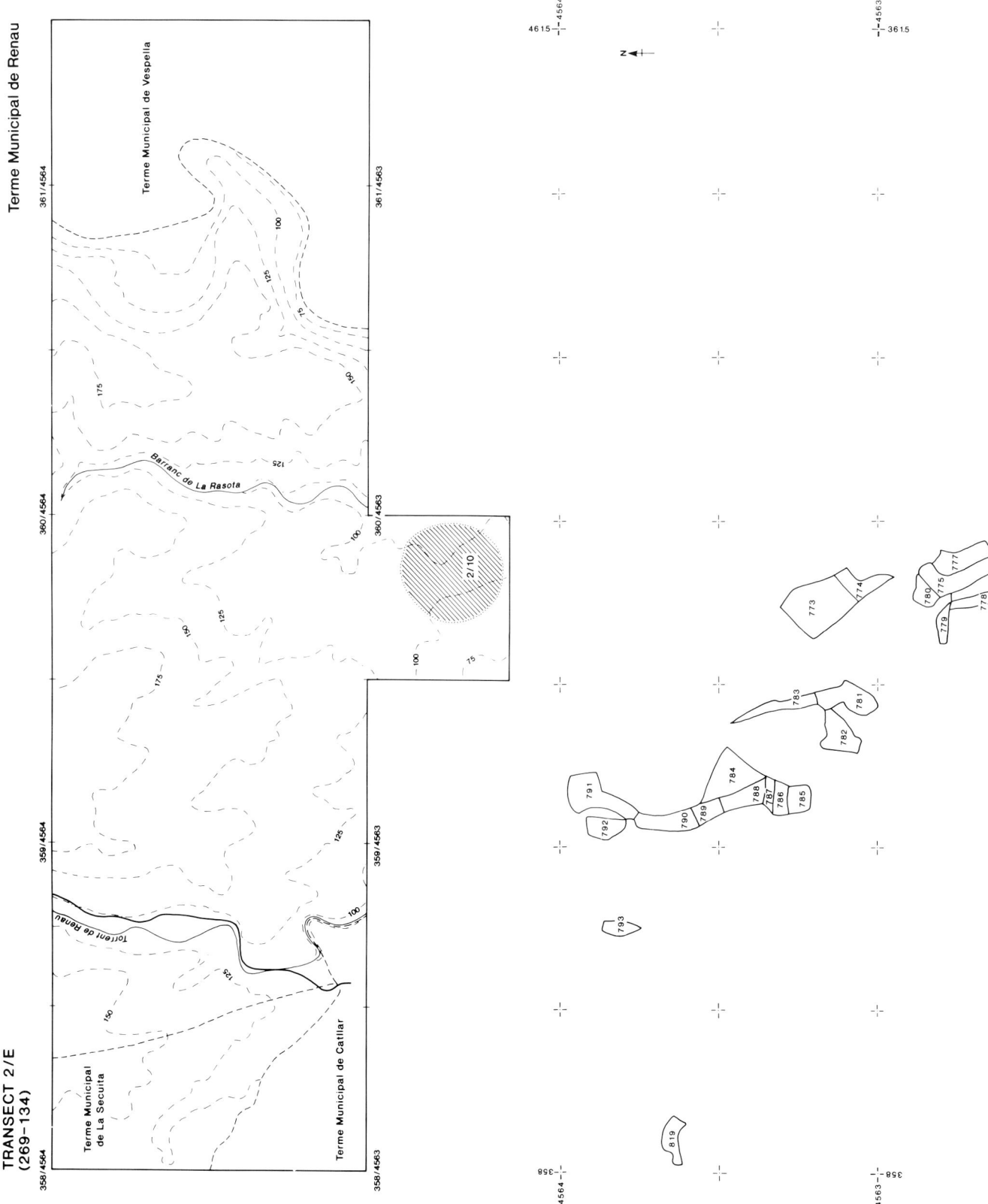

Fig.6.18. Transect 2/E: topography, site locations and field numbers.

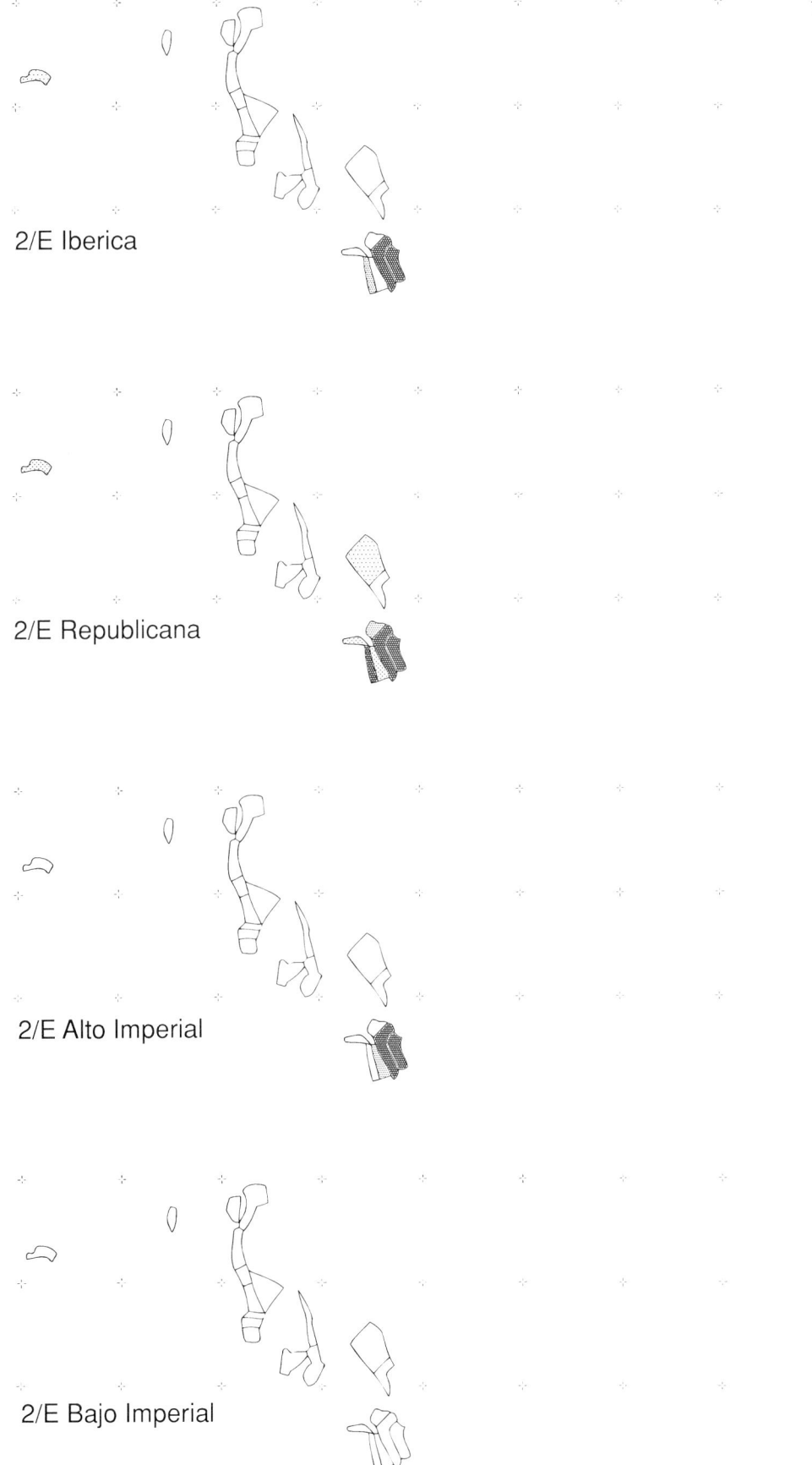

Fig.6.19. Transect 2E: densities of pottery.

Transect 3/A (figs. 6.20-6.21)

This sector lies within the Depressió Valls-Reus. It comprises land which generally slopes gently from W to E at an elevation of *c*.150-200 m. To the E is a scarp above the terrace of the Francolí, marked approximately by the 150-m contour. The Picamoixons-Morell road runs N-S near the W limit of the terrace. The ground falls away steeply to the river at its E edge. In the N part of the sector a tributary of the Francolí, the Barranc de Font Major, flows W to E. Its valley is deeply incised, especially where it cuts through the cliff above the river terrace. The area was heavily cultivated, with open arable fields on the plateau and a predominance of hazelnuts on the terrace and beside the Barranc de Font Major. It was possible to walk a good proportion of the land. A dense concentration of sites was located:

*Site 3.1*

A small, tightly clustered 'adabs', confined to the Iberian phase. The pottery spans the period from the 5th to the 1st c. B.C. No tile was associated. The concentration is consistent with the presence of a small settlement located on the edge of the plateau above the valley on the N side of the barranc.

*Site 3.2*

A small, tightly clustered 'adabs' which covers the Iberian and early imperial phases. The ceramic forms span the period from the late 3rd c. B.C. to the late 2nd/early 5th c. A.D. No tile was associated. This concentration is consistent with the presence of a small settlement, located overlooking the barranc on its N bank.

*Site 3.3*

Another small, tightly defined 'adabs', evident only in the Iberian phase. A light scatter of Republican and early imperial material provides little evidence for continuity into those phases. The pottery identified dates to the 5th-1st c. B.C. No tile was associated. The evidence supports the identification of another small settlement located on the plateau immediately S of the valley of the barranc.

*Site 3.4*

A small 'adabs' which was rather more diffuse than the others because of poor visibility in fields under stubble. It was probably a small settlement which has been dispersed by agricultural erosion. The material is confined to the Iberian and Republican phases. The pottery forms are limited to the 5th-1st c. B.C. No tile was associated. The site is situated on a bluff which overlooks both the barranc to the SW and the terrace of the Francolí to the E.

*Site 3.5*

A small 'adabs' which began in the Republican period and continued into the early imperial phase. The pottery forms span the period from the mid 2nd c. B.C. to the early 5th c. A.D. A substantial amount of tile was found in the same field. The site is small although well-defined in an area of good visibility. It is certainly a settlement. It is located on the edge of a plateau on its S side overlooking the barranc, in a position similar to that of site 3.4.

*Site 3.6*

A small but consistent 'adabs' present from the Iberian to the early imperial phases. It lacks associated tile. The only pottery form recovered dates to the late 2nd to mid 1st c. B.C. The 'adabs' is situated on the terrace just below the bluff on which Site 3.4 is located. It is possible that it represents redeposited material at the foot of the slope but more probably it was a small settlement.

*Site 3.7*

A very small 'adabs' comprising a very light scatter which reaches the top 10 percentile only in the early empire. No dated pottery forms or tile were recovered. It was located near the upper margin of the river terrace in a position similar to that of Site 3.6. Its identification as a settlement is very dubious even though ground conditions were not good.

*Site 3.8*

A small 'adabs', confined to the early imperial period located on the terrace just above the confluence of the Barranc de Font Major with the Francolí. No dated pottery forms were recovered and no tile. As the visibility in this area was good, the very low density of material makes its identification as a potential settlement very doubtful.

Transect 3/B (figs. 6.22-6.23)

The W edge of this sector is marked by the Francolí which has a broad terrace on its E side. The ground rises up a long, broken, and partially terraced slope to the edge of the plateau where the elevation is just over 200 m. The plateau continues to the E edge of our sector but is cut on the S by a series of small valleys. The Francolí terrace is cultivated for hazelnuts and arable crops. The land to the E is dominated by almonds and vines. Only one site was located even though reasonably good coverage was obtained.

*Site 3.9*

A reasonably well defined 'adabs' is evident here from the Iberian to late imperial phases (although the latter was represented by only one sherd). The dated pottery forms range from the 5th c. B.C. to the early 5th c. A.D. A small amount of tile was associated. The dispersed character of the site is probably the result of variable ground conditions but there is little doubt that it was a settlement. It was located on the edge of the plateau at the point where the ground begins to fall away to the SE to the valley.

*Possible sites*

In view of the overgrown nature of field 20 and the large quantity of undiagnostic pottery it is likely to conceal a site. The slight concentration in fields 1182, 1184, 1185 and 1186 may also indicate a site nearby whose focus was not located.

Transect 3/C (figs. 6.24-6.25)

As the mapping of the W end of this sector is incomplete, fields have been plotted from vertical air photographs. The ground dips down to the valley of the Torrent d'Hospitalet which flows NE-SW. Then there is a long slope up to the plateau (*c.*225 m asl), on the edge of which sits the village of Bellavista. The plateau continues E, rising gently to a maximum elevation of just over 250 m. A slight ridge running NE-SW lies towards the E end of our sector. It is marked by a farm track which leaves the map near its NE corner. The area is widely cultivated with tree crops and vines, allowing good coverage. A total of 10 sites was located:

*Site 3.10*

This 'adabs' was evident from the Iberian to late imperial phases. It was evidently a settlement but rather poor coverage in the adjacent fields makes it difficult to define its boundaries with certainty. The dated ceramic types range from the 5th c. B.C. to the early 5th c. A.D. Only a few pieces of tile were associated. The site was situated on the SE slope above the Torrent, overlooking the valley.

*Site 3.11*

A small but not very clearly defined 'adabs' falls in the top 10 percentile from the Iberian to the late imperial phases. Dated pottery forms are confined to the 5th to later 1st c. B.C. Only very small quantities of tile were found. Despite problems, this concentration almost certainly represents a small settlement on the slope NW-facing above the Torrent.

194

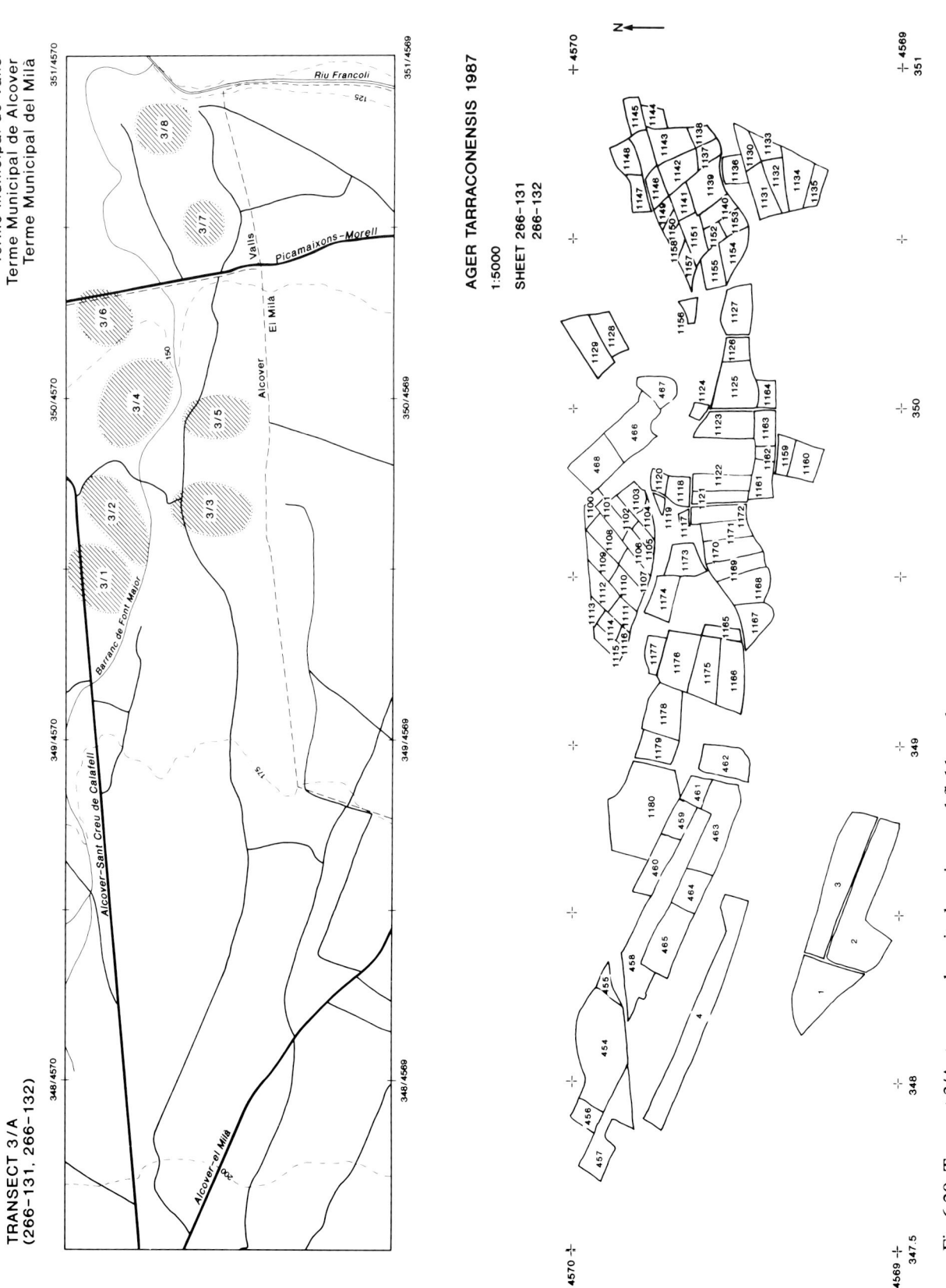

Fig.6.20. Transect 3/A: topography, site locations and field numbers.

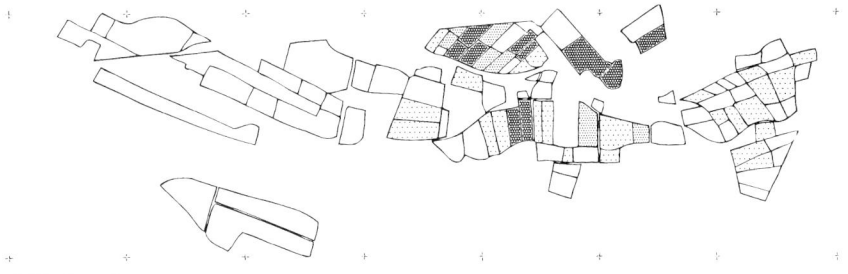

3/A Iberica

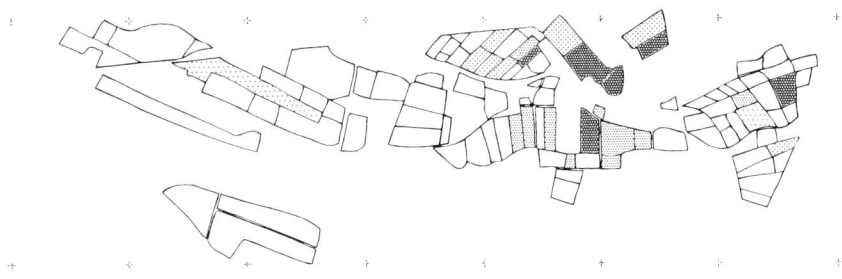

3/A Republicana

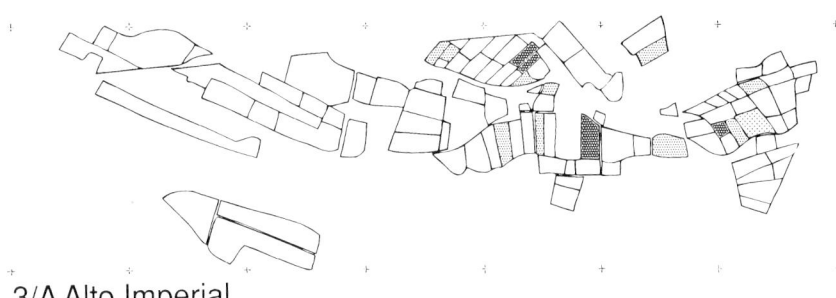

3/A Alto Imperial

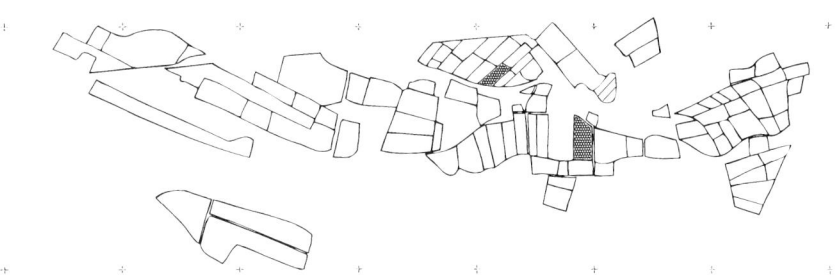

3/A Bajo Imperial

Fig.6.21. Transect 3A: densities of pottery.

196

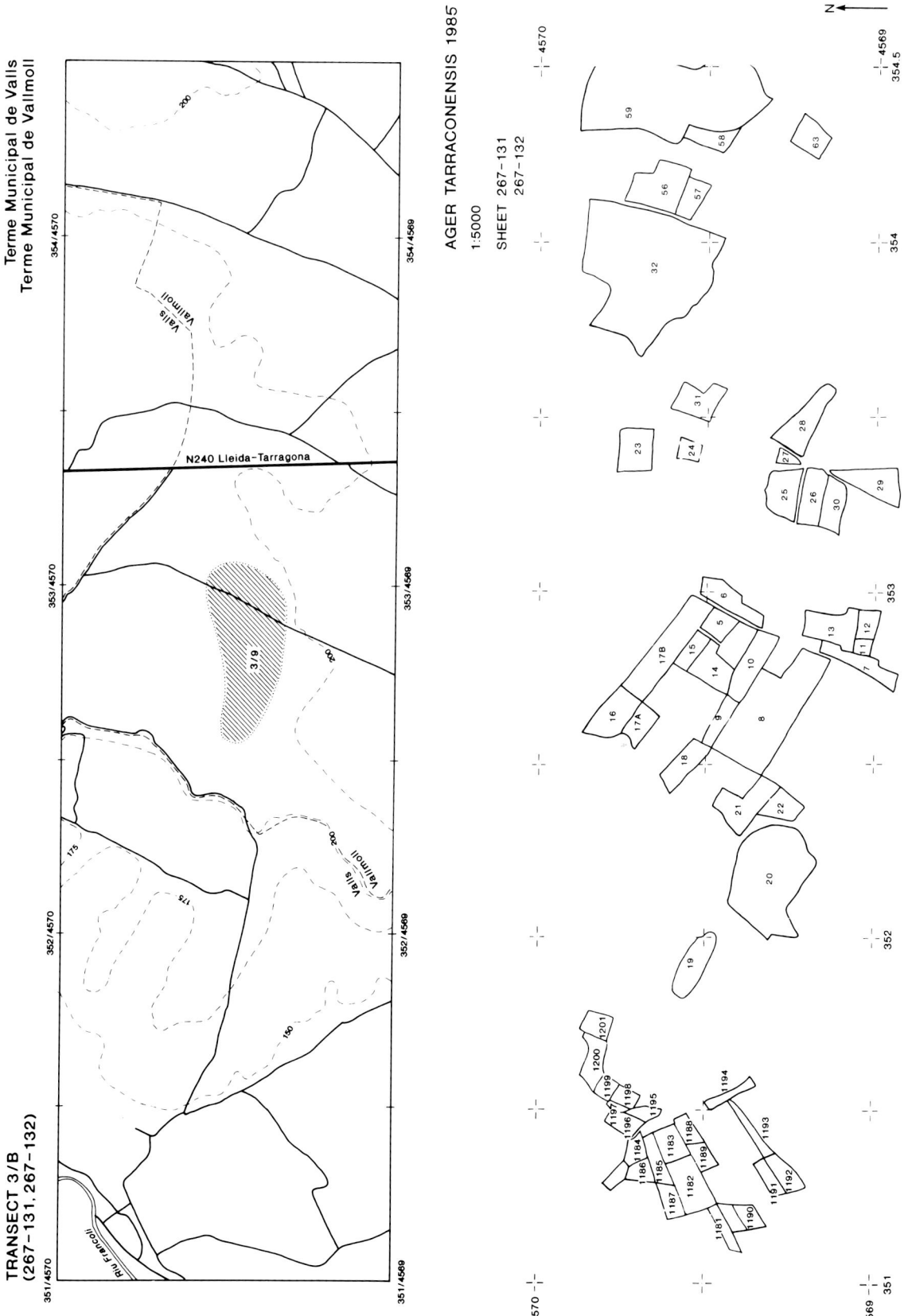

Fig.6.22. Transect 3/B: topography, site locations and field numbers.

197

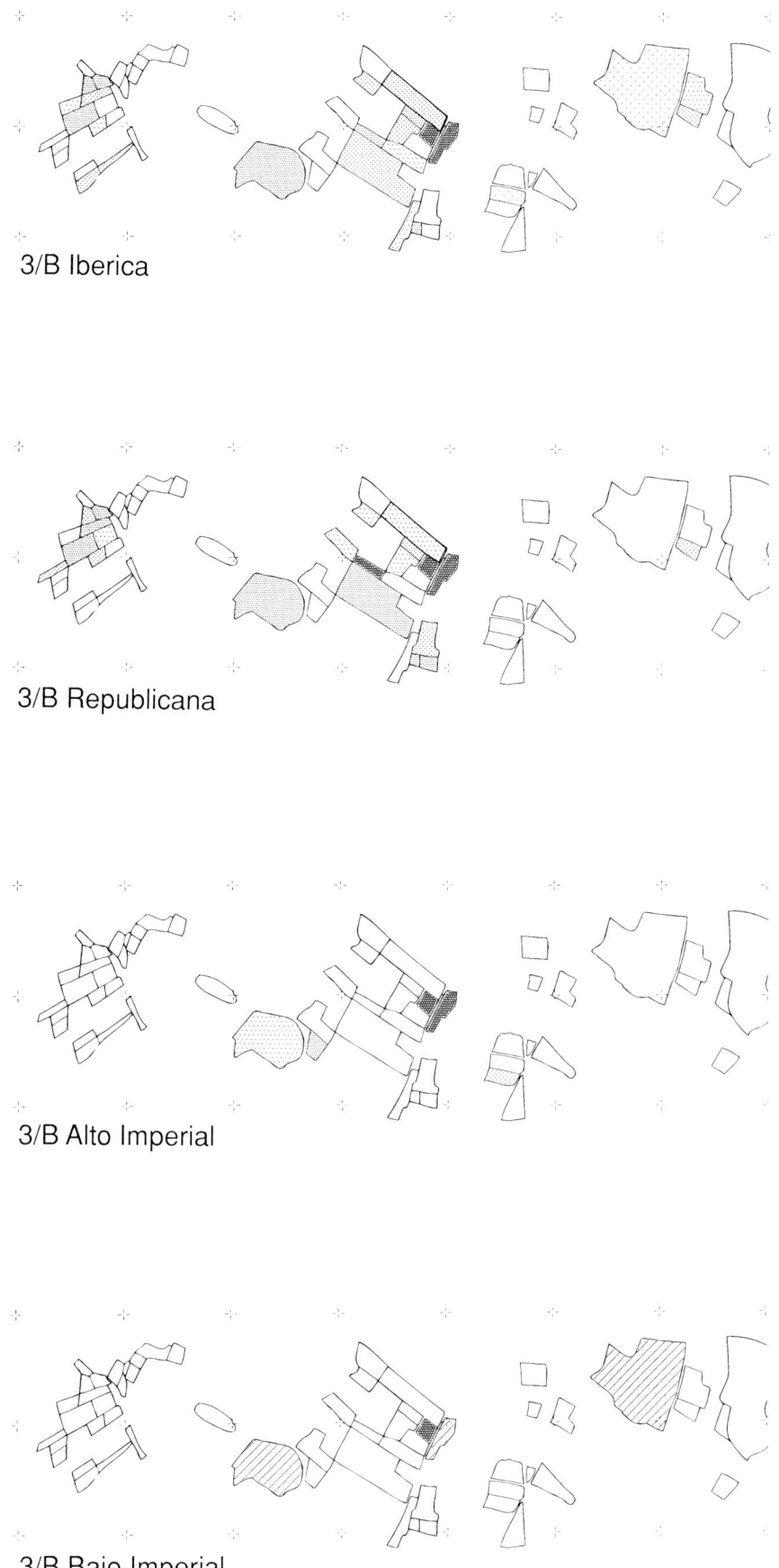

3/B Iberica

3/B Republicana

3/B Alto Imperial

3/B Bajo Imperial

Fig.6.23. Transect 3B: densities of pottery.

198

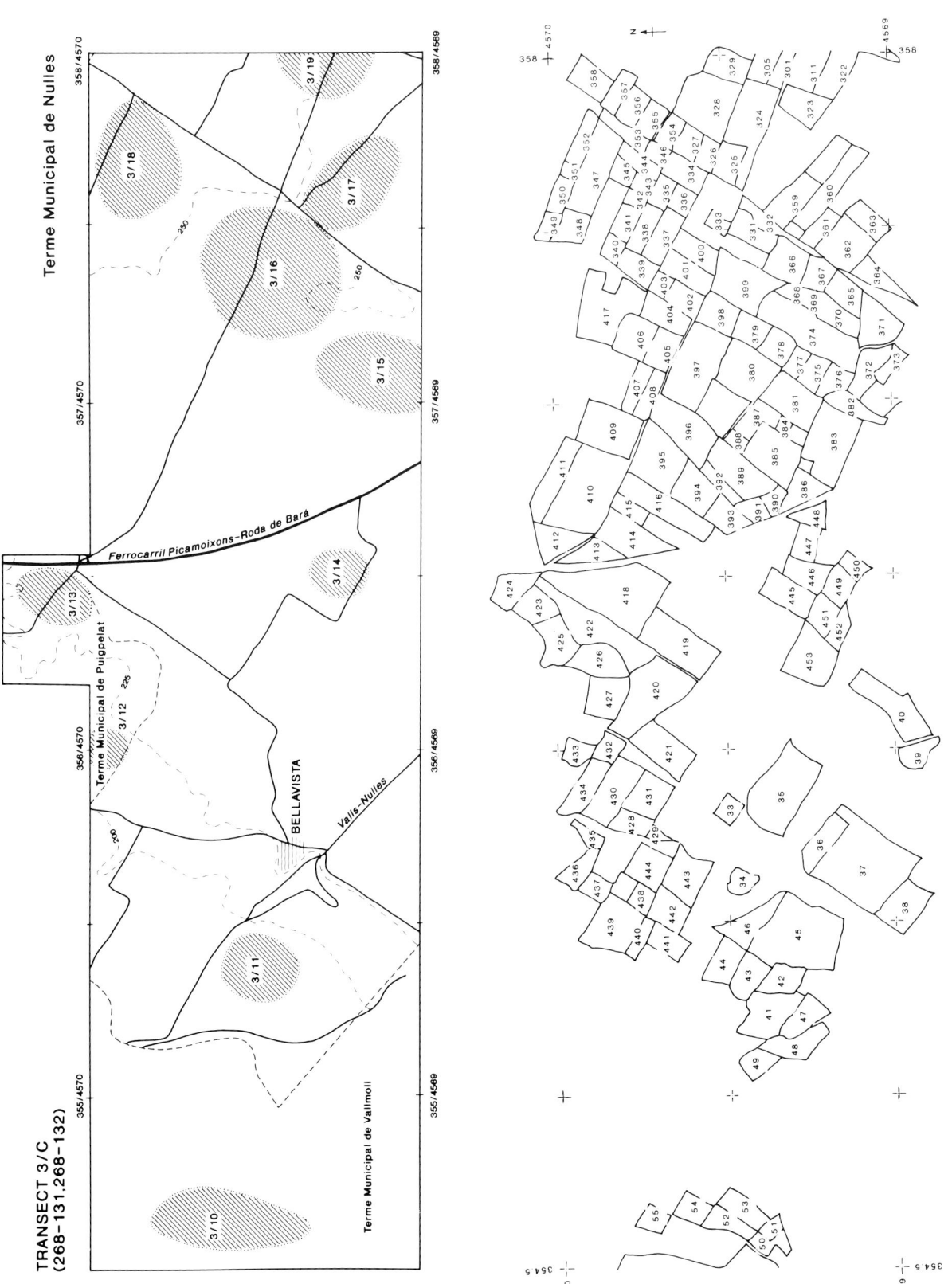

Fig.6.24. Transect 3/C: topography, site locations and field numbers.

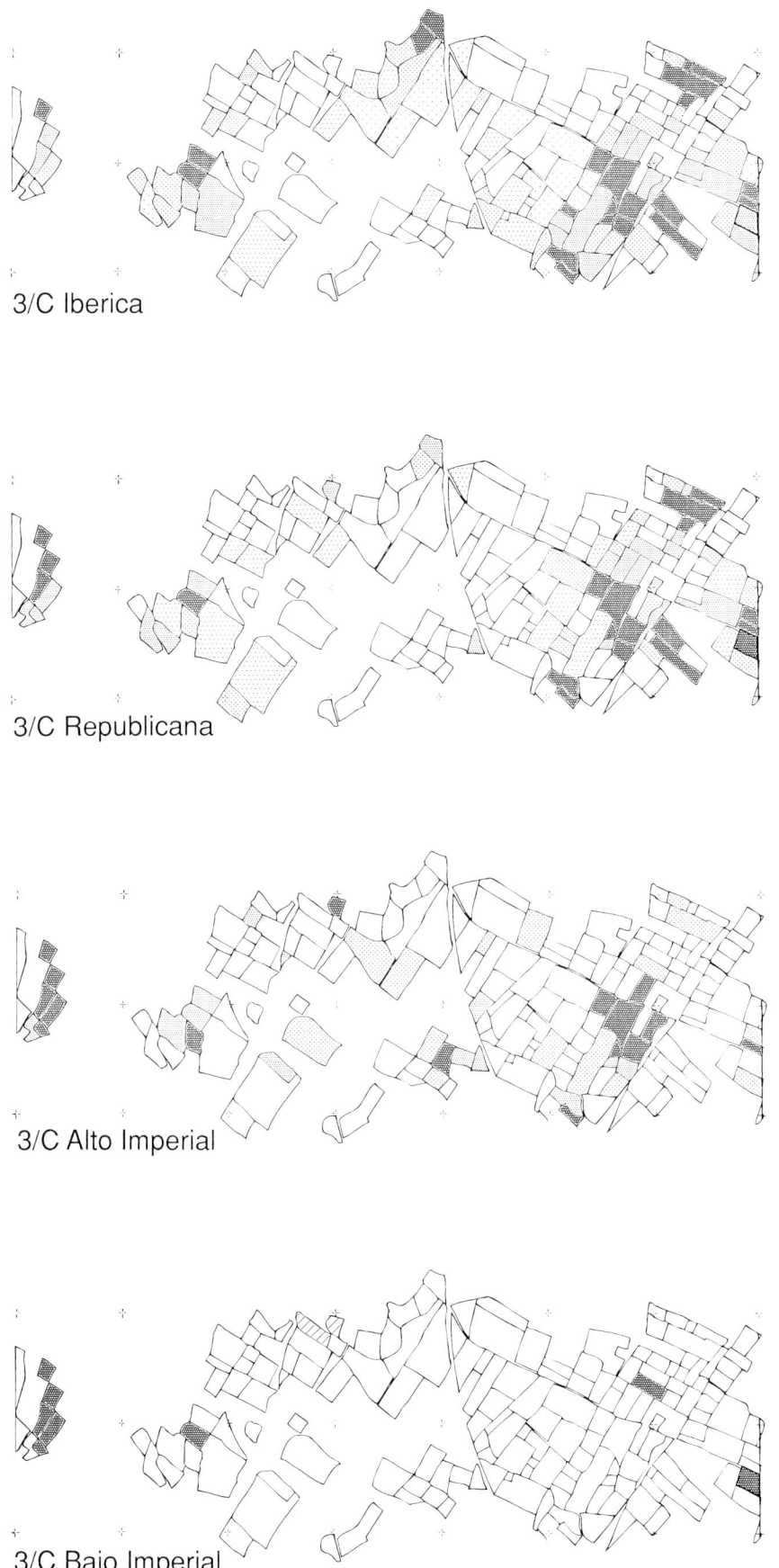

3/C Iberica

3/C Republicana

3/C Alto Imperial

3/C Bajo Imperial

Fig.6.25. Transect 3C: densities of pottery.

*Site 3.12*

A poorly defined and somewhat doubtful 'adabs', evident only in the early and late imperial phases. It had almost no associated tile. The pottery forms date from the 1st to early 5th c. A.D. The visibility was not particularly good in this field but it probably does not account for the poor definition of the scatter. Thus the identification as a settlement is doubtful. It lies on a spur part of the way down the slope overlooking the valley of the Torrent on the NW.

*Site 3.13*

A clearly defined 'adabs' of high density almost entirely confined to the Iberian phase. There is no associated tile. The dated pottery forms range from the 6th to the mid 1st c. B.C., with a strong emphasis on the period before the 3rd c. There is little doubt that it represents a small settlement. It is located on a spur at the edge of the plateau overlooking the valley of the Torrent on the NW.

*Site 3.14*

A very small 'adabs' which is evident only in the early imperial period. There are a few pieces of tile. No dated pottery forms were recovered. It was located in the centre of the plateau in an area of good visibility. The identification as a settlement is doubtful.

*Site 3.15*

A clearly identifiable 'adabs' which was evidently a settlement in the Iberian, Republican and early imperial phases. There is one sherd of late imperial date. The pottery spans the period from the 5th to the 1st c. B.C. A few pieces of tile were associated. It is located on the W side of the ridge with the ground falling away to both W and S.

*Site 3.16*

A very diffuse 'adabs' is evident through the Iberian to late imperial phases. The recovered pottery dates to between the 5th c. B.C. and the 1st c. A.D. A small quantity of tile was confined to fields 398 and 399. There is little doubt that the scatter represents a settlement focused upon fields 368, 398, and 399, that appears to have been dispersed through agricultural activity. It is located at the NW end of the ridge and in a hollow just to the N. Terracing perhaps accounts for the dispersion of the material. Some of the finds in the E part of the scatter may be derived from Site 3.17.

*Site 3.17*

A small and fairly well defined 'adabs' is evident only during the Iberian and Republican phases. The ceramic forms date to between the 5th and 1st c. B.C. Only a couple of pieces of tile are associated. The concentration seems to represent a settlement. It lies on the E side of the ridge overlooking the slope on the SE.

*Site 3.18*

A rather dispersed but defined 'adabs' is evident only during the Iberian and Republican phases. The pottery forms date from the 5th to 1st c. B.C. Almost no tile was associated. The site lies in an area of good visibility although the ground has been terraced, which may have caused the dispersion of the pottery. There seems little doubt that it was a settlement lying just below the top of the W side of the ridge, facing SW.

*Site 3.19* is described below under Transect 3/D

Transect 3/D (figs. 6.26-6.27)

Fieldwork was confined to the area within the *terme municipal* of Nulles since only a very small part of this sector was mapped at 1:5,000. It was dominated by a knoll, Puig Ferré, which marks the SE end of the ridge. From that point the ground falls away to N, S and E. This hill was entirely cultivated for trees; crops with vines occupy the surrounding fields. A single site was located:

*Site 3.19*

The top of Puig Ferré was covered with an 'adabs' which ran from the Iberian to the late imperial phase. Agricultural erosion appears to have spread this material over adjacent fields. The dated pottery spans the 5th c. B.C. to the 3rd c. A.D. The main focus of the site is in fields 301, 302, 303, 304, and 305 with a moderate concentration of tile in fields 301, 302 and 304. There is little doubt that it represents a substantial settlement located on the hill-top and dominating much of the surrounding area (fig. 10.2).

Transect 4/A (figs. 6.28-6.29)

The W end of Transect 4 in the foothills of the mountains rises as high as 500 m at the NW. The ground falls steeply to the Riera de Guixeres before rising again to form a lower ridge. At the E end of the sector it slopes less steeply to the SE. Most of the land was overgrown with *maqui* or woodland and inaccessible. A pocket of land in the valley of the Riera de Guixeres used for arable agriculture permitted a small sample to be walked. It did not reveal any sites.

Transect 4/B (figs. 6.30-6.31)

In this sector there is a distinct difference in terrain on either side of a geological boundary marked approximately by the Lleida-Tarragona road N-240. To the W the broken foothills of the mountains continue, sloping gently from over 375 m at the NW to about 300 m at the SE. On the E is a plateau which slopes gently towards the S. Its surface is undulating because of a series of valleys with seasonal streams which flow S. The area to the W was cultivated in a series of small fields amongst the hills which allowed a reasonable sample to be walked. On the E arable agriculture is widespread, with cereals, almonds and vines. Good coverage was obtained here except at the far E end where the outskirts of the Valls industrial estate are occupied by recently abandoned and overgrown fields. Four sites were located:

*Site 4.1*

A clearly defined 'adabs' runs from the Iberian to the early imperial phase. The concentration was smaller in the Iberian phase than later. Dated pottery forms range from the 5th c. B.C. to the mid 3rd c. A.D. It included two Dressel 1 amphora handles with stamps in Iberian script (figs. 5.68-5.69 and p.83). The pottery was associated with a light concentration of tile. Despite the relatively poor surface visibility, the boundaries of this site seemed clear. Its identification as a small settlement is confirmed by the geophysical survey (see Chapter 7). It lies on top of a ridge dominating the land to S, E and W.

*Sites 4.2, 4.3 and 4.4*

This 'adabs' has been divided into three because the concentration is cut by the Rosa de Cap Negre and another seasonal stream. Each represents a substantial area which has large quantities of pottery from the Iberian to the early imperial phase. Sites 4.2 and 4.4 continue into the late empire.

The principal focus of Site 4.2 lay in fields 942, 943, 944 and 945 where there was also a moderate concentration of tile. The pottery dates from the 5th c. B.C. to the earlier 5th c. A.D.

Site 4.3 was less concentrated than the other two 'adabs', the highest density of material being in field 949 where there was also a small quantity of tile. The pottery forms range from the 5th c. B.C. to the 2nd c. A.D.

The heart of Site 4.4 lay in fields 957 and 959. The former had the highest concentration of pottery in the whole survey as well as a dense concentration of tile. The identified ceramic forms span the period between the 5th c. B.C. and the 5th c. A.D.

202

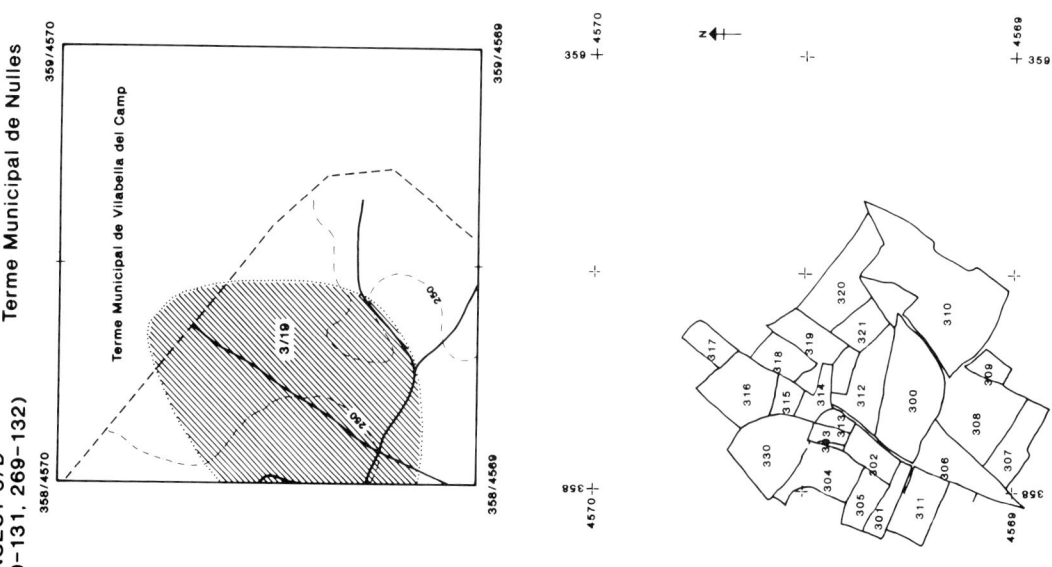

Fig.6.26. Transect 3/D: topography, site locations and field numbers.

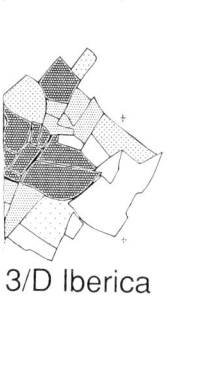

3/D Iberica

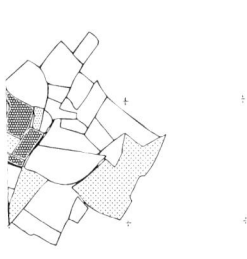

3/D Republicana

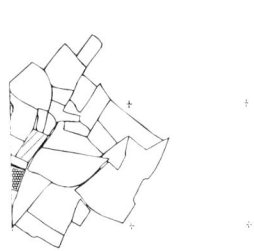

3/D Alto Imperial

3/D Bajo Imperial

Fig.6.27. Transect 3D: densities of pottery.

204

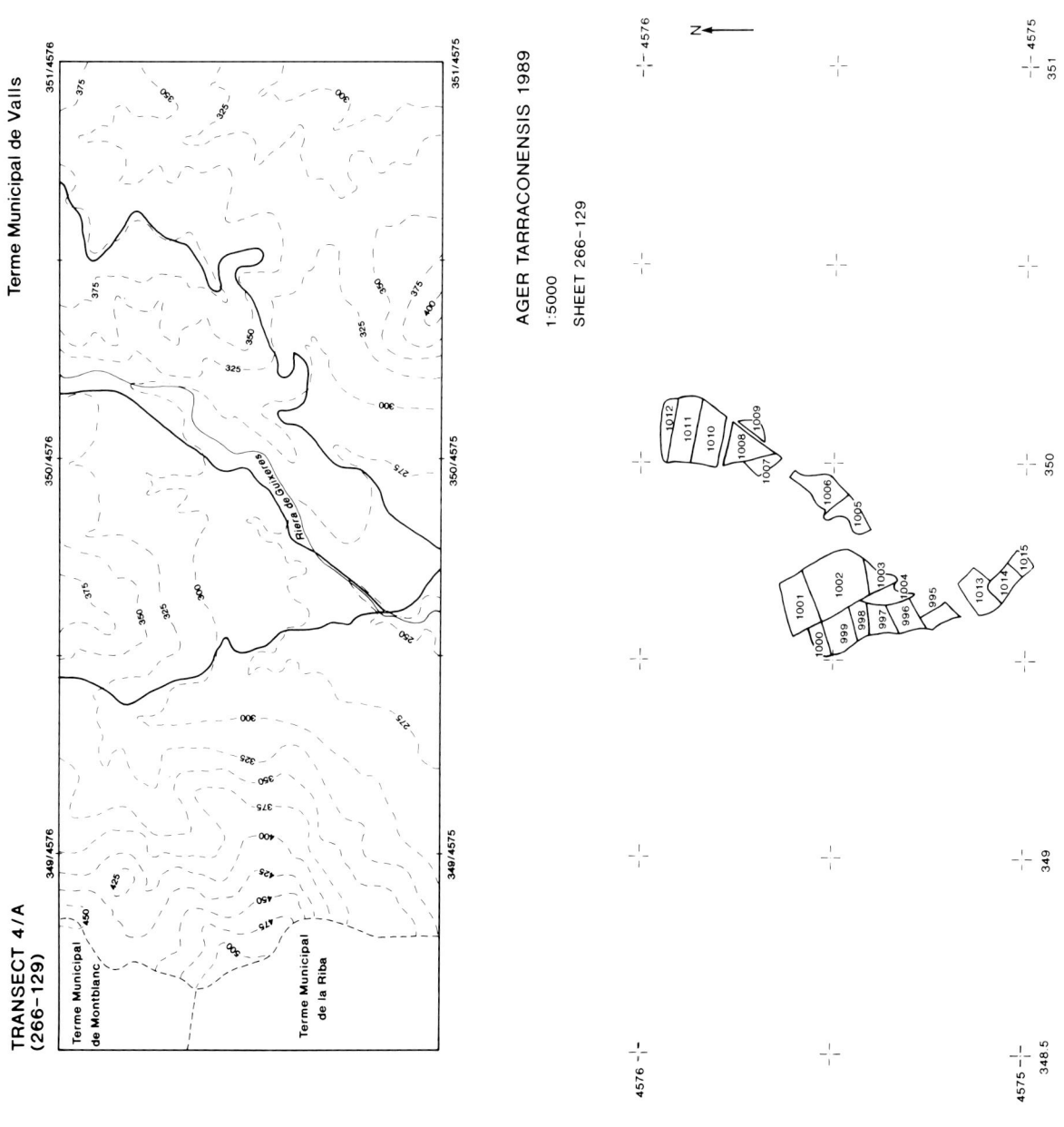

Fig.6.28. Transect 4/A: topography, site locations and field numbers.

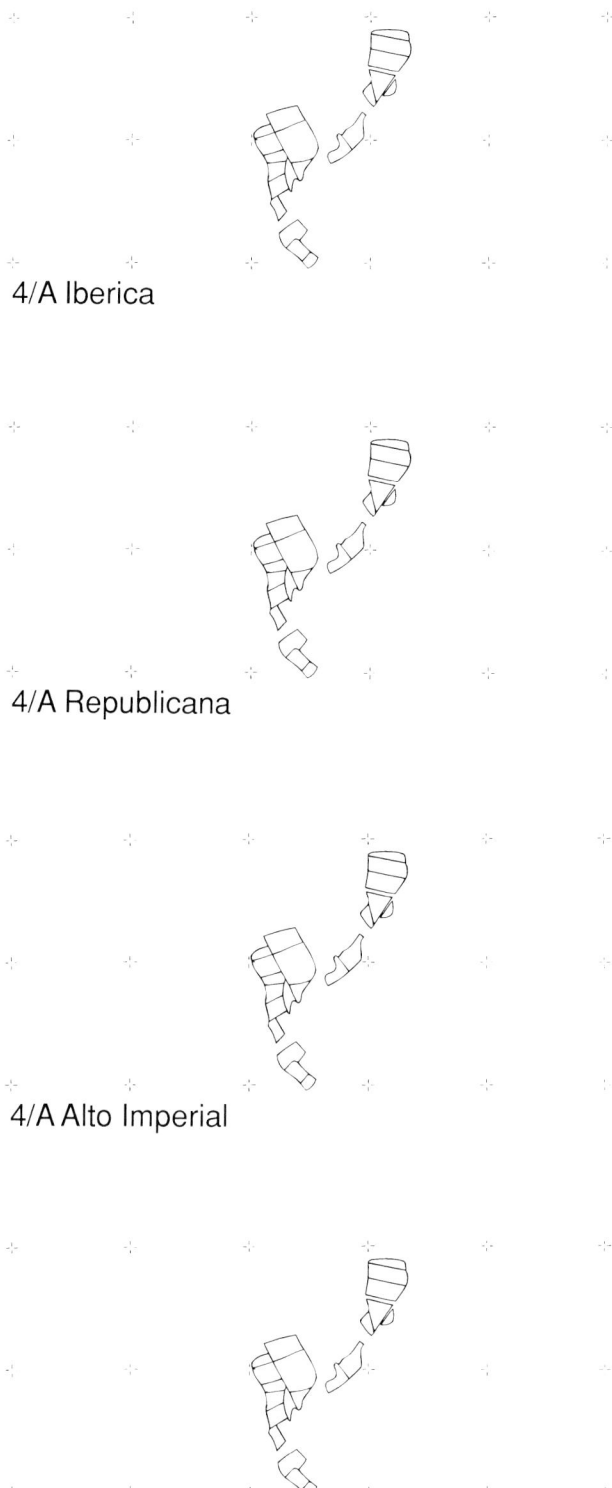

4/A Iberica

4/A Republicana

4/A Alto Imperial

4/A Bajo Imperial

Fig.6.29. Transect 4A: densities of pottery.

206

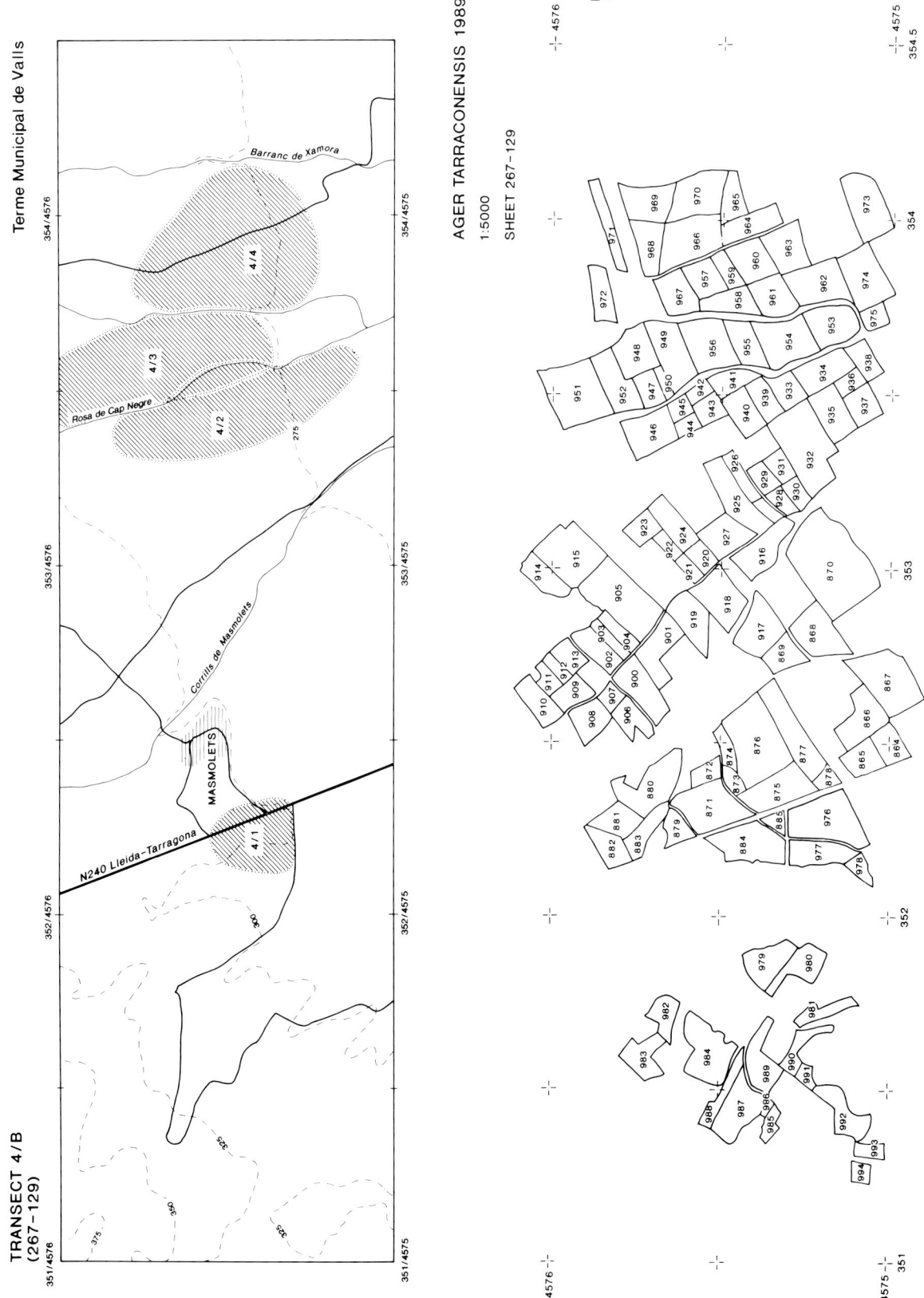

Fig.6.30. Transect 4/B: topography, site locations and field numbers.

207

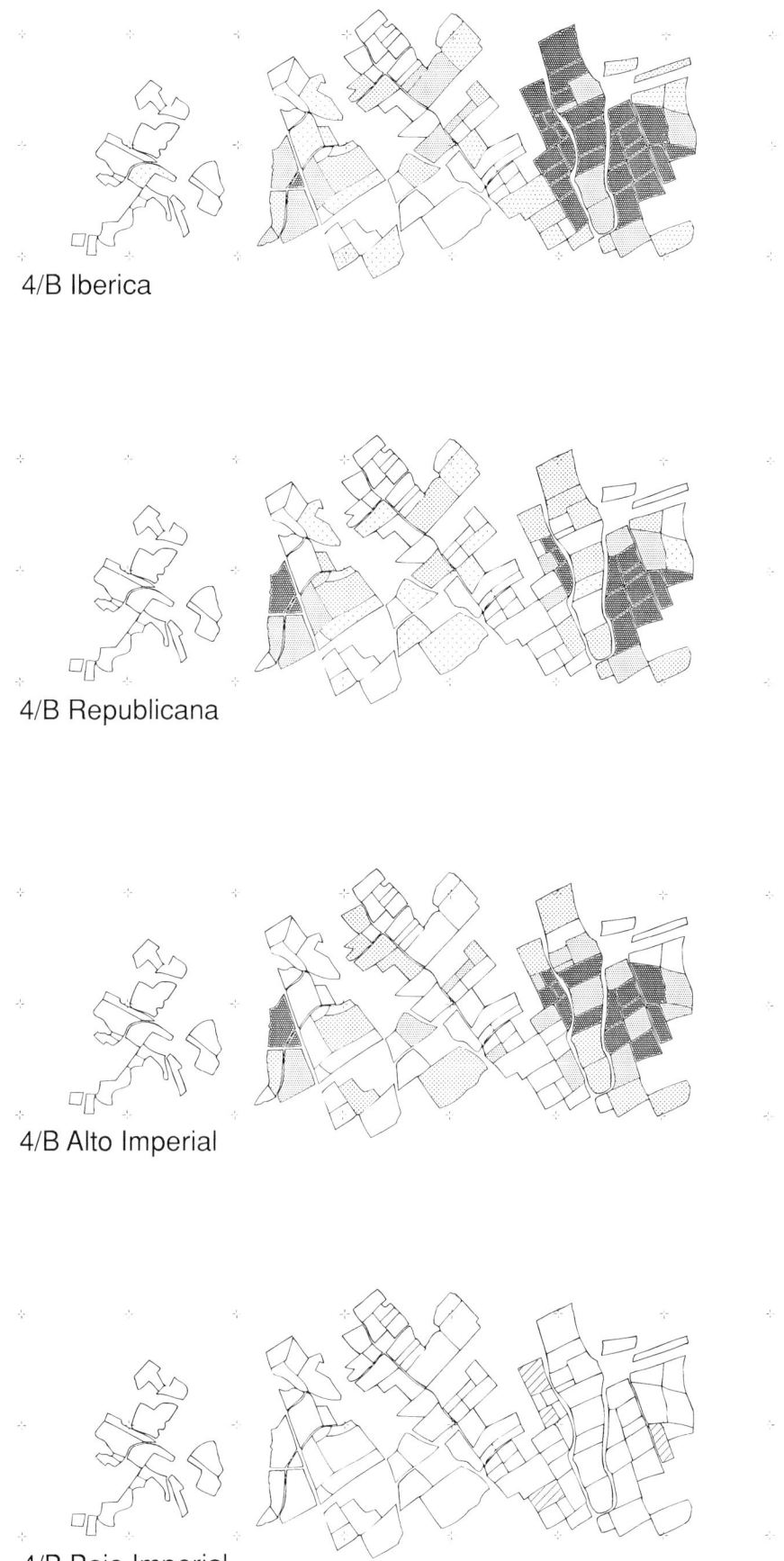

4/B Iberica

4/B Republicana

4/B Alto Imperial

4/B Bajo Imperial

Fig.6.31. Transect 4B: densities of pottery.

208

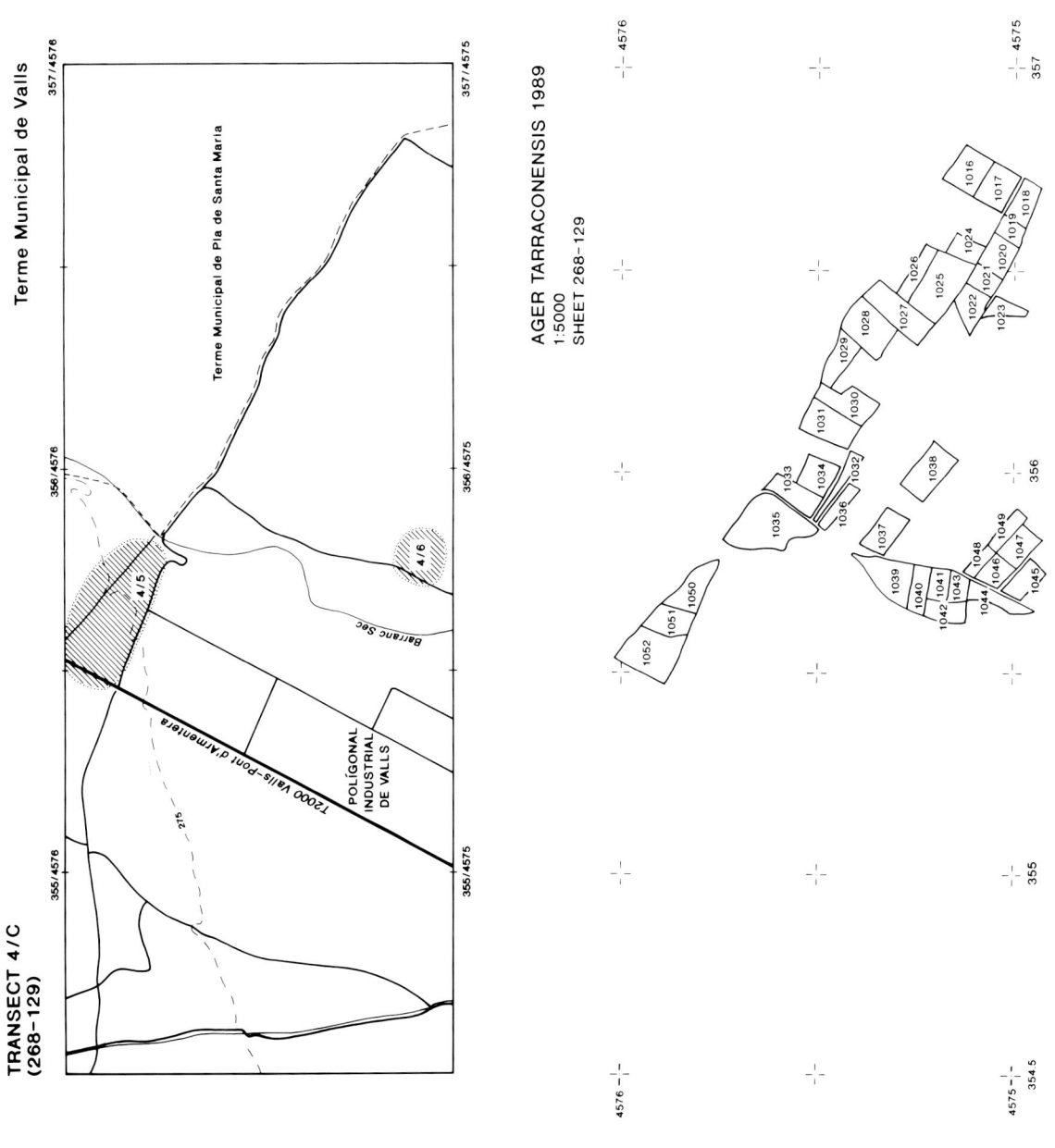

Fig.6.32. Transect 4/C: topography, site locations and field numbers.

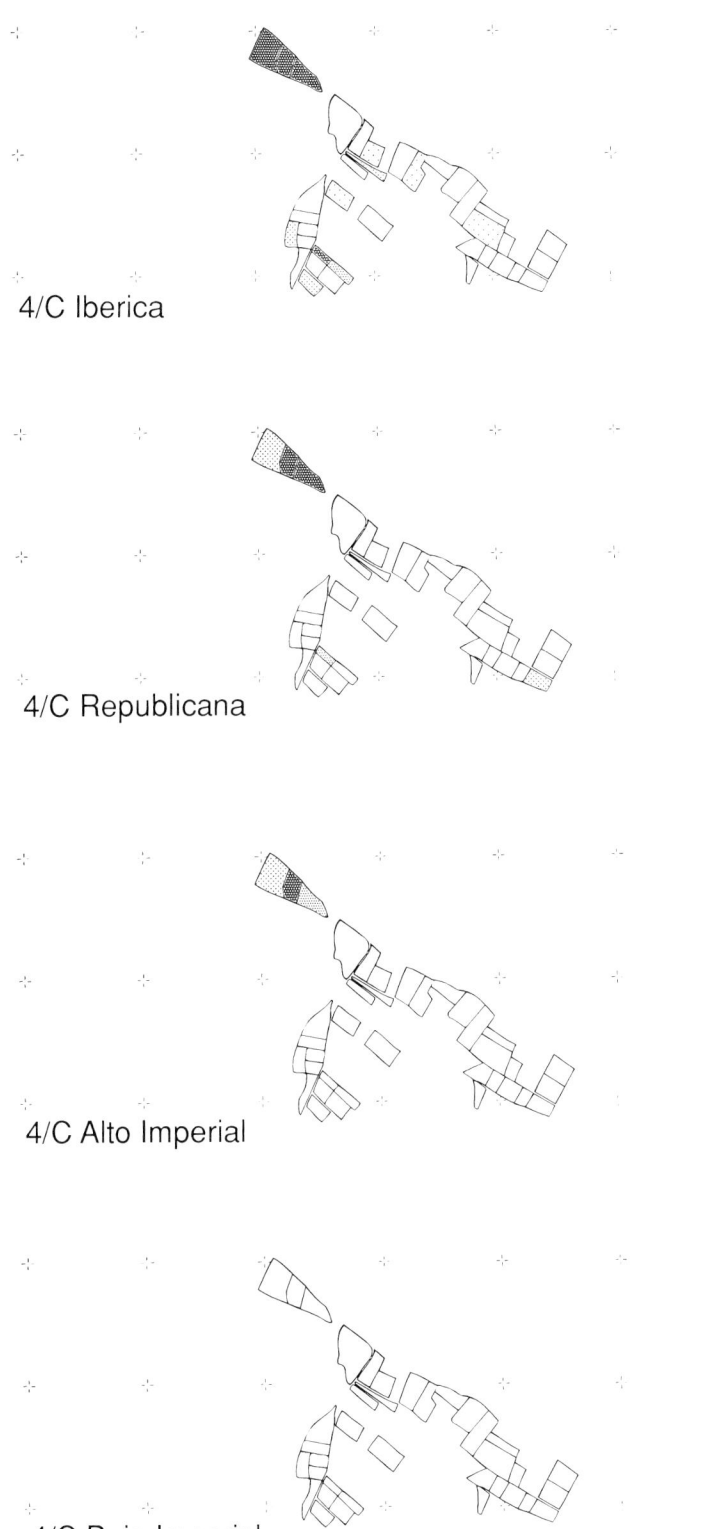

4/C Iberica

4/C Republicana

4/C Alto Imperial

4/C Bajo Imperial

Fig.6.33. Transect 4C: densities of pottery.

There can be no doubt that these are settlements, perhaps part of a single large village, or they may represent buildings situated along the streams, focused on a major building at the core of Site 4.4 (although a longer chronological range is suggested by the pottery from Site 4.2). The range of Iberian amphorae and finewares, and the presence of some overfired body-sherds, suggest that it might have been a kiln site. It may even have manufactured Dressel 1 amphorae (Types 7, 8 and 9). The land covered by the whole cluster slopes gently, providing a good aspect facing SE.

Transect 4/C (figs. 6.32-6.33)

The plateau here slopes down evenly to the S from an elevation of just over 275 m to 260 m. It is deeply cut by the Barranc Sec. The E part of the sector had not been mapped at the 1:5,000 scale. The W part lies beneath the Polígon Industrial de Valls and contained little land suitable for walking. In the intervening areas a small amount of land cultivated for almonds was available. Two sites were located:

*Site 4.5*

This is a small and reasonably well-defined 'adabs' even though the surrounding areas could not be walked. There is a strong concentration of material running from the Iberian to early imperial phases, with a single late-imperial sherd. The pottery dates from the 5th c. B.C. to the early 5th c. A.D. The core of the distribution lies in field 1050 where there was also a light scatter of tile. There is little doubt that it is a small settlement, located on the edge of the plateau just above the stream bed.

*Site 4.6*

This very small 'adabs' is evident only in the Iberian phase. The only dated forms are 5th/1st c. B.C. Almost no tile is associated. The 'adabs' is confined to a single field even though visibility was good in adjacent plots. Its identification as a small settlement seems certain and is confirmed by the geophysical survey (see Chapter 7). It is situated on the S side of the Barranc on the very edge of the valley.

Fig.6.34 summarizes the overall distribution of sites located in the survey and gives their numbering. Details of their sizes and phases of occupation are provided in Tables 6.1-6.4.

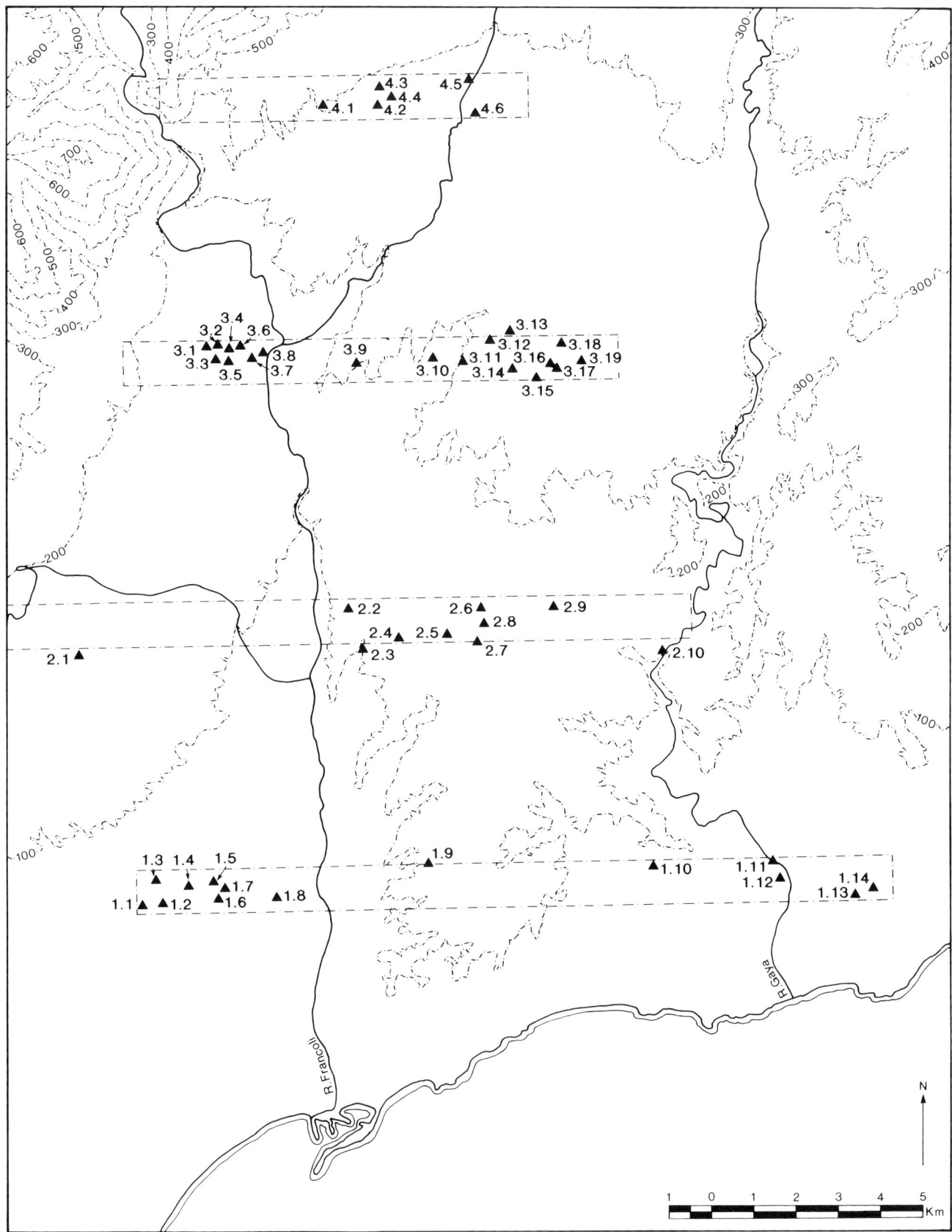

Fig.6.34. Summary map of the territory of Tarraco, showing the sites discovered in the survey and the numbering used.

Table 6.1:

Transect 1 - Fields included within sites and site areas

| Ceramic Phase | SITE: | 1.1 | 1.2 | 1.3 | 1.4 | 1.5 | 1.6 | 1.7 | 1.8 | 1.9 | 1.10 | 1.11 | 1.12 | 1.13 | 1.14 |
|---|---|---|---|---|---|---|---|---|---|---|---|---|---|---|---|
| Iberian | Fields: | | 122<br>144<br>145 | | 154<br>162 | 166 | 60<br>61<br>100<br>197 | | 199<br>200 | 276 | 270 | 109<br>110 | 118<br>120 | 250 | 234<br>235 |
| | Area (ha): | 0.31 | 3.55 | | 1.73 | 0.33 | 2.29 | | 1.38 | 0.42 | 0.67 | 0.68 | *1.00 | 1.74 | 1.43 |
| Republican | Fields: | 130 | 122<br>144<br>145<br>146 | 134 | 154<br>162 | 166 | 60<br>61<br>100<br>101<br>104<br>106<br>197 | | 199<br>200<br>205<br>206 | 275<br>276 | 269<br>270<br>271 | | | 244 | 234<br>235<br>236<br>238 |
| | Area (ha): | 0.31 | 5.48 | 0.26 | 1.73 | 0.33 | 5.61 | | 2.69 | 1.01 | 2.67 | | | 0.48 | 2.43 |
| Early Imperial | Fields: | | 149<br>152 | | 160<br>162 | | 60<br>61<br>100<br>101<br>104<br>106<br>108<br>197 | 168<br>169<br>170<br>177<br>179<br>183 | 198<br>199<br>200<br>205 | 276 | 269<br>270<br>271 | | | | 234<br>235<br>236<br>238 |
| | Area (ha): | | 0.94 | | 1.52 | | 6.52 | 3.10 | 2.75 | 0.42 | 2.67 | | | | 2.43 |
| Late Imperial | Fields: | | | | | | 60<br>61<br>100<br>*101*<br>*102*<br>*103*<br>*106*<br>*191*<br>*196* | 170<br>173 | | 276 | | | *118*<br>*120* | | 236 |
| | Area(ha): | | | | | | *1.85 | 2.05 | | 0.42 | | | *0 | | 0.28 |

*1.85

KEY:
*Italics* = single sherd
 * = estimated

Table 6.2  Transect 2 - Fields included within sites and site areas

| Ceramic Phase | | SITE: | 2.1 | 2.2 | 2.3 | 2.4 | 2.5 | 2.6 | 2.7 | 2.8 | 2.9 | 2.10 |
|---|---|---|---|---|---|---|---|---|---|---|---|---|
| Iberian | Fields: | | 860 | 734 | 758, 759, 760, 761, 762 | 648 | | 497 | 525, 526, 527 | | 690, 696, 697, 698 | 775, 777 |
| | Area (ha): | | 1.28 | 0.65 | 2.16 | 0.19 | | 0.66 | 0.98 | | 3.90 | 2.40 |
| Republican | Fields: | | 860 | 734 | 758, 759, 760, 761, 762 | 637 | | 495, 496, 497, 498, 500, 501 | 524, 525, 526, 527, 534 | | 683, 688, 690, 691, 693, 696, 697, 698, 700 | 775, 777, 778 |
| | Area (ha): | | 1.28 | 0.65 | 2.16 | 1.36 | | 3.14 | 2.54 | | *5.00 | 2.98 |
| Early Imperial | Fields: | | 860 | 730, 731, 733, 734 | 757, 758, 759, 760, 761, 762 | 637 | 533 | 495, 496, 497, 498, 499, 500, 501, 505, 508 | 524, 525, 526, 527, 534 | 512, 516, 517, 518, 519 | 696, 697, 698, 700 | 775, 777 |
| | Area (ha): | | 1.28 | 4.00 | 2.16 | 1.36 | 1.15 | 5.13 | 2.54 | 2.02 | 3.74 | 2.40 |
| Late Imperial | Fields: | | 860 | | 756, *758*, 759, 760, 761 | | 533 | | 524, 525, 526, 527, 534, 535 | 512, 515, 517, 518, 519, 520, 521, 522, 523 | 691, 693, 696 | |
| | Area(ha): | | 1.28 | | 5.87 | | 1.15 | | *4.00 | *3.00 | *2.21 | |

KEY:  
*Italics* = single sherd  
* = estimated

---

Table 6.4  Transect 4 - Fields included within sites and site areas

| Ceramic Phase | | SITE: | 4.1 | 4.2 | 4.3 | 4.4 | 4.5 | 4.6 |
|---|---|---|---|---|---|---|---|---|
| Iberian | Fields: | | 885 | 933, 934, 939, 940, 941, 942, 943, 944, 945, 946 | 947, 949, 951, 952, 955, 956 | 957, 958, 959, 960, 961, 962, 963 | 1050, 1051, 1052 | 1048 |
| | Area (ha): | | 0.29 | 6.74 | 7.29 | 7.97 | 3.06 | 0.29 |
| Republican | Fields: | | 884, 885 | 941, 942, 945 | | 957, 958, 959, 960, 961, 963 | 1050, 1051 | |
| | Area (ha): | | 2.12 | 1.72 | | 7.07 | 0.76 | |
| Early Imperial | Fields: | | 884, 885 | 941 | 949 | 957, 958, 959, 961, 963 | 1051 | |
| | Area (ha): | | 2.12 | 1.14 | 1.33 | 10.05 | 1.63 | |
| Late Imperial | Fields: | | | *935*, *943*, *946* | | 964 | | |
| | Area(ha): | | | *1.83 | | 1.24 | | |

KEY:  
*Italics* = single sherd  
* = estimated

Table 6.3

**Ceramic Phase**

Transect 3 - Fields included within sites and site areas

| | | 3.1 | 3.2 | 3.3 | 3.4 | 3.5 | 3.6 | 3.7 | 3.8 | 3.9 | 3.10 | 3.11 | 3.12 | 3.13 | 3.14 | 3.15 | 3.16 | 3.17 | 3.18 | 3.19 |
|---|---|---|---|---|---|---|---|---|---|---|---|---|---|---|---|---|---|---|---|---|
| **Iberian** | **SITE:** Fields: | 1110, 1111, 1112 | 1101, 1102 | 1171, 1172 | 466, 467 | | 1128 | | | 5, 6 | 55 | 43, 44 | | 423, 424 | | 372, 373, 377 | 366, 367, 368, 369, 398, 399 | 359, 360 | 345, 347, 351, 352 | 300, 301, 302, 303, 304, 305, 312, 313, 316 |
| | **Area(ha):** | 1.73 | 0.80 | 1.55 | *1.50 | | 0.76 | | | 1.81 | 0.14 | 2.01 | | 1.89 | | 1.77 | 5.76 | 1.59 | 3.22 | 10.63 |
| **Republican** | Fields: | | 1102 | | 466, 467 | 1123 | 1128 | | 1143 | 5, 6, 9 | 52, 54, 55 | 43 | | | | 372, 373 | 366, 367, 368, 398, 399 | 359, 360 | 345, 347, 352 | 301, 302, 303, 304, 305, 311, 312, 313, 314, 316, 318 |
| | **Area(ha):** | | 0.31 | | *1.50 | 1.25 | 0.76 | | 1.08 | *2.00 | 0.52 | 0.98 | | | | 1.30 | 5.47 | 1.59 | 3.22 | 13.54 |
| **Early Imperial** | Fields: | | 1101, 1102 | | | 1123 | | 1152 | | 5, 6 | 51, 52, 53, 54, 55 | 42 | 433 | | 446 | 373 | 331, 366, 368, 398, 399, 400 | | 345, 347, 352 | 301, 302, 304 |
| | **Area(ha):** | | 0.80 | | | 1.25 | | 0.33 | | 1.81 | 1.93 | 0.87 | 0.54 | | 0.97 | 0.31 | 6.55 | | 3.11 | 13.54 |
| **Late Imperial** | Fields: | | 1106 | | 467 | 1123 | | | | *6* | 51, 52, 53, 54, 55 | 43 | *433, 434* | | | | 337 | | *302* | 302, 311 |
| | **Area(ha):** | | 0.56 | | *0 | 1.25 | | | | *0.70 | 1.93 | 0.98 | *0.54 | | | | 1.03 | | 3.02 | 1.42 |

**KEY:**
*Italics* = single sherd
\* = estimated

# Chapter 7: EVALUATION OF THE EVIDENCE

Having presented the information for each transect together with conclusions about which ceramic concentrations represent settlement sites, we must evaluate the results. Three complementary approaches have been used. First, the potential biases recorded in the field are explored statistically to determine how far they might have influenced the quality and reliability of the data. Second, the relationship between surface distributions and the buried archaeology is studied through the detailed survey of a single site. Third, the results of geophysical surveys on a selection of identified sites are presented.

## 1. STATISTICAL ANALYSES OF BIAS

Perhaps the most difficult problem facing those wishing to evaluate the results of a survey is assessing the extent to which collection bias has affected the results. Although some attempt was made during the discussion of the identification of sites to take into account variations in surface visibility, they have not been discussed systematically. Previous studies (notably Shennan 1985) have shown that biases can have an important effect on the results of surface survey. The approach followed here is different from that of Shennan. Because of the much larger volume of finds from this survey, it was felt that differences in the quantities of material collected (for example, as a result of variation in surface visibility) would be of marginal importance.[1] As our methodology involved aggregating finds made by individual walkers by field, it seems likely that variations in efficiency between walkers will be reduced. Since the survey collected information about the varying surface conditions (figs. 3.7-3.8), it seemed worth undertaking a limited investigation of the relative importance of various biases.[2]

The first experiment investigated variations between individual walkers in Field 276 towards the end of the 1986 season. Without informing the walkers beforehand, a record was made of who had walked each line in a field where a heavy concentration of pottery had been found. The pottery collected was then counted and weighed before being sorted to establish variations in sherd size collected by each individual. The pottery from this field was almost entirely Iberian. Table 9.7 shows that the average sherd-size for this phase across the survey was 13.04 g; the mean for this field was 15.61 g. Table 7.1 shows the results of the experiment:

Table 7.1      Variations in collection between walkers in Field 276

| Walker | Number of Sherds | Weight of Pottery | Average Sherd size | Deviation from survey average |
|---|---|---|---|---|
| 1* | 189 | 2605g | 13.78 | +0.74 |
| 2 | 120 | 2068g | 17.23 | +4.19 |
| 3 | 334 | 4644 | 13.90 | +.086 |
| 4* | 77 | 1108 | 14.39 | +1.35 |
| 5 | 108 | 2110 | 19.54 | +6.50 |
| 6* | 71 | 1640 | 23.10 | +10.06 |
| 7 | 105 | 1433 | 13.65 | +0.61 |
| 8* | 93 | 1288 | 13.85 | +0.81 |
| 9* | 173 | 2500 | 14.45 | +1.41 |
| 10 | 34 | 960 | 28.23 | +15.19 |

---

1     For example, in Shennan's survey in East Hampshire the largest quantity of Romano-British pottery collected from any one field was 66 sherds (Shennan 1985, 117-21). With such a low density of finds, poor visibility, or a walker who misses sherds, will have a proportionately greater affect on the collected sample than on the densities noted than in our area where finds were generally much more common. For us such factors would be of most consequence for the late imperial phase, but there was so little pottery of this period that statistical analysis was itself problematical.

The walkers who were the most experienced members of the team are indicated by *. The results show a range of values, although the extent to which they result from walker bias rather than variations in the material is difficult to judge. The likelihood that it was variation in the surface material is suggested by two pieces of evidence. First, one of the most experienced walkers (no. 6) collected sherds of the largest average size. Second, in no case was the mean sherd-size for any walker less than the overall survey average. However, three of the four largest deviations from the mean were produced by inexperienced walkers, demonstrating that some variation did result from their lack of skill. In general a narrow range of values was produced by the majority of the team. If we exclude walker 10, who not only collected large sherds but was also less successful in finding pottery, we can derive reasonable reassurance from these data. Such variations between walkers will have relatively little impact on the data once it was aggregated into totals for the field as a whole.

The second experiment used data from the whole survey to investigate how far the time of day during which walking took place affected the results. This analysis was undertaken because there was concern that varying light conditions and fatigue might have an important effect upon the quality of data collected. The time of day at which each field was walked was noted using the following three categories:

08.00 - 11.00;          11.00 - 13.30;          16.30 - 19.30

Total sherd numbers and weights per ha for each ceramic phase from all fields were compared with the time of day when the fields were walked using Pearson's rank correlation co-efficient on SPSSX at Durham University. This showed that there was almost no correlation between the variables (-0.0046 for total sherd number; -0.0042 for total sherd weights). Although this is not a particularly sophisticated analysis, it provides little support for the suggestion that the time of day and light conditions had a serious impact on our results.

## 2. DETAILED SURVEY OF A SINGLE SITE

*Introduction*

The method for identifying sites adopted in this survey assumes that surface scatters reflect the existence of buried remains. It was felt that this key relationship warranted more detailed investigation. During 1989 it was noticed that the newly-constructed Vallmoll by-pass had cut through a series of Roman walls and floors (fig. 7.1). The exposed section was drawn at that time (figs. 7.2A-B). Although the site lay outside our Transects, it was felt that it could usefully provide information about the effectiveness of the survey methods used. The field received number 1254 in the survey records.

The objective was to assess how surface evidence was related to the buried deposits exposed in the section. The field was walked and geophysical surveys undertaken. In order to give closer spatial control than obtained by our ordinary methods of line walking, the field was divided into 5-m squares and each square thoroughly searched by a single walker. The finds from each square were collected and processed in the same way as material from the other fields.

There was an obvious density of surface material across most of the field. Although adjacent fields were not available for walking, a cursory examination suggested that they had significantly lower concentrations of finds. The totals of pottery recovered are listed in Appendix 4. The field area was approximately 0.21 ha. The densities recorded for the field as a whole were:

---

2    Further data are available on request for any researcher who wishes to undertake further research on these problems.

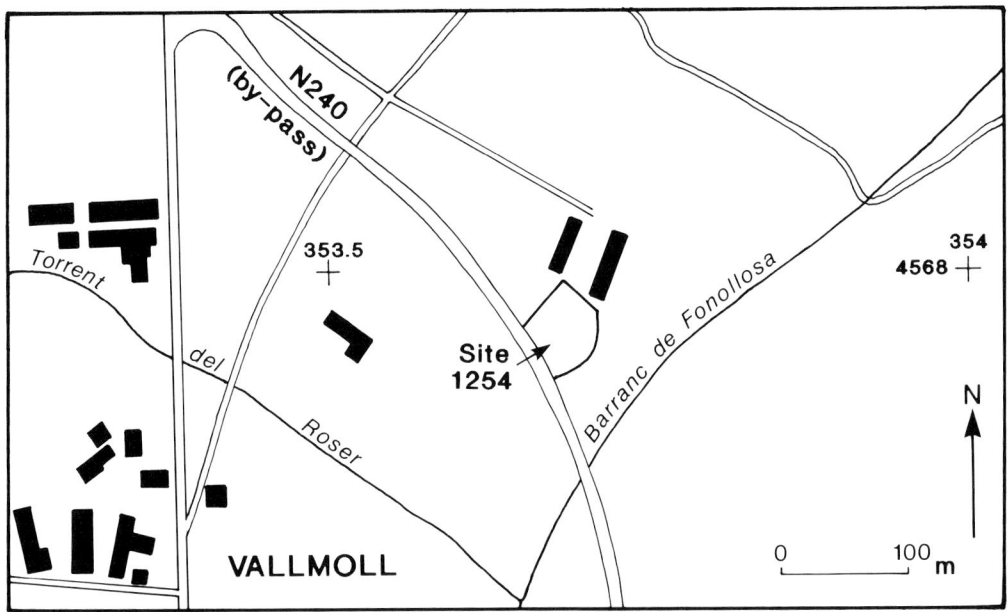

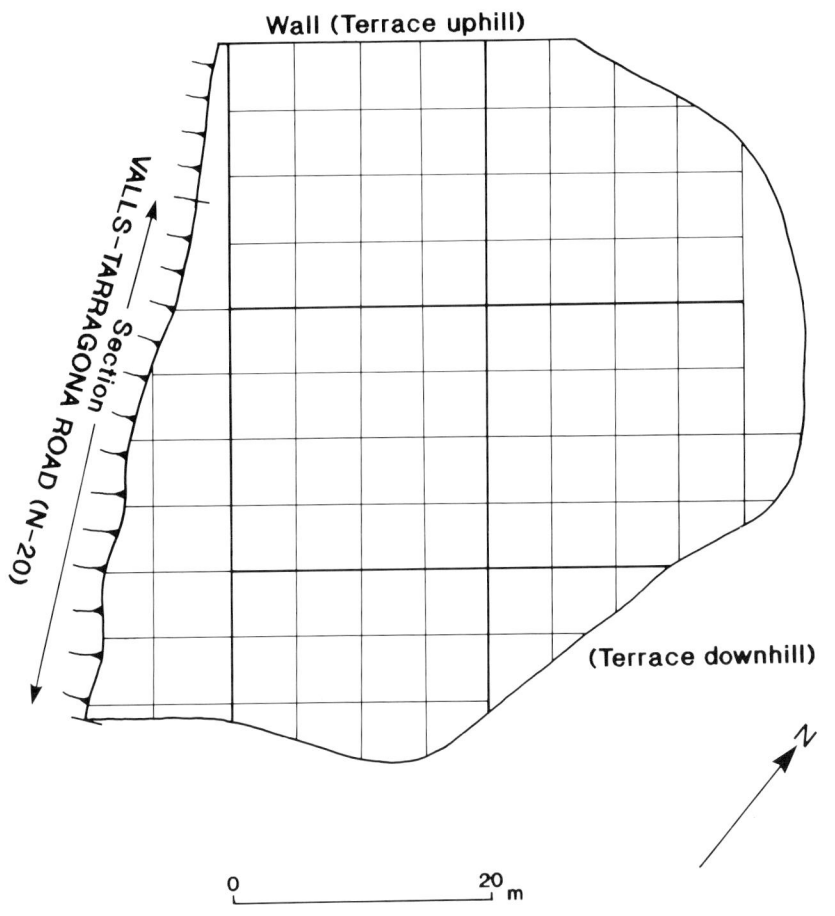

Fig.7.1. Situation and layout of the Vallmoll by-pass site (Field 1254); for location see fig.6.34.

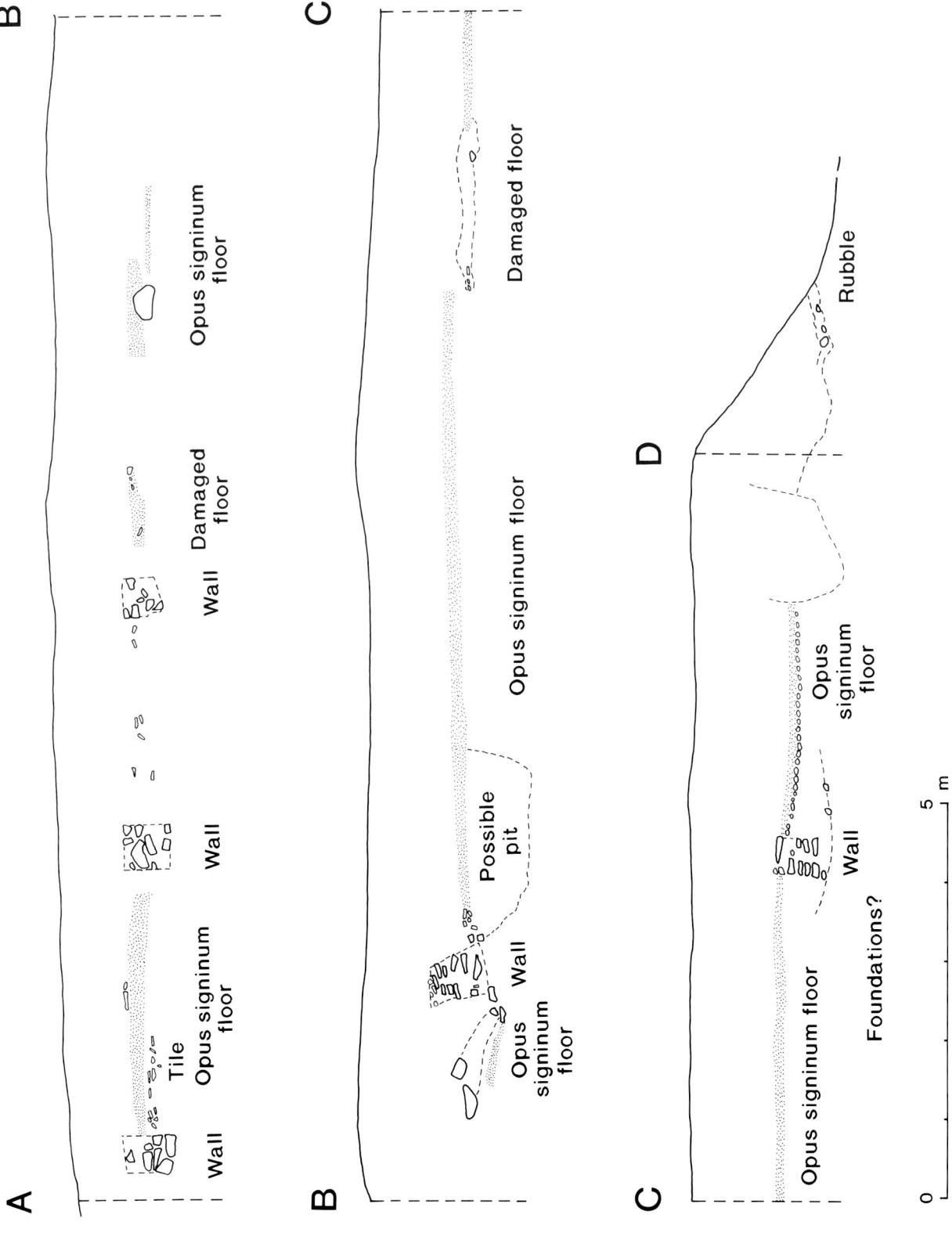

Fig.7.2A. Section exposed in the cutting for the Valmoll by-pass. For location see fig.7.1. For the relationship to the geophysical survey see fig.7.3. (Note: the cutting has been raked at an angle of 30° from the vertical, but in the drawing the perspective has been corrected to allow for it.)

Fig.7.2B. Part of the section shown in fig. 7.2A.

| Ceramic phase: | Number of sherds | Sherds per ha | Adjusted value |
|---|---|---|---|
| Iberian | 3 | 14.28 | 5.71 |
| Republican | 14 | 66.67 | 26.67 |
| Early empire | 106 | 504.76 | 201.90 |
| Late empire | 42 | 200 | 80 |

As the material was collected from within a grid which was thoroughly searched, the figures need to be adjusted for comparison with those obtained from line walking. It was estimated in Chapter 4 that line walkers at 5 m intervals cover 40-50 % of the surface. Thus the values for the totals from Field 1254 have been adjusted to 40% of the recorded density values for comparison. When compared with the scales used for identifying 'adabs' (Table 4.2), it will be seen that Field 1254 lies in the top 10 percentile in all phases except the Iberian. It would thus have been considered a potential site from the Republican to late imperial phases. The limited amount of stratified pottery recovered from the section is consistent with this dating. The substantial quantity of tile from the surface also supports its identification as a settlement. To this extent the experiment provides reassurance about the validity of our methods, despite the rather deep soil cover exposed in the section (fig. 7.2A) which might have been thought to make its identification from the surface difficult. In terms of site classification (Chapter 8) it would have been classified as size A and of higher status.

*The Geophysical Survey, by Jeremy Taylor*

The road section (fig. 7.2A) showed that soil depth in Field 1254 was far greater than on most of the other sites surveyed using geophysical techniques (see p.223 ff.). At 'A' on the section the archaeological features lay *c*.0.9 (top of feature) to 1.7 m (bottom of feature) below the surface, gradually increasing to 1.5-2.2 m at 'D'. In the N corner of the field, however, soil depth was c.0.4 m. Surface conditions in the field were good but rows of long-established hazelnut trees occasionally prevented readings from being taken.

A series of features make interpretation of the survey results from Field 1254 problematic. Along the line of the road section and the terrace, exposure of the soil profile on two sides had led to considerable drying near the margins of the field. Thus the value of resistivity survey within c.4 m of these boundaries was negated by the masking effect of high superficial resistance, part of which can be seen at 'A' on fig. 7.3. Interpretation of the resistivity survey was further complicated by the localized effect of the irrigation for the hazelnut trees. In the immediate vicinity of each tree root systems draw water from depth, helping to retain moisture near the surface and thereby causing lower localized soil resistance. The trees cause intermittent patches of lower soil resistivity along the main lines of planting that occasionally mask anomalies related to archaeological structures directly beneath them.

The magnetometer survey was severely hampered by the low levels of magnetic enhancement. This was probably due both to the low magnetic susceptiblity of the underlying geology and to climatic effects such as those investigated by Tite (1975). The depth of burial of the features in Field 1254 also limited the results. As Clark (1990, 79) has noted, the sensitivity of both proton magnetometers and gradiometers falls off rapidly between 1 and 2 m, to the extent that a feature giving an anomaly of 3 nT at 1 m would give only c.0.3 nT at a depth of 2 m. Consequently, the results of the gradiometer survey were disappointing, producing no interpretable anomalies. The resistivity results, however, were promising. A series of linear and broadly rectangular areas of high soil resistance were identified. They can be largely interpreted as the remains of the walls and floors of three probable buildings ('B', 'C' and 'D' on fig. 7.3).

The S side of building B is quite well defined. The interpretative drawings indicate the existence of a small room S of a larger rectangular structure that consists of at least two further rooms. The slightly higher than average soil resistance inside this room is probably due to the presence of an extant floor surface. It corresponds well with the northernmost structure visible in the road section (near 'A' on fig. 7.3). The difficulty in identifying the N corner of building B is caused by a diffuse high resistance anomaly (at 'B1') which may be due to the destruction of this part of the building or to the presence of a spread of artefactual and structural débris above. This interpretation is supported by the results of fieldwalking which show a particularly high density of tile in this part of the site.

The anomalies shown as building C are difficult to interpret as they make an irregular outline and become weaker in the S corner of the survey grid as the depth of overburden reaches c.1 m. The N part of 'C' appears clearly as a rectilinear structure aligned SW-NE and joined on the S by at least two more rooms. At 'C1', however, there is a strong high-resistance anomaly that obscures the general outline of building B. It may be related to a further dump of débris but its clearly rectangular outline suggests that it may be another structure such as an olive press, possibly not necessarily contemporary with building C.

The area within the two southernmost rooms of building C shows higher than average levels of resistivity. If, as seems possible, they are linked to the features identified in the road section (between 'B' and 'D' in fig. 7.3), they are likely to be the remains of opus signinum floors.

Building D was identified from relatively clear high-resistance anomalies on its N and W sides; they faded quickly along the S side and probably extend beyond the E edge of the survey. The poor resolution of the S side of the building was probably due to the direct superimposition of a row of hazelnut trees and their localized effect on soil moisture, rather than to destruction of the feature itself.

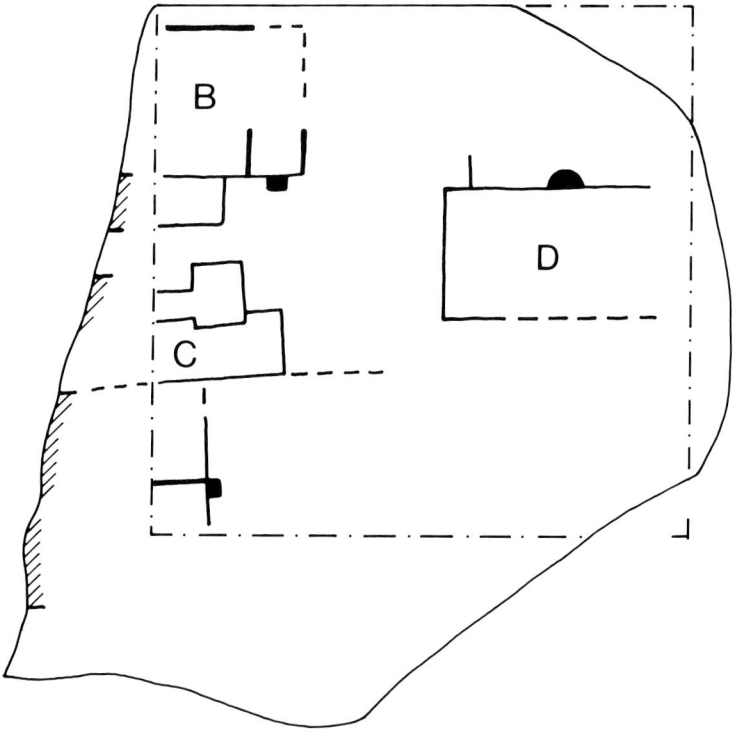

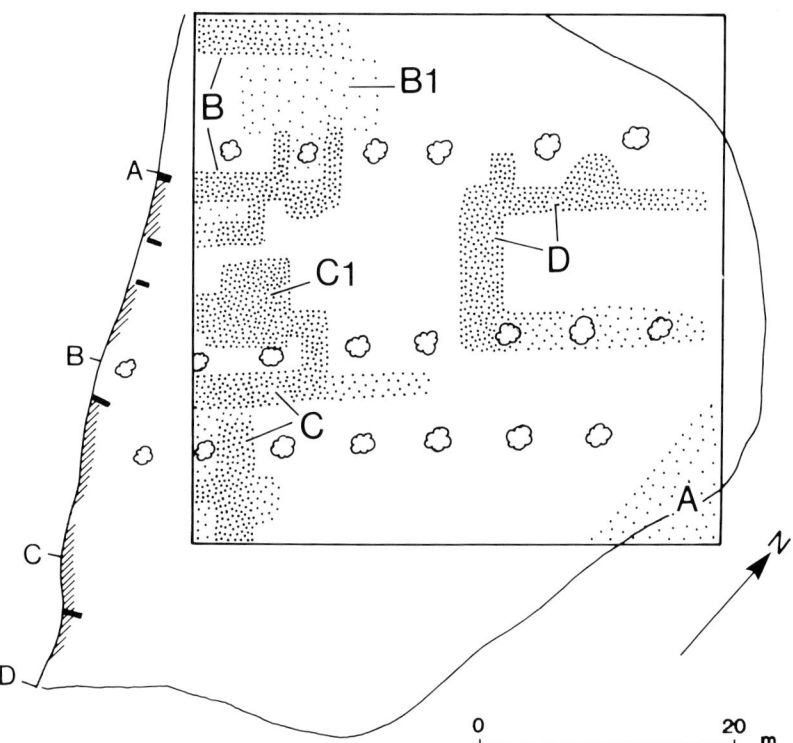

Fig.7.3. Geophysical survey of the Vallmoll by-pass site. Upper plan shows interpretation; lower plan shows the evidence. For key see fig.7.5.

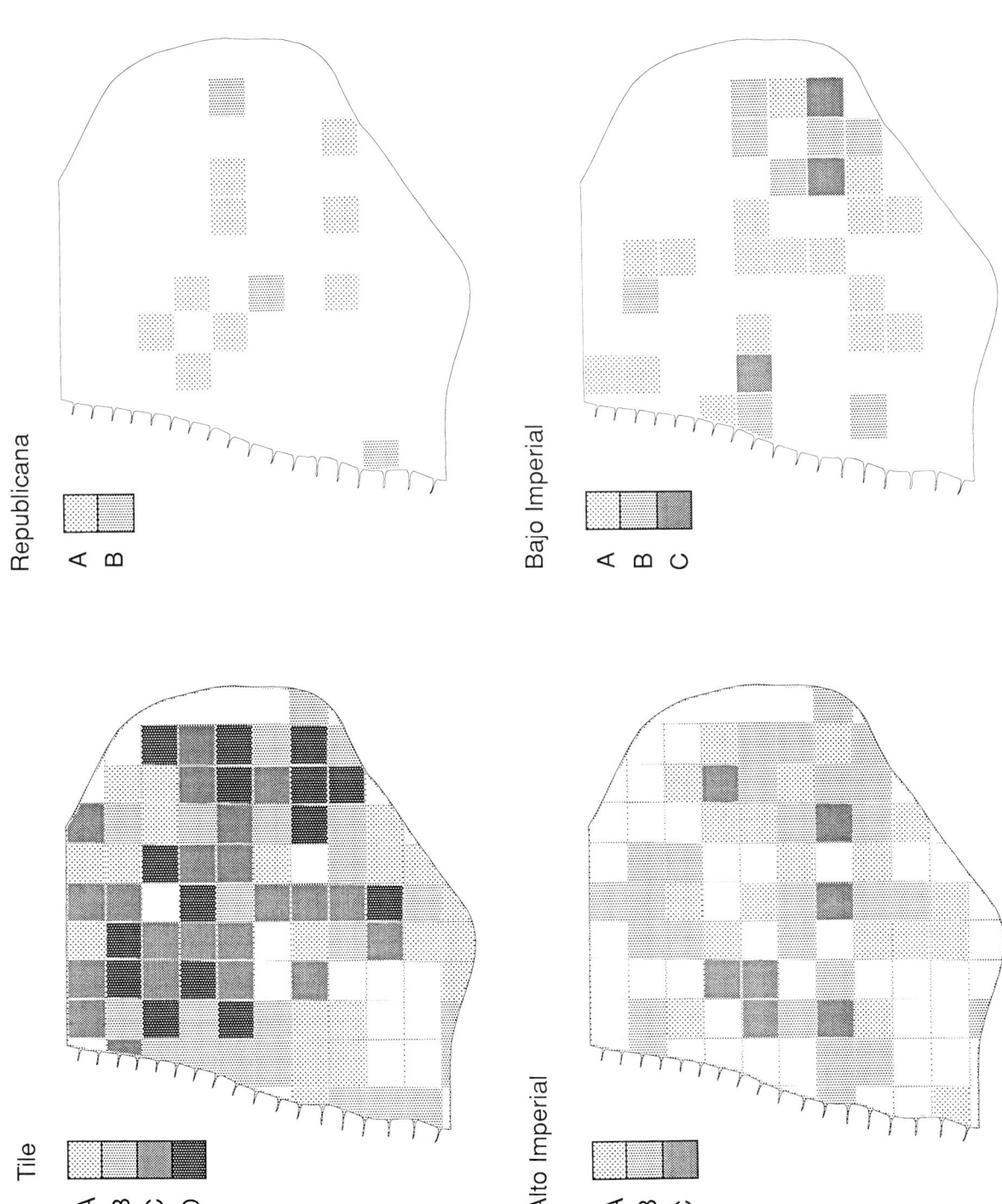

Fig. 7.4. Surface survey evidence from the Vallmoll by-pass site (Field 1254).
  A. Tile: scales, A = 1-2 fr. per square; B - 3-5 fr. per square; C = 6-8 fr. per square; D = 9 or more fr. per square.
  B. Republican pottery: scales, A = 1 sherd per square; B = 2 sherds per square.
  C. Early imperial pottery: scales, A = 1 sherd per square; B = 2-3 sherds per square; C = 4-6 sherds per square.
  D. Late imperial pottery: scales, A = 1 sherd per square; B = 2 sherds per square; C = 3 sherds per square.

Field-walking results

The exercise of grid-walking the site also provided the opportunity both to make comparisons between the distribution of surface finds and the geophysical results, and to examine details of the distributions of finds across the site. The small grid-size used in relation to the densities of material means that for some finds the recorded values are relatively low. Four sets of data have been plotted (fig. 7.4) using scales based on the density variations revealed within the field.[3]

The tile density (fig. 7.4A) was high across the whole field, with a maximum recorded value of 17 fragments per square (the equivalent of 6800 fragments per ha). The highest densities were concentrated across the N part of the field. There is a reasonable correspondence with the results of the geophysical surveys except in two places. At the S end of the field the geophysics and the section of the road cutting reveal the presence of buildings which are not apparent in the distribution of tile, probably because of the greater depth of topsoil in this area. On the other hand, there is a concentration of tile in the E part of the site which does not correspond to any of the buildings revealed by the geophysics although there was an amorphous anomaly ('A' on fig. 7.3). It may be the remains of another building less clearly defined than the others, a hypothesis which would be supported by the concentration of tile. An alternative explanation is a midden containing tile lying to the rear of the other buildings.

The Republican pottery (fig. 7.4B) is sparse. Its distribution largely mirrors that of the tile. Given the shallower soil depth at the N end of the field one might have expected more earlier pottery in this area since ploughing would have cut into earlier deposits but, as is clear from the density plots, this is not the case. Pottery of the early empire is more prolific and covered the same general area as the tile (fig. 7.4C). The slight concentration in the pottery distribution over Building C perhaps suggests that this building may be of Republican date. In contrast the late imperial pottery (fig. 7.4D) is less profuse but tends to concentrate away from the modern road, especially just S of Building D. This concentration coincides with the amorphous geophysical anomaly (A) and with one of the peaks in the density of tile. Whether it is a midden or a building, the evidence suggests a late imperial date.

Although these conclusions can be only tentative, the work on Field 1254 demonstrates the potential of integrated survey strategies for obtaining reasonably detailed evidence from such sites (cf. Keay *et al.* 1992). The overall plan does not resemble that of a classic villa. It may be either the *pars rustica* of a villa largely destroyed by the road-cutting or a nucleated settlement located at the junction of a route along the E side of the Francolí with one following the valley of the Torrent d'Hospitatet from the NW.

## 3. GEOPHYSICAL SURVEYS OF FIELD-WALKED SITES, *by Jeremy Taylor*

The above evidence points to the potential of geophysics to investigate surface scatters identified as rural settlements. In order to assess the physical relationship of the 'adabs' to any surviving structural remains below ground, a small sample of fields within some of the 'sites' was surveyed using a Geoscan FM18 Fluxgate Gradiometer and RM 4 Soil Resistivity Meter. Data from the surveys were stored and processed using the Geoplot version 1.2 software. The figures produced below are interpretive plans based on a composite of both the gradiometer and resistivity results from each site. For reasons of space, and to allow a synthetic view of the anomalies from each site to be discussed, the original plots are not presented but are available

---

3    In each of the plots the recorded densities of part squares have been rounded up to allow for their size.

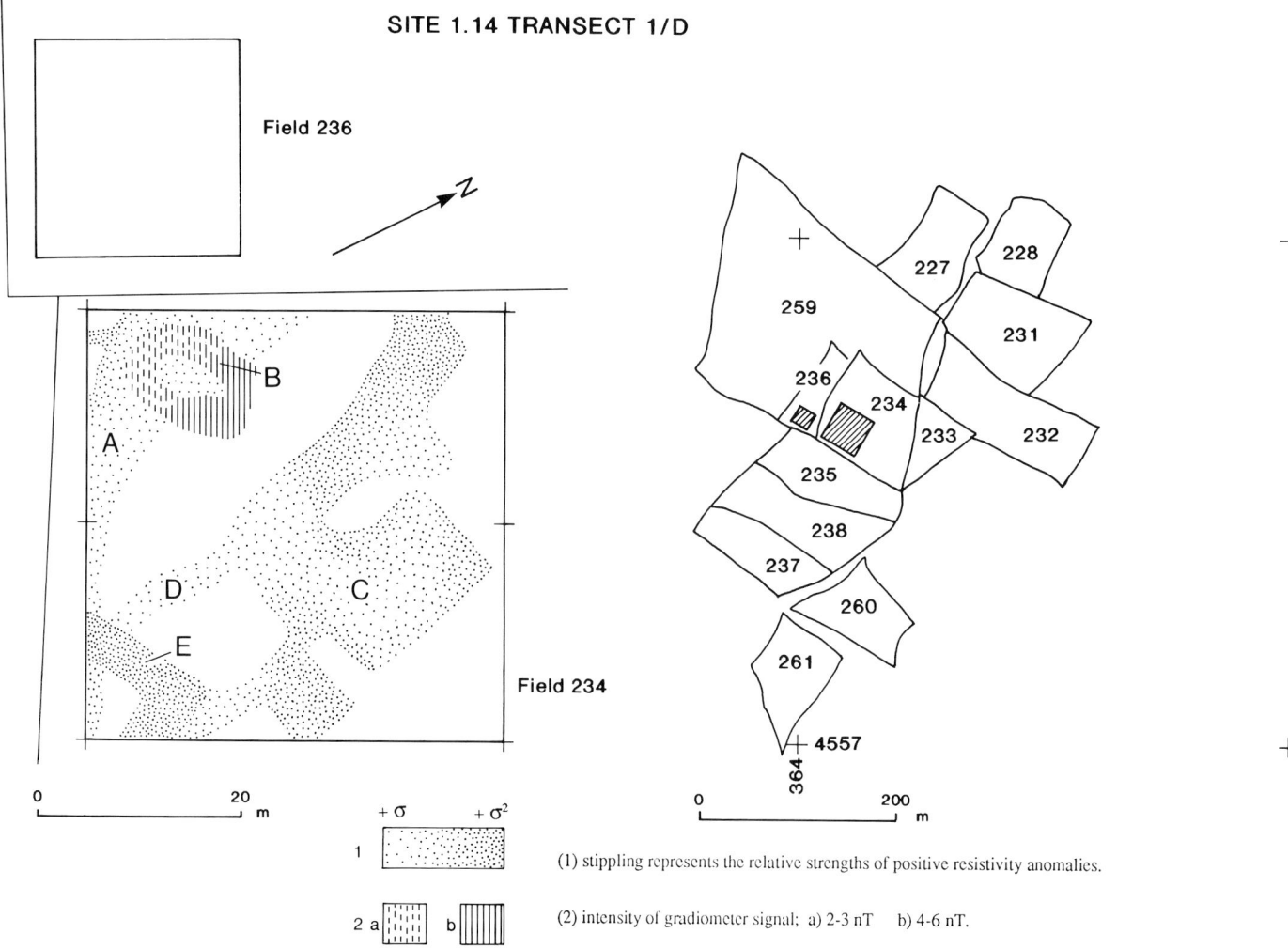

SITE 1.14 TRANSECT 1/D

Fig.7.5. Geophysical survey of site 1.14.

for consultation. Some impression of the strength and clarity of definition of each anomaly is provided by the intensity or type of shading used in conjunction with the figure legends.
The surveys were devised to investigate
1. whether high densities of localized surface ceramics relate broadly to the existence of settlement foci;
2. to study the form of subsurface archaeological remains in the sample fields and their state of preservation, and
3. to consider the viability of using magnetometry and resistivity for archaeological survey in the region.

In all, four sites identified by field walking were investigated (Sites 1.14, 2.9, 4.1 and 4.6), in addition to that at Vallmoll (Field 1254, see p.219 ff.) which lay outside the main transects. The overriding intention was to choose sites that represented much of the topographical, chronological and size-range of field scatters. The local and background context for each site is described and comments on ground conditions at the time of the surveys are provided.[4] Wider implications of the individual surveys are discussed at the end.

---

4    The information for this aspect of the survey was largely provided by Dr Romola Parish to whom I am particularly grateful.

**Site reports**

*Site 1.14* (Transect 1/D, see p.176)

The site consisted of Fields 234, 235, 236 and 238 (see fig. 7.5). For ease of access and continuity, Fields 234 and 236 were selected for survey. Both were small terraced fields on the valley side facing ESE. Soil depth was 100-150 mm, the deepest point lying on the lower edges of both terraces. Field 234 was under olive cultivation and surface conditions were good though dry. Field 236 was an abandoned olive grove with poor surface conditions and much thorny scrub.

Artefact collection indicated significant densities of material throughout, with the focus in Field 235 during the Iberian, Republican and early imperial phases, and in 236 during the late Roman phase. Field 234 showed consistently high densities of ceramics through all the periods mentioned.

The survey covered an area of 40 x 40 m in the W corner of Field 234. The interpretation of the results is shown in fig. 7.5. The area of generally higher soil resistance in the SW corner of the survey ('A') was the result of localized soil denudation. The effects of this process on the surviving archaeology are indicated by the marked weakening of a magnetometer anomaly, presumably due to its partial destruction ('B'). It is difficult to infer the archaeological origin of the anomaly at 'B' particularly as, at best, it had a contrast of only 4 nT from background. However, it may well represent the eroded remains of a roughly rectangular structure orientated NE-SW. A brief test survey in Field 236 suggested that a combination of surface conditions (particularly the development of a thick calcareous crust) and erosion made further survey here impractical.

The very shallow soil depths in Fields 234 and particularly 236 mean that any surviving feature is likely to have been levelled by the plough or cut into the underlying bedrock. The majority of the area is covered by a series of fairly well defined broad linear or rectangular areas of markedly higher soil resistance ('C'). They are probably the remains of floor surfaces within buildings and possibly (at 'D') the course of a path or road between them. Only one part of the site showed a slightly greater soil depth, where a well-defined linear anomaly may represent the survival of the corner of a building ('E').

*Site 2.9* (Transect 2/D, see p.187)

The site consisted of Fields 683, 688, 690-91, 693, 696-98 and 700 covering the crest and sides of a bluff overlooking the main valley (fig. 7.6) and a tributary running ESE and SE. Field 696 was chosen for survey as it was a reasonable size and lay at the centre of the ceramic cluster. Field collection had indicated particularly high densities of ceramics of all phases except late Roman with only a few sherds.

The field surveyed lay on the top of the bluff and sloped down gradually to the SE, though its NE edge reached a retaining terrace wall. Soils at the top of the slope were thinner (c.100-150 mm), with far more chalky pebbles and gravel and poor vegetation cover. On the slope by the terrace-edge grass cover was thicker and more continuous, and both the clay fraction (40%) and soil depth (c.270 mm) were higher. The geomorphological field assessment suggested that both soil fines and ceramics had been washed from the upper parts of the slope and accumulated between the break of slope and the wall of the terrace, leaving stones and larger artefacts near the crest.

The survey covered a roughly L-shaped area of c.2200 m$^2$ mostly along the E side of the bluff (fig. 7.6). The magnetometer survey identified very little of significance except for two poorly defined anomalies (c.2-5 nT) c.3-4 m across ('A' and 'B'). Their interpretation is difficult but they may represent localized dumps of ceramics or other magnetized material incorporated in structural débris.

226

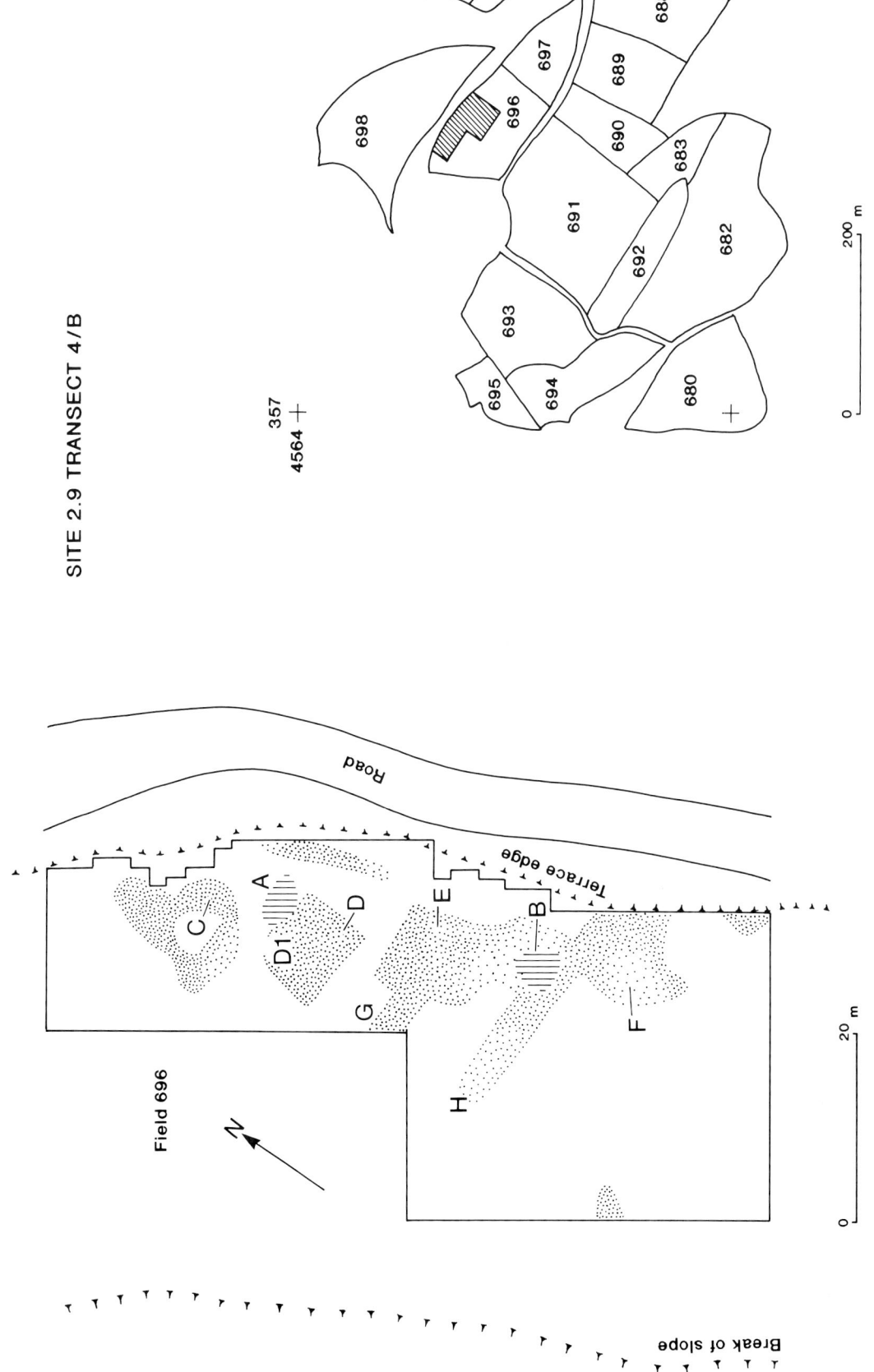

Fig.7.6. Geophysical survey of site 2.9. For key see fig.7.5.

The resistivity survey identified a number of clear, broadly rectangular anomalies arranged E-W along the E edge of the field. These high-resistance anomalies ('C', 'D', 'E', and 'F') almost certainly represent the eroded remains of floor surfaces surviving under the slightly deeper soil in the lee of the terrace wall. This was confirmed by the exposure of an *opus signinum* floor at 'D1'. Its exposure coincides with the point at which anomaly 'D' becomes more difficult to define and it probably represents the beginnings of the erosion of this surface. The almost total absence of resistivity anomalies along the centre of the bluff is best explained by soil denudation. Examination of the field surface in parts of the S quarter of the site revealed the mouths of rock-cut storage pits sealed with stone covers. Further support for the idea of almost total soil erosion along the field crest is given by the gradual fading of the two main linear high-resistance anomalies as they head E across the site ('G' and 'H').

*Site 4.1* (Transect 4/B, see p.201)

Site 4.1 covered two relatively flat fields (884 and 885) which were under vines and recently cultivated at the time of survey (fig. 7.7). Field 885 was selected for survey as it was the principal focus for deposition except during the Republican period. It lay on a slight S-facing slope on the plateau beyond Valls. Soil depth was better than on most sites within the survey (*c*.300 mm) and had well defined A-C horizons. The underlying geology was different from the predominantly limestone bedrock lower down the valley, and the soil matrix contained quartz, basalt and limestone cobbles (Parish, pers. comm.). There was no evidence for local drainage.

Preliminary soil evaluation suggested that the site was better preserved than most of the others. The presence of metamorphic intrusions in the soil might have been expected to cause problems of 'noise' for the magnetometer survey, but examination of the plots proved otherwise. The higher magnetic susceptibility of such minerals in the soil matrix may help to explain the stronger anomalies produced in the plot, particularly in connection with the linear feature running diagonally across the survey ('A'). It is interpreted as the line of a wall or drain, probably of tile or brick (though possibly stone if local rock with magnetic susceptibility is employed). The line of the magnetometer anomaly is matched by a corresponding area of generally lower-than-average resistivity, perhaps supporting the view that it is a brick or tile structure. It may contain more clay, creating differential moisture retention and thereby lowering soil resistivity. (Open structured stone walls, on the other hand, tend to retain little moisture and thus have higher resistivity.)

Higher levels of soil resistivity inside the area delimited by the linear anomaly ('B' and 'C') are likely to represent the remains of floor surfaces and débris within a building running E out of the survey area. Localized magnetometer anomalies at 'D' and 'E' are, to judge by experience at Peñaflor, Sevilla, probably the result of spreads of ceramics and amphorae (Jordan, pers. comm.), though they can sometimes be caused by concentrations of structural débris (Taylor, in prep.). It should be noted that Dressel 1 amphorae with Iberian stamps and other material had suggested the possible presence of kilns in the vicinity of the site. It is unlikely however that 'D' and 'E' are kilns, due to the poor strength and definition of their anomalies.

*Site 4.6* (Transect 4/C, see p.210)

Field 1048 comprised all of Site 4.6 (fig. 7.8) which surface collection suggested was of Iberian and Republican date. The field was covered by young almond trees and ground conditions were generally good. There was no evidence for local erosion or deposition, and the ground surface was almost perfectly flat. There was a chalky bed-rock and soil depth was reasonable (*c*.200 mm). The presence of small quantities of granite erratic pebbles created some signal 'noise' for the magnetometer survey but did not obscure anomalies.

The gradiometer survey identified an intermittently stronger (*c*.5-6 nT) and weaker (2-4 nT) linear anomaly delimiting a broadly rectangular area orientated E-W and extending beyond

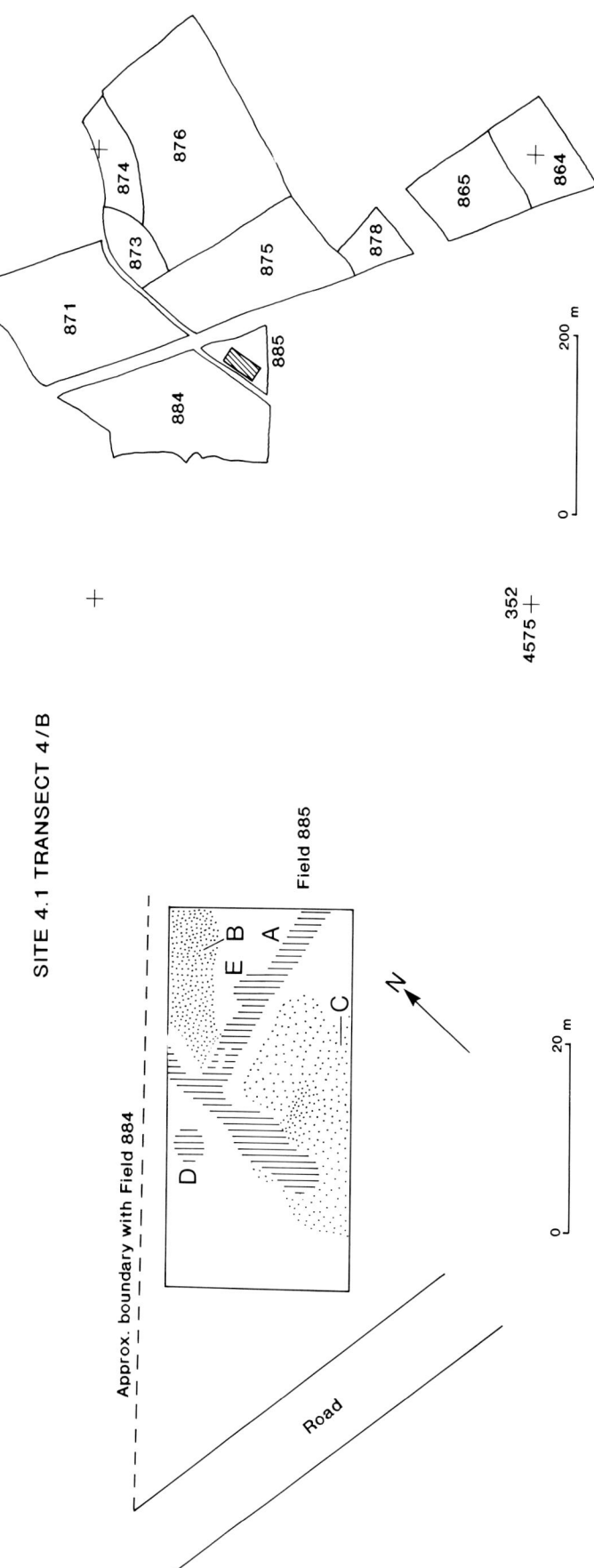

Fig.7.7. Geophysical survey of site 4.1. For key see fig.7.5.

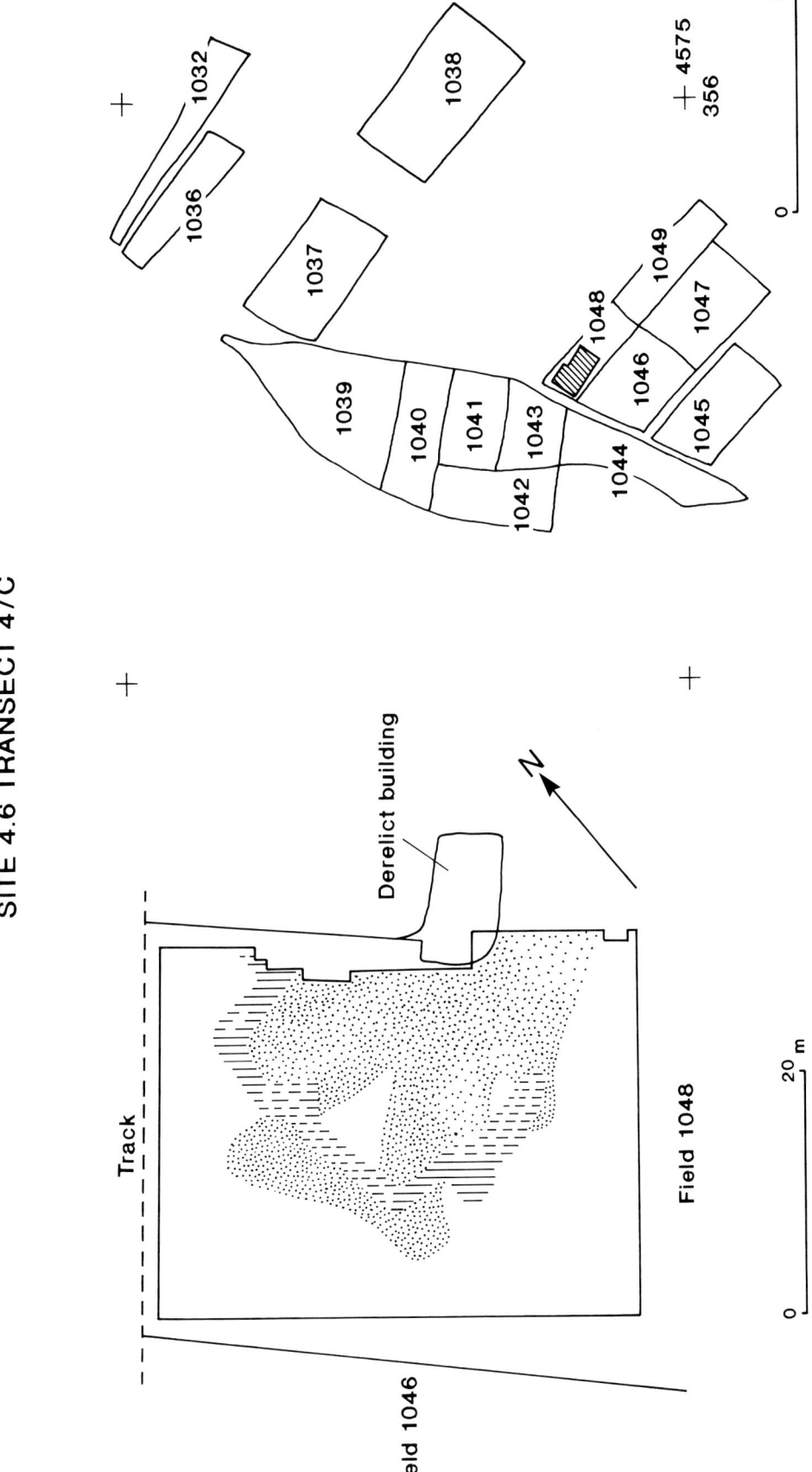

SITE 4.6 TRANSECT 4/C

Fig.7.8. Geophysical survey of site 4.6. For key see fig.7.5.

the NE boundary of Field 1048. It probably represents the line of a partly destroyed wall which, as it encloses an area of over 600 m$^2$, is less likely to be a building than an enclosure wall, possibly for a yard. The resistivity survey indicates that within this anomaly there was higher-than-average resistivity almost throughout. It was probably caused by the survival of a floor surface and/or extensive spreads of artefacts and structural débris. If this were the case, the building to which it would have been attached probably lay outside Field 1048 in an unsurveyed area to the E or, more probably, there was a timber structure within the enclosure.

The small size of the collection from this site and the nature of the plot from the geophysical survey suggest that it belongs to a small enclosure of Iberian and Republican date.

Discussion

The four surveys discussed and that at Vallmoll (p.219) provide a very limited sample on the basis of which to discuss the issues raised at the start. They do, however, provide some useful insights into some of the problems and possibilities of evaluating artefact scatters.

Most promisingly, all the geophysical surveys identified some surviving structural remains, suggesting that the classification of these scatters as 'sites' (or foci of activity) was valid. What form these sites took, and whether they were all parts of settlements, is a more complicated issue that is not easily resolved on the basis of the limited sampling surveys carried out. Some suggestions about the nature of occupation at each site have been made above, but a more detailed consideration of their form would require fuller surveys of each scatter and trial excavations to evaluate problems of interpretation or dating.

The combination of geomorphological evaluation in the field with geophysical surveys also enabled the very variable and often severe erosion across the region to be assessed. Fields 234, 236 (Site 1.14) and 696 (Site 2.9) were particularly badly eroded, and the surveys suggested that little would remain other than floor surfaces and features cut into the underlying bedrock. The majority of artefacts on these sites will already have been incorporated into the ploughsoil, and few if any pockets of stratigraphy will survive. Although fields such as these may be common within the region, it is not as severe a problem as was first thought. The survival of A-C horizons at Sites 4.1, 4.6, and the Vallmoll by-pass show that some of the scatters collected come from fields where some limited stratigraphy remains along with some standing architectural features. The great depth of stratigraphy at Vallmoll creates its own problems for interpretation but clearly shows that some buried sites in the region are still detectable from the surface.

Magnetometry was not generally well suited to conditions within the region, and by and large results were poor. In lowland areas the underlying geology and soils generally have very low magnetic susceptibility and surviving archaeological materials appear to show little contrast. The latter can partly be explained by the use of locally available limestone as building material. It is exacerbated by the effect of climatic conditions on soil magnetic susceptibility noted above and elsewhere in Spain (Taylor, in prep.). Better results were obtained further inland where the underlying geology and soils included metamorphic intrusions with higher magnetic susceptibility. Even here, however, anomaly contrast was weak, and on sites with deeper soil profiles, such as Vallmoll, any signal from archaeological features could be too attenuated to be detectable.

The resistivity surveys, by contrast, were largely successful. They often detected clear anomalies of significance. Problems arose only where the surviving archaeological deposits were themselves poorly preserved or masked by débris. Only occasionally, as in Field 236 (Site 1.14) and at Vallmoll, did local surface conditions or drainage cause difficulties. The small size of fields and terracing in the region often created problems where field walls or terraces created bands of higher resistance or obstructed survey of a large site. In lower lying areas, however, this should not prove too great an obstacle to further survey.

# Chapter 8: CLASSIFICATION OF SITES

Information on the distribution of ceramics across the survey area has been collated and certain concentrations have been identified as likely settlements. Before analysing the distribution of the sites, we should attempt to classify them since there are clearly significant differences between them. Other surveys have attempted to identify certain sites as villas through the presence of diagnostic finds, particularly architectural fragments. In this survey only one site (1.10) produced significant architectural decoration. Although others produced fragments of *opus signinum,* most of the 49 sites yielded none of the materials that would have enabled us to produce a classification solely on the basis of their architecture. Our classification is thus based primarily on size. Similar approaches have been used in other surveys but it is important to clarify the methods used, their limitations, and implications.

The approach followed here has been to examine each proposed site, taking field conditions into account. The aim was to ensure that the area of the scatter belonging to the defining top 10 percentile gave a reasonable estimate of its size. No systematic attempt has been made to adjust the sizes of the areas recorded in light of any additional material that might have lain outside the walked fields. Estimated values have been provided only in cases where there were difficult circumstances. For example, at Site 1.12 only that part of Field 120 recorded in the field notes has been included as part of the area counted, because the field was very large and to have taken its whole area would have given an overestimate.

The areas finally calculated (Table 8.1) thus represent the total *walked* area covered by the most dense pottery scatters. This has several implications. First, in the cases where only part of a site was accessible, the figure underestimates its size. Second, as our collection units were the individual fields, the average size of which was around 1 ha, the area of smaller sites will have been overestimated. Third, the method leads to an overestimate of size in cases where very large concentrations of material have been spread by agricultural activity or erosion. Finally, the method used for defining 'adabs' tends to normalize the results between phases, minimizing any distinctions. Little can be done to compensate for this. Its impact may not be too serious as there is some variation between phases of the total proportion of the surveyed area included within sites:

| Phase: | Iberian | Republican | Early Empire | Late Empire |
|---|---|---|---|---|
| % of total area included within sites: | 7.6% | 7.9% | 6.9% | 2.9% |

It does not seem sensible to try to compensate for these factors, although they need to be borne in mind when discussing the results. The first two problems perhaps balance each other out, but the general conclusion is that the data are imperfect, never likely to be susceptible to precise classification.

With these problems in mind, the sizes of the sites identified in each of the 4 broad chronological phases were plotted on graphs (fig. 8.1). The majority of the scatters were small, most being less than 2 ha. They have been further divided to separate those under 1 ha. A second group clusters between 4 and 8 ha. They too have been subdivided to separate those between 2 and 4 ha. Finally, a few sites were larger than 8 ha in extent. On this basis 5 size classes have been defined for further analysis:

| Class | Size range |
|---|---|
| A | < 1 ha |
| B | 1-2 ha |
| C | 2-4 ha |
| D | 4-8 ha |
| E | > 8 ha |

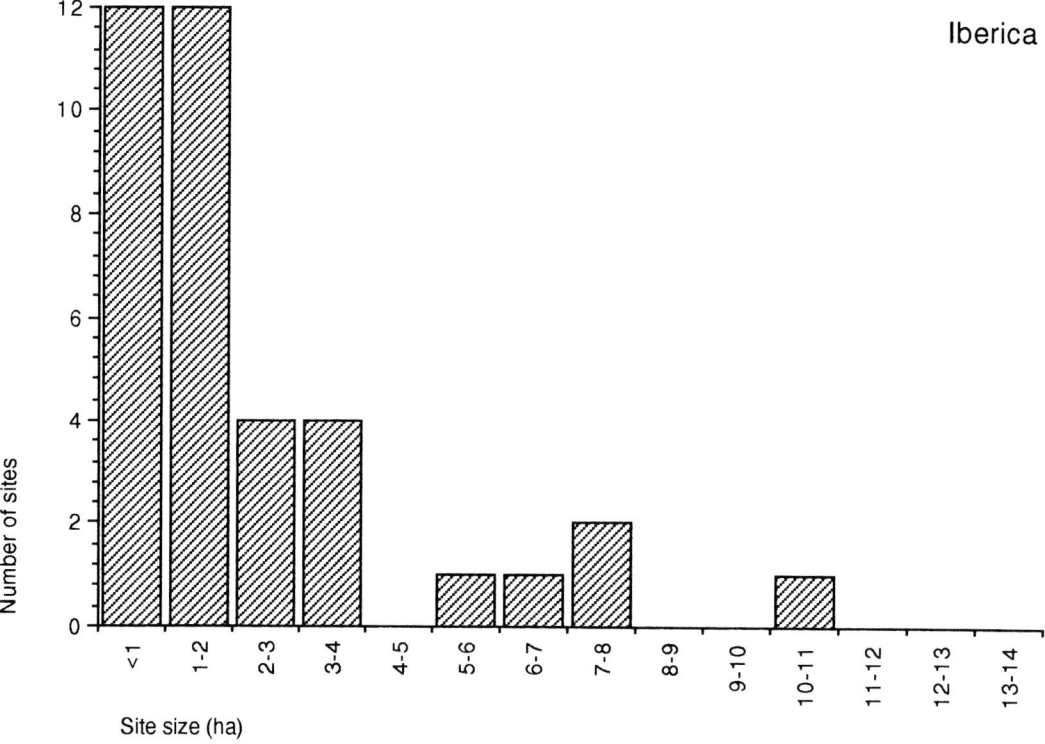

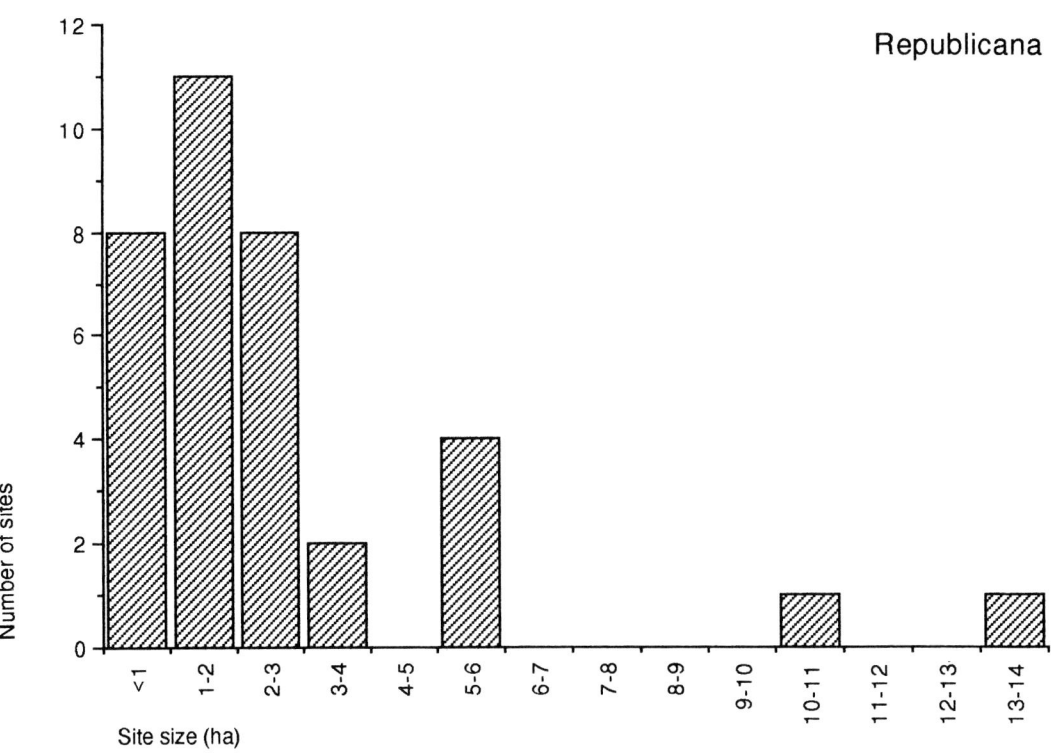

Fig.8.1. Changing size of sites through time.

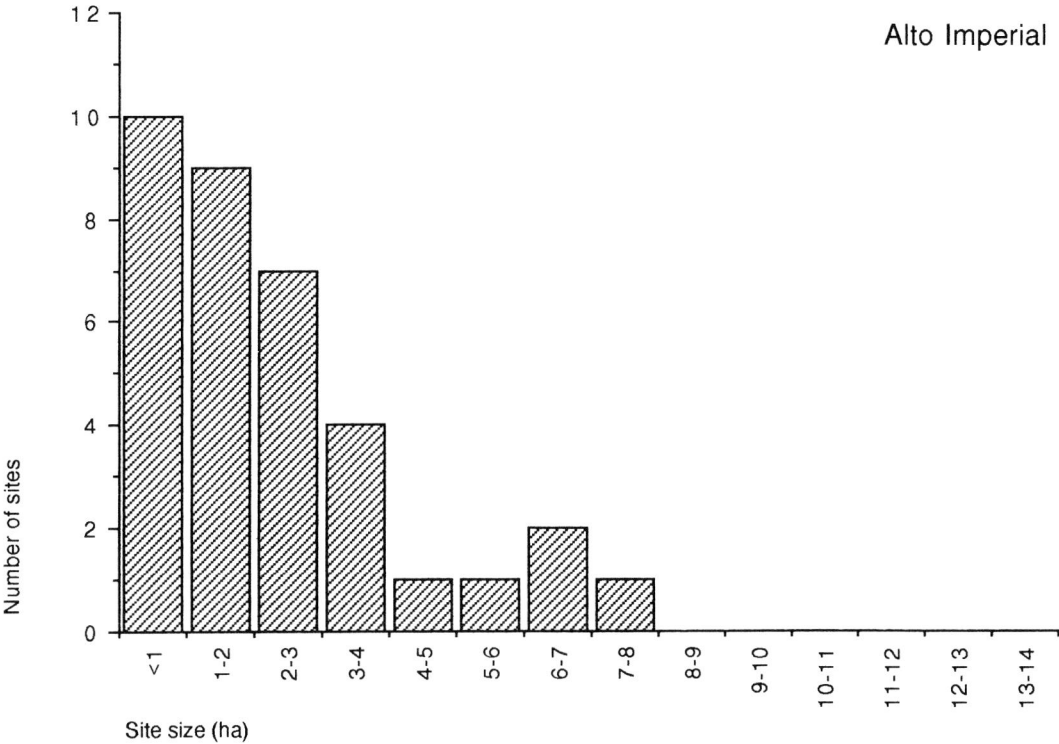

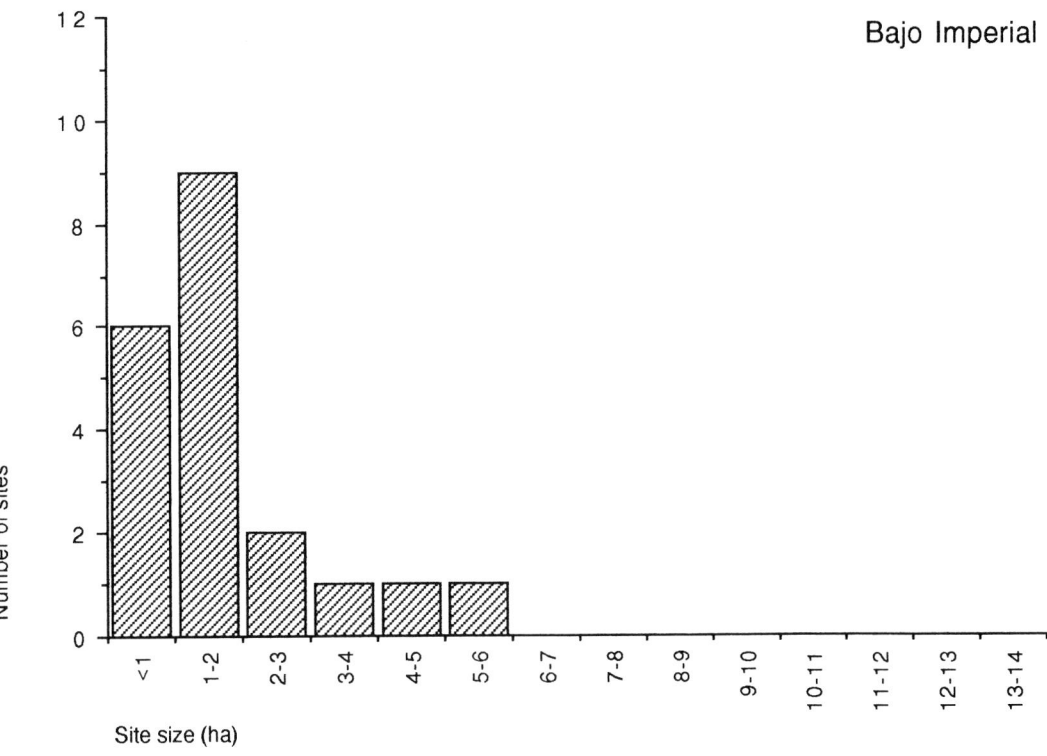

Fig.8.1 (continued). Changing size of sites through time.

# Chapter 8

Table 8.1    Size and classification of sites through the four ceramic phases

**Transect 1**

| Site | 1.1 | 1.2 | 1.3 | 1.4 | 1.5 | 1.6 | 1.7 | 1.8 | 1.9 | 1.10 | 1.11 | 1.12 | 1.13 | 1.14 |
|---|---|---|---|---|---|---|---|---|---|---|---|---|---|---|
| Iberian | A | C | | B | A | C | B | B | A | A | A | B | B | B |
| Republican | | D | A | B | A | D | C | C | B | A | A | B | A | C |
| Early Imperial | | A | | B | | D | C | C | A | C | | | | C |
| Late Imperial | | | | | | B | | | A | C | | | | A |
| Tile | | yes | | yes | | yes | yes | yes | | yes | | | | |
| Opus signinum | | | | | | yes | yes | | | yes | | | | |
| Dolia | | | | | | yes | yes | | | yes | | | | yes |
| Architectural stone | | | | | | | | | | yes | | | | |

**Transect 2**

| Site | 2.1 | 2.2 | 2.3 | 2.4 | 2.5 | 2.6 | 2.7 | 2.8 | 2.9 | 2.10 |
|---|---|---|---|---|---|---|---|---|---|---|
| Iberian | | | C | A | | A | A | | C | C |
| Republican | B | A | C | B | B | C | C | | D | C |
| Early Imperial | B | D | C | B | B | D | C | C | C | C |
| Late Imperial | B | | D | | | | D | C | C | |
| Tile | | | yes | | | yes | yes | | yes | |
| Opus signinum | | | | | | | yes | | yes | |

**Transect 3**

| Site | 3.1 | 3.2 | 3.3 | 3.4 | 3.5 | 3.6 | 3.7 | 3.8 | 3.9 | 3.10 | 3.11 | 3.12 | 3.13 | 3.14 | 3.15 | 3.16 | 3.17 | 3.18 | 3.19 |
|---|---|---|---|---|---|---|---|---|---|---|---|---|---|---|---|---|---|---|---|
| Iberian | B | A | B | B | B | A | | | B | A | C | | B | | B | D | B | C | E |
| Republican | | A | B | B | B | A | | B | C | A | A | | | | B | D | B | C | E |
| Early Imperial | | A | | | B | | A | | B | A | A | A | | A | A | D | | | C |
| Late Imperial | | A | | | B | | | | A | B | A | A | | | | B | | | B |
| Tile | | | | | yes | | | | | | | | | | | | | | yes |
| Opus signinum | | | | | | | | | | | | | | | | | | | |
| Dolia | | | | | | | | | | [yes] | | [yes] | | | | [yes] | | | [yes] |

**Transect 4**

| Site | 4.1 | 4.2 | 4.3 | 4.4 | 4.5 | 4.6 |
|---|---|---|---|---|---|---|
| Iberian | A | D | D | D | C | A |
| Republican | C | B | | E | B | |
| Early Imperial | C | B | B | D | A | |
| Late Imperial | | B | | B | | |
| Tile | | yes | | yes | | |
| Opus signinum | | | | | | |
| Dolia | yes | yes | [yes] | yes | | |

Key:

yes = present

[yes] = only one sherd

D = "Lower status"

*D* = "Intermediate status"

**D** = "Higher status"

This classification provides a useful basis for analysis, although it does not take account of the full range of evidence available. Although insufficient architectural material was available to form the basis of the classification, there were three kinds of material which can supplement the information on site area. First, as only a proportion of the sites produced more than a few pieces of tile, its presence is a potentially useful method for distinguishing between sites. Second, it has sometimes been suggested that the presence of *dolia* might allow farms engaged in larger-scale agricultural production to be identified, as *dolia* were used for the storage of large volumes of agricultural produce. Finally, a few sites produced fragments of *opus signinum* flooring that demonstrate a basic level of architectural elaboration.

The principal difficulty with using these three sets of finds is that none can be dated and the unstratified character of the material rules out dating by association. Thus, although the dated pottery can be used to provide some information about changing site sizes through time (fig. 8.1), it is not possible to assign the tile, *dolia*, or *opus signinum* to a particular period in the occupation of a site. Thus it becomes difficult to judge whether these materials were widely spread between sites of different sizes through time, or whether they were confined to sites of a particular size or period. Some of these questions will be addressed when we assess changing settlement patterns (see Chapter 9). Here, however, we have compared the occurrence of tile, *opus signinum*, and *dolia* with each site's maximum area (fig. 8.2). The graphs show a higher incidence of each class of material on the medium-sized and larger sites. Some chronological patterning is implied, since none of the sites which disappeared during the Iberian and Republican phases was associated with tile, suggesting that it was probably characteristic of the imperial period. The graphs provide some support for the notion that larger site size was correlated with both architectural elaboration (as measured through the presence of tile and *opus signinum*) and the storage of agricultural surpluses.

This approach is limited, as the presence of tile, *dolium* and *opus signinum* is compared only with maximum site sizes, not with particular sites or the occurrence of the characteristic materials on them. Table 8.1 shows that these diagnostic materials do often occur together, suggesting that there was a hierarchy of sites related to their size. Not every large site had indicators of higher status, but they were almost entirely absent from the smallest sites. Given the contrasts between the sites found and the more spectacular villas known previously (see Chapter 1), it would be extravagant to claim that even our larger, higher-status sites were major villas. Instead, it seems more appropriate to draw a distinction between different categories of farmstead. A dual method of classification has been adopted, where each phase of a site is assigned to a class according to its size (see above) and is graded as of 'Lower', 'Intermediate' or 'Higher status' on the basis of other finds, using the following criteria:

| | |
|---|---|
| Lower status | Neither tile, **nor** *opus signinum* **nor** *dolia* |
| Intermediate status | Tile, **or** *opus signinum* **or** more than one fragment of *dolium* present. |
| Higher status | More than one of these materials present |

The term 'Highest status' is reserved for those previously known sites which were clearly substantial villas (see Chapter 1). Our classification of the individual sites found in the survey is shown in Table 8.1. It shows that there is a correlation between increased size and enhanced status. Although it is not a perfect system of classification, it forms a basis both for the analysis of the distribution of sites and for comparisons with pottery distribution. The geophysical surveys (Chapter 8) have demonstrated that even the smallest sites of lower status (e.g., Site 4.6) contained defined structures. This supports the idea that the methodology of the surface survey is sufficiently sensitive to locate relatively insubstantial settlements. Nevertheless, seasonally occupied structures such as shepherds' huts may have been missed.

# Chapter 8

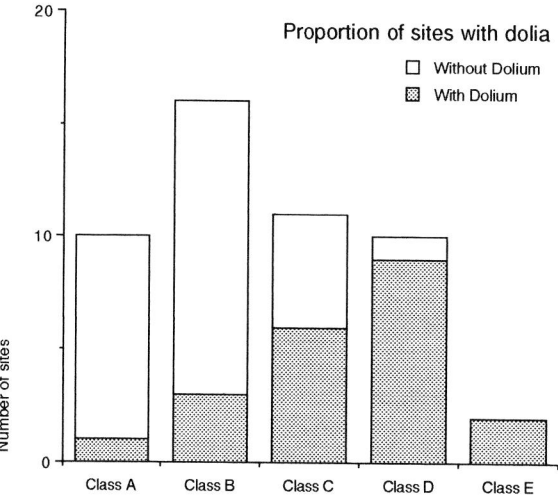

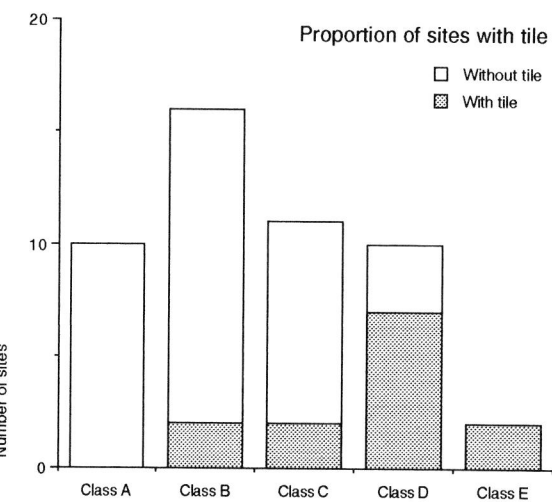

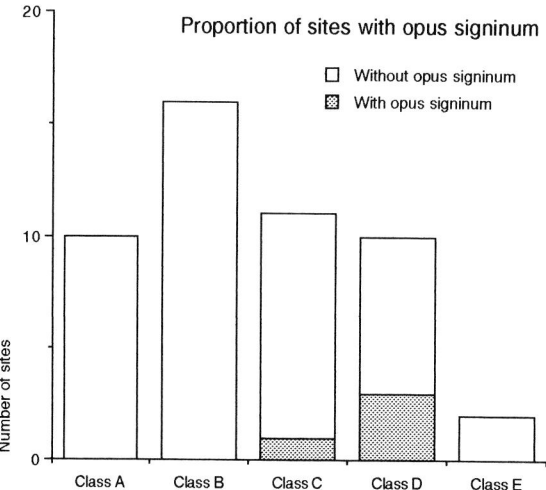

Fig.8.2. Proportions of sites in different size categories with tile, *dolia*, and *opus signinum*. For definition of the size categories see p.231.

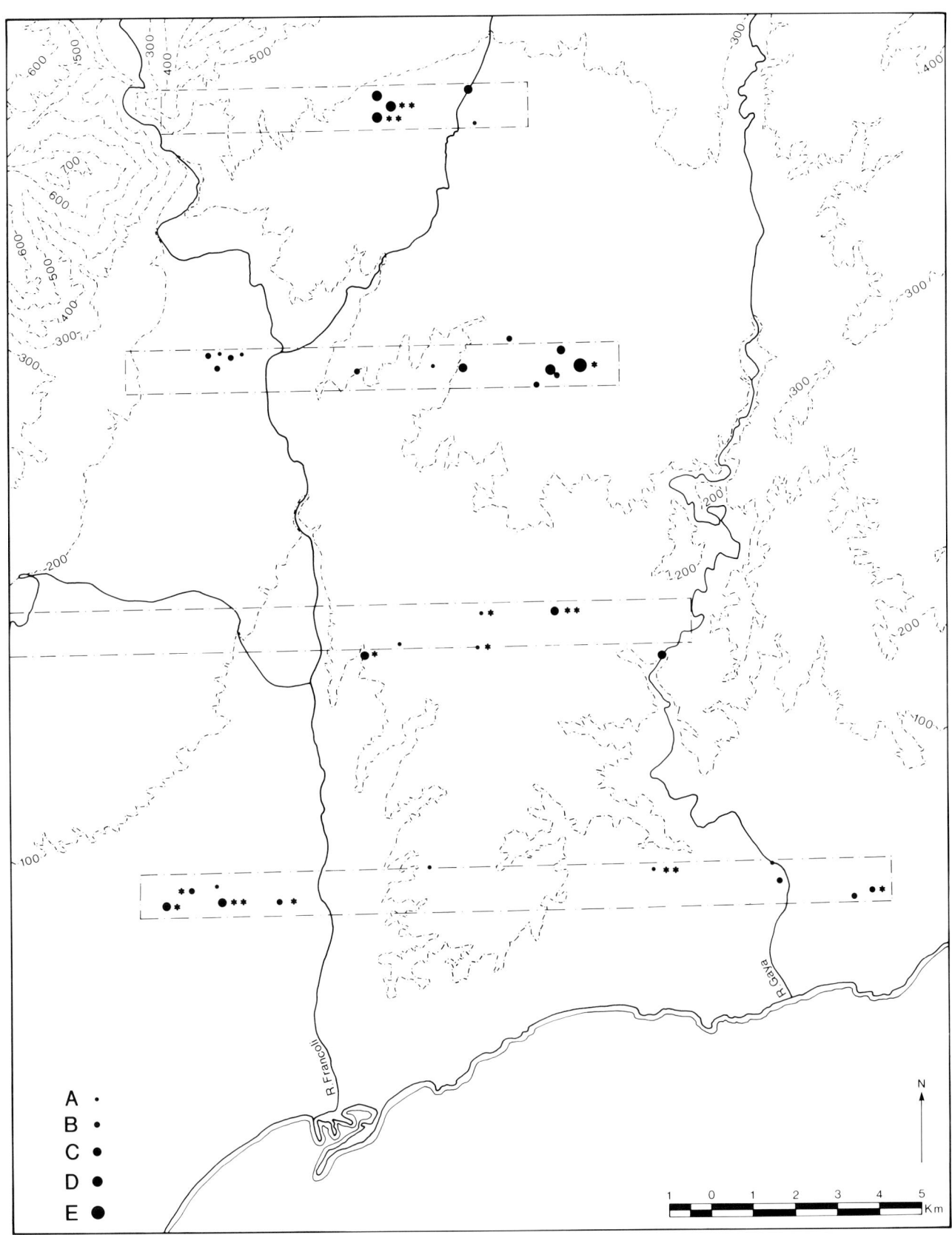

Fig.9.1. Distribution of sites with Iberian pottery located in the survey; for classification see p. 235.

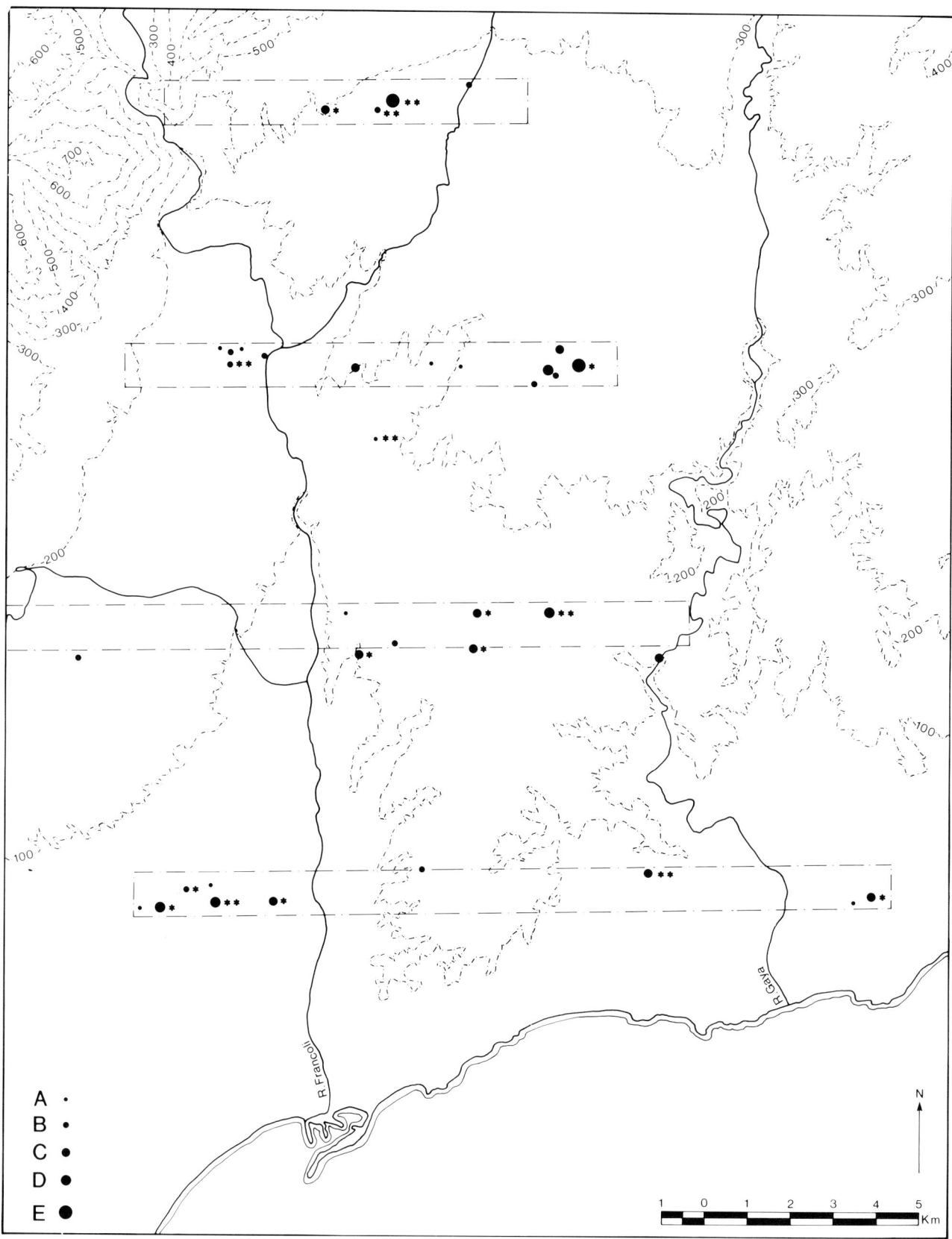

Fig.9.2. Distribution of sites with Republican pottery located in the survey; for classification see p. 235.

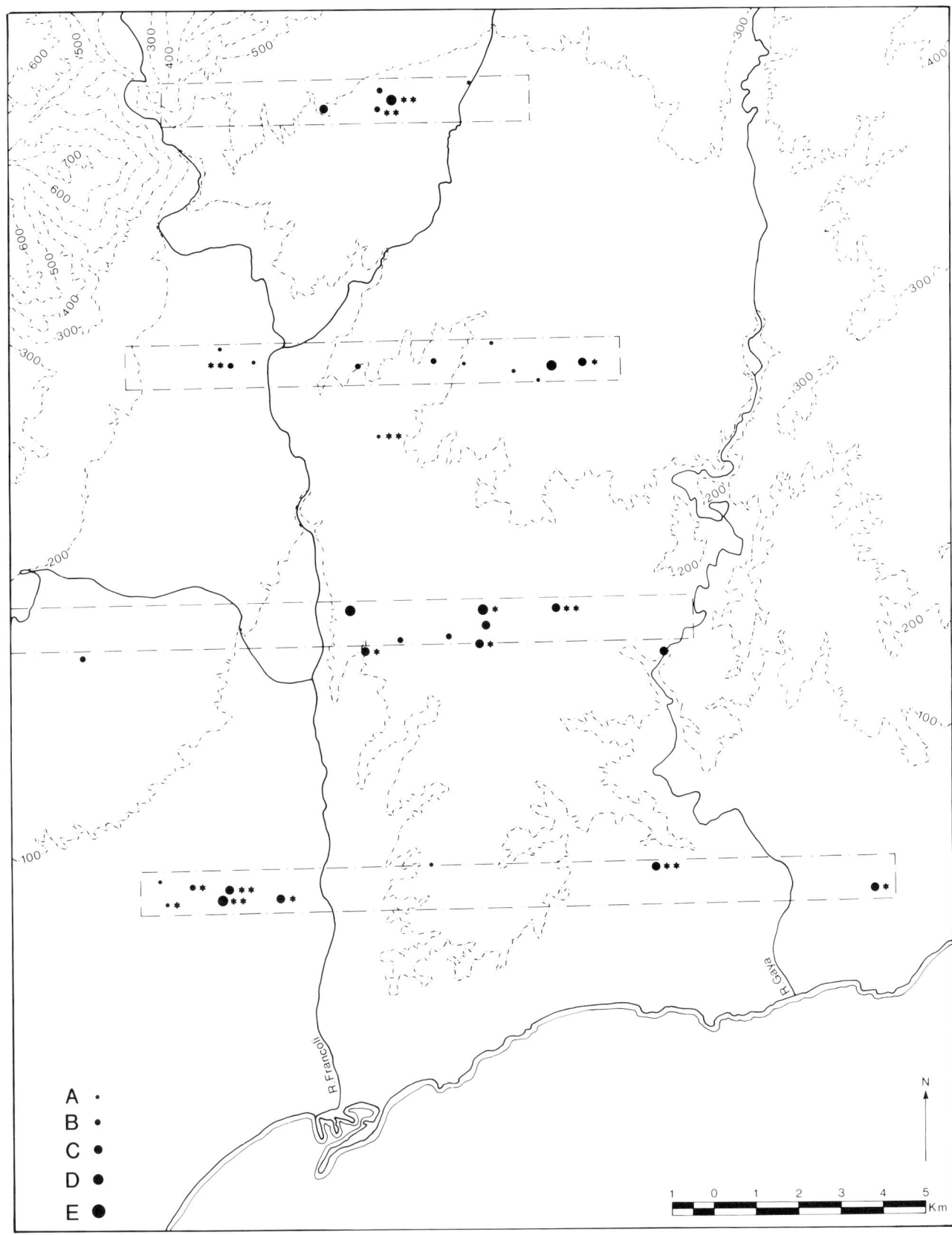

Fig.9.3. Distribution of sites with early imperial pottery located in the survey; for classification see p. 235.

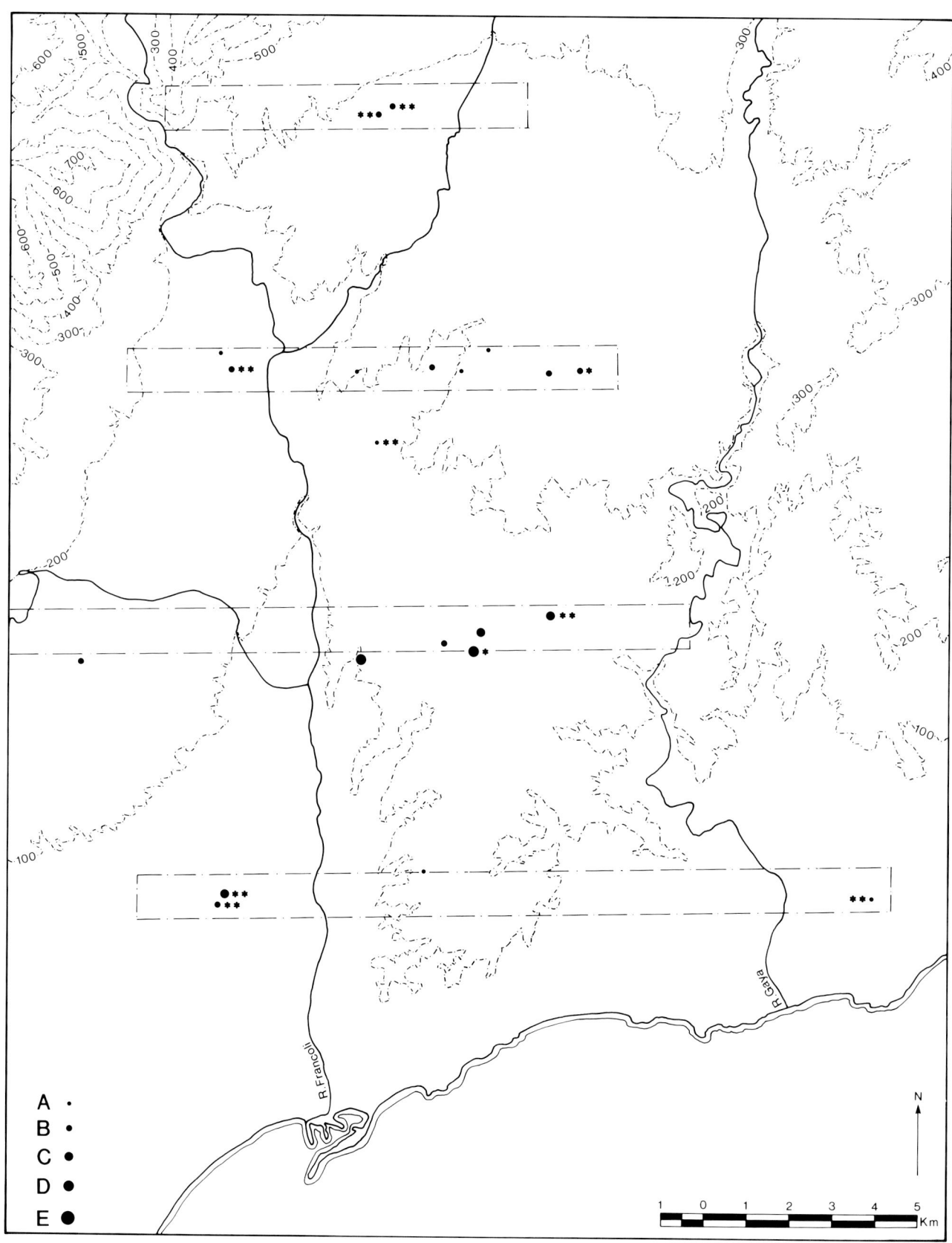

Fig.9.4. Distribution of sites with late imperial pottery located in the survey; for classification see p. 235.

# Chapter 9: ANALYSES OF PATTERNS OF SETTLEMENTS

This chapter is divided into two parts. In the first, the information collected is used as the basis for analyses of site location and for discussing aspects of the changing relationship between town and country. In the second, issues related to the patterns of off-site pottery distributions are explored.

## 1. PATTERNS OF LOCATIONS OF SETTLEMENTS

First aspects of site location are explored and comparisons made with sites known prior to our survey. We consider particularly the influence of natural topography and that of the Roman town, but, as a variety of different factors influenced location of settlement, it is rarely possible to identify discrete causes for the observed patterns.

The supply of pottery upon which our results are based is not always a reliable indicator of the presence or absence of settlement (see Chapter 4). This is particularly important for the beginning and end of the classical period in this part of Spain. The quantity of pottery found in the area of the survey varies through time (fig. 4.2), a point which has been taken into account in the method in processing the results. Despite careful searching, there is virtually no identified pottery pre-dating the Iberian period or post-dating the later Roman. It is unlikely that this resulted from the desertion of the countryside; it is more likely to have resulted from limited access to pottery or its poor survival. In any case it is most unlikely that the massive increase in pottery from the Iberian period results from either a sudden increase in the population or from any major colonization of the landscape. Such an explanation would also be at odds with current understanding of the genesis of the Iberian peoples. It is more likely to be a result of earlier settlement sites becoming visible archaeologically as they started to be supplied with pottery on a large scale (cf. Aquilué *et al.* 1992, 99). Excavation of a range of sites is the only way to test this hypothesis, to establish whether sites of this period with pottery have earlier, virtually aceramic phases. Similarly, it is unlikely that the decline of pottery finds in the later Roman period resulted from a wholesale desertion of the countryside; it seems more plausible that a decline in the availability of pottery meant that some sites became virtually aceramic and thus less visible archaeologically. This hypothesis too could be tested by careful excavation of a sample of sites.

Although these conclusions are open to debate, they form the starting-point for our analyses. We hold the view that, since absence of pottery cannot be taken to indicate an absence of settlement, it is possible to comment on the changes in settlement pattern only within the periods and sites which did produce pottery. This creates problems, especially during the later Roman period when it seems possible that pottery was available only at a limited range of sites.

### Settlement and landscape

In order to investigate the distribution of sites identified in Chapter 6 in relation to the landscape, we will analyse their locations in terms of geology, soils and topography. Geological information is available for the whole of the survey area (fig. 3.4). Soils information is less satisfactory (fig. 3.5) since it is available only for Transects 1 to 3 and even within them some blanks exist. The locational characteristics of sites involve a more subjective assessment. The landscape within the survey area is variable and important local features influenced the choice of particular places for settlement. They are often obvious only when visiting sites, as even the 1:5,000 maps are insufficiently sensitive to record slight knolls or ridges. Our first-hand knowledge of the landscape has led us to classify each site's locations by one of the following characteristics:

Table 9.1     Sites in relation to geology, soils and topography

| Site number | Classification Iberian | Republican | Early Imperial | Late Imperial | Geology Illus.3.4 | Soils Illus.3.5 | Situation see text |
|---|---|---|---|---|---|---|---|
| | | (from Table 8.1) | | | | | |
| 1.1 | | A | | | 3 | 4D | E |
| 1.2 | C | D | A | | 3 | 4D | G |
| 1.3 | | | A | | 3 | 3C | E |
| 1.4 | B | B | B | | 3 | 3C | D |
| 1.5 | A | A | | | 2 | 3C | A |
| 1.6 | C | D | D | B | 2 | 4D | D |
| 1.7 | | | C | C | 2 | 4D_3C | D |
| 1.8 | B | C | C | | 3_6 | - | B |
| 1.9 | A | B | A | A | 7 | - | D |
| 1.10 | A | C | C | | 7 | - | G |
| 1.11 | A | | | | 7 | - | D |
| 1.12 | B | | | | 7_10 | - | D |
| 1.13 | B | A | | | 5 | 4C | F |
| 1.14 | B | C | C | A | 5 | 4C | F |
| 2.1 | | B | B | B | 3 | 3C | G |
| 2.2 | | A | D | | 6 | 4D | F |
| 2.3 | C | C | C | D | 5 | 4D | B |
| 2.4 | A | B | B | | 6_5 | 4D | F |
| 2.5 | | | B | B | 5 | 4D | F |
| 2.6 | A | C | D | | 5 | 4D | C |
| 2.7 | A | C | C | D | 7_5 | 3C | G |
| 2.8 | | | C | C | 7_5 | 3C | G |
| 2.9 | C | D | C | C | 5_7 | 4D | G |
| 2.10 | C | C | C | | 7 | - | G |
| 3.1 | B | | | | 3 | 4D | D |
| 3.2 | A | A | A | A | 3 | 4D | D |
| 3.3 | B | | | | 3 | 4D | E |
| 3.4 | B | B | | | 3_1 | 2B | G |
| 3.5 | | B | B | B | 1 | 2B | D |
| 3.6 | A | A | | | 1 | 2B | B |
| 3.7 | | | A | | 1 | 2B | B |
| 3.8 | | B | | | 1 | 2B | B |
| 3.9 | B | C | B | A | 6_5 | 3C | D |
| 3.10 | A | A | B | B | 5 | 3C_4B | C |
| 3.11 | C | A | A | A | 6 | 4D | C |
| 3.12 | | | A | A | 6_5 | 4D | G |
| 3.13 | B | | | | 6_5 | 4D | G |
| 3.14 | | | A | | 5 | 4D | E |
| 3.15 | B | B | A | | 6_5 | 4D | D |
| 3.16 | D | D | D | B | 5 | 4D | F |
| 3.17 | B | B | | | 5 | 4D | D |
| 3.18 | C | C | | | 5 | 4D | F |
| 3.19 | E | E | C | B | 6_5 | 4D | G |
| 4.1 | A | C | C | | 3 | - | G |
| 4.2 | D | B | B | B | 3 | - | E |
| 4.3 | D | | B | | 3 | - | E |
| 4.4 | D | E | D | B | 3 | - | E |
| 4.5 | C | B | A | | 3 | - | D |
| 4.6 | A | | | | 3 | - | D |

| | |
|---|---|
| A | Valley floor |
| B | River terrace |
| C | Valley side |
| D | Break of slope |
| E | Plateau, or more or less featureless ground |
| F | Hillslope |
| G | Knoll, ridge-top or hill-top |

For each of the sites found in the survey this information is shown in Table 9.1; for those known before the survey began, it is given in Table 1.1. Where sites were found to lie at, or very near, the boundary between two geological formations or soil types, both are listed. In the case of previously known sites, too much reliance should not be placed on the data for two reasons: first, the precise locations of a number of these sites are uncertain, and there is uncertainty about the soils and geology on which they were located; second, as it has not been possible to visit all previously known sites, our knowledge of their locational characteristics is less reliable. These factors make close comparisons between the two sets of data problematical. For this reason, the newly-discovered sites are discussed first and information about those discovered earlier is introduced only by way of comparison. The patterns considered are those of the locations of the settlements; the areas farmed by the settlements may have had very different characteristics (see further p. 248).

Table 9.2          Sites in relation to geology

| Geology (Illus.3.4) | Area walked (ha) | Number of sites | ha walked per site found |
|---|---|---|---|
| 1 | 64.09 | 4.5 | 14.24 |
| 2 | 70.90 | 3 | 23.63 |
| 3 | 349.08 | 15 | 23.27 |
| 4 | 2.74 | 0 | |
| 5 | 384.77 | 14.5 | 26.53 |
| 6 | 146.01 | 5.5 | 26.54 |
| 7 | 89.38 | 6 | 14.89 |
| 8 | 0 | 0 | |
| 9 | 4.77 | 0 | |
| 10 | 9.66 | 0.5 | 19.32 |
| 11 | 0 | 0 | |
| 12 | 0 | 0 | |
| 13 | 26.11 | 0 | |
| 14 | 0 | 0 | |
| 15 | 11.79 | 0 | |

## Geology

The geological information for the area of the survey is collated in Table 9.2 where the total area walked on each of the geological types is compared with the numbers of sites found (taken from Table 9.1). Sites which occur on the boundaries between geological formations have been counted as half a site in each category. This shows that, despite the variation in the total areas walked on the different geologies, there is remarkably little variation in the density of sites. There is a marginal preference for geologies 1 (Quaternary gravels and clayey silts) and 7 (Tertiary limestones), while the absence of sites on 13 (Carboniferous deposits) may be significant despite the small area walked. In general, however, there appears insufficient variation to suggest that geology was an important determinant in the location of settlements. Analysis of the changing patterns of settlement also failed to indicate that geology had any influence on the 'success' or 'failure' of sites insofar as it is reflected in their growth in size or disappearance through time. In the absence of information about the representativeness of the sample of previously known sites or the total areas of the different geologies, it is difficult to make satisfactory comparisons with the sites located in the survey. An approximate comparison (ignoring the proportion of the area on each geology) can be made by comparing the percentage of sites in each sample on the various geological formations:

| Geological formation | 1 | 2 | 3 | 4 | 5 | 6 | 7 | 8 |
|---|---|---|---|---|---|---|---|---|
| Previously known sites (n=102) | 12 | 16.5 | 17 | 1.5 | 20 | 16 | 16 | 1 |
| Survey sites (n=49) | 9 | 6 | 30 | - | 29 | 11 | 12 | - |

| Geological formation | 9 | 10 | 11 | 12 | 13 | 14 | 15 |
|---|---|---|---|---|---|---|---|
| Previously known sites | 0.5 | 0.5 | - | 2 | - | - | - |
| Survey sites | - | 1 | - | - | - | - | - |

In general terms these figures show a strong similarity between the two sets of figures. Allowing for variations in sample sizes, the only marked divergences are between formations 2 (Quaternary angular gravels), 3 (Quaternary conglomerates), and 5 (Quaternary crust, silts and soils). The difference on formation 2 results from a concentration of previously-known sites in the SW part coupled with the comparatively small sample of this rock type walked in our transects. The difference between proportions of sites on formations 3 and 5 in the two samples cannot be explained by any obvious pattern, except that previous intensive work did not cover as much of these classes of rock as did the survey sample. In the light of these observations there seems to be little evidence of any major difference between the samples.

The combined evidence of both sets of data shows clearly that there was a more or less uniformly high density of occupation over most of the low-lying areas within the transects. By contrast, areas of older rocks (8-15) and the calcareous crust (4) are generally avoided by settlement.

## Soils

Soils are more difficult to assess because of the large number of gaps in the evidence and the absence of accurate figures for the proportions of the different soil types in the sample areas. However, the proportions of the sites found on each soil formation can be compared with the figures given for the proportions of each soil in the whole of the Tarragonès (Cobertera 1986, 159). Even though our survey area does not exactly correspond to the *Comarca*, the areas beyond it broadly correspond to those where the soils were not mapped, with the exception of a very small part of the Baix Camp (cf. Cobertera 1986, 154).

The table below therefore compares the proportions of sites on each soil type with the proportions of the landscape within the Tarragonès represented by the different soils:

| Soil Class | Tarragonès (17,687.5 ha) | Survey sites (n=37) | Previously known sites (n=56) |
|---|---|---|---|
| 1 | 6.3% | 0 | 3.6% |
| 2 | 11.8% | 13.5% | 13.4% |
| 3 | 16.9% | 21.6% | 15.2% |
| 4 | 64.2% | 64.8% | 67.9% |
| 5 | 0.8% | 0 | 0 |

These figures show that there is generally little difference between the proportions of sites on the different soils and the total land of each soil type available within the landscape. The two variations from this pattern concern the land in categories 1 and 3.

Although the survey transects included a substantial block of the best land of class 1, it did not produce any sites. In contrast, there was almost the expected number in the sample of previously-known sites. As fig. 3.5 shows, almost all the land of category 1 within the transects lay in Transect 2, where there was a substantial blank in the distribution of sites. This area on the W bank of the Francolí lay very close to the substantial villa of Parets Delgades (see p.20 fig.1.5, and p.272). This large establishment seems likely to have controlled some of the best agricultural land in the survey area, with the result that other settlement was excluded. The slight over-representation of sites on soils of class 3 within the sample transects seems, by contrast, to result from a slightly larger proportion of this soil walked, especially in Transect 3. Finally it should be noted that there is no discernible difference between the 'success' or 'failure' of sites located on the different soil types.

The evidence from the soils is thus analogous to that from the geology. It shows little evidence in the location of settlement for preference for particular soil types, although the absence of large tracts of the poorest land from the survey area should temper this conclusion. The density of settlement on the poor soils of class 4 suggests that the landscape in the territory was very densely occupied. As one would expect in this part of Spain, by the Iberian period settlement was already so dense that all available land apart from the mountains was heavily settled. This suggests that occupation continued from previous periods and was not the result of new, large-scale settlement activity.

**Location of sites**

The soils and geological evidence suggest that, as this was a landscape which was almost wholly settled, there might have been little scope for the exercise of choice in siting settlements. This is not the case, however, for there remained some choice for deciding the exact locations of settlements according to the nature of the local terrain. In the absence of much more detailed geographical evidence about the local topography, it is possible to examine only the two samples of sites to assess whether particular patterns of settlement preference prevailed. The most obvious feature of both groups of sites is the number of cases where there is uncertainty about the soil or geology on which they were located. This suggests some preference for locations at, or near, ecological boundaries, which might have enabled the inhabitants to utilize complementary agricultural strategies attuned to differences in the potential of the land.

A second pattern can be seen from a comparison of the two groups of site according to the nature of their locations:

|   |   | survey sites (n=49) | previously known sites (n=102) |
|---|---|---|---|
| A | Valley floor | 2% | 2% |
| B | River terrace | 10% | 21% |
| C | Valley side | 6% | 8% |
| D | Break of slope | 29% | 16% |
| E | Plateau, or more or less featureless ground | 14% | 27% |
| F | Hillslope | 14% | 13% |
| G | Knoll, ridge-top or hill-top | 24% | 14% |

The sites discovered during the survey show a clear preference for dominant positions in the landscape, either on hill-tops or at a break of slope, where the site overlooks the surroundings. These locations are not always easy to identify without visiting a site, and it is probably for this reason that the classification of the previously known sites shows a different pattern, with greater emphasis on the plateau and terrace. In reality, some of the sites in these categories may be situated in locally prominent positions. One of the implications is that water supply was not a perceived problem, so seasonal rainfall was presumably captured in cisterns. This echoes the pattern found by survey in the Penedès to the N (Sanmartí, Santacana and Serra 1984).

Both sets of results clearly demonstrate how known sites usually avoid the sides and floors of valleys. This is most likely due to the threat of flooding during seasonal downpours. The possibility remains that alluviation or erosion has buried or obscured sites in these locations. However, the geomorphological information from the survey suggests that this is unlikely, although it cannot always be ruled out.

The patterns of site location show no discernible chronological patterning although the previously-known villa sites lie in lowlands. We may note, however, that many of the existing villages in the region are located in a similar manner; this raises the possibility of some continuity from antiquity.

## Town and country

It is clear that the overall pattern of settlement was not heavily affected by ecological constraints although the precise points chosen for the building of settlements was influenced by a preference for certain types of location. Such a pattern is largely a product of a landscape that was fully exploited.

Within this settlement pattern, other factors, especially changing human geography, were perhaps most influential in the development of the landscape. We will examine how the development of Tarraco might have had an impact on its *territorium*. This will be done first through an examination of the settlement patterns and then by analysis of the changing supply and distribution of pottery. Broader conclusions will be suggested in Chapter 10. We begin from the assumption that the changing character of the town is likely to have had both an economic and social impact on the surrounding landscape (see Chapter 3). Any increase in the size of its population may have raised demands for food produced in the hinterland. As the city rose to the status of provincial capital at the end of the 1st c. B.C. an increasing number of the rich and politically powerful found it desirable to reside within easy reach of the political centre.

## The settlement data

Since the data for sites found during the survey are more detailed than for those previously known, we will begin with the survey. The distribution of sites by ceramic phase is shown in figs. 9.1-9.4 where the sites are classified according using the criteria set out in Chapter 8 (Table 8.1). The maps show a generally high density of sites across the landscape with no very drastic changes in the pattern through time. The occurrence of a range of sites of different sizes through the four phases also suggests that existing settlement patterns evolved rather than resulted from any single phase of rural implantation. This is especially evident in the Iberian phase where there already existed several larger settlements as well as many smaller farm-steads. If we examine the data for the continuity or discontinuity of sites (fig. 9.5 A-C), a clear pattern emerges. All the sites first appear in the Iberian phase (due to absence of identifiable earlier ceramics). After this, *c.*20% of sites first appear in the Republican[1] and early imperial phases, but no new sites have been identitied as established in the late imperial phase. The total number of sites also remains remarkably constant until the late empire:

| Phase | Iberian | Republican | Early empire | Late empire |
|---|---|---|---|---|
| Total number of sites | 37 | 35 | 35 | 20 |

---

1    As noted above (p. 57), the distinction between Iberian and Republican may reflect a preference for Roman ceramics by the inhabitants of some settlements, rather than a chronological distinction.

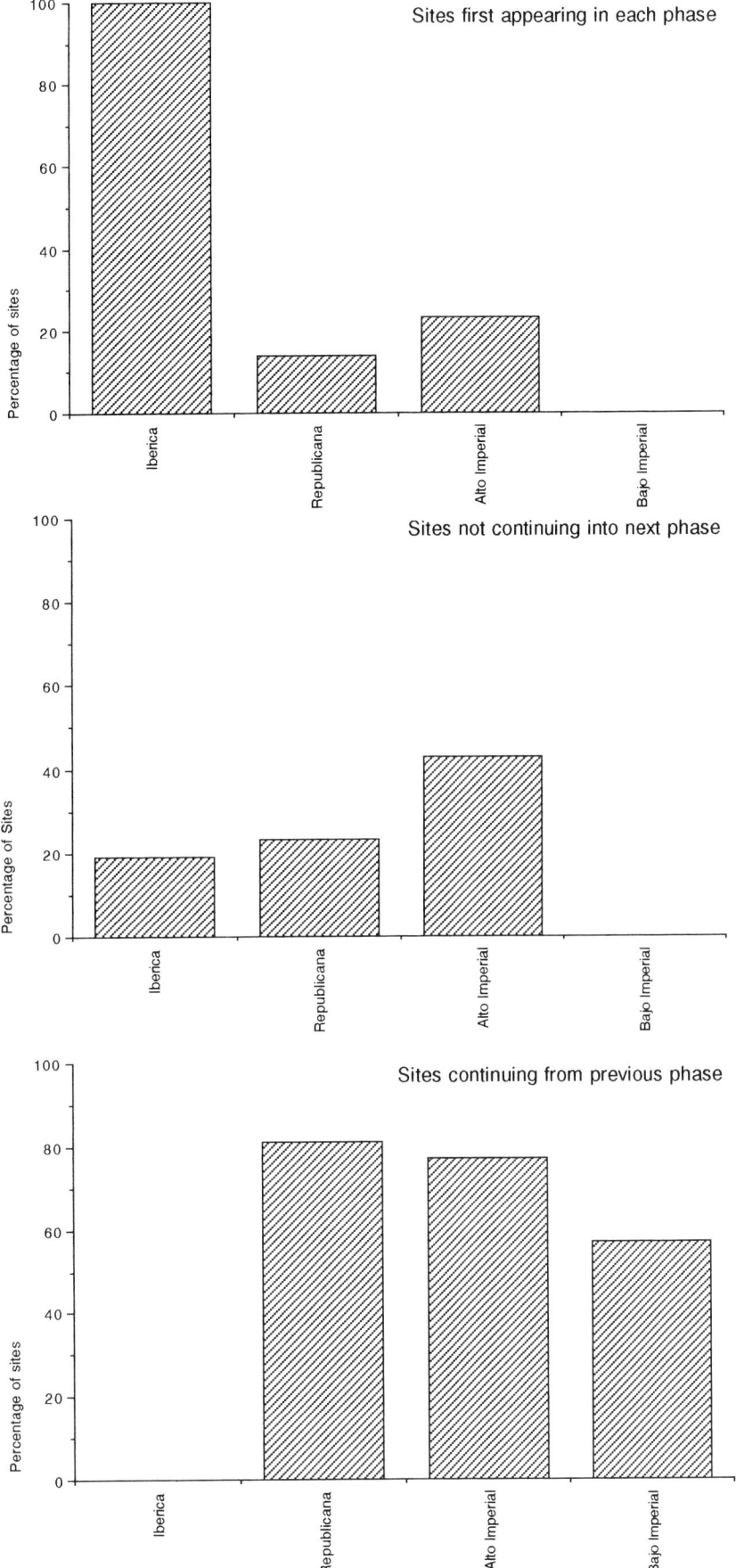

Fig.9.5. Graphs showing continuity and discontinuity of sites.

The sites which disappear are thus balanced by the appearance of new sites except in the final phase (fig. 9.5B). It has already been noted (Chapter 4) that this strong pattern of continuity may be overemphasized by the method used to define sites, so some caution should be exercised. However, the information from the survey shows a strong pattern of settlement continuity, especially when taken in conjunction with the evidence for topographical continuity.

A series of changes provide insights into settlement dynamics and reveal differences across the survey area. The first is that the density of sites within the areas walked varies between the four transects. The density of sites may be expressed by dividing the area walked by the number of sites found to arrive at the number of hectares walked in order to find a single site. The data from the survey are as follows:

|  | Iberian | Republican | Early empire | Late empire |
|---|---|---|---|---|
| Transect 1 | 18 ha | 20 ha | 22 ha | 50 ha |
| Transect 2 | 64 ha | 48 ha | 39 ha | 64 ha |
| Transect 3 | 27 ha | 29 ha | 34 ha | 47 ha |
| Transect 4 | 29 ha | 43 ha | 34 ha | 86 ha |
| Overall | 31 ha | 32 ha | 32 ha | 57 ha |

These data show that in the area nearest Tarraco (Transect 1) there is a consistently higher density of sites than elsewhere. By contrast, Transect 2 remains above average (although this is probably the result of the proximity of the Parets Delgada villa). The transects further inland are near the average except in the late empire. This suggests a general preference for settlement in proximity to Tarragona, presumably as a result of its social and economic importance. It should be noted, however, that this trend does not become any greater through time, although the variations within the late imperial phase probably result partly from our difficulties in identifying sites of this period.

These results allow us to estimate the average size of an estate farmed from each settlement. It would appear to have been in the region of 30 ha, if we assume that the whole landscape was farmed without tracts of unused territory. Two other problems should be noted before accepting this figure at face value. First, as Gregson (1982, 231) has pointed out, linear surveys tend to overestimate numbers of sites because they count each site discovered whether or not the transect passed directly through its centre. Gregson calculated that this increases the number of sites recorded by a factor of about three. On this basis the figure quoted for estate size might perhaps be increased to 90 ha. Second, the figure provides an average. Given the variations in size and status of the sites encountered, the mean is a highly unreliable measure for any particular estate. Lesser sites may have relied on smaller parcels of land while the largest of the villas probably farmed much larger areas, although they need not have formed a single block of land or have been in the immediate vicinity of Tarragona. Powerful landowners often held several estates in different areas and lands farmed by bailiffs are not distinguishable archaeologically. This serves to remind us that the patterns we are examining are those of settlement sites rather than of farming or land-ownership.

The classification of sites discovered in the survey was based on the two characteristics of size and the presence of possible indicators of status. The numbers of sites within each class appear to reveal patterns of change through time and across the area of the survey. Fig. 9.6 and Table 9.3 show how the sites changed in size through time. The overall pattern (fig. 9.6) shows the numbers of sites which changed from one size category to another between ceramic phases. The predominant pattern is one of continuity, with the largest single group remaining the same size between each of the phases. The period which saw the greatest increase in size of sites was the Iberian to Republican, when over 30% of sites grew. By comparison, the proportion decreasing in size was at its greatest in the Republic to early empire and early to late empire, although we may note from Table 9.3 that only during the former does the proportion decreasing in size equal the number that disappear. It is evident that unsuccessful sites were more likely to disappear from the landscape than decrease in area.

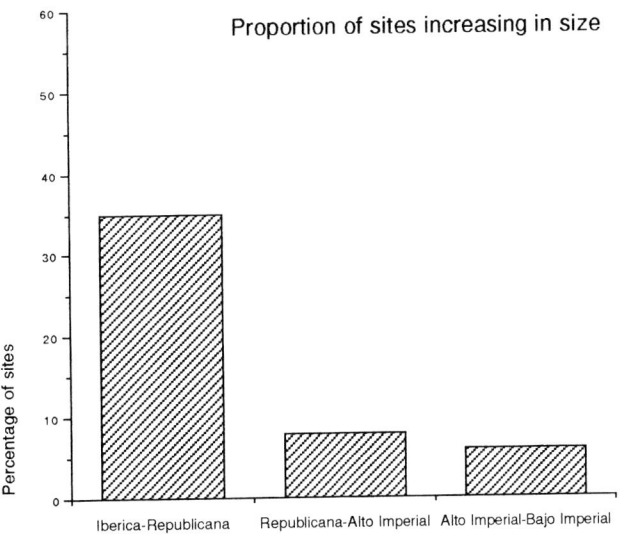

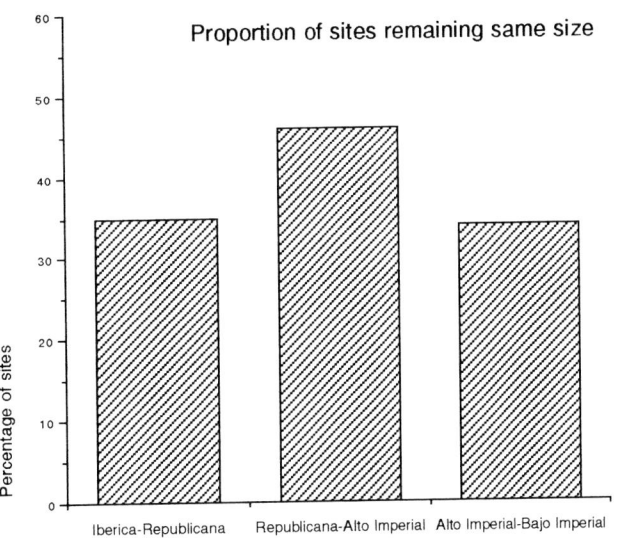

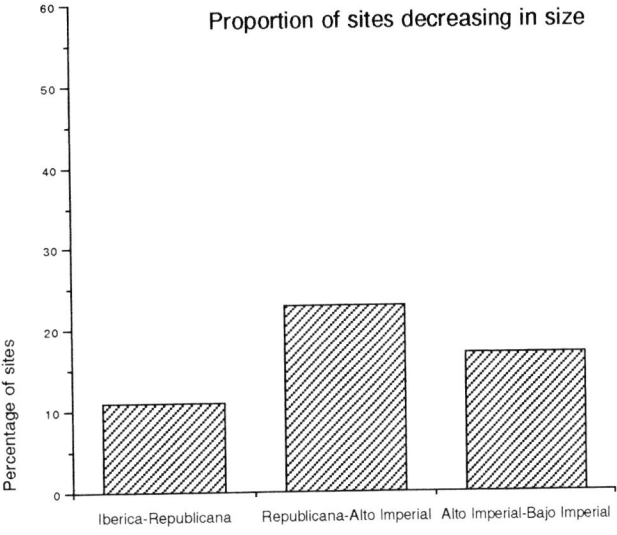

Fig.9.6. Graphs showing changes in size of site through time.

Table 9.3          Numbers of sites changing in size through time

| Ceramic Phase | | Size increase | Same size | Size decrease | Disappears |
|---|---|---|---|---|---|
| **Iberian-Republican** | Transect 1 | 6 | 2 | 1 | 2 |
| | Transect 2 | 4 | 2 | 0 | 0 |
| | Transect 3 | 1 | 9 | 1 | 3 |
| | Transect 4 | 2 | 0 | 2 | 2 |
| | Total | 13 | 13 | 4 | 7 |
| | % | 35 | 35 | 11 | 19 |
| **Republican-Early Imperial** | Transect 1 | 0 | 5 | 2 | 3 |
| | Transect 2 | 2 | 5 | 1 | 0 |
| | Transect 3 | 1 | 4 | 3 | 5 |
| | Transect 4 | 0 | 2 | 2 | 0 |
| | Total | 3 | 16 | 8 | 8 |
| | % | 8 | 46 | 23 | 23 |
| **Early Imperial-Late Imperial** | Transect 1 | 0 | 2 | 2 | 5 |
| | Transect 2 | 2 | 4 | 0 | 4 |
| | Transect 3 | 0 | 5 | 3 | 3 |
| | Transect 4 | 0 | 1 | 1 | 3 |
| | Total | 2 | 12 | 6 | 15 |
| | % | 6 | 34 | 17 | 43 |

The overall patterns of settlement change mask a series of differences between phases (Table 9.3), although the small numbers of sites make the trends ambiguous. The information in that Table can be supplemented by information about the average sizes of sites in the different Transects:

| | *Iberian* | *Republican* | *Early empire* | *Late empire* |
|---|---|---|---|---|
| Transect 1 | 1.38 ha | 2.27ha | 2.29 ha | 1.15 ha |
| Transect 2 | 1.71 ha | 2.38 ha | 2.67 ha | 2.91 ha |
| Transect 3 | 2.51 ha | 2.57 ha | 1.67 ha | 1.05 ha |
| Transect 4 | 4.27 ha | 3.74ha | 2.60 ha | 1.53 ha |
| Average | 2.33 ha | 2.58 ha | 2.25 ha | 1.68 ha |

Thus the increase in size of site within the Iberian and Republican phases was most marked in Transects 1 and 2, although the size of the sites in these areas remained below the average. This contrasts with Transects 3 and 4, where there was more stability although the average site size declined in the latter. The transition from the Republic to the early empire is more stable but again reveals some distinction between the same two pairs of Transects. Transects 1 and 2 show marginal increases in average size of site, but 3 and 4 both show a decline. It is accompanied by a significant decrease in the numbers of sites in Transect 3. The transition to the late empire shows a large number of sites disappearing and the average size decreases in all Transects except 2. These variations in the patterns can be summarized by saying that changes in settlement size and number were most marked in the areas closest to Tarragona. The areas within Transects 3 and 4 showed changes but they were more gradual and resulted in a steady decline in site numbers and average size. In other words, proximity to Tarragona resulted in more varied fortunes of sites.

The evidence for status of sites is more ambiguous as sites have been classified only according to a three-fold division and there is no way to establish the period during which a site's status changed. Equally, the relatively small numbers preclude any definitive conclus-

Table 9.4          Status of sites found within the survey

|  |  | Lower | Intermediate | Higher |
|---|---|---|---|---|
| Transect 1 | All | 7 (50%) | 4(29%) | 3(21%) |
|  | Iberian | 5 | 4 | 2 |
|  | Republican | 4 | 4 | 2 |
|  | Early Imperial | 2 | 4 | 3 |
|  | Late Imperial | 1 | 1 | 2 |
| Transect 2 | All | 6(60%) | 3(30%) | 1(10%) |
|  | Iberian | 2 | 3 | 1 |
|  | Republican | 4 | 3 | 1 |
|  | Early Imperial | 6 | 3 | 1 |
|  | Late Imperial | 3 | 2 | 1 |
| Transect 3 | All | 17(89%) | 1(5%) | 1(5%) |
|  | Iberian | 13 | 1 | - |
|  | Republican | 11 | 1 | 1 |
|  | Early Imperial | 9 | 1 | 1 |
|  | Late Imperial | 6 | 1 | 1 |
| Transect 4 | All | 3(50%) | 1(17%) | 2(33%) |
|  | Iberian | 3 | 1 | 2 |
|  | Republican | 1 | 1 | 2 |
|  | Early Imperial | 2 | 1 | 2 |
|  | Late Imperial | - | - | 2 |

ions. If we allow for these problems, the data (Table 9.4) permit some general conclusions. First, the greatest proportion of sites of higher status were found in Transects 1 and 4 (although the total numbers in the latter are very small). This is consistent with the idea that sites of higher status might tend to be concentrated near Tarragona. Second, sites of lower status consistently decline in frequency — a pattern created by the differential survival of sites in the intermediate and high-status categories. It suggests that sites of higher status were less susceptible ɔ declining pottery supply than those of lower status, and points to social competition within the landscape.

In order to assess the impact of Tarraco on its surroundings, the density of sites in the survey area was measured in a series of bands 1 km wide. The data used comprised both the previously-known sites (Table 1.1) and those discovered in the survey. In compiling the graph (fig. 9.7) it was not possible to differentiate sites by period because of uncertainties about the chronologies of many of the sites known before the survey began. This lack of chronological differentiation means that the data are only of the most general value.

There is considerable variation in density, most of which results from the varying intensity of fieldwork. But a few underlying trends are of greater interest. First, a zone around the town seems to be largely devoid of settlement. It seems that this gap in the distribution is largely real and corresponds to a zone which was exploited from the city. Similar patterns of low intensity of settlement have been identified around other towns in the NW provinces (Hodder and Millett 1980) and elsewhere (see Chapter 10). Secondly, an apparent peak in the density of sites occurs at 4 km from the city. It exists in both the previously-known sites and those discovered in the survey. It may result from intensive fieldwork around Constantí, although it seems improbable that the pattern is entirely a result of such bias. A higher density of sites within easy reach of Tarraco is not unexpected, given the inherent advantages to urban-based élites engaged in political activity and to farmers with crops to sell. Beyond this band the density declines to the normal rural intensity. In the zones where our survey was concentrated this effect is less rapid than is suggested by the sample of previously known sites. Thus Tarraco

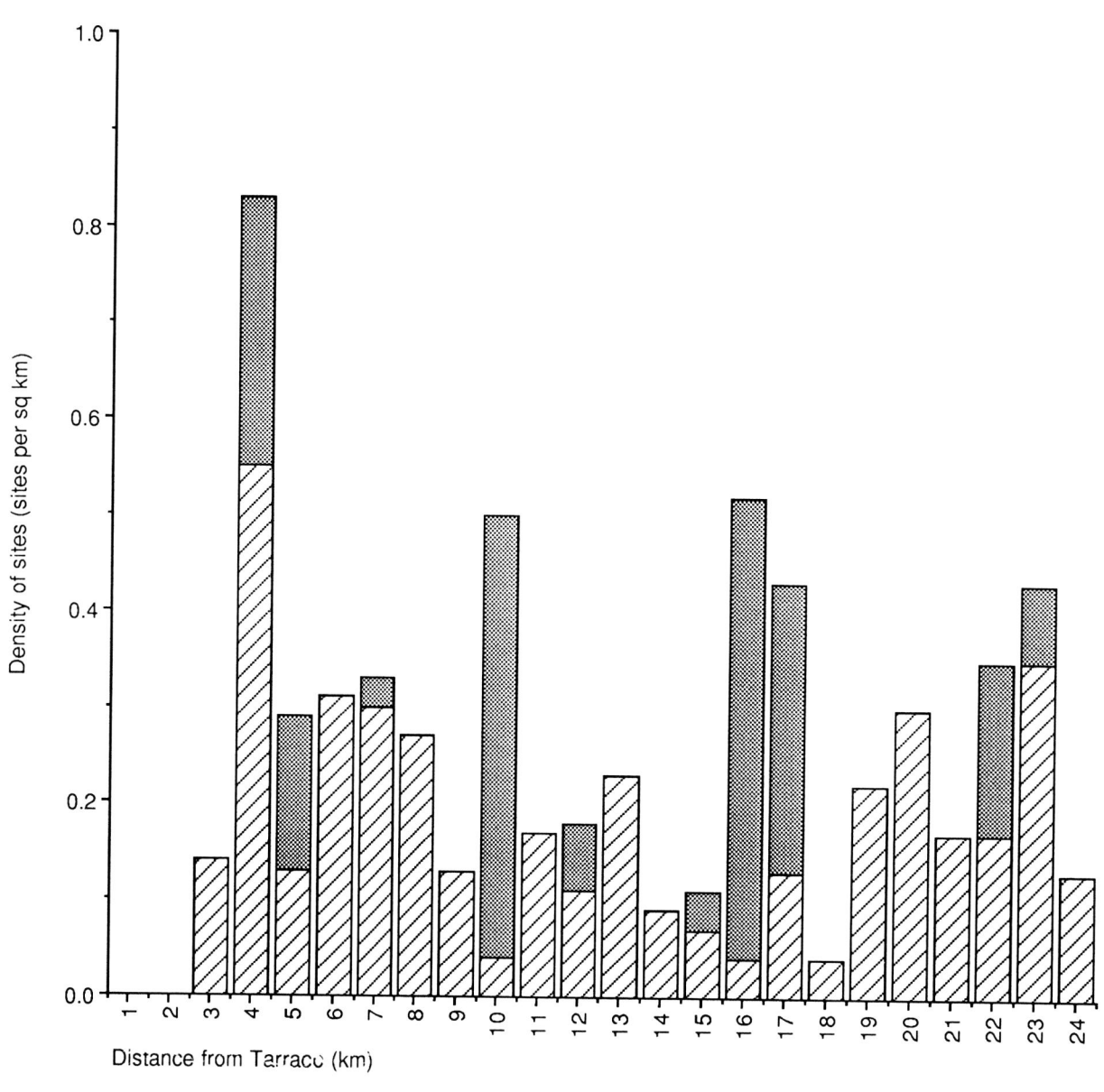

Fig. 9.7. Graphs showing the density of sites in 1-km bands moving out from Tarraco. The cross-hatched part of each column shows previously known sites (Table 1.1); the stippled part shows sites found in the survey.

had a very localized effect on density of settlement because it was high everywhere within the survey area. Its principal effect seems to have been in attracting higher-status sites to cluster around it.

*Summary*

Individually these different aspects of the settlement data do not present very striking patterns but taken together they reveal a consistent pattern. The area closest to Tarragona was the most densely settled and had the highest proportion of sites of higher status. In this area too the settlement pattern was most susceptible to change. By contrast, the areas further inland began with a high density of settlements, including a number of large size. They remained more stable in their patterns but show a gradual decline in density and size of site through time. This implies that the presence of Tarragona had less impact in these areas, which were eclipsed only gradually by the areas nearer the town. The patterns are interpreted here in terms of the relationship between town and country although they may equally result from a contrast between inland and coastal zones. These distinctions will now be examined through an investigation of the distribution of pottery.

## Pottery distribution

There are two fundamental problems in using the large volume of quantified pottery to investigate the changing relationship between town and country. Both result from the pottery being unstratified. The pottery cannot be dated by stratigraphic association, and it is difficult to make comparisons between the assemblages from different sites because ploughsoil assemblages are of mixed date. Any direct comparisons must rely on the use of external dating to assign the pottery to broad ceramic phases or to the more narrowly defined typological groups defined in Chapters 4 and 5. Even within this framework, variations in size and composition of collections make the comparison of individual sites problematic. It is difficult to assess the importance of absences of individual types. Also, conventional comparisons of percentages of fabrics are meaningless as the assemblages are of mixed date.

Given the very large quantity of material from the survey it was felt desirable to develop a new approach to what is an increasingly common archaeological problem. The method devised is based on the simple idea that each site is treated as an assemblage which can be compared with the total pottery assemblage from the whole survey. This enables the quantity of each fabric found at a particular site to be seen in relation to the overall pattern of supply and thus provides a tool for comparing individual sites and fabrics.

The procedure followed is summarized in Table 9.5. The graphs produced by this method (e.g., fig. 9.8) show the deviations of the percentage value of a fabric at each site from the mean percentage for the survey. Thus, those sites at or close to the centre line (zero value) have a percentage close to the mean value (66.53% in the case of fig. 9.8 — Iberian amphora fabric 14/16). Those with negative values have less than the survey mean, and those with positive values have more than that mean. In each case the proportion of pottery at a particular site is compared with the survey mean for the requisite ceramic phase.

Table 9.5    Method used for the computation of figures for comparing pottery assemblages from survey sites.

1.    Establish the **total** number of sherds of each fabric within the whole survey area

2.    Establish the percentage represented by each fabric within
      (a) the total survey assemblage, and
      (b) the assemblage from each ceramic phase for the whole survey

3.    Total the sherd numbers for each of the fields within each site

4.    Establish the percentage represented by each fabric within
      (a) that whole site, and
      (b) the ceramic phase to which it belongs on that site

5.    Compare the percentage of each fabric on the site (from 4) with the equivalent value for the whole survey (from 2)

Interpretation involves seeking explanations for patterns observed in the deviations. As the graphs are ordered by Transect with increasing distance from the coast (the Vallmoll by-pass [Field 1254] is listed in its geographical position between Transects 2 and 3), any basic location-

Chapter 9

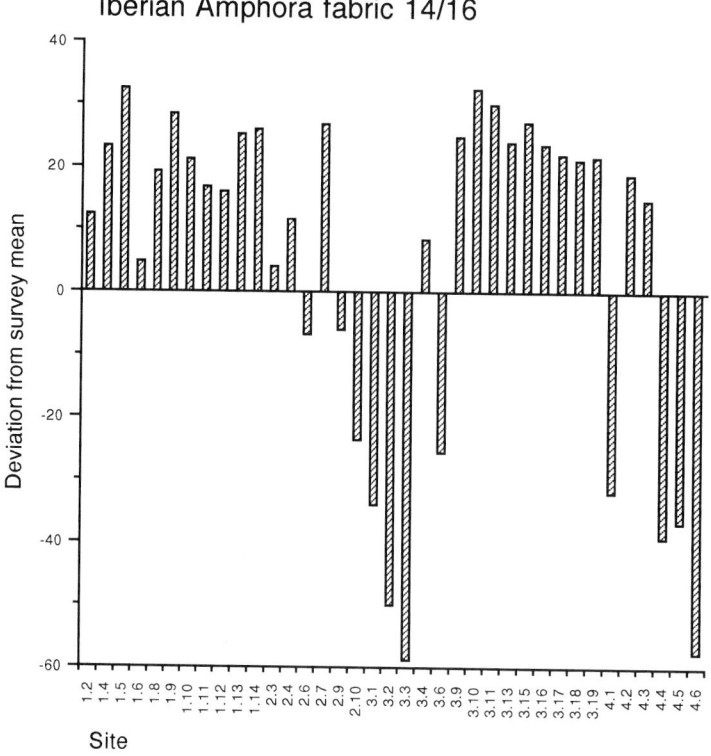

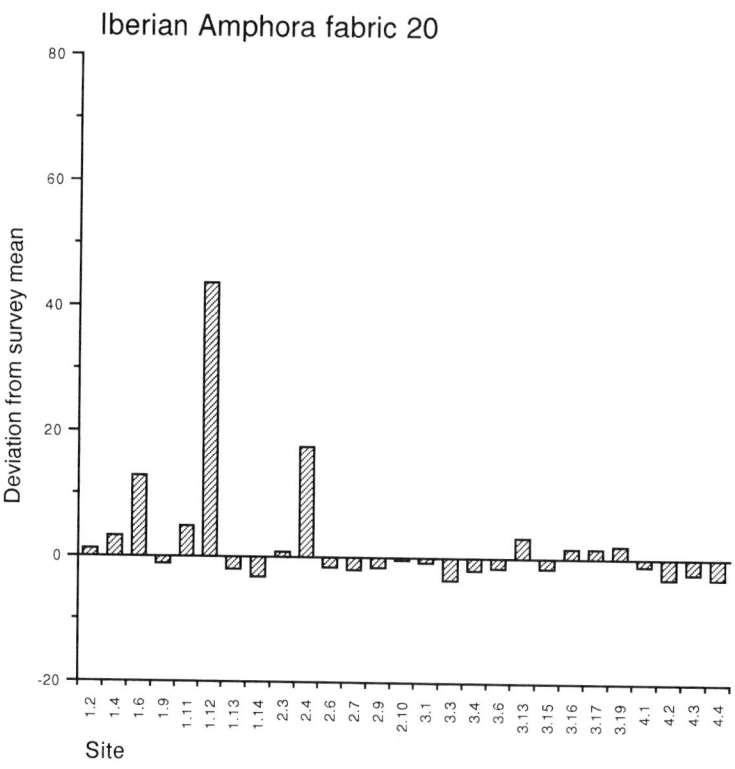

Fig.9.8. Graphs showing deviations from the mean for site ceramic assemblages of the Iberian phase. a = Iberian amphora fabric 14/16; b = Iberian amphora fabric 20.

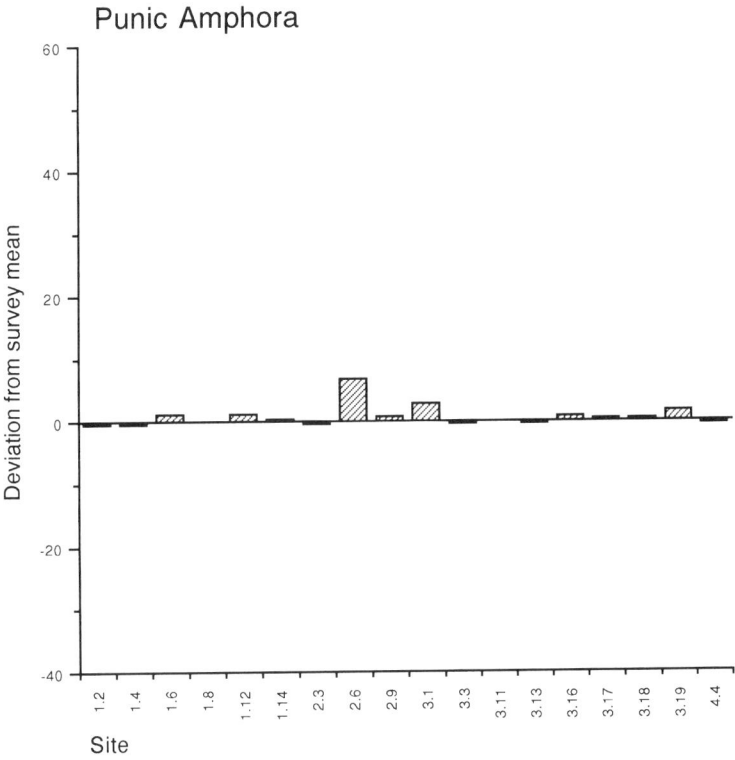

Fig.9.8 (continued). Graph showing deviations from the mean for site ceramic assemblages of the Iberian phase. c = Punic amphora.

al distinction should be obvious. Distinctions resulting from factors such as differences in size or status of site can be assessed by examining the graphs to see whether particular classes of sites show similar patterns of deviation from the mean. However, before seeking to explain patterns in archaeological terms one must establish whether biases in the data provide more likely causes. For example, aberrant values might be expected in cases where the assemblages are very small or where there was only a small range of values for a particular fabric.

The data for each site are listed in Appendix 5; the sum totals for each of the fabrics from the whole survey shown in Table 9.6. They form the basis for the following discussion. Interpretation is founded on two propositions. First, it is clear that worthwhile conclusions can be reached only where clear patterns can be identified. Sites with small assemblages and fabrics occurring infrequently offer limited information. Second, as the causes of variation between pottery assemblages are interconnected and complex, it will not always be possible to establish which particular factors are responsible for patterns noted (Millett 1987). To explain the causes of observed patterning it is necessary to consider a variety of possible causes. Equally, the complexity of the causes of variation may be such that the data in aggregate will appear to be random (Hodder and Orton 1976, 9-10).

An initial sorting of the pottery fabrics was undertaken, examining only the more common fabrics from each ceramic phase. The results have been compared with site locations and classifications in order to detect any obvious explanations for the patterns observed.

*Iberian types*

There were only three widely distributed fabrics: the Iberian amphora fabrics 14/16 and 20 and the Punic amphora. All these distinctive fabrics are amphorae. Graphs showing the deviations of these fabrics from the survey mean are shown in fig. 9.8.

Table 9.6                                                                 Totals of pottery fabrics from the survey

| | | Total (n) | Total (wt) | % n(period) | % wt(period) | % n (total) | % wt (total) |
|---|---|---|---|---|---|---|---|
| **IBERIAN** | | | | | | | |
| Fine ware | Iberian | 11625 | 128.44 | 28.65 | 3.08 | 12.18 | 2.22 |
| Coarse ware | Fabric A | 274 | 3.52 | 0.68 | 0.08 | 0.29 | 0.06 |
| Amphorae | Massiliote | 9 | 0.3 | 0.02 | 0.01 | 0.01 | 0.01 |
| | Iberian (14/16) | 27394 | 365.97 | 67.51 | 8.77 | 28.70 | 6.34 |
| | Iberian (20) | 1460 | 30.31 | 3.60 | 0.73 | 1.53 | 0.52 |
| | Punic | 214 | 5.82 | 0.53 | 0.14 | 0.22 | 0.10 |
| | sub-total | 40976 | 534.36 | | | 42.92 | 9.25 |
| **REPUBLICAN** | | | | | | | |
| Fine ware | Thin walled | 1 | 0.01 | 0.01 | 0.00 | 0.00 | 0.00 |
| | Black Gloss (A) | 63 | 0.98 | 0.57 | 0.18 | 0.07 | 0.02 |
| | Black Gloss (B) | 84 | 1.15 | 0.77 | 0.22 | 0.09 | 0.02 |
| | Black Gloss (C) | 3 | 0.03 | 0.03 | 0.01 | 0.00 | 0.00 |
| | Black Gloss (indet.) | 15 | 0.29 | 0.14 | 0.05 | 0.02 | 0.01 |
| | Gris Ampuritana | 32 | 0.24 | 0.29 | 0.04 | 0.03 | 0.00 |
| Coarse ware | Italian (6) | 378 | 9.96 | 3.44 | 1.87 | 0.40 | 0.17 |
| Amphorae | Italian (6) | 8247 | 379.71 | 75.14 | 71.13 | 8.64 | 6.57 |
| | Italian (Others) | 1044 | 87.09 | 9.51 | 16.31 | 1.09 | 1.51 |
| | Tarraconensian (9) | 736 | 39.49 | 6.71 | 7.40 | 0.77 | 0.68 |
| | Tarraconensian (12) | 3 | 0.38 | 0.03 | 0.07 | 0.00 | 0.01 |
| | Tarraconensian (13) | 1 | 0.13 | 0.01 | 0.02 | 0.00 | 0.00 |
| | African | 27 | 1.78 | 0.25 | 0.33 | 0.03 | 0.03 |
| | Ebussitanian | 342 | 12.58 | 3.12 | 2.36 | 0.36 | 0.22 |
| | sub-total | 10976 | 533.82 | | | 11.50 | 9.24 |
| **EARLY IMPERIAL** | | | | | | | |
| Fine ware | Pompeian Red | 2 | 0.02 | 0.02 | 0.01 | 0.00 | 0.00 |
| | Thin walled | 60 | 0.56 | 0.67 | 0.21 | 0.06 | 0.01 |
| | Sigillata Italica | 54 | 0.18 | 0.60 | 0.07 | 0.06 | 0.00 |
| | S. Gaulish Sigillata | 1151 | 9.31 | 12.81 | 3.51 | 1.21 | 0.16 |
| | Sigillata Hispanica | 280 | 1.58 | 3.12 | 0.60 | 0.29 | 0.03 |
| | Oriental Sigillata | 3 | 0.02 | 0.03 | 0.01 | 0.00 | 0.00 |
| | Sigillata Clara A | 663 | 2.79 | 7.38 | 1.05 | 0.69 | 0.05 |
| | Sigillata Clara B | 4 | 0.05 | 0.04 | 0.02 | 0.00 | 0.00 |
| | Imit.Clara | 3 | 0.02 | 0.03 | 0.01 | 0.00 | 0.00 |
| Coarse ware | Tarraconensian (12) | 151 | 4.36 | 1.68 | 1.64 | 0.16 | 0.08 |
| | Tarraconensian (13) | 607 | 9.3 | 6.75 | 3.51 | 0.64 | 0.16 |
| | Tarraconensian (K) | 718 | 7.68 | 7.99 | 2.90 | 0.75 | 0.13 |
| | Tarraconensian (L) | 92 | 1.35 | 1.02 | 0.51 | 0.10 | 0.02 |
| | Fabric B | 4 | 0.06 | 0.04 | 0.02 | 0.00 | 0.00 |
| | Fabric ZD | 313 | 2.37 | 3.48 | 0.89 | 0.33 | 0.04 |
| | Fabric ZL | 333 | 4.07 | 3.70 | 1.53 | 0.35 | 0.07 |
| | Fabric ZM | 238 | 1.91 | 2.65 | 0.72 | 0.25 | 0.03 |
| | African | 393 | 4.07 | 4.37 | 1.53 | 0.41 | 0.07 |
| Amphorae | Tarraconensian (12) | 1444 | 71.11 | 16.07 | 26.81 | 1.51 | 1.23 |
| | Tarraconensian (13) | 2297 | 129.96 | 25.56 | 49.00 | 2.41 | 2.25 |
| | Baetican (Dr 20) | 23 | 2.2 | 0.26 | 0.83 | 0.02 | 0.04 |
| | Baetican BI-IV (32) | 136 | 11.28 | 1.51 | 4.25 | 0.14 | 0.20 |
| | Gallic | 13 | 0.64 | 0.14 | 0.24 | 0.01 | 0.01 |
| | Italian | 2 | 0.06 | 0.02 | 0.02 | 0.00 | 0.00 |
| | Tarraconensian (18) | 3 | 0.16 | 0.03 | 0.06 | 0.00 | 0.00 |
| | Tarraconensian (33) | 1 | 0.09 | 0.01 | 0.03 | 0.00 | 0.00 |
| | sub-total | 8988 | 265.2 | | | 9.42 | 4.59 |
| **LATE IMPERIAL** | | | | | | | |
| Fine ware | Palaeochristian | 3 | 0.05 | 0.20 | 0.13 | 0.00 | 0.00 |
| | Sigillata Lucente | 3 | 0.06 | 0.20 | 0.16 | 0.00 | 0.00 |
| | Sigillata Clara C | 59 | 0.22 | 4.02 | 0.57 | 0.06 | 0.00 |
| | Sigillata Clara D | 125 | 1.25 | 8.51 | 3.23 | 0.13 | 0.02 |
| Amphorae | African | 1183 | 31.9 | 80.59 | 82.47 | 1.24 | 0.55 |
| | Oriental | 1 | 0.01 | 0.07 | 0.03 | 0.00 | 0.00 |
| | Spanish | 94 | 4.29 | 6.40 | 11.09 | 0.10 | 0.07 |
| | sub-total | 1468 | 37.78 | | | 1.54 | 0.65 |
| **UNDIAGNOSTIC** | | | | | | | |
| | Coarse ware | 19178 | 161.2 | | | 20.09 | 2.79 |
| | Mortaria | 1 | 0.16 | | | 0.00 | 0.00 |
| | Amphora | 11393 | 336.87 | | | 11.93 | 5.83 |
| | African Amphora | 1579 | 46.74 | | | 1.65 | 0.81 |
| | Tripolitanian Amph. | 1 | 0.01 | | | 0.00 | 0.00 |
| | Amphorae stopper | 1 | 0.11 | | | 0.00 | 0.00 |
| | Dolia | 1054 | 217.24 | | | 1.10 | 3.76 |
| | Sigillata Clara Indet. | 243 | 1.12 | | | 0.25 | 0.02 |
| | Red Slip Ware | 5 | 0.04 | | | 0.01 | 0.00 |
| | Tegula | 13708 | 5735.47 | | | | |
| | Brick | 87 | 8.79 | | | | |
| | Opus Signinum | 5 | 7.68 | | | | |
| | Lamps | 2 | 0.02 | | | | |
| | Glass | 2 | 0.02 | | | | |
| | sub-total | 33455 | 763.49 | | | 35.04 | 13.22 |
| | Total | 95863 | 2134.65 | | | | |

The most prolific fabric (Iberian amphora fabric 14/16) shows a wide range of variation which seems to have a clear geographical distribution. Sites in the S and SE of the survey show a strong pattern of positive deviations, whilst those in the N and NW show equally strong negative values. The whole of Transect 1 falls into the former grouping, but in Transects 2 - 4 the boundary line approximates to the river Francolí and the Baranc Sec. This clear cut distinction was not expected but it surely reflects a difference in the distribution of Iberian amphorae between the two areas.

The Iberian amphora fabric 20 shows a pattern with most of the sites very close to the survey mean, illustrating a more even pattern of supply. There are a number of larger positive deviations, in Transects 1 and 2. As none of these is immediately explainable in terms of small sample size, they suggest a distribution either introduced from the coast or from a distribution centre at Tarragona.

Punic amphorae are found at fewer sites and, although there is a range of variatiᴐns from the mean, these do not fall into any easily interpretable pattern.

The Iberian material as a whole reveals no variation which can be related to differences in settlement size, although the two varieties of Iberian amphora show clear geographical patterning. These suggest two separate supply zones, to SE and NW. The former, quite possibly the distribution zone of a centre at Tarragona, is marked by the presence of high proportions of both fabrics. The zone in the NW, dominated by other Iberian coarse and fine wares, might be viewed as within the distribution zone of another centre. These fabrics, some of which may have been made at the Fontscaldes kilns (Table 1.1, site 1), were perhaps distributed via the large site of El Vilar (Table 1.1, site 32, see p.19). These two zones cannot be distinguished on the basis of distribution of imported Punic amphorae. As is common elsewhere in coastal areas of eastern Spain, all of the survey area had ready access to external exchange networks and developed systems which brought imports to a wide range of sites. This supports the idea that the settlement pattern was already well established by the time that there is sufficient pottery for it to be mapped.

*Republican types*

This material includes imported fine wares, imported amphorae, and a locally-produced amphora fabric. The two varieties of Campanian ware (= Black Gloss A and B) show slight contrasts in their patterns. The values for Campanian A ware are generally close to the mean (fig. 9.9). There are few negative values (as a result of the low mean percentage) but there is a slight tendency for the larger positive anomalies to be found away from the coast in Transects 3 and 4. This is not sufficiently strong to bear an interpretation, especially as the number of sherds is rather small. The Campanian B ware shows a larger range of variations. They too probably result from the small numbers of sherds, and no distinct pattern emerges.

The principal amphora fabric is the Italica 6 (from Campania) which was found very widely within the survey area, demonstrating a large volume of imports within a well developed exchange-network. The graph (fig. 9.10) shows a range of variations from the mean, with the negative values tending to cluster away from the coast in Transects 3 and 4. In contrast, the positive anomalies are more common in Transects 1 and 2. It would be tempting to relate this to patterns of trade between the growing city of Tarraco and its hinterland. However, a close scrutiny of the data shows that the majority of the negative values are the reciprocal of high contentrations of other amphora fabrics in the N of our area.

The principal local Dressel 1 amphora fabric (Tarraconensian fabric 9) was probably manufactured somewhere in the region of Transect 4, possibly at the kilns of Fontscaldes (Table 1.1, site no. 2). Thus it is gratifying that the graph (fig. 9.10) shows a clear pattern of positive anomalies confined to Transect 4. The overall distribution shows a scatter of sites, with the fabric present over the whole area of the survey, although it may be noted that the findspots

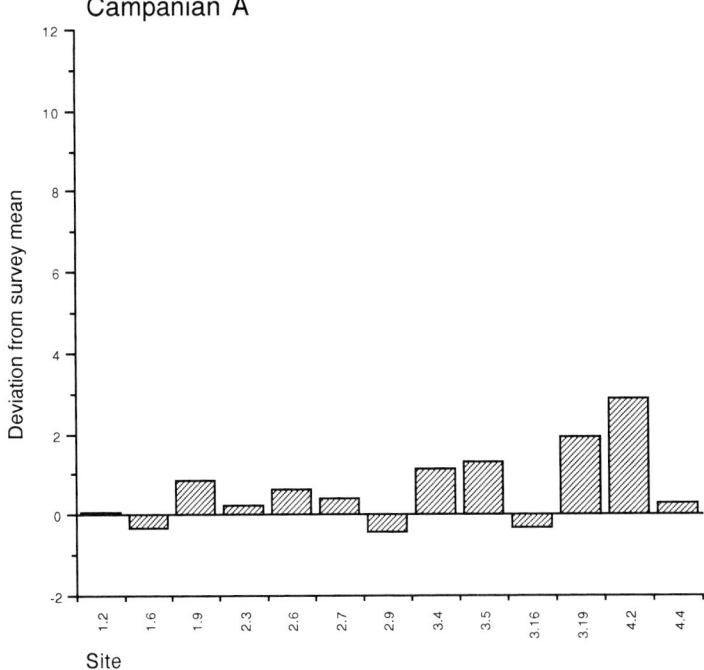

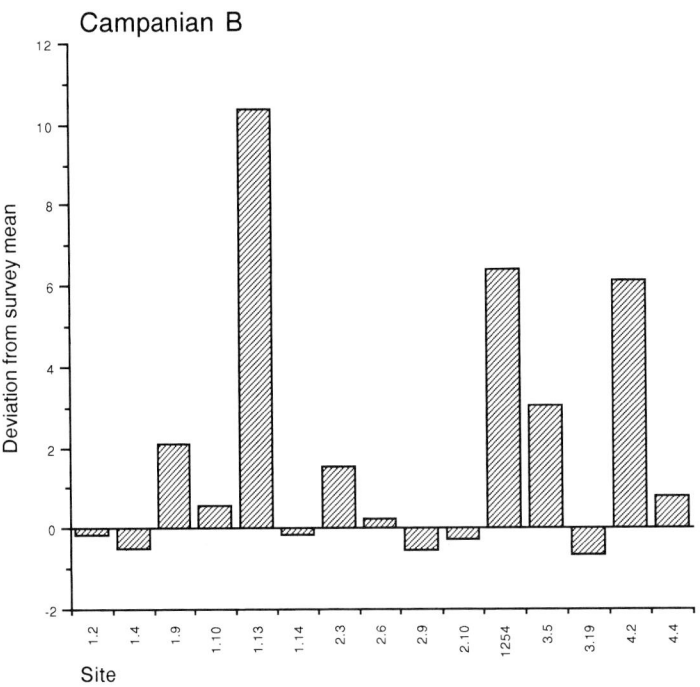

Fig.9.9. Graphs showing deviations from the mean for site ceramic assemblages of the Republican phase. a = Campanian A ware; b = Campanian B ware.

in Transects 1 and 2 are confined to sites within easy reach of the Roman road which followed the Francolí valley to Tarraco. It provides reasonably good evidence for the transport of these amphorae (and presumably their contents) to the town via the expected route.

The imported Ebusitanian amphorae (fig. 9.10) are also widely distributed, with a range of positive and negative deviations from the survey mean. The only apparent pattern is the group of positive anomalies in Transect 3. One or two of them may result from the small size of the group, but the sites concerned cluster at the E end of the transect and may imply redistribution from a centre hereabouts.

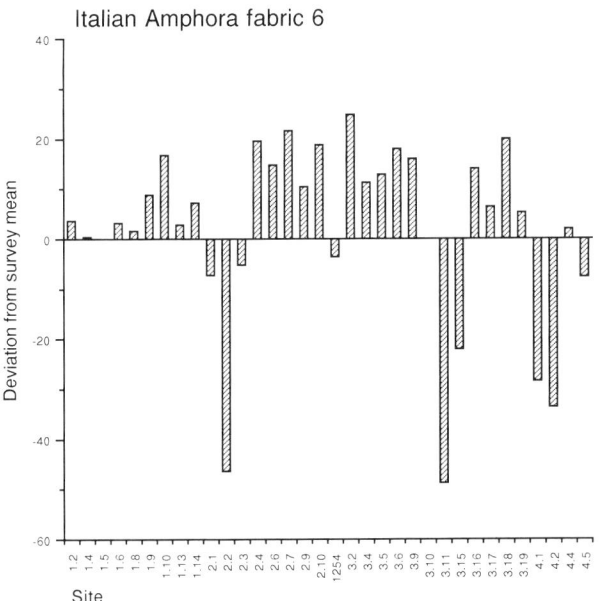

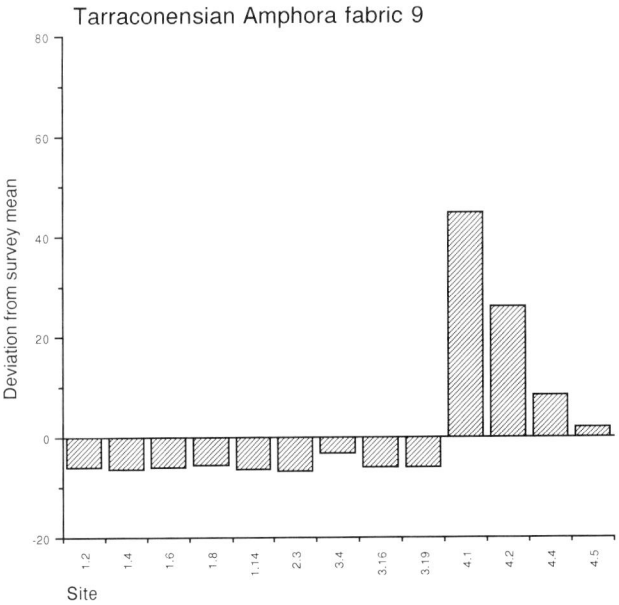

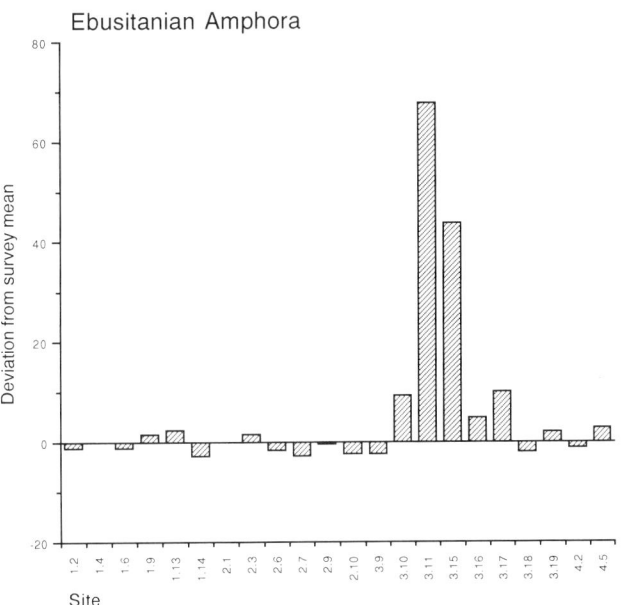

Fig.9.10. Graphs showing deviations from the mean for site ceramic assemblages of the Republican phase. a = Italian amphora fabric 6; b = Tarraconensian amphora fabric 9; c = Ebusitanian amphora.

The overall pattern of the Republican types reflects an increased range of ceramics with a predominance of imports whose widespread distribution demonstrates the effectiveness of the exchange networks. Amphorae dominate most of the assemblages, outnumbering coarse and fine wares by about 9 to 1 sherds on all sites. The distribution of 'local' amphorae is limited to their production area and sites along to the route to Tarraco. There is no evidence of any differentiation between the ceramic assemblages that can be related to the size or status of sites.

*Early imperial types*

This phase has a much broader range of pottery coming from a wider variety of sources. Four different classes of sigillata and three amphora fabrics are sufficiently common for their distributions to be analysed. This increased ceramic range is itself an important indicator of economic developments in the countryside of Tarraco under the principate.

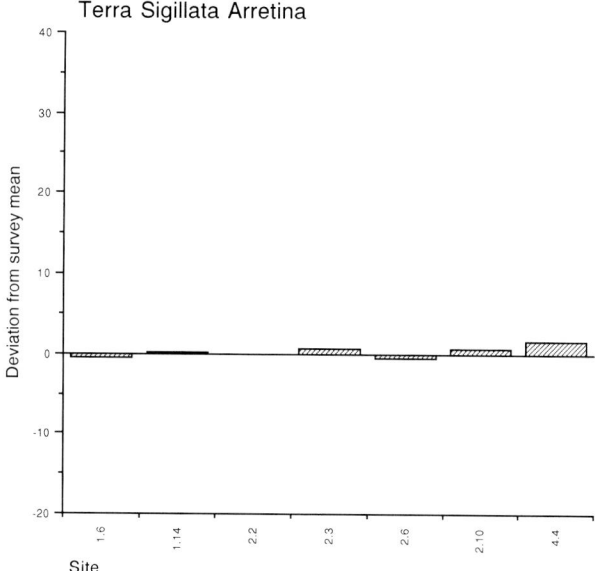

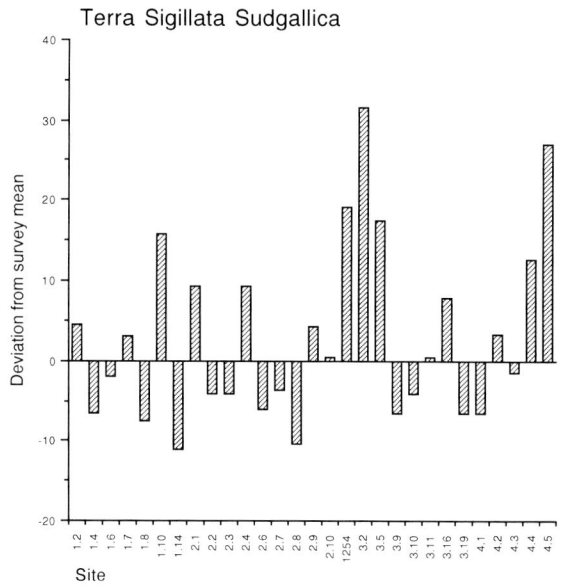

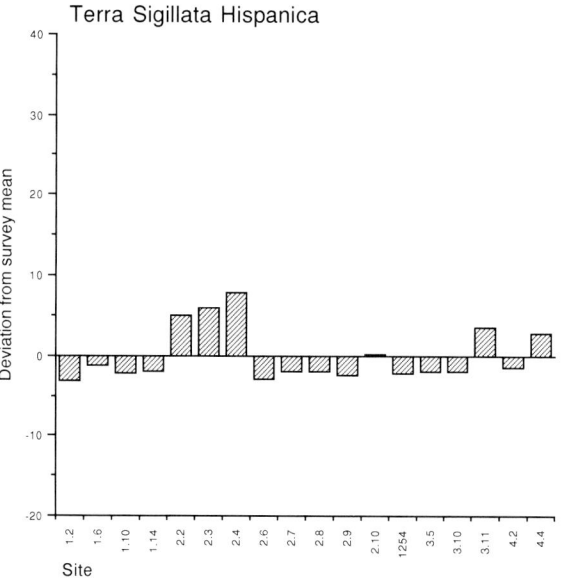

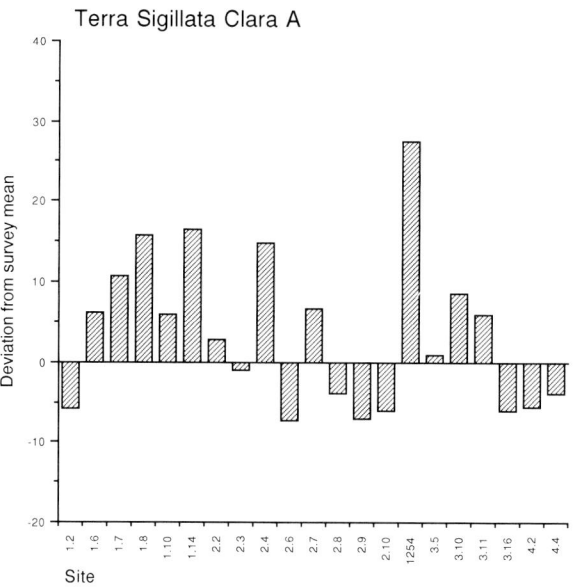

Fig.9.11. Graphs showing deviations from the mean for site ceramic assemblages of the Early imperial phase. a = Arretine ware; b = South Gaulish ware; c = Terra Sigillata Hispanica; d = African Red Slip ware (Terra Sigillata Clara A).

The sigillata shows a certain amount of variation in pattern. The Arretine ware (fig. 9.11) was confined to a narrow range of sites, suggesting a limited availability that contrasts with the earlier Campanian wares (see above), and the later South Gaulish and African products. The sites on which it is found are all of the larger size (C and above) and all but one are of intermediate or higher status. Given the small sample too much reliance should not be placed on this, although it may suggest that differences in ceramic assemblage related to status were beginning to emerge. The quantities of Arretine found on those sites which received it all lie very close to the survey mean.

South Gaulish ware reached a much larger number of sites that are quite evenly distributed across the area (fig. 9.11). There is no very obvious geographical pattern in deviations from the mean. The only pattern tentatively identified relates to status, with all sites of higher status showing positive anomalies. This was not an exclusive pattern, since some lower status sites also show positive anomalies, but some differentiation of status is evident.

Terra Sigillata Hispanica (fig. 9.11) was less widely distributed, although it occurs across the whole survey. The deviations from the mean cannot be related to either location or status.

The African Red Slip ware (Terra Sigillata Clara A) has a wide distribution similar to that of the earlier South Gaulish production (fig. 9.11). Most of the sites cluster near the mean. Although there is no evidence of variations between sites of different status, two points can be made. First, sites receiving this fabric are concentrated near Tarragona. The sites nearer the city also tend to have larger positive anomalies than sites further away, which tend to show negative values. Second, the Vallmoll by-pass site (Field 1254) has a particularly strong concentration of this fabric. As will be seen from discussion of the other fabrics (below), this site stands out as different from the others.

The most common amphorae are the two main Tarraconensian fabrics (fabrics 12 and 13). The most commonly occurring import is the Baetican *garum* amphora fabric 32. The graph for Tarraconensian fabric 12 (fig. 9.12) shows a very wide range of deviations, some of which are not readily explicable. There is, however, a general trend that positive anomalies are concentrated inland, in Transects 4 and to the E of the Francolí in Transect 3. This circumscribed area is curious in view of the fact that this fabric is typical of production in the Barcelona region. Fabric 13 is also widely distributed and has a wide spread of both positive and negative anomalies. They are mostly reciprocal to those of fabric 12, although the pattern is less clear. The trend is consistent with this fabric having been produced near the coast or brought to the area from outside via the coast. Neither fabric shows any clear pattern of distribution in relation to the size or status of sites.

The Baetican *garum* amphora (fabric 32) (fig. 9.12) is more thinly distributed. It has a marked concentration nearest the coast in Transects 1 and 2. Most of the sites fall near the mean; the largest anomalies are a product of small size of assemblage. They are strongly concentrated on larger sites, but the majority occur on those of intermediate or higher status.

The overall pattern of early imperial finds suggests a strong relationship between the status of sites and the presence of imported pottery. This pattern, which is not unexpected, may appear during this period only because the criteria set for the identification of settlements of intermediate and higher status were chronologically biased towards this period (see Chapter 8). Without excavation this question cannot be tested, but the pattern supports the idea that there was increasing differentiation between settlements in this period.

One of the more obvious general features of the early imperial pottery is its wider range and the increased presence of fine wares. The range of fabrics on any site reaches its maximum at between 12 and 15 when the assemblage size approaches 100 sherds. It is thus not possible to undertake very detailed comparisons between any sites except for the half dozen largest. Nevertheless, the differences between broader fabric groups, even in the smaller assemblages, offer the possibility of distinguishing between different types of site. One analysis demonstrates the potential of this type of study. The ratio of total numbers of sherds of amphorae to coarse and fine wares combined provides a potentially useful method of differentiating between assemblages.[2] Those with higher proportions of fine and coarse wares may represent domestic/consumer sites. Fig. 9.13 gives this information for all the sites of this phase. The graph shows the ratio of coarse and fine ware sherds to amphora sherds; the higher the number, the higher the proportion of coarse and fine wares in the site assemblage. Less than half the sites examined have more coarse and fine ware sherds than amphorae. The

---

2    There are evidently problems with this type of analysis caused by the methods of quantification. These and the method in general will be discussed further elsewhere (Millett forthcoming).

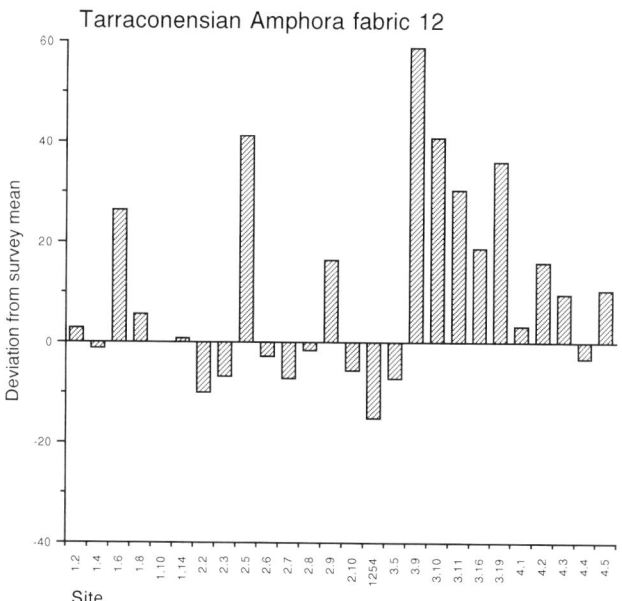

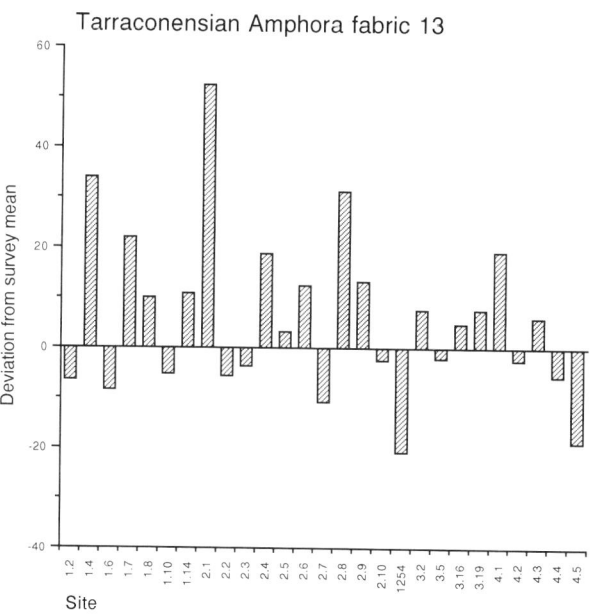

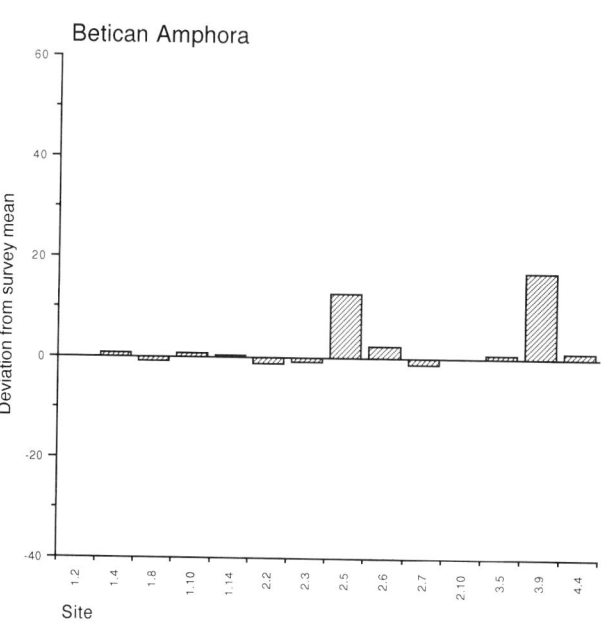

Fig.9.12. Graphs showing deviations from the mean for site ceramic assemblages of the early imperial phase. a = Tarraconensian amphora fabric 12; b = Tarraconensian amphora fabric 13; c = South Spanish (Baetican) amphora (fabric 32).

most extreme case is the Vallmoll by-pass (Field 1254) which has a value of more than 16:1. This site must be classed differently from those where amphorae predominate. An analysis of other sites with a ratio of more than 1:1 shows that they are widely distributed geographically and have no very strong correlation with sites of high or intermediate status. This suggests that the pottery can be used to distinguish domestic 'consumer' settlements. Although one would not wish to press this too far, the results demonstrate how pottery assemblages may be used to differentiate between different types of site from surface evidence alone. They also illustrate how the pattern of rural settlement was increasingly varied during the early empire.

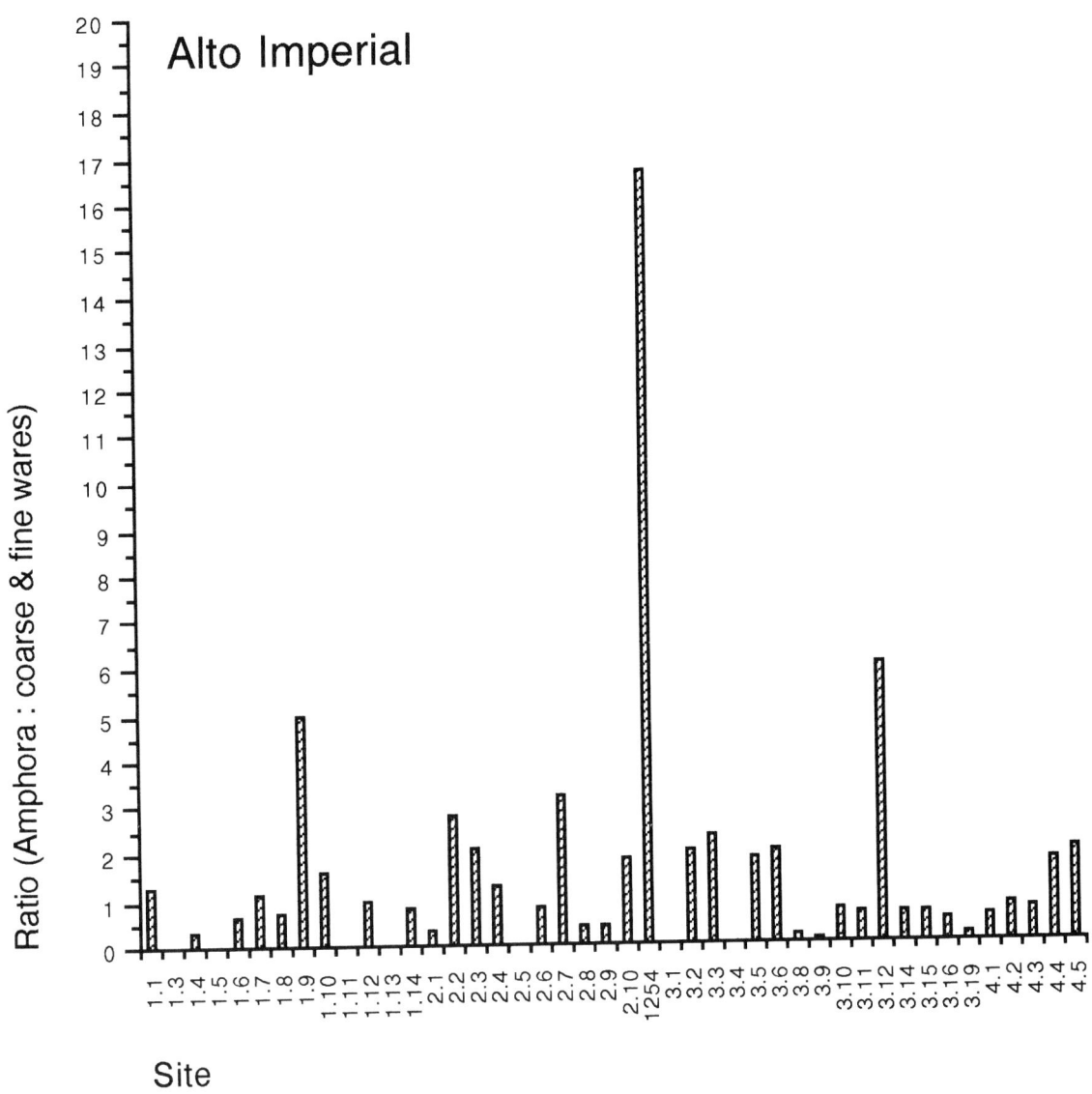

Fig.9.13. Graph showing the ratio of amphorae to coarse and fine ware fabrics for sites of the early imperial phase.

*Late imperial types*

In this phase the decreased volume of pottery in circulation means that even the most common fabrics are scarce. As a result, only 4 fabrics can be used in this analysis.

Terra Sigillata Clara C (fig. 9.14) is found on only 3 sites, at two of which the values are very close to the mean. This illustrates one of the problems with the period: as Site 2.7 produced the bulk of the finds of this period, it almost defines the mean by itself. The only site to deviate is the Vallmoll by-pass (Field 1254) which, as in the previous phase, has a major preponderance of fine wares. Sigillata Clara D (fig. 9.14) is slightly more widely distributed, but most of the assemblages are also near the mean. The only aberrant value is Site 1.6 where the assemblage is small, and the small number of amphorae exaggerates the percentage of other fabrics.

The most common amphorae are the African and Spanish (Baetican) types, but even these are much less widely distributed than those of earlier phases. The African fabrics (fig. 9.14)

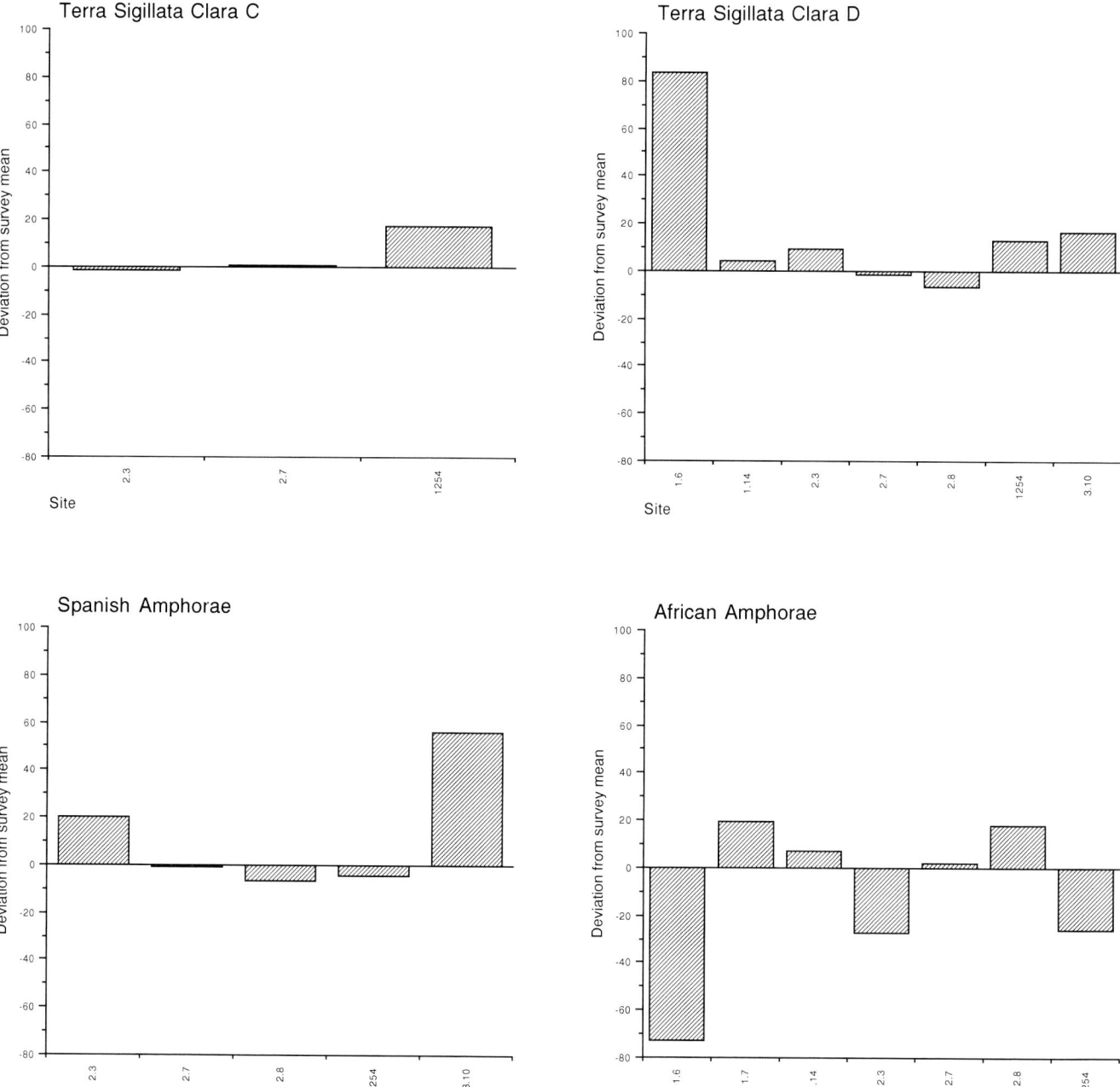

Fig.9.14. Graphs showing deviations from the mean for ceramic assemblages of the late imperial phase. a = Terra Sigillata Clara C; b = Terra Sigillata Clara D; c = Spanish amphorae; d = African amphorae.

occur most widely, but there is no strong pattern to the deviations from the mean. The Baetican types (fig. 9.14) also show no clear pattern.

Overall the results from this phase reveal few patterns. However, one distinctive and consistent feature is the location of the sites where larger pottery assemblages of this period were found. They were predominantly in the transects nearest to Tarragona. A similar pattern of imported material spreading inland from the coast has been noted in earlier phases. In this period it may be fortuitous, but given the number of possible sites in Transects 3 and 4 one might conclude that it represents a real pattern by which the bulk of the pottery circulated only in networks near to the town and at a few larger sites like 2.7. This raises the possibility that there was a population elsewhere with only intermittent access to pottery, and thus fails to appear in the archaeological record. This would be consistent with an overall decline in the volume of exchange in the later Roman world, with the idea of an increased separation between town and country, and possibly with increased social distinctions between landlords and tenants.

**Summary**

The evidence from this analysis of the pottery distributions has provided information about broad changes in distribution through time. More detailed analyses of particular fabrics and forms will be carried out later. However, a broad picture is evident and it demonstrates the value of collecting and analysing the pottery from surveys.

There was evidently an exchange network in place in the region before the first use of pottery in bulk in the Iberian phase. The distribution of the earliest pottery allows two broad zones to be identified, one connected to the coast or the indigenous settlement at Tarragona, the other perhaps centred on the site of El Vilar at Valls (Table 1.1, site 32). The bulk of imported Republican ceramics reinforces this pattern. A new local amphora production was established, centering on the inland area and using a route down the Francolí valley to Tarraco.

The early imperial phase witnessed a much increased use of pottery. Differentiation between the assemblages found points to clear distinctions in status and perhaps differences in economic rôles. There is a marked decline in the distribution of pottery in the late empire, which implies a reduction in the volume of exchange. Sites which continued to receive pottery were generally those in the immediate hinterland of Tarraco.

The change suggests that the foundation of Tarraco as a Roman town at first distorted and then dominated the surrounding area, before distributions declined in late antiquity. However, there was no total dominance by the town before the late empire since none of the distributions show strong patterns of decreasing density with increasing distance from the city. Ceramic evidence thus lends support to the view that the Roman countryside was not simply an adjunct to the town. There was a densely-populated rural landscape producing and consuming large volumes of goods. This should serve to remind us of the essentially symbiotic nature of the relationship between town and country.

## 2. OFF-SITE DISTRIBUTIONS

Finds not found in association with particular settlement sites are often referred to as 'off-site' distributions. In the study of prehistoric communities off-site distributions are particularly important as many human activities (e.g., hunting) took place away from settlements and communities were not always sedentary. A considerable literature is concerned with the interpretation of such distributions. There has been less discussion of the interpretation of off-site distributions from periods following the emergence of settled agricultural systems. This survey provides a rich source of data for exploring and interpreting the changing character of off-site distributions.

There are a range of ways in which objects found in off-site scatters may have reached their findspots. Some are likely to have been accidental losses by people working in or passing through the area; others may result from the presence of structures like shepherds' huts too small to have been recognized as settlements in the survey. Others may result from the movement of the finds with soil, either in antiquity or more recently. However, since much of the area examined was 'carpeted' with low densities of pottery (see figs. 6.3-6.33), more general explanations are needed.

Some of the pottery was probably spread out from inhabited settlements as a result of a combination of activities. Rubbish accumulates around the margins of both ancient and modern settlements and is spread into the surrounding areas by a variety of random actions — the activities of animals, the playing of children, and the day-to-day movements of the inhabitants. The result is a 'halo' of finds surrounding most settlements. It is especially obvious to archaeologists around centres which were most richly supplied with durable goods. In our survey these processes seem likely to account for the intensity of off-site finds surrounding site 1.6 (fig. 6.3) or 2.9 (fig. 6.17).

Another possible explanation is that objects were spread into the countryside as a by-product of the agricultural manuring of fields. Intensive arable agriculture requires the fertility of the land to be maintained by the addition of nutrients to the soil. This can be achieved through a variety of methods, including the rotation of crops, which permits animal grazing and thereby the natural addition of dung to the fields. Alternatively, settled communities who maintain a pattern of intensive arable land-use of the same fields may choose to add collected manure. Such manure is often collected in middens beside the settlements at which animals are stalled. It often includes both human faeces and other domestic refuse from the settlement. Such rubbish tips have been identified by detailed fieldwork on sites like Maxey in England (Crowther 1983; Crowther and Pryor 1985). When such middens incorporate archaeologically durable materials such as pottery it too becomes dispersed across regularly manured areas. The distribution of archaeological finds across the landscape in this manner has been documented in various contexts. A careful survey of the landscape at Maddle Farm in S. England has enabled archaeologists to reconstruct details of the farming pattern around a villa from the distribution of manured material (Gaffney and Tingle 1989). Their study makes it clear that the interpretation of manuring patterns is dependent upon a good understanding of the agricultural practices in a particular area. The archaeologists at Maddle Farm were fortunate in studying a landscape where the densities of finds were comparatively light and could be attributed to a single period of relatively short duration. In the case of our survey the superimposition of a series of phases of occupation over a wide area makes analysis more difficult, although it does seem very likely that deliberate manuring was an important contributor to the distributions observed.

The data from this survey enable us to consider off-site patterns but we should be aware of their limitations as well as their potential. It is important to note that the mapped patterns are the aggregate of both the depositional processes and subsequent activities. Each of our ceramic phases covers a considerable period and the densities of off-site pottery recovered are, by definition, low. Even allowing for the fact that the samples collected represent only a proportion of the pottery in the ploughsoil in a particular field, densities of a few sherds per hectare over several hundred years may be as likely to result from the random factors discussed above as from systematic and regular manuring. If they do derive from manuring, it is difficult to distinguish between constant activity over time and that which was intermittent or whose focus shifted. Finally, variations in the volume of pottery in circulation through time (see p.57 ff.) make it is easier to identify potential areas of manuring in some phases than in others. This acts as a reminder that manuring may have been taking place even when we cannot identify it through the inclusion of artefacts. The relative abundance of durable objects included in the manure was not simply a result of chronological factors. On larger agricultural estates it is likely that the greater distance between animal stalls and human habitation and the larger areas farmed resulted in less pottery being distributed onto the fields than was the case with land intensively cultivated close to small farms.

These issues provide a background against which to examine the results from the survey. The basic information on the densities of finds across the landscape has been presented in figs. 6.3-6.33 and Appendix 4. The maps show the distributions of dated pottery. They are supplemented by figs. 9.15-9.18 which illustrate the average sherd-size for all pottery recovered from each field (including the undated material). The maps mask a wide range of variation in the average sherd-sizes of the different fabrics (see Table 9.7).[3]

---

3    More detailed studies of the variations in sherd size through time and across the landscape might be informative but are beyond the scope of this report.

Average sherd size of pottery fabrics from the survey

Table 9.7

| | | Av Sherd size |
|---|---|---|
| **IBERIAN** | | |
| Fine ware | Iberian | 1.10 |
| Coarse ware | Fabric A | 1.28 |
| Amphorae | Massiliote | 3.33 |
| | Iberian (14/16) | 1.34 |
| | Iberian (20) | 2.08 |
| | Punic | 2.72 |
| | | 1.30 |
| **REPUBLICAN** | | |
| Fine ware | Thin walled | 1.00 |
| | Black Gloss (A) | 1.56 |
| | Black Gloss (B) | 1.37 |
| | Black Gloss (C) | 1.00 |
| | Black Gloss (indet.) | 1.93 |
| | Gris Ampuritana | 0.75 |
| Coarse ware | Italian (6) | 2.63 |
| Amphorae | Italian (6) | 4.60 |
| | Italian (Others) | 8.34 |
| | Tarraconensian (9) | 5.37 |
| | Tarraconensian (12) | 12.67 |
| | Tarraconensian (13) | 13.00 |
| | African | 6.59 |
| | Ebussitanian | 3.68 |
| | | 4.86 |
| **EARLY IMPERIAL** | | |
| Fine ware | Pompeian Red | 1.00 |
| | Thin walled | 0.93 |
| | Sigillata Italica | 0.33 |
| | S. Gaulish Sigillata | 0.81 |
| | Sigillata Hispanica | 0.56 |
| | Oriental Sigillata | 0.67 |
| | Sigillata Clara A | 0.42 |
| | Sigillata Clara B | 1.25 |
| | Imit.Clara | 0.67 |
| Coarse ware | Tarraconensian (12) | 2.89 |
| | Tarraconensian (13) | 1.53 |
| | Tarraconensian (K) | 1.07 |
| | Tarraconensian (L) | 1.47 |
| | Fabric B | 1.50 |
| | Fabric ZD | 0.76 |
| | Fabric ZL | 1.22 |
| | Fabric ZM | 0.80 |
| | African | 1.04 |
| Amphorae | Tarraconensian (12) | 4.92 |
| | Tarraconensian (13) | 5.66 |
| | Baetican (Dr 20) | 9.57 |
| | Baetican BI-IV (32) | 8.29 |
| | Gallic | 4.92 |
| | Italian | 3.00 |
| | Tarraconensian (18) | 5.33 |
| | Tarraconensian (33) | 9.00 |
| | | 2.95 |
| **LATE IMPERIAL** | | |
| Fine ware | Palaeochristian | 1.67 |
| | Sigillata Lucente | 2.00 |
| | Sigillata Clara C | 0.37 |
| | Sigillata Clara D | 1.00 |
| Amphorae | African | 2.70 |
| | Oriental | 1.00 |
| | Spanish | 4.56 |
| | | 2.57 |
| **UNDIAGNOSTIC** | | |
| | Coarse ware | 0.84 |
| | Mortaria | 16.00 |
| | Amphora | 2.96 |
| | African Amphora | 2.96 |
| | Tripolitanian Amph. | 1.00 |
| | Amphorae stopper | 11.00 |
| | Dolia | 20.61 |
| | Sigillata Clara Indet. | 0.46 |
| | Red Slip Ware | 0.80 |
| | Tegula | 41.84 |
| | Brick | 10.10 |
| | Opus Signinum | 153.60 |
| | Lamps | 1.00 |
| | Glass | 1.00 |
| | | |
| | | |
| | Overall average | 2.23 |

The variations in sherd-size largely result from differences in the robustness and wall thickness of the different wares (Taylor, in prep.). Our data were also constrained by the precision of the weighing apparatus used, which generally allowed measurement only to 10 g, or occasionally and at best 5 g. Where there were many sherds, the average size was more reliably measured than in fields where only a few pieces were found. Nevertheless, the mapping of this information provides results relevant to the debate about the character of off-site finds. Sherd-size may be used as a measure of the degree of abrasion to which sherds have been subjected, correlations might be expected between smaller sherd-sizes and areas of intensive agricultural activity, or between larger sherd-size and settlement foci. In reality the processes are far more complex (Taylor, in prep.), and it seems that many sherds in the ploughsoil are fragmented until they reach a size determined by their robustness and wall-thickness. Modern agricultural activity has affected most of the areas fieldwalked, thus reducing any distinctions that might have existed between on-site and off-site distributions at the time of deposition.

The maps (fig. 9.15-9.18) show three principal patterns. First, there is a similar pattern of average sherd-size in the majority of fields which produced pottery. Although there were some fields with larger sherds, most fell in the middle of the range, supporting the idea that agricultural activity has reduced most of the material in the ploughsoil to a minimum size where further breakage is less likely (Taylor, in prep.). This suggests that the average sherd-size for the different fabrics shown in Table 9.7 provides a useful index of their robustivity. Our results also imply that modern agricultural practice is having less effect in bringing fresh material to the surface than has sometimes been suggested.

Second, those fields which have larger sized sherds are not generally associated with identified sites but are isolated fields. This absence of patterning probably results from the small quantities of material found in those fields, rendering their average values less reliable. In a field on a settlement site an occasional amphora handle that is large and resistant to further breakage will not greatly increase the average sherd-size because it is only one of a large number of pieces contributing to that average. In contrast, a similar piece in a field where it is the only sherd will create an extreme value.

Transect 1A

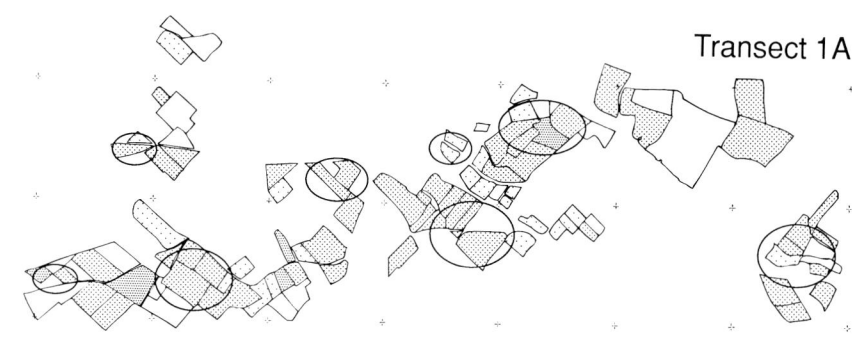

Transect 1B

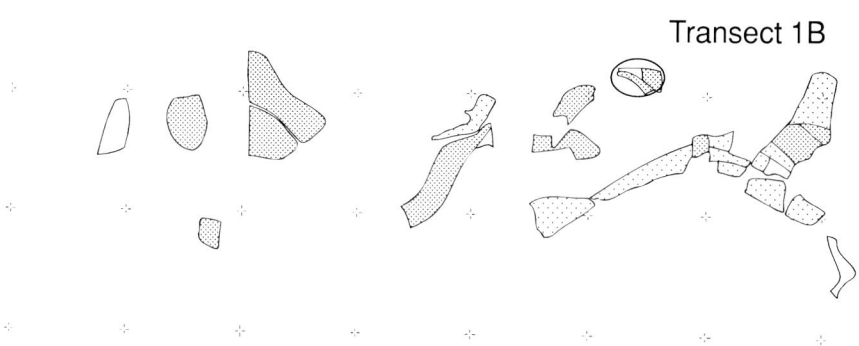

Transect 1C

Transect 1D

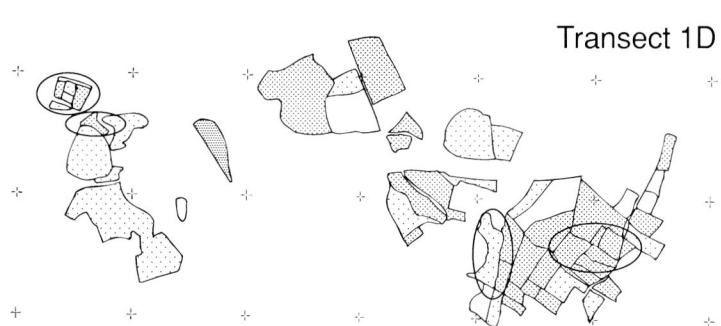

Fig.9.15. Map showing average sherd-size of pottery recovered from Transect 1. Scales: blank = no pottery; Lowest = less than 20 g per sherd; Medium = 20-50 g per sherd; Highest = more than 50 g per sherd. Sites identified in Chapter 6 are outlined by ellipses.

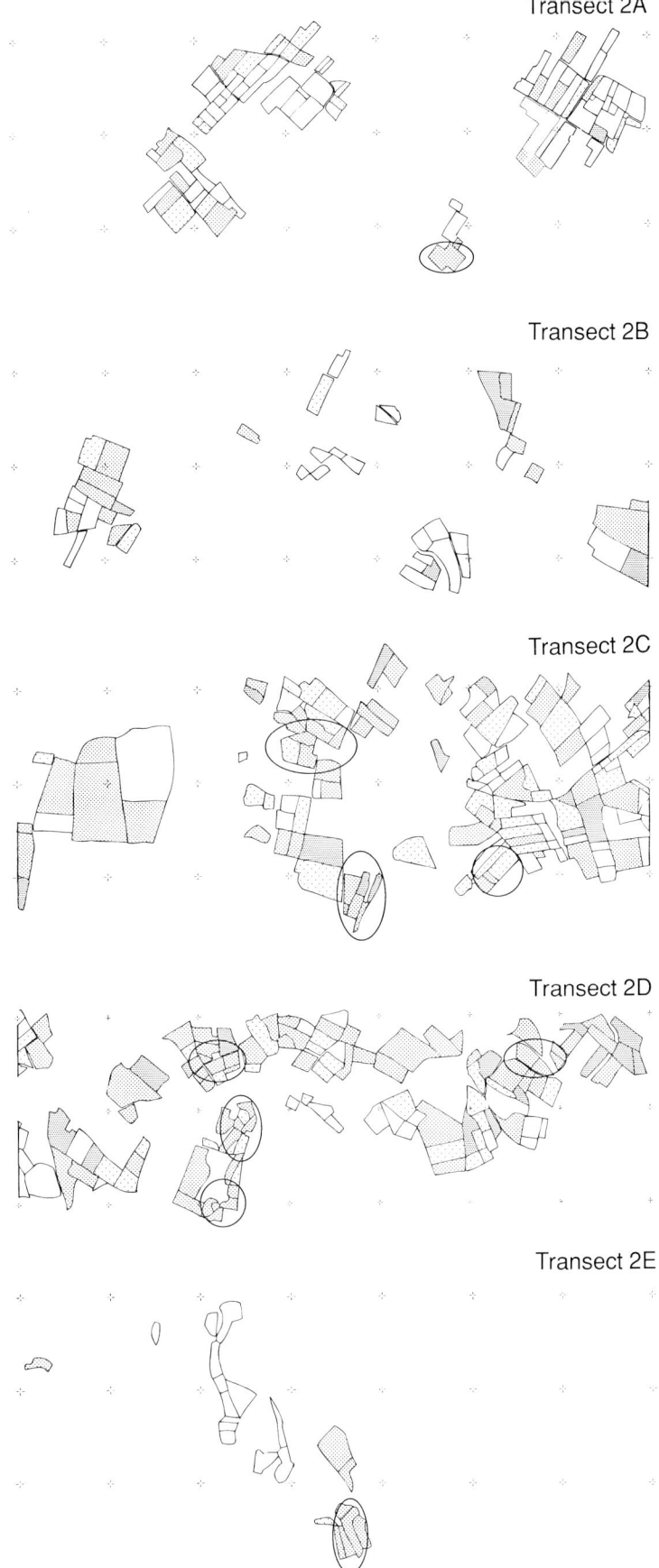

Transect 2A

Transect 2B

Transect 2C

Transect 2D

Transect 2E

Fig.9.16. Map showing average sherd-size of pottery recovered from Transect 2. Scales: blank = no pottery; Lowest = less than 20 g per sherd; Medium = 20-50 g per sherd; Highest = more than 50 g per sherd. Sites identified in Chapter 6 are outlined by ellipses.

Transect 3A

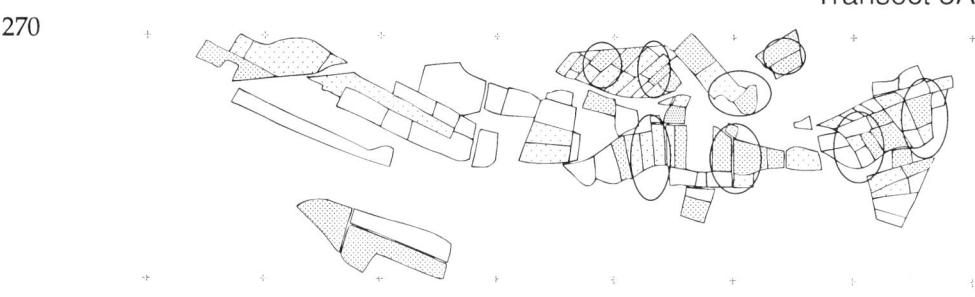

Transect 3B

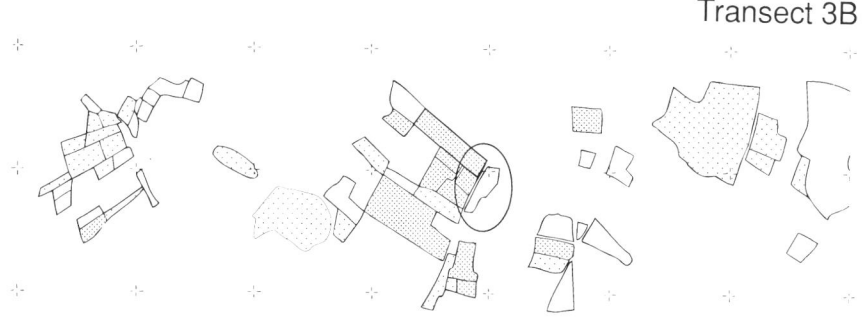

Transect 3C

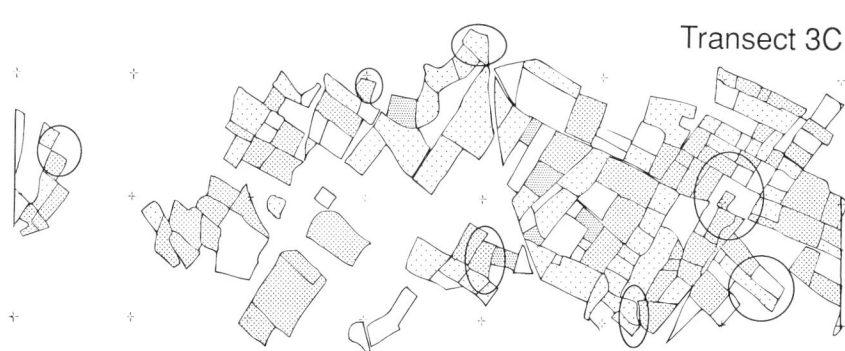

Transect 3D

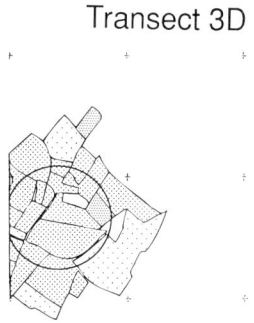

Fig.9.17. Map showing average sherd-size of pottery recovered from Transect 3. Scales: blank = no pottery; Lowest = less than 20 g per sherd; Medium = 20-50 g per sherd; Highest = more than 50 g per sherd. Sites identified in Chapter 6 are outlined by ellipses.

Transect 4B

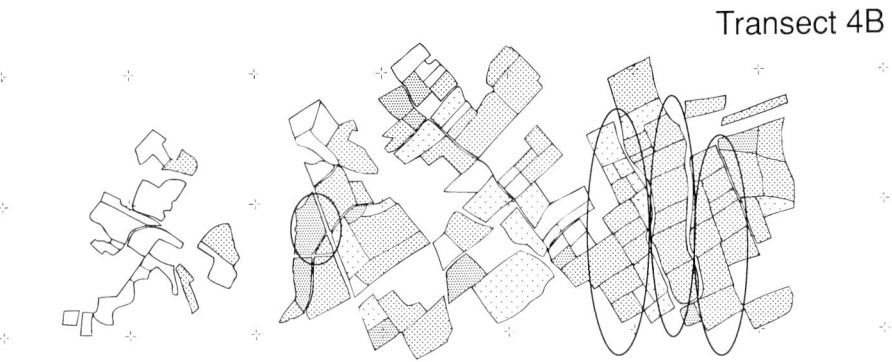

Transect 4C

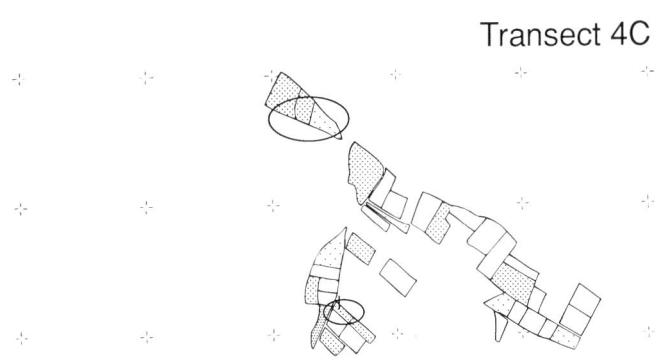

Fig.9.18. Map showing average sherd-size of pottery recovered from Transect 4. Scales: blank = no pottery; Lowest = less than 20 g per sherd; Medium = 20-50 g per sherd; Highest = more than 50 g per sherd. Sites identified in Chapter 6 are outlined by ellipses.

Finally, there is no evidence that the average sherd-size of material from settlement sites is higher than that from off-site distributions. In several cases, contrary to expectations it is rather smaller. This may be explained by two factors. First the sites with a low average sherd-size are most often those with a predominantly Iberian assemblage which has a lower average sherd-size than other phases (Table 9.7). Second, there may be a tendency for the fieldwalkers to have been more successful in collecting the smallest sherds in areas where there were higher densities of finds, since they may have searched more carefully.

**Fields without finds**

Certain of the fields which did not produce any pottery were scattered across the whole survey area and are simply a random product of a low-density distribution. However, in a few areas absences are more consistent and there seems to be a pattern of negative evidence that deserves explanation.

The western end of Transect 2 (sectors A and B) has a large number of such empty fields. The area is also sparse in settlement sites. It may simply be that the absence of farms resulted in an absence of a 'halo' of rubbish and of manuring scatters. However, the presence of the large villa of Parets Delgada (see p.20, fig. 1.5; Table 1.1, site 42), which lay just outside the transect to the north, should not be ignored. It is very likely that much of the area walked lay within the estate of this villa, but was at a sufficient distance from it not to have had its rubbish deposited as part of any manure which was spread on the land. It may be no coincidence that the land in this part of the transect is amongst the most fertile in the survey area (fig. 3.5). Thus it may not have needed manuring, or perhaps was used differently for agriculture.

The second area with a significant cluster of fields without pottery is at the E end of the same transect (2/E). The upland landscape suggests that an absence of finds results from either a lack of manuring or the low-density of settlement, or a combination of the two. The absence of finds does not necessarily imply that the land was not used. Different types of non-arable agriculture more suited to the terrain and which did not require manuring may have been practiced.

Transect 3/A has a variety of different patterns which suggest that the absence of pottery from the fields at its W end was the result of variations in agricultural practice. The best land in this sector (fig. 3.5) lay on the terrace of the Francolí where pottery is found on most fields. In contrast, much of the inferior ground on the plateau to the W produced no pottery. Between the two areas there is a remarkable concentration of small settlements which suggests that the various types of land were used for different and complementary agricultural purposes. It should perhaps be noted that the geology underlying the fields on which there was no pottery was Quaternary angular conglomerate (fig. 3.4, no. 3), the same as that beneath the sparsely carpeted area at the W end of Transect 2. The same geology is found at the E end of Transect 4. There were also a number of fields without pottery lying away from the 'halo' surrounding the major sites in Transect 4/B. Although soils information is not available for Transect 4 (and the soil quality varies between Transects 2 and 3), it might be suggested that the Quaternary conglomerates were used for different agricultural purposes from the other land in the survey. Perhaps the higher lands on this geology were used for pasture rather than arable farming; that would have removed any necessity for artificial manuring.

Finally, in the mountains in the NW corner of the survey (Transect 4/A and part of 4/B) outcropped the oldest rocks encountered (fig. 3.4). Neither settlements nor off-site pottery distributions were found. The slopes are not heavily farmed today and are perhaps unlikely to have been used for extensive arable farming in antiquity. This contrasts with their relatively intensive exploitation in earlier prehistory, as represented by the distribution of flints (Schofield et al., forthcoming).

# Chapter 10: DISCUSSION AND CONCLUSIONS

The objectives of the survey were detailed in Chapter 3. In the following discussion we take the questions outlined there as our starting point before turning to other issues that have emerged during the analysis of the data. The basic framework of the first part of the chapter is chronological. Despite the problems in dating the Iberian ceramics (see Chapter 4), the Iberian and Republican periods are treated separately.

## Prehistoric period

The primary question concerning the relationship between the Iberian settlement pattern and that of the preceding late Bronze Age was not satisfactorily answered by the survey since we found almost no material of pre-Iberian date. It is generally considered that Bronze Age settlement was on a small scale (see Chapter 2), but the lack of evidence from the survey cannot be used to sustain this conclusion. The absence of finds may result from a lack of settlement, or a scarcity of material culture used by the population, or a failure of finds to survive in the ploughsoil as a result of their poor quality manufacture. These possibilities confirm the danger of assuming a direct and simple correlation between densities of finds and population levels.

The prehistoric lithic distributions (Schofield *et al.*, forthcoming) show that the area was intensively exploited by the Neolithic period, and the evidence presented in this volume demonstrates that by the Iberian/Republican period the settlement pattern was dense across the whole area. It seems unlikely that the landscape was depopulated during the intervening periods and that the main settlement pattern first developed after the 6th c. B.C., as is often held to be the case in other parts of the Iberian region. Thus we infer that the origins of the Iberian settlement pattern lie largely in the preceding period. We suspect that there was a developed Bronze Age settlement pattern which field-survey has been unsuccessful in identifying. This hypothesis needs investigation through the careful excavation of selected rural sites.

## Iberian phase

The dated pottery from sites identified in the survey can be used as an index of when sites first become archaeologically visible. It is clear that a majority of the sites located in the survey first appear from the 5th c. B.C. onwards.

*Earliest date range for the pottery at each survey site*

| 6th c. B.C. | 5th c. | 4th c. | 3rd c. | 2nd c. | 1st c. | Early empire |
|---|---|---|---|---|---|---|
| 1 | 33 | 0 | 4 | 5 | 1 | 2 |

The overwhelming impression created is one of a densely settled landscape by the Iberian period. Allowing for variations in the chronology of individual forms, which range over a period of up to two centuries, the pattern appears to show most sites first receiving pottery at about the same time. This established pattern was consolidated through the 4th to 2nd c. B.C. Within the transects the density of sites with Iberian pottery is just over one per km$^2$ (after an adjustment has been made for the linear nature of the sample, see p.248). This implies a total of about 545 sites if the size of the survey area is taken into account and the mountains are excluded.

This evidence represents a change from earlier periods. It is notable that Iberian pottery was the most common found. Almost the whole landscape was covered with sites. There was also a considerable off-site scatter of ceramics. The only area where an absence of material was noted was on the uplands in Transect 4, suggesting that the area was uninhabited, or used as upland grazing, or for woodland. This pattern contrasts with both the earliest prehistoric evidence in this area (Schofield *et al.*, forthcoming) and with other parts of the coastal region

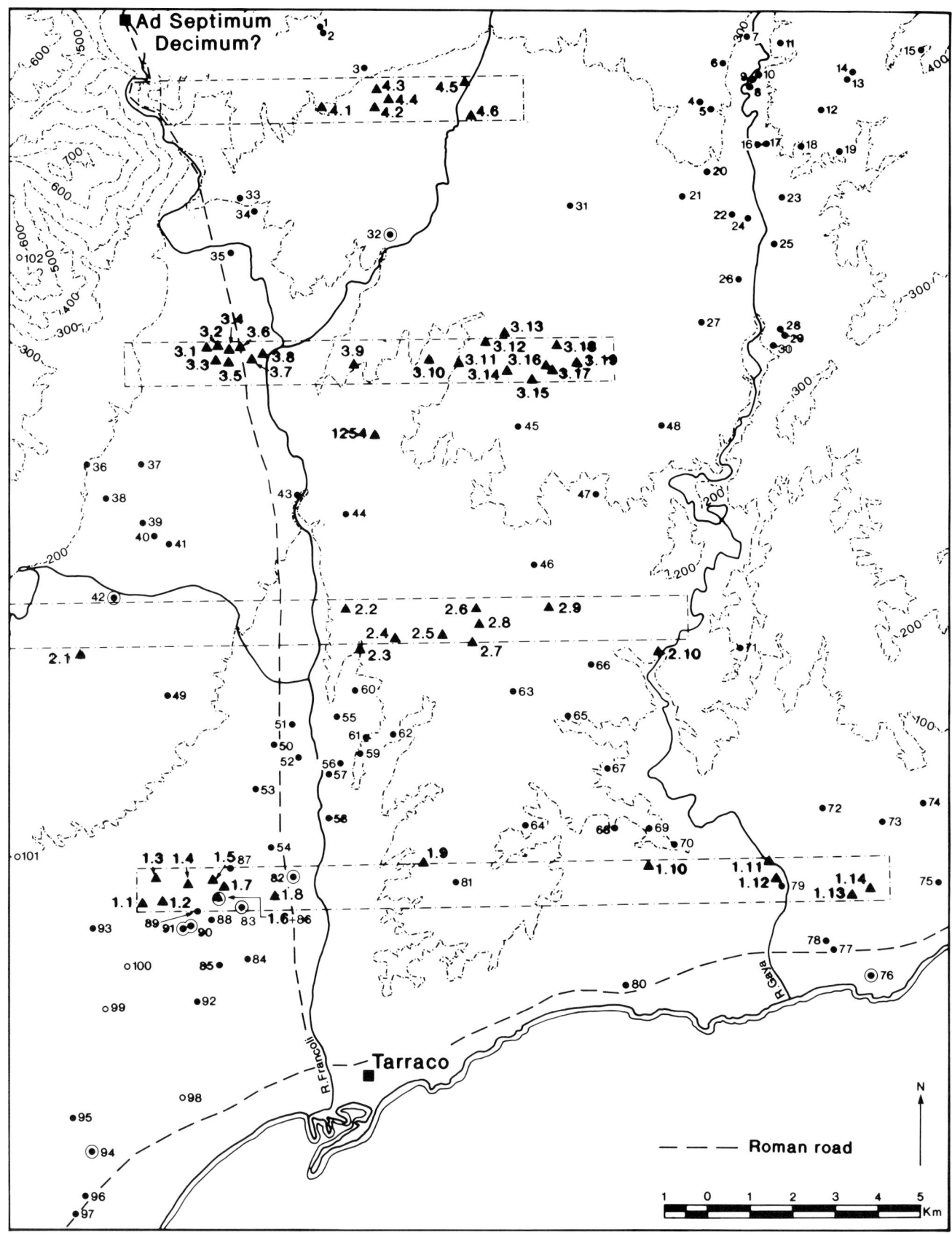

Fig.10.1. Map showing sites found in the survey together with those known previously.

Fig.10.2. Site 3.19 (Puig Ferré) from the SE, showing its location on a low hill.

of NE Spain where Iberian hill-top settlements are well known. From this period onwards the landscape was intensively exploited and there is little evidence for preference in location according to soil or geology. However, the exact position chosen for a settlement was commonly determined by a preference for locally elevated positions (fig. 10.2). This combination of occasional hill-top settlements and more common lowland sites on small prominences is typical of other parts of NE Spain, such as the Alt and Baix Empordà and the Gironès (see Chapter 2; Nolla and Casas 1984).

The density of pottery found within the survey area shows that there was a major increase in the availability of material in the exchange networks at this period. There is little evidence to suggest any localized variability in access to goods within these networks, as there are no evident distinctions in the types of pottery found on different sites. Nevertheless, there is a hierarchy in the size of sites. The majority of the sites found were in the region of 1-2 ha in extent, but ranged up to about 10 ha (fig. 8.1). Such a range is comparable to that of other sites within the Iberian region (Almagro-Gorbea 1986b), although evidence for other areas has not been collected systematically (Ruíz and Molinos 1992). The largest site of this period found (Site 3.19; fig. 10.2) is comparable in size to the two known major Iberian sites in the region, at El Vilar (fig. 10.1, site 32; fig. 1.3) and Tarragona (fig. 2.1), which, although imperfectly known, each cover c.10 ha. There are problems in making such comparisons because of the ways in which the areas of our sites have been measured, but the general impression is that of a hierarchy by size with a number of local centres each about 10 ha. In addition there is some evidence for the specialization of production. Pottery production is suggested at Sites 4.2 to 4.4 in Transect 4. These sites are just south of the kilns at Fontscaldes (fig. 10.1, sites 1 and 2), although recent work suggests that the latter may date to the 2nd c. B.C. (Lafuente 1992).

A tentative model for settlement before the Roman arrival in 218 B.C. can be proposed. The largest known sites, at Tarragona, El Vilar, and Site 3.19, were perhaps dominant. The first two, where there is excavated evidence, have produced imported Greek pottery which is apparently absent from other settlements in the survey. (Comparable material might be found if Site 3.19 were excavated.) Other sites of the period include specialist production centres (Sites 4.2-4.4). Further exploration might distinguish other types of settlement beyond simple farmsteads. We would argue that the three largest sites were at the top of the settlement hierarchy, with the others dependant upon them. On empirical archaeological grounds there is little evidence to distinguish Tarragona from the other two sites, but two alternative models may be suggested. A minimalist interpretation would see these three sites (and perhaps others yet to be discovered) as of approximately equal status, although drawing upon the varied resources of their contrasting locations. Tarragona drew upon the agricultural lowlands, coastal resources and maritime traffic. The other two sites exploited the agriculture of the interior (including upland pastures), produced some ceramics, and commanded communication routes with the interior via the Francolí. An alternative explanation sees Tarragona as having a more dominant rôle in the region because of its coastal location and by virtue of privileged access to high-status imported goods. Such a key rôle has been invoked for other centres such as Elche in SE Spain and perhaps Ullastret in the hinterland of Emporion.

**Roman Republican phase**

The figures quoted above demonstrate that there was no significant alteration to the settlement pattern during the Republican period and certainly provide no evidence for a phase of colonization. The presence of imported Italic wine amphorae and other pottery cannot be taken as evidence for the presence of Italic settlers. Despite the difficulties in distinguishing between sites occupied before and after Roman conquest, strong continuity seems to characterize the landscape. Most sites appear to continue in occupation. There is no evidence for any substantial dislocation. Equally the density of previously established settlement seems not to have increased during the Republican period. This is probably because there was little spare capacity within the landscape. It suggests that there was no substantial increase in rural production stimulated by the Roman presence. Against this background, it is not surprising that no archaeological evidence was found to support the recent suggestion that the territory of Tarraco was centuriated during this period (*contra* Gurt and Marquès 1988).

We have no evidence for the character of the rural settlements of this period although earlier work suggests that native-style (Sanmartí, Santacana and Serra 1984) and Romanized (Terré 1987) farmsteads may have co-existed from around the late 2nd c. B.C. onwards. Within the transects the adjusted density of sites recorded was approximately one per km², implying a total of about 500 sites within the survey area. If this density can be extrapolated to the suggested extent of the whole territory (as shown on fig. 1.1), it would imply a total of about 3,300 rural settlements.

The main characteristic noted was a great increase in the volume of imported pottery entering the region, especially from Italy from the later 2nd c. B.C. onwards. The variety and volume of imports at rural sites is greater than previously known; they are found on almost every site throughout the survey area. They evidently arrived via the coast and it is arguable that Tarraco's strategic military rôle stimulated trade in the region (Keay 1990). The finds from the Roman military camps around Numantia show that the troops were amply supplied with Italic wine (E. Sanmartí 1985b), and since we know that Tarraco acted as winter quarters for the Roman army during the Celtiberian wars it is reasonable to suppose that it remained a military supply base during the later 2nd c. B.C. Few ceramic deposits of Republican date have yet been excavated at Tarragona (Aquilué 1993b, 69-77; Vegas 1984-85) but Italic imports are present and we would expect future excavations to confirm their presence on a large scale. As a supply base Tarraco would have been a 'captive market' for Italian merchants.

A link between military demand and the widespread distribution of Italic fine wares and, by implication, amphorae throughout the western empire in the Republican period has been postulated by Woolf (1992), but the widespread distribution of Italian amphorae throughout the western Mediterranean and beyond (cf. Tchernia 1983; 1986; Fitzpatrick 1985) suggests that other factors, such as the broader commercial interests of Roman Republican landowners, shippers and merchants, might also have been responsible. This should caution against too specific an explanation for our particular region.

One of the most notable features of the ceramic distribution is the absence of differentiation in the rural distribution of Italic pottery. In view of the size of the survey area and the distance from the coast of the areas furthest inland, some evidence for a fall-off in the density of imported finds might have been expected. However, such a pattern is not visible. It is likely that the volumes of imported goods were so large that the supply networks in the region were saturated, with the result that all sites had equal access to imports regardless of their status or location with respect to Tarraco. We suggest that these goods were distributed through the native networks which had continued since at least the 5th c. B.C. This hypothesis is supported by the Iberian wares which continued in use during this period. They show that inland centres continued to play an important rôle in redistribution. The locally-produced Graeco-Italic and Dressel 1 amphorae (Types 6-9 of fabric 9) have a distribution that is largely confined to Transect 4; whilst apparently absent from Tarraco, they are also known at Iberian sites further north in the Maresme between the Llobregat and Tordera rivers (Comas *et al.* 1987). The distribution of Ebussitanian amphorae provides further evidence, suggesting that some material may have been entering the region from the NE via the Penedès rather than from Tarraco.

These different patterns of distribution hint at the development of parallel exchange systems — one based on the Roman town, representing the penetration of the imperial economy, the other continuing the indigenous traditions of inland exchange. The increasing variety of ceramics dated to after *c.*50 B.C. perhaps marks a shift in emphasis towards Tarragona as a supply axis.

Despite the uncertainty about the status of the settlement at Tarragona in relation to the other two large Iberian sites, it is clear that Tarraco achieved pre-eminence, particularly from the later 2nd c. B.C. (see Chapter 2). There is little evidence for the size of the urbanized area within the walled enclosure of the pre-Augustan town, although it was certainly larger in size than its Iberian predecessor. While Tarraco was undoubtedly growing, El Vilar and Site 3.19, which had been of equal area in the preceding phase, were not — and in the case of El Vilar became abandoned. It demonstrates the increasing dominance of Tarraco in the region during the Republican period. It is evident that Rome's purposes for Tarraco determined its success in relation to these other centres. However, it is not yet clear whether the Iberian settlement there was already dominant in the region when it was used by Rome as a military base during the Second Punic War.

### Early imperial period

The growth of Tarraco during the early empire is not reflected in any increased intensity of settlement within the survey area, largely because it was already densely exploited. There remains a strong pattern of continuity. The density of sites discovered remained more or less equal to that of the Republican period at roughly 1 per km². This implies a total number of rural sites in the town's *territorium* of approximately 3,300. Although it would be unwise to build too much on this estimate, it is instructive to compare this total with the size of Tarraco. The size of the early imperial town (fig. 2.1) was *c.*70 ha, of which perhaps 25% was occupied by major public buildings. Comparative figures for the areas of most towns in Spain are not available but in a dozen scaled plans published by Pfanner (1990) Tarraco's area is equalled only by that of Augusta Emerita (Mérida), another provincial capital. Comparative data from Gaul show Tarraco to be in the upper part of the range, although less than half the size of the four largest centres, which cover more than 150 ha (Pounds 1969, 153, table 8). It contrasts with them, however, because of the exceptionally large proportion of its area given over to public buildings (cf. plans in Pfanner 1990 and Bedon *et al.* 1988).

Converting such figures into population estimates is notoriously problematical but we may take two approaches in order to gain a perspective on the dynamics of settlement. First if we extrapolate the average size of rural sites from the survey to the whole of the *territorium*, we can suggest that the total area covered by rural settlements amounted to at least 5,000 ha. This would mean that the town represents perhaps only 1.4% of the land occupied by settlements. Alternatively (but more problematically) if we suggest that the population of each rural site averaged 20 people, we reach an estimate for the rural population of 66,000. This estimate relies on the idea that the sizes of the communities that occupied rural sites needed to be relatively large. Comparisons with recent agrarian societies in which the countryside was fully exploited without the use of machinery illustrate the need for a considerable pool of labour. It has recently been argued that most Roman families, even below the élite, were nuclear rather than extended and had perhaps 5-6 children (Garnsey and Saller 1987, 129, 143). But an estimate based on 7-8 people per site would ignore the need for agricultural workers, whether servile or free, probably also resident within the household (ibid. 127). Given the demand for labour on estates, which perhaps averaged 90 ha (see Chapter 9), a household size of 20 seems not unreasonable.

This figure for the rural population may be compared with that of the town by employing Hassan's figures for urban population densities as ranging from 137 to 216 per ha (Hassan 1981). Such a range, drawn from cross-cultural parallels, is not inconsistent with estimates for Classical Mediterranean cities (cf. Pounds 1969, 142; Duncan-Jones 1982, 276-77), and with an estimated range for Pompeii of 123 to 184 persons per ha (Jongman 1991, 111). Hassan's figures produce an estimate for Tarraco's population in the early empire at between 9,590 and 15,120. Such a modest population may be smaller than might have been expected for an important provincial capital, although it is not incompatible with figures derived for other Roman towns through a variety of means (Duncan-Jones 1982, 273, Table 7). Also, the figures for Tarragona ought to be maxima, as no account has been taken of the substantial area of public buildings.

Using these tentative estimates we may suggest that the population of Tarraco represented a maximum of between 13 and 20% of the total population of the territory. Although approximate, this proportion is comparable with recent estimates for Roman Italy (Jongman 1991, 66). This is only a very broad estimate, but it does support the impression already gained that the bulk of the population was rurally based, and it provides an important counter to the widely-held view that towns were dominant in the Roman world.

In Chapter 9 our survey identified a lightly settled zone for up to 4 km from Tarraco. Some suburban buildings have been found relatively close to the town walls, as at the Parc de la Ciu-tat (TED'A 1987) and at the centre of what would become the early Christian cemetery (Serra Vilaró 1928-35), but they cannot have farmed the whole of this zone. It may have been an area of market gardens farmed from the town, perhaps to be identified with the *hortos coherentes sive urbanum* mentioned in an inscription found at the town (*RIT* 366). Similar unoccupied zones are not uncommon around other classical cities in Hispania, such as at Astigi in Baetica (Durán and Padilla 1990, 127, mapa VI) and elsewhere in the Mediterranean. One of the best documen-ted examples is found around Iol Caesarea (Cherchel) in Algeria where villas are largely absent from a radius of up to 4 km from the town (Leveau 1984, figs. 214 and 222). Despite this, there can be no question that Tarraco was an 'agro-town' (cf. Duncan-Jones 1982, 260). The archaeological and epigraphic evidence suggests that Tarraco, like other provincial capitals and major towns, was primarily a political centre and a place of élite consumption. Such a rôle perhaps helps to explain the suggested population estimates, which at first sight appear low.

The only strong evidence for the impact of the town within the area of the survey is to be found in the concentration of more elaborate villas in its immediate surroundings. The major concentration of villas, which are predominantly of early imperial date, is in the SW part of the study area and along the coastal strip. Their presence may be symptomatic of the great wealth of the élites based at Tarraco, known to us from recorded benefactions (Alföldy 1975). The political importance of the provincial capital will equally have attracted a population from further afield (Etienne and Fabre 1979). For example, the presumed owner of the villa at Els Munts (Chapter 1, fig. 1.7), C. Valerius Avitus (*RIT* 923), was transferred to Tarraco from Augustobriga in central Spain on the orders of Antoninus Pius.

The areas most commonly occupied by high-status villas also coincide with those of the greatest agricultural potential. The best known is the early imperial farm which precedes the late imperial complex at Centcelles (Chapter 1, fig. 1.8). Most of our knowledge of such sites is derived from previously gathered information, not from our own field walking, and the variable quality of the evidence restricts the inferences which can be drawn. On the one hand, it could be argued that the villas were located to take advantage of the best quality land and that this accounts for the wealth. Alternatively, it could reflect the wealth that élites expended at Tarraco but produced elsewhere. A similar distribution pattern is seen in the hinterland of Iol Caesarea (Cherchel) where too it is uncertain whether the deciding factor was proximity to the provincial capital or access to the best agricultural land (Leveau 1984, fig. 214).

If the distribution of the more elaborate sites in the territory was determined by the richness of soils, it may well be that the area covered by the survey underestimates villas. The greatest area of rich soils lies in the Baix Camp around Reus, just outside our survey. If the densities of richer sites in the SW part of the survey area continued into that region, the number of villas will have been much greater than our sample suggests.

The principal feature of the pottery assemblages of this period is their increased variety and the range of their sources — a general characteristic of most rural sites along the Mediterranean coast of Spain (cf. Prevosti 1991). This was a period of economic success with rural settlements having widespread access to the extended exchange networks focused at Tarraco. Against this background, however, it is important to note that the overall quantity of pottery found on sites is less than in the earlier periods. In particular there is a decline in the numbers of amphorae, which may suggest an increasing reliance on locally-produced rather than imported foodstuffs. Since most amphorae were intended for long-distance transport, it is possible that their relative scarcity may reflect an under-representation characteristic of production areas. It is notable that the two Tarraconensian amphora fabrics typical of the area have complementary distributions, with one focused on Tarraco, the other apparently continuing the NE link to the Penedès already noted for the Republican period. This suggests that, despite the importance of Tarraco, the area over which it was the dominant local market remained circumscribed. The principal fabric that can be shown to have been distributed via the town is Tarraconensian amphora fabric 13 (see p.261). The zone over which this locally produced fabric predominates stretches for c.10 km inland from the town. It appears that some of the local wine carried in these amphorae (most of which was presumably destined for export) was redistributed from Tarraco to rural sites in its hinterland.

It would not be unreasonable to use the distribution of this fabric as indicative of the district served by the town. The radius of its distribution is closely comparable to that noted by Hodder (1974, fig. 19) for certain other low-value and bulky archaeological artefacts and it coincides with the distance over which it was possible to go to town and back easily within a day. If this can be taken as the main inland marketing area for the town, it represents only a portion of the area of the survey and is no larger than the zones served by most settlements in less developed provinces. This is not to say that other goods marketed from Tarraco did not reach a much broader area; it simply indicates the possible extent of its rôle as the principal local market used day to day. It supports the notion that the marketing rôle of major Roman towns has sometimes been overstressed. If this is the case, Tarraco served as a primary market for only a limited area, while minor centres, perhaps road stations, served the everyday needs of other parts of the *territorium*. This has important consequences for our understanding of the economic infrastructure of Roman Spain.

Although the settlement pattern in this period is strongly dominated by Tarraco, this should not obscure the increased range of settlement types located. In addition to the emergence of villas, there are indications of other types of site as well as the rural farmsteads typical of previous periods. Of particular note is the tight concentration of smaller sites around Site 1.6 near Constantí at the W end of Transect 1; they may represent a loosely nucleated village (fig.

6.3). Similarly, the geophysical survey of Field 1254 produced a plan (fig. 7.3) which cannot be readily understood as either a farmstead or villa. It too might have been a small but tightly nucleated settlement. Although no recorded ancient place-names are recorded in the region, these sites may be examples of villages like those elsewhere in the empire discussed by Whittaker (1991). They suggest increasing differentiation within the hierarchy of settlement during the early imperial period.

### Late imperial period

The problem in the survey area is a lack of pottery. This problem has also been noted in the Penedès in the most northerly part of the territory (Járrega 1992), in the vicinity of Baetulo and Iluro (Prevosti 1991), perhaps in hinterlands of Gerunda and Emporiae (Nolla and Casas 1984, 228-29), and further afield (Fernández Corrales 1988, 252-61). It is a feature of the period which deserves explanation, but the consequence is that it is both difficult to identify sites and to obtain reliable results.

Overall the scarcity of sites bears out impressions gained from earlier published evidence (see Chapter 2) but our survey also shows high-status sites to have been scarce. The lack of material demonstrates that exchange-networks were contracting and perhaps left some sites with almost no access to pottery. It is uncertain whether the change in pottery distribution was a result of a lack of supply or a decrease in demand. However, the presence of a wide range of imported pottery in 5th- and 6th-c. deposits at Tarraco (Keay 1984; Remolà 1989; 1993) suggests that the latter is more likely to have been the case. It is almost certain that some small sites have been missed by the survey. With this caveat in mind, it should be noted that the density of sites recorded was approximately one site per 1.6 km$^2$, implying a total of about 300 sites within the survey area, or just over 2,000 sites if extrapolated to the whole territory. This decrease in numbers of identified sites is less marked than that suggested by other surveys in the western Mediterranean (Millett 1992) although this may be due to variations in survey methodologies (see below). However, it is dense compared to Astigi in Baetica, for example, where it has been suggested that the 5th-c. settlement density was in the region of one site per 10 km$^2$ (Durán and Padilla 1990, 129).

Against the background of changing ceramic supply and decline in the number of sites occupied, there is evidence for increased differentiation between the remaining settlements. A number of the sites in the region, including Site 2.7 and villas such as Els Munts (Table 1.1 no. 76), continued as major settlements and produced assemblages of highly varied finds. They are largely dominated by North African amphorae and fine wares, together with some possible late-Roman coarse wares. Other sites are identified only by an occasional sherd. This might be taken to support the notion that there was increased differentiation of settlement, with the concentration of power and wealth in the hands of a limited number of individuals at larger sites (Keay 1991b; forthcoming). These sites tend to be clustered near to Tarraco, although the coincidence of this zone with the best agricultural land remains an issue. It should also be noted that if imported goods were entering the area via Tarraco, areas outside her primary distribution zone might have had less access to them and so be less easy to locate through surface survey. However, the excavation of a mid 5th-c. rubbish deposit at Tarraco has yielded comparatively large quantities of cattle bones (TED'A 1989, 403-14). If these animals were raised in the upland areas further west, we can tentatively suggest that the town's zone of supply extended at least as far as the posited limit of its *territorium* in the mountains (fig. 1.1).

Those sites which remained in occupation show no signs of disruption during the major political changes. The latest amphora forms found on sites in the survey can be dated to the later 6th or early 7th c. The 7th-c. African Red Slip ware forms that are rare at Tarraco are absent from the survey, although this may be more apparent than real given the small size of the sample. Ceramics of the later 7th and 8th c. are generally absent from both town and country throughout NE Spain. The survey shows continuity of some rural settlements well into the period of the Ostrogothic interregnum in Visigothic Spain, but subsequent developments and continuity into the 7th-c. Visigothic kingdom and beyond are impossible to assess.

The evidence from the town itself shows that although its character changed it remained important during the later empire. Its development into an ecclesiastical centre and the concentration of burials around the martyrium and later basilica in the Early Christian cemetery suggests that it exercised a great attraction as a regional centre. If some rural sites in the region were abandoned, there is nothing to suggest any resultant increase in the size of the town. It is possible that population was gradually attracted away from the town to some of the larger rural sites (like site 2.7), although there appear to be too few to account for a wholesale movement of population. The limited presence of such larger sites in the survey makes it impossible to judge. One possible explanation suggested by the location of sites like 2.7 and 2.9 is that successful later Roman nucleated sites lie beneath mediaeval villages. This is an hypothesis which ought to be investigated; it may support the idea of population nucleation in the countryside.

The total absence of pottery datable to after the beginning of the 7th c. A.D. seems unlikely to be due to desertion of the landscape. We would prefer to see the major change as the contraction of exchange networks, with the result that poorer sites gradually ceased to be supplied with pottery and thus disappear from the survey record. At some stage after the 6th and prior to the 12th c., sites in the survey seem to have been abandoned as the later mediaeval settlement pattern became established (Recasens 1975, 69-85).

**Chronological summary**

The survey has demonstrated that the analysis of pottery scatters can make a positive contribution to a study of the relationship between Tarragona and its hinterland in antiquity. In its territory the Roman period exhibits strong continuity with the preceding Iron Age landscape, which was already densely occupied. This is epitomized by the difficulty in distinguishing between sites of Iberian and Roman Republican date. The impact of Tarraco became clear from the later 2nd c. B.C. when Italic imports first appeared on rural sites in volume. Modifications in the settlement pattern became evident only in the early imperial period. In the course of the first two centuries A.D. the enhanced political importance of Tarraco appears to be one factor that stimulated the construction of élite villas in close proximity to the town. The overall density of settlement remained largely the same with the whole lowland landscape fully exploited. The ceramic evidence illustrates that the rural economy was now integrated with that of the town. The late imperial period is characterized by a marked decrease in the quantities of pottery found on rural sites. Despite this limitation, the sites identified continued from previous periods. Sites of the early empire which lack late imperial ceramics may have been abandoned or else ceased to be fully integrated with the networks supplying imported pottery. The nature of the town also changed; it decreased in size and its remaining public buildings were transformed. Nevertheless, it continued to receive large volumes of imported pottery and remained a significant population centre. Social differentiation evidenced at Tarraco and elsewhere in the empire may perhaps be reflected by the concentration of imported ceramics at fewer larger sites in the survey area. With the demise of imported pottery in the course of the 6th c., surface survey no longer allows us to chart changes in the patterns of settlement.

**Comparisons with other surveys**

The information presented in this volume is based on a set of methodologies developed in response to the experience of some other field surveys. It has been argued elsewhere that the methods adopted by other surveys overemphasize changes through time (Millett 1991a; 1992), although it is equally possible that the methods used here underestimate them (see p.61-62). Any attempt to draw general comparisons with the changing settlement-patterns of other regions must take account both variations in the volume of pottery supply, which we have sought to incorporate within our methodology, and the different character of the evidence from regions where there is better survival of upstanding structures. These problems can be overcome but detailed reanalysis, comparable with Alcock's (1993) synthesis of the data from the eastern empire, would be required. It should be the subject of further work.

However, it may be worth making two general comparisons here. First, as in virtually all other published surveys, our work has shown that the Roman landscape was heavily populated and densely exploited (cf. the papers in Barker and Lloyd 1991). The densities noted here (averaging 1 site per km$^2$) are comparable with figures recently proposed for the area around Augusta Emerita (Mérida) (Fernández Corrales 1988, 209). This figure is not as high as that in some other areas of NE Spain. For example, it has been calculated that there was a mean density of 1.25 sites per km$^2$ in the hinterlands of Baetulo and Iluro to the north (Prevosti 1991, 137). Yet even rural densities of 1 site per km$^2$ have considerable implications for our overall estimates of the population of the western empire. They also provide an important new source of comparative data to complement analyses of the census figures (cf. Lo Cascio 1994).

Secondly, the proportions of different types of site discovered in the survey show a predominance of smaller farmsteads over villas. Although the methods of classifying sites vary, the same general pattern seems to be emerging across recent surveys (cf. Barker and Lloyd 1991). It confirms the idea that the Roman landscape should not be thought of as merely comprising villas and towns. It had a more complex structure with only a relatively small number of high-status villas, presumably occupied by the élite, and a variety of other kinds of ordinary rural settlement. Unfortunately, archaeological evidence alone does not permit us to reconstruct complete patterns of land tenure. We cannot tell whether the smallest settlements represent the farms of free peasants or the tenants of larger estates. Yet just because they were small, we need not think of them as unsophisticated. The presence of quantities of imported pottery on even the smallest sites demonstrates that they were partially integrated into wider exchange networks.

## Retrospect on methodology

The success of our methods is best illustrated by the five-fold increase in the numbers of sites known in the survey transects, although this crude measure does not in itself indicate how appropriate our methods were to address the questions posed. Yet we believe that the methods have proved worthwhile as a step along the road to fuller realization of the potential of survey data. The collection and quantitative analysis of a fully representative sample of ceramics provided a valuable tool for moving beyond the practice of placing dots on distribution maps to permit a broader consideration of settlement and exchange systems. The limited work we have done also illustrates the value of combining field-walking with techniques of geophysical survey.

Our methods do not have a universal applicability; they were a response to the questions posed. Our work has illustrated their limitations in periods like the late empire where there was a shortage of surface pottery. Given the 5-m spacing between walkers, the only way in which we might have recovered larger samples of material would have been by rewalking the fields concerned (although this would have reduced the total area covered). Equally we recognize that in some situations the quantity of surface finds might demand a selective sampling approach. However, we would argue that any such sampling would not succeed if it did not aim to collect and analyse a fully representative cross-section of all surface material. Methods that select only 'diagnostic' sherds or those of known date are certain to lead to spurious interpretations. We also recognise that the collection of surface material can only provide a limited amount of information about past utilization of the landscape and that there are limitations to the inferences that can be drawn. We hope that this report will stimulate others to undertake new work and question our conclusions.

# BIBLIOGRAPHY

*Abbreviations:*

AIEC = Anuari d´l'Institut d'Estudis Catalans
IRC = Fabre, G., Mayer, M. & Rodà, I. 1984 *Inscriptions romaines de Catalogne. I. Barcelone (sauf Barcino)* (Paris)
MMAP = Memorias de los Museos Arqueológicos Provinciales
RIT = Alföldy, G. 1975 *Römische Inschriften von Tarraco* (Berlin)


AA.VV. 1993 *Anuari d'intervencions arqueològiques a Catalunya. Època romana. Antiguitat tardana. Campanyes 1982-89* (Col·lecció Anuaris d'Intervencions Arqueològiques a Catalunya 1, Barcelona)

Adserias, M., Burès, L., Miró, M. & Ramón, E. 1994 "L'assentament pre-romà de Tarragona," *Revista d'arqueologia de Ponent* 3 (Lleida) 177-227

Agraz, J., Carreté, J.-M. & Macias, J. M. 1993 "Las cerámicas de los niveles alto imperiales," X. Dupré & J.-M. Carreté (eds.), *La 'Antiga Audiència': un acceso al foro provincial de Tarraco* (Excavaciones Arqueológicas en España 165, Madrid) 87-116

Aguarod, M. C. 1991 *Cerámica romana importada de cocina en la Tarraconense* (Institución Fernando El Católico, Zaragoza)

Aguarod, M. C. 1992 "Un àmfora Tarraconense I / Layetana I con selo Ibérico procedente de Salduie," *Museo de Zaragoza, Boletín* 11, 109-16

Alcock, S. 1993 *Graecia capta: the landscapes of Roman Greece* (Cambridge)

Alföldy, G. 1969 *Fasti hispanienses: senatorische Reichsbeamte und Offiziere in den spanischen Provinzen des römischen Reiches von Augustus bis Diokletian* (Wiesbaden)

Alföldy, G. 1973 *Flamines provinciae Hispaniae citerioris* (Anejos del Archivo Español de Arqueología 6, Madrid)

Alföldy, G. 1975 *Die römische Inschriften von Tarraco* (Berlin)

Alföldy, G. 1990 "Dues inscripcions monumentals de l'Amfiteatre de Tarraco (estudi preliminar)," TED'A, *L'amfiteatre romà de Tarragona, la basílica visigòtica i l'església romànica* (Memòries d'Excavació num. 3, Tarragona) 130-37

Alföldy, G. 1991 *Tarraco* (Fòrum 8, Tarragona)

Alföldy, G. 1993 "Tarraco y la Hispania romana: cultos y sociedad," M. Mayer (ed.), *Religio deorum. Actas del Coloquio Internacional de Epigrafia Culto y Sociedad en Occidente* (Madrid) 7-26

Almagro Basch, M. 1955 *Las necrópolis de Ampurias* (Barcelona)

Almagro Gorbea, M. 1986a "Bronze Final y Edad de Hierro," F. Jordá, M. Pellicer Catalán, P. Acosta & M. Almagro Gorbea (eds.), *Historia de España I: Prehistoria* (Madrid) 431-545

Almagro Gorbea, M. 1986b "El área superficial de las poblaciones ibéricas," *AA VV, Los asentamientos ibéricos ante la romanización* (Madrid) 21-34

Almagro Gorbea, M. & Ruiz Zapatero, G. 1993 "Palaeoethnology of the Iberian peninsula: state of knowledge and future perspectives," M. Almagro Gorbea & G. Ruiz Zapatero (eds.), *Palaeoetnologia de la península ibérica* (Madrid) 501-7

Aquilué, X. 1993a "Las cerámicas finas de los niveles tardo-romanos," X. Dupré & J.-M. Carreté (eds.), *La 'Antiga Audiència': un acceso al foro provincial de Tarraco* (Excavaciones Arqueológicas en España 165, Madrid)

Aquilué, X. 1993b *La sede del Col.legi d'Arquitectes. Una intervención en el centro histórico de Tarragona* (Tarragona)

Aquilué, X. & Dupré, X. 1986 *Reflexions entorn de Tarraco en època tardo-republicana* (Fòrum 1, Tarragona)

Aquilué. X., Dupré, X., Massó, J. & Ruiz de Arbulo, J. 1991 *Tarraco. Guía arqueológica* (Tarragona)

Aquilué. X., Dupré, X., Massó, J. & Ruiz de Arbulo, J. 1992 *Tarraco: an archaeological guide* (Tarragona)

Aquilué. X., Mar, R., Ruiz de Arbulo, J., & Sanmartí, E. 1984 *El Fòrum romà d'Empúries* (Monografíes Emporitanes 7, Barcelona)

Aranegui, C. 1987 "Las ánforas Dr 2-4 de Saguntum," *El vi a l'antiguitat. Economia, producció i comerç al Mediterrani occidental* (Badalona) 100-3

Aranegui, C. & Pla, E. 1981 "La cerámica ibérica," *La baja época de la cultura iberica* (Actas de la mesa redonda celebrada en conmemoración del decimo aniversario de la Asociación Española de Amigos de la Arqueología, Madrid) 73-114

Arbeiter, A. & Korol, D. 1988-89 "El mosaico de la cúpula de Centcelles y el derrocamiento de Constante por Magnencio," *Butlletí Arqueològic de Tarragona* 10-11, 193-244

Arbeloa, J.-V. M. 1990a, "Poblat ibèric d'El Vilar, Valls (Alt Camp)," *Butlletí Arqueològic* V 12, 150-52

Arbeloa, J.-V. M. 1990b "Prospeccions i excavacions arqueològiques," *Butlletí Arqueològic* V 12, 119-323

Arce, J. 1988 *España entre el mundo antiguo y el mundo medieval* (Madrid)

Arteaga, O., Padrò, J. & Sanmartí, E. 1990 *El poblado iberico del Tossal del Moro de Pinyeres Batea, Terra Alta, Tarragona* (Barcelona)

Arthur, P. 1983 "Roman amphorae and the Ager Falernus under the Empire," *PBSR* 50, 22-33

Balil, A. 1973 *Casa y urbanismo en la Hispania antigua* (III) (Studia Archaeologica 20, Valladolid)

Barbara i Camafort, A. & Cabellé i Busquets, J. 1982 *Guía de Alcover* (Els Llibres de la Medusa 16, Tarragona)

Barker, G. & Lloyd, J. 1991 *Roman landscapes: archaeological survey in the Mediterranean region* (Archaeological Monographs of the British School at Rome 2)

Baudoux, J. 1992 "Production d'amphores dans l'Est de la Gaule," F. Laubenheimer (ed.), *Les amphores en Gaule: production et circulation* (Paris) 59-69

Bedon, R., Chevallier, R. & Pinon, P. 1988 *Architecture et urbanisme en Gaule romaine. Tome 2. L'urbanisme en Gaule romaine* (Paris)

Beltrán Lloris, M. 1970 *Las ánforas romanas en España* (Zaragoza)

Beltrán Lloris, M. 1976 *Arqueología e historia de las ciudades del Cabezo de Alcalá de Azailla (Teruel)* (Zaragoza)

Beltrán Lloris, M. 1977 "Problemas de la morfología y del concepto histórico-geográfico que recubre la nocion tipo," *Méthodes classiques et méthodes formelles dans l'étude des amphores romaines* (CollEFR 32) 97-132

Berges, M. 1969-70 "La villa romana dels Munts," *Boletín Arqueológico de Tarragona* 69-70, 140-50

Berges, M. 1970 "Notas sobre 'Els Munts' (Altafulla)," *Información Arqueológica* 3, 81-87

Berges, M. 1977 "Nuevo informe sobre Els Munts," *Estudis Altafullencs* 1, 24-27

Berges, M. 1982 "Teatro romano de Tarragona," *Actas del Simposio 'El teatro en la Hispania romana' (Mérida 1980)* (Badajoz) 139-52

Bonifay, M. 1986 "Observations sur les amphores tardives à Marseille d'après les fouilles de la Bourse," *RANarb* 19, 269-305

Borras i Querol, C. 1988 "Mas d'Arago, Cervera del Maestrat, Baix Maestrat," *Memòries Arqueològiques a la Comunitat Valenciana*, 1984-85 (Valencia) 147-51

Burnett, A. M., Amandry, M. & Ripollés, P. P. 1992 *Roman provincial coinage* vol. 1. *From the death of Caesar to the death of Vitellius (44 BC-AD 69)* (London/Paris)

Callender, M. H. 1965 *Roman amphorae* (London)

Carandini, A. (ed.) 1981 "Ceramica africana," *Atlante delle forme ceramiche I. Ceramica fine romana nel bacino mediterraneo (medio e tardo impero)* (EAA, Roma)

Carbonell, E. *et al.* 1986 "El centre d'intervenció prehistorica de Picamoixons," *Butlletí Arqueològic* V 8-9, 3-14

Carreras, C. and Williams, D. (forthcoming) "Spanish olive-oil trade in late Roman Britain: Dressel 23 amphorae from Winchester," *Journal of Roman Pottery Studies* 7

Carreras, J. & Garriga, E. 1991 *El Medol* (Tarragona)

Casas, J., Castanyer, P., Nolla, J. M. & Tremoleda, J. 1990 *Ceràmiques comunes i de producció d'època romana I: materials Augustals i alto imperials a les comarques orientals de Girona* (Centre d'Investigacions Arqueològiques de Girona. Sèrie monogràfica num. 12)

Castells, J. 1986 "L'inventari del patrimoni arqueològic de Catalunya," *Tribuna d'Arqueologia 1984-85* (Barcelona) 106-13

Cherry, J. F., Gamble, C. & Shennan, S. (eds.) 1979 *Sampling in contemporary British archaeology* (BAR 50)

Cintas, P. 1950 *Céramique punique* (Paris)

Cipriano, M. T. & Carre, M. B. 1989 "Production et typologie des amphores sur la côte adriatique de L'Italie," *Amphores romaines et histoire économique* (CollEFR 114) 67-104

Clark, A. J. 1990 *Seeing beneath the soil* (London)

Cobertera, E. 1986 *Los suelos cultivados de la Provincia de Tarragona* (Tarragona)

Collins, R. 1983 *Early medieval Spain. Unity in diversity, 400-1000* (Oxford)

Collis, J. 1984 *The European Iron Age* (London)

Colominas Roca, J. 1915-20 "El forn ibèric de Fontscaldes," *Anuari de l'Institut d'Estudis Catalans* 602-5

Comas, M., Martín, A., Matamoro, D. & Miró, J. 1987 "Un tipus d'àmfora Dr.1 de producció laietana," *Primeres Jornades Internacionals d'Arqueologia Romana (Museu de Granollers 5-8 de Febrer de 1987)* 372-78

Cortés, R. 1988 "El aprovisionamiento de agua en Tarraco: un proyecto de investigación," *Acta Arqueològica de Tarragona* 1, 1987-88

Cortés, R. 1993 "Els aqüeductes de Tàrraco," *Anuari d'intervencions arqueològiques a Catalunya. Època romana. Antiguitat tardana* (Barcelona) 264-65

Cortés, R., Bermúdez, A. & Lucena, A. M. 1985 "Aportaciones al estudio del Columbario de Vila-Rodona," *XVII Congreso Nacional de Arqueología (Logroño 1983)* (Zaragoza) 755-58

Courtoise, L. & Velde, B. 1978 "Une amphore à grenat jaune du Latium à Amathonte," *BCH* 103, 977-81

Crawford, M. 1985 *Coinage and money under the Roman Republic. Italy and the Mediterranean economy* (London)

Crowther, D. R. 1983 "Old land surfaces and modern ploughsoil: implications of recent work at Maxey, Cambs.," *Scottish Archaeol. Rev.* 2.1, 31-44

Crowther, D. R. & Pryor, F. M. M. 1985 "The surface (field-walking) survey," F. M. M. Pryor & C. A. I. French (eds.), *Archaeology and environment in the Lower Welland Valley* (East Anglian Archaeology 27) 44-53

D'Abadal i de Vinyals, R. 1974 *Dels Visigots als Catalans. La Hispània visigòtica i la Catalunya Carolíngia* (Barcelona)

del Amo, M. D. 1979-89 *Estudio critico de la necrópolis palaecristiana de Tarragona*, 3 vols. (Tarragona)

Dore, J. & Schinke, R. 1992 "First report on the pottery," N. Ben Lazreg & D. Mattingly (eds.), *Leptiminus (Lamta): a Roman port city in Tunisia. Report no. 1* (JRA S4) 115-56

Duncan-Jones, R. P. 1982 *The economy of the Roman empire* (2nd ed., Cambridge)

Dupré, X. 1986 "Els capitells corintis de l'Arc de Berà," *Empúries* 45-46 (1983-84) 308-15

Dupré, X. 1994 *L'arc romà de Berà (Hispania Citerior)* (Institut d'Estudis Catalans Monografies de la Secció Històrico-Arqueològica 3, Barcelona)

Dupré, X. & Carreté, J. M. 1993 *La 'Antiga Audiència': un acceso al foro provincial de Tarraco* (Tarragona)

Dupré, X. & Julià, M. 1984 "Un edifici de planta basilical a Villalonga del Camp (Tarragonès)," *Informació Arqueològica* 42, 58-61

Dupré, X., Massó, J., Palanques, L. & Verduchi, P. 1988 *El circ romà de Tarragona, I. Les voltes de Sant Ermenegild* (Excavacions Arqueològiques de Catalunya 8, Barcelona)

Dupré, X. & Subias, E. 1993 "Els antecedents de l'Anomenat Pretori de Tarragona," *Homenatje a Miquel Tarradell* (Barcelona) 603-9

Durán, V. & Padilla, A. 1990 *Evolución del poblamiento antiguo en el Término Municipal de Écija* (Sevilla)

Dyson, S. L. 1978 "Settlement patterns in the Ager Cosanus," *JFA* 5, 251-68

Enguix, R. & Aranegui, C. 1977 *Taller de anforas romanas de Oliva (Valencia)* (Trabajos Varios del Servicio de Investigaciones Prehistoricas 54, Valencia)

Esco, C., Giralt, P. & Senaca, P. 1989 *Arqueología islámica en la Marca superior de Al-Andalus* (Huesca)

Etienne, R. & Fabre, G. 1979 "L'immigration à Tarragone, capitale d'une province romaine d'Occident," *Homenaje a García y Bellido* IV = *Revista de la Universidad Complutense* 18, 95-116

Ettlinger, E. *et al.* 1990 *Conspectus formarum terrae sigillatae italico modo confectae* (Bonn)

Fabra i Salvat, M. E. & Burguete i Recasens, S., 1983 "El jaciment del Vilar, una questió inconclosa," *Revista Cultura* (Valls) 24-29

Fabra i Salvat, M. E. & Burguete i Recasens, S. 1986 "Introducciò a l'estudi del jaciment Ibèric de 'El Vilar'," *Quaderns de Vilaniu* 9, 55-78

Fàbrega, X. 1989 "Les ceràmiques comunes de producció local o indeterminada," TED'A, *Un abocador del segle V d.C. en el Fòrum Provincial de Tàrraco* (Memòries de Excavació num. 2, Tarragona) 205-32

Fasham, P. J., Schadla-Hall, R. T., Shennan, S. J. & Bates, P. J. 1980 *Field walking for archaeologists* (Hampshire Field Club and Archaeological Society)

Fernández Corrales, J. M. 1988 *El asentamiento romano en Extremadura y su análisis espacial* (Cáceres)

Fishwick, D. 1982 "The altar of Augustus and the municipal cult of Tarraco," *MM* 23, 222-33

Fitzpatrick, A. P. 1985 "The distribution of Dressel 1 amphorae in NW Europe, " *OJA* 4/3, 305-40

Flórez, H. 1769 *España sagrada* XXIV (Madrid)

Flórez, H. 1770 *España sagrada* XXV (Madrid)

Foley, R. 1981 "A model of regional archaeological structure," *PPS* 47, 1-18

Fulford, M. G. 1987 "Economic interdependence among urban communities of the Roman Mediterranean," *World Archaeology* 19.1, 58-75

Gaffney, V. & Tingle, M. 1989 *The Maddle Farm Project: an integrated survey of prehistoric and Roman settlement on the Berkshire Downs* (BAR 200)

Garabito, T. 1978 *Los alfares romanos riojanos. Producción y commercialización* (Bibliotheca Praehistorica Hispana 16, Madrid)

Garnsey, P. & Saller, R. 1987 *The Roman empire: economy and society* (London)

Genera, M. 1980 *Evolució del poblament prehistòric i protohistòric a les comarques de la Ribera d'Ebre i del Priorat* (Resum Tesi doctoral, Barcelona)

Gibert, A. M. 1900 *Ciutats focenses del litoral Cosetà*, Barcelona (reissue with *A. Callipolis Salauris. Aplec documentat de notícies històriques: Solcina (Vila-seca), La Pineda, Port de Salou, Platja de Barenys i Vilafortuny* (Monografíes de Vila-seca i Salou núm. 13, 1988)

Gibert, A. M. 1921-24 "Aplec documentat de noticies históriques Solcina (Vilaseca), La Pineda, Port de Salou, Platja de Barenys i Vilafortuny," *Butlletí Arqueològic* (Tarragona 1921, 1922, 1923, 1924) (reissue with Monografíes de Vila-seca i Salou núm. 13, 1988)

Gisbert, J. A. 1987 "La producció de vi al territori de Dianium durant l'Alt Imperi: el taller d'àmfores de la vil.la romana de l'Almadrava (Setlamirarrosa-Miraflor)," *El vi a l'antiguitat. Economia producció i comerç al Mediterrani occidental* (Badalona) 104-18

Gorges, J.-G. 1979 *Les villas hispano-romaines* (Publications du Centre Pierre Paris 4)

Goudineau, C. 1968 "La céramique arretine lisse," *Fouilles de l'École Française de Rome à Bolsena (Poggio Moscini) 1962-67*, IV (MEFR Suppl. 6, Paris)

Grácia, F., Munilla, G. & Pallarès, R. 1988 *La moleta del Remei. Alcanar-Montsia* (Tarragona)

Greene, J. A. 1992 "Une reconnaissance archéologique dans l'arrière-pays de la Carthage antique," A. Ennabli (ed.), *Pour sauver Carthage* (Paris) 195-97

Gregson, M. S. 1982 "Linear archaeology," K. Ray (ed.), *Young archaeologist: collected unpublished papers of M. S. Gregson* (Cambridge) 215-37

Guitart, J. 1936 "Descubrimientos romanos a Paret Delgada," *Boletín Arqueológico de Tarragona* III 5, 137-41

Gurt, J. M. & Marquès, A. M. 1988 "La conquesta cadastral de l'espai," *Espais, Revista del Departament de Política Territorial i Obres Públiques* núm. 12, juliol-agost, 46-51

Haselgrove, C. C. 1985 "Inference from ploughsoil artefact samples," C. Haselgrove, M. Millett & I. M. Smith (eds.), *Archaeology from the ploughsoil* (Sheffield) 7-30

Hassan, F. A. 1981 *Demographic archaeology* (London)

Hauschild, Th. 1988 "Excavaciones en la muralla romana de Tarragona," *Butlletí Arqueològic* 6-7, 11-38

Hauschild, Th. & Arbeiter, A. 1993 *La vil.la romana de Centcelles* (Tarragona)

Hauschild, T., Mariner, S. & Niemeyer, H. G. 1966 "'Torre de los Escipiones' Ein römischer Grabturm bei Tarragona," *MM* 7, 162-88

Hauschild, T. & Schlunk, H. 1986 *La vil.la romana i el mausoleu constantinià de Centcelles* (Forum 5, Tarragona)

Hayes, J. 1972 *Late Roman pottery: a catalogue of Roman fine wares* (London) (with *Supplement*, 1980)

Heron, C. & Pollard, A. M. 1988 "The analysis of natural resinous materials from Roman amphorae," in E. A. Slater & J. O. Tate (eds.), *Science and archaeology: Glasgow 1987* (BAR 196) 429-47

Hesnard, A. & Lemoine, C. 1981 "Les amphores du Cecube et du Falerne: prospections, typologie, analyses," *MEFRA* 93, 243-95

Hodder, I. 1974 "Regression analysis of some trade and marketing patterns," *World Archaeology* 6.2, 172-89

Hodder, I. & Millett, M. 1980 "Romano-British villas and towns: a systematic analysis," *World Archaeology* 12.1, 69-76

Hodder, I. & Orton, C. R. 1976 *Spatial analysis in archaeology* (Cambridge)

IGME 1973a [Instituto Geológico y Minero de España] *Mapa Geológica de España E. 1:50.000: Valls* (Ministerio de Industria, Madrid)

IGME 1973b [Instituto Geológico y Minero de España] *Mapa Geológica de España E. 1:50.000: Tarragona* (Ministerio de Industria, Madrid)

Izquierdo, P. 1988-89 "Un tram de Via Augusta al Perellò i una preposta de dinamitzaciò," *Butlletí Arqueològic* V 10-11, 169-91

Jannoray, J. 1955 *Ensérune. Contribution à l'étude des civilisations préromaines de la Gaule méridionale* (Paris)

Járrega, R. 1992 "Aproximació a l'estudi de l'antiguitat tardana a Les Comarques del Garraf, Alt Penedès i Baix Penedès," *Olerdulae* 17, 53-112

Jongman, W. 1991 *The economy and society of Pompeii* (Amsterdam)

Juan Tovar, L. C., Bermúdez, A. Massó, J. & Ramón, E. 1987 "Medio natural y medio económico en la industria alfarera: el taller iberorromano de Fontscaldes (Valls, Alt Camp, Tarragona)," *Butlletí Arqueològic* V 8-9, 59-85

Junyent, E. 1972 "Los materiales del poblado ibérico de Margalef en Torregrossa (Lérida)," *Pyrenae* 8, 89-132

Keay, N. 1989, "The amphorae," M. Fulford & M. Hall (eds.), *Excavations at Sabratha 1948-51. Vol. II. The finds* (London) 5-85

Keay, S. J. 1981 "The Conventus Tarraconensis in the third century AD: crisis or change?" A. King & M. Henig (eds.), *The Roman west in the third century* (BAR S109) 451-86

Keay, S. J. 1984 *Late Roman amphorae in the Western Mediterranean. A typology and economic study: the Catalan evidence* (BAR S196)

Keay, S. J. 1987 "The impact of the foundation of Tarraco upon the indigenous settlement pattern of the Ager Tarraconensis," *Primeres Jornades Internacionals d'Arqueologia Romana (Museu de Granollers 5-8 de Febrer de 1987)* 53-58

Keay, S. J. 1990 "Processes in the development of the coastal communities of Hispania Citerior in the Republican period," T. Blagg & M. Millett (eds.), *The early Roman empire in the west* (Oxford) 120-50

Keay, S. J. 1991a "New light on the Colonia Iulia Urbs Triumphalis Tarraco (Tarragona) during the late Empire," *JRA* 4, 387-97

Keay, S. J. 1991b "The Ager Tarraconensis in the late empire: a model for the economic relationship of town and country in eastern Spain," G. Barker & J. Lloyd (eds.), *Roman landscapes* 79-87

Keay, S. J. forthcoming "Tarraco-Tarracona in late antiquity," N. Christie & S. Loseby (eds.), *Towns in transition* (Leicester)

Keay, S. J., Carreté, J.-M. & Millett, M. 1989 "Ciutat i camp en el mòn romà: les prospeccions l'Ager Tarraconensis," *Tribuna d'Arqueologia* 1988-89, 121-29

Keay, S. J. & Jones, L. 1982 "Differentiation of early imperial amphora production in Hispania Tarraconensis," I. Freestone, C. Johns & T. Potter (eds.), *Current research in ceramics: thin section studies* (British Museum Occasional Paper 32) 45-61

Keay, S. J. & Millett, M. 1991 "Surface survey and site recognition in Spain: the Ager Tarraconensis and its background," A. J. Schofield (ed.), *Interpreting artefact scatters* (Oxford) 129-40

Keller, D. R. & Rupp, D. W. 1983 *Archaeological survey in the Mediterranean area* (BAR S155)

Koppel, E. 1985 *Die römischen Skulpturen von Tarraco* (Berlin)

Koppel, E. 1988 *La schola del collegium fabrum de Tarraco y su decoraciòn escultórica* (Faventia Monografíes num. 7, Barcelona)

Koppel, E. 1990 "Relieves arquitectónicos de Tarragona," W. Trillmich & P. Zanker (eds.), *Stadtbild und Ideologie: Die Monumentalisierung hispanischer Städte zwischen Republik und Kaiserzeit* (Bayerische Akademie der Wissenschaften. phil.-hist. Klasse. Abhandlungen N.F. Heft 103, Munich) 327-40

Laborde, A. de 1806 *Voyage pittoresque et historique dans l'Espagne* (Paris)

Lafuente, A. 1992 "La producció de la ceràmica ibèrica del Taller de Fontscaldes (Valls, Alt Camp)," *Les ceràmiques de tècnica ibèrica a la Catalunya Romana* (Barcelona) 47-77

Lamboglia, N. 1958 "Nuove osservazioni sulla terra sigillata chiara, tipi A e B," *RStLig* 24, 227-30

Lamboglia, N. 1963 "Nuove osservazioni sulla terra sigillata chiara (ii), tipi C, lucente e D," *RStLig* 29, 145-212

Laubenheimer, F. 1985 *La production des amphores en Gaule Narbonnaise* (Paris)

Laubenheimer, F. 1989 "Les amphores gauloises sous l'empire: recherches nouvelles sur leur production et leur chronologie," *Amphores romaines et histoire économique* (CollEFR 114) 104-38

Leveau, P. 1984 *Caesarea de Maurétanie. Une ville romaine et ses campagnes* CollEFR 70)

Lo Cascio, E. 1994 "The size of the Roman population: Beloch and the meaning of the Augustan census figures," *JRS* 84, 23-40

López, A 1977 "Cerámicas romanas de paredas finas," *Butlletí d'Informació Arqueológica* 24, 162-68

López, A. & Fierro, X. 1988 "Darreres intervencions a l'assentament ibèric i la vil.la romana de Darrò (Vilanova i la Geltru, Garraf)," *Tribuna d'Arqueologia* 1987-88, 53-68

López i Vilar, J. 1990 "Localitzaciò d'un tram de la Via Tarraco-Ilerda al Puig Cabrer," *Butlletí Arqueològic* V 12, 103-9

Macias, J. M. & Ramón, E. 1994 "La vil.la romana de la Llosa (Cambrils, Baix Camp)," *Tribuna d'Arqueologia* 1992-93, 125-33

Macready, S. & Thompson, F. H. 1985 *Archaeological field survey in Britain and abroad* (London)

Maluquer, J. 1968 *Epigrafía prelatina de la Peninsula Ibérica* (Barcelona)

Mañà, J. M. 1950 "Sobre tipologia de las anforas púnicas," *VII Congreso de Arqueología del Sudeste Español* 203-10

Manacorda, D. 1977 "Anfore," *Ostia IV* (Studi Miscellani 23) 117-254

Mar, R. & Ruiz de Arbulo, J. 1986 *La Basílica de la Colonia Tarraco. Una nueva interpretación del llamado Foro Bajo de Tarragona* (Forum 3, Tarragona)

MARC-7 1986 "Reorganitzaciò i nous impulsos, 1975-1985. L'arqueologia Catalana - III," *L'Avenç* 92, 47-53

Martin-Kilcher, S. 1983 "Les amphores romaines à huile de Bétique (Dressel 20 et 23), d'Augst (Colonia Augusta Rauricorum) et Kaiseraugst (Castrum Rauracense). Un rapport préliminaire," J. M. Blázquez & J. Remesal (eds.), *Producción y comercio del aceite en la antigüedad, II Congreso* (Madrid) 337-47

Martínez, J. 1982-83 "Tarragona y los inicios de la romanización de Hispania," *Butlletí Arqueològic* V 4-5, 73-86

Martínez Larriba, M. 1979 *Prehistoria de Vila-rodona* (Museu de Vila-rodona)

Martínez Larriba, M. 1980 *El món ibero-romà Vila-rodona* (Museu de Vila-rodona)

Martínez Larriba, M. 1982 *El món ibero-Roma a Vila.Rodona* (Museu de la Villa)

Massó, J. 1978 *Reus, prehistoria i antiguitat* (Reus)

Massó, J. 1985 "Les activitats arqueològica i museística de l'Agrupació excursionista de Reus, 1915-25," J. Massó *et al.* (eds.), *Miscel.lania en homenatge a Salvador Vilaseca i Anguera (1975-1985)* (Reus)

Massó, J. 1987 "El terme d'Alcover a l'Antiguitat," *Alcover, estat de la questió* (Alcover) 37-56

Massó, J. 1990a *Notes per a l'estudi del terme de Constantí a l'Antiguitat* (Constantí)

Massó, J. 1990b *El terme de cambrils a l'Antiguitat. Una aproximació arqueològica* (Cambrils)

Massó, J. & Soberanas, A. J. 1992 *Bibliografía impresa de B. Hernández Sanahuja* (Institut d'Estudis Tarraconenses Ramon Berenguer IV.20, Tarragona)

Mata, C. & Bonet, H. 1992 "La cerámica ibérica: ensayo de tipología," *Estudios de Arqueología Ibérica y Romana. Homenaje a Enrique Pla Ballester* (Servicio de Investigación Prehistórica, Serie de Trabajos Varios num.89, Valencia) 117-73

Mayer, M. & Rodà, I. 1986 "La romanitzaciò de Catalunya. Algunes questions," *Protohistoria Catalana. 6e Col.loqui Internacional d'Arqueologia de Puigcerdà* (Puigcerdà) 339-51

Mayet, 1975 *Les céramiques à parois fines dans la Péninsule Ibérique* (Paris)

Mezquiriz, M. A. 1961 *Terra sigillata hispanica* (Valencia)

Miles, G. C. 1952 *The coinage of the Visigoths of Spain, Leovigild to Achila II* (New York)

Millett, M. J. 1985 "Field survey calibration: a contribution," C. Haselgrove, M. Millett & I. M. Smith (eds.), *Archaeology from the ploughsoil* (Sheffield) 31-37

Millett, M. J. 1987 "A question of time? Aspects of the future of pottery studies," *Bull. Univ. London Inst. Arch.* 24, 99-108

Millett, M. J. 1991a "Pottery: population or supply pattern? The Ager Tarraconensis approach," G. Barker & J. Lloyd (eds.), *Roman landscapes* 18-26

Millett, M. J. 1991b "Roman towns and their territories: an archaeological perspective," J. Rich & A. Wallace-Hadrill (eds.), *City and countryside in the ancient world* (London) 169-89

Millett, M. J. 1992 "Rural integration in the Roman West: an introductory essay," M. Wood & F. Queiroga (eds.), *Current research in the Romanization of the western provinces* (BAR S575) 1-8

Miret, M. forthcoming "Dades sobre el poblament a La Comarca de Garraf durant la Baixa Romanitat i els inicis de l'Alta Edat Mitjana," *XXIX Assamblea Intercomarcal d'Estudiosos (Sitges, 27-28 Octubre de 1994)*

Miret, M., Sanmartí, J. & Santacana, J. 1988 "La evolución y el cambio del modelo de poblamiento ibèrico ante la romanización: un ejemplo," *Los asentamientos ibéricos ante la Romanización* (Madrid) 79-88

Miret, M., Sanmartí, J. & Santacana, J. 1991 "From indigenous structures to the Roman world: models for the occupation of central coastal Catalunya," G. Barker & J. Lloyd (eds.), *Roman landscapes* 47-53

Miró, J. 1985 "Algunas consideraciones sobre las ánforas ibéricas Maña B-3," *Pyrenae* 17-18, 335-42

Miró, J. 1988 *La producción de ánforas romanas en Catalunya* (BAR S473)

Miró, J. M. 1990 "El neolític a la Catalunya meridional: una aproximació espacial," *Acta Arqueològica de Tarragona* III, 21-31

Miró, M. 1988 "Restes ibériques al carrer Caputxins (Tarragona)," *Butlletí Arqueològic* 6-7, 3-9

Montón Broto, F. 1976-77 "El miliario de Morell," *Boletín Arqueológico de Tarragona* 133-34, 45-47

Morel, J.-P. 1981 *La céramique campanienne: les formes* (Paris)

Morote, J. 1979 "El trazado de la Via Augusta desde Tarracona a Cartagine Spartaria," *Saguntum* 14, 139-64

Navarro, F. 1969-70 "Enterramiento tardo romano en Montferri," *Boletín Arqueológico de Tarragona* 127-58

Nierhaus, R. 1964 "Baedro - Topografische Studien zum Territorium des Conventus Cordubensis in der Mittleren Sierra Morena," *MM* 5, 185-212

Nolla, J. M. & Casas, J. 1984 *Carta arqueológica de les Comarques de Girona. El poblament d'epoca romana al Nord-Est de Catalunya* (Girona)

Nolla, J. M., Padró, J. & Sanmartí, E. 1980 "Exploració preliminar del forn d'àmfores de Tivisa, Ribera d'Ebre," *Cypsela* 3, 193-218

Nolla, J. M. & Solias, J. M. 1984-85 "L'Àmfora Tarraconense 1. Característiques, procedència, àrees de producció, cronologia," *Butlletí Arqueològic de Tarragona* 6-7, 107-44

*Ostia* III = *Ostia, Terme del Nuotatore. Scavo dell ambiente V e un saggio nell'area SO* (StMisc 21, Rome 1973)

Oswald, F. & Pryce, T.-D. 1920 *An introduction to the study of terra sigillata* (London)

Padró, J. & Sanmartí, E. 1993 "Areas geográficas de las etnias prerromanas de Cataluña," M. Almagro-Gorbea & G. Ruiz Zapatero (eds.), *Paleoetnologia de la Peninsula Iberica* (Complutum 2-3) 185-94

Pallí, F. 1985 *La Via Augusta en Catalunya* (Faventia Monografías 3, Barcelona)

Palol, P. de 1953 *Tarraco hispanovisigoda* (Tarragona)

Papiol, L. 1973-74 "Noticias sobre hallazgos romanas en el término de Constantí," *Boletín Arqueológico de Tarragona* 121-28

Pascual, R. 1977 "Las anforas de la Layetania," *Méthodes classiques et méthodes formelles dans l'étude des amphores romaines* (CollEFR 32) 47-96

Passi, S., Rothschild-Boros, M. C., Fasella, P., Nazzaro-Porro, M. & Whitehouse, D. 1981 "An application of high performance liquid chromatography to analysis of lipids in archaeological samples," *Journal of Lipid Research* 22, 778-84

Peacock, D. P. S. 1971 "Roman amphorae in pre-Roman Britain," M. Jesson & D. Hill (eds.), *The Iron Age and its hill-forts* (Southampton) 161-88

Peacock, D. P. S. 1977a "Ceramics in Roman and medieval archaeology," D. P. S. Peacock (ed.), *Pottery and early commerce* (London) 21-34

Peacock, D. P. S. 1977b "Pompeian red ware," D. P. S. Peacock (ed.), *Pottery and early commerce* (London) 147-62

Peacock, D. P. S. 1977c "Roman amphorae: typology, fabric and origins," in *Etudes classiques et études formelles* (CollEFR 32) 261-78

Peacock, D. P. S. 1986 "Carthage and Spain: the evidence of the amphorae," *Cahiers des Etudes Anciennes* 14, 101-13

Peacock, D. P. S., Bejaoui, F. & Ben Lazreg, N. 1990 "Roman pottery production in Central Tunisia," *JRA* 3, 59-85

Peacock, D. P. S. & Williams, D. F. 1986 *Amphorae & the Roman economy* (Harlow)

Pensabene, P. 1993 "La decorazione architettonica dei monumenti provinciali di Tarraco," *Els monuments provincials de Tàrraco. Noves aportacions al seu coneixement* (Documents d'Arqueologia Clàssica 1, Tarragona) 33-105

Pereira, J. 1988 "La cerámica ibérica de la cuenca del Guadalquívir I: propuesta de clasificación," *Trabajos de Prehistoria* 45, 143-73

Pfanner, M. 1990 "Modelle römischer Stadtentwicklung am Beispiel Hispaniens und der westlichen Provinzen," W. Trillmich & P. Zanker (eds.), *Stadtbild und Ideologie* (Munich) 59-116

Pons d'Icart, L. 1572 *Libro de las grandezas y cosas memorables de metropolitana insigne i famosa ciudad de Tarragona* (reissued Tarragona 1981)

Ponsich, M. 1974 *Implantation rurale antique sur le Bas-Guadalquivir* I (Paris)

Ponsich, M. 1979 *Implantation rurale antique sur le Bas-Guadalquivir* II (Paris)

Potter, T. W. 1979 *The changing landscape of South Etruria* (London)

Pounds, N. J. G. 1969 "The urbanization of the classical world," *Annals of the Association of American Geographers* 59.1, 135-57

Prevosti, M. 1981 *Cronologia i poblament a l'àrea d'Iluro* (Mataró)

Prevosti, M. 1991 "The establishment of the villa system in the Maresme (Catalonia) and its development in the Roman period," G. Barker & J. Lloyd (eds), *Roman landscapes* 135-41

Puerta i López, C. 1989 *Baetulo. Ceràmica de parets fins* (Badalona)

Puig y Cadafalch, J. 1931, "Sepulcres d'Alcover," *AIEC* 7 [1921-26] 88-90

Py, M. 1978. "Quatre siècles d'amphores massilètes. Essai de classification des bords," *Figlina* 3, 1-23

Rafel, N. & Blasco, M. 1994 *El Coll de Moro, Un recinte ibèric fortificat. Campanyes 1982-83* (Memòries d'Intervencions Arqueològiques a Catalunya 8, Barcelona)

Ramallo, S. 1985 "Envases para salazón en el Bajo Imperio," *VI Congreso Internacional de Arqueologia Submarina. Cartagena 1982* (Madrid)

Ramón, E. 1988 *El poblamiento ibèrico en la comarca del Baix Camp* (Tesi de llicenciatura, Universitat de Barcelona, inèdita)

Ramón, E. 1989 "El poblament d'època ibèrica a la comarca del Baix Camp: estat de la questió," *Acta Arqueològica* 2, 1988-89, 55-67

Ramón, E. 1990 "Dos jaciments d'època ibèrica en el terme de Reus," *Revista Lligalls* 2, desembre

Ramón, E. & Massó, J. 1994 *El poblat ibèric de Santa Ana* (Memòries d'Intervencions Arqueològiques a Catalunya 11, Barcelona)

Ramón, J. 1981 *La producción anfórica punico-ebussitana* (Eivissa)

Recasens, J. M. 1975 *La ciutat de Tarragona* Volum 2 (Barcelona)

Remesal, J. 1986 *La annona militaris y la exportación del aceite betico a Germania* (Madrid)

Remolà, J. A. 1989 "Les amfores," TED'A, *Un abocador del segle V d.C en el Fòrum Provincial de Tàrraco* 249-320

Remolà, J. A. 1993 "Las anforas de los nievels tardo-romanos," X. Dupré & J. M. Carreté, *La 'Antiga Audiència': un acceso al foro provincial de Tarraco (Tarragona)* 151-65

Revilla, V. 1993 *Producción cerámica y economía rural en el Bajo Ebro en època romana. El Alfar de l'Aumedina, Tivissa (Tarragona)* (Barcelona)

Ribera, A. 1982 *Las anforas prerromanas valencianas (Fenicias, Ibericas y Punicas)* (Servicio de Investigaciones Prehistóricas, Serie de trabajos varios num. 73, Valencia)

Rich, J. & Wallace-Hadrill, A. 1991 *City and countryside in the ancient world* (London)

Richardson, J. S. 1986 *Hispaniae. Spain and the development of Roman imperialism 218-82 BC* (Cambridge)

Riley, J. 1979 "The coarse pottery from Berenice," J. Lloyd (ed.), *Excavations at Sidi Khrebish (Berenice)* II (Tripoli) 91-467

Rodà, I. 1990 "Sarcofagi della bottega di Cartagine a Tarraco," *L'Africa Romana* VII (1989) 727-36

Rodríguez-Almeida, E. 1984 *Il Monte Testaccio* (Rome)

Roldán, J. M. 1973 *Itineraria Hispana* (Madrid)

Romero, V. 1984 *Aportació al coneixament de la població prehistorica de Riudoms* (Riudoms)

Ros Sala, M. M. 1989 *La pervivencia del elemento indígena: la cerámica ibérica* (La ciudad romana de Carthago Nova: fuentes y materiales para su estudio no. 1, Murcia)

Rothschild-Boros, M. C. 1981 "The determination of amphora contents," G. Barker & R. Hodges (eds.), *Archaeology and Italian society* (BAR S102) 79-89

Rouillard, P. 1991 *Les grecs et la péninsule ibérique du VIIIe au IVe siècle avant Jésus-Christ* (Paris)

Rovira, J. & Santacana, J. 1982 *El yacimiento de La Mussara (Tarragona). Un modelo de asentamiento pastoril en el Bronce Final de Catalunya* (Monografíes Arqueològiques 2. Institut de Prehistoria i Arqueologia, Barcelona)

Ruiz, A. & Molinos, M. 1992 *Los iberos. Análisis arqueològico de un proceso histórico* (Barcelona)

Ruiz de Arbulo, J. 1990 "El Foro de Tarraco," *Cypsela* 8, 119-38

Ruiz Zapatero, G. 1985 *Los campos de urnas del NE de la Peninsula Iberica* (Madrid)

Sabir, A., Laubenheimer, F., Leblanc, J. & Widemann, F. 1983 "Production d'amphores vinaires républicaines en Gaule du sud," *Doc. Archeol. Méridionale* 6, 109-13

Sánchez Real, J. 1957 "Las invasiones germanicas," *Boletín Arqueológico de Tarragona* 57-60, 6-12

Sanmartí, E. 1978 *La cerámica campaniense de Emporion y Rhode* (Barcelona)

Sanmartí, E. 1985a "Sobre un nuevo tipo de ánfora de época Republicana, de origen presumiblemente hispánico," M. Picazo & E. Sanmartí (eds.), *Ceràmiques gregues i helenístiques a la Península Ibérica* (Barcelona) 133-41

Sanmartí, E. 1985b "Las anforas romanas del campamento numantino de Peña Redonda (Garray, Soria)," *Empúries* 47, 130-61

Sanmartí, E., Nolla, J. M. & Aquilué, X. 1987 "Les excavacions a l'àrea del pàrking al sud de la neàpolis d'Empúries," *Empúries* 45-46, 110-53

Sanmartí, E. & Padrò, J. 1976-78 "Ensayo de aproximación al fenomeno de la iberización en las comarcas meridionales de Cataluña. Simposi Internacional: els origens del mòn ibèric," *Ampurias* 38-40, 157-85

Sanmartí, E. & Santacana, J. 1987 "La jerarquia de núclis en el poblament ibèric de la costa del Penedès," *Protohistoria catalana. 6ᵉ Col.loqui Internacional d'Arqueologia de Puigcerdà* 227-43

Sanmartí, J. 1992 "Les ceràmiques del període ibèric tardà al Penedès," *Les ceràmiques de tècnica ibèrica a la Catalunya Romana (segels II a.C. - I d. C.)* (Societat Catalana d'Arqueologia, Barcelona) 32-46

Sanmartí, J. & Santacana, J. 1992 *El poblat ibèric d'Alorda Park. Calafell, Baix Penedès* (Excavacions Arqueològiques a Catalunya 11, Barcelona)

Sanmartí, J. Santacana, J. & Serra, J. 1984, *El jaciment ibèric de l'Argilera i el poblament protohistòric al Baix Penedès* (Quaderns de Treball 6, Barcelona)

Savory, M. 1968 *Spain and Portugal. The prehistory of the Iberian peninsula* (London)

Schlunk, H. 1988 *Die Mosaikkuppel von Centcelles* (MM Beiträge 13)

Schlunk, H. & Hauschild, Th. 1962 "Informe preliminar sobre los trabajos realizados en Centcelles," *Excavaciones Arqueológicas en España* 18

Schofield, A. J., Millett, M., & Keay, S. J. forthcoming "Prehistoric settlement in the Ager Tarraconensis "

Serra Ràfols, J. de C. 1941 "El poblado ibérico del castellet de Bañolas," *Ampurias* 3, 15 ff.

Serra Vilaró, J. 1928 *Excavaciones en la necrópolis romano-cristiana de Tarragona* (Memorias de la Junta Superior de Excavaciones y Antigüedades núm. 93)

Serra Vilaró, J. 1929 *Excavaciones en la necrópolis romano-cristiana de Tarragona* (Memorias ... núm. 104)

Serra Vilaró, J. 1930 *Excavaciones en la necrópolis romano-cristiana de Tarragona* (Memorias ... núm. 111)

Serra Vilaró, J. 1932 *Excavaciones en Tarragona* (Memorias ... núm. 116)

Serra Vilaró, J. 1935 *Excavaciones en la necrópolis romano-cristiana de Tarragona* (Memorias ... núm. 133)

Shennan, S. J. 1985 *Experiments in the collection and analysis of archaeological survey data: the East Hampshire Survey* (Sheffield)

Subias, E. & Remola, J. A. 1989 "La ceràmica grollera," *Un abocador del segle V d C en el Fòrum Provincial de Tàrraco* (Memòries de Excavació num. 2, Tarragona) 233-46

Tchernia, A. 1983 "Italian wine in Gaul at the end of the Republic," P. Garnsey, K. Hopkins & C. Whittaker (eds.), *Trade in the ancient economy* (London) 87-104

Tchernia, A. 1986, *Le vin de L'Italie romaine* (BEFAR 261)

Tchernia, A. & Zevi, F. 1971 "Amphores vinaires de Campanie et de Tarraconaise à Ostie," *Recherches sur les amphores romaines* (CollEFR 10) 35-67

TED'A 1987 [Taller Escola d'Arqueologia], *Els enterraments del Parc de la Ciutat i la problemàtica funerària de Tarraco* (Memòries d'Excavació num. 1, Tarragona)

TED'A 1989, *Un abocador del segle V d C en el Fòrum Provincial de Tàrraco* (Memòries de Excavació num. 2, Tarragona)

TED'A 1990, *L'amfiteatre romà de Tarragona, la basílica visigòtica i l'església romànica* (Memòries d'Excavació num. 3, Tarragona)

Terré, E. 1987 "La vil.la romana de 'El Moro' (Torredembarra): un exemple de poblament rural al camp de Tarragona," in *Jornades Internacionals d'Arqueologia Romana, Museu de Granollers 5-8 Febrer de 1987*, 217-24

Tite, M. S. 1975 "The effect of climate on the magnetic susceptibility of soils," *Nature* 256, 565-66

Tovar, L. C. J., Bermúdez, A., Massó, J. & Ramón, E. 1986-87 "Medio natural y medio economico en la industria alfarera: el taller iberromano de Fontscaldes (Valls, Alt Camp, Tarragona)," *Butlletí Arqueològic* V 8-9, 59-85

Van der Werff, J. H. 1978 "Amphores de tradition punique à Uzita," *BABesch* 52-53, 171-200

Vegas, M. 1973 *Cerámica común romana del Mediterraneo occidental* (Barcelona)

Vegas, M. 1984-85 "Estudio de algunos hallazgos ceramicos de la Muralla de Tarragona, Torre de Cabiscol," *Butlletí Arqueològic* V 6-7, 45-54

Velaza, J. 1991 *Lexico de inscriciones ibéricas (1976-89)* (Aurea Saecula 4, Barcelona)

Velde, B. & Courtoise, L. 1983 "Yellow garnets in Roman amphorae – a possible tracer of ancient commerce," *JArchSci* 10, 531-39

Vidal i Rosich, C. 1897 *Alcover, monografia històrica* (reissued 1973)

Vilaseca, S. 1936 *La industria del silex a Catalunya. Les estacions tallers del Priorat i Extensions* (Reus)

Vilaseca S. 1943 *El poblado y la necrópolis prehistoricos de Mola, Tarragona* (Acta Arqueologica Hispanica 1, Madrid)

Vilaseca, S. 1953 *Las industrias del silex Tarraconenses* (Madrid)

Vilaseca, S. 1968 "Tarragona. Notas de arqueología de Cataluña y Baleares," *Ampurias* 30, 348-65

Villaronga, L. 1983 *Les monedes ibèriques de Tàrraco* (Tarragona)

Vives, J. 1963 *Concilios visigóticos e hispano-romanos* (Barcelona)

Vives i Porta, M. nd. *Reculls històrics de la vila de Brafim* (Brafim)

Whittaker, C. R. 1991 "The consumer city revisited: the *vicus* and the city," *JRA* 3, 110-18

Will, E. L. 1982, "Greco-Italic amphoras," *Hesperia*, 51, 338-56

Williams, D. F. 1981 "The Roman amphora trade with late Iron Age Britain," H. Howard & E. Morris (eds.), *Production and distribution: a ceramic viewpoint* (BAR S120) 123-32

Woolf, G. 1992 "Imperialism, empire and the integration of the Roman economy," *World Archaeology* 23.3, 283-93.

# Appendix 1
# Fabric descriptions

This is a detailed description of all the amphora and coarseware fabrics from the survey. As in the case of the typology it is hoped that it will form the base for a fabric series for the region in the Iberian and Roman periods. To this end a reasonably full description of each fabric has been attempted along the lines of the suggestions by Peacock (1977a). The aim has been to facilitate future identification in the field, both in Tarragona and in the surrounding country. All the sherds were identified with the aid of a x10 hand-lens. In addition a limited range of fabrics was thin-sectioned (see Appendix 2).

All individual fineware productions were identified by the established fabric descriptions of Morel (1981), Oswald and Pryce (1920), Mezquirez (1961) and Hayes (1972). As these are well known it was thought unneccessary to repeat them and no attempt was made to produce a fabric series.

AMPHORAE

*Fabric 1*

A light buff brown coloured clay, which was hard with a somewhat rough feel and a smooth fracture. The fabric was characterized by having only a few distinctive inclusions, not easily distinguishable in hand-analysis. They included a few specks of mica and some dark-coloured and well sorted sub-rounded fragments (0.2-0.8 mm). They are probably of argillaceous origin.

On the basis of the thin-section report (Appendix 2) it is likely that this fabric is Italian in origin, although its exact location is not known.

*Fabric 2* not used

*Fabric 3*

A light buff brown coloured clay, which was soft with a somewhat soapy feel and a smooth fracture. The fabric was well sorted, characterized by having only a few distinctive inclusions. They included frequent flecks of mica, both biotite and muscovite, together with grains of quartz (0.2 mm) and some limestone (0.5 mm).

On the basis of the thin-section report (Appendix 2, sample 20) it is likely that this fabric is of Ibizan origin.

*Fabric 4*

A red-brown (ochre) coloured clay, which was hard with a somewhat rough feel and a smooth fracture. The fabric was relatively well sorted and characterized by moderate inclusions. They consisted of frequent grains of quartz (0.2 mm), fragments of limestone (1 mm), some flecks of mica and phyllite.

It was thin-sectioned (Appendix 2) but the source remains unknown.

*Fabric 5*

A light orange brown coloured clay, which was hard with a rough feel and a smooth fracture. The fabric was well sorted and characterized by abundant inclusions. They consisted of frequent grains of quartz (0.1-0.2 mm), with some fragments of limestone (0.2 mm), augite (0.2 mm), sanidine, felspar (1 mm), and some lava.

On the basis of the thin-section report (Appendix 2, sample 21) it is likely that the origin of this fabric is the Italian volcanic tract.

*Fabric 6*

A buff brown coloured clay, which was hard with a smooth feel and a smooth fracture. The fabric was relatively well sorted and characterized by the inclusion of fragments of a black mineral (0.2 mm) known as 'black sand' and yellow garnet.

On the basis of the thin-section report (Appendix 2, sample 22) it is likely that this fabric is of Campanian origin.

*Fabric 6A*

A dark orange brown coloured clay, which was hard with a rough feel and a hackly fracture. The fabric was relatively well sorted and characterized by the inclusion of a green/black mineral (>0.5 mm).

On the basis of the thin-section report (Appendix 2) it is likely that this fabric is of Campanian origin.

*Fabric 7*

A dark orange brown coloured clay, which was hard with a smooth feel and a smooth fracture. The fabric was poorly sorted and characterized by the moderate inclusion of quartz (0.2 mm), some limestone (0.1-0.3 mm), augite, and lava.

On the basis of the thin-section report (Appendix 2, sample 23) it is likely that this fabric is of Campanian origin.

*Fabric 8*

An orange brown coloured clay, which was hard with a rough feel and a hackly fracture. The fabric was characterized by the inclusion of frequent flecks of mica, quartz (>0.4 mm), some limestone (0.2 mm), felspar, and augite (>0.3 mm).

On the basis of the thin-section report (Appendix 2, sample 24) it is likely that this fabric originated along the Italian volcanic tract.

*Fabric 9*

A medium fine soft, 'sandwich'-coloured clay whose colour characteristically varies from sandy/buff (outer face) to sandy/grey (inner face), or is sandy buff with a pinkish core. It has a rough feel and smooth/rough fracture. It is relatively well sorted and characterized by sparse quartzite inclusions (0.5 mm), quartz (0.1 mm to 0.5 mm), and moderate white limestone (0.07 mm). The latter is clearer in the reduced version.

This fabric was produced locally and is discussed in the thin section report (Appendix 2, samples 2A, 2B, and 3). It is the same as amphora fabric 48.

*Fabric 10*

A light orange buff brown coloured clay, which was hard with a slight smooth feel and a smooth fracture. The fabric was ill-sorted and characterized by the inclusion of some quartz grains (>0.4 mm), limestone (0.5-1 mm), and flecks of mica.

The source of this fabric remains unknown.

*Fabric 11*

A bright orange-coloured clay, which was hard with a rough feel and a hackly fracture. The fabric was well sorted and was characterized by the frequent inclusions of quartz (0.2-0.4 mm) and some limestone (most 0.1 mm, some up to 0.6 mm).

On the basis of the thin-section report (Appendix 2, sample 25) the source of this fabric is thought to be North Africa.

*Fabric 12*

A dark orange-coloured clay, which was hard with a rough feel and a hackly fracture. The fabric was ill-sorted and characterized by moderate inclusions of quartz (>0.5 mm) with some flecks of mica, limestone (0.7-0.8 mm), felspar (1.5 mm), and granite.

On the basis of the thin-section report (Appendix 2, sample 7) it is likely that this fabric is local.

*Fabric 12A*

A dark orange-coloured clay, which was hard with a rough feel and a hackly fracture. The fabric was characterized by moderate inclusions of quartz (>0.5 mm) with some flecks of mica, limestone (0.7-0.8 mm), felspar (1.5 mm), and granite.

On the basis of the thin-section report (Appendix 2) it is likely that this fabric is local.

*Fabric 13*

A fine and light orange-coloured clay, which was hard with a rough feel and a hackly fracture. The fabric was well sorted and characterized by moderate inclusions of quartz (0.4-0.7 mm) and felspar (0.8-0.9 mm) and some inclusions of limestone (0.1-0.2 mm), hornblende, mica flecks, and granite.

On the basis of the thin-section report (Appendix 2) it is likely that this fabric is local.

*Fabric 14/16*

A fine clay, whose colour varied from orange to grey, often within the same sherd, giving it a 'sandwich' texture. It was soft with a smooth slightly soapy feel and a smooth fracture. The fabric is well sorted and characterized by moderate inclusions of limestone (>0.1 mm), some quartz, and felspar. (Some sherds with a more uniform colour fabric are labelled as fabric 14.)

On the basis of the thin-section report (Appendix 2, samples 4, 5 and 8) it is likely that this fabric is local.

*Fabric 17*

A fine and light buff-coloured clay, which was soft with a smooth feel and a smooth fracture. The fabric was ill-sorted and characterized by moderate inclusions of quartz (0.2-0.3 mm), some limestone (0.2 mm), and augite.

The origin of this fabric is not certain.

*Fabric 17A*

A light buff-coloured clay, which was soft with a smooth feel and a hackly fracture. The fabric was characterized by moderate inclusions of quartz (>0.5 mm), limestone (0.2-0.8 mm), and some black iron ore (0.4 mm).

The origin of this fabric is not certain but may be Italian.

*Fabric 18*

A medium fine, dark red/orange-brown coloured clay, which was soft-hard with a rough feel and a hackly fracture. The fabric was medium sorted and characterized by moderate quartz inclusions (>0.1 mm), some limestone (>0.5 mm), felspar, and flecks of mica.

The origin of this fabric is local or regional.

*Fabric 19*

A light buff-coloured clay, which was hard with a rather smooth fracture. This fabric was generally well sorted but had occasional flecks of lime (0.01 mm) and, possibly, ironstone. It seems to be a slightly coarser version of Fabric 20.

It is probably local.

*Fabric 20*

A very fine, light orange-coloured clay, which was soft with a smooth feel and a smooth fracture. The fabric was ill-sorted and characterized by sparse inclusions. They included some limestone (0.1-0.2 mm), quartz (>0.4 mm) and red-black minerals, possibly iron ore.

On the basis of the thin section report (Appendix 2, sample 6) it is likely that this fabric was of local or regional origin.

*Fabric 21*

A medium fine, orange-coloured clay, which was hard with a rough feel and a hackly fracture. The fabric was relatively well sorted and characterized by a sparse number of inclusions. They included a moderate amount of quartz (>0.2 mm), some felspar (>0.8 mm), and angular grey inclusions (>0.2 mm).

The origin of the fabric is to be sought in SE Italy.

*Fabric 22*

A medium fine, dark orange-coloured clay, which was hard with a rough feel and a hackly fracture. The fabric was well sorted and characterized by a number of common inclusions: quartz (0.1-0.7 mm), felspar/limestone (0.1-0.2 mm), black subrounded metasediment/flint (0.3-0.4 mm), and some flecks of mica.

The origin is to be sought in Italy.

*Fabric 23*

A medium fine, dark red-orange coloured clay, which was hard with a rough feel and a hackly fracture. The fabric was well sorted and characterized by a moderate inclusion of quartz (>0.2 mm), some limestone flecks (with one inclusion 1.0 mm across), and a small quantity of subrounded red glassy quartz/felspar inclusions.

This fabric was probably manufactured in North Africa.

*Fabric 24*

A relatively fine, dark orange-coloured clay, which was hard with a rough feel and a hackly fracture. The fabric was characterized by a moderate number of ill-sorted inclusions. They included some subrounded limestone (0.3-1.0 mm), some grey/black subrounded inclusions (0.3 mm), possibly quartz/augite, and a moderate inclusion of mica flecks.

The origin of this fabric is not certain but is probably local.

*Fabric 25*

An alternately grey/brown, dark red/orange coloured clay, which was hard with a rough feel and a hackly fracture. The fabric was characterized by a moderate number of relatively well sorted inclusions. They consisted of some quartz (0.2-0.3 mm), some limestone (0.3-0.4 mm), and possibly one large subrounded inclusion of felspar (0.8 mm).

The origin of this fabric is unknown but may be Italian.

*Fabric 26*

A coarse light brown-buff coloured clay, which was hard with a smooth soapy feel and a hackly fracture. The fabric was characterized by a number of moderately well sorted inclusions. They included a moderate amount of limestone/felspar (0.1 mm), quartz (0.2-0.4 mm), and some dark brown subrounded metasediment/clay pellets.

The origin of this fabric is not known.

*Fabric 27*

A buff-cream coloured clay, which is soft with a rough feel and a hackly fracture. The fabric was characterized by a moderate number of inclusions. They included flecks of mica (>0.5 mm), some rounded black iron ore (>0.1 mm), ferromagnesian minerals (up to 2.0 mm), quartz (1.0 mm), a long lath-like mineral softer than quartz (5.0 mm), and a single dark brown igneous rock inclusion.

The origin of this fabric is not certain but may be South Spanish.

*Fabric 27a*

A dark buff-coloured clay, which was hard with a smooth feel and a smooth fracture. The fabric was characterized by a moderate number of inclusions. They included a moderate inclusion of limestone/felspar (0.1 mm to 0.6 mm), some quartz (0.5 mm), and a moderate quantity of subrounded black iron ore (>0.2 mm).

The origin of this fabric is not certain.

*Fabric 28*

A fine light orange-brown coloured clay, which was hard with a smooth feel and a smooth fracture. The fabric was characterized by a number of common well sorted inclusions. They included a moderate inclusion of quartz (0.3-0.4 mm), a sparse subrounded white mineral (0.2 mm), possibly limestone/felspar, occasional subrounded black minerals (0.4-0.5 mm), and elongated white/cream limestone or shell (0.2 mm).

The origin of this fabric is not certain.

*Fabric 29*

A fine light brown-buff coloured clay, which

was hard with a soft feel and a hackly fracture. The fabric was characterized by a sparse number of well sorted inclusions. They included a sparse number of limestone inclusions (>0.8 mm), some white mineral inclusions (0.2 mm), possibly quartzite/felspar, and occasional flecks of mica.

The origin of this fabric is not known.

*Fabric 30*

A relatively coarse, orange-coloured clay, which was hard with a rough feel and a smooth fracture. The fabric was characterized by a sparse number of ill-sorted inclusions. They included a sparse number of quartz inclusions (0.2 mm) and angular black basic igneous rock fragments (0.2 mm).

The origin of this fabric is not known.

*Fabric 31*

A relatively coarse, dark orange-brown-coloured clay, which was hard with a rough feel and a hackly fracture. The fabric was characterized by a number of ill-sorted inclusions. They included a moderate number of quartz inclusions (0.4 mm), sub-angular black iron ore inclusions (0.1 mm), a sparse number of large angular red inclusions (felspar?), occasional limestone inclusions (0.1 mm), occasional quartz inclusions (1.8 mm), and some mica flecks.

The origin of this fabric is not known.

*Fabric 32*

A relatively fine, orange-buff coloured clay, which was hard with a rough feel and a smooth fracture. The fabric was characterized by sparse well-sorted rounded white inclusions up to 0.1 mm across (almost impossible to identify without a hand-lens). There were also occasional mica flecks and sparse to moderate sub-rounded quartz inclusions up to 0.1 mm across.

The origin of this fabric is to be sought in southern Spain.

*Fabric 33*

A coarse orange-brown coloured clay, which was hard with a rough feel and smooth fracture. The fabric was characterized by poorly-sorted sparse angular inclusions of calcite or limestone between 0.4 and 0.1 mm across. There were also rare flecks of mica between 0.1 mm and 0.22 mm across, as well as sparse sub-rounded inclusions of a dark-coloured iron ore.

It has an origin in NE Spain.

*Fabric 34*

A relatively coarse, dark red to orange-coloured clay, which was hard with a rough feel

and hackly fracture. The fabric was characterized by relatively well-sorted, moderate rounded quartz inclusions (up to 0.2 mm across), as well as sparse to moderate small flecks of limestone. There were occasional specks of mica and elongated inclusions of a ferro-magnesian mineral, 0.5 mm across.

It may have a North African origin.

*Fabric 35*

A coarse dark red to orange-coloured clay which was hard with a rough feel and hackly fracture. The fabric was characterized by relatively well-sorted, moderate angular quartz inclusions up to 0.5 mm across, and angular limestone inclusions up to 0.5 mm across. There were also sparse to moderate angular inclusions of iron ore.

It may have an Italian origin.

*Fabric 36*

A coarse cream to buff-coloured clay with a soft smooth feel and a hackly fracture. The fabric is well sorted and characterized by tiny (0.05 mm) red to brown inclusions of iron ore or grog: some may be voids. There were sparse pieces of black iron ore or a ferro-magnesian mineral (0.2 mm), as well as moderate angular inclusions of quartz of *c.* 0.2 mm.

The origin of this fabric is not known.

*Fabric 37*

A coarse light orange-coloured fabric, which is hard with a smooth feel and fracture. The fabric is well sorted and characterized by common rounded white inclusions (0.05 mm), possibly felspar, and large (0.3 mm - 0.4 mm) angular inclusions of limestone. There are sparse rounded inclusions (0.2 mm) of limestone. There are also sparse, angular inclusions of a shiny dark iron ore (0.2 mm - 0.3 mm), as well as sparse to moderate flecks of mica.

This fabric may be South Gaulish.

*Fabric 37A*

A hard brown to buff-coloured clay, with a smooth feel and hackly fracture. The fabric is characterized by sparse to moderate tiny specks of mica, and sub-rounded quartz (0.2 mm). In addition there are sparse, sub-rounded inclusions of a black iron ore (0.2 mm).

The origin of this fabric is not known.

*Fabric 38*

A coarse dark orange to red-coloured clay, which is hard, with a rough feel and a hackly fracture. The fabric is characterized by being ill-sorted and having a long strip of limestone running across its face. Above it were moderate, angular (irregular) inclusions of limestone. There were also sparse to moderate angular inclusions of iron ore (0.5 mm), moderate flecks of mica, sparse sub-rounded inclusions of quartz 0.8 mm across, and sparse, angular pink inclusions (0.7 - 0.8 mm) of felspar.

The origin of this fabric is not certain but may be Italian.

### Fabric 39

A fine light brown to buff-coloured clay, with a soft smooth feel and smooth to hackly fracture. The fabric is well sorted and characterized by sparse tiny flecks of mica, sparse rounded inclusions of a white mineral (0.1 mm), sparse angular quartz inclusions, and occasional tiny inclusions of a black iron ore.

The fabric is South Gaulish in origin.

### Fabric 40

A coarse soft, orange-coloured clay with a rough feel and hackly fracture. The fabric is ill-sorted and characterized by moderate to common angular inclusions of quartz of varying sizes (up to 0.9 mm - 1.0 mm). In addition there were sparse to moderate sub-rounded inclusions of black iron ore, sparse sub-rounded inclusions of various sizes (up to 0.9 mm) of a pink felspar, sparse angular white inclusions (0.2 mm), large rounded inclusions of a deep orange red colour (up to 1.0 mm across), sparse rounded glassy brown inclusions (0.8 mm), and large rounded limestone inclusions (3.0 mm across).

The origin of this fabric is not known.

### Fabric 41

A coarse hard, light brown to buff-coloured clay, with a smooth feel and hackly fracture. The fabric is ill-sorted and characterized by sparse rounded white glassy felspar inclusions (0.2 mm), dull white limestone inclusions (0.1 mm - 0.2 mm), and angular inclusions of quartz (0.3 mm). There were also sparse angular inclusions of black iron ore (up to 0.8 mm), and sub-rounded brown inclusions (0.1 mm).

The origin of this fabric is not known.

### Fabric 42

A coarse hard, dark red to orange-coloured clay, with a rough feel and hackly fracture. The fabric is ill-sorted and characterized by sparse to moderate irregular limestone inclusions, sparse, angular black iron ore, and a sparse angular white and glassy mineral (0.5 mm).

The origin of this fabric is not known.

### Fabric 43

A fairly coarse hard, brown to buff-coloured clay, with a smooth feel and hackly fracture. The fabric is well sorted and characterized by sparse sub-rounded black iron ore inclusions (0.15 mm), sparse flecks of mica, and sparse angular quartz (0.3 mm).

The origin of this fabric is not known.

### Fabric 44

A coarse soft, orange to red coloured clay, with a rough feel and hackly fracture. The fabric is ill-sorted and characterized by sparse, rounded black iron ore or ferro-magnesian inclusions (0.5 mm), sparse irregular inclusions of limestone (2.5 mm long), sparse rounded white felspar inclusions (0.2 mm), sparse angular pink/brown felspar inclusions (0.3 - 0.4 mm), and occasional flecks of mica.

The origin of this fabric is not known.

### Fabric 45

A fine soft, orange to buff-coloured clay, with a rough feel and hackly fracture. The fabric is ill-sorted and characterized by moderate, angular quartz inclusions (up to 1.0 mm), sparse to moderate angular felspar inclusions (0.5 mm), common plate-like mica inclusions (up to 0.8 - 1.0 mm), sparse to moderate angular dark iron ore (?) (0.5 mm), sparse to moderate angular brown inclusions (up to 0.9 mm), sparse to moderate angular brown inclusions (up to 0.9 mm), sparse sub-rounded dark red inclusion (possibly haematite) (1.3 mm), elongated rods of a ferro-magnesian mineral (1.0 mm), and occasional large volcanic rock fragments (5.0 mm).

The fabric is South Gaulish.

### Fabric 46

A coarse hard, light orange to buff-coloured clay, with a rough feel and smooth fracture. The fabric is ill-sorted and characterized by sparse angular quartz inclusions (up to 1.0 mm), sparse sub-rounded iron ore inclusions (0.5 mm), sparse angular brown inclusions (up to 0.5 mm across), and occasional flecks of mica.

The origin of this fabric is not known.

### Fabric 47

A moderately fine hard, orange-coloured clay, with a smooth feel and hackly fracture. The fabric is well sorted and characterized by sparse rounded white felspar inclusions (0.1 mm), large irregular inclusions of limestone (1.2 mm), rare shell fragments (0.7 mm across), and rare tiny flecks of mica.

The origin of this fabric is not known.

*Fabric 48*

A coarse clay, its colour varying in bands from grey/brown to dark orange/red, to grey/brown, and to brown. It is hard with a rough feel and a smooth yet slight hackly fracture. The fabric is ill-sorted and characterized by moderate sub-rounded white felspar or limestone inclusions (0.2 mm across), sparse sub-rounded black iron ore inclusions (up to 0.2 mm across), moderate, sub-rounded/rounded quartz inclusions of quartz (0.3 - 0.4 mm), and sparse flecks of mica.

This fabric is probably the same as amphora fabric 9.

*Fabric 49* not used

*Fabric 50* not used

*Fabric 51*

A coarse hard, light orange-coloured clay, with a rough feel and hackly fracture. The fabric is well sorted and charcterised by sparse flecks of mica, moderate to common inclusions of sub-rounded quartz (up to 0.5 mm), occasional large irregular inclusions of limestone (0.5 - 0.7 mm), sparse sub-rounded inclusions of an unidentified brown mineral (0.2 - 0.3 mm), and sparse angular black iron-ore inclusions (0.3 mm).

The origin of this fabric is not known.

*Fabric 52*

A fairly fine hard, orange-coloured clay, with a rough feel and hackly fracture. The fabric is medium well sorted and characterized by sparse, angular white limestone inclusions (0.2 - 0.3 mm), larger (0.5 mm) rounded limestone inclusions, sparse angular black iron-ore or ferro-magnesian inclusions (0.4 - 0.5 mm), sparse to moderate and sub-rounded to angular quartz inclusions (0.1 - 0.2 mm), and sparse flecks of mica.

The origin of this fabric is not known.

*Fabrics 53-59* not used

*Fabric 60*

A coarse hard, light brown-coloured clay, with a rough feel and hackly fracture. The fabric is ill-sorted and characterized by sparse flecks of mica, sparse to moderate angular quartz inclusions (up to 0.5 mm), sparse irregular inclusions of limestone (up to 1.0 mm), occasional large rounded inclusions of limestone (3.5 - 4.0 mm), sparse rounded black iron ore inclusions (0.5 mm), and ferro-magnesian minerals (1.0 mm).

This fabric may have an Italian origin.

*Fabric 61*

A medium fine soft, cream to buff-coloured clay, with a rough feel and hackly fracture. The fabric is ill-sorted and characterized by moderate sub-rounded quartz (up to 0.5 mm), sparse sub-rounded white felspar inclusions (0.1 - 0.2 mm), sparse flecks of mica, sparse sub-rounded pink orthoclase felspar inclusions (0.2 mm across), and sparse black iron-ore inclusions (up to 0.5 mm).

The origin of this fabric is not known.

*Fabric 62*

A coarse hard, dark orange-coloured clay with a rough feel and hackly fracture. The fabric is ill-sorted and characterized by moderate sub-rounded/rounded limestone inclusions (up to 4.0 mm), sparse rounded white felspar(?) inclusions (up to 0.4 to 0.5 mm), sparse sub-rounded black/brown iron ore (0.5 mm), sparse angular quartz inclusions (up to 0.3 mm), sparse angular rounded red/brown inclusions (0.6 mm), some possible volcanic inclusions (0.6 mm), and moderate flecks of mica.

The origin of this fabric is not known.

*Fabric 63*

A fine soft, dark cream to buff-coloured clay, with a rough feel and smooth fracture. The fabric is well sorted and characterized by sparse sub-rounded quartz inclusions (0.4 - 0.6 mm), very small black inclusions or voids, and rare tiny flecks of mica.

The origin of this fabric is not known.

*Fabric 64*

A coarse hard, dark red to orange-coloured clay, with a rough feel and hackly fracture. The fabric is ill-sorted and characterized by sparse sub-rounded white felspar inclusions (0.1 mm), rare inclusions (0.6 - 0.7 mm) of shell or possibly calcite, sparse to moderate angular quartz inclusions (0.4 mm), and moderate specks of mica.

The origin of this fabric is not known.

*Fabric 65*

A coarse hard, dark orange to brown-coloured clay, with a rough feel and hackly fracture. The fabric is ill-sorted and characterized by sparse sub-rounded brown/black iron-ore inclusions (1.0 mm), very rare elongated limestone inclusions (3.0 mm), sparse angular/irregular limestone inclusions, sparse shell (0.5 mm) inclusions, sparse rounded white felspar (0.3 mm), sparse sub-rounded/angular quartz inclusions (0.6 mm), sparse round brown clay pellets (0.5 mm), and occasional specks of mica.

The origin of this fabric is not known.

*Fabric 66*

A coarse hard, orange-coloured clay, with a

rough feel and hackly fracture. The fabric is ill-sorted and characterized by moderate angular red inclusions (up to 0.6 - 0.7 mm), moderate to common angular black/grey iron ore (up to 1.0 mm), moderate angular quartz (0.1 - 0.2 mm), sparse to moderate sub-rounded/angular white felspar (0.3 mm), rare elongated streaks of white limestone, occasional specks of mica, and sparse sub-rounded, white calcite inclusions (0.2 mm).

The origin of this fabric is not known.

### Fabric 67

A coarse soft, orange-coloured clay, with a rough smooth feel and a smooth fracture. The fabric is ill-sorted and characterized by occasional sparse flecks of mica, moderate to common irregular/angular inclusions of limestone (up to 0.2 mm), sparse angular sub-rounded black iron ore (0.2 mm) and an angular rock fragment (1.0 mm).

The origin of this fabric is not known.

### Fabric 68

A medium fine, very soft orange-coloured clay, with a smooth feel and a smooth fracture. The fabric is ill-sorted and characterized by sparse to moderate angular off-white inclusions (up to 1.0 mm) of limestone or calcite.

The origin of this fabric is not certain, although its occurrence in association with Type 21 suggests that it may be an Ibizan fabric.

### Fabric 69

A coarse hard, dark brown/buff coloured clay, with a rough feel and hackly fracture. The fabric is ill-sorted and characterized by sparse angular sedimentary rock (up to 2.0 mm), sparse sub-rounded/rounded dark iron ore (0.2 mm), sparse to common angular quartz inclusions (0.2 mm), sparse sub-rounded/rounded white felspar (0.2 - 0.3 mm).

The origin of this fabric is not known, although it may be Italian.

### Fabric 70

A coarse soft, dark orange/brown coloured clay, with a rough feel and hackly fracture. The fabric is ill-sorted and characterized by moderate angular quartz (0.7 mm across), occasional large (up to 2.0 mm) brown sub-rounded rock fragments with a ground scatter of pieces of about 0.2 mm, sparse sub-rounded white felspar (0.2 mm), sparse angular inclusions of a white limestone (0.4 - 0.5 mm), and occasional flecks of mica.

The origin of this fabric is not known, although it may be Italian.

### Fabric 71

A fine hard, light orange to brown grey coloured clay, with a smooth feel and smooth to hackly fracture. The fabric is well sorted and characterized by sparse sub-rounded white felspar (0.1 mm), and sparse rounded black iron ore (up to 0.3 mm).

The origin of this fabric is not known.

### Fabric 72

A coarse hard, dark orange-coloured clay, with a relatively soft feel and smooth fracture. The fabric is ill-sorted and characterized by moderate to common angular limestone (0.2 - 0.4 mm), sparse angular orthoclase felspar (0.4 mm), moderate sub-rounded angular quartz (0.05 - 0.1 mm), and sparse angular/rounded black iron ore (0.2 mm).

It may be a local fabric.

### Fabric 73

A coarse soft, dark orange-coloured clay with a dark brown-coloured layer in its centre; it has a rough feel and smooth fracture. The fabric is ill-sorted and characterized by sparse rounded limestone (up to 1.2 mm), large (1.7 mm) rounded glassy/grey igneous rock(?) inclusions, moderate angular quartz (up to 0.2 - 0.3 mm), sparse to moderate pink angular felspar angular (up to 1.5 mm), sparse sub-rounded black (0.2 mm) iron ore and sparse sub-rounded/angular white felspar.

The origin of this fabric is not known.

### Fabric 74

A very coarse hard, dark brown/red coloured clay, with a rough feel and a hackly fracture. The fabric is ill-sorted and characterized by moderate angular glassy black ferromagnesian minerals (up to 2.5 mm), sparse angular (rhombs) of a soft clear calcite, sparse sub-rounded white felspar (0.3 mm), sparse large (1.5 mm) irregular limestone, and sparse angular quartz (0.2 mm).

The origin of this fabric is not known but it may be Italian.

### Fabric 75

Quite a coarse hard, deep red/orange coloured clay, with a smooth feel and smooth yet hackly fracture. The fabric is well sorted and characterized by abundant common angular to sub-rounded white inclusions (up to 0.1 mm across) of uncertain identity, sparse irregular limestone (0.5 mm), and rare pink orthoclase (1.5 mm).

The origin of this fabric is not known but it may be North African.

*Fabric 76*

A medium fine hard, dark orange/brown coloured clay, with a rough feel and smooth yet slightly hackly break. The fabric is ill-sorted and characterized by sparse angular black iron ore (0.4 - 0.7 mm), sparse to moderate angular quartz (0.3 - 0.4 mm), sparse irregular orthoclase (1.0 mm), and sparse tiny white felspar.

It is a regional fabric.

*Fabric 77*

A coarse hard, dark grey/brown coloured clay, with a rough feel and hackly fracture. The fabric is ill-sorted and characterized by common to abundant angular white felspar (up to 1.0 mm in size), common to abundant angular quartz (0.5 - 0.8 mm), and sparse to moderate irregular/sub-rounded limestone (up to 1.0 mm).

The origin of this fabric is not known.

*Fabric 78*

A slightly coarse hard, bright orange-coloured clay, soapy to the touch and with a smooth to hackly fracture. The fabric is ill-sorted and characterized by sparse sub-rounded white calcite or limestone (up to 0.8 mm in size), and sparse sub-rounded black iron ore (0.1 - 0.2 mm).

The origin of this fabric is not known.

*Fabric 79*

A relatively fine hard, brown/buff coloured clay, with a rough feel and smooth/hackly fracture. The fabric is well sorted and characterized by moderate angular quartz (up to 0.3 mm), sparse sub-rounded brown clay pellets (0.2 mm in size), sparse sub-rounded brown iron ore (up to 0.4 mm), and sparse sub-rounded white felspar (up to 0.3 - 0.4 mm).

The origin of this fabric is not known.

*Fabric 80*

A coarse hard, dark and grey/brown coloured clay, with a rough feel and hackly fracture. The fabric is relatively well sorted and characterized by common to abundant sub-rounded/angular quartz inclusions (0.2 - 0.3 mm), sparse angular white limestone (up to 0.1 mm), and sparse angular brown/red clay pellets (0.3 mm).

This fabric was manufactured in Tripolitania.

*Fabric 81*

A relatively coarse soft, cream/buff coloured clay, with a slightly rough feel and hackly fracture. The fabric is ill-sorted and characterized by sparse to moderate sub-rounded black iron ore (up to 1.5 mm), moderate angular quartz inclusions (up to 0.7 mm), sparse rounded light brown/

ochre iron ore (up to 1.0 - 1.5 mm), sparse angular white felspar (up 1.8 mm), and sparse sub-rounded dull brown clay pellets (up to 0.8 mm).

The origin of this fabric is not known.

*Fabric 82*

A fine soft, light orange/buff coloured clay, with a smooth, soapy, powdery feel and a smooth fracture. The fabric is ill-sorted and characterized by sparse, moderately sorted, rounded black iron ore (0.2 mm), sparse rounded white felspar (0.1 mm), sparse to moderate angular/sub-rounded quartz (0.4 mm), occasional mica flecks, and sparse rounded orange rock (up to 1.0 mm).

The origin of this fabric is not known.

*Fabric 83*

A relatively coarse hard, orange buff coloured clay, with a rough feel and a hackly fracture. The fabric is ill-sorted and characterized by occasional to moderate flecks of mica, moderate angular quartz inclusions (0.2 mm), sparse tiny white inclusions, possibly felspar (0.05 mm), sparse angular black iron ore, sparse angular brown clay pellets (0.1 mm), and several sub-rounded red/brown rock fragments (up to 3.0 mm).

The origin of this fabric is not known.

*Fabric 84*

A coarse hard, brown-coloured clay, with a rough feel and hackly fracture. The fabric is ill-sorted and characterized by moderate sub-rounded quartz inclusions (up to 0.5 mm), sparse rounded white felspar(?) (0.5 mm), medium sized (0.7 mm) rounded white powdery limestone inclusions, rare large (2.0 mm) sub-rounded brown rock fragments, and sparse sub-rounded black/brown black iron ore (0.1 mm).

The origin of this fabric is not known.

*Fabric 85*

A coarse hard, dark red/orange coloured clay, with a rough feel and hackly fracture. The fabric is ill-sorted and characterized by sparse to moderate angular white felspar (0.05 - 0.1 mm), sparse sub-rounded brown clay pellets (up to 0.5 mm), sparse sub-rounded limestone inclusions (up to 0.5 mm), sparse angular black iron ore (0.3 mm), and sparse to moderate quartz inclusions (up to 0.4 mm).

This fabric is possibly Italian.

*Fabric 86*

A relatively coarse soft, light brown/orange coloured clay, with a slightly rough feel and smooth fracture. The fabric is ill-sorted and characterized by sparse sub-rounded white felspar (0.5 - 0.8 mm), sparse sub-rounded black inclusions, and sparse to moderate angular quartz inclusions (up to 0.8 mm).

The origin of this fabric is not known.

*Fabric 87*

A coarse hard, dark orange/brown coloured clay, with a rough feel and hackly fracture. The fabric is ill-sorted and characterized by sparse angular white quartzite (up to 1.0 mm), moderate angular quartz inclusions (0.5 mm), sparse angular softer white felspar (0.3 mm). sparse irregular limestone inclusions (various sizes up to 1.0 mm), sparse sub-rounded dark brown/grey glassy inclusions, sparse sub-rounded black iron ore (0.6 mm), and laminated angular brown buff meta-sediment (2.5 mm).

The origin of this fabric is not known.

*Fabric 88*

A coarse relatively soft, hard cream/buff coloured clay, with a smooth feel and hackly fracture. The fabric is well sorted and characterized by occasional flecks of mica, sparse sub-rounded brown iron ore or clay pellets (0.3 mm), sparse sub-rounded black iron ore (0.2 mm), and sparse sub-rounded white felspar or limestone (0.2 mm).

The origin of this fabric is not known.

*Fabric 89*

A coarse hard, cream/buff coloured clay, with a slightly rough feel and smooth fracture. The fabric is well sorted and characterized by sparse sub-rounded quartz inclusions (up to 1.0 mm), sparse sub-rounded black iron ore (0.1 mm), occasional flecks of mica, and sparse orange/brown inclusions (0.1 mm).

The origin of this fabric is not known.

*Fabric 90*

A relatively coarse hard, light brown/buff coloured clay, with a rough feel and slightly hackly fracture. The fabric is ill-sorted and characterized by sparse to moderate flecks of mica, sparse sub-rounded dark/black iron ore (0.1 - 0.2 mm), sparse elongated dark ferro-magnesian mineral (1.0 mm), and very rare angular quartz inclusions.

The origin of this fabric is not known.

*Fabric 91*

A very coarse soft clay with a dark red/brown coloured band and a dark grey/brown band. It is soft with a rough feel and a hackly fracture. The fabric is ill-sorted and characterized by sparse sub-rounded limestone (up to 1.0 mm), moderate to common angular quartz inclusions (up to 0.8 mm), and sparse angular white felspar (up to 0.1 - 0.2 mm).

The origin of this fabric is not known.

*Fabric 92*

A fine soft, light red/brown clay, which feels rough to the touch. The fabric is well sorted and characterized with occasional indeterminate inclusions which were moderately well sorted (less than 0.1 mm), and sparse (0.01 mm) voids.

The origin of this fabric is not known.

*Fabric 93*

A coarse soft, light brown/dark sandy-coloured clay, with a rough feel and fracture. The fabric is poorly sorted and characterized by moderate ill-sorted quartzite (0.1 - 0.5 mm), moderate dull brown inclusions (0.5 - 1 mm) and a moderate number of voids (0.1 to 1 mm).

The origin of this fabric is not certain but it may be South Spanish (Guadalquivir valley).

*Fabric 94*

A fine soft, light grey/red coloured clay, with a rough feel and hackly fracture. The fabric is characterized by sparse rounded white inclusions (0.1 mm) and sparse rounded dark quartz grains, with relatively frequent air holes.

The origin of this fabric is not known.

*Fabric 95*

The colour of the clay varies from light grey (interior) to grey/pink (exterior) and is coarse and hard with a hackly fracture. The fabric is characterized by occasional ill-sorted quartzite (up to 1.5 mm), moderate quartz, rare mica specks, and air holes.

The origin of this fabric is not certain but it may be South Spanish (Guadalquivir valley).

*Fabric 96*

A fine soft sandy clay, with a rough feel and a smooth to rough fracture. The fabric is ill-sorted and characterized by sparse dull white felspar (1.0 mm), quartz (1.0 mm), and rare iron stone(?) (4.0 mm).

It may be a local or regional fabric.

*Fabric 97*

A medium fine soft, light red/sandy coloured clay, with a rough feel. The fabric is ill-sorted and characterized by sparse quartz (1.0 mm), lime (usually 0.01 mm but occasionally up to 2.0 mm) and ironstone (up to 1.0 mm).

The origin of this fabric is South Spanish (Guadalquivir).

*Fabric 98* not used

*Fabric 99*

A fine hard, yellowy/buff coloured clay, with a rough feel. The fabric is well sorted and characterized by sparse quartzite (0.1 mm) and voids (0.1 mm).

The origin of this fabric is not known.

*Fabric 100*

A medium fine soft, light sandy/buff coloured clay with a rough feel. The fabric is well sorted and characterized by moderate plate-like white inclusions (0.1 - 0.5 mm) of uncertain identification, and occasional quartz.

This fabric is of Rhodian origin.

*Fabric 101*

A medium fine soft, yellowy/buff coloured clay, with a rough feel and hackly fracture. The fabric is fairly well sorted and characterized by sparse, white quartzite (0.1 - 0.5 mm), and more frequent lime (0.1 - 0.4 mm).

The origin of this fabric is not known.

*Fabric 102*

Quite a hard, orange to dark red clay with an irregular fracture. The fabric was quite well sorted with quite common quartz crystals (up to 0.2 mm), occasional limestone reaction rings, and clay pellets.

The origin of this fabric is Tunisian.

*Fabric 103*

A hard, orangey red to brown buff clay with an irregular fracture. The fabric was poor to medium sorted, with very common limestone reaction rims and lime (up to 2.0 mm), and moderately common quartz.

This fabric was probably manufactured in Tripolitania.

*Fabric 104*

A hard, dull orange to light brown clay with a rough fracture. The fabric is medium-sorted with quite common quartz and calcite crystals, together with occasional mica.

The origin of this fabric is South Spanish.

## COARSE WARES

*Fabric A*

A coarse brittle and crumbly, ochre/grey/black clay with a hackly fracture. The fabric is poorly sorted and characterized by common mica specks, moderate angular quartz (1.0 - 2.0 mm), quartz (1.0 - 2.0 mm) and felspar (1.0 - 2.0 mm).

It is probably a local fabric.

*Fabric B*

A very fine and hard, light buff to light brown clay, with a hackly fracture. The fabric is ill-sorted and characterized by subangular moderate quartzite (up to 2.0 mm), moderate calcite (up to 2.0 mm), moderate quartz (up to 0.5 mm), and specks of mica and moderate mudstone (up to 6.0 mm).

The origin of this fabric is not known.

*Fabric C*

A fine very hard, light orange (outer surface) to dark grey (inner face) coloured clay, with smooth to conchoidal fracture. The fabric is characterized by rare to moderate lime particles (less than 0.1 mm).

The origin of this fabric is not known.

*Fabric D*

A fine hard and slightly powdery, brown/buff to orange/pink coloured clay, with a smooth to conchoidal fracture. The fabric is well sorted and characterized by abundant lime particles (0.1 - 1.0 mm), occasional subangular quartz (0.4 mm), and rare subangular clay pellets (0.02 mm).

The origin of this fabric is not certain.

*Fabric E* not used

*Fabric F*

A very fine hard, light ochre to grey clay with a smooth fracture. The fabric is very well sorted and characterized by fairly common lime particles (0.1 mm) and rare subangular quartz (0.1 mm) and calcite (0.2 mm).

The origin of this fabric is not known.

*Fabric G*

A medium fine very hard, ochre/brown clay with a greyish core and a smooth/hackly fracture. The fabric is ill-sorted and characterized by moderate lime particles (0.2 mm) rarer inclusions of subangular/rounded quartz (0.01 - 0.5 mm), rare limestone reaction rings (0.01 - 0.05 mm), and rare clay particles (0.01 - 0.05 mm).

The origin of this fabric is not known.

*Fabric H*

A fine hard, greyish clay with an irregular fracture. The fabric is well sorted and characterized by moderate lime particles (0.1 mm), rare quartz (less than 0.1 mm), and grog.

It is almost certainly of regional origin.

*Fabric I*

A hard, light grey clay with smooth to conchoidal fracture. There are no visible inclusions.

It is almost certainly of regional origin.

*Fabric J*

A medium fine hard, buff to ochre clay with an irregular to hackly fracture. The fabric is quite well sorted and characterized by moderate air holes (up to 0.5 mm), rare specks of mica, rare iron ore, rare subangular quartz (up to 0.05 mm), and rare grog.

The origin of this fabric is not known.

*Fabric K*

A fine and very hard, light pink clay with an irregular/hackly fracture. The fabric is ill-sorted and characterized by frequent angular/ subangular quartz/quartzite grains (up to 2.0 mm), rare limestone reaction rings, rare mica specks, and rare calcite.

It is almost certainly local.

*Fabric L*

A coarse medium hard/crumbly, light brown to ochre clay with a hackly fracture and laminar cracks. The fabric is ill-sorted and characterized by common quartz (0.1 mm), common lime specks, and common ironstone.

It may well be local.

*Fabric M*

A medium fine hard, pinky/orange clay with smooth/irregular fracture and occasional air-holes. The fabric is ill-sorted and character-ized by abundant yellow lime particles and reaction rims (up to 0.1 mm), and rarer calcite (up to 1.5 mm) and quartz (0.1 mm).

The fabric probably has a North African origin.

*Fabric N*

A fine medium hard, light yellow/light buff clay with smooth conchoidal fracture. The fabric is quite well sorted and characterized by moderate clay pellets and grog (up to 3.0 mm) and rare dark plate-like inclusions.

The origin of this fabric is not known.

*Fabric O*

A medium fine very hard, chocolate brown clay with irregular/hackly fracture. The fabric is poorly sorted, characterized by common subangular quartz (up to 1.5 mm), subangular calcite (up to 1.5 mm), and occasional lime.

The fabric is probably of local or regional origin.

*Fabric P not used*

*Fabric Q*

A medium fine very hard, orangey red clay with hackly fracture. The fabric is characterized by abundant subangular black volcanic minerals (up to 1.5 mm), rare quartzite, rare lime specks, and rare orangey grog.

The fabric is similar to Amphora fabric 6 and is Italian in origin.

*Fabric R*

A medium grained hard, light buff to light brown clay with irregular/smooth fracture and occasional air holes. The fabric is medium-sorted and characterized by rare specks of lime (up to 1.0 mm), grog (up to 1.0 mm), and ironstone (up to 1.0 mm).

The fabric is almost certainly local in origin.

*Fabric S*

Medium or fine grained hard, dirty brown/ black clay with an hackly fracture. The fabric is quite well sorted and characterized by moder-ate/common lime (up to 0.5 mm), moderate/ common calcite (0.2 mm), and rare quartz (up to 0.5 mm). They are poorly sorted and subangular.

The origin of this fabric is not known but it is almost certainly local or regional.

*Fabric T*

A fine hard, light cream-coloured clay, with a smooth feel and smooth fracture. The fabric is well sorted and characterized by sparse, angular black iron ore (0.1 mm), sparse angular brown clay pellets (0.1 mm), occasional elongated voids filled with a white mineral, perhaps limestone or shell (3.0 mm), sparse white felspar (angular and 0.2 mm), and sparse angular quartz (up to 0.1 - 0.2 mm).

The origin of this fabric is not known but it is presumably local or regional.

*Fabric U*

A very fine hard, light orange-coloured clay with a smooth feel and smooth fracture. The fabric is very well sorted and characterized by moderate, angular white inclusions (0.05 - 0.1 mm), sparse black angular iron ore (0.2 mm), occasional flecks of mica, and possible voids (0.7 mm) containing limestone.

The origin of this fabric is not known but it is presumably local or regional.

*Fabric V*

An extremely fine soft, bright orange-coloured clay, with a smooth feel and smooth fracture. The fabric is very well sorted and characterized by sparse flecks of mica, moderate tiny white inclusions (0.05 mm), and sparse angular quartz (0.1 mm).

The origin of this fabric is not known but it is presumably local or regional.

*Fabric W*

A hard fine, dark orange-coloured clay, with a smooth feel and smooth fracture. The fabric is well sorted and characterized by sparse irregular limestone (0.7 - 0.8 mm), moderate sub-rounded white inclusions (0.05 - 0.2 mm), sparse angular black iron ore (0.1 - 0.2 mm), and sparse angular brown clay pellets (0.2 mm).

The origin of this fabric is not known but it is presumably local or regional.

*Fabric X*

A soft fine, light orange/brown coloured clay with grey brown centre, a rough feel and smooth fracture. The fabric is well sorted and is characterized by sparse to moderate sub-rounded white felspar (0.1 mm), rare flecks of mica, sparse angular quartz (0.1 - 0.2 mm), sparse limestone (up to 0.7 mm), and sparse black iron ore (0.05 mm).

The origin of this fabric is not known but it is presumably local or regional.

*Fabric Y*

A medium fine hard, light orange-coloured clay, with a rough feel and smooth fracture. The fabric is ill-sorted and characterized by moderate sub-rounded limestone (up to 1.0 mm), sparse angular black/brown iron ore (up to 2.0 mm), sparse angular white felspar (up to 1.2 mm), and angular quartz/quartzite (1.0 mm).

The origin of this fabric is not known but it is presumably local or regional.

*Fabric Z*

A very fine, orange/brown/grey coloured clay, with a smooth feel and hackly fracture. The fabric is well sorted and characterized by moderate angular limestone (2.0 - 2.4 mm), sparse angular limestone (0.1 mm), and sparse sub-rounded white felspar (0.1 - 0.2 mm).

The origin of this fabric is uncertain but it may be Italian.

*Fabric ZA*

A fine soft, light orange/red to buff coloured clay, with a smooth powdery feel and smooth fracture. The fabric is ill-sorted and characterized by sparse sub-rounded white limestone or calcite (1.0 mm), sparse angular black/brown laminar slate or iron ore (0.8 mm), and sparse angular/irregular bright red/orange rock (up to 0.8 - 0.9 mm). The upper surface has a brown glaze.

The origin of this fabric is not known.

*Fabric ZB*

A relatively fine soft, light orange (interior)/buff (exterior) coloured clay, with a smooth powdery feel and fracture. The fabric is ill-sorted and characterized by sparse flecks of mica, sparse elongated ferro-magnesian mineral (up to 1.8 mm), sparse sub-rounded limestone or calcite (1.0 mm), sparse/moderate sub-rounded brown clay pellets/iron ore (up to 0.5 mm), sparse sub-rounded quartz (up to 0.5 mm), sparse sub-rounded angular black glassy inclusions, rare flecks of mica, and sparse white felspar.

The origin of this fabric is not known but it is presumably local or regional.

*Fabric ZC*

A medium coarse soft, light orange-coloured clay, with a relatively smooth feel and smooth/hackly fracture. The fabric is ill-sorted and characterized by sparse/moderate angular inclusions of calcite (up to 1.0 mm), sparse sub-rounded limestone (up to 1.3 mm), sparse angular black iron ore (0.2 - 0.8 mm), sparse sub-rounded quartz (0.4 mm), sparse sub-rounded red iron ore (up to 0.8 mm), and occasional flecks of mica.

The origin of this fabric is not known but it is presumably local or regional.

*Fabric ZD*

A medium fine hard, grey (inner face)/orange (outer face) clay, with a smooth feel and smooth fracture. The fabric is medium and characterized by moderate sub-rounded brown/glassy iron ore (up to 0.5 mm), sparse flecks of mica, moderate sub-rounded to angular black iron ore (up to 0.3 mm), sparse rounded white limestone (up to 0.3 mm), sparse quartz (0.3 mm), and sparse elongated ferromagnesian (0.5 mm) inclusions.

The origin of this fabric is not known but it is presumably local or regional.

*Fabric ZE*

A fine soft, buff-coloured clay, with a smooth powdery feel and smooth fracture. The fabric is relatively well sorted and characterized by sparse sub-rounded cream/white limestone/calcite (0.8 mm), sparse tiny white felspar (0.1 - 0.2 mm), sparse angular quartz (0.2 - 0.3 mm), sparse angular black/grey ferro-magnesian mineral (up to 0.6 mm), and occasional sparse flecks of mica.

The origin of this fabric is not known but is presumably local or regional.

*Fabric ZF*

A fine soft, orange-coloured clay, with a smooth powdery soapy feel and smooth fracture. The fabric is well sorted and is characterized by large sub-rounded white calcite (0.1 mm), large angular white (felspar?) and black/grey (igneous rock?) and sparse sub-rounded grey inclusions (up to 0.1 mm).

The origin of this fabric is not known but it presumably is local or regional.

### Fabric ZF

An exceptionally fine hard clay, orange/buff to cream in colour with a rough feel and hackly fracture. The fabric is relatively well sorted and characterized by sparse to moderate mica flecks, sparse to moderate (0.05 - 0.2 mm) white inclusions, and sparse black iron ore (0.1 mm).

The origin of this fabric is not known but it is presumably local or regional.

### Fabric ZG

A medium fine hard, light orange/buff coloured clay, with a rough feel and hackly fracture. The fabric is medium-sorted and characterized by sparse to moderate sub-rounded limestone (up to 0.9 mm), sparse to moderate sub-rounded quartz (up to 0.5 mm), sparse flecks of mica, sparse rounded black/grey iron ore (0.2 - 0.7 mm), sparse sub-rounded white felspar/calcite (up to 0.3 - 0.4 mm), and sparse sub-rounded bright red/brown iron ore.

The origin of this fabric is not known but it is presumably local or regional.

### Fabric ZH

A fine soft, dark red brown coloured clay, with a smooth/powdery feel and smooth fracture. The fabric is very well sorted and is characterized by sparse tiny white inclusions, sparse angular quartz (0.5 mm), and sparse sub-rounded black iron ore (0.1 - 0.2 mm).

The origin of this fabric is not known but it is presumably local or regional.

### Fabric ZI

An exceptionally fine hard, grey-coloured clay, with a slightly smooth/powdery feel and hackly fracture. The fabric is very well sorted and characterized by sparse tiny white (lime?) inclusions and occasional sparse flecks of mica.

The origin of this fabric is not known but it is presumably local or regional.

### Fabric ZJ

A medium fine hard, orange buff/cream coloured clay, with a rough feel and hackly fracture. The fabric is ill-sorted and characterized by sparse angular white limestone (1.0 mm), sparse to moderate sub-rounded quartz (up to 0.4 mm), sparse rounded brown iron ore/clay pellets (0.1 - 0.2 mm), and sparse sub-rounded white felspar (0.1 mm).

The origin of this fabric is not known but it is presumably local or regional.

### Fabric ZK not used.

### Fabric ZL

A soft, grey/green coloured clay, with a rough feel and hackly fracture. The fabric is ill-sorted and characterized by sparse angular white felspar (between 0.1 and 1.0 mm), sparse angular black iron ore (up to 2 mm in length), sparse sub-rounded limestone (0.6 mm), and sparse angular quartz (0.4 - 0.6 mm).

The origin of this fabric is not known but it is presumably local or regional.

### Fabric ZL Var.

A medium soft, grey/green coloured clay, with a rough feel and hackly fracture. The fabric is coarse textured and ill-sorted and characterized by sparse to moderate angular quartz (up to 1.0 mm), sparse sub-rounded black iron ore (up to 0.5 mm), sparse sub-rounded dull grey inclusions (0.8 mm), sparse sub-rounded white felspar (0.1 - 0.2 mm), and sparse flecks of mica.

The origin of this fabric is not known but it is presumably local or regional.

### Fabric ZM

A medium fine soft, buff-coloured clay, with a smooth feel and smooth fracture. The fabric is quite well sorted, and is characterized by sparse to moderate sub-rounded black iron ore (0.05 - 0.1 mm), sparse irregular limestone (0.6 mm), and sparse sub-rounded brown iron ore (0.1 mm).

The origin of this fabric is not known but it is presumably local or regional.

### Fabric ZN

A medium hard, beige/brown coloured clay with a medium smooth feel and hackly fracture. The fabric is quite well sorted and characterized by occasional to medium angular/subangular quartz grains (0.1 mm).

The origin of this fabric is not known but it is presumably local or regional.

### Fabric ZO

A hard grey coloured fabric with a smooth feel. The fabric is quite well sorted and characterized by common mica flakes (0.001 mm) and common quartz ground-scatter.

The origin of this fabric is not known but it is presumably regional.

### Fabric ZZ

A light brown to reddish coloured fabric with a medium smooth feel and smooth/hackly fracture. The fabric is medium-sorted with few visible inclusions apart from the occasional subangular calcite (0.1-0.2 mm) grains and very occasional mica flakes.

# Appendix 2
# A petrological note on amphora fabrics from the survey and along the eastern Spanish coast
## David Williams

**Introduction**

In recent years much work has been done on the study of amphorae, particularly those that were in use during the Roman period. Detailed studies have been made, for example, on the *tituli picti* occasionally found, especially on Dressel 20 (Rodríguez-Almeida 1984); name stamps (Remesal 1986, following on from Callender 1965); residue analysis (Rothschild-Boros 1981; Passi *et al.* 1981; Heron and Pollard 1988); and, above all, on the typology (Keay 1984; Laubenheimer 1985; Peacock and Williams 1986).

Central to much of this work is the accumulation of sound information as to the origins of the various types. A growing number of kilns producing amphorae are known, but they almost certainly represent only a very small percentage of the total (Peacock and Williams 1986, chapter 6 — now a little out of date as additional sites have been discovered). It seems that few of the popular amphora forms were made in restricted areas. Accordingly it is not always possible to predict the origin of a particular amphora based on 'nuances' of form alone. The Dressel 2-4 is a good example, for the type was undoubtedly made at a variety of places in the western Roman Empire (Peacock and Williams 1986, Class 10). The late Republican types Dressel 1A and 1B, which were once thought to have been made exclusively in Italy, now appear to have been made also in France, albeit on a small scale (Sabir *et al.* 1983). Even the distinctive globular form of Dressel 20, produced in great numbers along the Guadalquivir and its tributaries in Baetica (Ponsich 1974; 1979), was copied in Germany, though the distribution seems to have been fairly localized (Baudoux 1992).

Fortunately, an appreciation of the materials used to make amphorae (i.e. the mix of local clay and occasional tempering constituents) can in certain cases allow amphorae to be tied down to particular regions or even individual kilns if the fabric is distinctive enough. This can be particularly useful for assigning incomplete vessels, where it is not possible to examine the whole form. Scientific analysis along these lines has been done largely through the application of petrological and chemical methods (see Peacock and Williams 1986 for references).

In the present study the petrological technique of thin-sectioning has been applied to all the samples examined. It involves fixing a comparatively small sample of pottery (*c.*10 x 10 mm) to a glass slide. The sample is ground down until the majority of the inclusions become transparent (at *c.*30 microns thickness). The precise determinations and texture of the minerals and rock fragments present in the clay (occurring naturally in the paste or as added temper) can be given by use of the polarizing microscope. This method is doubly useful, for it allows the texture of the non-plastic inclusions in known kiln material to be characterized (i.e. the size, shape, and frequency of the mineral grains) and in those cases where an unusual or exotic range of inclusions is present it enables the probable geographical areas to be identified.

In the present programme of analysis, a range of amphora sherds found on the survey was examined. The geographical area in question covers roughly the coastal zone of Catalunya, which in its northern section is largely granitic, and the Levantine lowlands, much of which is covered by Cretaceous limestone and Quaternary formations. The initial aim of this report is to characterize amphora fabrics that seemed to have originated in the Tarragona region during the Iberian, Republican and early imperial periods. It was done with reference to an analysis of material from the known and suspected kiln sites in the Tarragona region and against a survey of amphora fabrics from kiln sites in the provinces of Girona, Tarragona, Castellon, Valencia,

Alicante and Murcia (petrological work has been done on amphora fabrics from Barcelona: see Peacock 1977c; Williams 1981). It was hoped that this would permit products from the Tarragona region to be identified more easily and possibly allow 'fabric zones' for amphora production in this region of Spain to be defined. The second aim was to identify possible production areas for a range of imported amphora fabrics found.

**Petrology**

*Characterization of amphora fabrics found in the course of the survey*

  *Locally produced fabrics*

1. Fontscaldes: material from surface collection at this known kiln site (Table 1.1, site 1):
   **A** Sample taken from a pre-imperial Type 9/Dressel 1C: Amphora Fabric 9
   **B** Sample taken from a miscellaneous sherd: Fabric 9
2. Site 4.1, Campo 884:
   **A** Sample taken from a pre-imperial Type 8/Dressel 1B rim with an Iberian stamp: Fabric 9
   **B** Sample taken from a miscellaneous sherd: Fabric 9.
3. Site 4.4, Campo 959:
   **A** Sample taken from a pre-imperial Type 7/Dressel 1A rim: Fabric 9.

All of the above 5 sherds are in a similar fairly coarse-textured fabric. They are in a fairly hard, somewhat rough sandy fabric containing many small white inclusions of limestone scattered throughout the clay. The surface colour tends to be light red to yellowish-yellow (Munsell 2.5YR 6/8 to 5YR 7/6), with slightly darker tones in section achieving a light reddish-brown (5YR 6/4) colour at the core. Thin-sectioning shows frequent, generally well-sorted subangular quartz grains normally under 0.40 mm in size, although a few sparse grains reach 1 mm and over, together with small irregular pieces of cryptocrystalline limestone or reaction-rims surrounding voids which once held limestone, some chert, quartzite, flecks of mica, and a little fine-grained argillaceous material.

The fabric points to an area of origin close by sedimentary formations and is entirely compatible with a source in the survey area, which is composed largely of Tertiary limestones cut by quaternary terraces of the river Francolí and its tributaries, with Palaeozoic deposits just to the west. Moreover, an examination of other amphora sherds from the area of the survey shows that this is a common local fabric type.

4. Site 3.6, Campo 1128: sample taken from pre-imperial Type 4/Dressel 1A vessel in an 'Iberian' fabric: Fabric 14/16.

Under the microscope was visible a groundmass of frequent silt-sized quartz grains, some small irregular pieces of cryptocrystalline limestone, flecks of mica, and a little iron oxide.

5. Site 3.3, Campo 1171: sample taken from pre-imperial Type 4/Dressel 1A vessel in an 'Iberian' fabric: Fabric 14/16.

It exhibited a groundmass of frequent silt-sized quartz grains, with a few slightly larger quartz grains, flecks of mica, a little cryptocrystalline limestone, and a few grains of quartzite and plagioclase felspar.

6. Site 4.2, Campo 945: sample taken from pre-imperial Type 1/Boca Plana amphora: Fabric 20.

A fairly coarse, hard fired fabric, with small pieces of cryptocrystalline limestone and plentiful reaction rims surrounding voids which once held limestone, a moderate amount of quartz grains generally under 0.30 mm in size, and some flecks of mica.

The fabric of the above sherds is entirely in keeping with a local source or sources within the area of the survey. It is worth noting that included in the sherds sampled above are what must surely be regarded as Iberian versions of the late Republican forms Dressel 1A, 1B and 1C. Two of the 'Iberian fabric' sherds, sample 4 and 5, are in a somewhat finer-textured fabric than the rest.

Some of the amphora sherds sampled above are slightly sandier than others in the group, but on the whole they display a fairly uniform range of inclusions, suggesting that they were all made in the same general area. Indeed, slight nuances of texture between some of the sherds could point to a number of different production centres within the region. This situation has been noted before, for example in surveys that have been carried out around Barcelona (Pascual 1977) and in Italy in the areas of the *Ager Falernus* (Arthur 1983) and the *Ager Caecubius* (Hesnard and Lemoine 1981), in each of which a number of amphora kilns operating at roughly the same period have been discovered.

*Fabrics with an origin in eastern Spain*

**7**  Site 1.6, Campo 60: early imperial amphora Type 23 (Pascual 1): Fabric 12
Site 1.6, Campo 60: early imperial amphora Type 25 (Dressel 2-4 handle): Fabric 13
Site 1.6, Campo 60: pre-imperial amphora Type 1/Boca Plana: Fabric 12

All 3 samples contain inclusions of granite, together with grains of quartz, orthoclase felspar, mica (both biotite and muscovite) and a little hornblende, with some fragments of limestone and occasional metamorphic rocks. In texture, the sample of Fabric 13 stands out from the other two, as it is fairly fine-textured compared with the frequent inclusions present in the two sherds of Fabric 12. The granitic inclusions present in all 3 sherds suggest an origin in the Barcelona region.

**8**  Site 3.9, Campo 6: pre-imperial amphora Type 1/Boca Plana: Fabric 14/16
Campo 29 (off-site): pre-imperial amphora Type 1/Boca Plana: Fabric 14/16
Campo 8 (off-site): pre-imperial amphora Type 1/Boca Plana: Fabric 14/16

All 3 sherds are fairly fine-textured and contain predominantly limestone inclusions with a little quartz and the odd discrete grain of felspar. This range of inclusions agrees well with that found by Peacock (forthcoming) in his examination of Iberian amphorae.

*Comparative 'Tarraconensian' fabrics from kiln sites in the provinces of Girona, Tarragona, Castelló, Valencia, Alicante and Murcia*

Province of Girona

**9**  Ermedas kiln site (unpublished):
Sample from an early imperial Type 23/Pascual 1 amphora:

A reasonably coarse-textured fabric containing ill-sorted subangular quartz grains ranging up to 1 mm across in size, some discrete grains of potash and plagioclase felspar, quartzite, small fragments of granite and gneiss, a little chert and some flecks of mica and iron oxide. The site is situated on Eocene formations but close by two scattered outcrops of granite to the north, while gneiss is to be found not far away in the upper Pyrenees.

Province of Barcelona

**10**  A series of Roman kilns produced the forms Pascual 1 (Type 23) and Dressel 2-4 (Type 25) in the Barcelona area (Pascual 1977; see also Keay and Jones 1982). No new samples were analysed since the fabric associated with these types is particularly distinctive in the hand-specimen. It contains large discrete grains of white felspar and quartz, the 'points blancs' noted some time ago by Tchernia and Zevi (1971). Petrological analysis by Peacock (1977) on examples of Dressel 2-4 and by the writer (1981) on Pascual 1, both from this region, confirmed the granitic nature of the clay (much of the area is covered by granite formations) and suggested two broad fabric divisions (see also Peacock and Williams 1986, Class 6). Fabric 1 is dark red to reddish-brown in the hand-specimen (Munsell Soil Colour Chart 10R 4/4 to 4/6), and contains frequent discrete grains of quartz and felspar (mainly potash, but with some plagioclase), together with fragments of granite and a little mica. In contrast, Fabric 2 tends to be creamy-white in the hand-specimen (between 7.5YR 8/2 and 7/4). It contains the same range of inclusions, although with less mica, but is somewhat finer-textured.

Province of Tarragona

**11** Pla D'Aumedina (Tivissa) kiln site (Revilla 1993; Miró 1988, 54-56)

**A** Sample from a Type 25/Dressel 2-4 amphora:

A fairly coarse-textured fabric with tightly-packed subangular quartz grains under 0.30 mm in size and small pieces of generally rounded cryptocrystalline limestone, together with reaction rims surrounding voids which once contained limestone, and some flecks of mica and a little iron ore.

**B** Sample from a Type 23/Pascual 1 amphora:
Similar to A, but slightly finer-textured and not as hard fired.

The site of Pla d'Aumedina (Tivissa, Ribera d'Ebre) lies in an area of Upper Cretaceous, Quaternary and Trias formations. Both of these samples compare well with previous thin-sectioning of the products of this kiln (Keay and Jones 1982).

**12** Vilaseca kiln site (unpublished)

**A** Sample taken from an early imperial Type 23/Pascual 1 amphora:

A reasonably fine-textured fabric, with a groundmass of silt-sized quartz grains, a few larger quartz grains, frequent small pieces of cryptocrystalline limestone, a little calcite, a moderate amount of mica (both muscovite and biotite), a few small discrete grains of potash and plagioclase felspar, and some iron oxide. The site lies on Quaternary deposits.

**B and C.** Samples taken from Type 23/Pascual 1 amphorae:

Somewhat coarser-textured than sample A, with more frequent and some slightly larger quartz grains but still containing plentiful limestone.

**13** Mas D'Antoni Corts (Riudoms, Baix Camp) kiln site (Miró 1988, 54):
Sample taken from an early imperial Type 25/Dressel 2-4 amphora:

The fabric exhibited a moderate groundmass of silt-sized quartz grains and small pieces of cryptocrystalline limestone, flecks of mica, a little iron ore and a sparse but distinctive number of large subangular grains mainly of quartz but with some potash felspar, up to 1.60 mm across. The site lies on Quaternary formations but with granite outcrops close by, which would account for the large quartz and felspar grains present in the sample. This is visually similar to fabric 13.

**14** El Vendrell kiln site (unpublished)

**A** Sample taken from a pre-imperial Type 1/Boca Plana amphora:

A fine-textured dense clay matrix, containing a moderate amount of ill-sorted subangular quartz grains ranging up to 0.80 mm across, a scatter of irregular-shaped cryptocrystalline limestone, reaction rims surrounding voids which once held limestone, a little fine-grained metamorphic material, and some flecks of mica.

**B and C.** Samples taken from pre-imperial Type 1/Boca Plana amphora:

A much coarser fabric than sample A, with frequent grains of subangular quartz generally under 0.30 mm across and irregular-shaped pieces of cryptocrystalline limestone, together with some flecks of mica (including a few long strands of biotite), some iron oxide, and the odd small grain of plagioclase felspar.

Province of Castelló

**15** Mas D'Arago kiln site (Borras i Querol 1988):

**A** Sample taken from an early imperial Type 25/Dressel 2-4 amphora:

A micaceous fabric, with plentiful flecks of mica (both muscovite and biotite). Also present are a moderate amount of quartz grains under 0.30 mm in size, a little cryptocrystalline limestone with reaction rims surrounding voids which once contained limestone, and some iron oxide.

**B** Sample taken from an early imperial Type 27 or 28/ Dressel 7-11 amphora:

A somewhat finer-textured fabric than sample A and not quite so micaceous.
**C and D** Samples taken from two early imperial Type 23/Pascual 1 amphorae:
Even finer-textured than sample B.

The kiln lies in an area of Quaternary and Lower Cretaceous formations, and it is difficult at present to account adequately for the frequent mica flakes in sample A. There appears to be some variation in fabric between the different amphorae types present, and it would be interesting to see how representative the micaceous Dressel 2-4 is with respect to other kiln products.

Province of Valencia

**16** Deposit at the Grau Vell (Saguntum) (Aranegui and Mantilla 1987):
There is no evidence of a kiln here although it is thought that stamped early imperial Type 25/Dressel 2-4 amphorae were manufactured in the vicinity.

**A** Sample taken from a Type 25/Dressel 2-4 amphora rim stamped M P M:
A fine-textured fabric with a moderate amount of small quartz grains under 0.20 mm in size, some small pieces of cryptocrystalline limestone, a few reaction rims surrounding voids which once held limestone, flecks of mica, and some iron oxide. The Grau Vell is situated in an area of Quaternary deposits, close by to Triassic rocks.

**17** Oliva kiln site (Enguix and Alemany 1977):
**A** Sample taken from an amphora sherd of unspecified type.
**B** Sample taken from a bifid-handled sherd.

Both samples are in a moderately fine-textured fabric containing a groundmass of small silt-sized quartz grains and fairly frequent flecks of mica (mostly muscovite but with some biotite), irregular-shaped pieces of cryptocrystalline limestone with reaction rims surrounding voids which once held limestone, a scatter of larger-sized quartz grains generally up to 0.40 mm across, and a little iron oxide.

The site is situated in an area of Quaternary and Upper Cretaceous formations. Samples A and B appear to lack the inclusions of hornblende and clinopyroxene that were mentioned in a previous petrological analysis of certain pottery thought to have been made at this kiln (Keay and Jones 1982).

Alicante

**18** Almadrava (Denia) kiln site (Gisbert 1987):
**A** Sample taken from an early imperial Type 25/Dressel 2-4 amphora:
**B** Sample taken from the spike of a possible early imperial Type 25/Dressel 2-4 amphora:
Both samples contain a groundmass of moderately frequent silt-sized quartz grains, a scatter of larger quartz grains generally up to 0.30 mm across, irregular-shaped pieces of cryptocrystalline limestone, a few reaction rims surrounding voids which once held limestone, a moderate amount of mica, and some iron oxide.

The site is situated in an area of Quaternary and Eocene deposits.

Province of Murcia

**19** Aguilas (Cartagena) kiln site (Ramallo 1985):
Sample taken from a late imperial spatheion of Keay XXV1 type:
This is an extremely micaceous fabric, containing plentiful flecks of mica (mostly muscovite but with a little biotite). Also present are a moderate amount of quartz grains, some irregular-shaped pieces of cryptocrystalline limestone, a few fragments of quartz-mica-schist, and some iron oxide. Schist formations are situated close by the site, which probably explains the large amount of mica present in the fabric of the sample.

*Fabrics with an origin outside eastern Spain*
**20** Site 1.6, Campo 60: pre-imperial Type 21 or 22 amphora: Fabric 3.

This fabric is characterized by frequent flecks of mica (both muscovite and biotite), together with some grains of quartz and a little limestone. It is difficult to be certain of a local Ibizan source when dealing with such common inclusions, but it is worth noting that mica is a noticeable feature of Ibizan pottery (Peacock, forthcoming).

**21** Site 1.6, Campo 60: pre-imperial amphora Type 17-19/Dressel 1: Fabric 5.

This fabric was characterized by frequent grains of quartz, together with grains of augite and sanidine felspar and some fragments of limestone and lava. A source along the Italian volcanic tract is suggested (Peacock 1971).

**22** Site 3.9, Campo 5: pre-imperial amphora Type 15-17/Dressel 1A/Greco-Italic: Fabric 6
Site 1.6, Campo 60: pre-imperial amphora Type 36/Dressel 2-4: Fabric 6
Site 1.6, Campo 60: pre-imperial amphora Type 17-19/Dressel 1: Fabric 6

All three sherds are in a distinctive 'black sand' fabric. An origin in Latium has been suggested for this fabric on the basis of the presence of yellow garnet when viewed in thin-section (Courtois and Velde 1978). However, yellow-brown garnet is also a feature of the sands further south, and a Campanian origin, in particular the area around Pompeii and Herculaneum, has been suggested by Peacock (1977b). Further analysis by Velde and Courtoise (1983) using an electron microprobe has distinguished two separate compositional groups of yellow (melanitic) garnet, one of which they propose is from near Rome and the other in the region of Vesuvius. The latter proposal agrees with Peacock's (1977b) suggestion, but as yet there is no archaeological evidence for an origin near Rome for the 'black sand' fabric. In view of this a Campanian origin seems most likely, especially since examples of bricks and tiles in the Pompeii and Herculaneum region are in an identical fabric.

**23** Site 1.6, Campo 60: pre-imperial amphora Type 17/Dressel 1A: Fabric 7.

The most prominent non-plastic inclusions are grains of augite, together with some quartz, and pieces of limestone and lava. Texturally, this sample appears very similar to material from Campania studied by the writer.

**24** Site 1.6, Campo 60: pre-imperial amphora Type 19/Dressel IC: Fabric 8.

Frequent grains of quartz are present, together with some flecks of mica, felspar, a little augite, and fragments of limestone. A source along the Italian volcanic tract is probably indicated (Peacock 1971).

**25** Off-site scatter: pre-imperial amphora Type 10/Cintas 315: Fabric 11.

The non-plastic inclusions consist mostly of frequent quartz grains rounded by Aeolian action together with rounded pieces of limestone. The sample falls within the range of North African fabrics, the generally-accepted source for this form of amphora (Van der Werff 1978).

### Conclusions

A consideration of the petrological results outlined above allows a number of useful points to be made. However, some must be regarded as tentative, having regard to the lack of kiln material available in some cases or the relatively small number of sherds employed to represent regional fabrics.

1. The predominant local Roman amphora fabric of the survey area in the Republican period is Fabric 9, which is fairly coarse and contains predominantly quartz and limestone. The remainder of the samples tend to be in slightly finer-textured fabrics. Italian wine in Dressel 1 amphorae was undoubtedly being imported into the region, but the petrological analysis shows that there was also a local production of this form. It remains to be seen to what extent local wine was distributed in these vessels.

2. The previous macroscopic (Tchernia and Zevi 1971) and microscopic (Peacock and Williams 1986) work on amphorae from the Barcelona region indicates a distinctive granitic fabric.

3. The sample from Ermedas, just north of Girona, contains some granite, but in a quite different texture to the Barcelona material, and also a small piece of gneiss(?). Both inclusion types probably originate from the granite and gneiss outcrops located N of the site.

4. The sherd from Cartagena is highly micaceous, no doubt a reflection of the local schist formations.

5. It has been possible to section only one sherd from Mas D'Antoni, Corts, Riudoms, but this sample differs markedly from the rest of the Tarragona material, which are basically quartz-limestone fabrics. The sherd from Mas D'Antoni contains quartz and limestone and also has a scatter of unusually large and distinctive grains of quartz and felspar, both probably deriving from the nearby granite outcrops.

6. In the northern and southern parts of the region the fabrics appear to be quite distinctive. However, much of the remaining material is basically of a quartz-limestone fabric. Certain nuances of difference can be observed in some of the sherds, both comparing site-to-site assemblages and also some of the different amphorae forms made at particular kilns. Caution is advised in pressing these differences too far at present, since it is difficult to be certain how representative of the area and individual kilns the samples are.

# Appendix 3: Gas-chromatographic analysis of amphora sherds

## John Evans

### Preparation

The sherds were microscopically inspected but no adhering organic residues were discernable. The outer surfaces of the sherds were carefully abraded to remove any surface contamination. The sherds were then pulverized and subjected to the following analytical scheme.

### Procedure

The sample was extracted, sequentially, with hexane, chloroform and 2-propanol. Each extract was evaporated to dryness. Any residues so obtained were examined by infra-red spectroscopy (I.R.). These extracts, where sufficient, were then investigated by thin-layer chromatography (T.L.C.). This technique is especially useful for the hexane (oils and fats) and chloroform (resins) extracts, as it enables major constituents to be detected. For example, fats and oils are composed partially of triglycerides that are usually unique to a particular fat or oil.

In the next stage the extracts were subjected to gas (G.L.C.) and high-performance liquid (H.P.L.C.) chromatographies. Procedure depended upon the nature of the extract. For instance, the hexane residues were hydrolysed and any free acids methylated prior to G.L.C. Thus it was possible to identify the fatty acids present. This information, when coupled with that from the T.L.C., enabled any oils present to be identified with reasonable certainty.

After completion of the extraction procedure, the sample was divided. One part was refluxed with 6M hydrochloric acid to release amino acids from any proteinaceous material present. The second part was refluxed with alcoholic potassium hydroxide to decompose any 'dried' oils present. Any resulting products from these procedures were then subjected to appropriate chromatographic investigation.

### Results

*Sample 1*

A sherd of pre-imperial amphora Type 8/Dressel IB in Fabric 9 from Site 4.1, Campo 884. Contents: Fish products, possibly *garum* (I.R., G.L.C.)

*Sample 2*

A sherd of pre-imperial amphora Type 1/Boca Plana in Fabric 14/16 from Site 3.3, Campo 1171. Contents: Fish oil/products (I.R., T.L.C., G.L.C.)

*Comments*

Samples 1 and 2 both seem to be associated with fish, but sample 2 seems to be protein/amino acid-rich.

THE MICROFICHES IN THE POCKET INSIDE THE BACK COVER COMPRISE:

Microfiches 1 and 2: Appendix 4.  Field by Field Quantified Pottery Records

Microfiche 3: Appendix 5.  Site Pottery Summaries

and Appendix 6.  Dating Evidence of Ceramic Forms from Sites

Copies of the material appearing on the microfiches can be obtained from Martin Millett, Department of Archaeology, University of Durham, 46 Saddler Street, Durham DH1 3NU, England. Copies are available on disk or on paper.